D1284031

HANDBOOK OF REGIONAL
AND URBAN ECONOMICS
VOLUME II

HANDBOOKS
IN
ECONOMICS

7

Series Editors

KENNETH J. ARROW
MICHAEL D. INTRILIGATOR

NORTH-HOLLAND
AMSTERDAM · NEW YORK · OXFORD · TOKYO

HANDBOOK OF REGIONAL AND URBAN ECONOMICS

VOLUME II
URBAN ECONOMICS

Edited by

EDWIN S. MILLS
Princeton University

1987

NORTH-HOLLAND
AMSTERDAM · NEW YORK · OXFORD · TOKYO

ISBN North-Holland for this volume 0 444 87970 6
ISBN North-Holland for this set 0 444 87971 4

Publishers
ELSEVIER SCIENCE PUBLISHERS B.V.
P.O. Box 1991
1000BZ Amsterdam
The Netherlands

Sole distributors for the U.S.A. and Canada
ELSEVIER SCIENCE PUBLISHING COMPANY, INC.
52 Vanderbilt Avenue
New York, N.Y. 10017
U.S.A.

PRINTED IN THE NETHERLANDS

INTRODUCTION TO THE SERIES

The aim of the *Handbooks in Economics* series is to produce Handbooks for various branches of economics, each of which is a definitive source, reference, and teaching supplement for use by professional researchers and advanced graduate students. Each Handbook provides self-contained surveys of the current state of a branch of economics in the form of chapters prepared by leading specialists on various aspects of this branch of economics. These surveys summarize not only received results but also newer developments, from recent journal articles and discussion papers. Some original material is also included, but the main goal is to provide comprehensive and accessible surveys. The Handbooks are intended to provide not only useful reference volumes for professional collections but also possible supplementary readings for advanced courses for graduate students in economics.

CONTENTS OF THE HANDBOOK

VOLUME II: URBAN ECONOMICS

E.S. MILLS, Editor

CONTENTS OF VOLUME II

Chapter 27
Urban Public Facility Location
CHARLES REVELLE

Chapter 28
Rural–Urban Migration in Developing Countries
DIPAK MAZUMDAR

PART 3 – URBAN GOVERNMENT BEHAVIOR AND ISSUES

Chapter 29

Theoretical Analysis of Local Public Economics

DAVID E. WILDASIN

Chapter 30

Financing Urban Public Services

RÉMY PRUD'HOMME

Chapter 17

ADVANCES IN URBAN ECONOMICS

EDWIN S. MILLS
Princeton University

PETER NIJKAMP
Free University, Amsterdam

1. Introduction

Papers in this volume survey the development of urban economics. By any reasonable standard, urban economics is a young specialty. As a subject of academic research with a coherent theoretical foundation, urban economics might be said to date from publication of Alonso's (1964) book *Location and Land Use*. Most of the following chapters survey a burgeoning volume of research, but research that has a history of only one or two decades. This short history is in contrast with other specialities, such as public finance, international economics or labor economics, that go back many decades.

Its short history means that surveys of urban economics can be relatively precise and comprehensive. Thus, the papers in this volume cover virtually all the conceptual developments in the speciality. There are of course many applied studies, especially in recent years, pertaining to and published in many countries around the world. Coverage of applied studies is inevitably much more selective in most of the papers in this volume. In terms of conceptual developments and applied studies that employ careful theoretical and econometric tools, the papers in this volume provide remarkably broad coverage.

2. Pre-history of urban economics

There were of course insightful publications on urban issues before Alonso's (1964) book. In fact, Adam Smith had a remarkably elaborate view of cities and their functions. Fifty years later von Thünen introduced theoretical concepts that urban economists borrowed heavily. Marshall and most other neoclassical writers had surprisingly little to say about urban areas, especially given the rapid pace of urbanization in countries in which they were writing.

Handbook of Regional and Urban Economics, Volume II, Edited by E.S. Mills
© *1987, Elsevier Science Publishers B.V.*

After World War II, given the rapid growth of economic research and the gradual increase in the amount and quality of data available, research concerned with urban issues inevitably grew.

Interestingly, one of the first important postwar contributions was an entirely empirical paper. In 1951, Clark published estimates on urban population density functions for a variety of cities around the world, some going back to the early 19th century. Although Clark's paper stimulated dozens of subsequent papers, nearly all were published after the appearance of large numbers of theoretical papers on the subject in the late 1960s and early 1970s.

An important precurser to the theoretical work after 1964 was Wingo's (1961) volume, part of a large research program on urban economics at Resources for the Future. It is also important to mention Niedercorn's (1963) theoretical and econometric paper, part of a second research program in urban economics, at the Rand Corporation.

Starting just after 1964, there was an explosion of theoretical research on urban economics.

There can be no doubt that theoretical research has been crucial to the development of urban economics from the beginning. Theoretical models provided a coherent framework within which to think about empirical issues. In addition, it posed specific hypotheses for estimation and testing with data. Equally important, it suggested conceptual issues that attracted to the subject fine theoreticians, whose relationship to urban economics was temporary – such as Dixit, Mirrlees and Solow. In this respect, urban economics stands in some contrast with some other applied specialities in economics. Labor economics, for example, grew as a recognized specialty with only a minor theoretical component, although much earlier than urban economics. Urban economics, having evolved only in the 1960s and 1970s, benefited from developments in micro economic theory that had occurred during earlier decades. Urban economists borrowed a rich set of tools in analyzing consumer, firm and market behavior. Indeed, the timing of early theoretical research in urban economics was in part the result of improvements in micro economic theory that took place during the early postwar period.

One additional factor in the early conceptual development of urban economics should be mentioned. Urban economic theory requires the use of the tools of micro economic theory in a special spatial context. Although most micro economic theoretical analysis was either written in English or quickly become available in English, virtually all the early theoretical work on spatial analysis was in German. Thus, the use of spatial models to analyze urban economies had to await the availability of German literature to economists who were well versed in modern micro theory but did not read German. The 1954 translation of Lösch's classic was the key event in the education of English language scholars on spatial analysis.

Finally, the relationship between positive and normative motivations in the early history of urban economics should be mentioned. It is more than coincidental that the surge of research on urban economics starting in the mid-1960s followed shortly the growth of concern with poverty in many countries and with racial issues in the United States. A desire to edify the growing government concern with poverty and racial issues motivated many economists to undertake research on urban problems. Urban economics shares this relationship with labor economics and some other specialties in economics.

This pre-history of urban economic analysis should not be concluded without reference to the work of Hoover. Most of his writing is more properly classified as regional than an urban economics. But this patient insistence on the use of the best micro economic tools available and on their confrontation with spatial data both educated and inspired scholars during a long career.

All applied specialties in economics develop through interactions within and between theoretical and empirical research. Urban economics is no exception. The work of Clark, Hoover and a host of authors associated with Resources for the Future and Rand attests to the importance of empirical research in the early history of urban economics.

3. Overview of the volume

It is accurate to characterize the decade or so between the mid-1960s and the mid-1970s as an explosive period in theoretical analysis of urban spatial models. During that decade, tools of modern micro economic theory were applied to urban spatial analysis. These and more recent contributions are surveyed in Part 1 of this volume.

By far the largest number of theoretical publications analyzed household location. This work is surveyed in Chapter 18 by Straszheim. Almost all such theoretical models analyze the interaction between housing demand and commuting in a utility maximization context. A key insight was the realization that the housing-price–housing-consumption pairs among identical consumers at different locations in an urban area trace out a compensated demand equation for housing. Also important were theorems as to the circumstances in which residents with particular incomes might cluster together in an urban area. On these and other issues, theoretical models had implications that could be tested with census and other data from many countries.

The second major strand of analysis concerns business location, analyzed by Stahl in Chapter 19. Such analysis long predates the birthdate of urban economics assigned above, but recent work has applied basic business location theory to a specifically urban context. That turns out to be quite complex because the spatial characteristics of urban areas differ markedly from those used earlier by

Lösch and others in analyzing business locations. Indeed, although Lösch had ingenious analyses about clustering of business locations, he wrote nothing about spatial structure within an urban area.

Household location choices are conditioned by, among other things, business locations; and business locations are conditioned by, among other things, household locations, since households are both the customers and the major input suppliers for most urban businesses. Therefore, the third strand of analysis is of general equilibrium models of a single urban area, analyzing simultaneous location determinants of both households and businesses. This subject is surveyed and unified by Brueckner in Chapter 20. Only in the 1980s did urban economists make progress with general equilibrium spatial models of an urban area that did not assume or imply that all business locations clustered together in the central business district.

Although spatial analysis is in some degree the essence of urban economics, spatial detail comes at a high price. Modest amounts of sectoral and spatial detail deprive theoretical analysis of most qualitative results. Researchers are therefore driven to numerical analysis. Models of household and firm behavior are specified and a program is written that will solve the models for a set of household and business locations. Typically, such models are solved for a given urban area for a given year conditional on a spatial specification of dwellings and business capital that the urban area inherits from earlier years. Such models may include various exogenous variables, most importantly those resulting from government infrastructure and housing programs. Then, computer models can be simulated to estimate the effects of possible government actions, such as transportation improvements or low income housing programs. Kain surveys the extensive history of computer models in Chapter 21. It is worth mentioning that this subject has a stronger European ancestry than has most urban modeling. Presumably, the reason is that there is more government planning of urban areas there than in North American or Japan.

Computer models are mostly dynamic in that they trace through time the changes in an urban area as markets respond to an exogenous shock. But, until recent years, most theoretical work in urban economics has been static. Starting in the late 1970s, sophisticated dynamic theoretical models of urban adjustment began to appear. Spatial detail makes such models very complex and intractable, but remarkable progress has been made. This work is surveyed by Miyao in Chapter 22. Indeed, most theoretical urban economic models are not only static but also long run. Simulation models, tracing year-to-year adjustments to shocks, emphasize short run phenomena resulting from durability of housing and other structures and from slow responses of economic agents. All available evidence suggests that urban spatial and other adjustments are very slow indeed.

Research and writing by economists on specific urban markets and issues long predate the mid-1960s birthdate of urban economics. Such work is the subject of Part 2.

Housing is by far the most important urban market, measured by asset or flow values, and it has long been studied by economists. Until the 1980s, and except for a spurt of mostly low quality work in the late 1960s, most housing analysis was apparently not motivated by concern with low income housing problems or with government programs to improve low income housing. That is surprising and in some contrast with early research on general demand analysis, which was strongly motivated by concerns with nutritional problems of the poor. The late 1970s and 1980s have witnessed a surge of high quality theoretical and empirical research. This work has resulted in part from improved and more flexible theoretical tools that have become available, in part from better econometric estimation and testing models, in part from the availability of inexpensive and powerful computing and, very importantly, from the availability of micro housing data.

Theoretical analysis of housing is surveyed in Chapter 24 by Arnott. An important motivation for much recent theoretical work has been to reduce the diversity of housing types to a manageable set of dimensions. Since a major source of housing diversity results from locational diversity within an urban area, some recent theoretical work has built on the spatial models whose analysis dominated the 1960s and 1970s. A second major motivation for theoretical housing analysis has been the important fact that housing services are an important and expensive component of consumer budgets, but housing equity is also the largest item in the asset portfolio of typical owner-occupiers. Consumption and investment aspects of housing could be analyzed quite separately except for tax advantages, in the U.S. and a few other countries, of owner-occupancy and the incentive effects of better maintenance and care that are associated with owner-occupancy. That the second is more important than the first is suggested by similar rates of owner-occupancy in countries that are otherwise similar, in terms of income levels and housing costs, but differ as to tax status of owner-occupancy vs renting. Canada and the U.S. provide good examples. Yet tax status has been analyzed exhaustively whereas incentives effects of owner-occupancy have hardly been studied.

Perhaps the most impressive recent development in urban economics has been the explosion of empirical studies of housing markets. In the U.S., such work has been stimulated by availability of comprehensive micro housing and other socio-economic data from the Annual Housing Survey, from private household surveys and from the government-sponsored housing allowances experiments. The vast majority of studies have been of housing demand, facilitated by the powerful identifying restriction that, because of houses' longevity, short run supply is virtually independent of prices and other contemporaneous conditions. Little work has been done on supply responses by construction, demolition and alterations. Olsen surveys empirical work on housing in Chapter 25.

Transportation economics also has a long history. Some of that history is associated with computer modeling and is surveyed by Kain. The entire subject is surveyed by Beesley and Kemp in Chapter 26. Transportation is inherently spatial and all research has had more or less spatial detail. Computer models for transportation planning were the first models intended to analyze an entire urban area with elaborate spatial detail. Much of the recent work has been on modal choice, stimulated strongly by the availability of stochastic utility and demand models, which are much better able to cope with discrete modal choice than is neo-classical demand theory. Such analysis frequently contains only minimal spatial detail.

There has also been considerable recent transportation policy analysis, basically benefit–cost studies of alternative urban modal mixes. Most recent have been positive studies of government transportation policy formation and execution.

Most fundamentally, transportation interacts with every aspect of urban development. Increases in real income and changes in relative prices of alternative modes affect modal choice. Increases in income also affect housing demand and hence transportation demand. Many issues have yet to be carefully studied. To take an important example, we do not yet have careful estimates of the extent to which faster and cheaper commuting has been responsible for the suburbanization of metropolitan areas that has occurred almost everywhere.

In Chapter 27, ReVelle surveys the remarkable operations research literature on public facility location. Many such facilities may be government or private, but share the characteristic that their locations of service production form a spatial network to which easy access by residents is valuable. Police, fire, hospital, library, school and other service facilities are examples. Spatial detail is at the core of such modeling. Otherwise, models differ as to the assumptions made about the demand side and those made about capital and variable services production costs and transportation costs.

The last paper in Part 2, Chapter 28 by Mazumdar, surveys rural–urban migration literature concerned with developing countries. Restriction to developing countries is justified because of the large amount of rural–urban migration there, because resources are limited and because much high quality work has been done on the subject during recent years. Although there is much migration in many developed countries, there is little net rural–urban migration in most high income countries. Regional migration is substantial and extensively studied, but tends to be mostly urban–urban. Although not strictly a market or a sector, rural–urban migration is a natural subject to survey both because much good work has been done on it and because it constitutes a large source of urban growth in developing countries. The subject is intrinsically spatial, and many studies estimate effects of distance on migration propensities. But few studies include detailed spatial representation.

Part 3 is concerned with specific government policy issues. Governments are deeply involved in both provision of services to urban residents and in regulation of urban activities in all countries.

In Chapter 29, Wildasin surveys the vast theoretical literature on urban public choice. Local public finance has been a small specialty in economics for decades. Much of the work before the late 1950s was descriptive, being little influenced by sophisticated tax and expenditure analysis that other public finance specialists were undertaking. That changed sharply after publication of Tiebout's (1956) classic. Tiebout's model forced economists to think about households' responses to local government taxes and their incentives to vote and lobby for specific kinds and amounts of taxes, and to place at least some spatial detail in the analysis. The result has been an outpouring of research on both positive and normative aspects of the subject. Although such research has much to say about incentives of residents with similar levels of demand for local government services to collect themselves into particular local government jurisdictions, almost no research inspired by the Tiebout hypothesis contains much spatial detail.

In Chapter 30, Prud'homme surveys empirical aspects of local public finance. The constitutional and political positions of local government vary considerably among Western European and North American countries. Yet the services provided by local governments, the financial relationships between local and higher governments, and the methods of financing local governments from local sources seem to vary less than one might expect. One suspects that such differences were greater in earlier decades and that some convergence process is at work.

Although there are important exceptions, one is left with a feeling that empirical research has lagged somewhat behind theoretical research on local public choice issues, in comparison with other areas surveyed in this volume. The reason can hardly be lack of data, since local government financial data are plentiful and easily available in many countries.

Smith and Bartik survey work on urban amenities in Chapter 31. Amenities are items of collective consumption among a set of proximate consumers. All are influenced by people's actions, and some are produced by purchased inputs. Services of local governments available to all residents of a jurisdiction are examples of produced amenity items. Air quality over a city or neighborhood is influenced by human actions, but is not produced by purchased inputs. Thus, collective consumption may be imposed by physical or technical relationships, or may be imposed by political or constitutional considerations. Smith and Bartik survey an enormous volume of research on amenities, most of it published since Rosen's (1974) paper laying out a conceptual foundation for economic analysis. Crucial issues are the representation and estimation of amenities and their effects on market behavior, and specification of their relationships to government actions. Although all amenities have spatial dimensions, spatial considerations play only a minor role in most analyses.

Amenities are important. A great deal of what is important to people in urban life is collective consumption: school quality, crime, neighborhood quality and pollution are examples. Although economists have long estimated effects of amenities on property values and wage rates using conceptually simple arbitrage models, inferring benefits from amenity improvements has proven to be difficult and contentious. Even more difficult is analysis of the ways government and private actions can optimize amenity provision, and whether a political system motivates governments to produce or influence amenities appropriately.

In Chapter 32, Hamer and Linn review the literature on urban problems in developing countries. Urban problems are more vexing in developing than in developed countries because the pace of urbanization is much faster, resources to deal with urban problems are scarcer, and governments are less motivated and less skillful in dealing with urban problems. Only the third reason is controversial, but it should not be. Most developed countries have democratic governments in which voting and lobbying contrain governments to further residents' interests. Most developing countries have little or no democratic restraints on governments, and governments are less motivated to further residents' interests. There are of course exceptions to this generalization.

Research on urban problems in developing countries has increased rapidly since the early 1970s, much of it sponsored by the World Bank. There are now fine studies for at least a small sample of countries on most important urban issues. Vastly more is now known about most problems than was known a decade ago.

One of the urban issues that receives vast attention in developing countries is the alleged excessive sizes of the largest cities. Unfortunately, virtually all the conceptual and quantitative research on the subject has been done in the developed world. Tolley and Crihfield survey this work in Chapter 33. The most obvious and best studied sources of excessive sizes of large cities are externalities, especially pollution and congestion. Tolley and Crihfield also discuss city size distortions that might result from the redistributive effects of uniform tax rates applied to high and low income residents of cities. They review ingenious methods to estimate such distortions. In developing countries, local government service provision and minimum wages and scale and agglomeration economies may also distort city sizes. Unfortunately, documentation has hardly begun in developing countries. Most difficult is the question of appropriate government policy. In principle, causes of distortions in city sizes should be attacked. For example, if pollution induces the largest cities to be excessively large, then pollution control programs are the first best response. Optimum pollution controls programs will generate optimum city sizes with no programs directly intended to affect city sizes. Circumstances under which it is justified for governments to have programs that directly attempt to alter city sizes are unknown.

4. Possible future trends in urban economics

On any reasonable designation of its birth date, urban economics is no more than a quarter of a century old in 1986. It was established as a recognized specialty in economics by spatial economics. Theories of consumer behavior, firms, market equilibrium and, more recently, dynamic analysis, were placed in a special spatial context that could provide understanding of the spatial structure of urban areas.

During the last decade or so, research by urban economists has shifted its emphasis somewhat from spatial analysis to sectoral and government policy analysis. Housing, public choice and transportation have been important foci of attention. During the same decade, a substantial body of research has appeared that applies the tools of urban economics to urban issues in developing countries. Although most such research is in a spatial context, spatial detail is frequently lacking.

An important implication of the recent trend has been a blurring of boundaries between urban economics and other specialties such as housing, public choice and transportation. Almost certainly, one future trend will be continued break- down of boundaries between urban economics and other specialties. There will, for example, almost certainly be more public choice analysis in a spatial context and more positive and normative analysis of local government behavior by urban economists. It would be difficult to doubt that this trend is both inevitable and desirable.

A second future trend can be predicted with confidence: rapid growth of empirical econometric research in an urban context. In urban economics, as in other specialties, economists' and governments' interest in applied research will be fed by much better and more plentiful data, by econometric tools carefully designed for the specific issues and data, and, most important, widespread availability to scholars of inexpensive and powerful computers. This trend is of course entirely beneficial in that it will permit more thorough estimation and testing of theories, more stimulation of theoretical work by empirical findings that do not fit existing theories and more relevant and thorough government policy analysis.

A third trend, less confidently predicted, is an increase in the research concerned with numerical simulation of spatially detailed models of entire urban areas. Such research is needed for some kinds of government policy analysis, for example planning urban transportation systems and analyzing direct and indirect effects of government housing programs. It will certainly be facilitated by more powerful and less expensive computers, and by more plentiful data. But such research is nevertheless expensive and availability of funds to support it will depend, in most countries, on government policy interests.

The most difficult trend to predict is of theoretical developments in urban economics. As the surveys in this volume show, theoretical analysis has proceeded at a substantial pace even during the recent period of increased applied research. Nor is there any scarcity of topics to be studied. Perhaps the most dramatic example is models that analyze carefully the interactions between residential and employment locations. Even in the mid-1980s, most theoretical models locate all employment at the urban center, either by assumption or by conclusion. Yet no more than about 10 percent of urban employment is located in the central business district in most urban areas. Furthermore, such monocentric models cannot possibly comprehend the extent of residential suburbanization that exists in many large urban areas, or the complexity of commuting patters. Despite a few fine papers, no theoretical models come close to an adequate analysis of this phenomenon. It might be added that the numerical simulation models have also made hardly any progress with the issue. Most scholars versed in urban spatial analysis have been aware of the situation and its importance for a decade or more. Lack of progress apparently stems mostly from the difficulty of the problem.

Finally, one wonders whether theoretical urban economists will again borrow tools of analysis from other specialties and use them to shed light on urban spatial issues. A couple of examples will provide concrete suggestions.

In the industrial organization literature, an enormous number of publications have analyzed the effects of uncertainty and asymmetrical information availability among and between firms and consumers on market behavior. Almost no such analysis is in a spatial context and none seems to have influenced urban economists. Yet the analysis may have important urban spatial implications. In many contexts, information becomes less plentiful and/or more costly at greater distance from relevant events. Thus, information availability and costs may affect location and market performance. Some papers have introduced such spatial considerations in job search models, but there is little evidence of any influence on urban business location analysis. Some writers have thought that technical and market information may be more available, especially to small firms, in high density central business district locations. This has led to the so-called incubator hypothesis. But the analysis has not been incorporated in formal models of firm behavior.

A second example of where urban economists might borrow is from financial market analysis. Such analysis has developed sophisticated models of the effects of risk on investment and portfolio decisions. Risk of asset price fluctuations is positively correlated with asset longevity. That suggests that dwellings and other structures such as offices and hotels are assets subject to unusually great risk.

Formal risk analysis has had no influence on housing demand analyses, and little or none on spatial analysis of structures of any kind.

It seems likely that theoretical urban economics will continue to thrive. Scholars familiar with the theoretical literature can think of problems that are challenging and important. The above examples are merely suggestive. Undoubtedly, some theoretical research will involve spatial detail and some will not. Probably, most of the easy spatial analysis has by now been done. To say that urban economists are by now aware of how difficult and time consuming additional spatial analysis will be is not to say that they will not undertake it; it is merely to predict that they will be more careful than in the past to introduce just the spatial detail needed to solve the problems they pose.

It is difficult to predict what kinds of applied research will predominate during coming years. If one asks where there are issues that urban economics can shed light on, where data are available and where government policy edification can improve people's lives in important ways, one naturally thinks of developing countries. Every subject surveyed in this volume could be studied in the context of developing countries. But such research depends on institutional support, and future trends for support in this area are difficult to predict.

In a developed country context, issues are less urgent, but funds, data and institutional understanding are easier to come by. Undoubtedly, applied research will grow in many directions. One area that is almost certain to be the subject of more applied research in the future than in the past is public choice studies of local governments. Much fine applied econometric research has been devoted to the estimation of residents' demands for local government services. But little research has been devoted to the study of how local governments work. There is considerable variety among countries and, at least in the United States, within the country. What accounts for the variety, how does it affect the private sector, and what can be done to enable local governments to function better? For example, most U.S. specialists would probably agree that suburban local governments function better than central city local governments. Why?

The most confident prediction is that the boundaries between urban economics and related specialties will become increasingly blurred.

References

Alonso, W. (1964) *Location and land use.* Cambridge: Harvard University Press.
Clark, C. (1951) 'Urban population density'. *Journal of the Royal Statistical Society,* Series, 114:490–496.
Hoover, E.M. (1984) *The location of economic activity.* New York: McGraw-Hill.
Lösch, A. (1954) *The economics of location.* New Haven: Yale University Press.
Marshall, A. (1946) *Principles of economics.* London: Macmillan & Co.
Niedercorn, J. (1963) *An econometric model of metropolitan employment and population growth.* Rand Corporation, RN03758–RC (1974).

Rosen, S. (1974) 'Hedonic prices and implicit markets product differentiation in pure competition', *Journal of Political Economy*, 82:34–55.

Smith, A. (1776) *The wealth of nations*. London: J.M. Dent & Sons.

Tiebout, C. (1956) 'A pure theory of local expenditure', *Journal of Political Economy*, 64:416–424.

Von Thünen, H. Johann (1826) *Der isolierte Staat in Beziehung auf Nationalökonomie und Landwirtschaft*. Stuttgart: Gustav Fischer.

Wingo, L. (1961) *Transportation and urban land*. Washington: Resources for the Future.

PART 1

LOCATIONAL ANALYSIS

Chapter 18

THE THEORY OF URBAN RESIDENTIAL LOCATION

MAHLON STRASZHEIM*

University of Maryland

1. Introduction

The theory of urban residential location is an application of the theory of the household. Utility maximizing households choose a spatial location, with associated location-specific amenities, and amounts of housing and land at that location. The existence of location-specific amenities implies that location is an argument in the consumption set. Since the costs of commuting to work and prices for land or housing generally depend on location, residential location also enters the budget constraint.

Spatial variation in land prices arising out of competition for the most desirable sites generally is a necessary condition for equilibrium in urban models. For example, if all jobs are located at the city center, more centrally located residences confer the advantage of reduced commuting costs. Competition for close-in sites increases their price, with differences in site rents representing the compensating variation which makes less or more attractive sites competitive with one another.

Since location decisions and housing or land prices are jointly determined, household location models are often incorporated into an equilibrium framework determining urban spatial structure (describing the location of all households, the rent gradient, population density, and city size). In order to obtain analytic solutions to equilibrium models, it is necessary to adopt very simple household location models which abstract from many of the complexities of real-world location decisions. While models of urban spatial structure models are the subject of Brueckner's paper (Chapter 20, this volume), the extent to which particular residential location models can be incorporated into tractable general equilibrium models of urban spatial structure is noted throughout this paper.

Section 2 of the paper describes the standard location models of Alonso, Mills, and Muth, the cornerstone of modern neoclassical urban location theory. (This paper does not consider housing "demand" models which do not contain an

* The author gratefully acknowledges support of the Sloan Workshop in Public Economics, University of Maryland.

Handbook of Regional and Urban Economics, Volume II, Edited by E.S. Mills
© *1987, Elsevier Science Publishers B.V.*

explicit location dimension; for example, studies of tenure choice.) The city is described as a featureless plain, with location represented by distance to the city center. Defining space in one dimension and other assumptions of continuity allow use of the calculus and traditional comparative static analysis. Households wish to be near their place of employment at the city center (the city is monocentric). The location decision entails weighing the cost of accessibility to the city center and land rents.

An extension of this model treats the production of transportation services as endogenous. Transportation production functions affect residential location choices both because land used for transportation is unavailable for residential use and because transportation prices may reflect land or congestion costs. When congestion exists, transportation costs, travel patterns, and location choices are jointly determined. The third section of the paper reviews Mills' seminal work describing transportation costs in urban models and subsequent extensions of this approach.

Section 4 examines several models of neighborhood choice, including models where neighborhood characteristics are multi-dimensional and location is represented in a rectangular coordinate system. The final section of the paper describes models with decentralized employment opportunities and where both residential location and work place location are endogenous.

2. The standard monocentric model

2.1. The Alonso land market model

The forerunner of modern urban location theory is Alonso's (1964) model of the land market. Households' choices of a location and a consumption bundle are described by a static utility maximization model. Households maximize utility $V(z, q, u)$, where u denotes distance from the household's residence to the city center, q is the amount of land, and z is the composite good (numeraire below). The utility function is assumed increasing, continuous, twice differentiable, strictly quasi-concave and decreasing in u, with marginal utilities as follows: V_q, $V_z > 0$, $V_u < 0$. The inclusion of distance in the utility function represents distaste for commuting. The household's transportation expenditures to the center, $T(u)$, increase with distance, while the price of land, $r(u)$, is a decreasing function of distance:

$$\frac{\partial r}{\partial u} < 0, \qquad \frac{\partial T}{\partial u} > 0.$$

Land prices must be lower at less central locations because less central locations entail greater commuting costs.

From the Lagrangian, $V(z, q, u) - \lambda[z + qr(u) + T(u) - y]$, the first order conditions are as follows:

$$V_z - \lambda = 0,$$

$$V_q - \lambda r(u) = 0,$$

$$V_u - \lambda \left(q \frac{\partial r}{\partial u} + \frac{\partial T}{\partial u} \right) = 0,$$

$$z + r(u)q + T(u) - y = 0, \tag{1}$$

where y denotes income and the subscripts denote partial derivatives. The first two conditions imply that at the optimal location the marginal rate of substitution between z and q equals the ratio of prices:

$$\frac{V_z}{V_q} = \frac{1}{r(u)} . \tag{2}$$

The third condition defines location equilibrium. The household's decision to locate nearer or farther from the center entails trading off commuting and land costs. Substituting for $\lambda = V_z$, the marginal utility of income,

$$\frac{\partial r}{\partial u} q = - \left(\frac{\partial T}{\partial u} - V_u / V_z \right) \tag{3}$$

The r.h.s. is merely the change in transport outlays plus the monetized value of the disutility of a longer commute, V_u / V_z, which at the optimal location must equal the change in outlays for land.

A similar model by Beckmann (1974) and Henderson (1985) illustrates how Alonso's distance term can be interpreted in terms of leisure time. Include leisure time, assumed inversely related to commuting time, in the utility function rather than distance. Monetary costs of commuting are omitted. The time constraint $(24 - L(u) - t(u) = 0)$ is included in the Lagrangian, where $L(u)$ denotes leisure and $t(u)$ travel time. Letting γ and λ denote the Lagrangian multipliers, the marginal utilities of leisure and income, respectively, maximizing with respect to u yields the location equilibrium condition:

$$\frac{\partial r}{\partial u} q = - \frac{V_L}{\lambda} \frac{\partial t}{\partial u}, \tag{4}$$

where V_L is the marginal utility of leisure. The r.h.s. is the monetized value of the change in leisure, the marginal rate of substitution of income for leisure, multiplied by the marginal change in leisure associated with increasing commuting distance. Location equilibrium occurs when decreased housing costs of a longer commute just are offset by the increased costs of foregone leisure. This is the equivalent condition as the Alonso model, eq. (3), where monetary commuting costs are zero.

2.2. Bid rents

An alternative view of the location decision presented by Alonso is that of a competitive land market in which households bid for available space, and land owners offer land to the highest bidder. Alonso defines a "bid rent function" as the set of amounts households would bid for land at alternative distances and achieve a given level of utility. The bid rent function is equivalent to a "price indifference curve." A family of non-intersecting bid rent functions exists, with the level of utility inversely related to the level of bid rents. How much households must bid and hence the level of utility depends on the extent of competition from other bidders, households offering a bid just sufficiently high to secure a location.

The properties of location equilibrium and the bid rent function can be derived analytically using the indirect utility function [Solow (1973)].[1] Substituting the ordinary demand equations given by the first order conditions (1) yields the indirect utility function, V^*.

$V[\bar{z}(I(u),r(u)), \bar{q}(I(u),r(u)), u] = V^*[I(u),r(u),u]$, where I(u) denotes income at location u net of transportation cost, $I(u) = y - T(u)$, bars over z and q denote the utility maximizing solution, and $V_I^* > 0$, $V_r^* < 0$, and $V_u^* < 0$. The indirect utility function implicitly defines land rents at every distance such that utility is everywhere the same.

A property of the indirect utility function used below to define bid rents is Roy's Identity. Partially differentiate the indirect utility function:

$$V_r^* = V_z\left(\bar{z}_r + \frac{V_q}{V_z}\bar{q}_r\right),$$

$$V_z^* = V_z\left(\bar{z}_I + \frac{V_q}{V_z}\bar{q}_I\right), \tag{5}$$

---

[1] Bid rent gradients can also be derived using the duality theory of consumption [Nelson (1972); Wheaton (1974); McDonald (1979)]. Consider as given the level of utility realized by households with given income making utility maximizing choices at a given location. At an alternative location there exists a rent level which leaves households just as well off, compensating for differences in transportation costs. Land rents at alternative sites are viewed as endogenous, conditional on income, prices of other goods and the level of utility. With prices of all other goods and income fixed, the derivation of compensating rent variation is equivalent to finding that set of land rents which maximizes payments to landlords at alternative locations, or to minimizing the amounts spent on goods other than land.

where subscripts r and I denote partial derivatives with respect to $r(u)$ and $I(u)$. Differentiating the budget constraint

$$q + r\bar{q}_r + \bar{z}_r = 0, \tag{6}$$

$$r\bar{q}_I + \bar{z}_I = 1, \tag{7}$$

and substitution of (6), (7), and the first order condition, $V_q/V_z = r(u)$, into (5) implies Roy's Identity:

$$\frac{V_r^*}{V_I^*} = -q, \tag{8}$$

Roy's Identity has a similar interpretation as in a non-spatial context. V_r is the increase in utility from a dollar decline in land prices at the optimal location: this must equal the marginal utility of a dollar times the change in dollars available at distance u, in this case the quantity of land consumed multiplied by the marginal utility of income.

The bid rent function is given by differentiating the indirect utility function:

$$dV^* = V_r^* \frac{dr}{du} - V_I^* \frac{dT}{du} + V_u^*. \tag{9}$$

Dividing by V_I^*, substituting Roy's Identity, and noting $V_I^* = V_z$, yields an expression for the slope of the bid rent gradient.

$$\frac{dr}{du} = \frac{1}{q}\left(\frac{V_u}{V_z} - \frac{dT}{du}\right). \tag{10}$$

The first order differential equation in $r(u)$ can be integrated to yield the bid rent gradient for any stated level of utility. Expression (10) is merely the first order condition describing location equilibrium. Because $V_u < 0$, both terms in parenthesis in the r.h.s. of (10) are negative, implying a declining bid rent gradient.

The bid rent gradient is conditional on the level of utility. A family of non-intersecting bid rent gradients will exist, each gradient corresponding to a given level of utility, with bid rents inversely related to utility. Specification of the initial conditions necessary to yield a particular solution to eq. (10) is discussed below.

The shape of the bid rent gradient can also be derived using the Envelope Theorem. According to the Envelope Theorem, if $V^*(\alpha)$ is the solution to maximizing $V(\alpha)$ subject to $g(\alpha) = 0$, and α is a parameter of interest, $\partial V^*/\partial \alpha$ is given by the derivative of the Lagrangian, L, of the maximization problem with respect to α. In this case, given the indirect utility function $V^*(u)$, and assuming $dy = 0$, the derivative of the Lagrangian is as follows:

$$V_u^* = L_u = V_u - \lambda \left(q \frac{dr}{du} + \frac{dT}{du} \right). \tag{11}$$

Totally differentiating the indirect utility function, noting $\lambda = V_z$, and substituting (11) yields the bid rent function:

$$dV^* = V_u^* \, du = 0,$$

$$\frac{dr}{du} = \frac{1}{q} \left(\frac{V_u^*}{V_r^*} - \frac{dT}{du} \right). \tag{12}$$

Further conclusions about the shape of bid rent functions, land consumption, and population density require additional assumptions about the utility function and commuting costs. Differentiating (12) again, the condition for bid rents to be convex $(\partial^2 r / \partial u^2) > 0)$ depends on the marginal rate of substitution of land and distance (leisure) and on the transportation cost function:

$$\frac{\partial^2 r}{\partial u^2} = -\frac{\partial q / \partial u}{q^2} \left(\frac{V_u}{V_z} - \frac{\partial T}{\partial u} \right) + \frac{1}{q} \left(\frac{\partial (V_u / V_z)}{\partial u} - \frac{\partial^2 T}{\partial u^2} \right).$$

The first term in parentheses is negative from the first order conditions. However, when u enters the utility function, the marginal rate of substitution of q and u will vary with distance, and no conclusion can be drawn about $(\partial q / \partial u)$, hence the entire first term is of indeterminate sign.

The second term also may be of either sign, and involves assumptions about travel outlays and the marginal rate of substitution of distance for other goods. The term in brackets is the marginal change in marginal commuting costs at any given distance, and includes the monetized value of time spent in a longer commute, which will likely increase as commuting time increases with distance.

Considerable attention has been devoted to analyzing the effect of income on bid rent functions, location, and consumption choices. In a competitive land market bidders with different bid rent gradients arrange themselves by the height of their bid rent gradient, with bidders with the steepest bid rent gradient occupying the most central location. For the slopes of bid rent gradients to decrease as income rises, $d(\partial r / \partial u)/dy > 0$. Again, qualitative conclusions about income effects on the steepness of bid rent gradients require additional assumptions about the utility function. It is likely that both land and leisure are superior goods. Differentiating the bid rent function with respect to income, and denoting the marginal rate of substitution of other goods and leisure by $\psi(u) = V_u / V_z$ yields:

$$\frac{d(\partial r/\partial u)}{dy} = -\frac{dq/dy}{q^2}\psi(u) + \frac{1}{q}\frac{d\psi}{dy} = \frac{\psi(u)}{qy}[\eta_{\psi y} - \eta_{qy}],\tag{13}$$

where $\eta_{\psi y}$ denotes the elasticity of the marginal rate of substitution of other goods for leisure with respect to income, and η_{qy} denotes the income elasticity of land. The sign of the derivative (13) will depend on the income elasticity of land and the income elasticity of the marginal valuation of distance. Both are assumed to be positive, hence the term in brackets in (13) can be of either sign. Thus the slope of the bid rent gradient decreases with income only when the income elasticity of land exceeds the income elasticity of the marginal valuation of distance.

Empirical evidence indicates that land is a superior good and that higher income households tend to live in more suburban locations in most cities in the United States [Wheaton (1977 a,b); Straszheim (1975)]. However, interpretation of actual location patterns must consider factors besides those in the simple Alonso model. Superior environmental amenities, public services, and better quality housing are the most frequently cited factors which would explain high income households' willingness to bid more for distant sites. Whatever the basis for preferring more distance sites, these outweigh the disutility to higher income households of longer commutes. These income location patterns are less pronounced in cities in other countries.

2.3. Simplifying the Alonso model

Simplifying the specification of the Alonso location model yields additional qualitative conclusions about bid rent functions, land consumption, and population density. One frequently used simplification omits distance from the utility function, representing all commuting costs as monetary outlays in the budget constraint.[2] [Muth (1969), Mills (1967, 1972), Wheaton (1974]. The location equation condition (3) and the slope of the bid rent gradient (10) simplify to

$$\frac{\partial r}{\partial u} = -\frac{1}{q}\left(\frac{\partial T}{\partial u}\right).\tag{14}$$

Land consumption patterns can be readily derived. Totally differentiating the indirect utility function and substituting Roy's Identity, the compensated (or Hicksian) demand for land at a given level of utility is the reciprocal of the partial

---

[2]The Muth–Mills models include housing rather than land in the utility functions, as described below. The exclusion of distance or time from the utility function is the simplification yielding many of the qualitative results of these models.

derivative of bid rent function with respect to income.

$$dV^* = V_I^* \, dI + V_r^* \, dr = 0,$$

$$q(u) = 1/(dr/dI). \tag{15}$$

Since the own substitution effect is negative, $(\partial q/\partial r) \leqslant 0$, and bid rents decline with distance, land consumption will be a non-decreasing function of distance: $\partial q/\partial u = (\partial q/\partial r)/(\partial r/\partial u) > 0$. Residential density, the inverse of land consumption, $1/q(u)$, must decline with distance. The population gradient can be readily derived knowing the supply of land: $n(u) = \theta u/q(u)$, where θ is the fraction of land at u available for housing, $(0 < \theta < 2\pi)$ and n is population.

Whether the bid rent function is a convex function of distance depends on transportation costs. Differentiating (14) again

$$\frac{\partial^2 r}{\partial u^2} = -\frac{(\partial^2 T/\partial u^2)}{q(u)} + \frac{(\partial q/\partial u)}{q(u)^2} \frac{\partial T}{\partial u}. \tag{16}$$

The second term is positive since $(\partial q/\partial u) > 0$. A sufficient condition for $(\partial^2 r/\partial u^2) > 0$ is that $(\partial^2 T/\partial u^2)$ be non-positive. If the transportation cost function is a linear or concave function of distance, the bid rent function will be convex.

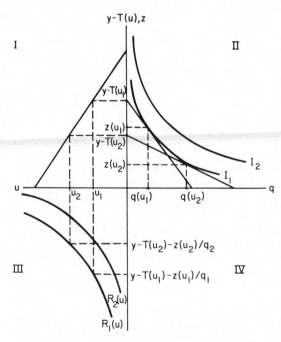

Figure 1. Consumption bundles and bid rents.

The solution to the simplified Alonso model is portrayed in Figure 1. In the illustration transportation outlays are assumed linear, hence net income available for consumption is linear, (upper left gradient, quadrant I), though this assumption can be relaxed. Households' utility maximizing consumption bundles at alternative locations are illustrated in quadrant II. At the close-in location u_1, households choose $z(u_1)$, $q(u_1)$, the budget line tangent to indifference curve I_1. Households' bid rent at u_1 is given by slope of the budget line portrayed in gradient III. At a more distant location u_2, by a lower price of land, tangency with the indifference curve is at a higher level of q. With convex indifference curves, the bid rent must be lower at u_2 than at u_1. The bid rent function R_1 is the locus of points defined by tangency at each point along the indifference curve, I_1. If a higher utility level is assumed, denoted by I_2, bid rents must be lower at every distance, as shown by R_2.

2.4. Muth–Mills housing models

A closely related class of residential location models [Mills (1967), Muth (1969)] includes a commodity "housing" rather than land in the preference set. Housing is produced with land and non-land inputs, hence households have a derived demand for land, dependent on both preferences for housing and the technical characteristics of the housing production function. Factor proportions and hence residential density reflect the elasticity of substitution in housing production. This formulation provides important insights into the source of declining gradients for density and capital–land ratios (building heights). (The Muth–Mills model is described by Brueckner, this volume.)

In Muth's original formulation, travel costs $T(u, y)$ depend on distance and income, the income variable representing value of time considerations, with higher income households perceiving higher travel costs, $(T_y > 0)$. Distance is omitted from the utility function. Households maximize utility subject to a budget constraint where q denotes housing, available at price $P(u)$, the Lagrangian is $V(z, q) - \lambda(z + P(u)q + T(u, Y) - y)$. The first order conditions are identical to those of the Alonso model, with the exception of the location equilibrium condition, which is now simplified:

$$-\frac{\partial P}{\partial u} q = \frac{\partial T}{\partial u}. \tag{17}$$

At the optimal location the increase in transport costs of a marginally longer commute must be offset by the associated saving in housing costs.

Muth's model can be used to infer a value of time from observed location choices. The location equilibrium condition can be rewritten:

$$-\frac{\partial P/\partial u}{P(u)} = \frac{\partial T/\partial u}{P(u)q}. \tag{18}$$

The l.h.s. and the denominator of the r.h.s. are observable, allowing calculation of marginal time costs. By subtracting marginal commuting outlays from $(\partial T/\partial u)$, the remaining marginal travel costs can be attributed to time costs.

The comparative statics of Muth's model have been presented by DeSalvo (1977). Considering only the effects of income changes, differentiating the first-order conditions yields the following linear system:

$$[B]\begin{pmatrix} dz \\ dq \\ du \\ d\lambda \end{pmatrix} = \begin{pmatrix} 0 \\ 0 \\ \lambda T_{uy}\,dy \\ -(1-T_y)dy \end{pmatrix},$$

where   (19)

$$B = \begin{bmatrix} V_{zz} & V_{zq} & 0 & -1 \\ V_{qz} & V_{qq} & -\lambda P_u & -P(u) \\ 0 & -\lambda P_u & -\lambda(P_{uu}q+T_{uu}) & 0 \\ -1 & -P(u) & 0 & 0 \end{bmatrix} < 0.$$

(Elements B_{43} and B_{34} are 0 because of the first order condition for location equilibrium.) The signs of the income effects are ambiguous, since a change in income has two opposite effects on location; higher incomes increase travel costs, encouraging households to choose a more close-in location, while increasing the demand for housing, encouraging households to locate at a greater distance, where housing is cheaper. If we assume income does not affect travel costs, then the income effect on distance can be determined.

$$[B]\begin{bmatrix} dz \\ dq \\ du \\ d\lambda \end{bmatrix} = \begin{bmatrix} 0 \\ 0 \\ 0 \\ -dy \end{bmatrix},$$

$$du = \frac{B^{*3}}{B} = \frac{D^{43}}{D}\,dy,$$

$$dq = \frac{B^{*2}}{B} = -\frac{D^{42}}{D}\,dy, \tag{20}$$

where B^{*i} is the determinant of the matrix replacing the ith column by the vector on the r.h.s. of (15) and D^{4i} is the value of the r, i cofactor of B. Using (20),

$$\frac{\partial u}{\partial y} = \frac{D^{43}}{D} = \frac{D^{43}}{(-dy\, D^{42})/dq} = -\frac{dq}{dy}\frac{D^{43}}{D^{42}}. \tag{21}$$

Examining the determinants shows $D_{43}/D_{42} < 0$; hence the income effect on distance has the same sign as the income effect on housing. This result is evident from the first order condition; those preferring more housing will choose a more distant location, absent any income effect on commuting costs.

If competitive conditions prevail in housing and land markets, housing and land prices will vary so profits are everywhere zero. Location advantages reflected in housing prices will be capitalized into the price of the fixed factor, land. Spatial variations in the price of housing $P(u)$ will be translated into variation in land prices, factor proportions, and population density. The following summarizes the theory of competitive equilibrium in the housing and land markets developed by Muth (1964, 1969).

Let housing supply be $q = f(k, l)$, where k is capital and l is land inputs. (Labour inputs are excluded, to preclude employment opportunities outside the city center.) Profits are given by $\pi = P(u)q - \delta k(u) - r(u)l(u)$, where δ is the constant rental rate of capital and $r(u)$ is land rents. The bid rent gradient for land which yields zero profits everywhere can be derived in an analogous fashion as in Alonso-type models. Totally differentiating the profit function and substituting the marginal productivity conditions implicitly defines a land rent gradient such that prices are everywhere zero. Alternatively, Henderson (1985) notes that the same result can be derived from properties of the unit cost function. Let $C(u)$ denote unit costs, which must equal the price in a competitive equilibrium with zero profit. Differentiating unit cost and substituting Shepherd's Lemma, $(\partial C(u)/\partial r(u)) = (l(u)/q(u))$, yields an expression in the bid rent gradient for land:

$$\frac{\partial P}{\partial u} = \frac{\partial C(u)}{\partial u} = \frac{\partial C}{\partial r(u)}\frac{\partial r(u)}{\partial u}$$

$$\frac{\partial r(u)}{\partial u} = \frac{q(u)}{l(u)}\frac{\partial P}{\partial u}, \tag{22}$$

(22) implies changes in housing expenditures at u must equal the change in land rents paid to housing producers.

Denoting land's share of total revenue as $\rho_l = l(u)r(u)/P(u)q(u)$, the bid rent gradient for land may be written as follows:

$$\frac{\partial r/\partial u}{r(u)} = \frac{1}{\rho_l(u)}\frac{\partial P/\partial u}{P(u)}. \tag{23}$$

Except in the special case where the production function has constant returns to scale and unitary elasticity of substitution, factor shares will vary with distance. Since ρ_l is likely small (e.g. 0.10), the slope of the bid rent gradient for land will be many times greater than the slope of the bid rent gradient for housing.

The capital-land ratio, a commonly employed measure of the intensity of urban land use, is also a negative function of distance. Let σ denote the elasticity of substitution in the production of housing:

$$\sigma = d(\ln(k(u)/l(u))/d(\ln(r(u)/\delta)).$$

Since δ is constant, the denominator simplifies to $d\ln(r(u)) = (\partial r/\partial u)/r(u)$. Factor proportions therefore vary with the slopes of the bid rent or housing price gradients:

$$\frac{\partial r/\partial u}{r(u)} = \frac{\sigma}{\rho_1(u)} \left[\frac{\partial P/\partial u}{P(u)} \right]. \tag{24}$$

Estimates of σ range from 0.5 to 1.0, hence the percentage change in factor proportions at any given distance will be many times greater than the percentage change in housing prices [McDonald (1979)]. Population density, the increase of land consumption per person at any distance, can be readily derived. Density depends on preferences and the production function, the latter affecting how much land is used to produce each unit of housing desired.

The most common specification of the traditional monocentric model uses logarithmic-linear functions [Henderson (1985)]. Let consumers maximize $V = A'z^b q(u)^c L(u)^d$, where $L(u)$ is leisure, subject to income and budget constraints: $y - z - P(u)q(u) = 0$, and $24 - L(u) - tu = 0$. Letting λ and γ denote the Lagrangian multipliers for the budget and time constraints, respectively, the location equilibrium is as follows:

$$q(u)\frac{\partial P(u)}{\partial u} = -t\frac{V\mathrm{d}}{\lambda L(u)} = t\frac{V_L}{V_z}. \tag{25}$$

At the optimal location, changes in housing outlays are offset by the monetized value of lost leisure. The demand for housing is $q(u) = (cy/(b+c+d))P(u)^{-1}$. Integrating the location equilibrium condition, and using rent at the outer boundary of the city, u_1, as the initial condition, yields the housing price gradient:

$$\frac{\partial P(u)}{\partial u} = -(td/c)P(u)(T - tu)^{-1},$$

$$P(u) = C(T - du)^{d/c} = P(u_1)(T - tu_1)^{-d/c}(T - tu)^{d/c}. \tag{26}$$

Assuming a Cobb–Douglas technology for housing, $q(u) = B'(u)^\alpha k(u)^{1-\alpha}$, housing producers' demand for land is

$$l(u) = \alpha q(u)P(u)r(u)^{-1} = (\alpha c/f)yr(u)^{-1}. \tag{27}$$

The unit cost function is:

$$P(u) = C(u) = B'\alpha^{-\alpha}(1-\alpha)^{(1-\alpha)}r(u)^{\alpha}r^{1-\alpha},$$

which when inverted yields the bid rent gradient:

$$r(u) = r(u_1)(T - tu_1)^{-d/c\alpha}(T - tu)^{d/c\alpha}. \tag{28}$$

The slope of the bid rent gradient is $1/\alpha$ times steeper than the price gradient.

More complicated specifications of preferences, transportation costs, and the production function for housing have also been used in urban models, and generally the resultant rent and density gradients must be approximated numerically. If longer commutes are more costly, land rent will be a declining function in distance, while density will be positively related to land rents and to the elasticity of substitution. Muth (1975) and Kau and Lee (1976) have analyzed a constant elasticity of substitution production function, and Kirmans, Kau and Lee (1979) used a variable elasticity of substitution production function. McDonald (1981) surveys empirical studies of housing production functions, discussing a number of econometric issues in interpreting estimates of the elasticity of substitution.

One extension of the Muth–Mills model involves a reinterpretation of the housing production function. Preferences may be rewritten as $V(z, q(k, l))$, households assumed indifferent to the capital-labor ratio chosen by producers. The consumer buys three goods, z, k, and l, with preferences for k and l weakly separable, the marginal rate of substitution of k and l independent of the amount of z purchased. McDonald (1979) notes that the housing production function is really acting to aggregate tastes, and that the assumption of a weakly separable utility function implies that the Allen partial elasticities of substitution of z for k and z for l are equal. If the "production" function is homogeneous of degree one, this implies that the income elasticities for k and l are equal. This assumption is quite restrictive, and there is some evidence that income elasticities for land may differ from elasticities of other characteristics of housing in the single family housing market. Brueckner (1983) introduces lot size explicitly in the utility function as well as including land as one of the "inputs" to produce housing.

The Muth–Mills approach using neoclassical production functions for housing is well suited to describing the multi-family housing market, where the output "housing" could be viewed as apartments of a given size, and where consumers might be considered indifferent to the land-capital (density) chosen by producers.

Another extension of the Muth–Mills approach recognizes the durability of the housing stock. In a static model with malleable capital the value of land always equals the value of its marginal product. A more realistic view would recognize that residential capital is durable and is costly to convert or replace. A putty-clay technology might better describe housing investments. The growth of an urban area can be viewed as a "layering" process in which new housing capital is continually added to past capital investments, which generally remain unmodified. Durable housing capital earns returns reflecting prevailing market competition for that capital.

The Muth–Mills model has been extended to cases in which housing capital is durable, with urban spatial structure viewed in dynamic context. (See Arnott's chapter, this volume.) Anas (1978) developed a dynamic version of the Alonso–Muth models in which the city's history is described by a series of time periods, each characterized by given population, income and transport costs. In each period additions are made to the housing stock. Prices of the fixed capital stock built in earlier time periods adjust so that all housing yields equal utility. Wheaton (1978a,b) has extended this model in two respects, by introducing perfect foresight on the part of developers and by allowing capital to depreciate. These extensions of the basic housing model capture an important characteristic of housing production functions, though at the cost of added complexity in modeling location and investment equilibria over time.

2.5. Equilibrium conditions

Bid rent functions for households and firms described above as differential equations in distance define bid rents up to a constant of integration. Determining a particular solution requires additional assumptions about bidding in the land market. The level of utility of bidders might be specified, which determines a bid rent level; or the number and types of bidders in the land market might be specified, in which case competition for available land determines each agent's bid for land and the associated level of utility. This latter approach is more ambitious since it entails specifying the conditions yielding an equilibrium solution to the location pattern for all agents, i.e. an equilibrium solution to urban spatial structure.

The simplest formulation of competitive equilibrium assumes all bidders have identical incomes and preferences, hence a common set of bid rent functions. In this circumstance land prices could not be such that any one location were a unique solution to the location problem, since insufficient land would be available at that location to satisfy all households, and land would be unutilized at other sites. Equilibrium in the land market results when market prices for land within the city coincide with households' common bid rent gradient, that set of prices such that households would be indifferent to any point along the gradient.

Two approaches have been used to define such an equilibrium, implying different assumptions about the dynamics of city size and migration [Wheaton (1974)]. The so-called "open city" model specifies a level of utility $\bar{V}$ which must be realized. It is assumed that land rent at the outer boundary of the city equals the rent for land in agricultural use, R_A, invariant with respect to distance. The outer boundary u_1 is such that all persons have a place to reside. These conditions are as follows:

$$r(u_1) = R_A,$$ (29a)

$$V^*(y - T(u_1), r(u_1)) = \bar{V},$$ (29b)

$$\int_0^{u_1} 2\pi u/q(u) = N,$$ (29c)

which uniquely determine rents at the center, $r(0)$, the outer boundary, and a city population, N, such that households achieve the given level of utility. The level of utility might be viewed as that prevailing in other cities, on the presumption that migration occurs until city size yields the level of utility realized elsewhere.

The alternative approach, the "closed city" model specifies city population, and hence equations (29) are solved for the boundary of the city, rents at the center, and the utility level.

Comparative static analyses of a simplified version of the Alonso model, omitting distance from the utility function, are presented by Wheaton (1974). By making assumptions about income elasticities he is able to fully describe how changes in income and transportation costs affect city size and the level of rents. Brueckner's chapter (this volume) follows this approach in describing an equilibrium solution to urban spatial structure using the Muth–Mills model.

An extension of the open city formulation treats income as endogenous, introducing a production sector in the city center which is the source of employment and earnings for city residents. A centrally located production sector "exports" to a national market and can sell any amount at the prevailing price. The export sector employs city residents who live outside the city center. The production sector is characterized by increasing returns to scale, which is the source of agglomeration economies necessary for a city of non-negligible size. [Mills (1967, 1972)]. The specification below follows Henderson (1985). Export production includes a Hicks neutral shift factor indicating economies of scale that are dependent on total city employment:

$$x(u) = G(N)x[l(u), k(u), n(u)]$$

where x is output, l is land, k is capital, n is labor, N is total city employment, and G is an agglomeration shift factor. Agglomeration economies are positive in N, and exhibit diminishing returns:

$$\frac{\partial G}{\partial N} > 0, \quad \frac{\partial^2 G}{\partial N^2} < 0.$$

Since all export output is shipped from the city center, export firms have a declining bid rent gradient for land, reflecting the transport cost advantages of being near the center. Denoting the price net of transport costs for firms located at any u by $P(u)$, bid rents depend on agglomeration effects and the net price: $r_f(u) = r(P(u), G(N))$, where the subscript f denotes export firms.

The conditions defining equilibrium can be easily summarized. First, the zero profit condition in the export sector implicitly defines a relationship between output price, land rents, and wages, W, at the city center:

$$\pi(P_x, r_f(0), W) = 0. \tag{30}$$

Second, at the boundary between centrally located export production and surrounding residences, (u_0), bid rents of the export sector and the residential sector coincide:

$$r_f(P(u_0), G(N)) = r_h(u_0), \tag{31}$$

where $r_h(u_0)$ denotes the household sector's bid rent for land at the boundary. As noted above, the household sector's bid rent gradient for land depends on income, the level of utility, preferences, transportation costs, and the production function for housing. Third, per capita income y, is the sum of wage income and a proportionate share of land rents distributed to all city residents:

$$y = W + \frac{1}{N}\left[\int_0^{u_0} r_f(u)\, du + \int_{u_0}^{u_1} rh(u)\, du\right]. \tag{32}$$

Fourth, all persons employed from the city center to distance u_0 must reside in the area from u_0 to the city's outer boundary, u_1.

$$\int_0^{u_0} 2\pi u(n_f(u)/l_f(u))\, du = \int_{u_0}^{u_1} 2\pi u\, l_h(u)^{-1}\, du, \tag{33}$$

where subscripts f and h denote the export and residential sectors' demands for land and labor. Each can be readily expressed from the marginal productivity conditions for the production of export and housing goods. The l.h.s. will depend on the endogenous variables N, w, u_0, and $r(0)$, while the r.h.s. will depend on the endogenous variables y, u_0, u_1. Equation (33) replaces eq. (25c) in the simpler formulation.

Equilibrium is defined by the solution of eqs. (30), (31), (32), (33), (29a), and (29b). These six equations jointly determine six endogenous variables, u_0, u_1, W, y, $r(0)$, and N, with utility in the city exogenous. The level of export and housing producers' bids for land at any distance can be determined knowing rents at the city center, $r(0)$. Total city output is readily determined from the aggregate production function.

City size and realized utility are determined by the extent of agglomeration economies and the costs of transport. In Henderson's formulation agglomeration economies exhibit diminishing returns, which limits the extent to which increases in export production and population allow firms to pay ever higher wages. In addition, transportation costs take an ever increasing share of total output as population and the size of the city increase. The latter results in a city of determinate size.

Another extension of the monocentric model introduces variation in bid rent functions across households. Each class of bidders maximizes utility by bidding the least possible, subject to the constraint that all members of each class of bidders secure a location within the city. Land will be sold to the highest bidder. Unless bid rent functions coincide, segregated land patterns will emerge, with boundaries between sectors dependent on the number of bidders of each class and the amount of land available at each location.

When there are multiple classes of bidders, finding an equilibrium solution analytically is generally complex. There are relatively few models presenting closed form solutions with multiple classes of bidders. One approach to such models represents variation among classes of bidders parametrically. For example, a common utility function is assumed, and a density function describes variation among households in income or parameters of the utility function. The solution specifies the distance from the center chosen by households with given incomes or tastes. Beckmann (1969) and Montesano (1972) present a model in which persons have a common utility function but income varies according to the Pareto distribution. This implies that there is continuous variation in bid rent gradients among persons, and persons of a given income will have a unique location in equilibrium. This is a problem in change of variable, a procedure introducing one (or more) additional differential equations into the model. While this procedure is very flexible in principle, in practice it is difficult to find realistic specifications of distribution functions which yield tractable results. Typically such models involve complex differential equations which require numerical solutions.

2.6. Optimum cities

In the equilibrium solutions described above, households with equal endowments or income are treated equally, and realize a common level of utility regardless of location. In the absence of externalities, such as congestion costs, this equilibrium is Pareto-efficient.

Optimal cities are a location pattern which maximizes a social welfare function $W(U_1 \ldots U_j \ldots)$, where U_j is the utility of the jth individual. The most frequently used welfare function is a Benthamite form of individual utilities:

$$W = \int_0^{u_1} V(z(u), q(u)) n(u) \mathrm{d}u$$

where $n(u)$ denotes the number of households residing at u. The most notable contribution of the literature on optimal cities, first noted by Mirrlees (1972), is the conclusion that a utilitarian planner could increase social welfare by treating households with identical tastes "unequally", for example, by altering the distribution of income so that some households are better off expost than others.[3] The planner will seek to redistribute income among households unless the marginal utility of income is everywhere constant. If the marginal utility of income varies with distance to the city center, social welfare could be increased by transferring income from those with low marginal utilities to those with high. Thus, the planner will not accept an equal utility outcome except in the special case where marginal utilities of income are constant for persons located at every distance.

Returning to the market equilibrium location patterns described in the previous section, it will generally be true that whereas utility is equal at every distance along the bid rent gradient, the marginal utility of incomes varies with location. This result has been noted by Wheaton (1974), Kanemoto (1980), and Wildasin (1984). Consider the special case where land and other goods appear in the utility function (but distance is omitted). Differentiating the indirect utility function:

$$V_r^* \frac{\partial r}{\partial u} + V_I^* \frac{\partial I}{\partial u} = 0,$$

$$\frac{\partial r}{\partial u} = -\frac{V_I^*}{V_r^*} \frac{\partial I}{\partial u}, \tag{34}$$

and differentiating Roy's Identity with respect to I,

$$-q_I = (V_{rI}^* + qV_{II}^*)/V_I^*. \tag{35}$$

Differentiating the marginal utility of income, and using (34) and (35):

$$\partial V_I^*/\partial u = V_{Ir}^* \left(\frac{\partial r}{\partial u} \right) + V_{II}^* \frac{\partial I}{\partial u}$$

$$= (V_{Ir}^* + qV_{II}^*) \left(\frac{\partial I}{\partial u}/q \right)$$

$$= q_I \frac{V_I^*(\partial I/\partial u)}{q}. \tag{36}$$

Equation (36) reveals how the marginal utility of income varies with location. As $\partial I/\partial u < 0$, the r.h.s. of (36) has the same sign as q_I, the income elasticity of demand for land. In the special case where the latter is zero, the marginal utility of income is constant. When q_I is positive, the marginal utility of income rises with distance.

---

[3] This result has also been analyzed by Riley (1973), Arnott and Riley (1977) and Levhari, Oron, and Pines (1978).

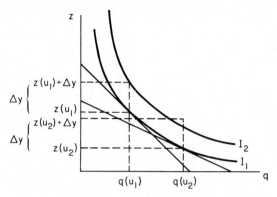

Figure 2. Marginal utility of income varies with location.

The result can be portrayed graphically (see Figure 2). The household residing at u_1 consumes the $z(u_1), q(u_1)$ pair: In the case considered here, with distance omitted from the utility function, its choices at a more distant location u_2 would be $z(u_2), q(u_2)$, the point of tangency with the flatter budget line implied by the lower bid rent. In this case, an increment of income, Δy, given to the first household would provide less of a gain in welfare than if given to the second household, reflecting the unequal marginal utilities of income. Only in the case of zero income elasticity of demand, or equal marginal utilities of income, will the transfer be worth the same to the two households, in which case indifference curves shift upward in "parallel" fashion.

This result, that social welfare maximization entails transferring income to those with the highest marginal utilities, yielding an outcome with unequal utilities among residents, is true for virtually all social welfare functions. The only specification which avoids this result employs a Rawlsian welfare function as the objective [Dixit (1973)]; maximizing the well-being of the least well off person permits no inequalities among person. The "equals treated unequally" result can be traced to a hidden non-convexity in location problems arising because no two households can simultaneously occupy the same location. Since commuting costs vary from different locations, some persons are able to realize higher utility than others. This characteristic of solutions, that of unequal utilities, could be eliminated only if all households could share all locations, hence confronting identical consumption possibilities.

3. Transportation production functions and accessibility

Urban models are considerably complicated when a realistic specification of the production function for transportation is included. Several characteristics of production functions for providing transport service must be considered. One of the necessary inputs in the provision of transportation services is the household's time, which must be incurred by each commuting household. Time costs often represent a large fraction of total travel costs.

Different technologies have widely varying factor proportions between land, time costs, and other inputs. The choice of the least cost technology depends on the density of trip ends, corridor volumes, and on the value of travellers' time. Whether public transit systems, which use less land and more of non-land inputs, are optimal depends critically on trip densities. Mass transit systems provide low cost service when many passengers move from one point to another. However, when trip origins are widely dispersed, public systems often prove noneconomic due to high time costs (added time is incurred in beginning a trip on a public system due to infrequent schedule or a long access trip to the public stop). Preferences for low density housing and high valuation on travel time imply that rail systems are not the least-cost mode except when the density of trip destinations and corridor volumes are very high. Car pooling is another means of substituting other inputs for land. However, widely dispersed trip origins or destinations also increase the costs of car-pooling, because of the costs of collecting the car pool. Thus, even when centrally located land commands a very high price, it may be uneconomic to adopt public transit systems which substitute other inputs for land. Automobile systems are the least cost mode for almost all urban trip making in American cities.

Another characteristic or urban transportation technology is that urban highway systems are often characterized by congestion. When traffic volumes affect travel time, transport costs become endogeneous, jointly determined with location choices and and land rents. The existence of congestion poses problems in obtaining Pareto-efficient location and investment decisions. Congestion costs represent a divergence between average and marginal costs of highway use which distorts location decisions in the absence of appropriate Pigovian taxes or tolls.

Similarly, automobile pollution externalities may distort location choices. Air pollution and air quality depend on traffic volumes, speeds, vehicle design, and geological factors which affect the diffusion of particulates. Air quality in particular neighborhoods is therefore jointly determined with location choices. Location choices will be distorted unless prices are charged which internalize these effects.

3.1. Models without congestion

Urban location models initially focused on the role of land in the production of transportation services. Mills (1967, 1970) noted that equilibrium conditions in the land market reflected the fact that land used for transportation was unavailable for consumption. In a monocentric city transportation service supplied at any distance u must accommodate all persons residing beyond that point who must commute to a more central employment site. Assume transportation supply is positively related to land devoted to transport, and that all land is used for transportation or housing. Equilibrium in the transportation market at every point beyond the boundary of central city requires that transport supply must be sufficient to meet demand:

$$S(G(u)) = \int_u^{u_1} D(u')(2\pi u' - G(u')) \, du',$$ (37)

where $D(u)$ is density at u, $G(u)$ is land devoted to transport, $S(\ )$ denotes the supply function for transportation. The transport sector's demand for land at any distance is perfectly inelastic at the quantity necessary to supply needed transport capacity.

Transportation prices confronting households will depend on the transportation production function as well. It is usually assumed that resource costs used in transportation are passed on to households. With fixed proportions, transport prices will vary proportionally with land rents, while if land and non-land factor substitution is possible, transport prices will vary less than proportionally with land rents.

The location equilibrium condition for households can be simply modified to reflect the relationship between transport costs and land rents. The marginal increment to transportation costs of locating at u will be an expression in land rents, $(\partial T/\partial u) = T(r(u))$. (In the absence of congestion, transportation cost is invariant to traffic volume.) As noted above, housing prices at distance u depend on land rents through the marginal productivity conditions. The location equilibrium condition is therefore a first order differential equation in land rents:

$$\frac{\partial P}{\partial r} \frac{\partial r}{\partial u} q(r(u)) + T(r(u)) = 0.$$ (38)

Given a particular solution to the land rent gradient, expressions for population and density gradients can be readily derived. The latter are also first order differential equations [Mills (1967)].

3.2. Congestion models

When congestion exists, travel costs are no longer invariant to traffic volume. Transport prices depend on both the supply and demand for transport capacity, the latter dependent on location decisions, housing, and land prices. The household location equilibrium condition in this class of models reflects the interdependency between congestion and transport prices, and hence location choices.

This dependency is easily illustrated. Assume transportation costs are positively related to demand and inversely related to capacity. Demand for transportation is equal to the number of people living beyond any point u who must commute past the point to the center. The most often used formulation of congestion costs in urban location models is due to Vickery (1965). Travel costs of traveling through point u rise more than proportionally with the ratio of demand to capacity:

$$\frac{\partial T}{\partial u} = \rho_0 + \rho_1 \left[\frac{D_t(u)}{S(G(u))} \right]^{\rho_2}. \tag{39}$$

D_t and S_t denote the demand and supply of transport at u, and $G(u)$ denotes the amount of land devoted to transport at distance u, $\rho_2 > 1$. Substitution of (39) into the location equilibrium condition results in a second order differential equation in land rents, with the transport land gradient $G(u)$ exogenous:

$$(\partial P/\partial u)q + \partial T/\partial u = 0,$$

$$-\frac{\partial P}{\partial r} r_u q(r(u)) = \rho_0 + \rho_1 \left\{ \left[\int_u^{u_1} D(r(u))(2\pi u - G(u)) du \right] \middle/ S[L_t(u)] \right\}^{\rho_2}. \tag{40}$$

In the models in the previous section without congestion, the location equilibrium condition was a first order differential equation in land rents. In the presence of congestion, a second order equation is obtained because of the interrelationship between locations and land rents at every distance, which enters the expression for the price of transportation, (39) above. Solution generally requires numerical methods. Once $r(u)$ is known, population locations and density gradients can be readily determined.

Mills' (1972) formulation assumed housing demand had a constant price elasticity, $q(u) = dP(u)^{\theta_2}$, and where d and θ_2 are parameters, and that housing was produced by a Cobb–Douglas technology with land coefficient α_2. The marginal productivity conditions imply: $P(u) = Cr(u)\alpha^2$. Housing demand at each u is related to land rents:

$$q(u) = d(Cr(u)^{\alpha_2})^{\theta_2}. \tag{41}$$

Equating demand for housing with supply at each distance defines equilibrium in the housing market, an expression in land rents and population:

$$n(u)q(u) = x(u),$$

$$n(u)d(Cr(u)^{\alpha_2})^{\theta_2} = a(r(u))^{1-\alpha_2}(2\pi u - G(u))^{\alpha_2}. \tag{42}$$

where $n(u)$ is persons residing at u, $q(u)$ is per capita housing consumption, $x(u)$ is total housing supplied, and $(2\pi u - G(u))$ is land available for housing at each distance u. Parameters of preferences and the production function appear in (42). Mills assumed transport costs depended on land devoted to transportation and traffic volume at u:

$$t(u) = \rho_1 \left[\left(\int_u^{u_1} n(u) du \right) \Big/ G(u) \right]^{\rho_2}, \tag{43}$$

(42) may be solved for $n(u)$ in terms of $r(u)$, and substituted into (43), yielding an expression in $r(u)$. Substitution of (41) and (43) into the location equilibrium yields a second order differential equation in $r(u)$, with $G(u)$ exogenous. The solution for $r(u)$ is used to determine population and density gradients. Extensions of Mills' model have modified the assumptions describing housing preferences, transportation production functions, and congestion cost relationships.

The existence of congestion externalities presents a standard welfare problem which has been analyzed in monocentric models. Congestion represents a divergence between average and marginal costs of commuting to and from different points. Location choices will be non-optimal in the absence of congestion tolls. Moreover, highway investment decisions based on benefit-cost calculations using market prices of land will be non-optimal, since land rents will not reflect the opportunity cost of land. When congestion costs vary continuously with distance, the appropriate pricing system requires a toll gradient, tolls varying continuously (under most assumptions) with distance to the city center [Oron, Pines, and Sheshinski (1973); Solow (1973a)[4]]. (The tax might be collected at one's place of residence.) When congestion tolls are employed, location choices will be optimal given the transport system in place; investment decisions regarding transportation capacity can be based on the usual benefit-cost calculations.

The derivation of optimal tolls and highway investments is a problem in control theory. Application of control theory to monocentric urban spatial models arises quite naturally, by treating distance to the city center as the continuous variable analogous to time in the standard dynamic optimization problem. The first applications of control theory to urban spatial models by Solow and Vickrey (1971) and Mills and de Ferranti (1971) showed that congestion resulted in suboptimal land use. Whereas the initial models were sufficiently simple that certain results could be derived analytically, the many subsequent applications of this methodology generally have required numerical methods. Capital-land substitution in the production functions for housing and transportation has been included [Sheshinski (1973), Livesey (1973), Kanemoto 1975, 1977), Legey et al. (1973)].

---

[4]The importance of continuous variation to tolls along a roadway was first noted by Strotz (1965) though his analysis was not imbedded in a formal spatial model.

3.3. Exhaust pollution externalities

Exhaust pollution is an externality posing many of the same analytic problems as congestion externalities. The general class of location models with neighborhood amenities is discussed in Section 4 below. The special case in which automobile pollution is included in the standard monocentric model can be quickly summarized [Oron, Pines and Sheshinski (1974); Robson (1976a,b)]. Air quality as affected by air pollution at any given distance is included as an argument in the utility function, hence affecting the equilibrium bid rent gradient. Air pollution at any distance is generally assumed to be directly related to vehicle emissions, which in turn depend on traffic volume and vehicle speed. Vehicle speed in turn depends on the amount of road capacity at each distance. Location decisions, traffic volume, speeds, and air quality are jointly determined. Differing assumptions regarding preferences, automobile technology, emissions diffusion processes, and highway capacity can be incorporated. Finding equilibrium solutions for rent, density and pollution gradients invariably requires numerical methods.

Just as in the case of congestion, when there are pollution externalities, location choices will be non-optimal in the absence of taxes which reflect the externality. Derivation of appropriate taxes is a control theory problem much like that of congestion. Robson (1976b) derives the optimal tax gradient which can be construed as a tax imposed when driving through each distance u. Duff and Straszheim (1982) have included both auto pollution and congestion externalities in a monocentric model. Pollution is related to vehicle design as well as speeds and traffic volumes, and several alternative engine designs are analyzed. Equilibrium rent, population, traffic volume and pollution gradients are derived and optimal taxes which reflect both congestion and pollution externalities are estimated. Comparisons are also made of the benefits of pre-mile taxes versus optimal toll gradients, and the effects of alternative pricing policies on the choice of an optimal engine design.

4. Neighborhood characteristics

The standard monocentric model focusing on land consumption and one-dimensional distance gradients ignores the role of neighborhood characteristics such as socioeconomic composition, population density, air quality, or public services in location decisions. The importance of neighborhood characteristics was first illustrated by empirical studies of housing prices. Housing services are defined as a multidimensional vector of attributes, including characteristics of both the structure and the neighborhood. In addition to valuing accessibility to the city center, households bid up the prices of housing which is located in more preferred neighborhoods. Relationships between observed housing prices and structure or neighborhood characteristics are called hedonic price equations.

The interpretation of hedonic price relationships rests on many assumptions about preferences, information and relocation costs, supply elasticites, the durability of the housing stock, and other variables which determine outcomes in the housing market. Nelson (1972) showed that competition among bidders for available sites would result in rent differentials, the necessary compensating variation for perceived advantages or disadvantages of particular sites. Under these assumptions housing prices will reflect preferences and need bear no relationship to the long run opportunity costs of providing housing. An alternative model assumes perfectly elastic supply functions and markets in long run equilibrium, in which case housing prices will reflect opportunity costs as well. Rosen's (1974) seminal paper showed that hedonic prices are derived from both preferences and supply functions, and that specific assumptions about both are necessary in order to interpret observed housing price data. Much controversy remains over the assumptions necessary to identify parameters of utility and production functions, and whether in particular applications hedonic price estimates can be interpreted as reflecting preferences or cost relationships [Brown and Rosen (1982)]. Nevertheless, there is an extensive empirical literature on hedonic prices, describing the amounts persons have paid for housing with particular neighborhood characteristics.[5]

Two approaches incorporate preferences for neighborhoods into residential location theory, employing differing assumptions defining "neighborhood" or the choice set. The simplest approach modifies the monocentric model by defining "neighborhood" as the immediate area centered at any given distance to the center. Neighborhood characteristics at any distance are included as arguments in the utility function. The second approach defines location by a rectangular coordinate systen. In some applications the choice set is defined as a set of discrete options which acknowledges discontinuities in consumers' choices. The elements of the choice set are typically types of housing units and neighborhoods, defined as distinct geographic areas in a rectangular coordinate system. Household choices are described in probabilistic terms, and econometric methods are employed. Equilibrium solutions can be obtained by linear programming or assignment methods, and simulation models have also been used (Kain's chapter, this volume).

4.1. Amenities in the standard location model

Defining a "neighborhood" as a small area centered at any given distance to the city center preserves all the analytic advantages of defining space by one dimensional distance gradients. Any number of neighborhood variables can easily

---

[5] Ridker and Henning (1967); King and Mieszkowski (1973); Harrison and Rubinfeld (1978); Goodman (1978); Linneman (1980).

be included. An essential feature of this class of models is that equilibrium rent gradients may no longer decline. In the traditional monocentric model proximity to the center reduces commuting costs, hence land rents must decline with distance. If neighborhoods at more distant locations have desirable features such as the absence of noise, air pollution, etc., people may value distant sites more highly in spite of the longer commute. Let amenities at any distance u be represented by a scalar, $a(u)$, which enters positively into the utility function, $V(z, q, a(u))$ [Polinsky–Shavell (1976)]. (We note below the significance of assuming a scalar.) Assume amenities are exogenous at each location and are available without "charge." Differentiating the indirect utility, $V^*(P(u), y - T(u), a(u))$, yields equilibrium rents such that households are indifferent to location.

$$\frac{\partial P}{\partial u} = \left(\frac{\partial V^*}{\partial P}\right)^{-1} \left(\frac{\partial V^*}{\partial(y - T(u))} \frac{\partial T}{\partial u} - \frac{\partial V^*}{\partial a} \frac{\partial a}{\partial u}\right). \tag{44}$$

Since $(\partial V^*/\partial r) < 0$, the sign of expression (44) will be opposite to the sign of the term in parentheses. While the transportation effect, the first term in brackets is positive $(\partial T/\partial u) > 0$, the second term will be positive if more distant locations have more desirable amenities. If amenities are sufficiently favorable at more distant locations, the amenities effect may exceed the transportation cost effect, and the land rent gradient will be positive.

This representation can be applied to any number of amenities defined by distance to the center, without restriction on the sign of $\partial V/\partial a$ or $\partial a/\partial u$. The slope of the bid rent gradient compensates for many attributes which vary over distance. If more than one amenity (including accessibility) is distance related, it becomes difficult to infer the relative weights which households place on particular distance-related variables. Even if the amenities variables themselves can be measured, the marginal utilities for each amenity generally are not identifiable since more than one amenity varies with the observed choice variable (distance).

One important special case of amenities is that of negative externalities arising when households reside near the centrally located production sector [Stull (1974), Robson (1976b), Henderson (1985)]. Henderson (1985) assumes air pollution is created at the center, emissions dissipating with distance from the production site. At close-in locations where the rate of decline in disamenities with distance may exceed the effects of changes in accessibility on utility, the equilibrium rent gradient may be positive. Henderson also shows that a discontinuity may arise in the rent gradient at the boundary between the two sectors, and in some circumstances business rents will exceed residential rents at the boundary. An efficient spatial configuration of businesses and households requires both a tax on producers and a zoning constraint prohibiting business entry into the residential portion of the city.

[6] King and Mieszkowski (1973); Daniels (1975); Yinger (1979); Schafer (1979).

4.2. Racial composition as a neighborhood characteristic

Household's racial preferences have been incorporated into location decisions with this approach. Becker (1957) and Bailey (1959) first suggested that race preferences of blacks and whites will affect location decisions or bid rent functions of each race. One such class of models defines race preferences in terms of distance to the border of neighborhoods comprised of persons of the opposite race, this distance term included as an argument in the utility function. [Rose–Ackermann (1975); Courant and Yinger (1977)]. The nature of equilibrium location patterns can be inferred by examining the bid rent functions of households of each race. Assuming one or both races prefer to live apart from the other yields a "segregated" spatial equilibrium, hence the term "border" models. For example, assume black households are assumed to have race neutral preferences, lower incomes than whites, and to occupy more central locations, while white households prefer living some distance away from black households. The bid rent function for white households may have positive slope at distances near the black–white border, reflecting the disutility of being near the black border [Daniels (1975), Little (1976), Schafer (1979)].

Border models are not well suited to describing cases in which variation in incomes or preferences within a given race results in widely differing bid rent gradients, since this implies there may be multiple borders or bands of white and black households. An appropriate measure of "distance" to blacks becomes more complex if white households perceive that accessibility to black borders must be measured with respect to many black neighborhood concentrations [Courant–Yinger (1977)]. Finding equilibrium solutions also becomes more complex as the number of types of bidders is multiplied.

An alternative formulation assumes that households care only about the racial composition of their immediate neighborhood, i.e. at the distance they reside from the center. [Yinger (1976), Kern (1981)]. The stability of integrated or segregated residential outcomes in this class of models depends on preference functions and supplier behavior. Inferences regarding stability of residential patterns can be drawn by examining bid rent functions of both races. Bid rent gradients which make whites and blacks indifferent to location can be readily derived from the indirect utility function, with neighborhood racial composition one of the arguments. Whereas Yinger suggests that a segregated solution will be stable only if sustained by discriminatory actions by sellers, Kern (1981) shows that complete segregation can exist if both whites and blacks prefer white neighbors, but preferences of whites for white neighbors are stronger than the preference of blacks.

Enriching urban location models to include race preferences entails a more elaborate specification of the role of the micro-motives of households, housing suppliers, and agents. The existence of racial prejudice on the part of some participants can affect the actions of others, for example, when landlords or real estate agents discriminate against blacks in response to prejudice of their white customers [Yinger (1975), Lee and Warren (1976), Yinger (1979)]. The dynamics of location choices over time is also affected by imperfect information and uncertainty. Schelling (1972) focuses on the role of uncertainty in describing neighborhood tipping in game-theoretic terms. Courant (1978) has shown that a simple signalling model will result in a segregated outcome in a competitive market in which only some white sellers are prejudiced. Black households limit their search to markets where success is likely to outweigh costs of search, which tends to be markets which are predominantly black. Anas (1980) also develops a model in which tipping occurs in the absence of racial discrimination.

4.3. Multi-dimensional attribute space and rectangular coordinates

A more realistic treatment of space defines "neighborhood" as a set of points in a rectangular coordinate system, with each such point characterized by a vector of neighborhood attributes. Assume preferences include an n dimensional vector, a, of neighborhood attributes, $V(z, q, a_1, \ldots a_n)$, and that the budget constraint includes the price of housing $P(q, a)$, which depends on neighborhood attributes. Denoting location by two (continuous) variables (u, v) denoting longitude and latitude, the consumer maximizes

$$V(z, q, a_1(u, v), a_2(u, v) \ldots a_n(u, v)),$$

choosing z, q and a location (u, v). The attribute functions $a_i(u, v)$ describe how attributes vary through space. The first order conditions defining location equilibrium reveal that the marginal change in housing price of altering location depends on the values which the market placed on the entire set of attributes:

$$\sum \left(\frac{\partial V}{\partial a_i}\right)\left(\frac{\partial a_i}{\partial u}\right) - \lambda \frac{\partial P}{\partial u} q = 0,$$

$$\sum \left(\frac{\partial V}{\partial a_i}\right)\left(\frac{\partial a_i}{\partial v}\right) - \lambda \frac{\partial P}{\partial v} q = 0, \tag{45}$$

where λ is the Lagrangian multiplier for the budget constraint.

Since attributes are acquired in bundles when location is altered, a new interpretation is required to define the "price" of any particular household consuming more of any one attribute. The "price" of consuming more of attribute i will reflect changes in all other attributes which would accompany a change in location increasing consumption of attribute i. The "price" to a household of any one attribute is the compensating variation needed to restore the household to its former level of utility where, among all possible location changes increasing consumption of the attribute in question one unit, that location change requiring the least compensating variation was selected. Such a location change may entail changes in the consumption of all other attributes. Since the "price" of each attribute depends on the utility function, it varies across individuals.

A recurring error in the theoretical literature on household location noted by Cropper (1984) arises when the location problem is formulated as a choice problem in "attribute" space, much like the standard model, but constraints on the availability of neighborhood attributes are ignored. The problem arises from a failure to distinguish between neighborhood attributes which are in fixed supply once location is chosen and housing attributes which the household may freely vary at any given location. The quality of public schools exemplifies the former, while certain structural features of one's house (e.g. interior decorating) may fit the latter. To illustrate this mistaken approach, assume all attributes are freely variable; utility maximization yields $(n+2)$ "usual" first order conditions (plus the budget constraint):

$$V_z = \lambda,$$

$$V_q = \lambda P(q, a),$$

$$(\partial V/a_i) = \lambda(\partial P/\partial a_i)q \quad (i=1, n), \tag{46}$$

according to this view. The first and last conditions imply that the consumer picks a point where the marginal value of each attribute, $(\partial V/\partial a_i)$, equals the increment in land costs. The "price" of an amenity is that increment to the price of land times the amount of land consumed. $(\partial P/\partial a_i)q$ [Linneman (1981); Diamond and Tolley (1982)].

Cropper (1984) observes that this formulation ignores a problem of dimensionality in mapping from attribute space to location space. The first order conditions (46) are correct only if households may choose the amounts of the attributes consumed at any location. Yet just the reverse applies for neighborhood characteristics; the household chooses one from among many locations, each of which is characterized by a fixed set of attributes. The existence of fixed bundles of attributes at each location implies the household confronts significant constraints on the set of attributes it may consume. These constraints exist even when location is continuously variable, and are not to be confused with constraints which arise when the choice set with respect to location is discontinuous, as when a finite set of neighborhoods is available.

The circumstances under which the location problem may be formulated as a utility maximization problem in attribute space, ignoring location constraints, are given by the Implicit Function Theorem. Suppose there are only two attributes, related to location as follows: $a_1 = a_1(u, v)$, $a_2 = a_2(u, v)$. If a_i are continuous functions possessing continuous first partial derivatives and the Jacobian of the transformation $J = |\partial a/\partial u, v| \neq 0$, then there exist unique inverse functions

$u = \phi_1(a_1, a_2)$, $v = \phi_2(a_1, a_2)$. Choosing a_1 and a_2 to maximize utility would yield a unique location (u, u). (Polinsky–Shavell's example of a scalar measure of amenities obviously falls in this category.) However, choosing a location (u, v) can only be translated into a choice problem in attribute space if all possible choices for a_i can be represented in two dimensions. In general, when attributes exhibit more than two distinct spatial patterns, the location problem must be solved in location space, by choosing a (u, v) pair.

Incorporating this treatment of the location problem, with space described by a rectangular coordinate system, into equilibrium models of urban spatial structure is complex. Finding spatial equilibrium when there are more than one class of bidders entails the solution of complex partial differential equations, which generally must be solved numerically. Relaxing the assumption that neighborhood characteristics are exogenous introduces an added complication. Many neighborhood amenities reflect the consequences of all households' location choices. Examples include public services, where the costs or quality of public services depend on who resides in the jurisdiction; air pollution, where emissions depend on travel patterns and location decisions; or socioeconomic or racial composition of the "neighborhood." Little progress has been made in finding general equilibrium solutions to such models.

4.4. Discrete choice models

To the extent that neighborhoods are defined by irregular boundaries (e.g. public sector jurisdiction boundaries), the assumption that location is continuously variable must be relaxed. Households might be viewed as choosing from among a set of discrete options, each such option defined as a bundle of housing services and neighborhood attributes and an associated price. These options are called "submarkets" below. Whereas in the Muth–Mills equilibrium models housing prices reflect marginal productivity conditions consistent with long run competitive equilibrium, discrete choice models are typically based on the assumption of durable housing capital. The durability of the stock implies that positive or negative quasi-rents may exist in particular submarkets, market prices differing from the long run cost of producing that unit. Using static utility maximization to describe household location choices, it is merely necessary to specify how these many characteristics defining submarkets affect utility of particular households.

In practice utility maximizing choices are modeled as a problem in random utility functions [Anas (1982)]. The utility a household realizes from a given unit in a submarket is defined by a utility function which includes a stochastic term to capture unspecified variation in household preferences, housing units or neighborhoods. Anas suggests several sources for the random term in the utility function, generally indistinguishable to the researcher: (a) deterministic variation in preferences that is unobservable to the researcher; (b) unmeasured attributes of the unit or neighborhood that imply variation exists in units within a submarket; (c) unobserved constraints on choices, imperfect information, or irrational behavior. Introducing stochastic terms in the utility function implies that only the probability distribution of each household's choice can be predicted. The probability function will include household characteristics or preferences as well as characteristics of units in different submarkets as its arguments.

The functional form of random utility models has generally been motivated by econometric considerations and computational costs. The frequency distribution of the stochastic terms enters into expressions for the probability that any particular submarket is chosen. Even the simplest specification of functional forms and probability functions entails non-linear estimation. Both probit and logit models have been used, the latter favored because of their ease of estimation.

The computational costs of finding maximum likelihood estimates increases more than proportionally with the number of alternatives in the household's choice set, and hence in practice it has been necessary to limit the number of house types and neighborhoods which may be included in the analysis. Early applications suppressed the location dimension, and defined choices of housing and neighborhood "types" (the latter defined by such characteristics as the population density of the neighborhood, or the tenure of units). Quigley's (1976) original application used 18 house types, and Williams (1979) considered 50 house and neighborhood types.

More recent applications [Lerman (1979); Anas (1982)] have widened the choice set by using a nested logit model, in which choices are represented by a sequential choice probability structure. In Anas' study the probability of choosing a house type and location is represented as a product of conditional probabilities – as the conditional probability of choosing a house type given the choice of location, times the marginal probability of choosing a location. This approach, motivated by computational considerations, imposes constraints on utility functions and choice behavior. An alternative approach randomly selects subsets of all possible housing and location choices, and than estimates the multi-nominal logit for the samples. This procedure yields consistent estimates [McFadden (1978); Quigley (1985)]. As computational costs are reduced, the specification of this class of logit models will become much more complex, allowing a more realistic description of choices.

5. Decentralized employment and location choices

An increasing fraction of employment opportunities occurs in non-central locations. Changes in manufacturing technology resulting in land-intensive production and increasing reliance on trucking rather than central city rail or port facilities have resulted in decentralization in manufacturing and wholesaling. Changes in information systems and communications permit decentralization of office activities. Suburbanization of residences has shifted the location of retailing and service markets.

The simplest approach introducing non-central employment into household location models assumes work site location is exogenous and treats space by distance gradients. More complex models permit work site location, wage income, transportation costs and residential location to be jointly determined. The difficulties in finding equilibrium solutions of urban spatial structure for this class of models are noted briefly below. (The role of employment locations in urban models is also described in the Stahl chapter, this volume.)

5.1. Exogenous work sites

If a household is employed at a single non-central work site, with both place of work and earnings exogenous, only a minor modification is necessary to the standard location model [Straszheim (1973)]. Transportation costs are defined with respect to place of work rather than the city center, and residential location and housing consumption can be derived in the usual manner. Absent neighborhood effects, the household's bid rent function must peak at its place of work and decline with distance from the work site in all directions. If market rents decline with distance from the city center, households will choose a residential location more distant from the city center than place of work, there being no incentive to commute "up" the rent gradient to reside nearer the city center, where land rents are higher than at (or beyond) their place of work.

Further conclusions about housing and commuting patterns rest on additional assumptions about housing price and transportation cost gradients. Assume the housing price gradient in convex to the origin and marginal transportation costs decline with distance to the center as speeds increase. For commutes of any given distance, the benefits of a marginal change in commuting distance from a more centrally located work site will be greater than the benefits of a marginal change in commuting distance from a more suburban work site. This implies that households with a given income working nearer the city center and confronting the highest and steepest portion of the housing price gradient will make longer commutes and consume less housing than households with the same income who work at a more suburban site. These inferences have been tested using data on commuting and housing patterns in San Francisco [Straszheim (1975)]. In cross section analysis of intra-metropolitan housing choices, households with different places of work confront different housing prices and transportation costs. Econometric estimation of price effects rest on a description of the variation in housing and transportation costs associated with different work sites, which is the source of different consumption and location choices.

One or more members of a household may commute to a second (non-central) work site. White (1977) describes a model of work-leisure and residential location choices when a household has one member working in the center and a second working in a ring a given distance to the city center. A preferred representation of two worker household location decisions is to regard both places of work as fixed points in a plane. Curran et al. (1982) analyze this case using polar coordinates. Assume the household has two workers, incurring commuting costs to the city center and to a second (suburban) place of work. The person working in the center commutes u_1 miles to place of residence, while the second worker works u_3 miles from the center and commutes u_2 miles to place of residence. Let θ denote the angle between the vectors connecting the center to the place of residence and second place of work respectively. The distance u_2 may be expressed in terms of u_1 and θ using the Law of Cosines, $u_2^2 = u_1^2 + u_3^2 - 2u_1 u_3 \cos\theta$. Assume a Cobb–Douglas utility function, $V = q^a z^b L_1^c L_2^d$; the two workers ($i = 1, 2$) earn wages w_i; incur constant marginal travel costs, t_i; and travel at constant speeds, s_i. The bid rent surface may be described in terms of θ:

$$P(\theta, u_1, u_3) = b(Vw_1^c w_2^d)^{-1/a}[k(w_1 + w_2) - r_1 u_1$$
$$- r_2(u_1^2 + u_3^2 - 2u_1 u_3 \cos\theta)^{1/2}]^{a'/a}, \tag{47}$$

where $r_i = t_i + w_i/S_i$, and $a' = a + b + c + d$, and b are constants. If travel costs are greater for worker two than worker one, $r_2 > r_1$, the bid rent surface may be positively sloped along a vector from the center, at a distance inside the suburban employment site. At points beyond the suburban employment site the bid rent gradient will have its usual negative slope. This model again illustrates the loss in analytic convenience when space is not defined by one dimensional gradients.

5.2. Endogenous place of work

Urban location models in which both place of work and place of residence are at choice are a relatively simple modification of the standard monocentric model. The complexity arises when this generalization is incorporated into equilibrium models of urban spatial structure. These extensions are discussed in turn.

An early discussion of models with endogenous work sites by Muth (1969) assumed that households both work and live at the same location, eliminating transportation costs from consideration. Consumers choose a work site and consumption bundle maximizing utility $V(z, q)$, subject to the budget constraint $r(x)q(x) + z = w(x)$, where $r(x)$ and $w(x)$ denote housing prices and wages at distance x. The slopes of the wage and rent gradients appear in the first order condition for location equilibrium:

$$-\lambda\left(q\frac{\partial P}{\partial x}-\frac{\partial w}{\partial x}\right)=0,$$

implying

$$\frac{\left(\frac{\partial w(x)}{\partial x}\right)\Big/w(x)}{\left(\frac{\partial P(x)}{\partial x}\right)\Big/P(x)}=\frac{P(x)q}{w(x)}.\tag{48}$$

At the optimal location the slope of the wage gradient will be a fraction of the slope of the rent gradient. If households possess identical utility functions, this condition describes bid rent and wage offer functions such that households will be indifferent to location, the condition for spatial equilibrium.

A more realistic formulation allows commuting between place of work and place of residence. Solow (1973b) and White (1978) introduce monetary commuting outlays in the analysis, while Sullivan (1983) and Straszheim (1984) add leisure time to the model. Let households choose a place of work x and a place of residence u, each measured as distance to the city center, with the utility function including leisure time (L) as one of the arguments: $V(z, q, L)$. Commuting costs from place of work to place of residence include travel time $t(x, u)$ and monetary outlays, $c(x, u)$. Leisure time is diminished by daily commuting time: $L(x, u)+t(x, u)=24$. The budget constraint includes wages $w(x)$ at the work site: $z+P(u)q+c(x, u)=w(x)$. The first order conditions defining work site and residence site equilibrium are as follows:

$$V_L\left(\frac{\partial L}{\partial x}\right)+\lambda\left(\frac{\partial w}{\partial x}-\frac{\partial c}{\partial x}\right)=0,\tag{49}$$

$$V_L\left(\frac{\partial L}{\partial u}\right)-\lambda\left(q\frac{\partial P}{\partial u}+\frac{\partial c}{\partial u}\right)=0,\tag{50}$$

where λ is the Lagrange multiplier, the marginal utility of money. Let $\psi=(\partial V/\partial L)/\lambda$, denoting the monetized value of the marginal utility of leisure time. (49) and (50) may be rewritten as:

$$\frac{\partial P}{\partial u}=-\frac{1}{q}\left(\frac{\partial c}{\partial u}+\psi\frac{\partial t}{\partial u}\right),\tag{51}$$

$$\frac{\partial w}{\partial x}=\frac{\partial c}{\partial x}+\psi\frac{\partial t}{\partial x}.\tag{52}$$

The first is the familiar condition for residential location equilibrium, while the latter states that at the place of work x, the marginal change in wages must offset the marginal change in transport costs, monetary outlays plus the monetized value on leisure of an incremental change in work site location.

The complexity in introducing decentralized employment opportunities and endogenous work place locations into a general equilibrium model of urban spatial structure arises because bid rent and wage offer gradients are interdependent. Households' bids for land at any given residential site will depend on their place of work, wages, and commuting costs; similarly, a household's willingness to accept any given wage at any work site will depend on its residential location, housing prices, and commuting costs. As noted above, deriving equilibrium location patterns and rent gradients is more difficult when there are many classes of bidders with differing endowments and bid rent functions.

This complexity is illustrated by examining the indirect utility function, which includes wages, housing and transportation prices, and leisure:

$$V^*[w(x)-c(x, u)), P(u), L(x, u)].$$

The indirect utility function implicitly defines wage and housing price gradients, respectively, such that households with a given residence are indifferent to marginal changes in place of work and households with given place of work are indifferent to marginal changes in residence. Denoting net income by $y = w(x) - c(x, u)$, differentiating the indirect utility function with respect to u and x respectively

$$\frac{\partial V^*}{\partial P}\frac{\partial P}{\partial u} + \frac{\partial V^*}{\partial y}\frac{\partial y}{\partial u} + \frac{\partial V^*}{\partial L}\frac{\partial L}{\partial u} = 0, \tag{53}$$

$$\frac{\partial V^*}{\partial y}\left(\frac{\partial w}{\partial x} - \frac{\partial c}{\partial x}\right) + \frac{\partial V^*}{\partial L}\frac{\partial L}{\partial x} = 0. \tag{54}$$

Noting that $\psi = (\partial V/\partial L)/(\partial V/\partial y)$, $\partial y/\partial u = -\partial c/\partial u$, $\partial L/\partial u = -\partial t/\partial u$, and Roy's Identity implies $q(u) = -(\partial V^*/\partial P(u))/(\partial V^*/\partial y)$, appropriate substitutions yields (51) and (52) above. The first order conditions thus define bid rent and wage offer functions that makes households indifferent to place of residence and place of work respectively.

The problem of finding an equilibrium solution is now apparent. Since a household's bid rent function for land (51) depends on its place of work and its wage, and there are many places of work, there will exist families of differing bid rent functions of households indexed by place of work. Similarly, the inclusion of travel time in the wage offer function (52) implies that wage offers will vary with place of residence. Persons with different places of residence who are prospective employees at any given work site have different amounts of time net of commuting, hence there will be families of wage offer functions indexed by place of residence. Market equilibrium gradients will be envelope functions. Rent-maximizing landlords will receive the upper envelope of intersecting bid rent functions of households, while cost-minimizing firms will pay the lower envelope of intersecting wage offer functions of households. Since workplace and residential locations of any one household will depend on market equilibrium, wage and rent gradients and location decisions of all households are interdependent. The introduction of endogenous work sites is a further analytic complication to that of deriving land rent envelope functions which are consistent with the bid rent functions of households with different incomes listed above.

A number of urban spatial models include non-central employment opportunities. Solow (1973b) first suggested that persons might be employed in a local-goods sector, whose output was produced and sold to households at the location where they reside. In Solow's formulation time costs are omitted, and hence the wage gradient making households indifferent to place of work can be readily calculated by netting out transport outlays. Transport outlays and hence the wage gradient are exogenous to the model. Others have adopted this same approach. White (1976, 1977) described cities with suburban export nodes (bands about the city center whose land was devoted solely to non-residential use). Households who worked at the suburban export nodes might commute from more central or less central residential locations, and the land rent gradient might have local peaks at these suburban export points. Brueckner (1978) presented a model similar to Solow, with some workers employed in a "local-goods" sector, whose output is not shipped. Most recently, Sullivan (1983) and Straszheim (1984) present solutions of a class of equilibrium models with "segregated" outcomes, employment and residences occupying separate parts of the city and where spatial wage variation exists within the employment sector.

All of these papers adopt assumptions about utility functions and commuting costs which avoid the analytic complexity of deriving envelope functions. In each of the models cited above, bid rent functions for land are independent of place of work, and wage offer functions are independent of place of residence. These simplifications are derived by assuming marginal time costs are constant (or that there are no time costs). The second term in (52) above therefore disappears, and the wage offer function is independent of u. The equilibrium wage gradient reflects transportation outlays which are exogenous to the model. Since households at a given residence u have the same disposable income regardless of place of work, rent gradients given by (51) are therefore independent of place of work. Wage offer and bid rent functions are identical for all households, and can be determined by solving the two differential equations (51) and (52) subject to certain boundary conditions. This class of models establishes that households commute to a workplace more central than their residence, but does not further describe commuting patterns [Straszheim (1984)].

If time costs appear in the utility function, and the assumption of constant marginal time costs is relaxed, differing families of wage offer functions and bid rent functions will exist, indexed by place of work and place of residence. Equilibrium wage and rent envelope functions will be endogenous, dependent on commuting patterns. Equilibrium conditions in the labor and land markets require the solution of complex differential equations describing commuting patterns. Models with this generality have not yet been developed.

6. Conclusions

Assumptions of continuity and treating space by one dimensional distance gradients yield models well suited to analyzing rent-transportation cost tradeoffs and characteristics of urban spatial structure in the long run, especially in circumstances where political jurisdictions and neighborhood effects are not important. The monocentric model can be readily extended to represent environmental or other neighborhood characteristics which continuously vary with distance. However, when there are fixed characteristics of housing units or neighborhoods and neighborhood boundaries assume importance at particular locations, discontinuities arise in the choice set and the conventional location models are less useful. Econometric and simulation techniques may prove more powerful in representing choices when discontinuities exist.

Considerations largely ignored in the traditional static models are the costs of relocation, imperfect information, and uncertainty. When changes occur in income, family size, place of work, preferences, or neighborhoods, a household's valuations of its current and alternative possible residences are affected. Yet search for a different residence is costly, moving entails monetary outlays and time and psychic costs, and there are inevitably uncertainties about the future course of other neighborhoods, the quality of units being contemplated, and the household's future income and housing preferences. A consequence of high moving costs is that households' decisions will reflect expectations over an extended period of time.

Little progress has been made in modelling relocation decisions in a dynamic context and in the presence of imperfect information. Studies relating mobility rates to characteristics of the household or its present housing consumption generally do not specify the important roles of uncertainty, search costs, and expenditures in the moving decision.[7] A static model of the decision to move by Weinberg, Friedman and Mayo (1981) related households' decisions to move to the cost of relocation, and to the divergence between the utility of their present housing bundle and the utility of an alternative "desired" bundle of services. Muth (1974) introduced uncertainty into the household's choice of housing by

---

[7]A survey of traditional mobility studies is Quigley and Weinberg (1977).

including a probability distribution on the date of a future move. This model could be extended by relating the probability of a move to the suitability of a household's present housing consumption relative to the satisfaction of alternative bundles and their costs, all of which might be described by probability distributions. These and other extensions will require that we learn far more how households form expectations and how they value uncertain future outcomes.

References

Alonso, W. (1964) *Location and land use*. Cambridge, Mass.: Harvard University Press.

Anas, A. (1978) 'Dynamics of urban residential growth', *Journal of Urban Economics*, 5:66–87.

Anas, A. (1980) 'A model of residential change and neighborhood tipping', *Journal of Urban Economics*, 7:358–370.

Anas, A. (1982) *Residential location models and urban transportation: economic theory, econometrics and policy analysis with discrete choice models*. New York: Academic Press.

Arnott, R. and J. Riley (1977) 'Asymmetrical production possibilities, the social gains from inequality and the optimum town', *Scandinavian Journal of Economics*, 79:301–311.

Bailey, M. (1959) 'Note on the economics of residential zoning and urban renewal', *Land Economy*, 35:288–290.

Becker, G. (1957) *The economics of discrimination*. Chicago: Univ. of Chicago.

Beckmann, M. (1969) 'On the distribution of urban rent and residential density', *Journal of Economic Theory*, 1:60–67.

Beckmann, M. (1974) 'Spatial equilibrium in the housing market', *Journal of Urban Economics*, 1:99–107.

Beckmann, M. (1976) 'Spatial equilibrium in the dispersed city', in: G. Papageorgiou, ed., *Mathematical land use theory*. Lexington, Mass.: Lexington Books. 117–125.

Brueckner, J. (1978) 'Urban general equilibrium models with non-central production', *Journal of Regional Science*, 18:203–215.

Brueckner, J. (1983) 'The economics of urban yard space: an "implicit market" model for housing attributes', *Journal of Urban Economics*, 13:216–234.

Brown, J. and H. Rosen (1982) 'On the estimation of structural hedonic price models', *Econometrica*, 50:765–768.

Courant, P. (1978) 'Racial prejudice in search models of the urban housing market', *Journal of Urban Economics*, 5:329–45.

Courant, P. and J. Yinger (1977) 'On models of racial prejudice and urban residential structure', *Journal of Urban Economics*, 4:272–91.

Cropper, M. (1984) 'Should the Rosen model be used to value environmental amenities?', University of Maryland, Sloan Workshop in Urban Public Economics, mimeo. College Park, Md.

Curran, C., L. Carlson and D. Ford (1982) 'A theory of residential location decisions of two-worker households', *Journal of Urban Economics*, 12:102–113.

Daniels, C. (1975) 'The influence of racial segregation on housing prices', *Journal of Urban Economics*, 2:102–122.

DeSalvo, J. (1977) 'Urban household behavior in a model of completely centralized employment', *Journal of Urban Economics*, 4:1–14.

Diamond, D., Jr. and G. Tolley (1982) *The economics of urban amenities*. New York: Academic Press.

Dixit, A. (1973) 'The optimum factory town', *Bell Journal of Economics and Management Science*, 4:637–51.

Duff, V. and Straszheim (1982) 'Auto pollution and congestion in an urban model: an analysis of alternative strategies', *Journal of Urban Economics*, 12:11–31.

Goodman, Jr., J. (1978) 'Housing consumption disequilibrium and local residential mobility', *Environment and Planning*, 8:855–74.

Harrison, D. Jr., and D. Rubinfeld (1978) 'Housing values and the willingness to pay for clean air', *Journal of Environment Economics Management*, 5:81–102.

Henderson, J.V. (1985) *Economic theory and the cities*. New York: Academic Press.

Kanemoto, Y. (1975) 'Congestion and cost-benefit analysis in cities', *Journal of Urban Economics*, 2:246–64.

Kanemoto, Y. (1976) 'Optimum, market, and second-best land use patterns in a von Thunen city with congestion', *Regional Science and Urban Economics*, 1:23–32.

Kanemoto, Y. (1977) 'Cost-benefit analysis and the second-best land use for transportation', *Journal of Urban Economics*, 4:483–503.

Kanemoto, Y. (1980) *Externalities in a spatial economy*. Amsterdam: North-Holland.

Kau, J. and C. Lee (1976) 'Capital-land substitution and urban land use', *Journal of Regional Science*, 16:83–92.

Kern, C. (1981) 'Racial prejudice and residential segregation: the Yinger model revisited', *Journal of Urban Economics*, 10:164–73.

King, T. and P. Mieszkowski (1973) 'Racial discrimination, segregation, and the price of housing', *Journal of Political Economy*, 81:590–606.

Kirmans, D.F., J.B. Kau and C.F. Lee (1979) 'The elasticity of substitution in urban housing production: a VES approach', *Journal of Urban Economics*, 6:407–415.

Lee, C. and E. Warren, Jr. (1976) 'Rationing by seller's preference and racial price discrimination', *Economic Inquiry*, 14:36–44.

Legey, L., M. Ripper and P. Varaiya (1973) 'Effects of congestion on the shape of the city', *Journal of Economic Theory*, 6:162–179.

Lerman, S. (1979) 'Neighborhood choice and transportation services', in: D. Segal, ed., *The economics of neighborhood*. New York: Academic Press, 83–118.

Levhari, D., Y. Oron and D. Pines (1978) 'A note on unequal treatment of equals in an urban setting', *Journal of Urban Economics*, 5:278–84.

Linneman, P. (1980) 'Some empirical results on the nature of the hedonic price function for the urban housing market', *Journal of Urban Economics*, 8:47–68.

Linneman, P. (1981) 'The demand for residence site characteristics', *Journal of Urban Economics*, 9:129–148.

Little, J. T. (1976) 'Residential preferences, neighborhood filtering, and neighborhood change', *Journal of Urban Economics*, 3:68–81.

Livesey, D. (1973) 'Optimum city size: a minimum congestion approach', *Journal of Economic Theory*, 6:144–161.

McDonald, J. (1979) *Economic analysis of an urban housing market*. New York: Academic Press.

McDonald, J. (1981) 'Capital land substitution in urban housing: a survey of empirical estimates', *Journal of Urban Economics*, 9:190–211.

McFadden, D. (1978) 'Modelling the choice of residential location', in: A. Karlquist, ed., *Spatial interaction theory and planning models*. Amsterdam: North-Holland.

Meyer, J., J. Kain and M. Wohl (1965) *The urban transportation problem*. Cambridge: Harvard University Press.

Mills, E. (1967) 'An aggregate model of resource allocation in a metropolitan area', *American Economic Review*, 57:197–210.

Mills, E. (1970) 'The efficiency of spatial competition', *Papers and Proceedings of the Regional Science Association*, 25:71–82.

Mills, E. (1972) *Studies in the structure of the urban economy*. Baltimore, Maryland: Johns Hopkins Press.

Mills, E. and D. De Ferranti (1971) 'Market choices and optimum city size', *American Economic Review*, 61:340–45.

Mirrlees, J. (1972) 'The optimum town', *Swedish Journal of Economics*, 74:114–35.

Mohring, H. and M. Harwitz (1962) *Highway benefits: an analytic approach*. Evanston, Illinois: Northwestern University Press.

Montesano, A. (1972) 'A restatement of Beckmann's model on the distribution of urban rent and residential density', *Journal of Economic Theory*, 4:329–354.

Muth, R. (1964) 'The derived demand curve for a factor of production and the industry supply curve', *Oxford Economic papers*, 56:221–234.

Muth, R. (1969) *Cities and housing*. Chicago: University of Chicago Press.

Muth, R. (1974) 'Moving costs and housing expenditures', *Journal of Urban Economics*, 1:108–125.

Muth, R. (1975) 'Numerical solutions of urban residential land-use models', *Journal of Urban Economics*, 2:307–332.

Nelson, R. (1972) 'Housing facilities, site advantages and rent', *Journal of Regional Science*, 12:249–259.

Oron, Y., D. Pines and E. Sheshinski (1973) 'Optimum vs equilibrium land use patterns and congestion tolls', *Bell Journal of Economics and Management Science*, 4:619–36.

Oron, Y., D. Pines and E. Sheshinski (1974) 'The effect of nuisances associated with urban traffic on suburbanization and land values', *Journal of Urban Economics*, 1:382–395.

Polinsky, M. and S. Shavell (1976) 'Amenities and property values in a model of an urban area', *Journal of Public Economics*, 5:119–130.

Quigley, J. (1976) 'Housing demand in the short run; an analysis of polytomous choice', *Explorations in Economic Research*, 3:76–102.

Quigley, J. (1985) 'Consumer choice of dwelling, neighborhood, and public service', *Regional Science and Urban Economics*, 15:41–63.

Quigley, J. and D. Weinberg (1977) 'Intra-urban residential mobility: a review and synthesis', *International Regional Science Review*, 2, 1:41–66.

Ridker, R. and J.A. Henning (1967) 'The determinants of residential property values with special reference to air pollution', *Review of Economics and Statistics*, 49:246–257.

Riley, J. (1973) 'Gammaville': an optimal town', *Journal of Economics Theory*, 6:471–483.

Riley, J. (1974) 'Optimal residential density and road transportation', *Journal of Urban Economics*, 1:230–49.

Robson, J. (1976a) 'Cost-benefit analysis and the use of urban land for transportation', *Journal of Urban Economics*, 3:180–91.

Robson, J. (1976b) 'Two models of urban air pollution', *Journal of Urban Economics*, 3:264–285.

Rose-Ackermann, S. (1975) 'Race and urban structure', *Journal of Urban Economics*, 2:85–103.

Rosen S. (1974) 'Hedonic prices and implicit markets: product differentiation in pure competition', *Journal of Political Economics*, 82:34–55.

Schafer, R. (1979) 'Racial discrimination in the Boston housing market', *Journal of Urban Economics*, 6:176–196.

Schelling, T. (1972) 'Neighborhood tipping' in: A. Pascal, ed., *Racial discrimination in economic life*. Lexington, Mass.: D.C. Heath.

Sheshinski, E. (1973) 'Congestion and the optimum city size', *American Economic Review*, 63:61–66.

Solow, R. and W. Vickrey (1971) 'Land use in a long narrow city', *Journal of Economic Theory*, 3:430–47.

Solow, R. (1973a) 'Congestion costs and the use of land for streets', *Bell Journal of Economics and Management Science*, 4:602–19.

Solow, R. (1973b) 'On equilibrium models of urban spatial structure', in: J. Perkins, ed., *Essays in modern economics*. London: Longmans.

Straszheim, M. (1973) 'Estimation of the demand for urban housing services from household interview data', *Review of Economics and Statistics*, 55:1–8.

Straszheim, M. (1975) *An econometric analysis of the urban housing market*. New York: Columbia University Press.

Straszheim, M. (1979) 'Assessing the social cost of urban transportation technologies', in: P. Mieskowski and M. Straszheim, eds., *Current issues in urban economics*. Baltimore: Johns Hopkins University Press.

Straszheim, M. (1984) 'Urban agglomeration effects and employment and wage gradients', *Journal of Urban Economics*, 16:187–207.

Strotz, R. (1965) 'Urban transportation parables', in: J. Margolis, ed., *The public economy of urban communities*. Washington, D.C.: John Hopkins Press.

Stull, W. (1974) 'Land use and zoning in an urban economy', *American Economic Review*, 64:337–347.

Sullivan, A. (1983) 'A general equilibrium model with external scale economies in production', *Journal of Urban Economics*, 13:235–255.

Vickery, W. (1965) 'Pricing as a tool in coordination of local transportation', in: J. Meyer, ed., *Transportation economics*. New York: National Bureau of Economics Research.

Weinberg, D., J. Friedman and S. Mayo (1981) 'Intra urban residential mobility: the role of transactions costs, market imperfections and household disequilibrium', *Journal of Urban Economics*, 9, 3:332–349.

Wheaton, W. (1974) 'A comparative static analysis of urban statial structure', *Journal of Economic Theory*, 9:223–237.

Wheaton, W. (1977a) 'A bid rent approach to housing demand', *Journal of Urban Economics*, 4:200–217.

Wheaton, W. (1977b) 'Income and urban residence: an analysis of consumer demand for location', *American Economic Review*, 67:620–631.

Wheaton, W. (1978a) 'Urban spatial development with durable but replaceable capital', *Journal of Urban Economics*, 12, 1:53–67.

Wheaton, W. (1978b) 'Urban residential growth under perfect foresight', *Journal of Urban Economics*, 12:1–21.

White, M. (1976) 'Firm suburbanization and urban subcenters', *Journal of Urban Economics*, 3:323–342.

White, M. (1977) 'A model of residential location choice and commuting by men and women workers', *Journal of Research Science*, 1:41–52.

White, M. (1978) 'Job suburbanization, zoning, and the welfare of minority groups', *Journal of Urban Economics*, 5:219–240.

Wildasen, D. (1984) 'Spatial variation of the marginal utility of income and unequal treatment of equals', *Journal of Urban Economics*, (forthcoming).

Williams, R. (1979) 'A logit model of demand for neighborhood', in: D. Segal, ed., *The economics of neighborhood*. New York: Academic Press.

Yinger, J. (1975) 'An analysis of discrimination by real estate brokers', Institute for Research on Poverty, Discussion paper, University of Wisconsin, Madison, Wisconsin.

Yinger, J. (1976) 'Racial prejudice and racial residential segregation in an urban model', *Journal of Urban Economics*, 3:383–396.

Yinger, J. (1979) 'Prejudice and discrimination in the urban housing market', in: P. Mieszkowski and M. Straszheim, eds., *Current issues in urban economics*. Baltimore: Johns Hopkins University Press.

Chapter 19

THEORIES OF URBAN BUSINESS LOCATION

KONRAD STAHL*

University of Dortmund

1. Introduction

Urban economics as a special field of economic science derives much of its justification from the fact that land is an essential input into any economic activity. The neglect of this feature typical of other branches of economics would be of little concern, if all these activities could be performed with convex technologies, with the implication that everything could be produced and consumed at the same cost everywhere within a geography homogeneously endowed with natural resources.

However, nonconvexities in these technologies make it worthwhile to perform these activities at only a few points in space. Costly interaction then necessary between them gives rise to the problem of optimal location for individual activities. It typically involves the consideration of attracting, as well as repelling forces. Consider, for instance, a retailer's location decision. He is primarily interested in locating his plant at points of maximal demand, i.e. as closely as possible to the consumers demanding his commodity bundle; and to retailers who, by supplying complementary commodity bundles, attract the desired clientele. By contrast, he desires to locate as far away as possible from his direct competitors, in order to enjoy as much of a monopolistic advantage as possible.

As another example, the producer of an export commodity will find it to his advantage to locate close to the input labor and to the firms supplying other intermediate inputs. Conversely, he will try to avoid competition between firms about inputs, especially about labor, thus enjoying a monopsonistic advantage over his competitors in the input market.

These are key forces used in the sequel to explain and to evaluate intraurban business location decisions, and the resulting location patterns. In principle, our theory should be powerful enough to answer questions such as: How does the spatial distribution of production, or of retailing and consumption activities come

*I am grateful to Jacques Thisse for perceptive comments.

Handbook of Regional and Urban Economics, Volume II, Edited by E.S. Mills
© *1987, Elsevier Science Publishers B.V.*

about, and change its structure in response to forces such as technical change in production and retailing, or changing population density, increasing incomes, and declining transportation costs? In particular, how do centers and subcenters of production and retailing activities form? Are number and locations of production and retailing centers efficient relative to the spatial distribution of the population? Can the bundles of commodities and services produced and/or retailed, and the prices charged in these be bettered from an efficiency, or an equity point of view? If so, what policies ought to be used in order to improve upon the efficiency and equality impacts of entry, location, product, and price choices?

There are hard conceptual and technical problems involved in the construction of models towards answering these questions. First of all, nonconvexities are the main cause of the phenomena to be explained, and therefore cannot be assumed away. Secondly, the framework of competitive analysis is not necessarily the most appropriate one, if we wish to explain the formation of agglomerations. The spatial concentration of businesses instrumental in the formation of the urban fabric involves, at least initially, a few enterprises only. We cannot presume them to act beforehand in an environment characterized by perfectly elastic demand or supply functions in all relevant markets.[1] Consider as but one example the supply of an intermediate input to a locating firm. Even if that input is supplied by many enterprises (say with identical technologies), there is almost always one firm closer than any other to any contemplated location, so trading with this firm is of potential advantage. This gives rise to a bilaterally monopolistic trading situation between the locator and this firm.

Thirdly, the decisions at the level of the individual firm are very complex. They involve choices of whether or not, and if so, with how many plants to enter the market; the choice of location(s); of the bundle of commodities and services to be offered; of the technique to be employed (in particular the degree of vertical integration); and finally about the prices offered for inputs, and charged for outputs. These encompass all the choices analyzed in the recent theoretical literature on industrial organization, *plus* additional ones, in particular those involving the number and location of plants within an imperfectly competitive environment! Badly enough, these choices are mutually dependent and cannot be separated without considerable loss of explanatory power.

Fourthly, most of the decisions considered above, and most prominently the entry and location ones involve an irreversible capital commitment and therefore are of a long term nature. This not only implies that expectations bear upon them in an important way. Since different agents take these decisions at different points

---

[1] I do not mean to say that the intraurban market arrangements in question are never (approximately) competitive. However, that they possibly end up having this property should be a result of the analysis rather than a presumption.

in time, it also follows that one firm's decision is conditioned on the historical evolution of the economic environment generated from other firms' and consumers' past decisions. A typical example is a firm's decision to adopt a capital increasing change in technique. This typically involves an expansion in the physical plant which sometimes can be accommodated by the acquisition of neighboring lots, and at other times only by developing a new location. However, the traditional tool kit of competitive ex ante analysis is not very appropriate for replicating such discrete decisions.

Fifthly, location-allocation decisions in production necessarily involve labor, and therefore their representation needs to be built on an adequate specification of a local labor market. Indeed, the location decisions themselves are instrumental in its formation. However, there is as of now no adequate paradigm of such a local labor market.

Finally, the influence of resource rents, in particular of rents on buildings and land, on decisions in production and retailing is not entirely clear. In the literature in von Thünen's spirit, land rent is most conveniently perceived as a residual. That is, land rent is not a determinant of (competitive) location decisions, but is determined as a result of these. Owing to the oligopolistic, and sometimes even monopolistic structure of the markets under consideration in this paper, this notion cannot be upheld at ease in the present context. A good case is the just contemplated expansion of the physical plant. The profitability of that expansion, viz. a relocation is dependent on the outcome of a bilaterally monopolistic bargaining game with a neighboring landlord, resulting in an a priori indeterminate distribution of profits, and therefore land rents.

In view of all these difficulties, it is not surprising that the scale of theoretical research on the determinants of urban business location has not been commensurate with the importance of the subject.[2] By comparison, much more research effort was spent on the economic structure of the urban housing market, and on urban transportation.[3] At any rate, the literature to date attacks these problems in various ways. The contributions relevant here evolve around several seminal paradigms, notably those of Weber (1909), von Thünen (1826), Hotelling (1929) and Lösch (1940). As it will turn out, the assumptions used within each string of literature are relatively idiosyncratic to the paradigm used. It is therefore difficult to give an integrated view.

More specifically, following these seminal paradigms the literature addresses quite different questions. The contributions in the spirit of Weber almost exclusively treat the location problem, and sometimes the choice of technique, for

---

[2] Incidentally, the same is claimed by Struyk and James (1975) for empirical research in this area.

[3] Recent surveys of the state of the art, such as Mieszkowski and Straszheim's (1979) very useful compendium give much room to analyses of the housing and the transportation sector, but no treatment of production nor of retailing, nor of important related markets such as the urban labor market.

a single plant. The assumptions employed here are of a nature such that the theory can be used at best to replicate individual producers', rather than marketeers' intraurban location decisions. The papers along von Thünen's paradigm primarily treat land use decisions for exporting perfectly competitive production activities. The production techniques used in these models are typically characterized by constant returns, so plants are of unidentifiable size. This limits the analysis of input interaction flows between plants.

Papers in the Hotelling and Lösch tradition mostly discuss the oligopolistic, or monopolistically competitive interaction in output markets between specialized firms. The terms of input acquisition are largely neglected.

These differences in orientation invite a separate treatment of input market oriented decisions modelled in the Weber and von Thünen tradition, and output market oriented decisions modelled in the spirit of Hotelling and Lösch. The former relate to basic activities producing for a perfectly competitive export market, that seek optimal locations and techniques in view of the differential availability of inputs in space. By contrast, the latter relate to nonbasic middlemen's activities receiving commodities from a perfectly competitive input market and distributing these commodities to final consumers.

This conceptual distinction is not only analytically convenient, but also reflects the present day organization of industry in a large class of cases. Most often, production and retailing are conducted in separate plants, if not by separate firms. The economic reason for this is that the economic forces acting on these two activities diverge to an ever increasing extent. In particular, technical change induces economies of scale in production (in one plant), that are not nearly matched by economies of scale in distribution (in one plant), so the scales of operation become incommensurate. Also, economies of scope in the distribution of commodities (and services) induce the distribution of very heterogeneous products within one retailing plant.

This motivates the division of this paper's presentation into two main sections. Section 2 is devoted to the treatment of the production, and Section 3 of the retail sector of the urban economy. The paper concludes with remarks on deficiencies of the analysis to date, and on its possible improvements.

2. Basic industries: Manufacturing

In this section, we study decisions of producers of commodities and services, and their interaction. We restrict our attention to the case where each firm produces in one plant only and competitively supplies one product to an export market. It is free to choose location and input quantities. Among the inputs we distinguish between land, labor and intermediate inputs.

Location decisions of such producers can hardly be understood without reference to two phenomena, namely decreasing costs and agglomeration economies. As is well known, decreasing costs at the plant level are responsible for production not everywhere to take place, which gives rise to costs in assembling labor as well as intermediate inputs. Furthermore, agglomeration economies are the driving force for the spatial concentration of productive activities. However, what exactly constitute agglomeration economies is not a question asked frequently, nor are their effects modelled precisely. Within the context of the intraurban location of production facilities, these economies are largely due to cost reductions in the exchange of intermediate inputs. Aggregatively this may find an expression via a production function subject to economies of scope.[4] Viewed this way, the exhaustion of agglomeration economies via close location is similar, and in many cases, a substitute to a vertical integration of production processes which also induces economies of scope.

However, the advantage obtained from close location cannot be enjoyed without cost. Cost increases are primarily due to increased competition in labor and land markets. They may be evaded to some extent by substituting away towards the intermediate input(s). But in as much there are limits to this substitution, there are limits to the agglomeration of production activity.

Several principal sources of inefficiency and of income inequality are related to the allocation decisions in question. A first one arises from indivisibilities associated with production at decreasing costs, together with the transportation costs of obtaining inputs: Each locator inflicts an "external effect" on other locators with whom he exchanges inputs, as long as he does not absorb all transportation costs generated from his location decision. A second one comes up under this proviso if the transportation activities so generated are subject to congestion. A third one occurs when the firms involved do not behave competitively in all input markets. This situation arises naturally from the fact that typically some input suppliers are located closer to any locator than others.

Given the obvious fact that the forces exercised by these inefficiencies are not unidirectional, the following principal questions emerge on the spatial distribution of business activity within urban areas, as generated by the market: Do the market forces lead to a correct spatial distribution of business activities; or are the agglomerative, or the deglomerative forces excessive from an efficiency point of view? Is the internal structure of clusters of business activity correct, or would a rearrangement of input-output flows lead to an improvement of the state of affairs? Finally, do market interactions lead to correct input pricing decisions, in particular in the labor market?

---

[4]This notion is developed in Baumol, Panzar and Willig (1982). See also Goldstein and Gronberg (1984).

The models developed so far are mostly too partial to give satisfactory answers to these questions. The impacts of imperfect competition on these allocation decisions are particularly little researched. At any rate, we have two long established paradigms within which some of the above questions are attacked, namely the location paradigm in the tradition of Weber, and the land use paradigm in the tradition of von Thünen. The former concentrates on the locational choice within a two dimensional geography, and sometimes the choice of technique of a single firm which is a price taker in all markets and in addition absorbs all the transactions costs involved in obtaining inputs and shipping outputs. The firm locates with reference to predetermined locations of markets for inputs and outputs. Typically, neither localized inputs – except for those provided ubiquitously at the same price and therefore of no impact on the location decision – nor the effects of competitive market interactions are considered. Thus, the relevant trade off involved in alternative locations is the decrease in transportation costs incurred for one input (or output) by moving towards the location of its market, vs their increase for other inputs or outputs from doing so.

By contrast, von Thünen type land use models focus on the effects of perfect competition for land as inputs into production and consumption activities. Location typically takes place with reference to just the location of the output market (or shipping point of output). Firms compete for land close to this market. The essential locational trade off involved here is the decrease in output transportation costs with a move closer to the market, vs the increase in the price of input land (or possibly of labor) involved in such a move. Thus, only the distance to the market is essential. Recently, an important variant of the von Thünen type land use models has emerged. Within these models, the business center is not formed on the basis of an exogenous export shipment point, but on the basis of agglomeration economies.

Given the quite substantive differences in their original analytical set up, Weberian and von Thünen type models cannot be easily merged into one framework.[5] Weberian models are more general than von Thünen ones in considering several reference points for the location decision in essentially a two dimensional geography. However, due to the peculiarities in the assumptions made, it turns out to be difficult to incorporate this paradigm into a more general market model.

By contrast, the land use models are more general in considering land – and possibly labor – as local inputs available under different conditions at different localities, and competitive interactions amongst firms in the land (and possibly labor) market. However, the geography is essentially one dimensional, a feature that for technical reasons is hard to overcome.

[5]An early and insightful statement on this problem is due to Alonso (1967).

In the sequel, we will discuss relatively briefly selected versions of Weberian location, and then in more detail von Thünen type land use models and their modern variants involving an endogenous formation of business centers. The latter models all involve a perfectly competitive world. The section continues with attempts to model business location within an imperfectly competitive world, and closes with remarks on possible future research.

2.1. *Individual producers' behavior*[6]

The set up for the individual producer's location problem originally stated by Weber (1909) is well known. A specialized one plant firm produces a given quantity of output with a two input fixed coefficients technology. The individual inputs are obtained from, and output is supplied to one location each. The firm is a price taker in all markets and has to bear all transportation costs which are proportional to Euclidian distance and quantity shipped. The firm seeks a location minimizing its costs, which is either at the vertex or in the interior of the "Weberian triangle" spanned by the three reference points.[7]

Formally speaking, let $\{y_1, y_2, y_3\} \subset R^2$ denote the two locations of input supplies, and that of the output market, respectively; x_i, $i = 1, 2, 3$ the given quantities of inputs and output to be shipped to, and from the plant; and t_i, $i = 1, 2, 3$ the associated transport costs per unit quantity and distance. If y is the plant location sought, then the original Weber problem consists of

$$\min_y \sum_{i=1}^{3} t_i x_i d(y, y_i),$$

where the $d(\cdot, \cdot)$ denote Euclidian distances. Quite naturally, the *locational pull* exercised by a location i varies with the shipment volume x_i and the unit transport costs t_i associated with that location.

The only economic variables relevant in this problem are the transportation costs and distances, and the input/output ratios. Since these, and output are fixed, prices have no role in the optimization process.

The economic appeal of the original Weber problem is greatly enriched by removing some of its rigid assumptions. The papers elaborating on these may be

---

[6]This survey concentrates largely on economic, rather than operations research models of the Weber problem. The latter primarily focus on numerical approaches to finding the optimal location of the firm, while the former establish its qualitative properties. Also, the survey will be informal. The reason will become obvious below. The contribution of Weberian models to the explanation and evaluation of intraurban business location decisions as of now is not very deep. Earlier surveys of the economic approach are found in Miller and Jensen (1978), Brown (1979), or Ponsard (1983).

[7]The Weber problem is succinctly restated and extended by Alonso (1967).

sorted into three groups. A first one largely sticks to the original Weberian framework; a second one considers the effects of uncertainty on location; and a third one incorporates local inputs and thereby establishes explicit links with the land use paradigm.

Within the first group, early important extensions of Weber's model are the incorporation of input substitution and of profit maximization over a variable quantity of output by Moses (1958), and of a finitely elastic output demand exercised at several market points by Alonso (1967). Hakimi (1964) considers location within a network of transportation lines. More general transportation rate structures are introduced by Woodward (1973), and Miller and Jensen (1978). Eswaran et al. (1981) approach the location–allocation problem using duality theory and employing a general production function.

Recent developments in the theory of the firm under uncertainty due to Sandmo (1971) or Leland (1972) are taken up in the second group of papers. The effects of uncertainty about the quantity demanded on the firm's location decision are taken up by Mai (1981); about input and output prices by Martinich and Hurter (1982); and about transportation rates by Alperovich and Katz (1983).

The authors of the third group of papers concentrate on the incorporation of local resources, in particular land in the model. While this is typically done on the cost of reducing the number of nonlocal resources employed by the firm, authors such as Clapp (1983) are able to link the Weberian model to the urban land use one.

The results derived in the first group of studies to which we now return fall into three categories: (1) characterization of cost minimizing vs (output constrained) profit maximizing locations, (2) derivation of conditions under which location and input choices are separable, and of those under which locational choices are independent of the (exogenously chosen) quantity of output, and (3) (other) comparative statics. The results are derived by alternatively considering a line or a plane as the space of locations.

The characterization of optimal locations under different criteria is somewhat blurred in Moses' (1958) original graphical analysis. This gave rise to most of the follow up papers comprising this first group of studies on the Weberian model. Sakashita (1967) clarifies matters for the one dimensional location case within a formal model employing a linearly homogeneous production function, and Woodward (1973) does so within a graphical analysis. They both show that minimum costs (maximum profits) as a function of location between points of demand for output and supply of inputs are strictly concave (strictly convex). Hence *the only locational candidates in the one dimensional Weber location problem are market locations.* This is also the case if an input is ubiquitously available at constant price, if transportation rates are decreasing in distance, and if, in the case of profit maximization, revenues are concave in quantities.[8]

---

[8] These points are reiterated by many other authors, such as Emerson (1973), Miller and Jensen (1978), Mathur (1979, 1982), or Mai and Shieh (1984).

modelled here is between transportation outlays for non-localized inputs and output. Now, for commodity shipments transiting the agglomeration's boundaries it may be safe to assume that transportation costs are relatively invariant in the choice of location within the agglomeration. Conversely, for commodities shipped within it, the fixed costs of loading and unloading tend to dominate the distance costs, which even increases the tendency towards locating at a Weberian vertex [Louveaux et al. (1982)]. The only counteracting force then is generated by competition about localized resources, such as land and labor, a force which is typically not considered within the Weberian paradigm.

Thus, in view of intraurban location decisions more emphasis should be devoted to the characterization of the typical firm's location decisions at input, or output market locations, and of the impact of competition about land and labor as a key force driving its optimum away from these locations. In view of a better understanding of intraurban location decisions, single firm location models could also account for additional features; for instance of the phenomenon that labor is spatially distributed in non-uniform densities, implying that the cost of drawing it to the plant varies in space; or that manufacturing processes of different sorts demand floorspace for production that can be supplied only in specific proportions of building capital and land; or that the performance of different functions within a firm makes attractive the choice of different intraurban locations for the different functions. Some of these features are developed upon in the land use models to be discussed next.

2.2. Perfectly competitive equilibrium in production

Production is treated in various ways in the land use models to date. In the sequel, we will first classify the models according to several criteria, and then selectively discuss some of the modelling approaches taken. The models may be distinguished according to the following considerations: A first distinguishing feature is the frame of reference for the location of production activities. The classical set up is proposed in Alonso's (1964) adaption of the von Thünen framework, in which an exogenously specified absorption point for output is the point of reference for production. Most land use models are built this way. Examples are Mills (1967, 1972, Chapter 5), Henderson (1977), Schweizer and Varaiya (1976, 1977) or Miyao (1981, Chapter 1). By contrast, in more recent models, the points of reference for one firm are the locations of all other firms in the city. Examples are Ogawa and Fujita (1980), Fujita and Ogawa (1982), Imai (1982) or Kanemoto (1985).

Secondly, production may be represented in one aggregate sector, in multisector aggregates or in a form in which individual plants are explicitly recognized. Examples for the first case include Mills (1967, 1969) and Odland

(1976, 1978); for the second case, Miyao (1981, Chapter 1), Mills (1972, Chapter 5) or Hartwick (1976); and for the third case Solow and Vickrey (1971), White (1976), Ogawa and Fujita (1980), Fujita and Ogawa (1982), Imai (1982) and Kanemoto (1985).

A third characterization concerns the restrictions imposed on the location of business. Many of the models allow for business location only in the center of town, such as Mills (1967), Henderson (1977, Chapter 1), or Sullivan (1983a). In fact, some models, such as Mills (1969), Solow and Vickrey (1971), Miyao (1981, Chapter 1), Tauchen and White (1984) or Sullivan (1984) do exclusively concentrate on land use decisions for production (and possibly transportation) within the business part of the city.

Other models do allow for the suburbanization of business within a von Thünen single center framework. In White's (1976) model, suburbanization is induced by the establishment of a suburban export node and the availability of cheaper labor there. In Mills (1972, Chapter 5), Solow (1973) or Hartwick (1976), industrial activities may coexist with residential ones, again because of the availability of cheaper labor. Business locations are modelled within a multicentric framework by Lave (1973), Fujita and Ogawa (1982), Imai (1982) and Miyao (1981, Chapter 13).

Fourthly, the models differ in their treatment of external economies in production. Alonso's (1964, Chapter 3), Mills' (1969) and White's (1976) contributions, for example, do not consider such externalities at all. In some models, externalities are introduced in aggregate form as Hicks neutral shift factors, indicating economies of scale as dependent on total city population [Henderson (1977), Straszheim (1984)], or total export output [Sullivan (1983a,b,c)].[12] In yet other models, externalities are specified more explicitly as interactions between firms. Examples are Solow and Vickrey (1971), O'Hara (1977) and Tauchen and White (1984). As mentioned before, in Fujita and Ogawa (1982), Imai (1982) and Kanemoto (1985), city centers are formed this way.[13]

Next, the models may be characterized by their consideration of producers' input choices in reaction to variations in input supply over space. In the most widely used standard model, exemplified by Mills (1969), Henderson (1977, Chapter 1) or Miyao (1981, Chapter 1), only land prices vary explicitly over space. In particular, capital and labor can be obtained everywhere at the competitive wage rate. Thus, the choice of technique varies across locations only in reaction to land price variations. In other models, the firm's location relative to that of the labor pool also plays a role in the determination of its labor supply,

[12]The basic reference for this formulation is Chipman (1970).
[13]Extreme cases within this class of models are Beckmann (1976), and Borukhov and Hochman (1977). Therein, every agent interacts with every one else in the city.

and therefore its wage payments [Capozza (1976), White (1976), Sullivan (1983a), Straszheim (1984)].[14]

There is also a class of models in which intermediate input interactions are explicitly accounted for. This is done in two groups of papers differing in objectives, and therefore modelling emphasis. In a first group consisting of Solow and Vickrey (1971), O'Hara (1977), Miyao (1981, Chapters 12 and 13), Fujita and Ogawa (1982), Imai (1982), Tauchen and White (1984) and Kanemoto (1985), symmetric interactions between identical indivisible business units are considered. By contrast, the second group emphasizes a more explicit representation of asymmetric intermediate input interaction flows. This group consists primarily of papers relating Koopmans' and Beckmann's (1957) seminal contribution to von Thünen type urban land use theory, such as Mills (1972, Chapter 5), Goldstein and Moses (1975), Hartwick (1976), Schweizer and Varaiya (1976, 1977), Starrett (1978) and Schweizer (1978).[15] Except for Schweizer and Varaiya (1977), none of the models considering intermediate input interaction allows for input substitution in reaction to input price variations.

Finally, the models can be grouped with respect to their objectives. These may be positive, explanatory, i.e. equilibrium oriented; or normative, i.e. efficiency oriented. Examples for the former are Mills (1969), Henderson (1977, Chapter 1), Fujita and Ogawa (1982) and Miyao (1981, Chapter 12); for the latter, Koopmans and Beckmann (1957), Odland (1976), Starrett (1978), Miyao (1981, Chapter 13), Imai (1982) and Kanemoto (1985).

Let us consider some of these models in more detail, and concentrate first on those involving exclusively the location of business (and possibly transport). The standard model of input choice and location within a von Thünen world is offered by Mills (1969). Urban output is produced with a technology described by a Cobb–Douglas production function involving land, labor and capital. Labor and capital are supplied in unlimited quantities at uniform rates, whereas the supply of land is limited at any given distance to the center of the city, where all output is absorbed. Output producers of undefined size – because of the assumption of constant returns – are price takers in all markets. They compete in the land market with the supplier(s) of transport services, required for the shipment of the output. All profits are absorbed in land rents. It follows quite readily that *in equilibrium land rents decrease in distance from the center* – a condition also derived by Solow (1973) using a unit cost function. Also, *output is produced the less capital and labor intensely, and the more land intensely the farther away from the center production takes place.* Thus, output per unit land is highest

---

[14]More general variants include differentiated labor [White (1978), Straszheim (1980)].

[15]There are also several computational models in which intermediate input exchanges are considered within an activity analysis framework. Examples are Hartwick and Hartwick (1974), and Mills (1976).

near the center. Finally, since transport is not subject to congestion, and since competitive producers internalize all transportation costs generated in this model, the allocation decisions to production are efficient in the sense of maximizing net output.

Miyao's (1981, Chapter 1) paper builds on Solow's (1973) and in some sense generalizes Mills' work by considering m constant returns industries, where industry i, characterized by a cost function $C^i[r, w]$, exclusively occupies ring i around the center of the city. Competition leads to an absorption of all profits in land rent. The bid rent per unit land is defined as the payment to land equating profit per unit land to zero. In equilibrium, it must hold that the bid rent in ring i, $r^i(y) \geq r^j(y)$ for all industries $j=1,\ldots,m$ and $y^{i-1} \leq y \leq y^i$ where y^{i-1} and y^i are the inner and outer radii of ring i. Denote by p^i the product price per unit of output i and by $t^i(y)$ its transport cost over distance y. It follows that in equilibrium

$$C^j[r^i(y), w] \geq p^i - t^j(y), \quad j=1,\ldots.\ m; \quad y \in [y^{i-1}, y^i], \tag{1}$$

with strict equality holding for $j=1$, in which case $r^i(y)$ can be interpreted as industry i's bid rent function.

Industry i's demand for labor per unit of input land is given by

$$n^i[r^i(y), w] = C_w^i / C_r^i, \tag{2}$$

where C_w^i and C_r^i are partial derivatives of C^i, representing the industry's demand for labor and land per unit of output, respectively, at y. Hence n^i can be interpreted as industry i's labor intensity at y. The region's total labor force N is exogenously given. In equilibrium, wages adjust to full employment. Hence

$$\sum_{i=1}^{m} \int_{y^{i-1}}^{y^i} n^i[r^i(y), w] \, g(y) \, 2\pi \, y \, dy = N, \tag{3}$$

where $g(y)$ represents the land available at y for prodution.

Finally, in equilibrium $r^i(y)$ must be a continuous function. In particular,

$$r^i(y^i) = r^{i+1}(y^i), \quad i=1,\ldots,m \quad \text{and}$$
$$r^m(x^m) = r^0, \tag{4}$$

where r^0 represents the exogenously given opportunity cost of land.

Assuming the existence of an equilibrium satisfying the set of conditions (1)–(4), Miyao demonstrates the stability of equilibrium in land and labor markets under the well known condition similarly derived for residential location models[16], that at every boundary between two rings the industry located in the inner

---

[16]For instance by Fujita (1985).

zone should have a higher ratio of marginal transport costs to land per unit of output than the industry in the outer zone.

Miyao then demonstrates the effects of an increase in the labor supply N, and of land $g(y, v)$ available for production in some strictly positive distance interval, with v a shift parameter such that $\partial g / \partial v > 0$.

He obtains

$$\frac{\partial w}{\partial N} < 0, \qquad \frac{\partial w}{\partial v} > 0,$$

$$\frac{\partial y^i}{\partial N} \gtreqless 0, \qquad \frac{\partial y^i}{\partial v} \lesseqgtr 0 \quad \text{iff} \quad n^i(y^i) \gtreqless n^{i+1}(y^i),$$

$$\frac{\partial y^m}{\partial N} > 0, \qquad \frac{\partial y^m}{\partial v} < 0,$$

with all variables evaluated at equilibrium.

Hence the effects of an increase in labor supply and in the supply of land are always opposite in sign. Quite obviously, the equilibrium wage will decrease with an increase in labor supply or a decrease in the supply of land, and the converse holds for the radius of the region in which production takes place. Much less obviously, these changes in input supplies will lead to an expansion of the ring occupied by the relatively more labor intensive industry against the relatively less labor intensive one. In other words, this implies that a relaxation in zoning regulations with a concomitant increase in land supply in a zone where the industry produces relatively less labor intensively than its neighbors will lead to an expansion, rather than a contraction of its land consumption in both inward and outward directions. Finally, an increase in the opportunity cost of land will have the same effect as an increase in the supply of labor on the equilibrium wage and on inner boundaries, but will lead to a decrease in the total area allocated to production.

So far, the supply of labor was determined exogenously, and was independent of the firms' locations. However, in a competitive labor market with un-differentiated labor, firms located more closely to residential districts face wages lowered by the laborers' savings on commuting costs. This idea was first captured by Mills (1972, Chapter 5) within a von Neumann type model.[17] This and the class of models building on it can be interpreted more generally in terms of intermediate input interaction. We return to it later.

An explicit account of the spatial structure of the labor market substantially enriches the possible location patterns for production even within the standard

---

[17] The idea was originally introduced by Moses (1962), but not used there for a discussion of firm location patterns.

single center model involving one production sector. The following principal
patterns may emerge: "Complete segregation", i.e. location of production exclusively in the area next to the city center, and of residences in an outer ring;
"partial segregation", i.e. location of production and residences in separate rings,
but with at least one activity in more than one ring; "partial integration", i.e.
some production concentrated near the city center, and some located together
with residences in one ring; and "complete integration", i.e. production in-
termingling with residences throughout.

The richness in possible patterns greatly complicates the analysis of the
equilibrium and efficient location decisions. In particular, the notion of equilibrium in the labor market becomes more intricate because the more individualized
representation of commuting patterns yields labor supply to change with the
location of production. It also complicates the determination and characterization of equilibrium in the land market. For instance, outward commuting of
labor may occur, with a concomitant increase in the rent gradient away from the
city center. It is therefore not surprising that the few analyses so far conducted
within this framework were restricted to only some of these cases.

Solow (1973) was the first to introduce a partially integrated pattern within a
neoclassical framework allowing for substitution in both the production and the
consumption sector. Together with a centrally located export sector modelled as
before, he considers a local service sector in each residential ring. Both sectors
operate at constant returns with inputs land and labor. The competitive wage
paid in the export sector is w, and in the service sector it is

$$w(y) = w - t^l y, \tag{5}$$

where $(-t^l y)$ reflects laborers' savings in the money costs of commuting from y
to the centrally located business if employed at their location of residence. The
function $w(y)$ is called the wage gradient.[18] Now, since both land and labor costs
decrease in distance, the price of local services also falls, a factor contributing to
the suburbanization of the residential population. How the share of land devoted
to local service production will change with increasing distance cannot be
determined in general. For the special case in which households' utility and local
service production are represented by Cobb–Douglas functions, this share remains constant.

In a suggestive, but not fully developed model, White (1976) analyses first a
completely segregated, and then a partially segregated land use pattern.[19] Inputs

---

[18]The wage profile $w(x)$ implies that laborers living at $x' > x$ are indifferent between jobs located in
the interval $[0,x]$. This is obviously not a general necessary condition for equilibrium in a labor
market with differentiated job locations.

[19]Its presentation here is modified to suit the framework developed thus far. In addition to
White, I assume for simplicity production at constant returns to scale.

into aggregate production are land, labor and ubiquitously available capital. Let the production process be described by the unit cost function $C[r, w]$ where r and w are defined as before. In the case where land uses are completely segregated, the industry bid rent $r(y)$ per unit land at y is determined by solving

$$C[r, w - t^l(y)] = p - t(y).^{20} \tag{6}$$

Differentiating $r(y)$ with respect to y, we observe two counteracting forces on that bid rent: An increase in y implies an increase in output transportation outlays, but a decrease in wage payments. Thus, bid rents for production may increase, or decrease in y. Within a multisectoral representation of production, this would imply a sorting of production activities such that those with high output transportation costs and highly capital intensive but labor and land extensive technique would locate near the center, and others farther away.[21]

The model is not closed by an explicit representation of labor supply as a fixed proportion of the residential population. However, as long as the land use pattern is restricted to be completely segregated, one can expect a standard von Thünen type equilibrium residential land use pattern.

White then induces the suburbanization of production by supposing that the production activities are confronted with transportation costs for export output from a suburban location y_s, equal to that from the center. This production sector's bid rent function $r(y)$ is determined by the solution to

$$C[r, w - t^l(y)] = p - t(\min\{y, |y_s - y|\}), \tag{7}$$

with all functions and variables defined as before. Differentiation yields

$$\frac{dr}{dy} = \frac{C_w t_y^l(\mp) t_y}{C_r^2} \quad \text{for} \quad y \in \left[0, \frac{y_s}{2}\right) \cup [y_s \infty) \quad \left(y \in \left[\frac{y_s}{2}, y_s\right)\right), \tag{8}$$

with all variables defined as before. It also can be verified that $r''(y) > 0$. A typical bid rent function is pictured in Figure 1 (in lines heavily drawn) for a given wage gradient and therefore a given household bid rent function $r^1(y)$, under the assumption that increases in output transportation costs in distance always dominate input cost decreases.

---

[20] An assumption implicit in White's formulation but explicit in Sullivan's (1983a) similar model is that wages in the business district just vary to compensate for commuting costs to the business district's boundary, rather than to the workers' residences. This implies that the labor market is not differentiated by residential locations of the laborers.

[21] The notion of "capital" is somewhat elusive in this class of models. It may refer to building capital which, together with land, is used to produce floorspace as an intermediate input; it may also refer to machines used in the production process; and it finally may include intermediate inputs stored for production. The statement in the text is appealing only if "capital" in the main refers to building capital. If it refers to machinery, it is much less so, since the elasticity of substitution between such machinery and land tends to be very low, implying that a production with machine intensive technique may well be driven away into zones with lower land prices.

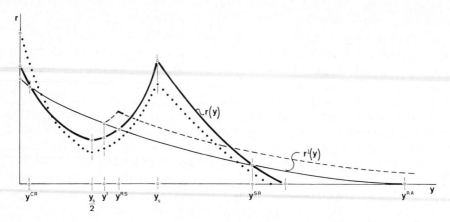

Figure 1. Bid rent functions $r(y)$ for a suburbanized export sector and $r^l(y)$ for a residential (labor) sector.

For obvious reasons, $r(\cdot)$ takes on peaks at $y=0$ and y_s. The latter must be higher because at y_s the wage is lower than at $y=0$. Also, the slope of the rent gradient must be steeper on $y\in[y_s/2, y_s)$ because here all cost components work in the same direction.

Observe that Figure 1 as drawn can only reflect an equilibrium in both labor and land markets if the labor force located in the two residential rings is exactly sufficient to satisfy, *by commuting inwards*, the demand for labor in the two business districts. In particular, any outward commuting of the labor force from the inner residential district characterized by the interval $[y^{CR}, y^{RS})$ towards the location of suburbanized business is left uncompensated, and therefore cannot occur.

Suppose now that the demand for labor from suburbanized business is not satisfied by the supply of labor obtained from the suburban residential zone. In order to draw labor from some distance interval $[y', y^{RS})$, business located at $y''\in[y^{RS}, y^{SR})$ must increase its wage payments to

$$w(y', y'')=w-t(y')+t(|y''-y'|).$$

If individual businesses cannot discriminate between laborers by residential location, then all suburban businesses have to pay the so inflated wages. Let y' denote the distance beyond which laborers commute to suburban workplaces. Self selection among laborers in terms of job locations closest to their residence leads workers living in $[y', y^{RS})$ to choose jobs in $[y^{RS}, y'']$, say. This induces a kink at y' in the residential bid rent $r^l(y)$, and possibly even a positive slope of that function over some distance interval. Finally, suburban business bid rents are deflated due to the increase in wage payments. If an equilibrium in land and labor markets exists at all in this case, then rents in an "open city"[22] are adjusted to a structure drawn in dotted and dashed lines in Figure 1. This suggests that the suburbanization of firms as induced by improved suburban export opportunities leads to an expansion of city size.

The suburbanization of firms in reaction to the suburban location of labor or of suppliers of another input is also modelled within a framework originally proposed by Mills (1970; 1972, Chapter 5), in which both types of agents produce or consume in fixed proportions, and all units are transported at costs proportional to distance. As earlier, the final commodity is exported only through the center. Due to the linearity of the model structure, only two land use patterns can be obtained, namely the completely segregated one in which the intermediate commodity (or labor) is always supplied from the suburban ring, and a completely integrated pattern. That latter pattern emerges if it is cheaper to transport units of output per unit input than input itself; or if an acre of land devoted to producing input is highly productive compared to an acre devoted to output production, and therefore an integration of land uses requires more shipment of a few units of output and less input shipment. It is intuitive that under the assumptions used here, the equilibrium land use pattern is also efficient, i.e. maximizes net output.

This two sector intermediate input model is generalized by Schweizer and Varaiya (1976) to a multisector one. A given vector of final demands is produced with fixed proportions of inputs, and shipped to the CBD. Under the restriction that land at each distance is devoted to production with one technique only, it is shown that an *efficient land use pattern* (supported by a linear price system) *involves a strict ordering of land uses by distance, and this ordering is independent of the levels of final demand.*[23] Furthermore, *goods for meeting intermediate and final demands are shipped only in the direction towards the* CBD, *and never outwards.*

While this latter conclusion holds for an efficient land use pattern also when production techniques are Leontief but substitutable, the former does not [Schweizer and Varaiya (1977)]. In particular, the ordering of rings by techniques and commodities produced changes with required output, and techniques employed in inner rings may reappear in distant outer ones. This "*reswitching*" *property* known from growth models involving Leontief techniques with substitution [Burmeister and Dobell (1970)][24] *defies commonly accepted stylized facts*

---

[22]Worker households migrate in or out until their well being in the city exactly equals some reference utility $\bar{u}$. Cf Straszheim (1985), or Arnott (1985), this volume.

[23]This is a spatial version of the nonsubstitution theorem [Nikaido (1968)]. Schweizer (1978) generalizes it by allowing for imports of factors of production and intermediate products through the CBD.

[24]See also Bruno, Burmeister and Sheshinski (1966).

such as the decline with distance of capital/land, or output/land ratios. It is also surprising that an efficient land use pattern with these properties can be sustained by a linear price system – which does not imply that equilibria are always efficient. At any rate, Schweizer and Varaiya (1977) offer a conceptual break-through in the sense that for the first time choices of technique are explicitly made dependent on the local availability of inputs.[25]

In the land use patterns derived thus far, production was characterized by constant returns to scale. Thus, individual firms were not identifiable, nor were their interactions with others at the individual level. However, if production takes place at decreasing costs, firms can be identified, and therefore also the (costly) interaction between them, that gives rise to agglomeration economies. This invites the *endogenous determination of centers of business activity*.

In the sequel, this idea is pursued within the simplest framework possible. Business firms are typically characterized as indivisible (but atomless) units generating a fixed quantity of output from fixed input requirements. In line with modern city structures, these firms don't ship their output via a predetermined center, but export it from their plant at costs nearly invariant in location. This leaves to the model the generation of the CBD as a region of culminating business activity, and the determination of its internal structure.

The group of papers initiated by Solow and Vickrey (1971) concentrates on the latter aspect. The general issue addressed is the equilibrium vs efficient distri-bution of business activities within the CBD. Solow and Vickrey do this by also accounting for land used in transportation. Land is available along a rectangular strip of length W and width L. Breadthwise transportation is disregarded. There are B businesses, each consuming one unit of land, and generating n tons of traffic per unit of time. Destinations are uniformly distributed over the entire business area B, whose shape is to be determined. Thus, at any strip from y to $y+dy$, $y \in [-L/2, +L/2]$, the space of width W has to be apportioned to business and to (crosswise) transportation, subject to congestion, so that for the decision to be efficient, the total transport costs involved in the business interactions are minimized. The solution to this calculus of variations problem characterizes, as one expects, a road profile narrowing with increasing rate as distance from the median point $y=0$ of the strip increases.

For obvious reasons, the interaction costs decrease as a business unit is located more closely towards $L/2$. Within a competitive allocation process, this must be reflected in land rents increasing towards $y=0$. Details depend on the in-stitutional arrangements for sharing these interaction costs. Solow and Vickrey

---

[25]However, competitive equilibrium with such input interactions is not discussed and compared to the efficient outcome(s). In view of the inefficiencies discussed below that arise in the presence of such interactions, one is tempted to argue that competitive equilibria are efficient only under peculiar institutional arrangements concerning the distribution of the transportation cost burden.

quite realistically assume that the sellers deliver to destinations at a uniform delivered price, and the transportation authority is unable to collect any congestion costs.

These two assumptions guarantee that, no matter the distribution of land between business and transportation activity, the *rent per unit land generated by business* at location *y does not reflect the social net benefits from devoting one more unit of land to transportation* across *y*. There are two reasons for this. The first well known one is the presence of unpriced congestion. A second one, however, arises even if congestion costs are properly accounted for; namely from the fact that upon locating, the typical business unit does not account for *all* transportation activity generated by its location decision. While it accounts for all delivery cost for its output to the other units, it neglects the costs of receiving output from the other ones. In conclusion, the rent profile rises less sharply than it should towards the locational median, because locational advantages are not fully reflected in private cost savings.[26]

The second source of inefficiency, due to an incomplete internalization of the transportation costs generated by the typical firm's location decisions, is the focus of Tauchen and White's (1984) paper, which extends O'Hara's (1977) equilibrium analysis to include efficiency questions. Here, transportation is not treated as a land using and congestion generating activity,[27] in lieu of a more refined treatment of the business sector.

Consider first the equilibrium location of an endogenously determined number *B* of business firms withing a square CBD of size *L* by *L*. Within that, providing *b* firms with one unit of floorspace each at a given location involves a cost *C(b)*, where *C(·)* is an increasing convex function. As in Solow and Vickrey, the individual firm is supposed to interact once per unit of time with every other firm in the CBD.[28] The monetized benefits resulting from this are characterized by the strictly increasing and concave function *q(B)*. The cost of interacting involves a travel outlay of *t* per unit distance. Travel takes place along a ubiquitous rectangular grid.

In equilibrium, business firms will have entered into the central business district until at all locations

$$(y_1, y_2) \in \left[-\frac{L}{2}, +\frac{L}{2} \right] \times \left[-\frac{L}{2}, +\frac{L}{2} \right],$$

---

[26]Solow and Vickrey's analysis is extended to a circular CBD by Kraus (1974) and to a square one by Miyao (1978; 1981, Chapter 12).

[27]The latter assumption can be defended by the observation that congestion takes place during rush hours when workers commute to and from the CBD, rather than during the hours where the interactions discussed here are realized.

[28]Relaxing this assumption and endogenizing interaction decisions does not substantially modify the results.

the typical firm's profits are zero. Hence its bid rent $r(y_1, y_2)$ is determined by

$$r(y_1, y_2) = q(B) - T(y_1, y_2),\tag{9}$$

where

$$T(y_1, y_2) = \int\!\int t(|y_1 - u| + |y_2 - v|) b(y_1, y_2)\, du\, dv,\tag{10}$$

is the typical firm's travel outlay. Also, the competitive outlay of floor space implies that at each location (y_1, y_2), the firm's rental payments equal the marginal costs of providing that space:

$$r(y_1, y_2) = C'(b(y_1, y_2)).\tag{11}$$

The model is closed by defining the total number of firms in the CBD:

$$B \equiv \int\!\int b(y_1, y_2)\, dy_1\, dy_2.\tag{12}$$

Suppose for a moment that $b(y_1, y_2) = B/L^2$; i.e. that the businesses are distributed uniformly over the square. Then an inspection of (10) reveals that despite rectilinear travel the isocost outlays are circular around $(y_1, y_2) = (0, 0)$. Furthermore, differentiating the land rent function

$$R(y_1, y_2) = b(y_1, y_2)\, r(y_1, y_2) - C[b(y_1, y_2)]\tag{13}$$

for a fixed b, we observe that *land rents decrease at an increasing rate from the center of the* CBD. For fixed b this results from the strict concavity of $r(y_1, y_2)$, the individual firm's bid rent. It is quite surprising that the strict concavity of r is sustained also for an arbitrary distribution of business in the CBD. However, it does not follow that the equilibrium land rent function is also strictly concave with an endogenously determined distribution of firms. In this case, both the density function of firms $b(y_1, y_2)$ and the land rent function $R(y_1, y_2)$ are concave near the origin, but may become convex towards the CBD boundaries [O'Hara (1977)]. At any rate, this result is at variance with the one derived earlier within the von Thünen framework, in which the equilibrium land rent function is strictly convex.

Let us now turn to a comparison of the equilibrium with the efficient outcome, where the latter is defined as the maximal value of output net of the cost of floorspace construction and of transportation costs; i.e. the maximum of

$$B q(B) - \int\!\int [C(b(y_1, y_2)) + T(y_1, y_2) b(y_1, y_2)]\, dy_1\, dy_2.\tag{14}$$

This is again a problem in the calculus of variations with instruments B and $b(y_1, y_2)$. Its solution [Tauchen and White (1984)] satisfies

$$q(B) - T(y_1, y_2) - C'(b(y_1, y_2)) + q'(B)B - T(y_1, y_2) = 0. \tag{15}$$

By contrast, inserting (11) in (9) reveals that in equilibrium only the first three terms must equal zero at all locations. The term $q'(B)B - T(y_1, y_2)$ which must additionally equal zero in the efficient allocation reflects the *net benefit to the other firms of the last firm locating in the CBD. The divergence between equilibrium and efficient allocations results from the individual firm's lack of accounting for this external net benefit.*[29]

How does the equilibrium land use pattern differ from the efficient one? An inspection of (15) suggests that an efficient allocation involves more firms in the CBD, and a stronger concentration of these firms around its center, for in this case the Marshallian external benefits are increased and the transaction expenditures are reduced. Such an efficient solution is supportable by either controlling the market for floorspace via bulk zoning and controls on floorspace rents, or by levying a locational tax adjusting for the terms in (15) not accounted for in equilibrium. However, in this interpretation care must be taken of the fact that this model is very partial. Not only are intra CBD congestion costs unaccounted for, but also the costs of labor commuting towards the CBD. This latter feature is taken up now.

Following Ogawa and Fujita (1980), and Fujita and Ogawa (1982)[30], we return to a representation of space via a long narrow strip of length L. This space houses N laborer-households. Each household consumes a units of land. Just as in White's (1976) paper, wages are indexed by business location. It is the household's objective to maximize the quantity z consumed of a numeraire commodity by choosing appropriate residential and work locations y' and y, respectively. The bid rent for a household living at y' which is maximal with respect to a choice of workplace y is given by

$$r^h(y') = \max_y \frac{1}{a} [w(y) - t(|y - y'|) - z], \tag{16}$$

where z must be uniform across households because of competition.

The B identical business units in this local economy produce one unit of output each with fixed amounts of land and labor, v and n, respectively. Agglomeration

---

[29] In addition to the inefficiencies discussed in Solow and Vickrey (1971), this model thus accounts for a third commonly observed inefficiency, which is the firm's lack of incorporating the external benefits of its entry decision on the other firms.

[30] Their work concentrates on the characterization of equilibria. Imai (1982) independently conducts an analysis of the efficient pattern in a very similar approach. His model is very close to the one of Mills (1972, Chapter 5) described earlier, with the exception that the city center is determined endogenously as a cumulation point of business interaction, rather than exogenously as an export terminal.

economies net of interaction costs are reflected in the function

$$q(y) = \int kb(z)\,e^{-\alpha(|y-z|)}\,dz, \tag{17}$$

where $b(z)$ reflects, as before, the density of firms at z, $b(z) \in \{0, 1/v\}$; k is a parameter characterizing the interaction benefits, and α is a parameter reflecting the rate of decay in interaction benefits with increasing distance. The economic meaning of (17) is equivalent to the expression $q(B) - T(y_1, y_2)$ used earlier. Indeed, $q(y)$ is also strictly concave for $\alpha > 0$ if all businesses are concentrated in one interval.

The entry of businesses is limited by the availability of labor. Thus, $B = N/n$. However, competition in the land market drives business profits to zero. The typical firm's bid rent function then becomes

$$r(y) = \frac{1}{v}[q(y) - w(y)n]. \tag{18}$$

An equilibrium in this model is described by the following conditions: Letting $R(y) = \max\{ar^h(y),\ vr(y),\ r^0\}$,

$$h(y) = 1/a \quad \text{if} \quad R(y) = ar^h(y), \text{ and } 0 \text{ otherwise}, \tag{19}$$

where $h(y)$ refers to the number of households at y;

$$b(y) = 1/v \quad \text{if} \quad R(y) = vr(y), \quad \text{and } 0 \text{ otherwise}; \tag{20}$$

$$h(y) + vb(y) < 1 \quad \text{and} \quad = 1 \text{ iff } R(y) > r^0; \tag{21}$$

$$b(y)n = \int h(z)\,\beta(y, z)\,dz; \tag{22}$$

where $\beta(y, z)$ refers to the share of households living at y that commutes to z;

$$\int h(y)\,dy \equiv N; \tag{23}$$

and

$$\int b(y)\,dy \equiv B \equiv N/n. \tag{24}$$

The meaning of these conditions is as follows. (19), (20) and (21) determine the land use pattern; (22) equilibrates the labor market; and (23) and (24) are accounting identities.

There is a rich set of possible equilibrium configurations which may be sorted

along the lines discussed earlier involving segregated or integrated or intermediate land use patterns. However, any equilibrium necessarily has the following properties [Ogawa and Fujita (1980)]: Firstly, cross commuting of households
cannot occur. Secondly, if commuting takes place, then the equilibrium wage
offered in the business district must be declining at rate t towards the closest
residential district. Thirdly, business never locates at the fringe of the city.

The equilibrium land use patterns may be parametrized along t, k and $(-\alpha)$.
We restrict ourselves to patterns symmetric about the median point $y=0$. The
complexity of the emerging possible patterns forbids an analytical solution. The
following numerically analyzed example may be illustrative [Fujita and Ogawa
(1982)]. A monocentric pattern results if the labor commuting costs are small
relative to the benefits resulting from interaction summarized in k, and the
interaction decay $(-\alpha)$. This example is characterized in Figure 2.

Of the many other patterns that may emerge, a less standard one is presented
in Figure 3. Business and residential activities are integrated near the median

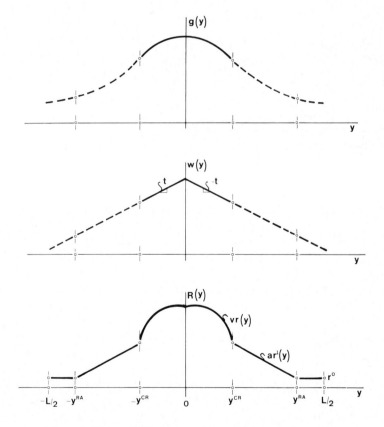

Figure 2. Monocentric land use pattern with business interaction.

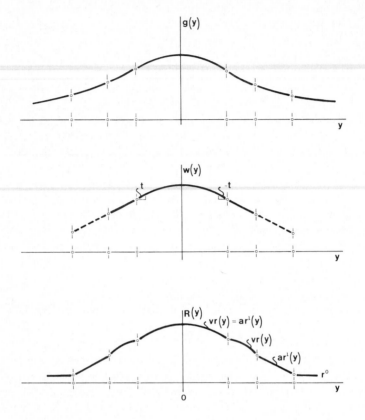

Figure 3. Partially segregated/integrated land use pattern with business interaction.

point $y=0$. Next to this are pure business districts, followed by pure residential districts.

It should finally be emphasized that marginal changes in the parameters may result in dramatic (long run) changes of the land use pattern, a feature which merits further analysis.

How does all this relate to an efficient outcome, i.e. an outcome maximizing the value of output net of all transactions costs? We can infer directly from our earlier discussion that *no equilibrium tends to be efficient*. Unfortunately, Imai's (1982) analysis of efficient patterns based on a very similar model is parametrized differently, and thus not directly comparable to the above equilibrium analysis. Kanemoto (1985) extends Imai's efficiency analysis by the firms' endogenous choice of interactions, and by a demonstration via a modified Henry George theorem, of the supportability of the efficient spatial configuration by a system of Pigovian taxes and subsidies. However, this support is insufficient when the number of activities varies. This is due to the fact that equilibrium cities may be too large, and nonconvexities impede the formation of a new city in the market [Henderson (1974)].

Finally, Miyao (1981, Chapter 13) determines an efficient number of business centers by means of a somewhat different paradigm. He further extends a square business center version of Solow and Vickrey's (1971) model to include agglomeration economies and businesses' demands for labor, and adds four rectangular residential zones to this business district. Then he asks for conditions under which such a configuration ought to be replicated to achieve the maximum net output, called the efficient outcome.

Intuitively speaking, an increase in the size of one, rather than a separation into several business centers is the favoured solution if the gains from local business interaction are large, both the output/land ratio and the costs of business interaction are high, and the costs of commuting to the suburban residences are small. These expectations can be verified without considering congestion [Lave (1983)]. With congestion in commuting and business traffic, an increase in the latter's costs will have an ambiguous effect on the efficient number of business centers.

At any rate, it is unknown whether or not such an efficient number of business centers, and the allocation decisions taking place within them, can be supported by a set of prices; and how equilibria relate to this efficient configuration.

We conclude the discussion of perfectly competitive location models by concentrating again on a problem central to the question of public policy, namely the efficiency of competitive equilibrium in an economy with costly transactions. This issue was addressed first by Koopmans and Beckmann (1957), and further by Starrett (1978).

Regarding this issue, the models presented hereto are but special cases. They nevertheless have revealed a fundamental reason for inefficiencies arising from individual maximizing behavior even under the condition of price taking. It is that *whenever an agent enters a market, locates, and establishes his trading relations without considering all transactions costs (and benefits) conferred on all other agents, he inflicts external effects on these.* Naturally these external effects are not mediated by the land market. Thus there is no reason to assume that competition about land and in particular, and landlords' quest for "highest and best (i.e. land rent maximizing) use" would lead to social efficiency. This is the key issue behind the inefficiencies, and in particular the nonexistence of efficient equilibria, addressed by the aforementioned authors.

The external effects causing this inefficiency would only be negligible if the agents would be able to economically act as self sufficient individuals each in an autarkic Robinson Crusoe economy, or if the agents would each occupy a very small space and interactions could economically be restricted to a very small set of other agents nonintersecting with other agents' respective sets. Both hypotheses are questionable the more, the farther technical change pushes both the division of labor and economies of scale (and scope) of producing large quantities of any product at one location. Hence the importance of these externalities tends to increase over time in as much technical change enforces increases in the volume of physical transactions between agents. It may decrease only insofar the transactions volume can be reduced, and substituted for by technically perfected telecommunication.

   This fundamental inefficiency arises even within a perfectly competitive spatial economy. However, its very source: the indivisibility of interacting production processes, is the source of another market failure, namely the agents' deviation from price taking behavior. We will now turn to approaches incorporating this phenomenon.

2.3. Imperfectly competitive equilibrium in production

The indivisibility of production units, and the nature of the spatial interaction between them both contribute to the difficulty of maintaining the assumption of price taking behavior in a spatial economy. In particular, if due to indivisibilities and the associated decreasing costs not everything is produced everywhere, and transactions costs are high, there is a natural source of imperfectly competitive behavior in all input markets. Of course, its impacts are constrained the more, the lower the transactions costs. Transactions costs are lowered with an agglomeration of interacting agents. However, in deriving principles of firms' location and agglomeration, it will be useful to resort to interaction among a few agents in the different input markets.

   There are only very few attempts to capture some of these market imperfections within formal models. In a first one, Fujita (1981) models the equilibrium location decisions of two firms trading inputs within a Weberian framework. More specifically, he considers a Weberian triangle spanned by the separate locations of markets for two inputs and one output. Each one of the two locating firms produces with a fixed coefficients technology involving two inputs: one supplied at a market, and the other one supplied by the second firm. Faced with given constant unit prices and transport rates for inputs and output, and bearing all input transportation costs together with the costs of transporting output sold to the market rather than to the other firm, each entrepreneur seeks a profit maximizing location, taking as given the other firm's choice. This implies for each firm solving Weber's original problem.

   A characterization of the Nash equilibrium solutions to this noncooperative game is difficult: generally, there is an infinite number of location patterns. All that can be said and indeed is a standard result from duopoly theory, that none of these equilibria is efficient relative to the locations resulting from the joint profit maximization of firms, unless the latter involve locations at vertices.[31] While equilibria efficient in that sense can be supported by taxes and subsidies on the transportation rates, they have to be earmarked by the firms' locations and thus are difficult to implement.

A second, quite different approach is chosen by Schulz and Stahl (1985a). Two firms, each producing output for a world market with two inputs, namely labor and the output supplied at world market price by the other firm, choose locations, input quantities and wages along a line uniformly populated by laborers of uniform grade. The latter are induced to work at the firm offering the higher wage net of commuting costs, provided the net payment exceeds some reservation wage. This induces a game in which the typical firm is confronted with the following locational trade off, together with appropriate choices of input quantity and wage: Either to locate closely to the other firm and thereby to save on transportation outlay for the nonlabor input, on the cost of increased competition in the labor market; or to establish a local monopsony in the latter market, on the cost of an increased outlay per unit of nonlabor input.[32]

More specifically, firm i's technique is specified by the production function $f(m^i, n^i)$, where m^i and n^i denote quantities of intermediate input and labor, respectively. Although the firms' products are different, their techniques f are identical,[33] and neoclassical except for additive separability. The costs of entering the market are sunk. World market prices for outputs are normalized to unity. The space of locations is a line of length L along which atomless labor is distributed with mass one. The boundaries of the line are assumed not to matter, so all that counts in terms of firms' location is the distance between them.

Each firm pays a uniform wage. It thus does not discriminate among laborers by residential location. Laborers' commuting costs are t^l per mile, and their reservation wages are zero. Intermediate input is transported at the receiver's cost at rate t per unit and mile. It is assumed that transporting intermediate input from the world market is always more costly than obtaining it from a local firm. Both firms contribute positive net supplies to the world market.

The firms' interaction is modelled within a two stage game. In its first stage, the firms choose a location, i.e. a distance d between them; and in the second one, they determine input quantities m^i and n^i and wage payments w^i. The solution

---

[31] One might also expect this result in view of the last subsection's conclusions.

[32] This set up is similar to Fujita's as far as the savings in input interaction costs as agglomerative force is concerned. It differs in the representation of deglomerative forces. In his model, these are the costs of obtaining a second input from a distant location; in ours, it is the quest for locally monopolistic power in the labor market. A further difference is that we allow for input substitution. Finally, both models dodge the issue of bilaterally monopolistic interaction in the intermediate input trade.

[33] This condition is necessary to guarantee the existence of equilibrium. See also Schulz and Stahl (1985b) for a broader discussion of this existence issue.

concept employed is Selten's (1975) concept of subgame perfectness in multistage games. According to this concept, an s-tuple of strategies is a perfect equilibrium if, after any stage, the subset of the firms' strategies that pertains to the remaining stages of the game forms a Nash equilibrium of that game. Applied to the present context, this implies that upon choosing a location, the firms anticipate Nash equilibrium input choices and wage payments. It also implies that we can work backwards and determine first Nash equilibrium choices of inputs and wages for any given distance between the firms, and then equilibrium locations conditional upon these.

Consider the second stage of this game. For a given distance, additive separability of the production techniques implies independent choices of intermediate input quantities. The latter are decreasing in distance between the firms because of increasing transactions costs. Furthermore, the firms' wage setting decisions uniquely determine their labor supplies (cf. Figure 4, where at given d, w^1 and w^2, firm 1 obtains $w^1/t^l + d/2 + (w^1 - w^2)/2t^l$ units of labor). Hence in this stage of the game, wages are the only relevant variables with interaction effects.

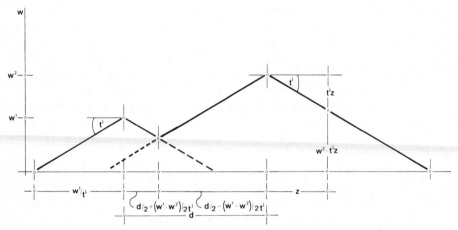

Figure 4. Duopoly in a spatial labor market.

An equilibrium in this wage game is characterized as follows.[34] For close distances between the firms, the firms compete in the labor market (cf. Figure 4). In this case, the wage equilibrium is unique and involves identical payments by

[34] For the construction of equilibria, we assume also that the advantages from bilateral input trades to either firm are higher than the disadvantages from competition in the labor market. In this case, outbidding the other ffirm, or setting entry deterring wages is not a dominant strategy.

the firms that, owing to decreased competitive pressure in the labor market, decrease in distance. Also, if the firms are located sufficiently far from each other, they are both local monopsonists, and obviously their wage payments do not vary with a marginal change in location. However, there is also an unexpected intermediate distance interval within which there is a continuum of equilibria, each with the property that wages are chosen so that the labor markets just touch. In this distance interval, the firms do not compete intensively, but extensively in the labor market: any (small) distance change results in an upward wage adjustment so that the labor markets again border each other. Thus, $w^1 + w^2 = t^l d$, where w^1, w^2 are equilibrium wages.

We now turn to the first stage of the game where the firms determine a profit maximizing distance, given a correct forecast of equilibrium wages and input choices for each contemplated distance. The typical firm's profits tend to be convex in the interval where the two firms compete intensively in the labor market. In that case the only candidates for equilibrium are the zero distance and a distance where the labor markets just touch.

It is surprisingly difficult to precisely determine the conditions under which either one of the equilibria obtains. One might expect, that decreases in labor commuting costs, or increases in the density of laborers per unit interval decrease the competitive pressure in the labor market and lead the firms to move closer to each other; or that decreases in intermediate input transactions costs have a decentralizing effect. However, while the latter expectation is correct, the former ones are not: both, decreases in commuting costs, and replications of the labor sector tend to have a decentralizing effect. This result is quite counterintuitive and merits further investigation. It is finally very surprising that even within this simple model, comparisons between equilibrium and efficient solutions, defined as solutions maximizing the sum of producers' and workers' incomes, are very difficult to obtain. In particular, it is unclear a priori whether the latter lead to a more concentrated, or a more decentralized location pattern.

It appears nevertheless worthwhile to pursue further research along the lines suggested by this paradigm. It accounts for the principal agglomerative and deglomerative forces, and the analysis along it can be pushed much further. For instance, agglomeration and deglomeration can be conditioned explicitly on the relative shares of, and the elasticity of substitution between the inputs used; and the (sequential) entry, and location–allocation decisions of further firms trading intermediate inputs can be studied within a framework where these inputs are substitutable. Most importantly, in this latter case the entry decision of firms is made dependent on local input supply conditions, which seems to be of central importance from an empirical point of view. A consideration of these aspects within the present framework is warranted even more in view of the following observation: while the perfectly competitive models discussed earlier elucidate well the aggregate efficiency problems involved in business location decisions when business interactions are present, they almost by nature cannot replicate in detail location choices conditional upon individual firms' characteristics and resultant market outcomes. Furthermore, it is open to question whether imperfect competition enhances, or mediates this principal inefficiency.

In conclusion, one therefore might want to speculate about whether the (realistic) introduction of imperfectly competitive behavior worsens, or improves upon the efficiency of equilibria. Oddly enough there appears to be a tendency towards an improvement of the state of affairs. As firms ascertain a significant market power in the local market, they tend to internalize more of the local effects external to perfectly competitive small firms. An example in the present case is the allocation of the input labor. Oligopolistic firms will tend to account for the effects of their wage setting on the supply of labor including commuting activities, and possible congestion effects. Competitive firms tend to do so much less.

3. Nonbasic industries: Retailing

In this section, we analyze decisions involved in local distribution and consumption. We focus on the distribution of commodities and services to final consumers; that is, on retailing, rather than on wholesaling, which involves the distribution of commodities to firms as demanders of intermediate product.

We begin by discussing consumer theory with transactions costs. The demand faced by retailers is deeply influenced by the structure of consumers' transactions outlays, and in particular by the savings in transactions costs enjoyed when jointly shopping several commodities at one location, or searching at that location for the preferred alternative among close substitutes. Thus, rather than looking for the lowest delivered price per commodity, the consumer chooses to patronize the market place offering a bundle of commodities whose purchase at quoted prices maximizes his (expected) utility net of the transactions costs incurred.

Since consumers differ in their locations relative to any marketplace, the market demands derived for such a marketplace exhibit a peculiar structure. The market demand for a given commodity is not only dependent on the consumers' preferences, but also on the local supply of all other commodities and the conditions under which they are offered, such as their suppliers' advertising outlays, or their reputation in terms of selecting and marketing commodities. At any rate, the consumer's economies of scope in transactions outlays induce complementarities in the market demand for commodities that are substitutes in the individual consumer's eyes.

All this would be of little consequence on allocation decisions in the retailing sector, were retailing itself not subject to economies of scale and scope. These result in retailer's reaction to this pattern of market demands, in supplying an often large bundle of heterogeneous commodities, and/or in agglomerating in marketplaces, thus seeking rather than evading competition. The system of marketplaces thus resulting is differentiated by size and structure, i.e. number and types of commodities offered. Since the market demand faced by any retailer is reflecting *local* market conditions typically differing across marketplaces, equilibrium in the retailing sector tends to be characterized by a permanently upheld price dispersion for physically identical commodities even in an a priori undifferentiated world.

Due to the nonconvexities critically entering this analysis, an explicit generation of this pattern within one integrated model turns out to be difficult even if informational problems are assumed away. Even more difficult is an evaluation of this pattern in terms of efficiency, or of equity criteria. Nevertheless, forgoing the elegance of convex analysis not only leads us to observing the specifics of allocation decisions in this sector, but also the possible welfare problems involved in them; and it therefore teaches us to ask some relevant policy questions, for instance: Is the pattern of commodity supplies generated by unrestricted market activities appropriate in terms of location, commodities offered and prices charged, relative to the spatial distribution of the consumer population? What is the impact of different modes of retailing (custom vs cash and carry vs mail order delivery), and of different modes of organizing the industry (single plant retailing and external wholesaling, vs chain store retailing with internalized wholesaling) on this pattern, and on the pattern of supplies forthcoming from the producing sector? Adding uncertainty and informational asymmetries between consumers and retailers, does the retail sector perform properly its selection and information transmission function? Again, how does this performance differ by mode of retailing, and of organizing the industry?

There are principal sources of inefficiency, that need to be analyzed in view of providing suitable answers to these questions. A key one is that in view of the transactions cost advantages consumers enjoy from joint shopping, retailers, upon joint location confer "demand externalities" onto each other, that typically are not all internalized. A second one is sellers' imperfectly competitive behavior that arises from economies of scale and scope in selling, and from an internalization of these "demand externalities". A third one is induced by the sellers' informational advantages over the buyers, which may be exploited especially within an imperfectly competitive situation.

As in the case of business location, we are not very far in our ability to give well founded answers to the questions raised above. Indeed there is only little positive, not to speak of normative analysis to date incorporating the peculiarities of the retailing sector at least inasmuch as they relate to space. That sector is accounted for only in rudimentary form within the land use models analyzed in Section 2. Therein, retailing typically takes place within the exogenously specified center of the city. Exceptions are Solow (1973) in the model discussed, White

(1975), and most recently Fujita and Thisse (1986).

In the recent wave of literature on oligopolies involving product differentiation, it has been taken for granted that Hotelling's (1929) classical pricing and location paradigm covers in essence the intricacies of retailing. This is not really the case. In particular, there is hardly an analogy in the world of product differentiation models to the important attractive force for any locating retailer exercised by clusters of retailing operations in space. We therefore will not consider large segments of this literature. It anyway has been competently reviewed elsewhere.[35]

Even Lösch's (1940) central place paradigm widely used among spatial economists does not explicitly capture the consumers' economies of scale and scope involved in shopping, which are basic to the evolution of his central place system. We therefore abstain also from a detailed review of the literature based on the classical central place paradigm. After all this, it is of no surprise that even in the standard textbook chapters the effects of the consumers' transactions costs involved in collecting commodities remain unanalyzed.

However, early attempts to capture these phenomena are due to Baumol and Ide (1957) within a model formulated somewhat ad hoc, and in an informal but very perceptive paper by Holton (1957).[36] Models formalizing consumer behavior under certainty are due to Reinhardt (1973), Stahl and Varaiya (1978a), Lentneck et al. (1981), Stahl (1982a), and Harwitz et al. (1983). A fairly exhaustive treatment of shopping cost minimizing consumer behavior is given by Bacon (1984). Implications on the oligopolistic interactions between retailers in terms of location are drawn by Niedercorn (1981), and Eaton and Lipsey (1982); and in terms of pricing by Stahl (1982a) and Weinberg (1985). Bliss (1985) develops a monopolistically competitive model based on consumer behavior with transactions costs.

While there is ample empirical demonstration of the existence of strong economies of scale and scope in selling commodities and services, e.g. by Dean (1942), Holdren (1960), Douglas (1962), Bucklin (1972), Arndt and Olsen (1975) and Nooteboom (1980, 1982), theoretical analyses so far consider only in a rudimentary form the economies of scale enjoyed by single product firms, and their effects on the spatial organization of these markets.[37] The contributions

[35]Good recent surveys are provided by Friedman (1983, Chapter 4) and Gabszewicz and Thisse (1984).

[36]Holton apparently was the first to recognize that the market demand faced by a multiproduct seller may exhibit complementarity even between products that are substitutes in terms of the consumer's preferences. This notion was later independently developed by Selten (1970) and Stahl (1982a).

[37]The literature on markets involving multiproduct firms producing with economies of scale and scope has only recently emerged even within a nonspatial context. The most comprehensive account to date is by Baumol, Panzar and Willig (1982).

taking off from Hotelling's and Lösch's seminal paradigms all fall into this class of models.

A second strand of literature takes off from Stigler's (1961) seminal contri-bution. Of particular interest here are the papers focussing on the consumers' search cost advantages from looking at several alternatives offered close by. An early paper not considering supply side effects is by Stuart (1979). Stahl (1981, 1982b) and Wolinsky (1983) developed models explicitly accounting for suppliers' interactions. A recent account of location, product choice and pricing decisions under alternative market arrangements is by Schulz and Stahl (1986). Finally, Stahl and Varaiya (1978b) study retail location within a context where the retailers themselves are imperfectly informed about the consumers' demand, and they orient themselves towards locations where previous entry has generated demand information.

The general lack of recognition of the impacts of consumers' transactions costs motivates the following relatively detailed treatment of consumer behavior under certainty. We then look at the sellers' reactions in terms of the location of retailing units, and of product choice and pricing.[38] We continue by sketching implications of consumer search behavior on retailers' strategies responding to this. Finally we give thought to further extensions of these models.

3.1. Consumer shopping behavior, and local market demand

Most acts of consumption are preceded by a shopping trip, during which the relevant commodities are purchased and transferred to the consumer's home; alternatively, services are consumed at the location of delivery. Such shopping trips, especially if conducted by car, are characterized by great *economies of scale* in the quantity of any commodity or service picked up, and *economies of scope* in the number of commodities and services jointly purchased or consumed.

The consumer could fully exhaust these economies by bundling all shopping activities in one trip if the commodities would not depreciate and their storage would be costless, and if the consumer had no interest in spreading the con-sumption of services over time. By contrast, the consumer is faced with a decision problem involving the optimal bundling of the commodities and services shopped jointly, and the determination of the optimal frequency for these shopping activities per period. However, it is illuminating and helpful for the later analysis of market interactions to concentrate first on the simplified case where the

---

[38] Proofs of the original results presented below are available from this author. However, the problems involved in ensuring the existence of equilibria are disregarded throughout. Their treatment is formally quite involved. On this issue, consult Gabszewicz and Thisse (1984), MacLeod (1985); Schulz and Stahl (1985b), Stahl (1985) and Weinberg (1985).

consumer is able to exhaust without restriction the aforementioned economies of joint shopping, and therefore bundles all shopping activities in one.

The impacts of the economies so incurred are demonstrated by means of the following simple model, taken from Stahl (1982a). Let our consumer be endowed with income R net of housing and work trip expenses, and with a preference ordering over $N+1$ commodities or services i, $i=0,\ldots,N$, $N\geq 2$. Let these preferences be representable by a utility index $u(x)$ where $x=(x_0,\ldots,x_N)$, $x\geq 0$. The commodities are considered physically different. They are not distinguished in terms of the consumer's preferences, if they only differ by the location of availability.[39] At any rate, that preference index is assumed to satisfy the usual properties, namely sufficient differentiability, strictly positive monotonicity, and strict quasiconcavity.

Fix our consumer's location at y. Suppose that at y he can purchase and consume commodities, such as mail order delivered goods, aggregated into the numeraire commodity 0. Options to purchase other commodities are available at two alternative marketplaces A and B located at y^A and y^B, respectively. Let the set of commodities offered at marketplace A be a strict subset, namely the first k commodities of the set of commodities offered at B. The consumer's transportation costs incurred in visiting these marketplaces, $t^A=t(y,y^A)$ and $t^B=t(y,y^B)$, respectively, are assumed to depend *only on the distance travelled*, and *not on the number and quantity of commodities hauled*.[40] The consumer is supposed to patronize at most one marketplace per period of time. His choice is dependent on the maximal utility obtained from an allocation of his budget R to transportation, and to the commodities available at the chosen marketplace and at home.

Suppose for a moment that the two marketplaces are equidistant from the consumer's location, and thus $t^A=t^B=t$; and furthermore, that the price charged for commodities 1 through k available in both marketplaces is the same at A and B, i.e. $p_i^A=p_i^B=p_i$.

Then the consumer has always a weak preference for a commute to marketplace B, where the larger commodity bundle is offered. Formally, $v(p_1,p_2^B,R-t)\geq v(p_1,\infty,R-t)$, where v denotes the consumer's indirect utility at given prices and transportation costs; p_1 is the price vector for commodities available at both A and B, p_2^B is the vector of prices for commodities available

---

[39] Although the latter distinction is customary in the general equilibrium literature since Debreu (1959), it is not very helpful. As is well known, such a differentiation may lead to nonconvexities in consumption sets and preferences as well as in production technologies, that are purely of a technical nature, and thus behaviorally unfounded.

[40] This is an assumption at variance with one customarily made since Lösch (1940). While not entirely realistic, it reflects the consumer's transaction costs at today's transportation and consumption technologies much more adequately than the received one of proportionality in transportation outlays in quantities of each and every commodity hauled.

only at *B*, and for simplicity of notation $p_2^A \equiv \infty$. This preference is strong if for some commodity *i* only offered at marketplace *B* the quoted price p_i^B satisfies $p_i^B < \tilde{p}_i$, where

$$\tilde{p}_i \equiv p_j \frac{\partial u/\partial x_i(\hat{x}^A)}{\partial u/\partial x_j(\hat{x}^A)},$$

for some commodity *j* offered in *A* (and *B*). This condition simply says that the price of at least one commodity exclusively offered in marketplace *B* should be low enough to induce the consumer's positive demand. A graphical example is given in Figure 5, where for simplicity the consumption of commodities at home is neglected.

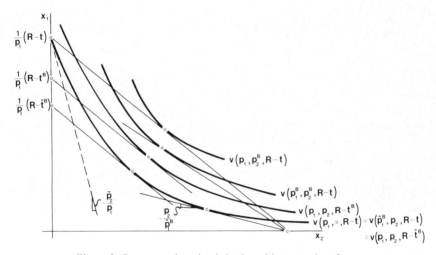

Figure 5. Consumer shopping behavior with economies of scope.

It follows readily that a strong preference for marketplace *B* may be upheld even if the prices for commodities available in both marketplaces are higher in that marketplace (in Figure 5: $v(p_1^B, p_2^B, R-t) > v(p_1^A, \infty, R-t)$), or if the costs t^B of patronizing marketplace *B* are higher than those of patronizing marketplace *A* (in Figure 5: $v(p_1, p_2^B, R-t^B) > v(p_1, \infty, R-t)$). The latter increase can be the larger, the lower the prices for the commodities offered in marketplace *B*, and − loosely speaking − the lower the elasticity of substitution between the commodities offered in marketplace *A*, and those offered uniquely in marketplace *B*.

Now, let a price, and a transportation cost configuration prevail so that our consumer is indifferent between patronizing either marketplace (in Figure 5: $v(p_1, \infty, R-t) = v(\tilde{p}_1^B, p_2, R-t) = v(p_1, p_2, R-t^B)$). What happens in this situation if his income increases or, for that matter, the transportation costs to both marketplaces fall in the same proportion? The consumer will remain indifferent if he is endowed with preferences described by a homothetic utility function. However, he will prefer to patronize the larger marketplace if, as eminently reasonable, his preferences are structured so that with increased income he even more prefers convex combinations of the larger set of commodities offered in B, rather than of the smaller one offered in A.

We so far have unrealistically assumed that our consumer has no explicit time preference for consuming services within the time period considered, nor that he incurs storage or depreciation costs for the physical commodities assembled at home for consumption. Building on Stahl and Varaiya (1978a) and Bacon (1984), let us concentrate on the consumption of physical commodities[41] and suppose that our household insists on maintaining a constant consumption flow of these commodities over the period in question. For any given quantity of commodities consumed during this period, the household is then faced with a trade off between frequent costly commuting for shopping, and a high cost of storage.

Let s_i be the cost of storing a unit of commodity i per unit of time,[42] and suppose for a moment that commodity i cannot be purchased jointly with any commodity j on one shopping trip. If that commodity is offered at marketplace A at price p_i^A, the consumer's cost of availing himself with x_i units of that commodity over the time period considered is minimized by minimizing $\varphi_i t^A + s_i x_i / 2\varphi_i$ with respect to the shopping frequency φ_i. Taking φ_i as continuous, we obtain an optimal shopping frequency $\varphi_i = (s_i x_i / 2t^A)^{1/2}$, which quite naturally increases in the quantity consumed and in the commodity storage cost, and decreases in the cost of the shopping trip. The uniqueness of this frequency is easily ascertained by observing that the total cost of obtaining x_i units of the commodity,

$$C_i(x_i, \varphi_i, p_i^A, t^A) = p_i^A x_i + \varphi_i t^A + (s_i x_i)/2\varphi_i, \tag{25}$$

is u-shaped in the frequency of the shopping commute (see Figure 6). Inserting $\hat{\varphi}_i$ in (25), we obtain

$$\hat{C}_i(x_i, p_i^A, t^A) = p_i^A x_i + (2s_i x_i t^A)^{1/2}. \tag{26}$$

Observe finally that increases in x_i or t^A lead to a less than proportional increase in the associated costs, for $\hat{C}_i$ increases in both x_i and t^A at a decreasing rate.

---

[41] The case of service consumption is briefly discussed in Stahl (1983).

[42] We use here the simplest formulation of the inventory problem of operations research. More explicit formulations would include a dependence of storage costs on the commodity price reflecting the capital cost of inventory; a commodity specific real depreciation term; and the cost of providing appropriate storage space – which in term may interact with the real depreciation of perishables. For an elaboration of this also involving the consumer's time commitment, see Harwitz et al. (1983).

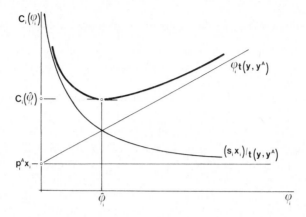

Figure 6. Purchase cost of one commodity with varying shopping frequency.

Let us now introduce again economies of scope in purchasing several commodities. The consumer may reduce his purchasing cost by jointly purchasing commodities i and j on one shopping trip. Let both i and j be offered at marketplace B, in addition to i being offered at A. Then our consumer will purchase both commodities jointly on shopping trips to B if

$$\hat{C}_i(x_i, p_i^A, t^A) + \hat{C}_j(x_j, p_j^B, t^B) > \hat{C}_{i+j}(x_i, x_j, p_i^B, p_j^B, t^B), \tag{27}$$

where the lhs (rhs) of inequality (27) refers to the cost of separate (joint) purchase, with all costs defined corresponding to (26). If $t^A = t^B = t$ and $p_i^A = p_i^B = p_i$, the purchases are conducted jointly at B, provided that

$$\sum_{i,j} [(s_k x_k)^{1/2}] > \left(\sum_{i,j} s_k x_k\right)^{1/2},$$

which always holds. Thus, under the prevailing conditions our consumer always bundles his purchases in shopping trips to B, and commutes with frequency $\hat{\varphi}_{i+j} \in (\hat{\varphi}_i, \hat{\varphi}_j)$ if at no loss of generality $\hat{\varphi}_i < \hat{\varphi}_j$.

How does he ever return to purchasing i at A? Only if the price p_i^A is much lower than p_i^B and/or t^A is much lower than t^B, and i is demanded in large quantities. However, in all such cases, our consumer may still decide not to purchase all of commodity i at marketplace A, but some quantities at A and some at B, whenever convenient.[43]

All these alternatives provide for a rich set of behavioral choices, which can at

[43]These conditions are ascertained by observing that purchases at A require

$$(p_i^B - p_i^A)x_i + (t^B - t^A)(\hat{\varphi}^A + \hat{\varphi}^B) = \frac{s_j x_j}{2\varphi^B}\left(\frac{\hat{\varphi}^A}{\hat{\varphi}^B} + 1\right).$$

best be modelled explicitly at the individual consumer's level.[44] However, we are primarily interested in the emergence of retail location patterns as a result of this behavior. We thus have to be satisfied with the simplest admissible description of individual behavior, and we therefore will resort in the sequel to the first model variant of consumer behavior.

Before moving on to an analysis of aggregate demand and of sellers' behavior, let us briefly relate the view of consumer behavior presented here to that of the classic writers such as Hotelling (1929) or Lösch (1940) and used in most of the follow up literature. In the spatial location interpretation of Hotelling's model, the typical consumer demands exactly one unit of one homogeneous commodity, and patronizes the marketplace for which commodity price plus hauling costs are lowest. In our nomenclature, he chooses to buy at A (B, respectively) if $p^A + t^A (\lessgtr) p^B + t^B$.

In this case, the model structure enforces an identical treatment of purchasing, and transportation costs. This treatment is upheld in Lösch's consumer model. Here, the individual consumer's transportation outlay is proportional in the quantity of each and every commodity hauled. Beyond this, the demands for different commodities are assumed independent of each other. Thus both, economies of scale and scope in hauling commodities are excluded in these formulations. While this simplifies all further analysis and especially that of retailers' reactions to the relatively simple structure of market demands, it also does away with the main economic reason for the formation of marketplaces as clusters of retailing activities.

What do patterns of *aggregate demand* look like when generated from the consumer behavior just described? We focus on two cases. First, the case where *physically different commodities are available within one marketplace*; and second, where only *identical commodities are offered, but at different locations*.[45]

For an analysis of the *first* case, let us return to the simplest model of consumer behavior discussed above, which involved shopping on just one trip. The exposition is simplified if the typical consumer's preferences are considered homothetic. Then his demand is multiplicatively separable in prices and income (net of transactions costs). Furthermore, his transport costs are assumed linear in distance. Formally,

$$x(p, R - tz) = (R - tz)x(p, 1), \tag{28}$$

is the consumer's demand vector if he lives z miles away from a marketplace. Thus the relative quantities demanded are invariant in income, and therefore in

---

[44]An analysis even of the simplest of these cases within a utility maximization framework involves non-convexities in the consumer's budget set. Cf Stahl (1983) or Bacon (1984) for examples.

[45]The general treatment where physically different commodities are available at different marketplaces is excluded here. It is formally very involved.

distance from the marketplace. Let the consumers be identical except for location, atomless, and uniformly distributed with mass one along a line of length L, with $y \in [-L/2, +L/2]$. L is sufficiently large, so that boundaries don't matter.

Suppose that at location y, n commodities are offered at prices $p = (p_1, \ldots, p_n)$. For the moment, other consumption opportunities are all local and reflected in an opportunity utility level v^0 invariant across locations. Then a consumer living z miles away from y will (not) demand commodities from there if $v(p, R - tz)(\gtreqless)v^0$. We obtain

$$\tilde{z}(p, v^0) = \{z \mid v(p, R - tz) = v^0\}, \tag{29}$$

as the unique distance at which a consumer is indifferent between patronizing and not patronizing the marketplace. Quite naturally, $\tilde{z}$ decreases in both p and v^0.

The market demand at y is given by

$$X(p, v^0) = 2x(p, 1) \int_0^{\tilde{z}(p, v^0)} (R - tz)\, dz. \tag{30}$$

This demand is continuous in all variables, and unchanging with small changes in y. Differentiating (30) we obtain as the typical expression

$$\frac{\partial X_i}{\partial p_j} = 2\frac{\partial x_i}{\partial p_j}(p, 1)\left(R - \frac{1}{2}t\tilde{z}\right)\tilde{z} + 2(R - t\tilde{z})x_i(p, 1)\frac{\partial \tilde{z}}{\partial p_j}. \tag{31}$$

The first term on the rhs of (31) refers to the standard *Marshallian substitution effect*. It determines the impact of a price change for commodity j on the individual consumer's demand for commodity i, aggregated over all consumers patronizing the marketplace. The second effect is new. It determines the effect of that price change on the size of the market area, i.e. on the mass of consumers itself. We term it the *market area effect*.[46] While this latter effect is always negative, the former is positive if i and j are Marshallian substitutes, $j \neq i$, and negative if they are complements.

Taken together, these effects imply that *the market demands for the two commodities i and j are complementary even if the commodities are Marshallian substitutes in the individual consumer's eyes, provided that the substitution effect is smaller* (in absolute terms) *than the market area effect.* In that case, a price decrease for commodity j not only increases the market demand for j, but also for its substitute i. By the same token, the introduction of an additional commodity k at location y at a price at which the typical consumer exhibits positive demand

---

[46]More specifically, the effect of the price change on the (standardized) demand per consumer is weighed by the consumer's average income after transactions costs, and multiplied by the mass of consumers patronizing the marketplace. Furthermore, the effect on the market area is weighed by the income of consumers located at its fringe of the market area. See Novshek and Sonnenschein (1979) for a similar disaggregation of effects within a product differentiation world.

will increase the market demand also for (not too close) substitutes as well as, of course, for complements. This is so because in both cases the number of consumers patronizing the market place increases.

Let us now turn to the *second* case where physically identical commodities are offered at two different marketplaces A and B located at y^A and y^B, $0 < y^A < y^B$. By assumption, consumers choose to patronize either marketplace A, or B, or none of the two. Given p^A and p^B, either the market areas don't touch – in which case the typical local market demand is given by (30); or the market areas touch – in which case there is a unique location $\tilde{y}$ at which the consumer is indifferent between buying at A or at B; or prices differ so dramatically that the low priced marketplace fetches the demand of all consumers patronizing a marketplace at all. The transitions between these cases are such that the *local market demands* $X^i(p^A, p^B, y^A, y^B, v^0)$, $i = A, B$ *are continuous in both, prices and locations.*

The continuity of local market demands comes as a surprise to any one versatile with the classical Hotelling/Lösch paradigm. Therein, market demands typically are discontinuous at price intervals at which the consumer located at y^B is indifferent between purchasing at A or B. The discontinuity of demand arises, because under the unrealistic specification of the transportation cost structure discussed before all consumers located to the right of y^B are also indifferent between patronizing y^A or y^{B}.[47] It disappears with the more realistic specification of consumers' transportation costs introduced here. Under this specification, the consumers located to the right of y^B strictly prefer to patronize B. This is due to the income effect of transportation expenditures, implying that the transportation cost increases are broken over a smaller bundle of commodities if purchased at A. Finally, as p^A is decreased (proportionally) relative to p^B, the interval in space from which market demands for y^B are generated moves to the right, and shrinks continuously to zero.[48] Figure 7 pictures a typical situation for the case where the consumers' utilities are linearly homogeneous, and therefore decrease linearly in distance from the respective marketplace. Observe that utility decreases in distance the faster, the lower (proportionally) the commodity prices.[49]

---

[47]The discontinuity also arises if a consumer located at y^A is indifferent between patronizing y^A and y^B. These discontinuities are demonstrated in d'Aspremont et al. (1979), and their consequences on the existence of equilibria are discussed in detail in Gabszewicz and Thisse (1984).

[48]Suppose that just one good is sold at both marketplaces. Then a consumer living at y^B is indifferent between patronizing y^A and y^B if $x^A(y^B) = [R - t(y^B - y^A)]/p^A = x^B(y^B) = R/p^B$. A consumer living at $y' > y^B$ is faced with reduced consumption opportunities because his income after transportation outlays is reduced. At y^B, he is thus able to buy only $x^B(y') = [R - t(y' - y^B)]/p^B$ units of x. Let the consumer be at y^B: Then, purchasing the same quantity at y^A would involve higher unit expenditures: $p^B < p^A + t(y^B - y^A)/x^B(y')$, which is easily shown by proper substitution. This result is due to Weinberg (1985). It generalizes to the case discussed here. A proof is available on request.

[49]Continuity of aggregate demand can also be obtained if the consumers' transportation costs per unit purchased are assumed to be strictly convex in distance. See d'Aspremont et al. (1979), and Gabszewicz et al. (1981). While this assumption is well applicable to the product differentiation world, it appears less realistic in the situation under study here.

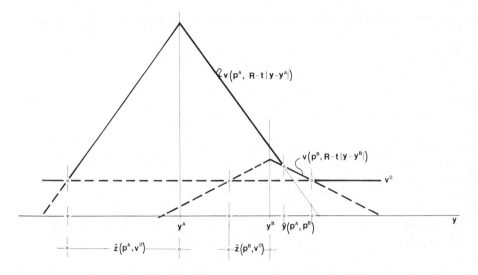

Figure 7. Market areas for identical bundles of commodities.

3.2. Equilibrium in retailing

Consumer purchasing behavior in space as discussed here implies that the structure of market demands is much different from the one derived in the classical models a la Hotelling and Lösch. In summary, their features are as follows. Firstly, consumer economies of scale in hauling larger quantities of one commodity insure that the *typical consumer is disproportionately attracted to marketplaces offering discounts*; he is willing to travel over a long distance and to engage in a bulk purchase, because travel costs are broken over that larger quantity of the commodity. Thus, market demands disproportionately increase with a (unilateral) price decrease. As a useful fringe benefit of introducing these economies, the market demands for physically identical commodities offered at different locations remain continuous in prices.

Secondly, and more importantly, consumer economies of scope in transportation outlays imply dependences in market demands for physically different commodities beyond those generated from consumer preferences. In particular, *the market demand for one commodity at a given location is not only dependent on its price, but also on the prices of other commodities available there.* To the individual consumer, larger marketplaces offering larger sets of commodities may be more attractive even if farther away, and this the more, the larger the difference in the size of the commodity bundle offered there. Furthermore, the utility increase obtained from the increased choice, or alternatively speaking, the decrease in the real cost of living, may be sustained even if the commodity prices are high relative to those prevailing in closely located smaller marketplaces. However, if the price of some arbitrary commodity in positive demand is shifted upwards too much, the consumer will cease to patronize that marketplace altogether. Such a price change thus affects the consumer's local demand for all other commodities, be they substitutes of, or complements to the commodity in question. In consequence the aggregate drawing power of a marketplace is a function of the entire price list of commodities offered there.

Thirdly, differences in the quantities demanded, and in storage and depreciation costs associated with different commodities induce differential *shopping trips at different frequencies for different commodity bundles*. Most notably, demands for perishable commodities such as groceries are more localized than demands for durable ones.[50]

All these conclusions are eminently reasonable from an empirical point of view. Furthermore, they have strong effects on the sellers' entry, location, product bundle and pricing decisions. For instance, consumer economies of scale ensure that "sales" become an attractive instrument of drawing customers to a marketplace. Consumer economies of scope imply that if sellers of different commodities agglomerate in a marketplace, they confer a "demand externality" upon each other by whatever local action taken, such as by changes in price, advertising or changes in the offered commodity bundle.[51] Alternatively speaking, they all contribute to a "local collective commodity" consisting of the market area from which consumers are drawn. Quite obviously, the individual seller's contribution to this collection commodity is felt, and internalized by himself the less, the more sellers partake in the marketplace.

At any rate, this *demand externality*, or local collective commodity, is due to the indivisibility involved in the consumers' choice of moving, and it takes on a nontrivial magnitude because of the indivisibilities involved in setting up retail outlets. Of course, that demand externality, as many others, invites internalization, which is one important reason for the emergence of multiproduct sellers.

The other reason is the existence of *economies of scope* sellers materialize when offering additional products. They mainly consist of cost reductions in sharing common overhead (plant, equipment and personnel); and of reductions in the cost of advertising, and in developing expertise for prepurchase advice to customers. In fact, it is hard to imagine bundles of commodities for which there

---

[50]This also explains the dramatic shifts in consumer grocery shopping behavior and consequently, the changes in the organization of retailing that occurred with the advent of cost reducing storage techniques such as the refrigerator and the freezer. Together with cost reducing bulk transportation techniques through the automobile, they led to a reduction of grocery shopping frequencies, and to purchases in larger bulks at locations offering commodities at reduced prices, even if farther away.

[51]This is not an externality in the customary sense. The notion of "externality" is clearly defined only within the context of perfectly competitive markets.

are absolutely no such economies. While recognized in the empirical literature on retailing, they thus far have not been considered in formalized treatments of the retailing sector.

A third factor bearing influence on retailers' behavior are *economies of scale* in selling additional quantities of the same commodity. They are due to several sources. First, the overhead costs are distributed over a larger quantity sold. Second, unit inventory costs decrease with increasing turnover. And third, retailers enjoy buying advantages from lot size economies passed on by producers or wholesalers. All these economies, and especially the latter ones can be exhausted by resorting to discount selling, and by establishing chain stores all selling the same product line.[52]

Apart from considering economies of scale as arising from fixed costs in setting up a retail outlet, there are virtually no analytical contributions concentrating on the effects of this peculiar cost structure on the organization of retailing. While incorporating the fixed costs of setting up a retail outlet, we therefore focus in the sequel on the impacts of the demand externalities on the behavior of sellers, and on equilibrium and efficiency in the retailing sector.

Even if we abstract from all these peculiarities in sellers' costs of providing commodities, a rich set of alternative market structures may emerge. The market may house the classical (imperfectly) competitive specialized single plant firm a la Hotelling, or Lösch. Alternatively, the single plant firm may supply several products; here we focus on the special case where this firm is a "spatial monopolist", offering as sole supplier at the chosen marketplace all products that can be profitably supplied. Finally, the firm may be specialized, but supply in several plants; we consider the special case of "commodity monopoly", where the firm has exclusive control over offering a particular commodity in as many plants as it wishes. Of course, the market may generate combinations between these types of firms, and the emergence of such types should be endogenous to a fully satisfactory model. However, this is beyond the scope of current research.

In principle, each potential seller is faced with the following choices: Whether or not to enter the market; given entry, which location(s) to choose; then, which products to offer; and finally, which prices to charge.[53] For the analysis of equilibria, we use the multistage game approach and subgame perfectness as equilibrium concept, as elucidated in Section 2.3. We again proceed backwards and begin our analysis with the *fourth stage of the game* involving the firms' pricing decisions, given the preceding choices. However, in this last stage, as well

---

[52]Set up costs are to some extent informational, and therefore subject to economies realized by increasing the number of establishments. Inventory costs may be saved by internalizing the wholesaler's functions.

[53]The space of decisions can be enriched even more by including the choice of capacity, or the choice of a sales technique such as custom, or cash & carry retailing.

as in the preceding stages we cannot elaborate on all cases. In line with the above analysis of aggregate demand, we will focus primarily on interactions between demands for, and sellers of imperfect substitutes at one marketplace, i.e. on competition in commodity space; and secondarily on the interaction of sellers of perfect substitutes across marketplaces, i.e. on spatial competition.

Let us first turn to the former case, involving the consequences on pricing of competition in commodity space at one marketplace. We compare the equilibrium prices adopted by the firms under alternative locational and organizational set ups.[54] Consider first a three commodity economy in which as before the numeraire commodity 0 is purchased and consumed at home, and let firm i, $i = 1, 2$, supply commodity i at marginal cost k_i in a plant located at y. The set up costs are sunk. Let the market demand be specified as in (30), but suppose for the moment that only firm i supplies at y. We account for this by setting p_{-i}, the price for the other commodity, to infinity. Then firm i maximizes

$$\pi_i(p_i, \infty) = (p_i - k_i) X_i(p_i, \infty, v^0) .$$

with respect to p_i. Assuming strict concavity of π_i and the existence of an optimal solution, the first order necessary condition determines the firm's profit maximizing price. Define $\eta_i(p) \equiv -(\partial x_i/\partial p_i) p_i/x_i$ to be the own price elasticity of the individual consumer's (standardized) demand, and $\mu_i(p) \equiv -(\partial \tilde{z}/\partial p_i) p_i/\tilde{z}$ as the price elasticity of the market area; and let $\tilde{w} \equiv R - t\tilde{z}$ be the marginal, and $\bar{w} \equiv R - t\tilde{z}/2$ the average consumer's income. Then the necessary condition can be written as

$$\frac{p_i - k_i}{p_i} = \frac{1}{\eta_i(p) + (\tilde{w}/\bar{w})\mu_i(p)} . \tag{32}$$

Thus, we obtain the usual rule that the firm's profit maximizing price-cost margin must be equal to the inverse of the own price elasticity of its market demand. That price elasticity is decomposable into the two elasticities just defined, with the market area elasticity weighed by the fraction of the marginal to the average consumer's income.

Obviously the necessary condition remains structurally the same when the second firm supplies its commodity also at y, and both firms behave as price setting Nash competitors, We wish to compare the resulting equilibrium price for firm i, p_i^C with the profit maximizing price p_i^M if the firm is the sole locator – a "one product spatial monopolist". In particular, we will show that possibly $p_i^C > p_i^M$ despite increasing competition.

To this end, suppose the two prices were the same, i.e. $p_i^C = p_i^M = p_i$. If the two commodities are imperfect Marshallian substitutes, the own price elasticity of the

---

[54]The following discussion is a further elaboration and generalization of Stahl (1982a).

individual consumer's demand increases,[55] and the weighed market area elasticity decreases with the introduction of the second commodity at a finite price. This is quite intuitive: the introduction of a second substitutable commodity at the marketplace increases the price sensitivity of the individual consumer's demand for *i*. Furthermore, it decreases the price sensitivity of the market area, because customers now are attracted by a larger list of commodities and prices, so that the influence of individual price changes is reduced. Now, $p_i^M < p_i^C$ is implied by $(p_i^M - k_i)/p_i^M < (p_i^C - k_i)/p_i^C$. Hence $p_i^M < p_i^C$ if, evaluated at $p_i^M = p_i^C = p_i$, $\eta_i(p) + (\tilde{w}/\bar{w})\mu_i(p)$ decreases with the introduction of the second commodity, which is the case whenever the increase in the own price elasticity of individual consumers' demand from introducing commodity $-i$ is more than outweighed by the decrease in the market area elasticity. That increase will be small whenever the two commodities offered jointly in the marketplace are not "too close" substitutes. It furthermore may be easily checked and it is intuitive that $p_i^M < p_i^C$ whenever the two commodities are Marshallian complements.

A second interesting comparison of pricing strategies is that between two competitive one product sellers located jointly, and a spatial monopolist selling the very same two products. Let us concentrate on strategic differences in pricing and therefore abstract from the economies of scope unquestionably enjoyed by such a spatial monopolist. He then maximizes

$$\pi(p_1, p_2) = (p_1 - k_1)X_1(p, v^0) + (p_2 - k_2)X_2(p, v^0),$$

with respect to p_1 and p_2. Assuming for simplicity that the typical consumer's preferences are symmetric in commodities 1 and 2 so that for each x_0 and $x_1 = x_2$ as well as $p_1 = p_2$, we have $\partial x_1/\partial p_1 = \partial x_2/\partial p_2$ and $\partial x_1/\partial p_2 = \partial x_2/\partial p_1$, and assuming again that the conditions relevant for an optimum are satisfied, the necessary conditions determining his profit maximizing pricing strategy are given by

$$\frac{p_i - k_i}{p_i} = \frac{1}{\eta_i(p) + \eta_{i,-i}(p) + 2(\tilde{w}/\bar{w})\mu_i(p)}, \tag{33}$$

where the new term $\eta_{i,-i}(p)$ refers to the cross price elasticity of the individual consumer's demand between the two commodities sold by the spatial monopolist. This term is negative if the two commodities are substitutes, and positive if they are complements. The two commodity spatial monopolist will charge lower prices than the two one product competitors, if, evaluated at equal prices,

$$\sum_{j \neq i} -\eta_{ij}(p) < (\tilde{w}/\bar{w})\mu_i(p); \tag{34}$$

that is, if the cross price elasticity is bounded above by the (strictly positive)

---

[55] If we assume, as eminently reasonable, that $\partial x_i/\partial p_i(p_i, \infty, 1) > \partial x_i/\partial p_i(p_i, p_{-i}, 1)$ for finite p_{-i}.

market area elasticity. Hence the two commodity *spatial monopolist will always charge a lower price for complementary commodities. But he will also do so for substitutes, provided that they again are not too close.*

The reason for this surprising difference in monopolistic vs competitive pricing behavior is that the competitive one product firms give insufficient account to the demand externality associated with price changes. *While both, the substitution and the market area effects of, say, a price increase on their own demand are correctly accounted for by each one of the competitors, the negative effect of the market area reduction on the competitor's sales is neglected. This effect is internalized by the spatial monopolist,* which results in lower monopoly prices unless strong competition about the demands for close substitutes forces competitive prices down even more.

The implications of all these results on product choices assigned to the *third stage of the game* are rather obvious. Given symmetry in demands, both the two one product sellers at one marketplace, as well as the spatial monopolist will choose to offer strict complements. In this case, the *spatial monopolist will always charge lower prices than the competitors will do,* no matter whether he sells one of the products or both.

Is this difference in behavior between spatial monopolist and competitors upheld if the number of commodities sold in the marketplace is increased? Presuming again that the demands for all these commodities will exhibit identical properties, this will be the case if

$$\sum_{j \neq i} -\eta_{ij}(p) < (n-1)(\tilde{w}/\bar{w})\mu_i(p),$$

where $n > 2$ is the number of commodities sold in the marketplace. This inequality can be upheld just as well as inequality (34). The decrease in $\mu_i(p)$ with an increasing list of commodities and prices is compensated by increases in the weighing factor $(n-1)$. However, it is quite likely that the list of complementary products and weak substitutes will at some point be exhausted with the successive introduction of products at the marketplace, which then leads to an increase of the lhs, and therefore a reversion of that inequality. We will return to this point, when it comes to discussing entry decisions of firms at that marketplace. For the moment, we observe that for both, competitive firms assembled at one marketplace, as well as the spatial monopolist, the list of commodities offered most profitably is worked "downwards" from the strictly complementary to the substitutable ones.

We now concentrate on the pricing implications of the second form of competition arising in geographical space between sellers of given homogeneous commodities. In view of the location decisions discussed hereafter, we will consider as binding the boundaries of the geographical space, i.e. our line. Otherwise, the sellers of perfect substitutes would always establish spatial monopolies.

Weinberg (1985) considers pricing aspects in a special version of the consumer model discussed hereto, in which consumers use all of R, $R > tL$ on transportation outlays and expenditures to purchase the maximal quantity of one composite commodity at one of two marketplaces A and B.

These marketplaces, in each one of which one firm supplies one commodity at marginal cost k, are located equidistant from the boundary of the market, hence $-y^A = y^B$. It is demonstrated that the location $\tilde{y}(p^A, p^B)$, at which consumers are indifferent between patronizing A and B, varies continuously in prices. This is a necessary condition to the demonstration of the existence and the uniqueness of Nash equilibria in prices for any given, symmetric locational configuration.

How do these prices vary with parametric changes in locations? One expects them to be highest when both firms locate at the market boundaries and lowest, namely at marginal cost, when they are arbitrarily close to the midpoint of the market.[56] This intuition is not correct, if the marginal cost k is strictly positive. In particular, *the firms charge the highest equilibrium price at less than the maximal distance, and they do not compete each other all the way down to the classical Bertrand prices as they are located arbitrarily closely.* All that goes with intuition is that equilibrium prices and profits strictly decrease as the firms move closer towards each other within a distance less than $L/2$.

The reason for this behavior is that the competitive pressure on prices due to a closer location may be more than offset by the fact that the total revenue obtained from a customer located in a firm's hinterland remains constant no matter the chosen price, but profits are reduced with a price decrease because of increases in sales per customer and therefore increases in total costs.

Thus, the maximal profit at equilibrium prices is obtained when the firms are located within the first and the fourth quartile of the line, respectively, a result which is at variance with all major modifications of the Hotelling model, such as by Smithies (1941), Eaton (1972), or d'Aspremont et al. (1979).[57]

We now consider the *second stage of the game* involving locational aspects, and first turn to the results of competition in differentiated products at one marketplace, again without effective boundaries on the market area. Suppose that the seller of commodity i has the choice of either establishing a local monopoly unrestricted by spatial competition at the price p_i^M determined according to (32), or to offer the same product by joining the seller of $-i$ in a marketplace. Then he will always do the latter if he is free to choose a complement to the commodity offered by $-i$, provided that the demands for the two commodities are again symmetric. *But he may also do so if offering a substitute.* This is not immediate

---

[56]This is suggested, for instance, from a variant of Hotelling's model offered by d'Aspremont et al. (1979).

[57]It would be natural to compare these results with the ones obtained for a "commodity monopolist" operating both stores. This is problematic within the present model. While the inelasticity of gross revenues per customer in prices is helpful in conducting the equilibrium analysis, it leads the profit maximizing chain store monopolist to increase prices without bounds.

from the preceding analysis, as possibly increased equilibrium prices in the competitive market, together with the presence of a substitute offer, may lead to substantial losses in the quantity sold there, relative to a monopolistic location.

However, in order to ascertain the latter result suppose for a moment that the cross price elasticities $\eta_{i,-i}$ between the two commodities are zero, and the price p_i^C charged in the competitive marketplace is *forced* to be equal to p_i^M, the price optimally charged in the monopolistic one. Then the individual consumer's standardized demands are equal in both sorts of marketplaces. But, owing to the availability of the second commodity, the typical consumer's utility from patronizing the larger marketplace increases, and with it the market area $\bar{z}$; thus the market demand increases for each commodity.

In this situation it is always profitable for firm i to join firm $-i$. However, since p_i^C is forced to equal p_i^M, the firm can only do better by optimally adjusting p_i^C which implies that a possible loss in market demand due to a price increase is more than compensated. Hence profits are unequivocally higher in the larger marketplace. Thus there is room for changing cross price elasticities from zero to positive while preserving the order of profitability. Hence the result.

Due to technical difficulties, it so far has not been possible to derive locational equilibria for the case where spatial competitors sell perfect substitutes. From the parametric results derived in the pricing stage of the game, however, we can expect equilibrium locations at a distance between the two firms larger than $L/2$, i.e. larger than the half of the length of the line.

Let us now turn to the *first stage of the game* involving the firms' entry decision. Now the set up costs associated with the establishment of a retail outlet become relevant. We concentrate on competitive entry at one marketplace, and neglect spatial competition. We will first show how entry decisions of one product sellers are dependent on each other. Suppose that firm i incurs set up costs K_i (converted to flows) invariant cross locations, and firm $-i$ is already in the market. Then whenever $\pi_i(p_i^C, p_{-i}^C) - K_i > 0 > \pi(p_i^M, \infty) - K_i$, a condition that appears highly realistic in many cases, the preceding entry of firm $-i$ has made profitable the entry of firm i! In this case, *the entry of firms spurs the entry of competitors.* Conversely, if firm $-i$ had not found it profitable to enter the market on its own, then firm i would not enter to begin with. However, if cooperating, it is very conceivable that both firms could profitably enter. In this case, *cooperation of competitors spurs entry, i.e. the opening of new marketplaces, in a spatial market.*

All these results are obviously due to the "demand externality" derived before. Of course, this demand externality invites as internalization. Thus the preceding discussion is empirically only relevant to the extent that there are limits to the horizontal merger of retailing activities at one marketplace. Armchair empiricism suggests, however, that there are strong limits to such a merger, or an internalization.

It is also illustrative to compare entry decisions of the two-product spatial monopolist and of the two specialized competitive firms. First of all, the monopolist's profits upon entry are always at least as high than is the sum of the two competitive firms' profits. This implies *that the monopolist is more likely to enter the market* even if his set up costs are $K_1 + K_2$, i.e. even if economies of scope in set up costs are disregarded. By the same token, after an unrestricted entry of one product sellers, and introduction of products by the spatial monopolist, respectively, the *monopolist is likely to offer more products in one market-place than the competitors do in that marketplace.* This is by virtue of completely internalizing the positive market demand effects generated from the introduction of an additional commodity.

In the extreme, complete internalization may lead the monopolist *to permanently offer a commodity at a price below marginal cost.* Pursuing this strategy of introducing a loss leader is profit maximizing if the losses incurred from selling that commodity are more than compensated by the gains from selling other commodities to the additional consumers so attracted. Introducing a commodity i this way is the more likely, the higher (in absolute terms) the market area elasticity for i, and the lower (in absolute terms) the price elasticity of the individual consumer's demand for i. The former leads to a large expansion of the market area through a lowered p_i and therefore a large positive demand externality; and the latter to a small quantity of i sold, and therefore small losses through sales below marginal (and average) costs. The introduction of a permanent loss leader could not be observed in a world with single product firms, nor without the market area effect generated from the demand externality.[58]

One might finally ask whether in a world with free entry of specialized single plant firms, competition will not take over upon (successive) entry of firms and will depress prices below the monopolistic level. This desirable state may, or may not obtain, depending on the structure of the set up costs relative to the profitability of the enterprises thereafter.

How can all these results be evaluated in terms of efficiency? Since all these models are far from complete in incorporating the essential features that bear upon on the structure and conduct of retailing, it is somewhat premature to conduct an efficiency analysis, and to derive policy implications. The following conclusions stand out quite firmly, however: First, spatial monopoly as a form of market organization appears to increase efficiency, relative to competition between specialized firms, in three senses. The spatial monopolist tends to open marketplaces where specialized competitive firms would not. Furthermore, he tends to offer a larger bundle of commodities at such a marketplace. And finally, he may set lower prices than competitive firms would do.[59] Indeed, if spatial competition between those spatial monopolists leads profits to decrease to zero,

---

[58] Loss leading behavior in this context is analyzed by Stahl and Weinberg (1986).

[59] It appears well worth to study empirically the differences between monopolistically and competitively structured marketplaces.

then the individual monopolist will choose prices according to the Ramsey inverse elasticity rule such that the price margin above marginal costs just covers his overhead [Bliss (1985)]. This is clearly a second best efficiency rule for allocation decisions in this economy. It is up to further analysis, however, how these conclusions are modified when, as is empirically often the case, spatial and product monopolies are combined.

A second conclusion is but a corollary to the first one. In as much as specialized one plant firms are the emerging form of retailing, firms of this type do form too few marketplaces. This leads to an excessive concentration of retailing activities at the marketplaces that indeed are formed. However, the formation of coalitions among these firms helps improving on efficiency, at least when it comes to the formation of new marketplaces; and it may help in the determination of efficient product bundles and prices within such marketplaces. The first, and to some extent the second of these objectives is pursued via the coalition enforced by the shopping center developer, However, he generally perceives it not as his task to intervene in pricing decisions, and therefore does not contribute to their efficiency.

While all these results are quite intuitive, one might ask to what extent they are sensitive to the assumptions underlying their derivation. Most of the results are developed under the assumption that competition was exercising force only within, rather than between marketplaces; critical may be also that the consumer population is assumed to be distributed uniformly and without effective bounds. Also, land does not figure as an input into retailing. And finally, sellers' economies of scale (in variable costs), and economies of scope have not entered the discussion.

The effects of spatial competition on these results can be detailed only within a model incorporating both forms of competition, competition in geographical and in commodity space. It appears technically difficult to handle this general case. Intuition suggests, however, that the principal results derived here are upheld. The novelty of the results is due to the market area effect. While this effect is obviously influenced by spatial competition, it does never vanish under this form of competition.

The market area effect does also not vanish if the consumer population is non-uniformly distributed, as long as the density of consumers does not go down to zero within areas where the market area effect is operative. Hence the results are upheld for a strictly positive consumer distribution. By contrast, the market area effect may vanish with effective bounds on the spatial market. However, it does so only if bounds are effective in *all* geographical directions, which appears to be an unrealistic assumption. If the market is unbounded in just one direction, the market area effect is preserved, and hence the principal results derived from it. Finally, as far as the location results is concerned, one should keep in mind that limiting the market has a positive effect on the spatial concentration of retailing activities, inasmuch as spatial concentration limits the impacts of boundaries for any given number of sellers.

What is the effect of introducing consumer heterogeneity? Consider two types of consumers, type A and B so that type A exhibits preferences with respect to goods 1 and 2 that are identical to those of type B for goods 2 and 1, and suppose that the consumer types each are distributed with mass $\frac{1}{2}$ each along the line. It is easy to show that this heterogeneity leads to a decrease in the cross price elasticity of market demand, resulting in an increased tendency towards the agglomeration of specialized firms, and elevated equilibrium price quotations relative to those of the spatial monopolist.

The prices of land as input into retailing are invariant in space, and therefore unimportant, as long as the consumer population is uniformly distributed by assumption. This changes with a realistic modification of the latter assumption. It is of interest not only to further study the changes in locational behavior due to this, but also possible changes in retailing technique; in particular from land extensive custom retailing to land intensive cash and carry retailing.

Economies of scale and scope need also further study in their effects on the choice of technique, and on the determination of the individual storeholder's product offer. There is now an explicit trade off between offering few commodities at very great economies of scale, viz. many such commodities at economies of scope. In the first case, the clientele is attracted primarily by low prices; in the second, by the large product bundle. A final important impact of these economies well worth further consideration is on the formation on chain stores, and on their effect on pricing, product choice, location and entry decisions.

Some of these aspects have been addressed within other modelling frameworks, which will be discussed presently. In the study of market equilibrium, we so far have used only the primitive version of the consumer model. What are the consequences of introducing details in shopping behavior, such as variable shopping frequencies? They lead naturally to a hierarchy of marketplaces in which commodities shopped at high frequencies are offered in a larger number of marketplaces than commodities shopped at low ones. This idea is detailed in a study by Eaton and Lipsey (1982). Two commodities are demanded inelastically, and marketed at given price in exogenously given bundles of different size. Households, uniformly distributed over a bounded line, accordingly organize their purchases to minimize their transportation costs. One product firms, producing with techniques described by the cost functions $C^i(X_i) = k_i X_i + K_i$ introduced before, are sales maximizing Nash competitors in locations. Locational equilibrium is studied with free entry of firms.

While this model generates a hierarchy of market places as expected, its set up is not suited as of now to study the emergence of equilibrium prices within such a system. It appears difficult to construct an appropriate analytically solvable model. However, it should be quite clear that the equilibrium prices for physically identical commodities will differ across marketplaces of different size as measured by the number of commodities offered, and structure as measured by the set of commodities supplied, simply because the elasticities (32) (or (33)) relevant for their determination will differ. This provides for yet another compelling *explanation of empirically observed strong price differences for identical commodities.*[60]

How does a system of spatially competitive retail stores evolve with a non-uniform distribution of the customer population? This is discussed by White (1975) for the special yet typical case that the population is distributed with negative exponential density around some city center. Under the Hotelling–Lösch assumption on consumer demand described before, and the assumption that firms can sell everywhere at the same fixed plus constant marginal costs, he derives an approximate distribution for profit maximizing firms that in equilibrium produce at zero profit.

In this situation, retailing is more centralized than the population, owing to the fact that the higher population density near the center can support a larger number of retailing units per unit area. White also predicts a spatial decentralization of retailing activity with decreasing population density, increasing incomes and falling transportation costs. The latter two conclusions are hard to sustain in light of the discussion conducted earlier around our model of consumers' choice of marketplaces. White finally derives that the f.o.b. price charged by the typical firm decreases in distance from the center, but the prices after transportation costs relevant to the consumers increase.[61] Finally, the size of the retailing plant measured in units of output sold must increase in distance, in order to support the overhead by sales at lower prices.

Let us return again to the impact of effective limits on the market size. De Palma et al. (1985) and Ben-Akiva et al. (1985) derive retail locations and prices for parametric numbers of specialized single plant firms selling given products. In the first model, the spatial concentration of these firms at one point is demonstrated under the proviso that products and consumers are sufficiently heterogeneous, and that firms cannot determine a priori differences in consumers' tastes. The second one is to some extent a variant of the first, in which a stochastic term representing the firms' uncertainty about consumer choice in the first model is replaced by an explicit utility representation of the heterogeneity of consumers' tastes.

The principal results derived from these models are that the agglomeration of firms into one marketplace is the more likely, the smaller the transportation rate

---

[60]For an empirical study, see Pratt et al. (1979). For a critique of received studies of price dispersion, and another analytical model, see Varian (1980, 1981).

[61]Although this result is not unreasonable, it is derived under the analytically somewhat foggy condition that the market area is given to the individual retailer, while it is really a function of the price set by him.

t, the smaller the market size *L*, the smaller the number *n* of firms in the market and the more heterogeneous the consumers' tastes. These results nicely reiterate our results derived earlier from a different model.

Heal's (1980) paper is the only study known that traces the effects of decreasing variable costs on the number of retail outlets. The economies discussed therein are due to cost reductions in transporting commodities in bulk between a producer and a middle-man – the retailer – rather than in small numbers between the producer and the individual consumer. Heal suggests the following set up. Consumers with inelastic demands are located in uniform density around the periphery of a circle. There is a single producer at the center. Each consumer may buy by either going directly to the center or by going to the next local shop located on the circumference. This shop in turn buys from the producer at the center, but in bulk and therefore at lower unit transport costs.[62] Heal demonstrates that relative to the number of shops minimizing total transportation costs, free entry equilibria tend to lead to an excessive number of shops in large markets (where demands per consumer are relatively high), but to an insufficient number of shops in small markets. In other words, large markets tend to be overserved and small markets underserved, relative to the efficient (cost minimizing) state.

Up to now, our discussion about retailing was conducted on the assumption that all agents are perfectly informed about the choices open to them. This assumption is not realistic for two reasons. Firstly, consumers tend to be imperfectly informed about the products offered, and the prices charged in different shops; and secondly, especially before establishing a shop firms are imperfectly informed about the demand prevailing for particular commodities at particular locations.

Some of the consumer's informational deficit is made up for by firms' advertising; its impacts will not be discussed here.[63] In great many cases, however, it is reduced by personal search. Quite obviously, an individual consumer's search costs are reduced and his expected utility from searching is increased if sellers of the desired product (variants) agglomerate in one marketplace. Indeed, the consumer's search cost schedule exhibits economies of scope just as modelled in Section 3.1.

Now, if the market would only house sellers of perfect substitutes, as in the many nonspatial models in the Stigler (1961) tradition, there would hardly be an

---

[62]The geometry suggested here can be easily reinterpreted within an von Thünen world, in which the commodity is produced, or at least provided at the center, and retailers are located within a ring around the center.

[63]See however Butters (1977) and Balcer (1981). These papers study consumer behavior in space in reaction to firms' advertising, and firms' equilibrium reactions to this reactions. No locational consequences are analyzed as of now.

agglomeration of retailing activity. For if sellers would concentrate in space, consumers would have nearly zero cost of arbitrage, and hence a Bertrand equilibrium would result with firms making nearly zero profits. By contrast, the firms tend to strive for a local monopoly induced by consumers' search costs, and therefore locate as far distant from each other as possible.

However, this tendency changes when the sellers offer imperfect substitutes, and consumers look for the alternative most suiting their preferences (and their budget), and in addition the consumers' tastes are heterogeneous. Then sellers may concentrate in space despite increased competition, because their agglomeration increases the attractivity of the marketplace to consumers. This is the situation independently modelled by Stahl (1981, 1982b) and Wolinsky (1983) within structurally very similar models. A most recent version of this class of models is by Schulz and Stahl (1986). They show results on retailers' entry, location, product choice and pricing behavior that are in spirit very similar to the ones derived earlier in this section from the model under certainty.[64]

This completes the survey of analyses of retailing behavior. Many interesting features with impacts on the structure, conduct and performance of the retailing sector are not discussed here and await further research. The impacts of economies of scale and scope enjoyed from selling large quantities of the same, and of different commodities are hardly touched upon. Not covered at all are the emergence of different retailing techniques: in particular of custom, cash & carry and mail order delivered retailing, and the competition between these different modes of organizing the marketplace.

There is no analysis of retailers' strategic behavior under threat of competitors' entry, or in view of forcing a competitor's exit. And a last interesting field not covered here, but also worth further investigation are the emergence and the implications of vertical restraints on retailers' behavior, such as of different sorts of franchising or licensing; or of resale price maintenance. Yet we hope the framework for these types of analysis is provided here.

4. Concluding remarks

Relative to other fields of microeconomics, research on urban business location and indeed, on business location decisions at large is far from having achieved a mature state. This is astounding, given the importance of business decisions on the general welfare in urban economies. Of the many deficiencies one might cite, two stick out clearly to this author. The first one is the general lack of analysis of

---

[64]Burdett and Malueg (1981), and Carlson and McAffee (1984) study consumer search behavior when search is conducted jointly for several commodities. Optimal search rules are developed. No consequences on retailer behavior are derived as yet.

imperfectly competitive behavior in production decisions involving location. The second, probably more important, one is the lack of "historical" analysis of business decisions.

As alluded to in the introduction to this paper, most decisions of the type discussed here are not taken simultaneously, but sequentially. Especially entry and location decisions are irreversible to a large extent, which implies that *all* agents' past decisions have a strong conditioning effect on *individual* agents' decisions taken presently and in the future. We probably will better understand the phenomena in question, if we model decisions in an ex post, rather than in an ex ante framework, thus suitably accounting for their intertemporal inter-dependences.

Approached this way, such decisions are by nature taking place in thin markets, and therefore have to be modelled within an imperfectly competitive framework. Modern game theory provides a good approach for this kind of analysis.

Incorporating locational analysis within such a framework implies linking it directly, and usefully, to the modern theory of industrial organization and more generally, to modern microeconomic theory. This will lead to a clarification of the assumptions taken, and the approaches chosen in spatial analysis. Furthermore, it will allow us to attack classes of location problems hardly discussed hereto, but nevertheless important for the understanding of business behavior in urban economies, and for the conduct of suitable business policy.

References

Alonso, W. (1964) *Location and land use.* Cambridge, Mass.: Cambridge University Press.

Alonso, W. (1967) 'A reformulation of location theory and its relation to rent theory', *Papers of the Regional Science Association*, 19:23–44.

Alperovich, G. and E. Katz (1983) 'Transport rate uncertainty and the optimal location of the firm', *Journal of Regional Science*, 23:389–396.

Arndt, J. and L. Olsen (1975) 'A research note on economies of scale in retailing', *Swedish Journal of Economics*, 77:207–221.

Arnott, R. (1985) 'Economic theory and housing', *this volume*.

d'Aspremont, C., J.J. Gabszewicz and J.F. Thisse (1979) 'On Hotelling's "stability in competition"'. *Econometrica*, 47:1145–1150.

Bacon, R.W. (1984) *Consumer spatial behavior.* Oxford: Clarendon Press.

Balcer, Y. (1981) 'Equilibrium distributions of sales and advertising prices over space', *Journal of Economic Theory*, 25:196–218.

Baumol W.J. and E.A. Ide (1957) 'Variety in retailing', *Management Science*, 3:93–101.

Baumol, W.J., J.C. Panzar and R.D. Willing (1982) *Contestable markets and the theory of industry structure.* New York: Harcourt Brace Jovanovich.

Beckmann, M.J. (1976) 'Spatial equilibrium in the dispersed city', in: G.J. Papageorgiou, ed., *Mathematical land use theory*. Lexington, Mass.: Lexington Books, 117–125.

Ben-Akiva, M., A. De Palma and J.F. Thisse (1985) 'Spatial competition with differentiated products', Louvain La Neuve: CORE Discussion Paper no. 8517.

Bliss, C. (1985) 'The economic theory of retailing', Paper presented at the 5th World Congress of the Econometric Society.

Borukhov, E. and O. Hochman (1977) 'Optimum and market equilibrium in a model of a city without a predetermined center', *Environment and Planning A*, 9:849–856.

Brown, D.M. (1979) 'Location decision of the firm: an overview of theory and evidence', *Papers of the regional Science Association*, 43:23–39.

Bruno, M., E. Burmeister and E. Sheshinsky (1966) 'The nature and implications of the reswitching of techniques', *Quarterly Journal of Economics*, 80:526–554.

Bucklin, L.P. (1972) *Competition and evolution in the distributive trades*. Englewood Cliffs: Prentice-Hall.

Burdett, K. and D.A. Malueg (1981) 'The theory of search for several goods', *Journal of Economic Theory*, 24:362–376.

Burmeister, E. and A.R. Dobell (1970) *Mathematical theories of economic growth*. New York: McMillan.

Butters, G. (1977) 'Equilibrium distributions of sales and advertising prices', *Review of Economic Studies*, 44:465–491.

Capozza, D. (1976) 'Employment/population ratios in urban areas: a model of urban land, labor and goods markets', in: G.J. Papageorgiou, ed., *Mathematical land use theory*. Lexington, Mass.: Lexington Books, 127–143.

Carlson, J.A. and R.P. McAffee (1984) 'Joint search for several goods', *Journal of Economic Theory*, 32:337–345.

Chipman, J.S. (1970) 'External economies of scale and competitive equilbrium', *Quarterly Journal of Economics*, 86:347–385.

Clapp, J. (1983) 'A general model of equilibrium locations', *Journal of Regional Science*, 23:461–478.

Cooke, T.W. (1983) 'Testing a model of intraurban firm relocation', *Journal of Urban Economics*, 13:257–282.

Dean, J. (1942) 'Department store cost functions', in: D. Lange et al., eds., *Studies in mathematical economics and econometrics in memory of Henry Schultz*. Chicago: University of Chicago Press, 222–254.

Debreu, G. (1959) *Theory of value*. New York: Wiley.

Douglas, E. (1962) 'Size of firm and cost structure in retailing', *Journal of Business*, 35:158–190.

Eaton, B.C. (1972) 'Spatial competition revisted', *Canadian Journal of Economics*, 5:268–278.

Eaton, B.C. and R.G. Lipsey (1982) 'An economic theory of central places', *Economic Journal*, 92:56–72.

Emerson, D.L. (1973) 'Optimum firm location and the theory of production', *Journal of Regional Science*, 13:335–345.

Eswaran, M., Y. Kanemoto and D. Ryan (1981) 'A dual approach to the locational decision of the firm', *Journal of Regional Science*, 21:469–490.

Friedman, J.W. (1983) *Oligopoly theory*. London: Cambridge University Press.

Fujita, M. (1981) 'Location of firms with input transactions', *Environment & Planning A*, 13:1401–1414.

Fujita M. (1985) 'Existence and uniqueness of equilibrium and optimal land use: boundary rent curve approach', *Regional Science and Urban Economics*, 15:295–324.

Fujita, M. and H. Ogawa (1982) 'Multiple equilibria and structural transition of non-monocentric urban configurations', *Regional Science and Urban Economics*, 12:161–196.

Fujita, M. and J.F. Thisse (1986) 'Spatial competition with a land market: Hotelling and von Thünen unified', *Review of Economic Studies*, forthcoming.

Gabszewicz, J.J. and J.-F. Thisse (1984) 'Spatial competition and the location of firms', *Fundamentals of Pure and Applied Economics*, Harwood Academic Publishers, forthcoming.

Gabszewicz, J.J., A. Shaked, J. Sutton and J.F. Thisse (1981) 'Price competition among differentiated products: a detailed study of Nash equilibrium', London School of Economics, ICERD Discussion Paper 37.

Goldstein, G.S. and T.J. Gronberg (1984) 'Economies of scope and economies of agglomeration', *Journal of Urban Economics*, 16:91–104.

Goldstein, G.S. and L.N. Moses (1975) 'Interdependence and the location of economic activities', *Journal of Urban Economics*, 2:63–84.

Hakimi, S.L. (1964) 'Optimum location of switching centers and the absolute centers and medians of a graph', *Operations Research*, 12:450–459.

Hartwick, J.M. (1976) 'Intermediate goods and the spatial integration of land uses', *Regional Science and Urban Economics*, 6:127–145.

Hartwick, P.G. and J.M. Hartwick (1974) 'Efficient resource allocation in a multinucleated city with intermediate goods', *Quarterly Journal of Economics*, 340–352.

Harwitz, M., B. Lentnek, and S.C. Narula (1983) 'Do I have to go shopping again? A theory of choice with movement costs', *Journal of Urban Economics*, 13:165–180.

Heal, G. (1980) 'Spatial structure in the retail trade: a study in product differentiation with increasing returns, *Bell Journal of Economics*, 11:565–583.

Heaps, T. (1982) 'Location and comparative statics of the theory of production; *Journal of Economic Theory*, 28:102–112.

Henderson, J.V. (1974) 'The sizes and types of cities', *American Economic Review*, 64:640–657.

Henderson, J.V. (1977) *Economic theory and the cities.* New York: Academic Press.

Holdren, B.R. (1960) *The structure of a retail market and the market behavior of retail units.* Ames, Iowa: The Iowa State University Press.

Holton, R.H. (1957) 'Price discrimination at retail: the supermarket case', *Journal of Industrial Economics*, 6:13–32.

Hotelling, H. (1929) 'Stability in competition', *Economic Journal*, 29:41–57.

Hsu, S.K. and C.C. Mai (1984) 'Production location and random input price', *Regional Science and Urban Economics*, 14:45–62.

Imai, H. (1982) 'CBD hypothesis and economies of agglomeration', *Journal of Economic Theory*, 28:275–299.

Kanemoto, Y. (1985) 'Optimal cities with indivisibility in production and interactions', Queen's University, Discussion Paper no. 597.

Katz, E. (1984) 'The optimal location of the competitive firm under price uncertainty', *Journal of Urban Economics*, 16:65–75.

Koopmans, T.C. and M.J. Beckmann (1957) 'Assignment problems and the location of economic activities', *Econometrica*, 25:53–76.

Kraus, M. (1974) 'Land use in a circular city', *Journal of Economic Theory*, 8:440–457.

Kusumoto, S.I. (1984) 'On a foundation of the economic theory of location – transport distance vs technological substitution', *Journal of Regional Science*, 24:249–270.

Lave, L. (1973) 'Urban externalities', in: Center for Environmental Studies, ed., *Papers from the Urban Economics Conference*, London, 1:37–95.

Leland, H.F. (1972) 'Theory of the firm facing uncertain demand', *American Economic Review*, 48:278–291.

Lentneck, B., M. Harwitz and S.C. Narula (1981) 'Spatial choice in consumer behavior: towards a contextual theory of demand', *Economic Geography*, 57:362–372.

Lösch, A. (1940) *Die räumliche Ordnung der Wirtschaft.* Jena: Fischer.

Louveaux, F., J.-F. Thisse and H. Beguin (1982) 'Location theory and transportation costs', *Regional Science and Urban Economics*, 12:529–595.

MacLeod, W.B. (1985) 'On the non-existence of equilibria in differentiated product models', *Regional Science and Urban Economics*, 15:245–262.

Mai, C.C. (1981) 'Optimum location and the theory of the firm under demand uncertainty', *Regional Science and Urban Economics*, 11:549–557.

Mai, C.C. and Y.N. Shieh (1984) 'Transport rate structure, optimum location, and theory of production: reexamination', *Journal of Urban Economics*, 16:225–231.

Martinich, J.S. and A.P. Hurter Jr. (1982) 'Price uncertainty and the optimal production-location decision', *Regional Science and Urban Economics*, 12:509–528.

Mathur, V.K. (1979) 'Some unresolved issues in the location theory of the firm', *Journal of Urban Economics*, 6:299–318.

Mathur, V.K. (1982) 'Erratum', *Journal of Urban Economics*, 9:368–369.

Mathur, V.K. (1983) 'Location theory of the firm under price uncertainty', *Regional Science and Urban Economics*, 13:411–428.

Mieszkowski, P. and M. Straszheim, eds. (1979) *Current issues in urban economics.* Baltimore: The Johns Hopkins University Press.

Miller, S.M. and O.W. Jensen (1978) 'Location and the theory of production, a review, summary and critique of recent contributions', *Regional Science and Urban Economics*, 8:117–128.

Mills, E.S. (1967) 'An aggregative model of resource allocation in a metropolitan area', *American Economic Review*, 57:197–210.

Mills, E.S. (1969) 'The value of urban land', in: H.S. Perloff, ed., *The quality of the urban environment*. Baltimore: The Johns Hopkins University Press, 231–253.

Mills, E.S. (1970) 'The efficiency of spatial competition', *Papers of the Regional Science Association*, 25: 71–82.

Mills, E.S. (1972) *Studies in the structure of the urban economy*. Baltimore: The Johns Hopkins University Press.

Mills, E.S. (1976) 'Planning and market processes in urban models', in: R.E. Grieson, ed., *Public and urban economics*. Lexington, Mass.: Lexington Books, 313–329.

Miyao, T. (1977) 'Some dynamics and comparative statics of a spatial model of production', *Review of Economic Studies*, 44:321–327.

Miyao, T. (1981) *Dynamic analysis of the urban economy*. New York: Academic Press.

Moomaw, R. (1980) 'Urban firm location: comparative statics and empirical evidence', *Southern Economic Journal*, 47:404–418.

Moses, L. (1958) 'Location and the theory of production', *Quarterly Journal of Economics*, 72:259–272.

Moses, L.N. (1962) 'Towards a theory of intra-urban wage differentials and their influence on travel patterns', *Papers of the Regional Science Association*, 9:53–63.

Niedercorn, J.H. (1981) 'Spatial monopoly in a single industry Löschian equilibrium framework', *Papers of the Regional Science Association*, 48:67–76.

Nikaido, H. (1968) *Convex structures and economic theory*. New York: Academic Press.

Nooteboom, B. (1980) *Retailing: applied analysis in the theory of the firm*. Amsterdam: Uithoorn.

Nooteboom, B. (1982) 'A new theory of retailing costs', *European Economic Review*, 17:163–186.

Novshek, W. and H. Sonnenschein (1979) 'Marginal consumers and neoclassical demand theory', *Journal of Political Economy*, 87:1368–1376.

Odland, J. (1976) 'The spatial arrangement of urban activities: a simultaneous location model', *Environment and Planning A*, 8:779–791.

Odland, J. (1978) 'The conditions for multi-center cities', *Economic Geography*, 54:234–244.

Ogawa, H. and M. Fujita (1980) 'Equilibrium land use patterns in a non-monocentric city', *Journal of Regional Science*, 20:455–475.

O'Hara, D.J. (1977) 'Location of firms within a square central business district', *Journal of Political Economy*, 85:1189–1207.

De Palma, A., V. Ginsburgh, Y.Y. Papageorgiou and J.F. Thisse (1985) 'The principle of minimum differentiation holds under sufficient heterogeneity', *Econometrica*, 53:767–781.

Ponsard, C. (1983) *A history of spatial economic theory*. Berlin: Springer.

Pratt, J.W., D.A. Wise and R. Zeckhauser (1979) 'Price differences in almost competitive markets', *Quarterly Journal of Economics*, 93:189–211.

Reinhardt, P.G. (1973) 'A theory of households grocery inventory holdings', *Kyklos*, 26:497–511.

Sakashita, N. (1967) 'Production function, demand function and location theory of the firm', *Papers of the Regional Science Association*, 20:109–122.

Sandmo, A. (1971) 'On the theory of the competitive firm under price uncertainty', *American Economic Review*, 61:65–73.

Schulz, N. and K. Stahl (1985a) 'Localisation des oligopoles et marchés du travail locaux', *Revue Economique*, 36:103–134. English Version in Working Papers in Economic Theory and Urban Economics, University of Dortmund, no. 8306.

Schulz, N. and K. Stahl (1985b) 'On the non-existence of oligopolistic equilibra in differentiated products spaces', *Regional Science and Urban Economics*, 15:229–243.

Schulz, N. and K. Stahl (1986) 'Consumer search and the spatial organization of markets for differentiated products', University of Dortmund, Working Papers in Economic Theory and Urban Economics, forthcoming.

Schweizer, U. (1978) 'A spatial version of the nonsubstitution theorem', *Journal of Economic Theory*, 19:307–320.

Schweizer, U. and P.P. Varaiya (1976) 'The spatial structure of production with a Leontief technology', *Regional Science and Urban Economics*, 6:231–251.

Schweizer, U. and P.P. Varaiya (1977) 'The spatial structure of production with a Leontief technology – II: substitute techniques', *Regional Science and Urban Economics*, 7:293–320.

Selten, R. (1970) *Preispolitik der Mehrproduktenunternehmung in der Statischen Theorie*, Heidelberg: Springer.

Selten, R. (1975) 'Reexamination of the perfectness concept for equilibrium points in extensive games', *International Journal of Game Theory*, 4:25–56.

Shieh, Y.N. and C.C. Mai (1984) 'Location and the theory of production: classifications and extensions', *Regional Science and Urban Economics*, 14:199–218.

Smithies, A. (1941) 'Optimum location in spatial competition', *Journal of Political Economy*, 41:423–439.

Solow, R.M. (1973) 'On equilibrium models of urban location', in: J.M. Parkin, ed.: *Essays in modern economics*. London: Longman, 2–16.

Solow, R.M. and W.S. Vickrey (1971) 'Land use in a long narrow city', *Journal of Economic Theory*, 3:430–447.

Stahl, K. (1981) 'Consumer search and spatial pricing under alternative market arrangements', University of California, Berkeley: Center for Research in Management, IP-306.

Stahl, K. (1982a) 'Location and spatial pricing theory with nonconvex transportation cost schedules', *Bell Journal of Economics*, 13:575–582.

Stahl, K. (1982b) 'Consumer search and the spatial distribution of retailing', *Journal of Industrial Economics*, 31:97–114.

Stahl, K. (1983) 'A note on the microeconomics of migration', *Journal of Urban Economics*, 14:318–326.

Stahl, K. (1985) 'Existence of equilibrium in spatial economies: presentation', *Regional Science and Urban Economics*, 15:143–147.

Stahl, K. and P.P. Varaiya (1978a) 'Spatial arrangement of markets with optimal shopping frequencies', University of Dortmund, Manuscript.

Stahl, K. and P.P. Varaiya (1978b) 'Economics of information: examples in location and land use theory', *Regional Science and Urban Economics*, 8:43–56.

Stahl, K. and J. Weinberg (1986) 'Loss leadership: a theoretical analysis', forthcoming.

Starrett, D. (1978) 'Market allocations of location choice in a model with free mobility', *Journal of Economic Theory*, 17:21–37.

Stigler, G. (1961) 'The economics of information', *Journal of Political Economy*, 69:213–225.

Straszheim, M.R. (1980) 'Discrimination and the spatial characteristics of the urban labor market for black workers', *Journal of Urban Economics*, 7:119–140.

Straszheim, M. (1985) 'The theory of urban residential location', this volume.

Straszheim, M.R. (1984) 'Urban agglomeration effects and employment and wage gradients', *Journal of Urban Economics*, 16:187–207.

Struyk, R. and F. James (1975) *Intrametropolitan industrial location: The pattern and process of change*. Lexington, Mass.: Lexington Books.

Stuart, C. (1979) 'Search and the spatial organization of trading', in: S. Lipman, and J.J. McCall, eds., *Studies in the economics of search*. Amsterdam: North-Holland, 18–33.

Sullivan, A.M. (1983a) 'A general equilibrium model with external scale economies in production', *Journal of Urban Economics*, 13:235–255.

Sullivan, A.M. (1983b) 'The general equilibrium effects of congestion externalities', *Journal of Urban Economics*, 14:80–104.

Sullivan, A.M. (1983c) 'Second best policies for congestion externalities', *Journal of Urban Economics*, 14:105–123.

Sullivan, A.M. (1984) 'Land use and zoning in the central business district', *Regional Science and Urban Economics*, 14:521–532.

Tauchen, H. and A.D. White (1984) 'Socially optimal and equilibrium distributions of office activity: models with exogenous and endogenous contacts', *Journal of Urban Economics*, 15:66–86.

v. Thünen, J.H. (1826) *Der Isolierte Staat in Beziehung auf Landwirtschaft und Nationalökonomie*. Hamburg.

Varian, H. (1980) 'A model of sales', *American Economic Review*, 70:651–659.

Varian, H. (1981) 'Errata', *American Economic Review*, 71:517.

Weber, A. (1909) *Über den Standort der Industrien*. Tübingen.

Weinberg, J. (1985) 'Bertrand oligopoly in a spatial context: the case of quantity independent transportation costs', *Regional Science and Urban Economics*, 15:263–275.

White, L.J. (1975) 'The spatial distribution of retail firms in an urban setting', *Regional Science and Urban Economics*, 5:325–333.

White, M.J. (1976) 'Firm suburbanization and urban subcenters', *Journal of Urban Economics*, 3:323–343.

White, M.J. (1978) 'Job suburbanization, zoning and the welfare of urban minority groups', *Journal of Urban Economics*, 5:219–240.

Wolinsky, A. (1983) 'Retail trade concentration due to consumers' imperfect information', *Bell Journal of Economics*, 14:275–282.

Woodward, R.S. (1973) 'The iso-outlay function and variable transport costs', *Journal of Regional Science*, 13:349–355.

Chapter 20

THE STRUCTURE OF URBAN EQUILIBRIA: A UNIFIED TREATMENT OF THE MUTH–MILLS MODEL*

JAN K. BRUECKNER

University of Illinois at Urbana-Champaign

1. Introduction

A principal challenge facing the urban economist is the formulation of a rigorous economic explanation for a variety of observed regularities in the spatial structures of real-world cities. The most obvious among these is the dramatic spatial variation in the intensity of urban land-use. Buildings are tall near the centers of most cities, while suburban structures embody much lower ratios of capital to land. Providing a precise explanation of this pattern is an important goal of urban economic analysis. Among other obvious regularities requiring explanation is building height variation among (as opposed to within) cities. Buildings near the centers of large urban areas appear to be much taller than those near the centers of small cities, and a successful economic model must be able to isolate the causes of this observed difference.

Urban economics has met the challenge of scientific explanation with considerable success. The last twenty years have seen the emergence and refinement of a simple yet powerful model of urban spatial structure that successfully explains the principal regularities observed in the urban landscape, including those mentioned above. This model, which derives from the work of Alonso (1964), Mills (1967, 1972b), and Muth (1969), is built around the key observation that commuting cost differences within an urban area must be balanced by differences in the price of living space. This compensating price variation, which reconciles suburban residents to long and costly commuting trips, has far-reaching implications for the spatial structure of the city. While Alonso explored these implications in a framework where individuals consume land directly, Muth and Mills analysed a more realistic model where land is an intermediate input in the production of housing, which is the final consumption good.

The purpose of the present chapter is to provide a unified treatment of the

*I wish to thank Mahlon Straszheim, Takahiro Miyao, and Edwin Mills for comments. Any errors are mine.

Handbook of Regional and Urban Economics, Volume II, Edited by E.S. Mills
© *1987, Elsevier Science Publishers B.V.*

Muth–Mills version of the urban model, deriving the well-known results on the internal features of cities in a framework which is then used for comparative static analysis. This unified approach offers clear insight into the structure of the urban equilibrium. We begin by deriving the model's implications regarding the intracity spatial variation of the important urban variables (the central city–suburban building height differential noted above is, for example, shown to be an implication of the model). While the approach is somewhat different, the conclusions of the analysis are familiar from Muth (1969). Next, we offer a comparative static analysis of the urban equilibrium, deriving results that are useful in comparing the spatial structures of different cities (the large city–small city building height differential noted above is derived from the model). This discussion generalizes Wheaton's (1974) comparative static analysis of the Alonso model to an urban economy with housing production (many mathematical details are relegated to an appendix). It should be noted that while the method of analysis (and many of the results) are familiar from Wheaton, comparative static analysis of the Muth–Mills model has not previously appeared in the literature.[1] Finally, the chapter concludes with a short survey of papers that attempt to modify in various interesting and realistic ways the basic assumptions of the model.

2. Intracity analysis

In the stylized city represented by the model, each urban resident commutes to a job in the central business district (CBD) along a dense radial road network. Commuting cost per round-trip mile equals t, so that commuting cost from a residence x radial miles from the CBD is tx per period (the CBD is a point at $x = 0$).[2] All consumers earn the same income y per period at the CBD, and tastes are assumed to be identical for all individuals. The common strictly quasi-concave utility function is $v(c, q)$, where c is consumption of a composite non-housing good and q is consumption of housing, measured in square feet of floor space. Note that although real-world dwellings are characterized by a vector of attributes, the analysis ignores this fact and focuses on a single important attribute: interior living space. While the price of the composite good c is assumed to be the same everywhere in the city (the price is taken to be unity for simplicity), the rental price per square foot of housing floor space, denoted p, varies with location.

Since consumers are identical, the urban equilibrium must yield identical utility

---

[1] While Mills (1967, 1972b) was the first to analyse the overall equilibrium of an urban economy, his analysis lacked generality.

[2] All the results of the analysis can be derived for a general commuting cost function $T(x)$, provided the function satisfies a rather weak requirement ($T'' < 0$ guarantees satisfaction of this requirement).

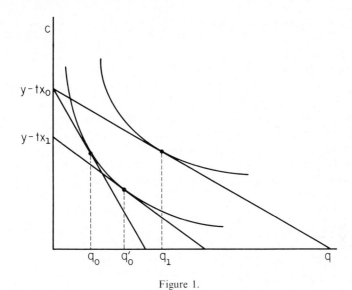

Figure 1.

levels for all individuals. Spatial variation in p provides the key to achieving equal utilities throughout the city. In particular, the price per square foot of housing will vary over space so that the highest utility level attainable at each location equals some constant u. Substituting for c in the utility function using the budget constraint $c + pq = y - tx$, the requirement that the maximized utility level equals u can be written

$$\max_{\{q\}} v(y - tx - pq, q) = u. \tag{1}$$

Eq. (1) reduces to two separate statements. First, since consumers choose q optimally conditional on p, the first-order condition

$$\frac{v_2(y - tx - pq, q)}{v_1(y - tx - pq, q)} = p, \tag{2}$$

must hold (subscripts denote partial derivatives). The key additional requirement is that the resulting consumption bundle must afford utility u, so that

$$v(y - tx - pq, q) = u. \tag{3}$$

The simultaneous system composed of (2) and (3) yields solutions for the unknowns p and q. The solution values depend on the parameters of the equation system: x, y, t, and u.

Figure 1 illustrates various solutions to (2) and (3). The indifference curve with the given utility level is plotted first. Then a budget line with c-intercept equal to

$y - tx$ is drawn so that it is tangent to the indifference curve. The absolute slope of the resulting line equals p, and q is read off from the tangency point. Note that this procedure is the reverse of normal consumer optimization, although the diagram is identical. Utility is fixed, then a price is determined, rather than vice versa. The determination of the urban utility level will be discussed below.

The nature of the dependencies of p and q on the parameters x, y, t, and u can be derived mathematically by totally differentiating (2) and (3). The results can also be inferred diagrammatically from Figure 1. For present purposes, the most important relationships are those between p and x and q and x. These relationships indicate the spatial behavior of housing prices (per square foot) and housing consumption within the city. Totally differentiating (3) with respect to x yields

$$-v_1\left(t + \frac{\partial p}{\partial x}q + p\frac{\partial q}{\partial x}\right) + v_2\frac{\partial q}{\partial x} = 0. \tag{4}$$

Since $v_2 = pv_1$ by (2), (4) yields

$$\frac{\partial p}{\partial x} = \frac{-t}{q} < 0. \tag{5}$$

Thus, the price per square foot of housing is a decreasing function of distance x to the CBD. This result, which is of fundamental importance, can be seen directly in Figure 1. An increase in x from x_0 to x_1 reduces the c-intercept of the budget line, as shown in the figure, so that reestablishing the tangency requires a counterclockwise rotation of the line around the new intercept. Since the budget line's absolute slope decreases, it follows that p declines as a result of the x increase.

As can be seen from Figure 1, the associated change in q (from q_0 to q_0') is positive, establishing that q is an increasing function of x. Concretely, this means that dwelling sizes increase moving away from the center of the city, a prediction which appears to be confirmed in the real world. Note that since utility is constant, the increase in q corresponds exactly to the substitution effect of the housing price decrease. Formally, it follows that

$$\frac{\partial q}{\partial x} = \eta\frac{\partial p}{\partial x} > 0, \tag{6}$$

where $\eta < 0$ is the slope of the appropriate income-compensated (constant-utility) demand curve.[3]

The intuitive explanation behind the spatial behavior of p and q is straightforward. Consumers living far from the CBD must be compensated in some fashion for their long and costly commutes (otherwise, no one would live voluntarily at great distances). Compensation takes the form of a lower price per square foot of

---

[3]Note that $\eta = \partial\text{MRS}/\partial q|^{-1}_{\text{utility}=u}$, a negative expression given the convexity of indifference curves ($\text{MRS} \equiv v_2/v_1$).

housing relative to close-in locations. The resulting decline with x in the price of housing causes consumers to substitute in its favor, leading to larger dwellings at greater distances.[4]

The influences of the parameters y, t, and u on p and q tell us nothing immediate about the internal structure of the city. However, since the various partial derivatives play a crucial role in the comparative static analysis presented below, derivation of their signs is helpful at this point. The discussion will make use of Figure 1. Since an increase in y has the same effect as a decrease in x on the c-intercept of the budget line, it follows that a rotation opposite to that discussed above is needed to restore a tangency. By the above arguments, it then follows that[5]

$$\frac{\partial p}{\partial y} > 0, \quad \frac{\partial q}{\partial y} < 0. \tag{7}$$

Similarly, since an increase in t has the same effect on the budget line's c-intercept as an increase in x, it follows that

$$\frac{\partial p}{\partial t} < 0, \quad \frac{\partial q}{\partial t} > 0. \tag{8}$$

Finally, an increase in u holding x, y, and t fixed raises the level of the indifference curve but leaves the c-intercept of the budget line unchanged. A counterclockwise rotation of the line around its fixed intercept is therefore required to restore the tangency, reducing p. The effect on q of the increase in u depends on whether housing is a normal good. If housing is normal, then rotation of the budget line leads to an increase in consumption, as shown in Figure 1 (housing consumption rises from q_0 to q_1). Therefore, when housing is a normal good, it follows that[6]

---

[4] Note that (6) together with (5) implies that $\partial^2 p / \partial x^2 > 0$, or that p is a convex function of x. The same conclusion would hold with a general commuting cost function $T(x)$ as long as $T'' < 0$. Also, note that while the price per square foot of housing declines with x, dwelling rent, which equals pq, may either rise or fall. This follows because $\partial(pq)/\partial x = (1 + \eta p/q) q \partial p/\partial x \equiv (1 + \sigma) q \partial p/\partial x$, where σ is the income-compensated price elasticity of demand. Note that $\partial(pq)/\partial x \gtrless 0$ as $\sigma \lessgtr -1$.

[5] Note that $\partial q/\partial y$ bears no relation to the regular income effect since utility is held fixed.

[6] The results in (7), (8), and (9) are derived mathematically by total differentiation of (2) and (3) with respect to y, t, and u. This yields

$$\frac{\partial p}{\partial y} = \frac{1}{q} > 0, \quad \frac{\partial p}{\partial t} = \frac{-x}{q} < 0, \quad \frac{\partial p}{\partial u} = \frac{-1}{q v_1} < 0$$

$$\frac{\partial q}{\partial y} = \eta \frac{\partial p}{\partial y} < 0, \quad \frac{\partial q}{\partial t} = \eta \frac{\partial p}{\partial t} > 0, \quad \frac{\partial q}{\partial u} = \left[\frac{\partial p}{\partial u} - \frac{\partial \text{MRS}}{\partial c} \frac{1}{v_1} \right] \eta > 0.$$

The sign of $\partial q/\partial u$ is derived using the inequality $\partial \text{MRS}/\partial c > 0$, which must hold for q to be a normal good. The inequality states that indifference curves become steeper moving vertically in Figure 1. Together with convexity, this property implies that a parallel upward shift in the budget line moves the tangency point to the right.

$$\frac{\partial p}{\partial u} < 0, \quad \frac{\partial q}{\partial u} > 0. \tag{9}$$

Turning now to the supply side of the housing market, it is assumed that housing square footage is produced with inputs of land l and capital N according to the concave constant returns function $H(N, l)$. This function gives the number of square feet of floor space contained in a building with the specified inputs.[7] Concavity of H means among other things that $H_{11} < 0$ (capital's marginal productivity diminishes), reflecting the fact that as buildings become taller, capital is increasingly consumed in non-productive uses such as stairways, elevators, and foundations.

An important feature of the model is that the issue of the durability of structures is avoided via the implicit assumption that housing capital is perfectly malleable. In effect, the analysis portrays producers as able to costlessly adjust both their capital and land inputs from period to period. Accordingly, producers are viewed as renting the inputs rather than purchasing them outright, an assumption which may appear particularly unrealistic for the capital input. It should be realized that the assumption of malleable capital is invoked to achieve analytical tractability. Models in which the durability of structures is explicitly recognized are more realistic than the present one but considerably more complex.[8]

Recalling that floor space is rented to consumers at price p, it follows that the revenue from a building is $pH(N, l)$. Note that the building is implicitly being divided up into dwellings (apartments) of the size demanded by consumers. Letting r denote land rent per acre (an endogenous variable) and i denote the spatially-invariant rental price per unit of capital, it follows that producer profit is $pH(N, l) - iN - rl$. Since H exhibits constant returns, profit may be rewritten as $l(pH(N/l, 1) - iN/l - r)$. To simplify notation, let S denote the capital-land ratio N/l, which is an index of the height of buildings (S will be referred to as structural density). Substituting S, profit can be rewritten as

$$l(ph(S) - iS - r), \tag{10}$$

where $h(S) \equiv H(S, 1)$ gives floor space per acre of land. The function h satisfies $h'(S) \equiv H_1(S, 1) > 0$ and $h''(S) \equiv H_{11}(S, 1) < 0$.

For fixed l, the producer chooses S to maximize profit per acre of land (the expression in parentheses in (10)), and land rent r adjusts so that profit per acre is zero. Since total profit is then zero regardless of the value of l, the scale of the

---

[7]It is easy to see that in order for this production function to be well-defined, the fraction of the land area covered by the capital must be specified in advance. For a model where the open space surrounding the structure gives utility to the consumer and consequently becomes a choice variable of the producer, see Brueckner (1983).

[8]For a survey of such papers, see the chapter by Miyao in this volume.

producer's building (represented by l) is indeterminate. From (10), the first-order condition for choice of S and the zero-profit condition are

$$ph'(S)=i, \tag{11}$$

$$ph(S)-iS=r. \tag{12}$$

Recalling that p is already a function of x, t, y and u from the solution to the consumer problem, it follows that (11) and (12) determine S and r as functions of these same variables and i. Totally differentiating (11) and (12) with respect to x, t, y, and u yields

$$\frac{\partial p}{\partial \phi}h' + ph''\frac{\partial S}{\partial \phi}=0, \tag{13}$$

$$(ph'-i)\frac{\partial S}{\partial \phi}+\frac{\partial p}{\partial \phi}h=\frac{\partial r}{\partial \phi}, \quad \phi=x,t,y,u. \tag{14}$$

Recalling (11), (14) and (13) yield

$$\frac{\partial r}{\partial \phi}=h\frac{\partial p}{\partial \phi}. \tag{15}$$

$$\frac{\partial S}{\partial \phi}=-\frac{h'}{ph''}\frac{\partial p}{\partial \phi}, \quad \phi=x,t,y,u. \tag{16}$$

The effect of a change in the capital cost parameter i is not considered in the analysis.

Since $h''<0$, (16) implies that $\partial S/\partial \phi$ has the same sign as $\partial p/\partial \phi$, while $\partial r/\partial \phi$ and $\partial p/\partial \phi$ also have the same sign by (15). Recalling (5), the important results

$$\frac{\partial r}{\partial x}<0, \quad \frac{\partial S}{\partial x}<0, \tag{17}$$

are then immediate. Thus, land rent and structural density are both decreasing functions of x, so that land is cheaper and buildings are shorter farther from the CBD. The latter result shows that the model successfully predicts the decline in building heights over distance that is observed in real-world cities. The intuitive explanation for the results in (17) is that lower land rents are required at greater distances to compensate producers for the lower price per square foot of housing. The resulting decline with distance in the relative price of land causes producer substitution in its favor, leading to lower structural densities.

An additional variable of interest is population density, denoted D. Assuming without loss of generality that households each contain one person, D is given by $h(S)/q$, which equals square feet of floor space per acre divided by square feet of floor space per dwelling, or dwellings (persons) per acre. Since $\partial q/\partial x>0$ and

$\partial S/\partial x < 0$, it follows immediately that $\partial D/\partial x < 0$; population density is a decreasing function of distance. The intuitive reason is that since buildings are shorter and the individual dwellings contained within them are larger at greater distances, fewer dwellings and hence fewer people fit on each acre of land. Note that the spatial behavior of population density is a joint result of consumer and producer decisions; consumer substitution in favor of housing and producer substitution in favor of land as x increases are together responsible for the decline of density.

Summing up, the analysis so far has yielded results on the internal structure of cities that appear to recapitulate reality. In particular, the model has predicted that the price per square foot of housing, land rent per acre, and structural and population density are all decreasing functions of distance to the CBD, with dwelling size an increasing function of distance. While these conclusions appear broadly consistent with the results of casual empiricism, systematic empirical tests of the model's predictions have focused mainly on the population density variable. A wealth of evidence has accumulated confirming the negative association between density and distance predicted by the model.[9]

3. Comparative static analysis

While we have seen that the Muth–Mills model does a good job of predicting observed regularities in the internal structures of cities, an equally important goal of the model is to explain intercity differences in spatial structures. For example, the model should be able to explain the building height differential between large and small cities noted in the introduction.

Intercity analysis requires development of the two conditions that characterize the overall equilibrium of the urban area. The first equilibrium condition requires that housing producers outbid agricultural users for all the land used in housing production. Letting $\bar{x}$ denote the distance to the urban–rural boundary, this condition translates into the requirement that urban land rent equals the agricultural rent r_A at $\bar{x}$. Since $\partial r/\partial x < 0$, urban rent will exceed r_A inside $\bar{x}$, as required, and fall short of r_A beyond $\bar{x}$. Recalling that r depends on y, t, and u in addition to x, the first equilibrium condition may be written[10]

$$r(\bar{x}, y, t, u) = r_A. \tag{18}$$

---

[9]See, for example, Muth (1969). For an analysis of the conditions under which the commonly-fitted negative exponential density function will be the correct specification, see Brueckner (1982).

[10]Recall that while r depends on the capital cost parameter i, this variable is not of interest in the present analysis.

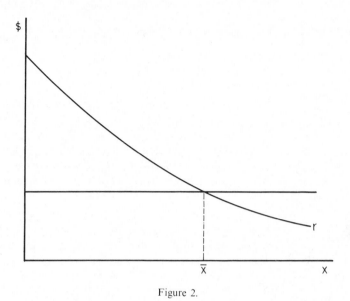

Figure 2.

Figure 2 presents a graphical representation of condition (18) (note that the level of the r function will depend on y, t, and u).[11]

The second equilibrium condition requires that the urban population exactly fit inside $\bar{x}$. To formalize this condition, let θ equal the number of radians of land available for housing at each x, with $0 < \theta \leq 2\pi$ (the remaining land will be consumed by the transportation network and topographical irregularities). Then, note that the population of a narrow ring with inner radius x and width dx will approximately equal $\theta x D(x, y, t, u) dx$, where the functional dependence of population density has been made explicit. The condition that the urban population L fit inside $\bar{x}$ may then be written

$$\int_0^{\bar{x}} \theta x D(x, t, y, u) \, dx = L. \tag{19}$$

The interpretation of the urban equilibrium conditions depends on whether the city is closed or open to migration. In the "closed-city" case, where migration

----

[11]The curvature of the land rent contour can be derived by using (15) to compute

$$\frac{\partial^2 r}{\partial x^2} = h' \frac{\partial S}{\partial x} \frac{\partial p}{\partial x} + h \frac{\partial^2 p}{\partial x^2}.$$

Since this expression is positive by previous results, the land rent contour is convex, as shown in Figure 2.

cannot occur, the population variable L is exogenous and the urban utility u is determined along with $\bar{x}$ by balancing of the supply and demand for housing, as expressed in conditions (18) and (19). These conditions constitute two simultaneous equations that determine equilibrium values for u and $\bar{x}$ as functions of the parameters L, r_A, y, and t. In the "open-city" case, costless migration ensures that the urban residents are neither better off nor worse off than consumers in the rest of the economy. In this case, the urban utility level is fixed exogenously, and population L becomes endogenous, adjusting to whatever value is consistent with the prevailing utility level. The boundary distance $\bar{x}$ remains endogenous, and r_A, y, and t remain as parameters. Note that in the open-city case, the system (18)–(19) is recursive instead of fully simultaneous. Eq. (18) determines $\bar{x}$ directly in terms of the parameters, and (19) then gives L.

With the urban equilibrium conditions established, the stage is now set for comparative static analysis.[12] The closed-city case is discussed first, with attention then turning to the open-city case.

3.1. The closed-city case

The goal of the analysis is to deduce the impacts of changes in the parameters L, r_A, y, and t on the spatial size of the city ($\bar{x}$), housing prices (p), land rents (r), dwelling sizes (q), and building heights (S). The first step in the analysis is total differentiation of the equation system (18) and (19), which yields the comparative-static derivatives $\partial u/\partial \psi$ and $\partial \bar{x}/\partial \psi$, $\psi = L, r_A, y, t$. While this calculation shows the impact of parameter changes on $\bar{x}$, more work is required to derive the effects on p, q, r, and S. Recalling that at a given x, each of these variables depends on y, t, and u, the sources of change are clear. When y or t increases, there is both a direct effect and an indirect effect operating through the induced change in u. When L or r_A increases, the indirect effect alone is felt since p, q, r, and S do not depend directly on population and agricultural rent. Since the analysis outlined above is quite complex, details are relegated to an appendix.

Before proceeding, it is important to realize that the discussion will focus on the impact of parameter changes on the equilibrium of a single city. Once the differences between the pre-change and post-change cities are known, the conclusions can be used to make intercity predictions (separate cities with parameter levels corresponding to the pre- and post-change values can be compared).

---

[12]A final point regarding the urban equilibrium concerns the disposition of the rent earned by urban land. Since urban residents subsist on wage income alone, it is clear that the analysis implicitly assumes that rent is paid to absentee landlords living outside the urban boundary. See Pines and Sadka (1986) for comparative static analysis of a model where land is internally owned.

3.1.1. The effects of an increase in L

It is shown in the appendix that $\bar{x}$ and u are respectively increasing and decreasing functions of L, or that

$$\frac{\partial \bar{x}}{\partial L} > 0, \quad \frac{\partial u}{\partial L} < 0. \tag{20}$$

A population increase thus causes the city to expand spatially and leads to a lower urban utility level. The population increase will also lead to changes in p, q, r, and S at each location. Since y and t are fixed, the impact of the increase in L is felt entirely through the induced change in u, as explained above. The impact on p is given by

$$\frac{dp}{dL} = \frac{\partial p}{\partial u}\frac{\partial u}{\partial L} > 0, \tag{21}$$

where the inequality follows from (20) and the fact that $\partial p/\partial u$ is negative (see (9)). Eq. (21) indicates that the price per square foot of housing rises at all locations as a result of the population increase.

The total derivatives of q, S, and r with respect to L are given by expressions analogous to (21), with p replaced by the appropriate variable. Since the sign of $\partial q/\partial u$ is positive by (9) and since $\partial r/\partial u$ and $\partial S/\partial u$ share the negative sign of $\partial p/\partial u$ by (15) and (16), it follows using (20) that

$$\frac{dq}{dL} < 0, \quad \frac{dr}{dL} > 0, \quad \frac{dS}{dL} > 0. \tag{22}$$

Thus, an increase in L leads to smaller dwellings, higher land rents, and higher structural densities (taller buildings) at all locations. Since q falls and S rises, it follows that population density rises everywhere ($dD/dL > 0$).

It is helpful to trace through the effects of the population increase using a heuristic approach. When the city starts in equilibrium and population increases, excess demand for housing is created at the old prices: the urban population no longer fits inside the old $\bar{x}$. As a result, housing prices are bid up throughout the city. On the consumption side of the market, this increase in prices leads to a decline in dwelling sizes at all locations. On the production side, the price increase causes land rents to be bid up everywhere, and higher land rents in turn lead producers to substitute away from land, resulting in higher structural densities. Since buildings are taller and dwellings smaller, population density rises everywhere, so that more people fit inside any given $\bar{x}$. Finally, the rise in the level of the land rent function leads to an increase in the value of $\bar{x}$ that satisfies (18) (Figure 3 shows the upward shift in the land rent contour (from r_0 to r_1) together with the increase in $\bar{x}$ (from $\bar{x}_a$ to $\bar{x}_b$)). The resulting spatial expansion of the city,

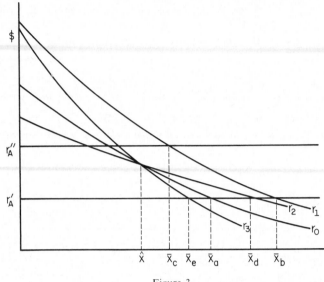

Figure 3.

together with the increase in population densities, tends to eliminate the excess demand for housing, restoring equilibrium.

By describing what appear to be instantaneous changes in the structure of the city as a result of the population increase, the above discussion ignores the fact that buildings are not easily or quickly replaceable. This, of course, is a reflection of the assumption that housing capital is perfectly malleable. Realistically, one would expect the adjustments described above to unfold over a long time period as buildings are torn down and replaced. Thus, the comparative static results are best viewed as predicting the long-run effect of a population increase.[13]

Although the appropriate time horizon must be considered in predicting changes in the spatial structure of a particular city, this issue does not arise when the comparative static results are used to predict intercity differences at a given point in time. The reason is that in a stationary or gradually changing world, the spatial structures of different cities will reflect equilibrium (or approximate equilibrium) outcomes, so that the comparative static results will give correct predictions in intercity comparisons. In the case of population differences, we would expect (holding r_A, y, and t constant) that larger cities would have bigger spatial areas. Moreover, at any given distance from the center, the larger city will have taller buildings and smaller dwellings, and thus a higher population density.

---

[13]A problem with this view is that the model is being interpreted in a dynamic sense even though producer decision-making has been modeled in a static context.

In addition, the price per square foot of housing and land rent per acre will be higher at a given distance from the center in a larger city. These predictions appear to be consistent with the observed features of cities in the real world.[14]

3.1.2. The effects of an increase in r_A

The effects on the closed-city equilibrium of an increase in the agricultural rent r_A are similar to those of an increase in population. The appendix establishes that

$$\frac{\partial \bar{x}}{\partial r_A} < 0, \quad \frac{\partial u}{\partial r_A} < 0, \tag{23}$$

indicating that an increase in agricultural rent reduces the spatial size of the city and lowers the urban utility level. Since r_A is not a direct argument of p, q, r, and S, the derivation of the impacts of the agricultural rent change on these variables proceeds as in the case of a population increase, with each total derivative equal to $\partial u / \partial r_A$ times the partial derivative of the relevant variable with respect to u (for example, $dp/dr_A = (\partial p/\partial u)(\partial u/\partial r_A)$). Using (9), (15), and (16) together with (23), the signs of the total derivatives are

$$\frac{dp}{dr_A} > 0, \quad \frac{dq}{dr_A} < 0, \quad \frac{dr}{dr_A} > 0, \quad \frac{dS}{dr_A} > 0. \tag{24}$$

Note that the directions of change in (24) are the same as in the case of a population increase. In particular, the price per square foot of housing, land rent, and structural density rise at each location, while dwelling sizes fall. Note that the movements of q and S raise population density everywhere, so that $dD/dr_A > 0$.

The intuitive explanation for the above results borrows from the explanation of the impact of a population increase. Proceeding heuristically, the first-round effect (holding u constant) of an increase in r_A is spatial shrinkage of the city, with land near the boundary returned to agricultural use (with u and hence r fixed, an increase in r_A from r'_A to r''_A reduces $\bar{x}$ below its original value of $\bar{x}_a$, as can be seen in Figure 3). This change, however, creates excess demand for housing, so that further adjustments unfold as in the case of a population increase. Note that while $\bar{x}$ expands from its first-round adjustment value (reaching $\bar{x}_c$ in Figure 3 in the case where the final land rent function corresponds to r_1), the variable never rises to its original level (since the city becomes denser, its population fits in a smaller area).

These results can be used to predict differences between otherwise identical cities facing different agricultural rents. For given values of L, y, and t, a city in a

---

[14]For empirical confirmation of the comparative static predictions regarding the spatial sizes of cities, see Brueckner and Fansler (1983).

region of low agricultural rent (a desert, for instance) will have a larger area than a city located amidst productive farmland. In addition, at a given distance from the center the low-rent city will have shorter buildings and larger dwellings, and thus a lower population density. Also, the price per square foot of housing and land rent per acre will be lower in the low-rent city at a given distance from the center. Real-world observation appears to confirm these predictions.

3.1.3. The effects of an increase in y

An increase in the urban income level raises the demand for housing, so that the city grows spatially. In addition, the utility level of urban residents rises. These results are established in the appendix, where it is shown that

$$\frac{\partial \bar{x}}{\partial y} > 0, \quad \frac{\partial u}{\partial y} > 0. \tag{25}$$

Deriving the impacts of a higher y on p, q, S, and r is more difficult than the analogous earlier calculations since the direct effect of y must be considered along with the indirect effect that operates through u. The total derivative of p with respect to y is given by

$$\frac{dp}{dy} = \frac{\partial p}{\partial u}\frac{\partial u}{\partial y} + \frac{\partial p}{\partial y}. \tag{26}$$

Using (25), (9), and (7), it is clear that the first term in (26) is negative while the second term is positive, so that the sign of the expression is not immediately apparent. However, calculations in the appendix show that

$$\frac{dp}{dy} \begin{smallmatrix} > \\ < \end{smallmatrix} 0 \text{ as } x \begin{smallmatrix} > \\ < \end{smallmatrix} \hat{x}, \quad \text{where } 0 < \hat{x} < \bar{x}. \tag{27}$$

That is, at locations inside some $\hat{x} < \bar{x}$, p falls as y increases, while p rises at locations beyond $\hat{x}$. Thus, an increase in y causes a counterclockwise rotation of the p contour. Moreover, since

$$\frac{dr}{dy} = \frac{\partial r}{\partial u}\frac{\partial u}{\partial y} + \frac{\partial r}{\partial y}$$

$$= h\frac{\partial p}{\partial u}\frac{\partial u}{\partial y} + h\frac{\partial p}{\partial y}$$

$$= h\frac{dp}{dy}, \tag{28}$$

by (16), it follows that the land rent contour rotates counterclockwise in step with the p contour (the point of rotation is the same $\hat{x}$). Figure 3 illustrates this outcome (r rotates from r_0 to r_2 and $\bar{x}$ increases from $\bar{x}_a$ to $\bar{x}_d$). Since

$$\frac{\mathrm{d}S}{\mathrm{d}y} = \frac{-h'}{ph''}\frac{\mathrm{d}p}{\mathrm{d}y}, \tag{29}$$

by (15), it follows (recalling $h'' < 0$) that the S contour rotates in the same fashion as the p and r contours. Thus, an increase in y lowers the price per square foot of housing, land rent, and structural density at central locations while increasing the levels of these variables at more distant points. These conclusions, as well as the results in (25), can be used as before to predict differences in the features of otherwise identical cities with different values of y.

It is easy to establish that q rises in response to the increase in y at any location where p falls. This follows because the new consumption bundle must lie on a higher indifference curve [recall (25)] at a point where the MRS is lower (the absolute slope of the budget line, p, has fallen by assumption). Such a point must lie to the right of the original bundle in Figure 1 given that housing is a normal good and indifference curves are convex. Thus, since p falls inside $\hat{x}$, dwelling sizes rise at central locations in response to the increase in income. Since S falls inside $\hat{x}$ from above, it follows that population density also falls at central locations.

By referring to Figure 1, it is easy to see that at locations where p rises, q may either rise or fall. Thus, at locations between $\hat{x}$ and the old $\bar{x}$, the change in q in response to the increase in y is ambiguous. Since it may be shown that the value of p at the new urban boundary is the same as at the old,[15] it follows that the new boundary value of q must be higher than the old boundary value. It is easy to see, however, that this conclusion is not inconsistent with a decline in q at some intermediate location.

To gain an intuitive understanding of the rotation of the p contour, consider the change in locational incentives caused by an increase in income. When income rises, desired housing consumption increases, and since housing is cheaper at greater distances, consumers have an incentive to move to less central locations. This desire to relocate drives up houses prices at distant locations and depresses prices in the now less-attractive central part of the city. These changes lead to sympathetic movements in r and S.

---

[15]To see this, note that r in (12) must be replaced by r_A when (11) and (12) are evaluated at $\bar{x}$. The two equations then serve to determine boundary values of p and S. Since $\bar{x}$ does not appear explicitly, it follows that the boundary values of both these variables are independent of $\bar{x}$. Note that this argument implies that the boundary values of S and p will also be invariant to changes in L and t (they will change with r_A, however).

3.1.4. The effects of an increase in t

When the commuting cost parameter t increases, commute trips of any given length become more expensive, and the city shrinks spatially in response. The urban utility level declines. These results are proved in the appendix, where it is shown that

$$\frac{\partial \bar{x}}{\partial t} < 0, \quad \frac{\partial u}{\partial t} < 0. \tag{30}$$

As in the case of an increase in income, the impacts of higher commuting cost on p, q, r, and S are complex. The appendix establishes that

$$\frac{\mathrm{d}p}{\mathrm{d}t} = \frac{\partial p}{\partial u}\frac{\partial u}{\partial t} + \frac{\partial p}{\partial t} \gtrless 0 \quad \text{as } x \lessgtr x^*, \quad \text{where } 0 < x^* < \bar{x}. \tag{31}$$

Thus, the housing price contour rotates in a clockwise direction, with p rising inside some $x^* < \bar{x}$ and falling beyond x^*. As in the earlier discussion, the r and S contours rotate in exactly the same fashion as the p contour (in this case, clockwise). An increase in t therefore raises the price per square foot of housing, land rent, and structural density at central locations while lowering the values of these variables at more distant points. These impacts, of course, are just the reverse of those generated by an increase in y. The rotation of the land rent contour from r_0 to r_3 and the resulting decline of $\bar{x}$ from $\bar{x}_a$ to $\bar{x}_e$ are shown in Figure 3 (for simplicity, the Figure assumes $x^* = \hat{x}$).

Applying the same argument as before, it follows that q falls at any location where p rises (recall that utility declines in the present case). Thus, dwelling sizes decrease in the central part of the city, although they may rise beyond x^*. Recalling that S rises inside x^*, it follows that central population densities rise.

An intuitive understanding of the rotation of the p contour comes from noting that the increase in t makes close-in locations more attractive given the original pattern of housing prices. The resulting desire of consumers to move toward the CBD bids up central prices and reduces prices at more distant locations, causing a clockwise rotation of the contour.

3.2. The open-city case

For the predictions of the closed-city model to be valid, urban populations must be captive, ruling out utility-equalizing migration flows. When such flows occur, the urban utility level is no longer determined internally, and the open-city model is appropriate. The discussion now turns to a comparative static analysis of this model.

As noted above, the exogenous parameters in the open-city model are u, r_A, y, and t. Holding u fixed, the goal of the analysis is to derive the impact of changes in the observable parameters r_A, y, and t on $\bar{x}$, L, p, q, r, and S (recall that population is now endogenous). The analysis is considerably simpler than in the closed-city case. First, since u is now a parameter, the impact of a changes in r_A, y or t on $\bar{x}$ follows immediately from (18). With the $\bar{x}$ impact thus determined, the effect of a parameter change on L can be read off directly from (19) (the system (18)–(19) is now recursive rather than simultaneous). In addition, the exogeneity of u means that indirect effects on p, q, r, and S (which figured prominently in the closed-city analysis) are absent. Direct effects are the sole sources of change.

An increase in the agricultural rent level has an especially simple impact on the open-city equilibrium. Since y, t, and u are fixed, the land rent function is unchanged as r_A increases (both direct and indirect effects are absent in this case). As a result, $\bar{x}$ must fall as r_A increases, as can be seen in Figure 3. Since p, q, and S are (like r) unchanged at a given x, it follows that the effect of the increase in r_A is simply to truncate the city at a smaller $\bar{x}$, reducing its population but not altering the structure of its remaining area. The model therefore predicts that an open city in a high-r_A region will be smaller spatially and have a lower population than an open city in a low-r_A region. At a given distance from the CBD, however, the cities will be identical.

An increase in y leads to more extensive changes in the open-city equilibrium since the increase in income alters p, q, r, and S at every location, with the impacts (direct effects) given by the partial derivatives in (7), (15), and (16). The signs of these derivatives indicate that the price per square foot of housing, land rent, and structural density rise at all locations in response to the increase in y, while dwelling sizes fall. The upward shift in r leads to an increase in $\bar{x}$, and since population density increases everywhere, L from (19) also increases. These results indicate that in an open urban system, a high-income city will have a higher population, a larger area, and will be denser and more expensive to live in than a low-income city. Note that the model predicts the positive correlation between income and city size noted in various empirical studies.[16]

The changes in the open-city equilibrium following from an increase in t are just the reverse of the impacts of higher income. From (8), (15), and (16), p, r, and S fall at all locations as t increases, while dwelling sizes increase everywhere. Since r falls, $\bar{x}$ declines in Figure 3. Lower population densities at all locations together with a smaller $\bar{x}$ lead to a smaller L by (19). Thus, a high-t city in an open system will have cheaper housing, a smaller area and population, and will be less dense than a low-t city.

To appreciate the connection between these comparative static results and

[16]See, for example, Hoch (1972).

those for a closed city, it is helpful to decompose the open-city changes into two parts. First, let the given parameter (r_A, y, or t) increase holding L fixed, and predict impacts using the closed-city analysis. Then, adjust population to cancel the utility change generated by the parameter increase, again inferring impacts using the closed-city model. The net impact of the two changes corresponds to the open-city effect of the given parameter change. Consider first the case of an increase in income. Holding L fixed, a higher y increases $\bar{x}$ and causes counter-clockwise rotations of the p, r, and S contours (recall Section 3.1.3). Since utility rises and since $\partial u/\partial L < 0$, it follows that an increase in population is required to restore the original utility level. The required increase in L raises $\bar{x}$ further and shifts the rotated p, r, and S contours upward while shifting the q contour downward. From above, the net changes relative to the starting point turn out to be an upward shift in each of the p, q, and S contours, and a downward shift in the q contour. Note that the changes holding L fixed could be interpreted as short-run adjustments, with the remaining impacts unfolding after migrants have begun to enter the city in response to the higher utility level.

While the decomposition of the effect of an increase in t parallels the above, an increase in r_A yields a somewhat different series of changes. Holding L fixed, a higher r_A lowers $\bar{x}$, raises the p, r, and S contours, and lowers the q contour. Since utility falls as a result of the higher r_A, a decline in population is required to restore the original utility level. The required decrease in L lowers the p, r, and S contours and raises the q contour, restoring their original positions. The decline in r drives $\bar{x}$ further below its original level. Again, the first-round impacts can be viewed as occuring before migration begins, with the second-round impacts capturing the effects of the outward migration flow induced by the decline in the city's standard of living.

In concluding this section, it is interesting to consider the question of whether cities in a national economy are best viewed according to the open- or closed-city model. On the one hand, the costs of migration (both pecuniary and psychic) are often high, so that utility differences between cities may persist over long periods. On the other hand, migration flows must ultimately eliminate intercity differences in standards of living, especially over a time horizon as long as one or two generations. Casual empiricism suggests that the predictions of both the open- and closed-city models are partly borne out in reality. For example, the real world appears to exhibit the positive correlation between income and city population predicted by the open-city model. Conversely, the low-density charac-ter of desert cities is consistent with predictions of the closed-city model but at variance with those of the open-city model. This kind of evidence suggests that utility levels in certain cities may diverge appreciably from the national norm at any point in time. Such differences, of course, are always in the process of being eliminated as consumers migrate.

4. Modifications of the model

Having gained an understanding of the properties of the Muth–Mills model, it is important to remember that its portrayal of the urban economy is highly stylized. While the good predictive performance of the model suggests that its simplifications are artfully chosen, capturing the essential features of real-world cities, it is nevertheless instructive to list the ways in which the model is unrealistic and note the attempts of various authors to add greater realism.

The assumption that the city is monocentric is perhaps the most obvious source of difficulty. While the assumption will be reasonably accurate for many urban areas, many cities have important secondary employment centers outside the CBD. By demonstrating that land-use patterns around such centers follow the predictions of the basic model, Muth (1969) showed that the lessons of the analysis are largely unchanged in a polycentric setting. In a different vein, White (1976) analyzed the forces leading to decentralization of employment by exploring the incentives that might lead a CBD firm to seek a suburban location. In more ambitious studies, Mills (1972a) and Fujita and Ogawa (1982) constructed models where the location of all employment within the city is endogenous and potentially decentralized.

The assumption that all urban residents earn the same income is also unrealistic. The effect of relaxing this assumption has been discussed by Mills (1972b) and extensively analyzed by Muth (1969), who offers a complete treatment of the effect of income differences on household location. In addition, Hartwick et al. (1976) and Wheaton (1976) present comparative static analyses of the equilibrium of a city with multiple income groups. The results of these studies show that many of the key properties of the model are unaffected by income heterogeneity.

While the Muth–Mills approach essentially ignores the urban transportation system by assuming an exogenous commuting cost function, the fact that urban traffic congestion (and hence the cost of travel) is endogenous has been stressed in a number of studies. Although the endogeneity of commuting costs has received most attention in normative models of city structure [see, for example, Dixit (1973)], early positive analyses recognizing the importance of investment in the transportation network were provided by Mills (1967, 1972a).

Another unrealistic feature of the model is its treatment of the housing commodity. As was noted in Section 2, the model's focus on a single housing attribute (floor space) is inconsistent with the fact that real-world dwellings are characterized by a vector of attributes. Although awareness of this fact gave birth to the empirical hedonic price literature in the early 1970s, incorporation of multiple housing attributes in urban spatial models has been more recent [see Büttler (1981) and Brueckner (1983)]. Interestingly, this modification leaves most of the important predictions of the model unchanged.

Modification of the Muth–Mills assumption that housing capital is perfectly malleable has been the goal of a growing new literature in urban economics. The resulting models, which stress the importance of spatial variation in the age of buildings, are considerably more complex than the basic malleable-capital framework (see Miyao, Chapter 22 in this volume, for a survey). The models do, however, generate the kind of spatial irregularities that are observed on a micro level in real-world cities (erratic local building height patterns, for example) but are not successfully explained by the Muth–Mills model.

Finally, a number of studies have introduced local public goods (which are absent in the Muth–Mills framework) into urban spatial analysis. While most studies assume that public consumption is spatially uniform, Schuler (1974) and Yang and Fujita (1983) add a new spatial element to the analysis by focusing on models where the public good level varies with location.

Appendix

This appendix derives the comparative static results cited in Section 3. While the analysis largely parallels that of Wheaton (1974), the derivations do not rely on Wheaton's assumption that the non-housing good is normal (more extensive substitutions in several expressions made avoidance of the assumption possible).

The first step is computation of the partial derivatives of r with respect to x, y, t, and u. Substituting for $\partial p/\partial \phi$ in (15) using (5) and footnote 6, it follows that

$$\frac{\partial r}{\partial x} = \frac{-th}{q} < 0, \quad \frac{\partial r}{\partial y} = \frac{h}{q} > 0, \quad \frac{\partial r}{\partial t} = \frac{-xh}{q} < 0, \quad \frac{\partial r}{\partial u} = \frac{-h}{qv_1} < 0. \tag{1a}$$

Then, noting that $D \equiv h/q = -(\partial r/\partial x)/t$, (19) may be rewritten as

$$-\int_0^{\bar{x}} x \frac{\partial r}{\partial x} \, \mathrm{d}x = tL/\theta. \tag{2a}$$

Integrating (2a) by parts then yields

$$-r_A \bar{x} + \int_0^{\bar{x}} r \, \mathrm{d}x = tL/\theta, \tag{3a}$$

where (18) has been used. Letting λ denote any one of the parameters (L, r_A, y, t), total differentiation of (3a) gives

$$\int_0^{\bar{x}} \left(\frac{\partial r}{\partial \lambda} + \frac{\partial r}{\partial u} \frac{\partial u}{\partial \lambda} \right) \mathrm{d}x = \frac{1}{\theta} \left(t \frac{\partial L}{\partial \lambda} + \frac{\partial t}{\partial \lambda} L \right) + \frac{\partial r_A}{\partial \lambda} \bar{x}, \tag{4a}$$

(note that the terms involving $\partial \bar{x}/\partial \lambda$ cancel and that since u is an endogenous variable, the effect of λ on the u argument of r must be taken into account). Since

$\partial u/\partial \lambda$ does not depend on x, this term may be brought outside the integral in (4a), yielding

$$\frac{\partial u}{\partial \lambda} = \frac{\dfrac{1}{\theta}\left(t\dfrac{\partial L}{\partial \lambda}+\dfrac{\partial t}{\partial \lambda}L\right)+\dfrac{\partial r_A}{\partial \lambda}\bar{x}-\displaystyle\int_0^{\bar{x}}\dfrac{\partial r}{\partial \lambda}\mathrm{d}x}{\displaystyle\int_0^{\bar{x}}\dfrac{\partial r}{\partial u}\mathrm{d}x}. \tag{5a}$$

Noting that $\partial L/\partial \lambda$ equals one for $\lambda = L$ and equals zero otherwise, and similarly for $\partial t/\partial \lambda$, and recalling the results of (1a), as well as $\partial r/\partial r_A = \partial r/\partial L = 0$, the following inequalities emerge simply from inspection of (5a):

$$\frac{\partial u}{\partial L}<0, \quad \frac{\partial u}{\partial r_A}<0, \quad \frac{\partial u}{\partial y}>0, \quad \frac{\partial u}{\partial t}<0. \tag{6a}$$

Computation of the derivatives of $\bar{x}$ makes use of (5a). Differentiating (18) yields

$$\frac{\partial \bar{r}}{\partial x}\frac{\partial \bar{x}}{\partial \lambda}+\frac{\partial \bar{r}}{\partial u}\frac{\partial u}{\partial \lambda}+\frac{\partial \bar{r}}{\partial \lambda}=\frac{\partial r_A}{\partial \lambda}, \tag{7a}$$

where the bar over r indicates that the function is evaluated at $\bar{x}$. Since $\partial \bar{r}/\partial x < 0$, the sign of $\partial \bar{x}/\partial \lambda$ is the opposite of the sign of

$$\frac{\partial r_A}{\partial \lambda}-\frac{\partial \bar{r}}{\partial u}\frac{\partial u}{\partial \lambda}-\frac{\partial \bar{r}}{\partial \lambda}. \tag{8a}$$

Since $\partial r_A/\partial L = \partial \bar{r}/\partial L = 0$ and $\partial \bar{r}/\partial u < 0$, and since $\partial u/\partial L < 0$ from (6a), it follows that (8a) is negative for $\lambda = L$, implying

$$\frac{\partial \bar{x}}{\partial L}>0. \tag{9a}$$

Setting $\lambda = r_A$, (8a) becomes $1-(\partial \bar{r}/\partial u)(\partial u/\partial r_A)$, which, using (5a) with $\lambda = r_A$, becomes

$$\frac{\displaystyle\int_0^{\bar{x}}\dfrac{\partial r}{\partial u}\mathrm{d}x-\bar{x}\dfrac{\partial \bar{r}}{\partial u}}{\displaystyle\int_0^{\bar{x}}\dfrac{\partial r}{\partial u}\mathrm{d}x}. \tag{10a}$$

The sign of (10a) is the opposite of that of its numerator, which, integrating by parts, becomes

$$\left[\bar{x}\frac{\partial \bar{r}}{\partial u}-\int_0^{\bar{x}}x\frac{\mathrm{d}}{\mathrm{d}x}\left(\frac{\partial r}{\partial u}\right)\mathrm{d}x\right]-\bar{x}\frac{\partial \bar{r}}{\partial u}=\int_0^{\bar{x}}x\frac{\mathrm{d}}{\mathrm{d}x}\left(\frac{h}{qv_1}\right)\mathrm{d}x, \tag{11a}$$

using (1a). Now $\partial(h/q)/\partial x \equiv \partial D/\partial x < 0$. Also, it may be shown that $dv_1/dx > 0$ holds as long as q is a normal good. These facts imply $d(h/qv_1)/dx < 0$ and yield positive signs for (10a) and (8a), giving

$$\frac{\partial \bar{x}}{\partial r_A} < 0. \tag{12a}$$

The positive sign of $dv_1/dx = v_{11}\partial c/\partial x + v_{12}\partial q/\partial x = (v_{12} - v_2 v_{11}/v_1)\partial q/\partial x$ is established by noting that the term multiplying the positive expression $\partial q/\partial x$ will itself be positive when q is a normal good. Note that $\partial c/\partial x = -(v_2/v_1)\partial q/\partial x$ since utility is constant over x.

When $\lambda = y$, (8a) becomes $-((\partial \bar{r}/\partial u)(\partial u/\partial y) + \partial \bar{r}/\partial y)$, which, substituting (5a), has the sign of

$$\frac{\partial \bar{r}}{\partial y}\int_0^{\bar{x}}\frac{\partial r}{\partial u}\,dx - \frac{\partial \bar{r}}{\partial u}\int_0^{\bar{x}}\frac{\partial r}{\partial y}\,dx. \tag{13a}$$

Gathering all terms under the same integral sign and substituting from (1a), (13a) becomes

$$\int_0^{\bar{x}}\frac{\bar{h}h}{\bar{q}q}\left(\frac{1}{\bar{v}_1} - \frac{1}{v_1}\right)dx, \tag{14a}$$

where the bar again indicates that the variable is evaluated at $\bar{x}$. Since $dv_1/dx > 0$, it follows that the integrand in (14a) is negative over the range of integration, making (13a) and (8a) positive and yielding

$$\frac{\partial \bar{x}}{\partial y} > 0. \tag{15a}$$

Computation of $\partial \bar{x}/\partial t$ is more difficult and proceeds in a reverse manner to the above. Eq. (19) is differentiated directly and then $\partial u/\partial t$ is eliminated using (7a). Differentiating (19) with respect to t yields

$$\overline{xD}\frac{\partial \bar{x}}{\partial t} + \int_0^{\bar{x}}x\left(\frac{\partial D}{\partial t} + \frac{\partial D}{\partial u}\frac{\partial u}{\partial t}\right)dx = 0. \tag{16a}$$

Rearranging (7a) to solve for $\partial u/\partial t$ and substituting in (16a) yields, after more rearrangement,

$$\frac{\partial \bar{x}}{\partial t}\left[\overline{xD}\frac{\partial \bar{r}}{\partial u} - \int_0^{\bar{x}}x\frac{\partial D}{\partial u}\frac{\partial \bar{r}}{\partial x}\,dx\right] = \int_0^{\bar{x}}x\left(\frac{\partial D}{\partial u}\frac{\partial \bar{r}}{\partial t} - \frac{\partial D}{\partial t}\frac{\partial \bar{r}}{\partial u}\right)dx. \tag{17a}$$

Using the definition of D,

$$\frac{\partial D}{\partial t} = \frac{h'}{q}\frac{\partial S}{\partial t} - \frac{h}{q^2}\frac{\partial q}{\partial t}. \tag{18a}$$

Substituting for $\partial S/\partial t$ and $\partial q/\partial t$ using (16) and footnote 6, (18a) becomes

$$\frac{\partial D}{\partial t} = -\left[\frac{(h')^2}{ph''q} + \frac{h}{q^2}\eta\right]\frac{\partial p}{\partial t} \equiv \Gamma\frac{\partial p}{\partial t}, \tag{19a}$$

with $\Gamma > 0$. To evaluate $\partial D/\partial u$, $\partial S/\partial u$ and $\partial q/\partial u$ from (16) and footnote 6 are substituted into an expression analogous to (18a). Since

$$\partial q/\partial u = (\partial p/\partial u - (\partial\,\mathrm{MRS}/\partial c)(1/v_1))\eta,$$

the result is

$$\frac{\partial D}{\partial u} = \Gamma\frac{\partial p}{\partial u} + \frac{h}{q^2}\frac{\partial\,\mathrm{MRS}}{\partial c}\frac{\eta}{v_1} \equiv \Gamma\frac{\partial p}{\partial u} + \Lambda, \tag{20a}$$

with $\Lambda \equiv (h/q^2)(\partial\,\mathrm{MRS}/\partial c)(\eta/v_1) < 0$ (see footnote 6). Since $\partial p/\partial u < 0$, it follows that $\partial D/\partial u$ is negative, which implies that the integral on the LHS of (17a) is positive, making the entire term multiplying $\partial \bar{x}/\partial t$ negative. Next, substituting (19a) and (20a) to evaluate the RHS of (17a), the expression reduces to

$$\int_0^{\bar{x}}\left[x\Gamma\left(\frac{\partial p}{\partial u}\frac{\partial \bar{r}}{\partial t} - \frac{\partial p}{\partial t}\frac{\partial \bar{r}}{\partial u}\right) + x\Lambda\frac{\partial \bar{r}}{\partial t}\right]\mathrm{d}x =$$

$$\int_0^{\bar{x}}\left[x\Gamma\frac{\bar{h}}{q\bar{q}}\left(\frac{\bar{x}}{v_1} - \frac{x}{\bar{v}_1}\right) + x\Lambda\frac{\partial \bar{r}}{\partial t}\right]\mathrm{d}x. \tag{21a}$$

The second term in the integrand of (21a) is positive while the first term is also positive since $\bar{x}/v_1 > x/\bar{v}_1$ holds over the range of integration by virtue of $\mathrm{d}v_1/\mathrm{d}x > 0$. Thus the RHS of (17a) is positive, and it follows that

$$\frac{\partial \bar{x}}{\partial t} < 0. \tag{22a}$$

The final results to be derived are the effects of an increase in y or t on p. Substituting in (26) using footnote 6 yields

$$\frac{\mathrm{d}\tilde{p}}{\mathrm{d}y} = \frac{1}{\tilde{q}}\left(1 + \frac{1}{\tilde{v}_1}\frac{\partial u}{\partial y}\right), \tag{23a}$$

where the $\tilde{\ }$ indicates that the variable is evaluated at some $\tilde{x}$ between 0 and $\bar{x}$. Substituting for $\partial u/\partial y$ from (5a) and factoring out $\int_0^{\tilde{x}}\partial r/\partial u\,\mathrm{d}x$, (23a) has the sign of

$$-\left[\int_0^{\tilde{x}}\frac{\partial r}{\partial u}\mathrm{d}x + \frac{1}{\tilde{v}_1}\int_0^{\tilde{x}}\frac{\partial r}{\partial y}\mathrm{d}x\right] \tag{24a}$$

$$= -\int_0^{\tilde{x}} \frac{h}{q}\left(\frac{1}{\tilde{v}_1} - \frac{1}{v_1}\right) dx, \tag{25a}$$

using (1a). When $\tilde{x} = \bar{x}$, so that $\tilde{v}_1 = \bar{v}_1$, (25a) is positive given $dv_1/dx > 0$. Conversely, when $\tilde{x} = 0$, so that $\tilde{v}_1 = v_1^0$, (25a) is negative. Furthermore, since (25a) is increasing in $\tilde{x}$, it follows that the expression changes sign just once, establishing that $d\tilde{p}/dy$ is negative for $\tilde{x}$ less than some $\hat{x}$ and positive beyond $\hat{x}$.

Substituting in (31) using footnote 6 gives

$$\frac{d\tilde{p}}{dt} = -\frac{1}{q}\left(\tilde{x} + \frac{1}{\tilde{v}_1}\frac{\partial u}{\partial t}\right). \tag{26a}$$

Substituting for $\partial u/\partial t$ using (5a), (26a) has the sign of

$$\tilde{x}\int_0^{\tilde{x}}\frac{\partial r}{\partial u}dx + \frac{1}{\tilde{v}_1}\frac{L}{\theta} - \frac{1}{\tilde{v}_1}\int_0^{\tilde{x}}\frac{\partial r}{\partial t}dx. \tag{27a}$$

Using (2a) to eliminate L/θ and replacing $\partial r/\partial x$ by $(t/x)(\partial r/\partial t)$ using (1a), (27a) reduces to

$$\int_0^{\tilde{x}}\frac{h}{q}\left[\frac{2x}{\tilde{v}_1} - \frac{\tilde{x}}{v_1}\right]dx, \tag{28a}$$

making further substitutions from (1a). For $\tilde{x} = 0$, (28a) is clearly positive. Although (28a) is ambiguous in sign for $\tilde{x} = \bar{x}$, the facts that the boundary value of p is invariant with t (see footnote 12) while $\partial\bar{x}/\partial t < 0$ together imply that $d\tilde{p}/dt < 0$ (recall $\partial p/\partial x < 0$). Thus (28a) must be negative for $\tilde{x} = \bar{x}$. The fact that its derivative with respect to $\tilde{x}$ is negative then means that (28a) changes sign just once between $\tilde{x} = 0$ and $\tilde{x} = \bar{x}$, implying that $d\tilde{p}/dt$ is positive inside some x^* and negative beyond x^*.

References

Alonso, W. (1964) *Location and land use*. Cambridge: Harvard University Press.

Brueckner, J.K. (1982) 'A note on sufficient conditions for negative exponential population densities', *Journal of Regional Science*, 22:353–359.

Brueckner, J.K. (1983) 'The economics of urban yard space: An "implicit-market" model for housing attributes', *Journal of Urban Economics*, 13:216–234.

Brueckner, J.K. and D. Fansler (1983) 'The economics of urban sprawl: Theory and evidence on the spatial sizes of cities', *Review of Economics and Statistics*, 55:479–482.

Büttler, H. (1981) 'Equilibrium of a residential city, attributes of housing, and land-use zoning', *Urban Studies*, 18:23–39.

Dixit, A. (1973) 'The optimum factory town', *Bell Journal of Economics*, 4:637–651.

Fujita, M. and H. Ogawa (1982), 'Multiple equilibria and structural transition of non-monocentric urban configurations', *Regional Science and Urban Economics*, 18:161–196.

Hartwick, J., U. Schweizer and P. Varaiya (1976) 'Comparative static analysis of a residential economy with several classes', *Journal of Economic Theory*, 13:396–413.

Hoch, I. (1972) 'Income and city size', *Urban Studies*, 9:299–328.

Mills, E.S. (1967) 'An aggregative model of resource allocation in a metropolitan area', *American Economic Review*, 57:197–210.

Mills, E.S. (1972a), *Studies in the structure of the urban economy*. Baltimore: Johns Hopkins University Press.

Mills, E.S. (1972b), *Urban economics*. Glenview, Illinois: Scott Foresman.

Muth, R.F. (1969) *Cities and housing*. Chicago: University of Chicago Press.

Pines D. and E. Sadka (1986) 'Comparative statics analysis of a fully closed city', *Journal of Urban Economics*, 20:1–20.

Schuler, R.E. (1974) 'The interaction between local government and urban residential location', *American Economic Review*, 64:682–696.

Wheaton, W.C. (1974) 'A comparative static analysis of urban spatial structure', *Journal of Economic Theory*, 9:223–237.

Wheaton, W.C. (1976) 'On the optimal distribution of income among cities', *Journal of Urban Economics*, 3:31–44.

White, M.J. (1976) 'Firm suburbanization and urban subcenters', *Journal of Urban Economics*, 3:323–343.

Yang, C. and M. Fujita (1983) 'Urban spatial structure with open space', *Environment and Planning A.*, 15:67–84.

Chapter 21

COMPUTER SIMULATION MODELS OF URBAN LOCATION

JOHN F. KAIN

Harvard University

1. Introduction

This paper critically examines efforts over a twenty-five year period to construct two kinds of policy-oriented computer models of urban-location–land-use forecasting models and computer simulation models of urban housing markets. The land use forecasting models were typically developed to provide 10–20 year forecasts of urban development patterns as part of the travel forecasting requirements of metropolitan transportation studies. The housing market models, in contrast, were developed to assist in the evaluation of a variety of housing and urban development programs and policies.

In spite of their different subject matters and orientations, i.e. long range forecasting versus program evaluation, these models have a number of common characteristics. First, both were inspired by actual planning and policy problems and were often carried out in conjunction with ongoing policy and planning studies. Second, recognition of the actual and potential power of computers was instrumental in their inception and design and computers were used extensively both for the estimation of model parameters and for model simulations. And, finally there was considerable intellectual cross-fertilization between the two streams of model development.

Space considerations make it necessary to ignore, or consider only in passing, several classes of urban location models including the highly interesting, optimizing models initiated by Mills (1972) and extended by Hartwick and Hartwick (1974), the monocentric numerical models of urban location by Mills (1972), Muth (1974), and by Arnott and MacKinnon (1977), the simulation models developed at the University of North Carolina [Chapin et al. (1962) and Donnelly (1964)], the Community Analysis Model (CAM) developed by David Birch and his associates at MIT [Birch et al. (1974, 1977)], and scores of individual empirical studies of residential location, urban densities, housing demand and prices, and employment location.

The next section of this paper critically examines the most notable of the hundreds of land use forecasting models. While the categories used, based on a

Handbook of Regional and Urban Economics, Volume II, Edited by E.S. Mills
© *1987, Elsevier Science Publishers B.V.*

somewhat idiosyncratic combination of chronological order and methodology, are somewhat difficult to sustain, land use forecasting models are grouped into three major categories: (1) Eclectic Empirical–Econometric Models; (2) Gravity Type Models; and (3) Integrated Land-Use Transportation Models. Many fewer housing market simulation models have been constructed, and thus the paper's third Section provides detailed consideration of only four: the ADL–San Francisco Model, the Urban Institute Model, the NBER Urban Simulation Model, and Harvard Urban Development Simulation Model (HUDS). The paper's final section examines the implications of further advances in computer technology and particularly the micro computer revolution on likely future developments in urban simulation models.

2. Land-use forecasting models

While the first attempt to construct computer simulation models to forecast land uses for metropolitan transportation studies emerged in the early 1960s, they were strongly influenced by earlier modeling efforts. The Detroit Metropolitan Area Transportation Study (1955–56) and the Chicago Area Transportation Study [CATS (1960)] were the most influential of these early studies. The Detroit study is usually credited with formulating what has come to be known as the UTP (Urban Transportation Planning) model. The UTP model operationalizes the concept, first articulated by Mitchell and Rapkin (1954), that urban tripmaking is a derived demand depending on land uses and that future travel could be derived from forecasts of future land uses.

The Detroit study relied on the land use plans prepared by the region's numerous city and regional planning agencies for its forecasts of future land uses. The inadequacy of these plan-based forecasts became apparent when the sum of the independent employment and population projections far exceeded any plausible projections of the region's aggregate growth. When J.D. Carroll, director of the Detroit Study, and his talented analysts moved to Chicago, they assigned a high priority to the collection and analysis of land use data. Analyses of Detroit origin and destination data had shown that trip generation and attraction rates per acre varied widely among zones, reflecting large differences in employment and population densities. Thus, the Chicago Area Transportation Study (CATS) made a major effort to collect floor area data and extensive historical information on population densities and vacant land. Using these data, John Hamburg and others [CATS (1960), Hamburg (1960), and Hamburg and Creighton (1959)] devised an ingenious land use forecasting model based on the concept of development capacity. Lowry (1967) provides an insightful discussion of both this and several other early land use forecasting models. CATS also pioneered in the use of computers as its analysts completed the first computer based assignment of trips to a metropolitan highway network.

Progress by CATS in developing more scientific methods of land use forecasting inspired even more elaborate modeling efforts in subsequent studies. Post-CATS efforts to construct land use forecasting model have tended to follow one of two approaches. Thus, the discussion that follows divides the post-CATS efforts to construct land use forecasting models into Econometric Models and Gravity Type Models, even though the distinction becomes increasingly hard to maintain.

2.1. Eclectic Empirical-Econometric Models

The most publicized proposal to use computer simulation methods to forecast future land uses involved efforts by Britton Harris and others [Herbert and Stevens (1960); Harris (1962a, b)] associated with the Penn–Jersey study to use linear programming to predict residential locations. The idea of using linear programing to predict residential location proved to be infeasible, given the avialable time and resources and the capabilities of available computers and computing methods. Harris and his students, however, continued to pursue the idea and subsequently developed a prototype model [Harris (1966) and Wheaton (1974)]. While the Herbert–Stevens model has yet to see its first use in an operational land use forecasting study, it has nonetheless influenced both theoretical and empirical research in urban economics. Its continuing appeal is evident from Senior (1977), and the efficient algorithm devised by Harris was used in the NBER Urban Simulation [Kain, Apgar, and Ginn (1977a)] and Harvard Urban Development Simulation (HUDS) [Kain and Apgar (1985)] models.

Although less widely publicized, Penn–Jersey's ambitious efforts to collect and analyze a variety of land use data and detailed information on household behavior may have been of even greater importance. Penn–Jersey analysts designed and executed an elaborate supplementary household survey that provided detailed information on household behavior and collected unprecedented amounts of data on employment by industry and location. These extensive employment and household data were used in developing and estimating an eclectic land use forecasting model [Seidman (1969)].

Employment data collected and analyzed by the Penn–Jersey, Puget–Sound [Graves (1964); Joshi (1964)], and other transportation studies greatly increased our empirical knowledge of urban spatial structure patterns since almost no spatially disaggregated employment data had existed. Unfortunately, the analyses of these employment data produced few useful generalizations and the cross-section and one shot nature of the data collection efforts inhibited meaningful analyses of changes in the spatial distribution of employment. As Kain (1968) demonstrates the employment location models developed by these land-use transportation studies seriously underestimate central area employment declines and the rate of employment dispersal because of their nearly total reliance on cross-section data. Limited availability of employment data on spatially disaggregate workplace locations remains a serious impediment to research on urban spatial patterns.

In the mid-1960s Donald Hill and others (1965, 1966) developed the "Empiric" model for the Boston area regional transportation study. In spite of unending and generally justified criticisms of its weak theoretical foundations and its rather casual use of simultaneous equation methods, variants of the EMPIRIC model have been used to forecast the spatial distribution employment and population in more than a dozen metropolitan areas including Boston, Atlanta, Denver, Puget–Sound, Minneapolis–St. Paul, and Washington, D.C. [Peat, Marwick, and Mitchell (1972)].

Empiric is a linear, simultaneous equation system designed to explain changes in regional population and employment shares, generally for four or five population categories by income and five or six industry sectors. While many of the explanatory variables used were similar from one city to the next, somewhat different explanatory variables were used, depending on which subset maximized each equation's R^2. EMPIRIC models typically explain large fractions of the variance of the share dependent variables, but nearly all of their explanatory power is accounted for by lagged dependent variables. Relying heavily on the persistence of land use patterns, the model provides very little insight about the forces causing changes in metropolitan structure and is nearly worthless in situations where conditional forecasts are required.

2.2. Gravity Type Models

In 1961, Ira S. Lowry, then an analyst with the Pittsburgh Metropolitan Area Study published a working paper describing what has come to be known as the "Lowry model" [Lowry (1964)]. The model begins with exogenous projections of so-called basic employment and zone-to-zone travel costs, and produces estimates of employment and population by geographic areas or zones. Improved variants of the model have served as the core the land use forecasting models employed in dozens of land-use transportation studies both in this country and overseas.

Much of the Lowry model's appeal is traceable to its, often misunderstood, iterative structure. While the iterations are no more than a solution technique for a single period model, they have frequently been endowed with behavioral significance, resulting from a tendency to confuse the model's iterative solution method and the conceptual distinction between population serving and basic (non-population serving) employment. There has also been a tendency to confuse the "basic", "non-basic" dichotomy used in economic base models with the "basic" and "population serving" employment categories used by Lowry. A less confusing terminology and one that is more faithful to Lowry's use of the concepts would be "population serving" and "non-population serving" employment.

In the first iteration, the Lowry model uses a journey-to-work function of the gravity type to distribute workers employed in basic industries in workplace zone j among residence zones i according to (1),

$$P_{ij} = (C_{ij})^{-1.32R},$$ (1)

where P_{ij} is the proportion of workers employed at j living at i, C_{ij} is the airline distance from zone i to j, and R is the number of residence zones at distance C_{ij}. The total number of basic workers assigned to each residence zone, obtained by summing over workplaces, is then converted to an initial estimate of resident population by use of a population/employment ratio.

After (1) has been used to allocate basic workers to residence zones, journey-to-shop functions are used to allocate three types of population serving employment to each zone j. The journey-to-shop function is analogous to the journey-to-work function except that population serving workers required to serve the resident population of each residence zone i are allocated among j workplace zones. Following the first round allocation of population-serving employment to zones, the journey-to-work function is again used to allocate population-serving workers at j among available residence zones i and the journey-to-shop function is used to allocate population-serving workers to residence zones. This iterative process continues until convergence is achieved. Maximum density constraints and minimum employment constraints to produce a clustering of population-serving jobs complete the model.

Crecine (1964) was the first of a large number of researchers that attempted to use the Lowry framework as the core of an operational forecasting model. Working as a consultant to the Pittsburgh Community Renewal Programing study, Crecine developed TOMM (Time Oriented Metropolitan Model). Crecine retained the distinction between basic and population serving employment and the gravity formulation, but provided for incremental, rather than single-year, solutions and suggested a number of other extensions. Crecine completed and ran a prototype model, but election-inspired changes in the management of Pittsburgh's Community Renewal Planning Program and dissatisfaction with the larger modeling project led to its cancellation before TOMM could be completely tested. Brewer (1973) provides a detailed discussion of this failed modeling effort.

Goldner's (1968) Projective Land Use Model (PLUM) is one of the earliest, and certainly one of the best documented, applications of the Lowry framework to an operational land use forecasting model. While PLUM's overall structure closely follows Lowry's original formulation, Goldner made a number of significant modifications and improvements, including programing changes to accommodate zones of different sizes (Lowry used a square mile grid), the use of travel time rather than airline distance, substitution of a rather different distribution function, and the use of somewhat different constraints. An improved version of the model, IPLUM, provided incremental solutions [Goldner (1972)].

Goldner's careful implementation and PLUM–IPLUM's unusually detailed documentation led Putman (1976) to use it as the protype gravity-type model in his highly useful comparison of predictive land use models. Putman originally planned to reestimate and compare versions of the PLUM–IPLUM and Empiric models using data for identical cities. Dissatisfaction with the estimation methods used in PLUM–IPLUM and improvements suggested by British research on gravity models, however, caused Putman to develop and use a modified version of PLUM–IPLUM, which he named DRAM (Disaggregated Residential Allocation Model).

Putman re-estimated EMPIRIC for Boston, Minneapolis–St. Paul, and Washington, D.C. and estimated DRAM for Minneapolis–St. Paul and Washington, D.C. Comparisons of model output indicated that while EMPIRIC tended to explain somewhat greater fractions of sample variance, the parameters of either model could be adjusted to obtain rather close statistical fits to baseline data. Putnam concluded, however, that while Empiric might perform slightly better than DRAM as a pure forecasting model, i.e. assuming no changes in policy, DRAM had a clear advantage whenever conditional forecasts were required. This result, of course, is due to EMPIRIC's lack of sensitivity to variables other than lagged employment and population.

At the same time Goldner was developing PLUM–IPLUM, researchers in the United Kingdom were attempting to improve the Lowry model and adapt it to British circumstances. In 1967 A.G. Wilson, a physicist by training and early research experience, published a seminal paper showing that both the gravity and intervening opportunities [Schneider, CATS (1960)] models of spatial distribution could be derived using entropy maximization principals adapted from statistical mechanics [Wilson (1970b, p. 2)]. Wilson demonstrated, for example, that the conventional gravity model could be represented by the trip matrix, T_{ij}, and three constraints: the sum of T_{ij}'s over i origins must equal total originating trips; the sum T_{ij}'s over j destinations must equal total destinations; and the sum of the product of T_{ij} and c_{ij}, i.e. generalized cost per trip, must equal total generalized cost C for the entire system [Wilson (1967, p. 258)].

Wilson's work on entropy maximization models provided a rigorous foundation for the gravity model – even the most ardent admirers of the Lowry model were bothered by the fact that its theoretical basis was a rather forced appeal to Newton's gravitational law. Without in any way diminishing Wilson's valuable contribution, it should be clearly understood that his early work did nothing to provide a behavioral or theoretical justification for these models. Rather Wilson's reformulation made the gravity model's structure more explicit and made it easier for researchers to introduce complications that could be endowed with behavioral interpretations. Notions about market and individual behavior provided a guide for disaggregating the distribution functions or choosing and specifying constraints, while a finely honed set of tools borrowed from statistical mechanics provided a rigorous accounting framework and suggested methods of estimating and solving ever more complex models.

During this same period several other British researchers sought to use the Lowry framework as the core of operational land use forecasting models. Batty (1971) describes these early efforts, distinguishing between models at the subregional scale and models at the town scale. Batty also discusses Garin's (1966) efforts in the United States to refine the Lowry model, crediting Garin with "explicitly incorporating spatial interaction models in place of the potential models used to allocate activities" and with "consistently integrating these models with the economic base methodology" [Batty (1971, p. 159)].

The Nottingham–Derbyshire model is representative of early British efforts to estimate gravity type models at the subregional scale [Batty (1971)]. The region was divided into 62 zones including three very large zones, the cities of Nottingham (305,050 persons), Derby (125,900 persons), and Chesterfield (79,080 persons), that accounted for nearly a third of the region's population. Because the zones used in the subregional models were so large, virtually all work and shopping trips were intrazonal, a feature that greatly reduced the applicability of the Lowry model.

Numerous constraints included in spatial distribution models greatly reduce the applicability of conventional estimation models; thus Batty (1970) and other British researchers [Batty and Mackie (1972)], guided by Wilson's restatement of these models in entropy maximization terms, devoted considerable effort to calibrating spatial allocation models, which previously had been calibrated by highly ad hoc and frequently questionable methods. The Nottingham–Derbyshire study, for example, employed an iterative procedure, described as a gradient search procedure, which resembles the simulation procedures used to calibrate the Urban Institute Housing model [DeLeeuw and Struyk (1975), Putman (1976)], in discussing U.S. efforts to implement gravity-type models, asserts that "in U.S. practice, with but one exception, no Lowry-type model had ever been successfull calibrated (in a statistical sense)." The exception identified to by Putman, a model developed by A.M. Voorhees and Associates (1972) for the North Central Texas Council of Government, is explained by the participation of a British transport analyst on the Voorhees team.

Batty (1971) also describes five models developed by Echenique and his colleagues at the Centre for Land-Use and Built-Form studies at the University of Cambridge. These models distinguish between the processes of allocating floor space (buildings) to sites and of allocating a particular activity group to the existing stock of structures, emphasizing in particular the differences in time scale between these two processes, and include a submodel for allocating floor space [Echenique et al. (1969)]. While the conceptual distinction is important, the floor space model has virtually no behavioral content; it serves simply as a capacity constraint on the residential and employment location models.

Rhodes implemented one of the first operational models to successfully disaggregate population by socio-economic group. Batty and other researchers at the Urban Systems Research Unit at the University of Reading meanwhile pioneered in the development of models disaggregating employment and population and in introducing dynamics. Cripps and Foot (1969), for example, developed a disaggregated model of the housing market employing several static disaggregated models of the residential sector.

Batty (1973), drawing on what he describes as both utility maximizing principles and entropy maximization, developed a housing market model for Reading that combines a primitive demand model with a gravity-type spatial distribution model. The Reading model partitions households into three occupational (income) groups and dwelling units into five house-types (large and small owner-occupied units, good and poor private rental units, and all public rented units). Using workplace and residence choice data, Batty estimates two variants of a simple demand model. Model I predicts the numbers of each type of household who occupy each type of unit in each residence zone using probabilities that vary by type of households, but are the same for all workplaces. Model II employs probabilities that vary for each type of household and workplace.

Model II's demand equations are similar to those estimated by Kain and Brown [Ingram, Kain, and Ginn (1972), Appendix B] for San Francisco as tests of the gross price hypothesis; Batty's overall model, moreover, resembles the submarket demand and residential location models used in the NBER–HUDS models, except that the NBER–HUDS submarket demand model employs more housing types and more categories of households and includes gross prices in the demand functions [Ingram, Kain, and Ginn (1972); Kain, Apgar, and Ginn (1977); and Kain and Apgar (1985)]. The residential location submodel used in the NBER–HUDS models uses linear programming to assign the participants in each housing submarket in each year, while Batty uses a gravity type distribution function to allocate all households.

Engle (1974) has shown that linear programming models of the type used in the NBER–HUDS models uses linear programming to assign the participants in each costs for a matrix defined by a fixed number of origins and destinations and zone-to-zone travel costs. Gravity models, fit to actual journey-to-work data, obtain intermediate solutions, a fact that many analysts interpret as meaning that households do not minimize journey-to-work costs or maximize utility. In fact, considerable confusion exists about the utility maximization assumptions used in monocentric models of residential location. Many non-economists confuse transport cost minimization and utility maximization in urban economic models, concluding that economic models assume households locate so as to minimize their journey-to-work costs. In fact, the central observation of these models is that households tradeoff increases in transport costs from longer journeys to work against savings in housing costs in such a way that maximizes their total utility. Recognition of heterogeneous preferences, a durable and heterogeneous housing stock, and transactions and moving costs go far in reducing the apparent inconsistency between allocations obtained from linear programing and gravity type models. In an important, but fugitive paper, Quigley (1972) demonstrates that recent movers, participating in fairly homogeneous rental submarkets, tend to chose residence locations that are very close to their minimum gross price (the sum of journey to work costs and location rents) residence locations.

Wilson and his colleagues also made considerable progress in implementing more sophisticated spatial distribution models as part of a comprehensive modeling effort for the West Yorkshire–Leeds region. These spatial distribution models are especially notable for their treatment of time and for their representation of moving behavior. Following suggestions by Wilson (1970b), Mackett and Mountcastle (1977) allow four types of moving behavior: (1) households with a new place of residence and a new place of work; (2) households with a new place of residence, but the same place of work; (3) households with the same place of residence, but a new place of work; and (4) households with the same places of residence and work. The addition of moving behavior permits filtering, defined in this study as the gradual decline in a zone's relative income.

In implementing their model for Leeds, Mackett and Mountcastle estimate separate distribution functions for three social (income) groups. Housing types are included in the model as zone-and social group-specific constraints. The model first allocates the highest social group among the entire stock of vacant units using a distribution function that includes both journey-to-work distance and each zone's stock of vacant houses, then the second social group is allocated according to its distribution function and the stock of remaining units, and so on.

As part of the same study, Senior (1977) describes efforts to estimate three kinds of residential location models:

Model 1, spatial allocation model of the social physics type proposed by Wilson (1970a), identifies workers by workplace location j, including a zero/one variable to distinguish between heads of households and dependent workers. Allocations of workers to residence zone i are derived by maximizing an appropriate entropy function.

Model 2, a version of the Herbert–Stevens model proposed by Wheaton and Harris (1972) and by Senior and Wilson (1974), assumes a fixed housing stock and thus obtains short run rather than long run solutions, explicitly represents multiple workplaces, and employs the same demand and supply constraints as Model 1. The crucial difference is that the Herbert–Stevens model uses the concept of bid rents/prices b_{ijkw} to describe the attractiveness of housetypes and locations to household groups. Model 2 also employs a demand model, initially proposed by Harris (1965) and implemented by Harris, Nathanson, and Rosenburg (1966) and Wheaton (1972), to estimate bid rents and to adjust them nonlinearly.

Model 3, a version of the Herbert–Stevens model cast within an entropy maximizing framework, is derived by maximizing the entropy function subject to demand and supply constraints, including the LP objective function as an additional behavioral constraint which may take on a suboptimal value which is determined at the calibration stage. [Senior and Wilson (1974)]. Senior argues this approach has the advantage avoiding the optimizing and associated perfect competition assumptions the LP procedure implies. Senior also derives terms for the entropy maximization model which he argues can be interpreted as the market price of housing and as the surplus or welfare term.

When empirically implemented, Model 3 does a relatively poor job of locating dependent workers, fails to allocate properly by tenure, and consistently understates the differences in locational behavior among social class groups. Senior concludes these failings are due in part to the coarseness of classifications schemes used, but adds that "the fundamental issues lie with the model's hypotheses and assumptions which do not capture, in sufficient detail or perhaps as accurately as desirable, the preferences and constraints which differentially condition the choice and opportunities of the worker groups" (p. 306). More specifically, he acknowledges that house price is an incomplete representation of the attractiveness of housing.

From his experience, Senior argues for a separate representation of the attractiveness of individual attributes in the residential environment to various worker groups, identifying this feature as a notable strength of the model proposed by Anthony and Baxter (1971). Finally, Senior, in discussing future work, gives as a medium term objective the completion of a more ambitious computer representation of Model 3 that would emphasize (a) the development of at least a quasi dynamic model; (b) a more comprehensive approach that pays particular attention to tenure constraints, eligibility conditions and housing supply; and (c) a greater attention to policy variables.

While efforts to develop entropy maximization models have been centered in Great Britain, a number of United States researchers have made important contributions as well. Their work, moreover, reflects the extensive data and computing resources available to them and the institutional settings in which they worked. Unfortunately, in contrast to the British experience, much of the United States research is poorly documented and, if available at all, is published only in difficult-to-obtain working papers and reports. Among the limited body of published work, Putman's (1978) is the most extensive; in addition to his careful comparisons of the PLUM–IPLUM and Empiric models, Putman and Ducca (1978a,b) estimated DRAM spatial distribution functions for at least 15 metropolitan areas and for different levels of zonal aggregation, and Putman (1980 and 1983) implemented the first fully integrated land use transportation model.

DRAM typically requires the estimation of nine parameters for four equations defined by income quartets. Each equation expresses the probability that a worker employed at j will reside in residence zone i as a function of the time and cost of traveling between zone i and j and the residential attractiveness of zone i. Attractiveness is represented by seven variables of which by far the most important are the fractions of each zone's residents belonging to each income quartet; the remaining variables for each residence zone are the amount of residential land, the amount of vacant, buildable land, and the share of buildable land that has been used. DRAM's parameters are estimated from a cross section sample of all workers, rather than only movers, using a gradient-search technique discussed in Putman and Ducca (1978a).

The resulting parameter estimates vary widely among 11 areas with comparable data and model specifications. While Beta, "a measure of people's willingness to make increasingly long (in time or cost) trips between work and home" [Putman and Ducca (1978b, p. 1003)] is negative in all 44 equations, its value for the lowest income quartets varies ranges from -0.15 (San Diego) to -2.42 (Vancouver) and for the highest income quartets from -0.12 (Denver and San Diego) to -1.38 (Philadelphia). Even larger and more inscrutable differences were obtained for the remaining explanatory variables. Thus, while Putman and Ducca's estimation of DRAM distribution equations for such a large sample of cities is a major achievement, DRAM, nonetheless, has limited behavioral content.

2.3. Integrated Land-Use Transportation Models

Putman's crowning achievement is development of ITLUP [Putman (1980) and 1983)], the first fully integrated transportation and land use package. While the interrelationship between land use and transportation has long been recognized and has been central to the methods used by transportation studies since at least the Detroit study, the feedbacks between urban development and transportation investments have seldom been adequately considered. The usual practice has been to project land uses with only the vaguest of reference to proposed transport investments and their impacts on journey times and costs and to design transport investments to serve the projected land use pattern. Puget Sound [Joshi and Utevesky (1964)] and a few other studies considered alternative land use and transportation plans, but the examination of feedbacks in even these studies has been incomplete at best.

It is well then to clarify the nature of Putman's achievement. The traditional UTP model consists of a series of interrelated models and computer programs: (1) land use forecasting models that project land use (employment and population by zone); (2) trip generation models that provide trip origins and destinations by origin and destination zones; (3) zonal interchange models that convert projected trip origins and destinations into forecasts of interzonal travel; (4) modal split models that assign interzonal trips to alternative transport modes; and (5) network assignment algorithms that provide assignments to public and private transport networks. Most recent studies, moreover, have used capacity-constrained assignment algorithms to obtain equilibrium assignments that are sensitive to network performance. While all of the UTP submodels should be affected by transport system characteristics and performance, the feedbacks from transport system performance to the remaining submodels were either ignored or were treated in a completely ad hoc way prior to Putman's work.

The delay in developing a fully integrated land-use transportation model is due to several interrelated factors. First, as Putman acknowledges, he was able to exploit several years of improvements in each of the several submodels. Second, the computers used by Putman were many times more powerful than those available to earlier analysts. Even so, the principal reason for the delay may have been a justified lack of confidence in available land use forecasting models and the insensitivity of these models to transport system performance. Since transport system performance had little or no effect on the forecasts produced by available land use forecasting models, it made little or no sense to incur the substantial trouble and expense required to achieve full consistency between the land use forecasts and transport system performance.

The difficulty and huge expense of model simulations, in turn, reflected the demands by transport engineers for excessive geographic disaggregation. Models with a thousand or more zones and thousands of links were commonplace. Yet it was obvious to all concerned that accurate land use forecasts were impossible at this level of geographic detail and it was generally believed that the effects of transport system improvements and performance on workplace and residence locations operated over a much wider area. If feedbacks were to be fully considered, it was clear that more manageable models, with fewer zones and less detailed networks, that could be used for large numbers of simulations would have to be developed. TASSIM a 100–200 zone land use-transportation model developed by Ingram and Fauth (1974) to study problems of air quality is an example of such a smaller model.

While TASSIM was subsequently used to study a variety of transport system management (TSM) policies and while Kain and Fauth (1974) used it to evaluate alternative transport and land use plans for Tehran, these analyses were much more ad hoc and lacked the well articulated linkages to transport system performance provided by Putman's fully integrated model. Still, TASSIM's size, integration, and cost per iteration were such that additional feedbacks between system performance and land uses could have been included fairly easily, if suitable land use forecasting models, that were sensitive to system performance, had been available.

Anas (1982, 1983) may have had the most success in developing a computer simulation model for studying the interrelationship between land use and transportation that is well rooted in economic theory. CATLAS consists of four behavioral submodels derived as multinomial logit models consistent with utility or profit maximization: (1) a demand submodel, (2) an occupancy submodel, (3) a new construction submodel, and (4) a demolition submodel.

The CATLAS demand submodel computes the probability that a worker employed at workplace j will live in residence zone i and the conditional probability he will commute by mode m, given the choice of residence zone i. The formal statement of the model includes specific dwelling units, but the empirical implementation employs zonal averages. The NBER–HUDS models [Kain and Apgar (1985)] estimate somewhat similar equations, except that they include individual dwelling unit characteristics as well as zone characteristics and determine mode split by minimizing travel costs, including both time and money costs. CATLAS also obtains a single equation for all households, while the NBER–HUDS models estimate separate equations for 96 types of households defined in terms of household characteristics (preferences) and incomes.

The occupancy or existing housing stock supply submodel calculates the probability that the average dwelling in each zone will be offered for rent in a particular year as a function of the average rents in that zone and various zonal attributes, interpreted as proxies for the differential maintenance cost of having the unit occupied rather than keeping it vacant. CATLAS simulates changes in the housing stock and in the rent of each zone as well as changes in the age distribution of the housing stock by zone. Anas assumes that both new construction and the demolition of existing units depend on the present value of profits that can be derived from a dwelling over its remaining lifetime and provides a theoretical framework that considers construction costs, expected future resale values, current and future taxes, operating costs, and land prices. Market clearing is achieved by solving for each year's clearing rent vector, assuming the number of households assigned to each residence zone must equal the number of units supplied in each year.

CATLAS's demand and supply submodels are estimated for only two work-places, the CBD and the rest of the Chicago SMSA. Anas contends only two workplaces are sufficient because CATLAS has been used to examine the impacts of radial rail transit lines serving the CBD and that these lines have almost all of their effects on CBD employment. The CBD multinomial logit model considers four modes (auto, commuter rail, rapid transit, and bus), while the non-CBD model considers only auto and bus. In addition to measures describing the service characteristics of each mode, the logit equations also include income, the log of travel time, the log of travel time plus rent, housing age, zone income, the zone's distance from the CBD, the zone's relationship to Lake Michigan, and three dummy variables indicating the zone's location in four distance rings around the CBD.

Anas obtains plausible elasticities from the demand and supply side models. They indicate that: (1) a one percent increase in the rent of an average zone (holding the rents of the other zones constant), would cause a 0.3 percent decrease in the demand of CBD commuters for that zone and a 0.2 percent decrease in the demand for non CBD commuters; (2) A one percent increase in travel cost to the average zone would result in a 0.25 percent decrease in the demand of CBD and non-CBD commuters for that zone; (3) A one percent increase in travel time to the average zone would result in a 1.7 percent increase in the demand of CBD commuters and in a 0.25 percent decrease in the demand on non-CBD commuters; (4) A one percent increase in a zone's average rent would result in a 0.24 percent decrease in the number of dwellings kept vacant by the owners in that zone; and (5) A one percent increase in the average zone's rent results in a 0.29 percent increase in the zones housing stock in one year.

3. Housing market models

Excepting recent attempts by Batty (1973), by Wilson et al. (1977), and by Anas (1982 and 1983), the land use-transportation models discussed above have attempted to simulate residential location decisions and urban development patterns without explicit recognition of the housing market, either changes in the characteristics of the housing stock or the determination of housing prices and their effect on the choice of housing type and location. Another, less numerous, class of numerical models have these questions as their central focus. This section considers four housing market simulation models starting with the earliest, the Arthur D. Little model for San Francisco; it then compares three more recent models, the Urban Institute (UI), the NBER, and the HUDS models. It does not discuss the promising modeling effort by Engle, Rothenberg, Bradbury, and Levin [Engle (1972) and Bradbury et al. (1977)] or the much earlier effort by Donnelly et al. (1964), as it appears these models were never fully implemented or used for policy studies. Ingram (1979), moreover, provides an excellent review of what he refers to as the Engle–Rothenberg model, comparing it to DRAM and the UI and NBER models.

Arthur D. Little (1966) made the earliest effort to develop a computer simulation model of an urban housing market for the San Francisco Community

Renewal Program (CRP). Brewer (1973) provides a detailed and unsympathetic description of ADL's pioneering efforts, which had to proceed without access to either well developed theory or much systematic empirical research, and which had to rely on, by today's standards, a primitive, slow, costly, and difficult-to-use computer for its data analyses and simulations.

The San Francisco model broke much new ground, both conceptually and empirically, and, in fairness to its creators, its problems and accomplishments should be compared to those of the several hundred other CRP studies conducted at about the same time. The research and policy issues addressed by the CRP studies were exceedingly complex and there is no evidence that the analyses and policy recommendations provided by the ADL team were inferior in any way to those provided by analysts in other cities. With the exception of the Pittsburgh and St. Louis studies, none of the more than 200 other CRP studies made any noticeable contribution to improving our understanding or urban housing markets. The contribution of the St. Louis CRP, furthermore, was indirect: its unusually comprehensive survey of St. Louis households, dwelling units, and living environments was the basis of several influential empirical studies of urban housing markets [Galster (1977); Kain and Quigley (1970); Kain and Quigley (1972); Kain and Quigley (1975); Peterson (1984); and Yinger (1978)] and the survey itself served as a model for a number of subsequent housing market surveys.

The San Francisco model [ADL (1966); Robinson (1965)] differed from the models developed for transportation studies in several respects. First, its emphasis was less on forecasting than on evaluating the impacts of a variety of housing and community development programs. Second, it was concerned principally with the central city, while the land use models developed for transportation studies encompassed the entire metropolitan area. One of the model's most serious deficiencies was its failure to simulate competition between the central city's housing market and those of the rest of the region; the San Francisco model required exogenous forecasts of population by household types defined by demographic characteristics and income. The model proposed for the Pittsburg CRP [Steger (1965)] would have encompassed the entire metropolitan area, but its representation of the housing stock was exceedingly primitive and it made no effort to simulate the behavior of housing suppliers.

The author's of the San Francisco modeling effort acknowledge that "the model did not become operational prior to the development of the Community Renewal Program" [ADL (1966, pp. 196–197)]. They added, however, that the "model building effort forced a unique discipline on all of our research efforts," ... that "the required investigations expanded our knowledge of the crucial determinants of San Francisco's housing," ... and that this "increased knowledge had its impact upon the program" [ADL (1966, p. 196)]. When pressed, model builders will usually acknowledge that much, if not the larger part, of the benefit from building computer simulation models in policy studies comes from the lessons learned in building them rather than from actual model simulations. Unfortunately, this point is seldom conveyed to or understood by the sponsors of modeling efforts, who frequently become impatient with unanticipated delays, by the difficulty of applying the models to new situations, and the model builders' seemingly insatiable appetites for further model improvements.

The most valuable contribution of the San Francisco modeling effort was undoubtedly its pioneering efforts to model the behavior of both housing demanders and suppliers and its attempts to incorporate their decisions in a rudimentary market clearing framework. The San Francisco model represented 114 types of households (defined in terms of income, family size, race, and age), 27 types of dwelling units (defined in terms of structure type, tenure, number of rooms, and condition), and 106 neighborhoods. Among the San Francisco model's most significant contributions was the development of housing supply models that assumed profit maximization by housing suppliers and made supply decisions dependent on projections of market rents and estimates of the cost of new construction and of renovation, anticipating the supply models that would be used in the UI and NBER–HUDS models more than a decade later.

In the end, the San Francisco model was used to complete only two nine-period (1960–78) computer runs, a baseline run and a simulation of the programs and policies that had been recommended as the Community Renewal Program. Comparison of the policy and baseline simulations indicated that the policies substantially reduced the number of substandard units and that code enforcement would induce private owners to spend 40 percent more on rehabilitation than they would in the absence of code enforcement. At the same time, the simulations also indicated that these housing stock improvements would not be free as lower quality units would experience sharp rent and price increases relative to the baseline.

The UI and NBER–HUDS models

Research on the UI and NBER models began nearly a decade after the San Francisco CRP study. While the UI model [DeLeeuw and Struyk (1975)] was intended to be a housing market model from the outset, the NBER modeling project had its roots in a proposal by Kain and Meyer (1961) to build a computer simulation model for the Rand study of urban transportation and its original charter was to develop a model to analyze land use transportation inter-relationships.

Variants of the UI model have been calibrated to at least eight actual United States metropolitan areas and a version was formulated for use in studying housing problems in less developed countries [Struyk (1976)]. The UI model, moreover, has been used to study a wide variety of housing and urban development programs and policies including housing allowances [Vanski (1976) and Marshall (1976)], the Section 8 Program, public housing, interest rate subsidies for new construction, and an expanded Section 312 Rehabilitation Loan program [Ozanne and Vanski (1980)]. Urban Institute researchers have steadily improved the model's original design and programming. In one of the most significant programing improvements, MacCrae (1982) devised a dramatically more efficient solution algorithm which greatly reduced the computational cost per simulation, permitting much more extensive testing and use of the model, and relaxing significantly the serious constraints on the number of zones, model dwelling units, and model households. Availability of extensive micro data from the Annual Housing Survey enabled Urban Institute researchers, moreover, to make further improvements in both the model's conceptual framework and calibration [Struyk (1983)].

The NBER–HUDS models comprise a family of at least three distinct models. The Detroit Prototype [Ingram, Kain, and Ginn, (1972)] is the oldest and best known of these models and nearly all published references to the NBER model have it as referent. A much improved and substantially different NBER model was used to study the market effects of housing allowances as part of the Experimental Housing Allowance Program (EHAP) [Kain, Ginn, and Apgar, (1977), Kain and Apgar (1977)], and, a third version, the HUDS (Harvard Urban Development Simulation) model was developed and used to evaluate the impacts of spatially concentrated housing improvement programs [Kain and Apgar (1981), Kain and Apgar, (1985)]. Most of the specific references to the NBER–HUDS models below refer to HUDS.

In spite of the fact that both the Urban Institute Model and the NBER–HUDS models are market models and have been used to evaluate a similar range of housing and urban development programs and policies, they are also quite different. Both models attempt to simulate market behavior and obtain market clearing prices and quantities. The Urban Institute model, however, uses a kind of Walrasian auction with recontracting to obtain end of decade quantities and prices that more or less correspond to long run equilibrium solutions. The NBER–HUDS models, in contrast, obtains annual market clearing solutions and employs a disequilibrium framework in which housing choices and location rents within 50 distinct housing submarkets are obtained using a linear programming assignment and the level of prices in each submarket is determined using an excess supply–excess demand framework.

The most striking difference between the Urban Institute and NBER–HUDS models, however, is the level of detail each employs. The UI model, for example, uses between 25 and 45 model households and dwelling units to represent the population and housing stock of the Chicago metropolitan area during 1960–70, while HUDS uses a random sample of between 72,000 and 85,000 households and dwelling units to represent the same area. Similarly, HUDS divides the

Chicago metropolitan area into just under 200 residence zones while the UI model uses only six zones.

Housing in the UI model is represented by model dwelling units that vary in terms of the quantity of services they provide. In this, and many other respects, the UI model seems to owe a substantial debt to Muth (1969). Housing units are located in particular residence zones and the utility functions of model households include arguments that represent zonal wealth, average journey-to-work travel times for each zone, and the racial composition of each zone. While these zonal attributes affect the choice of housing units by model households in the UI model they do not figure strongly in the analysis since the model includes only five or six zones.

HUDS employs a more elaborate representation of housing and neighborhood characteristics. Housing is a multidimensional bundle of housing services consisting of three types of housing services: structure type, neighborhood quality, and the quantity of structure services that households must consume as an indivisible package at a particular location. Housing services in HUDS are thus a heterogeneous quantity subscripted by structure type and neighborhood.

The UI model simulates the quantity of housing services supplied by each model dwelling at the end of a 10-year simulation period, given end of period rents and the quantity of housing services provided by the model dwelling at the start of the decade. Housing services are supplied by the owners of existing dwellings according to a production function that expresses the current level of housing services (Q) in terms of an initial level of services (Q^0) and a quantity of newly added capital inputs (K^*). The production function has the further property that, if an owner fails to add any new capital inputs to an existing dwelling, the level of services produced depreciates at an exogenously specified rate.

New capital inputs must be added to maintain or increase the level of housing services; the UI model assumes these additions to capital are most productive for units that have relatively large amounts of capital at the start of the decade and that the marginal productivity of new capital declines as the quantity of capital (K^*) increases for all dwellings. The end of decade quantities of housing services and the amounts of capital added during the decade are both determined by profitability calculations that take into account the costs of adding capital, operating inputs, the productivity of the added capital, and the end of period rents the owners of existing properties can obtain from supplying various quantities of housing services.

Profit maximization subject to the UI Model production function yields a two parameter supply function that is calibrated from historical data using an ingenious three stage simulation technique devised by deLeeuw and Struyk (1975). Briefly, the procedure involves a parametric search in which judiciously selected supply parameters are used with previously calibrated utility functions and actual end of period model households to simulate end of decade quantities of housing services and rents; the supply parameters that best replicate actual end of period distributions are then used in subsequent policy simulations.

HUDS also employs a housing services production function, but uses the term structure services to refer to only those services that are produced from structures using various combinations of capital and operating inputs, distinguishing structure services from the housing services that accrue to each unit by virtue of its location in a neighborhood of a particular quality level. HUDS makes this distinction because, while the rents a property owner can obtain from producing a particular quantity of structure services are greatly affected by the level of neighborhood quality, individual property owners cannot appreciably affect the level of neighborhood quality. The UI model does not decompose housing services in this way. It defines the relative wealth of each of the five or six residence zones identified by the model and includes a relative neighborhood wealth preference parameter in the utility functions of model households and dwelling units in neighborhoods with higher relative wealth scores (more neighborhood quality in HUDS terminology).

HUDS also subscripts rents, structure services, and the capital embodied in each model dwelling by structure type. Individual property owners can change the structure type of their dwellings by appropriate capital outlays, but absent difficult and expensive conversions, the quantities of structure services and the capital used to produce them belong to a particular structure type category. The UI production function includes operating inputs, but it does not allow substitution of capital and operating inputs. The HUDS production function, in contrast, includes operating inputs and two kinds of capital of different durability and permits property owners to substitute among them depending on both relative prices and expectations about changes in rents and neighborhood quality.

HUDS also contains an explicit and elaborate treatment of expectations. Investment decisions depend on expected future rents and costs and these, in turn, are strongly influenced by expectations about changes in neighborhood quality. HUDS projects rents for each type of structure, neighborhood quality level, and residence zone and uses these data, as well as projections of future neighborhood quality levels for each residence zone, in deciding whether to build new units or convert existing units to a different structure type as well as to decide about how much to spend on additions to each type of capital in each year. The UI model has no comparable treatment of expectations; builders and owners of existing units make their decisions about whether to provide new units or how much capital to add to existing units on the basis of a profitability calculation that assumes they know end of period rents and are able thereby to determine their profit maximizing quantity of housing services and capital investment.

The quantity of housing services demanded by model households in the UI model, which is derived from each model household's utility function and budget constraint, depends on the quantity of housing services consumed, the quantity of other goods consumed, and the employment accessibility, relative wealth, and racial composition of the zone in which the dwelling is located. The utility function used assumes that the optimum quantity of housing services demanded by a household is independent of neighborhood characteristics.

Recent versions of the UI model [Struyk (1983)] provide for an especially rich representation of the effects of federal taxes on housing demand, incorporating features that permit explicit representation of provisions allowing owner-occupants to deduct their mortgage interest and property tax payments as well as provisions allowing landlords to benefit for accelerated depreciation deductions. While it might be possible to modify HUDS to explicitly consider these factors, the existing version of HUDS does not.

The demand sector of HUDS model employs econometrically estimated multi-nomial logit demand functions in which 96 types of households (defined by race, age and head, family size, and income) choose among 50 types of housing bundles defined by five neighborhood quality levels and 10 structure types on the basis of the relative minimum gross prices of the fifty bundles. Gross prices, which vary by bundle type, residence zone, and the workplace and hourly wage of the household's primary worker, are the sum of a dwelling unit's market rent and the commuting costs a particular model household would incur to consume a particular type of housing in a specific residence zone. The commuting costs a model household would incur in consuming a particular dwelling unit, in turn, depend on the workplace location and hourly wage of the household's primary wage earner.

HUDS calculates 50 minimum gross prices for each model household parti-cipating actively in the housing market in each year (roughly 20 percent of all households) and uses these minimum gross prices to determine the bundle choice of each model household. After each housing market participant has been assigned to a housing submarket (one of the fifty housing bundles), a linear programing algorithm is used to assign them to residence zones. The same algorithm produces estimates of location rents which are used as price signals and in combination with other information are used to calculate market prices for each of the fifty housing bundles in each of the 200 residence zones.

Both the UI and HUDS models explicitly recognize the effects of racial discrimination on housing demand and residential location. The utility function used in the UI model assumes that whites prefer to live in neighborhoods with higher percentages of white households and that blacks are indifferent about the racial composition of their neighborhoods. These assumptions are implemented in the UI model by adding a parameter to the utility functions of white households that causes their utility to increase as the zone's percentage white increases; this racial preference parameter, the wealth preference parameter, and the employment accessibility parameter are calibrated simultaneously using a procedure similar to that described above for obtaining the UI model's supply parameters, except that the simulations involve assignments of actual start of period model households to actual start of period housing stocks.

In HUDS separate demand functions are estimated for black and non-black households and discriminatory markups are added to gross prices, both in estimating these demand models and in assigning households to specific residence zones in the market submodel. The discrimination markups used in HUDS, somewhat analogously to the procedures used to calibrate the racial preference parameter in the UI model, are obtained by determining the zone specific discrimination markups that when used in the linear programing assignment with actual start of decade black and white workplace distributions and housing bundle choices come closest to reproducing the start of decade patterns of residence by race. The discrimination markups are interpreted as representing both the higher search costs blacks incur in attempting to obtain housing outside of well established black areas and the effects of exclusion [Kain and Quigley (1975)].

As the preceding discussion should make clear, the UI and NBER–HUDS modeling projects were major research projects spanning several years, involving contributions by dozens of individuals, and requiring large amounts of data and financial resources. Still, it is easy to overstate the amount of resources that have been devoted to the building of these models, particularly when compared to the amounts spent on individual studies or other approaches to studying the same questions. The development of these models also placed heavy demands on available computer technology and at the same time made significant advances in the difficult task of harnessing the intrinsic power of computers to the needs of urban analysis. Continuing advances in computer technology are increasing the feasibility of computer simulation technology and, perhaps most importantly are dramatically reducing the barriers to entry by making computers both cheaper and easier to use.

4. Implications of the micro computer revolution

Efforts to develop land use-transportation and housing market models have been inspired by and have benefited from rapid advances in computer hardware and software and by the development of efficient computing techniques. Rapid advances in computer technology, however, have created a moving target: models that were infeasible or prohibitively expensive to solve 20 or even 10 years ago are trivial today.

Computer technology is continuing to evolve as computers are becoming cheaper and more powerful. The most recent advance, the micro computer revolution, is certain to stimulate further efforts to construct simulation models to replicate and analyze urban development patterns and the characteristics of this new technology will undoubtedly strongly influence the nature of these efforts. In assessing the probable impact of the micro computer revolution on urban analysis, it should be understood first that today's micros are considerably faster and more powerful than the mainframe computers available to model builders two decades ago, and second, that the trend towards cheaper and faster micro computers with more memory and greater storage capacity shows no sign of abating.

The trends in micro computer technology are such that within a decade or two every serious professional economist-researcher can be expected to own one or more micro computers having the speed and storage capacity of all but the largest and most powerful of today's mainframes. Specifically, he or she will own a 32 bit machine that is several times as fast as the current generation of MS–DOS machines, with several megabytes of random access memory, a hard disk or other high speed storage device with more than 100 megabytes of storage, and another somewhat slower device providing thousands or even millions of bytes of storage.

Improvements in software fostered by the micro computer revolution may be even more important. The most popular integrated spreadsheet now available, LOTUS 1–2–3, which had no parallel on mainframes, is only a promise of the software that will be developed as the speed, memory, and storage capacity of micro computers increase. Existing graphics and mapping packages are far better than anything previously available for mainframes and dramatic improvements are still being made. Faster micros with larger and higher resolution screens will permit even larger improvements in graphics and mapping programs.

The anticipated rapid development of micro computers, moreover, does not mean that technological improvements in mainframe computers will come to a halt. Mainframes will continue to become faster, to have greater and more accessible storage, and computational costs will continue to decline. Improvements in communications hardware and software, moreover, will permit economists and other quantitative researchers to connect their powerful micros to far more powerful mainframes and to access large quantities of data. Widespread acquisition of micro computers by various public and private organizations, moreover, will encourage and facilitate the creation and maintenance of more and better data on urban areas. These developments, of course, may be viewed as the continuation of trends of long duration, but it can also be argued that the growing availability of powerful micro computers will accelerate these trends and significantly affect the style of economic analysis.

Easy access to cheap (zero marginal cost) and powerful micro computers will enable urban economists to extend and elaborate the monocentric numerical models of urban location developed by Mills (1972), Muth (1974), and by Arnott and MacKinnon (1977). It is only a question of time, moreover, until a micro computer version of the UI model becomes available. Versions of the UTP model, including capacity restraints, are already available for micro computers. [Multisystems, Inc. (1975); PRC Engineering (1982)]. These programs, which formerly took hours of CPU time and cost several thousands of dollars per simulation, can now be run on a micro computer for up to 500 zones at zero marginal cost in less time than mainframe versions of the same programs required 10 or 15 years ago. The micro computer versions of the UTP model are also far easier to use and will soon come equipped with powerful screen oriented graphics. Similar graphics programs, invaluable tools for analyzing networks, were simply not available on mainframes. Output from these programs further can be analyzed with the aid of electronic spread sheets, data base managers, and graphics programs.

The available UTP modeling packages, initially adapted from mainframe FORTRAN programs for 64K CPM machines, have only recently been shifted to IBM compatible, MS-DOS machines, with their larger memories and greater storage. The limiting factor was the availability of a suitable FORTRAN compiler. A number of high quality FORTRAN compilers are now available for MS–DOS machines as are compilers for most other popular languages used on mainframes. The availability of these compilers will permit many programs originally written for mainframes to be shifted to micros.

The UTP packages currently available on MS-DOS machines, though easier to use and more powerful than early mainframe versions of the same programs, are still slow and difficult to use in comparison to other micro computer programs. As time passes, versions of the UTP model written in faster languages and modified to exploit the capabilities of second, third, and fourth generation micros will become available. At the same time micro computers will increase in speed and capacity, permitting the simulation of larger and more complex models. Micro computer versions of the UTP model are rapidly displacing mainframe versions of the same model for the analysis of modest size problems, i.e. less than 300 zones and 5,000 links, and, perhaps more importantly, are making the technology accessible to many individuals and organizations that formerly could not support mainframe versions of the same models – individual cities, less developed countries, and the like.

Development of a micro computer version of the UI model likely will create something of a cottage industry, as university based researchers, city planning agencies, and regional planning organizations in scores of metropolitan areas calibrate the UI model to their specific metropolitan areas. Experience with initial versions of the model will point to desirable improvements and enhancements and the more computer literate and adventurous of these analysts will customize the model to their areas, develop improved versions, or entirely new models. The resulting process will be very much like the one envisioned by the architects of the San Francisco CRP model over twenty years ago. It is certain that the ADL staffers will have been correct in their vision, but they will have missed their delivery date by something like thirty-five years.

It would be a mistake to assume that the micro computer revolution will encourage the development of only small computer simulation models. The biggest weakness of large computer simulation models, such as HUDS, is not, as widely believed, the expense of running model simulations. Rather, it is the time and expense of preparing model inputs and of analyzing and comprehending the huge quantities of detailed model output. The authors of the ADL book on the San Francisco modeling experience, for example, observe that a single run of their model "requires two and one-half hours of ultrahigh speed computer time," and "the evaluation team must analyze approximately 900 pages of computer output containing a half million bits of information" [ADL, p. 199)].

Advances in computer technology have trivialized the comment about ultrahigh speed computer time; the San Francisco model could easily be run on today's generation of micro computers in much less than an hour and it might require as much as a minute or two of CPU time on a contemporary mainframe. The observation about extensive model output remains valid, however. The HUDS model produces hundreds of pages of tightly packed summary statistics for each ten year simulation as well as a complete listing of all 60,000 or so model households and dwelling units and their characteristics, of units leaving the inventory, and of model households leaving the sample in each year because of death, family dissolution, and outmigration.

The computational expense of analyzing these model outputs on mainframes plus the programing and analyst time required have meant that only the most limited and superficial analyses of the extensive output produced by the HUDS model have been completed. The availability of zero marginal cost micro computers and of integrated analysis packages, such as LOTUS 1–2–3, and of graphics and mapping programs represent a major increase in our capacity to analyze these extensive model outputs. A typical HUDS summary table contains raw numbers pertaining to some dwelling unit characteristic or household, i.e. structure type, rent levels, household by race, mean neighborhood quality levels, mean neighborhood income, and the like, for each of the roughly 200 analysis zones included in the model. Meaningful analyses of these data, moreover, typically entail transformations of the raw numbers to more understandable indexes and comparisons of a policy and baseline run. Previously these analyses required either laborious, expensive, and error prone calculations with an electronic calculator or the preparation of expensive special purpose analysis programs.

With micro computers, model simulations can be carried out on the mainframe and model outputs can be downloaded to micros for further analysis. Files of detailed model outputs can then be read into Lotus 1–2–3 or some other integrated package and be analyzed in a fraction of the time and with far greater thoroughness than would have been possible previously. Time trends and other regularities, moreover, can be viewed instantaneously using on screen graphs and hard copy versions of selected graphs can be prepared in only slightly more time using inexpensive printers or plotters. After the raw output data have been transformed to more meaningful measures, moreover, they can be loaded into inexpensive mapping programs and color coded maps may be used to identify spatial regularities. Again it should be understood that these analysis tools are not only far cheaper and easier to use on micros than they were on a mainframe, but they are frequently far better than similar programs that were previously available on mainframes. Certain capabilities, such as graphics and mapping, were either not available at all on mainframes or were cumbersome to use and exceedingly primitive.

Efforts over the past 25 years to develop computer simulation models to forecast land uses and to evaluate the impacts of various programs and policies on housing markets and urban development patterns have been inspired by the continuing advances in computer technology and the hope that the computational power of these awesome machines would permit the development and use of more detailed and realistic models of urban growth and development and of housing market behavior. As the discussions in this paper have demonstrated, while considerable progress has been made towards this goal, the task has proved to be far more difficult than most early model builders expected or at least hoped. Still, solid advances have occurred and the most recent advance in computer technology, the development of increasingly powerful, easy to use, and inexpensive micro computers is certain to stimulate further interest in harnessing the power of computers to build complex, realistic, and conceptually sound computer simulation models of urban growth and development processes. The next decade or two will likely see the realization of the dreams and aspirations of models builders a decade or two ago.

References

Anas, A. (1973) 'A dynamic disequilibrium model of residential location', *Environment and Planning*, 5:633–647.

Anas, A. (1982) *Residential location markets and urban transportation*. Academic Press.

Anas, A. (1983) 'The Chicago area transportation – land use analysis system', Urban and Regional Planning Program, Department of Civil Engineering, Northwestern Univ., April.

Anthony, J. and R. Baxter (1971) 'The first stage in disaggregating the residential submodel', Working Paper 58, Land Use and Built Form Studies, University of Cambridge.

Arnott, R., J. and J.G. MacKinnon, (1977) 'The effects of the property tax: a general equilibrium analysis', *Journal of Urban Economics*, 4: no. 4, October 1977.

Batty, M. (1970) 'Some problems in calibrating the lowry model', *Environment and Planning*, 2: no. 1:95–114.

Batty, M. (1971) 'Design and construction of a subregional land use model', *Socio-Economic Planning Sciences*, 5:97–124.

Batty, M. (1971) 'Recent developments in land use modeling: a review of British research', *Urban Studies*, 9:151–177.

Batty, M. and S. Mackie. (1972) 'The calibration of gravity, entropy, and related models of spatial interaction', *Environment and Planning*, 4:205–233.

Batty, M. (1973) 'A probability model of the housing market based on quasi classical considerations', *Socio-Economic Planning Sciences*, 7:573–598.

Birch, D. et al., (1974) *The New Haven laboratory: a test bed for planning*. Lexington: Lexington Books, D.C. Heath and Co.

Birch, D. et al., (circa 1977) *The community analysis model*. U.S. Department of Housing and Urban Development Office of Policy Development and Research.

Bradbury, K. et al., (1977) 'Simultaneous estimation of the supply and demand for household location in a multizonal metropolitan area', in: G.K. Ingram ed., *Residential location and urban housing markets*. Cambridge, Mass.

Brewer, G.D. (1973) *Politicians, bureaucrats, and the consultant: a critique of urban problem solving*. New York: Basic Books.

Chapin, F. Stuart Jr. and S. F. Weiss (1962) *Some input refinements for a residential model*. Chapel Hill, N.C.: University of North Carolina, Center for Urban and Regional Studies, July.

Chicago Area, Transportation Study (CATS). 1960. *Chicago area transportation study, Vol. II. Data projections*, July.

Crecine, J.P. (1964) TOMM (Time Oriented Model). Pittsburgh, PA: Department of City and Regional Planning, CRP Technical Bulletin No. 6.

Cripps, E. and D. Foot. (1969) 'A land use model for subregional planning', *Regional Studies*, 3:243–268.

Cripps, E. and D. Foot. (1969) 'The empirical development of an elementary residential location model for use in sub-regional planning', *Environment and Planning*, 1:81–90.

DeLeeuw, F. and R.J. Struyk. (1975) *The web of urban housing: analyzing policy with a market simulation model*. Washington D.C.: The Urban Institute.

Detroit Metropolitan Area Transportation Study 1955–56. *Part I: Data summary and interpretation* and *Part II: Future traffic and a long range expressway plan*. Lansing, Michigan: Speaker-Hines and Thomas, Inc., State Printers.

Donnelly, T.G., F. Stuart Chapin Jr., and S.F. Weiss. (1964) *A probabilistic model for residential growth*. Chapel Hill, N.C.: University of North Carolina, Center for Urban and Regional Studies, May.

Echenique, M.D. Crowther and W. Lindsay (1969) 'A spatial model of urban stock and activity', *Regional Studies*, 3:281–312.

Engle R.F. (1972) 'An econometric simulation model of intra-metropolitan housing location: housing, business, transportation, and local government', *American Economic Review*, 62:87–97.

Engle R.F. (1974) 'Issues in the specification of an econometric model of urban growth', *Journal of Urban Economics*, 1:250–67.

Garin, R.A., (1966) 'A matrix formulation of the lowry model for intra-metropolitan activity location', *Journal of the American Institute of Planners*, 32:361–64.

Galster, G.C. (1977) 'A bid-rent analysis of housing market discrimination'. *American Economic Review* 67:144–55.

Goldner, W. (1968) 'Projective Land use mode' (PLUM). Berkeley, CA: Bay Area Transportation Study Commission, BATSC Technical Report 291.

Graves, C. (1964) 'Forecasting the distribution of 1985 population and employment to analysis zones for plan A', Puget Sound Regional Planning Commission, Seattle, Staff Report Number 15.

Goldner, W., S.R. Rosenthall and J.R. Meredith (1972) 'Projective land use model-PLUM: theory and application', Institute of Transportation and Traffic Engineering, University of California, Berkeley, CA.

Hamburg, J. (1960) *Land use forecasts: Chicago*. Chicago Area Transportation Study.

Hamburg, J.R. and R.L. Creighton. (1959) 'Predicting Chicago's land use pattern', *Journal of the American Institute of Planners*, 26, 2:67–72.

Harris, B.J. (1962a) 'Basic assumptions for a simulation of the urban residential housing and land market', Harrisburg, PA: State Department of Highways, Penn-Jersey Transportation Study.

Harris, B.J. (1962b) 'Linear programing and projecting of land uses', Harrisburgh, Pa: State Department of Highways, Penn-Jersey Transportation Study.

Harris, B. (1965) 'Notes on an approach to metropolitan housing market analysis', unpublished paper, Institute of Environmental Studies, University of Pennsylvania, Philadelphia, Pa.

Harris, B. et al., (1966) 'Research on an Equilibrium model of metropolitan housing and locational choice'. Interim Report, Univ. of Pennslyvania, Philadelphia.

Hartwick, J.M. and P.G. Hartwick (1972) 'Durable structures and efficiency in the development of an urban area', October (mimeo).

Hartwick, P.G. and J.M. Hartwick (1974) 'Efficient resource allocation in a multinucleated city with intermediate goods', *Quarterly Journal of Economics*, 88:340–352.

Herbert, J. and B.H. Stevens (1960) 'A model for the distribution of residential activity in urban areas', *Journal of Regional Science*, 2:21–3.

Hill, D.M. (1965) 'A growth allocation model for the Boston region', *Journal of the American Institute of Planners*, 31:111–120.

Hill, D.M., D. Brand and W.B. Hansen. (1966) 'Prototype development of statistical land use prediction model for greater Boston region', *Highway Research Record*, 114:51–70.

Ingram, K. Gregory and G.R. Fauth (1974) 'TASSIM: A transportation and air shed simulation model, Vol. II- Program user's guide, final report', Prepared for Department of Transportation, May. Report DOT-05-30099-6.

Ingram, K. Gregory, J.F. Kain and J.R. Ginn (1972) *The detroit prototype of the NBER urban simulation model.* New York: National Bureau of Economic Research.

Ingram, K. Gregory (1979) 'Simulation and econometric approaches to modeling urban areas', in: Peter Mieszkowski and Mahlon Staszheim, eds., *Current issues in urban economics.* Baltimore and London: Johns Hopkins Press, 130–165.

Joshi, R.N. (1984) 'Distribution of 1985 population and employment to analysis zones for land use plan B', Puget Sound Regional Planning Commission, Seattle, Staff Report Number 17.

Joshi, R.N. and R. Utevesky (1964) 'Alternative patterns of development – Puget Sound region', Puget Sound Regional Planning Commission, Seattle, mimeo.

Kain, J.R. and J.R. Meyer (1961) 'A first approximation to a RAND model to study urban transportation', Santa Monica, California: The RAND Corporation, RM-2878-FF.

Kain, J.F. (1968) 'Distribution and movement of jobs and industry', in: J.Q. Wilson, ed., *The Metropolitan Enigma.* Cambridge: Harvard University Press.

Kain, J.F. and J.M. Quigley (1970) 'Evaluating the quality of the residential environment', *Environment and Planning*, 2:23–32.

Kain, J.F. and J.M. Quigley (1972) 'Housing market discrimination, home ownership, and savings behavior', *American Economic Review*. 62:263–77.

Kain, J.F. and G.R. Fauth (1974) 'Transport planning for Teheran: transport and land use alternatives', Report prepared for the National Plan and Budget Organization, Teheran, September.

Kain, J.F. and J.M. Quigley (1975) *Housing markets and racial discrimination.* New York: National Bureau of Economics Research.

Kain, J.F., W.C. Apgar, Jr., and J.R. Ginn (1977a) 'Simulation of the market effects of housing allowances. Vol. I: Description of the NBER model', Harvard University, Kennedy School of Government, Program in City and Regional Planning, Research Report R77-2.

Kain, J.F. and W.C. Apgar, Jr. (1977b) 'Simulation of the market effects of housing allowances. Vol. II: baseline and policy simulations for Pittsburgh and Chicago', Harvard University, Kennedy School of Government, Program in City and Regional Planning, Research Report R77-2.

Kain, J.F. and W.C. Apgar, Jr. (1981) 'Market responses to spatially concentrated housing and neighborhood improvement programs', Cambridge, Mass.: John F. Kennedy School of Government, Research Report to the U.S. Department of Housing and Urban Development.

Kain, J.F. and W.C. Apgar, Jr. (1985) *Housing and neighborhood dynamics: a simulation study.* Cambridge: Harvard University Press.

Little, A.D. (1966) *Community renewal programing.* New York: Frederick A. Praeger.

Lowry, I.S. (1964) 'Model of a metropolis', Santa Monica, California. The RAND Corporation, RM-4036-RC.

Lowry, I.S. (1967) 'Seven models of urban development: a structural comparison', the RAND Corporation, P-3673.

MacCrae, C.D. (1982) 'Urban housing with discrete structures', *Journal of Urban Economics*, 11:131–47.

Marshall, S.A. (1976) 'The urban institute housing model: application to South Bend, Indiana', Washington, D.C.: Urban Institute Working Paper 216–26.

Mills, E.S., (1972) 'Markets and efficient resource allocation in urban areas', *The Swedish Journal of Economics*, 74:100–113.

Mills, E. (1977) 'A critical evaluation of the community analysis model'. U.S. Department of Housing and Urban Development, Office of Policy Development and Research.

Mackett, R.L. and G.D. Mountcastle (1977) 'Developments of the lowry model', in: A.G. Wilson et al., eds., *Models of cities and regions: theoretical and empirical developments*. Chichester: John Wiley and Sons, 201–281.

Mitchell, R. and C. Rapkin (1954) *Urban traffic: a function of land use*. New York.

Multisystems, Inc., (1975) 'Transportation network analysis packages for microcomputers: draft final report', prepared for the U.S. Department of Transportation Urban Mass. Transportation Administration.

Muth, R. (1969) *Cities and housing*. Chicago: University of Chicago Press.

Muth, R. (1974) 'Numerical solution of urban residential land use models', *Journal of Urban Economics*, 2, no. 4:307–33.

Ozanne, L. and J. Vanski (1980) 'Rehabilitating central city housing: simulations with the urbans institute housing model'. Washington D.C.: The Urban Institute, Contract Report 266-01.

PRC Engineering (1982) 'MicroTRIPS users Manual', Mclean, Va.

Peat, Marwick, Mitchell and Co. (1972) 'Empiric', Activity Allocation Model: Application to the Washington Metropolitan Region, Washington, D.C.: Metropolitan Washington Council of Governments, December.

Peterson, G.E. (1984) 'Housing prices and tenant characteristics', The Urban Institute Working Papers 785-01.

Putman, S.H. (1976) 'Laboratory testing of predictive land-use models: some comparisons', Washington, D.C.: U.S. Department of Transportation.

Putman, S.H. and F. Ducca (1978a) 'Calibrating urban residential models 1: procedures and strategies', *Environment and Planning A*, 10:633–50.

Putman, S.H. and F. Ducca (1978b) 'Calibrating urban residential models 2: procedures and strategies', *Environment and Planning A*, 10:1001–1014.

Putman, S.H. (1978) 'Development of an improved integrated transportation and land use model package, report of results', NSF Grant APR 73-07840-A02, Urban Simulation Laboratory, University of Pennsylvania, Philadelphia PA.

Putman, S.H. (1980) 'Integrated policy analysis of metropolitan transportation and location', Washington, D.C.: U.S. Department of Transportation, Report DOT-P-30-80-32, August.

Putman, S. (1983) *Integrated urban models*. Pion.

Quigley, J.M. (1972) 'The influence of workplace and housing stock on residential choice: a crude test of gross price hypothesis', Presented at the Annual Meeting of Econometric Society, Toronto.

Robinson, I.M., H.B. Wolfe and R.L. Barringer (1965) 'Simulation model for renewal programing', *Journal of the American Institute of Planners*, 31:126–134.

Rhodes, T. (1969) 'Computer models in subregional planning', *Regional Studies*, 8:257–265.

Seidman, D.R. (1969) 'The construction of an urban growth model', Plan Report No. 1, Technical Supplement, Vol. A. Delaware Valley Regional Planning Commission, Philadelphia.

Senior, M.L. and A.G. Wilson (1974) 'Explorations and synthesis of linear programing and spatial interaction models of residential location', *Geographical Analysis*, 6:209–238.

Senior, M.L. (1977) 'Residential location', in: A.G. Wilson et al., eds., *Models of cities and regions: theoretical and empirical developments*. Chichester: John Wiley and Sons, 283–318.

Steger, W.A. (1965) 'The Pittsburgh urban renewal simulation model', *Journal of the American Institute of Planners*, 144–150.

Struyk, R. (1976) 'A simulation model of urban housing markets in developing countries', Washington, D.C.: Urban Institute Working Paper 5062-1.

Struyk, R.J., S.A. Marshall, and L.J. Ozzane (1978) *Housing policies for the urban poor*. Washington, D.C.: The Urban Institute.

Struyk, R.J. and M.A. Turner (1983) 'The urban institute housing market simulation model: revised theory and solution process', Washington, D.C.: Urban Institute Discussion Paper, 3156-05-01.

Vanski, J. (1976) 'The urban institute housing model: application to Green Bay, Wisconsin', Washington, D.C.: The Urban Institute Working Paper 216–27.

Voorhees, A.M. and Associates, (1972) 'Application of the urban systems model (USM) to a region-north central Texas', Prepared for the North Central Texas Government.

Wheaton, W. Jr. and B. Harris (1972) 'Linear programing and locational equilibrium: the Herbert-Stevens model revisited', unpublished paper, MIT and University of Pennsylvania.

Wheaton, W. Jr. (1974) 'Linear programing and locational equilibrium: The Herbert-Steven's Model revisited', *Journal of Urban Economics*, Vol. 1, pp. 278–87.

Wilson, A.G. (1967) 'A statistical theory of spatial distribution models', *Transportation Research*, 1:253–269.

Wilson, A.G. (1969) 'Developments of some elementary residential location models', *Journal of Regional Science*, 9, 3:377–385.

Wilson, A.G. (1970a) 'Disaggregating elementary residential location models', *Papers, Regional Science Association*, 24:103–125.

Wilson, A.G. (1970b) *Entropy in urban and regional modeling*. London: Pion.

Wilson, A.G. et al. (1977) *Models of cities and regions: theoretical and empirical developments*. Chichester: John Wiley and Sons.

Yinger, J. (1978) 'The black–white price differential in housing: some further evidence', *Land Economics*, 54:187–206.

Chapter 22

DYNAMIC URBAN MODELS

TAKAHIRO MIYAO*

University of Southern California
University of Tsukuba

Introduction

It is sometimes argued that one of the most remarkable phenomena in this century is the rapid growth and development of large cities throughout the world. Especially in the postwar period major metropolitan areas have registered impressive economic growth, showing the vigorous trends of urbanization and suburbanization in many industrialized nations. Economists, among others, have long been aware of this phenomenon, and acknowledged the importance of urban economic development in the overall growth process of the national economy [e.g., Friedman and Alonso (1964)]. In view of the strong dynamism exhibited by the economy of cities, some observers even define a city as a "settlement that consistently generates its economic growth from its own local economy" [Jacobs (1970, p. 262)].

Despite the long-standing recognition of the role of urban growth and dynamics among economists, most urban models in the economic literature have been completely static in nature, and very little has been done to formulate dynamic urban models. It seems that the main reason for the delay in developing dynamic models of urban growth is because the theoretical foundations of urban economic analysis had not been solid enough to withstand a further elaboration of the system for dynamization until very recently. Only after the heavy groundwork done by such pioneers as Alonso, Beckmann, Mills, and Muth in the field of urban economics, dynamic urban models which pay explicit attention to both time and space have been appearing in the literature. Currently, more and more urban economists are working on the dynamics of urban systems in order to shed light on the complex phenomenon of urban economic growth.

This survey covers recent developments in the following two areas: (1) dynamic urban models of production and employment, and (2) dynamic urban models of residential land and housing. In both areas the main focus is on the dynamic

*The author is grateful to Jan Brueckner for his helpful comments on an earlier version of this paper.

Handbook of Regional and Urban Economics, Volume II, Edited by E.S. Mills
© *1987, Elsevier Science Publishers B.V.*

process of urban growth, although dynamic adjustment-stability analysis is also taken up. Section 1 covers urban production–employment models, and Section 2 reviews urban residential models. Because most models specialize in the analysis of either production or residential activity, there turn out to be very few models which are mentioned in both Sections 1 and 2. By taking advantage of this, otherwise unfortunate, division in the literature, the survey is organized in such a way that the reader who is interested only in urban residential models may directly proceed to Section 2 without reading Section 1.

1. Dynamic urban production models

In the literature, a majority of urban growth models are concerned with production, employment, and income. These models may be called "dynamic urban production models," which focus on the production activity of a city or a metropolitan region, while largely ignoring the residential aspect of urban growth. Most of the dynamic urban production models are spatially aggregated, as they are intended to study the causes of urban growth rather than its spatail patterns. Recently, however, some production models which deal with both time and space have been developed in the literature.

First, we take up non-spatial dynamic models, which attempt to analyze the causes and processes of production and employment growth. Depending on their assumption regarding the causes of growth, these models can be classified into three categories: demand-oriented, supply-oriented, and demand-supply interactive models. Then, we review spatial dynamic models, which are based on the classic von Thunen model of production. There are two kinds of spatial dynamic models in the literature, that is, dynamic adjustment models and dynamic growth models. In what follows, these non-spatial and spatial production models are examined in turn.

1.1. Non-spatial production models

Many dynamic models of urban production and employment are direct applications of the aggregative analysis of economic growth, and do not explicitly incorporate spatial aspects. These non-spatial models can be classified into three categories. First, "demand-oriented models" regard the demand for the city's products as the main cause of urban growth, whereas "supply-oriented models" emphasize the supply of factors of production in the city. These two extreme cases are reconciled by "demand-supply interactive models," which take account of the interaction of demand and supply in generating long-run urban growth and development.

1.1.1. Demand-oriented models

Demand-oriented growth models assume that urban economic growth is primarily caused by the growth of demand for the city's products and not by the growth of supply of factors in the city. At each point in time, the city's output and employment are constrained by the exogenous demand which is growing over time, while the supply of factors will fully respond to meet the growing demand.

The most popular hypothesis of this sort in the literature is called the export base theory or economic base theory. In its crudest form, the export base theory maintains that the city's employment is determined solely by the level of export demand, and the total population of the city grows over time as the export demand for its output increases exogenously. Some of the representative studies of the export base theory can be found in Pfouts (1960) and Friedman and Alonso (1964). According to this theory in its static version [e.g., Czamanski (1964)], the city's population P is an increasing function of its total employment E

$$P = a_1 + b_1 E, \quad b_1 > 0, \tag{1.1}$$

and total employment consists of the amount of employment in the export sector E_1 and that in the local, non-export sector E_2,

$$E = E_1 + E_2, \tag{1.2}$$

where E_2 is a function of the city's total population P,

$$E_2 = a_2 + b_2 P, \quad b_2 > 0. \tag{1.3}$$

The linear system (1.1)–(1.3) yields

$$P = \frac{a_1 + b_1 a_2 + b_1 E_1}{1 - b_1 b_2}, \tag{1.4}$$

which states that the total population of the city is determined by the level of employment in the export sector, and the city grows as exports increase, i.e.

$$\frac{dP}{dE_1} = \frac{b_1}{1 - b_1 b_2} > 0, \tag{1.5}$$

provided that

$$b_1 b_2 < 1. \tag{1.6}$$

While the export base theory remained essentially a static model in the 1950s and the early 1960s, many authors such as Czamanski (1964) and Thompson (1965) called it a model of urban growth. In fact, it was not until the mid 1960s that Czamanski (1965) formulated the first dynamic model of the export base type. In essence his dynamic model can be written as follows:

$$P(t) = a_1 + b_1 E(t-2), \tag{1.7}$$

$$E(t) = E_1(t) + E_2(t), \tag{1.8}$$

$$E(t) = a_2 + b_2 P(t-1), \tag{1.9}$$

which together lead to

$$P(t) - b_1 b_2 P(t-3) = a_1 + b_1 a_2 + b_1 E_1(t-2). \tag{1.10}$$

By setting the right-hand side of (1.10) equal to zero, the complementary function $p(t)$ can be obtained as

$$p(t) = C_1 \lambda_1^t + C_2 \lambda_2^t + C_3 \lambda_3^t, \tag{1.11}$$

where

$$\lambda_1 = (b_1 b_2)^{3/2}, \quad \lambda_2 = (b_1 b_2)^{3/2} \left\{ -\frac{1}{2} + i\frac{(3)^{1/2}}{2} \right\},$$

$$\lambda_3 = (b_1 b_2)^{3/2} \left\{ -\frac{1}{2} - i\frac{(3)^{1/2}}{2} \right\}, \tag{1.12}$$

and C_1, C_2, and C_3 are constants. Since $b_1 b_2 > 0$, we have the property of oscillatory convergence with $p(t) \to 0$ as $t \to \infty$, provided that

$$b_1 b_2 < 1, \tag{1.13}$$

which is the same condition as (1.6). This means that, given (1.13), $P(t)$ will converge to a stationary solution if the right-hand side of (1.10) is stationary over time, or will converge to a steady growth path if the right-hand side of (1.10) is growing at a constant rate.

A somewhat different version of dynamic export base analysis is offered by Paelinck (1970), where part of the demand for the city's exportable goods is endogenously generated by those industries which are attracted to the city's "local labor pool",

$$E_1(t) = E_{10} + b_0 E(t-1), \quad b_0 > 0, \tag{1.14}$$

where E_{01} is exogenously given. Assuming that (1.1)–(1.3) hold with $P(t), E(t), E_1(t)$, and $E_2(t)$ together with (1.14), we find

$$(1 - b_1 b_2) P(t) - b_0 P(t-1) = a_1 (1 - b_0) + b_1 a_2 + b_1 E_{10}. \tag{1.15}$$

This first-order linear difference equation has a stationary solution

$$\bar{P} = \frac{a_1 (1 - b_0) + b_1 a_2 + b_1 E_{10}}{1 - b_0 - b_1 b_2}. \tag{1.16}$$

For the denominator to be positive, the following condition should be met:

$$b_0 + b_1 b_2 < 1. \tag{1.17}$$

It turns out that (1.17) ensures the monotonic convergence of $P(t)$ to $\bar{P}$ in (1.15), since (1.17) implies that $0 < b_0/(1 - b_1 b_2) < 1$. Note that (1.17) is a little stricter than (1.13). If, on the other hand, we have $b_0 + b_1 b_2 > 1, P(t)$ will grow at a positive rate of

$$\frac{b_0}{1 - b_1 b_2} - 1 > 0. \tag{1.18}$$

In this case, urban growth is generated not by the growth of export demand, but by endogenous demand growth, and the model ceases to be of the export base type.

Other kinds of dynamic export base models include the model of Moody and Puffer (1970) which introduces an adaptive adjustment of local service employment and that of Harvey (1974) which takes account of long-run productivity growth in the export sector as well as in the local service sector. Although both models, treating time explicitly, are dynamic, the Moody–Puffer model has only an adjustment mechanism with no growth factors, whereas the Harvey model focuses only on a long-run steady state, but does not provide any dynamic stability analysis. It should be noted that an adjustment mechanism similar to the one adopted by Moody and Puffer will be mentioned later in the context of spatial models, and productivity growth due to technical progress, which is discussed by Harvey, will be part of the supply-oriented models in the next section.

In addition to the models reviewed above, there have been a number of demand-oriented dynamic models of metropolitan growth used in econometric studies. These metropolitan growth models generally focus on the determination and growth of income and output rather than employment in a metropolitan area. Two types of such income growth models may be identified: the export base type and the Keynesian type. Based on Bell's regional econometric model which has a strong flavor of the export base theory [Bell (1967)], Glickman (1971) and Hall and Licari (1974) build metropolitan income growth models in which the growth of output in the export-oriented sector is directly linked to the growth of GNP. On the other hand, Moody and Puffer (1969) and Anderson (1970) follow the tradition of Keynes [Klein (1969)], and set up dynamic versions of the Keynesian metropolitan/regional econometric model.

While the Keynesian type of income growth model is more aggregated in terms of output than the export base type, not only exports but also other demand items such as autonomous investment and government spending are treated as exogenous growth elements in the Keynesian model. For example, a simplified version of Anderson's model is as follows:

$$Y(t) = C(t) + I(t) + G(t) + X(t) - M(t), \tag{1.19}$$

$$C(t) = a_1 + b_1 V(t) + c_1 V(t-1), \tag{1.20}$$

$$I(t) = a_2 + b_2 R(t) + c_2 R(t-1) + A(t) + d_2 A(t-1), \tag{1.21}$$

$$W(t) = a_3 + b_3 Y(t) + c_3 t, \tag{1.22}$$

$$M(t) = a_4 + b_4 Y(t), \tag{1.23}$$

$$V(t) = W(t) + R(t), \tag{1.24}$$

$$Y(t) = V(t) + D(t), \tag{1.25}$$

where Y is income, C is consumption, I is investment, G is government spending, X is exports, M is imports, V is disposable income, R is non-wage income, A is autonomous investment, W is wage income, and D is depreciation plus taxes. All the variables are for the metropolitan region in question, and G, X, A, and D are exogenously given at each t. The system (1.19)–(1.25) then reduces to

$$[1 - b_1 - b_2(1 - b_3)]Y(t) - [c_1 + c_2(1 - b_3)]Y(t-1)$$
$$= a_1 + a_2 - c_2 a_3 + a_4 - c_3[b_2 t + c_2(t-1)] - (b_1 + b_2)D(t)$$
$$- (c_1 + c_2)D(t-1) + G(t) + X(t) + A(t) + d_2 A(t-1). \tag{1.26}$$

It is obvious by comparing (1.26) and (1.15) that Anderson's model behaves in much the same way as Paelinck's. If the absolute value of

$$\frac{c_1 + c_2(1 - b_3)}{1 - b_1 - b_2(1 - b_3)}. \tag{1.27}$$

is less than unity, $Y(t)$ converges to a stationary value when the right-hand side of (1.26) is stationary, or converges to a steady growth path when the right-hand side of (1.26) is growing at a constant rate over time.

As pointed out by Thompson (1965), Winger (1969), Richardson (1971, 1973), Engle (1974), Conroy (1975), Miron (1979), and others, the demand-oriented urban growth models ignore the supply of factors of production by assuming in effect that the supply of factors is completely elastic. Despite some argument otherwise by North (1955), Moody and Puffer (1970), McNulty (1977), and Gerking and Isserman (1981), it should be clear, at least from the theoretical point of view, that these models which take account of the demand side only are inadequate as long-run urban growth models. The availability of factors of production such as labor migration and capital inflow into the city should be an important determinant of its capacity to grow in the long run. We shall, therefore, turn to supply-oriented dynamic urban models.

1.1.2. Supply-oriented models

Supply-oriented dynamic models regard the growth of factors of production as the main cause of urban growth. It is assumed that the availability of inputs in the city, but not the demand for its products, limits the level of the city's output and income, and that the supply of inputs can increase internally and/or through inflows of factors such as labor and capital in-migration to the city. Most supply-oriented models of urban/regional growth are neoclassical in nature, and are based on neoclassical economic growth theory or international trade theory. Those models often incorporate neoclassical production functions and invariably emphasize the role of factor movements in determining the growth of urban/regional income and output. Here we review only non-spatial dynamic models of this kind.

A regionally disaggregated, but yet non-spatial, version of the typical neoclassical growth theory is set up in Borts and Stein (1964), where labor migration is regarded as a crucial determinant of regional growth patterns. Romans (1965) and Borts (1971) stress the importance of interregional capital movements, whereas Siebert (1965) considers the growth of capital, labor, and technology from internal as well as external sources. Smith (1974, 1975) and Rabenau (1979) rigorously analyze the dynamic property of the neoclassical urban growth model with emphasis on labor and capital movements. The Smith model, which also assumes technological progress, is expressed as follows:

$$Y = K^a M^{1-a}, \quad 0 < a < 1, \tag{1.28}$$

$$M = N e^{gt}, \quad g \geqslant 0, \tag{1.29}$$

$$\dot{K} = sY + v \cdot (r - r_A) \cdot K - \delta K, \quad 0 < s < 1, \quad v > 0, \quad \delta \geqslant 0, \tag{1.30}$$

$$\dot{N} = nN + m \cdot (w - w_A) \cdot N, \quad n > 0, \quad m > 0, \tag{1.31}$$

where Y is output, K is capital, N is labor, r is the rental price of capital, and w is the wage rate. The rate of technical progress g, the savings ratio s, the depreciation rate δ, the natural growth rate n, and the coefficients $a, v,$ and m are all constants. The dot indicates differentiation with respect to time, and the subscript A means the national value. The second terms of (1.30) and (1.31) represent capital and labor movements, respectively, responding to factor price differentials. It is assumed that the national economy is growing steadily with constant values of Y_A/K_A and $Y_A/M_A (= Y_A/N_A e^{gt})$ and, therefore, the values of Y_A/N_A and w_A are growing at the constant rate g. Given all these assumptions, however, the Smith model fails to have a steady growth equilibrium for $g > 0$. It turns out that if (1.30) is replaced with

$$\dot{N} = nN + m \frac{w - w_A}{w_A} N, \quad n > 0, \quad m > 0. \tag{1.32}$$

we can easily find a unique steady-growth equilibrium which is globally stable. In this case, the fundamental dynamic equation becomes:

$$\widehat{(K/M)} = \hat{K} - \hat{M} = [(s + va)(K/M)^{-(1-a)} - (vaY_A/K_A + \delta)]$$
$$- [m(K/M)^a (K_A/M_A)^{-a} - m + n + g], \tag{1.33}$$

where $\hat{x} \equiv \dot{x}/x$. The existence, uniqueness, and global stability of a steady growth equilibrium with the value $(K/M)^*$ can be shown as in Figure 1.1. Rabenau (1979) proves these properties in the absence of technological progress.

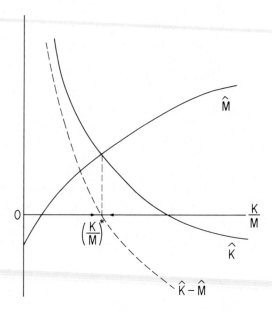

Figure 1.1.

The Smith model assumes constant returns to scale and does not take account of agglomeration economies or diseconomies. Agglomeration economies, however, can be regarded as an important aspect of urban growth, and are even considered by some authors to be the main cause of urban concentration, i.e., the very existence of cities. In the literature there are a number of supply-oriented growth models which incorporate urban agglomeration economies and/or diseconomies. Notably, Rabenau (1979) introduces a production function with agglomeration effects in the context of urban growth and decay. Specifically, his model has the production function

$$Y = A(N)K^a N^{1-a}, \quad 0 < a < 1, \tag{1.34}$$

(b>0)

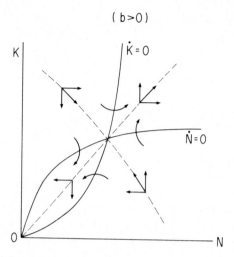

Figure 1.2.

and

$$A(N) = N^b, \quad 0 < 1 - a + b < 1, \tag{1.35}$$

where Y is output, K is capital, N is labor, and b is positive *or* negative, depending on whether there are agglomeration economies *or* diseconomies in urban production activities. K and N will change over time, according to (1.30) and (1.31), where the depreciation rate δ is assumed to be zero. Then, there are two possible cases which are illustrated in Figures 1.2 and 1.3, in which the curve

(b<0)

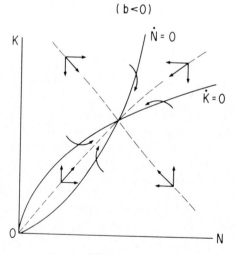

Figure 1.3.

for $\dot{K}=0$ is given by

$$K=\left(\frac{s+va}{vr_A}\right)^{1/(1-a)} N^{(1-a+b)/a},$$

(1.36)

and the curve for $\dot{N}=0$ by

$$K=\left(\frac{mw_A-n}{m(1-a)}\right)^{1/a} N^{(a-b)/(1-a)}.$$

(1.37)

In the case of agglomeration economies $(b>0)$, the city will either explode without limit, or reduce to zero, depending on initial conditions. In the case of diseconomies $(b<0)$, the economy is shown to converge to an equilibrium with constant values of K and N. Rabenau further takes up a more complicated case with both agglomeration economies and diseconomies, where $b>0$ for small values of L and $b<0$ for larger values of L. In this case, it is proved that with initial values of K and N being sufficiently large, the economy will grow and eventually converge to a stationary state.

Dendrinos (1982) supposes agglomeration economies as well as "congestion", which affects population dynamics as

$$\dot{N}=m\cdot(w-w_A)\cdot N-hY^2, \quad h>0,$$

(1.38)

in place of (3.4). In the presence of agglomeration economies and congestion externality, his analysis shows the possibility of oscillatory cycles around a stationary equilibrium. Rabenau and Hanson (1979), based on Rabenau's simple optimal growth model of a factory town (1976), develop an urban growth model with public capital in the form of urban infrastructure, say, Z, which enters a production function as

$$Y=A(Z/N)K^a N^{1-a}, \quad A'(\ )>0,$$

(1.39)

where public capital per worker Z/N provides essentially the same effect as agglomeration economies. They also suppose that private capital moves instantaneously to equate the urban rate of return r to the national rate r_A, and labor migrates into and out of the city as represented by (1.31). Given that the urban government uses a payroll tax to finance the urban public capital so as to maximize the present value of the future stream of utility for its average resident, the city is shown to approach a steady growth path with private capital and labor growing at a constant rate which is equal to the sum of the natural rate and the migration rate. If this long-run growth rate is strictly positive, relatively large initial values of Z/N will ensure self-sustained urban population growth, whereas relatively small values of Z/N will yield some initial period of population decay before sustained growth appears in the city.

Supply-oriented urban growth models of the neoclassical type have been criticized by several authors in the literature, most notably by Richardson (1971, 1973), who questioned the validity of the underlying assumptions of neoclassical growth theory, such as perfect competition and full employment, in the context of urban and regional economic growth. It is fair to say that the neoclassical approach with its exclusive emphasis on the supply side may be less appropriate for the growth analysis of the urban economy than for that of the national economy. Even in the long run, the effect of supply responses to the demand side seems as important as demand responses to the supply side in determining the dynamic process of urban growth.

1.1.3. Demand-supply interactive models

Criticisms of both demand- and supply-oriented growth models naturally lead to the third kind of dynamic urban models which take into account the interaction of demand and supply. Here we review non-spatial models of this kind.

A simple way of incorporating the interaction of demand and supply in the context of urban growth is to extend the export base model so as to consider the effect of urban population (labor force) on the level or growth of employment in the city's basic industry. In fact, Paelinck's model (1970) which was explained in Section 1.1.1 could be interpreted as such a model, since the city's labor force is assumed to influence the demand for exportable goods in his model. In the literature, one of the earliest attempts to develop this kind of model is made by Niedercorn and Kain (1963) and Niedercorn (1963). Their model is intended to be an extension of the export base model, and assumes that an "equilibrium" level or normal level of manufacturing employment E^e is an increasing function of urban population P. More specifically,

$$E^e = aP, \quad a > 0. \tag{1.40}$$

And the actual level of manufacturing employment E is assumed to change in response to the relative deviation of the actual level of employment E from its normal level E^e, as well as the rate of change of E in the previous period, i.e.,

$$\frac{\Delta E}{E} = b \frac{E^e - E}{E} + h \left(\frac{\Delta E}{E} \right)_{-1}, \quad b > 0, \quad h \geqslant 0, \tag{1.41}$$

Furthermore, the rate of change of urban population is a linear function of the rate of change of employment:

$$\frac{\Delta P}{P} = c \frac{\Delta E}{E} + d, \quad c > 0, \quad d > 0. \tag{1.42}$$

As pointed out by Mills (1972) and Miron (1979), this system (1.40)–(1.42) does not have a long-run steady growth equilibrium. It is, however, possible to prove

that in a special case with $h=0$ in (1.41) the model does have a steady growth
equilibrium which is unique and globally stable, if the system is written in the
following differential equation form:

$$\hat{E}=b\frac{E^e-E}{E}=b\frac{aP-E}{E},\tag{1.43}$$

$$\hat{P}=c\hat{E}+d,\tag{1.44}$$

where $\hat{x}\equiv\dot{x}/x$. (1.43) and (1.44) lead to

$$\left(\frac{\hat{P}}{E}\right)=\hat{P}-\hat{E}=-ab(1-c)\frac{P}{E}+b(1-c)+d.\tag{1.45}$$

It is clear that this system is globally stable and yields a unique steady growth
equilibrium, provided that

$$c<1.\tag{1.46}$$

On the other hand, there have been similar attempts made by "neoclassicists".
Muth (1968, 1971, 1972) emphasizes the importance of both demand and supply
in urban growth, as opposed to purely demand-oriented export base models, and
proposes the following demand-supply interactive model:

$$\hat{E}=a\hat{P}+b,\quad a>0,\quad b>0,\tag{1.47}$$
$$\hat{P}=c\hat{E}+d,\quad c>0,\quad d>0,\tag{1.48}$$

where employment growth $\hat{E}$ is affected by population growth $\hat{P}$ in (1.47), and
vice versa in (1.48). The system (1.47)–(1.48) can be solved for $\hat{E}$ and $\hat{P}$ as

$$\hat{E}=\frac{ad+b}{1-ac}>0,\tag{1.49}$$

$$\hat{P}=\frac{bc+d}{1-ac}>0,\tag{1.50}$$

provided that

$$ac<1.\tag{1.51}$$

Similar models are set up by Okun (1968), Lewis and Prescott (1972), and
Greenwood (1973), which also take into consideration the interaction of demand
and supply through wage/income variables which influence population or employment growth.

As criticized by Mazek and Chang (1972), however, the Muth model has a
serious weakness as a long-run growth model, because $\hat{E}$ and $\hat{P}$, as given by (1.49)
are not equal to each other unless $ad+b=bc+d$. This means that the model does
not in general yield a steady growth equilibrium and cannot maintain the growth

path characterized by (1.49) and (1.50) in the long run. One possible way out of this difficulty is to reformulate the Muth model in line with the Niedercorn–Kain model by assuming that $\hat{E}$ is some increasing function of P/E rather than of $\hat{P}$:

$$\hat{E} = f(P/E), \quad f'(\ ) > 0, \tag{1.52}$$

$$\hat{P} = c\hat{E} + d, \tag{1.53}$$

which will give

$$\left(\frac{\hat{P}}{E}\right) = -(1-c)f(P/E) + d, \tag{1.54}$$

whose behavior is essentially the same as (1.45), so long as $0 \leqslant c < 1$. Alternatively, the Muth model could be modified by supposing that $\hat{P}$ is an increasing function of E/P rather than of $\hat{E}$:

$$\hat{E} = a\hat{P} + b, \tag{1.55}$$

$$\hat{P} = h(\dot{E}/P), \quad h'(\ ) > 0, \tag{1.56}$$

which will yield

$$\left(\frac{\hat{E}}{P}\right) = -(1-a)h(E/P) + b. \tag{1.57}$$

This system has a steady growth equilibrium with a long-run value of $(E/P)^*$, which is dynamically stable, provided that $0 \leqslant a < 1$. A special case of this model with $a = 0$ is studied by Todaro (1969), where E/P is interpreted as the rate of urban employment.

While the Niedercorn–Kain model and the Muth model can be regarded as extensions of the traditional models of neoclassical growth and export base growth, respectively, there is another type of demand-supply interactive models based on the principle of "cumulative causation", first suggested by Myrdal (1957). This principle emphasizes the existence of increasing returns to scale or agglomeration economies in manufacturing industries, and is intended to explain the cumulative advantages of fast-growing regions over slow-growing regions. These "cumulative causation models" which are adopted and refined in Kaldor (1970), Richardson (1973, 1978), and Dixon and Thirlwall (1975), take account of the interaction of demand and supply along with increasing returns to scale in the form of productivity growth in manufacturing. More specifically, the model assumes the endogenous growth of labor productivity which depends on the rate of output growth and particularly export growth, an assumption which is known as the Verdoorn Law. This means that the growth of (export) demand for output affects the supply side through labor productivity growth. On the other hand, productivity growth tends to reduce the cost and price of output, which in turn will lead to demand growth in manufacturing and exports.

In Richardson (1973, 1978) and Dixon and Thirlwall (1975), the Verdoorn Law is expressed as the growth rate of labor productivity r being a linear function of the growth rate of output g,

$$r = ag + b, \quad a > 0, \ b > 0, \tag{1.58}$$

where g is assumed to be proportional to the growth rate of export demand x,

$$g = cx, \quad c > 0, \tag{1.59}$$

and x is a decreasing function of the rate of export price increase $\hat{p}$, which is equal to the rate of nominal wage increase z minus the rate of productivity growth r,

$$x = h - d \cdot \hat{p} = h - d \cdot (z - r), \quad h > 0, \ d > 0, \ z > 0. \tag{1.60}$$

Combining (1.58)–(1.60), we find

$$g = acdg + c(h + bd - zd), \tag{1.61}$$

which can be solved for g as

$$g^* = \frac{c(h + bd - zd)}{1 - acd}, \tag{1.62}$$

provided that $acd \neq 1$. Furthermore, a one-period time lag can be introduced into (1.60) so that

$$x_t = h - d \cdot \hat{p}_{t-1} = h - d \cdot (z - r_{t-1}), \tag{1.63}$$

as in Dixon and Thirlwall, or more generally, as Richardson assumes, the rate of output growth in period t, g_t, depends on the lagged value of itself g_{t-1} because of a one-period time lag in (1.58), (1.59), or (1.60), that is,

$$g_t = acdg_{t-1} + c(h + bd - zd). \tag{1.64}$$

Then the dynamic system (1.64) will converge to a steady growth rate of output g^* or will diverge from it, depending on whether $acd < 1$ or $acd > 1$. The convergent case with $acd < 1$ and $c(h + bd - zd) > 0$ is illustrated in Figure 1.4, and the divergent case with $acd > 1$ and $c(h + bd - zd) < 0$ in Figure 1.5. Dixon and Thirlwall (1975) and Richardson (1978) conclude that the convergent case is more likely to hold empirically than the divergent case, although the latter may be closer to what some advocates of the cumulative causation principle have in mind.

Although many important dynamic elements are taken into consideration in the demand-supply interactive models, those models as well as the demand- and supply-oriented models examined above have a serious weakness in common, that is, the lack of explicit analysis of spatial and locational aspects. Without such analysis, the dynamic process of urban growth and adjustment cannot be fully

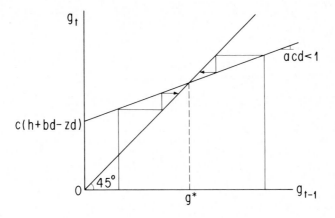

Figure 1.4.

understood. Even for the purpose of studying the causes of urban production growth only, it is necessary to consider the spatial patterns of production and employment as well as the locational choice of industries and individual firms explicitly. We are now ready to turn to spatial dynamic models of urban production.

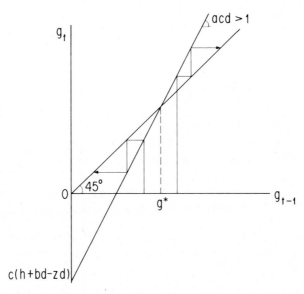

Figure 1.5.

1.2. Spatial production models

Let us examine dynamic production models which explicitly deal with the spatial and locational aspects of urban activity. It turns out that most of these models are based on von Thunen's spatial model of production in a monocentric region. We first take up dynamic adjustment models in which the stability of spatial equilibrium is analyzed. Then, we review dynamic growth models which treat spatially expanding cities in the long run, and discuss the relationship between those spatial growth models and the non-spatial growth models surveyed in the previous section.

1.2.1. Dynamic stability analysis

First, we summarize a monocentric city model of the von Thunen type with many industries, as reformulated in Beckmann (1972), Solow (1973), Miyao (1977a, 1981), and others.

In a city characterized by von Thünen's homogeneous plane with a single central market, there are assumed to be a number of industries producing different kinds of products subject to constant-returns-to-scale production functions of the neoclassical type, using land and labor as inputs. All producers in the same industry have identical production functions and identical transport cost functions, whereas those functions may differ between industries. Producers must transport all their products to the central market to sell at an exogenously given price. In equilibrium, industries are located in concentric rings, or zones, around the central market in such a way that each zone is filled exclusively with producers in a single industry. Both zones and industries are numbered in ascending order of distance from the center so that zone i is occupied by industry i ($i = 1, \ldots, m$).

A producer in industry i, located at distance x from the central market, operates at the minimum cost per unit of product, which can be written as $C_i[r(x), w]$, where $r(x)$ is the land rent at x and w is the wage rate. In equilibrium under perfect competition and constant returns to scale, industry i's unit production cost C_i must be equal to the price of its product p_i minus unit transport cost c_i:

$$C_i[r_i(x), w] = p_i - c_i(x) \quad (i = 1, \ldots, m), \tag{1.65}$$

which defines industry i's "bid rent" $r_i(x)$, that is, the maximum rent that producers in industry i are willing to pay for location x without incurring a loss. Since zone i is occupied by industry i, it should be the case that

$$r(x) = r_i(x) \geqslant r_j(x) \quad \text{for all } j \quad \text{for } x_{i-1} \leqslant x \leqslant x_i, \tag{1.66}$$

where x_{i-1} and x_i are the inner and outer boundaries (radii) of zone i, respectively. (1.66) means that industry i's bid rent is the highest or at least equal to the bid rent of any other industry everywhere in zone i and, therefore, industry i's bid rent function becomes the prevailing market rent function in zone i.

Then, the equilibrium system is derived as follows. Industry i's bid rent at x is found by solving (1.65) for $r_i(x)$ as

$$r_i(x) = r_i[p_i - c_i(x), w] = r_i(x, w) \quad \text{for } x_{i-1} \leqslant x \leqslant x_i \quad (i = 1, \ldots, m). \tag{1.67}$$

Industry i's labor-land ratio at x can be expressed as

$$n_i(x) = n_i[r_i(x, w), w] = n_i(x, w) \quad \text{for } x_{i-1} \leqslant x \leqslant x_i \quad (i = 1, \ldots, m). \tag{1.68}$$

Assuming that at each distance x, a fraction $g(x)$ of the land area is available for industrial use, the full employment condition for the city as a whole is

$$2\pi \sum_{i=1}^{m} \int_{x_{i-1}}^{x_i} g(x) n_i(x) x \, dx = N, \tag{1.69}$$

where N is the total population (labor force) which is a given positive constant and $x_0 = 0$. Finally, the market rent condition requiring the market rent function to be continuous everywhere, particularly at every boundary, is written as

$$r_i(x_i) = r_{i+1}(x_i) \quad (i = 1, \ldots, m-1), \quad r_m(x_m) = r_0, \tag{1.70}$$

where r_0 is the opportunity cost of land, e.g., agricultural land rent, which is assumed to be given exogenously. The model consists of (1.67)–(1.70), which can determine the equilibrium values of w and $x_i (i = 1, \ldots, m)$ and the equilibrium functional forms of $r_i(x)$ and $n_i(x)$ $(i = 1, \ldots, m)$.

Miyao (1977a, 1981) introduces two alternative processes of dynamic adjustment in this system, that is, a gradual adjustment of the boundaries responding to rent differences in the land market, and a gradual adjustment of the wage rate responding to the excess demand for labor in the labor market. First, in the presence of some frictional elements in the land market, each boundary between industries is assumed to be adjusted through time in such a way that the position of a boundary will move outward *or* inward, according as the bid rent of the industry located inside the boundary is higher *or* lower than that of the industry outside the boundary, i.e.,

$$\dot{x}_i = f_i[r_i(x_i) - r_{i+1}(x_i)] \quad (i = 1, \ldots, m-1),$$
$$\dot{x}_m = f_m[r_m(x_m) - r_0], \tag{1.71}$$

where $f_i'(\ ) > 0$ and $f_i(0) = 0$ $(i = 1, \ldots, m)$. To show the dynamic stability property of the system (1.71), note that w can be expressed as a function of x_i's $(i = 1, \ldots, m)$ from (1.68) and (1.69): $w = w(x_1, \ldots, x_m)$. This, together with (1.67) and (1.71), gives

$$\dot{x}_i = f_i[r_i\{x_i, w(x_1, \ldots, x_m)\} - r_{i+1}\{x_i, w(x_1, \ldots, x_m)\}] \quad (i = 1, \ldots, m-1),$$
$$\dot{x}_m = f_m[r_m\{x_m, w(x_1, \ldots, x_m)\} - r_0]. \tag{1.72}$$

In a small neighborhood of equilibrium, (1.72) may be approximated by the following linear differential equation system,

$$\dot{z} = FAz, \tag{1.73}$$

where z is a column vector whose ith element is $x_i - x_i^* (i = 1, \ldots, m)$, F is a diagonal matrix whose ith diagonal element is $f_i'(0)$ $(i = 1, \ldots, m)$, and A is an $m \times m$ matrix with the following property: For any choice of positive diagonal matrix F, there exists a positive diagonal matrix D such that DA is symmetric and negative definite, if

$$-\partial r_i(x_i^*)/\partial x > -\partial r_{i+1}(x_i^*)/\partial x \quad (i = 1, \ldots, m-1), \tag{1.74}$$

or equivalently,

$$c_i'(x_i^*)/h_i(x_i^*) > c_{i+1}'(x_i^*)/h_{i+1}(x_i^*) \quad (i = 1, \ldots, m-1), \tag{1.75}$$

where $h_i(x)$ is industry i's land-output ratio at x, and x_i^* denotes the equilibrium value of $x_i (i = 1, \ldots, m)$. According to Arrow and McManus (1958), the differential equation system (1.73) is stable for any positive diagonal matrix F under the assumption (1.75) which may be called the "von Thunen condition".

Second, Miyao assumes that the wage rate will increase or decrease, according as the excess demand for labor is positive or negative, whereas all the other variables including x_i's are instantaneously adjusted so as to satisfy (1.67), (1.68), and (1.70). At each point in time, (1.67) and (1.70) yield

$$r_i(x_i, w) = r_{i+1}(x_i, w) \ (i = 1, \ldots, m-1), \quad r_m(x_m, w) = r_0, \tag{1.76}$$

which can be solved for x_i's as functions of $w: x_i = x_i(w)$. Then, in view of (1.68), the left-hand side of (1.69) becomes a function of w as

$$G(w) = 2\pi \sum_{i=1}^{m} \int_{x_{i-1}(w)}^{x_i(w)} g(x) n_i(x, w) x \, dx, \tag{1.77}$$

which may be interpreted as the total labor demand function. The dynamic process of wage adjustment can thus be expressed as

$$\dot{w} = f[G(w) - N], \tag{1.78}$$

with $f'(\ ) > 0$ and $f(0) = 0$. This system is shown to be locally stable for any positive speed of adjustment $f'(0) > 0$, if the von Thünen condition (1.75) is met. This follows from the property that $G'(w) < 0$ in a small neighborhood of equilibrium, given (1.75). It should be noted that a similar adjustment process is discussed verbally in Solow (1973) with only one industry surrounded by a homogeneous group of households in a monocentric city.

A somewhat different version of the von Thunen model with multi-products is studied in Day and Tinney (1969), Day and Kennedy (1970), and Day, Kennedy, and Tinney (1978), and the dynamic stability of land use patterns in examined by using a recursive programming method. Their assumption that product prices are endogenously determined so as to clear the product market in each period and that production decisions are based on the lagged value of product prices tends to yield a rich variety of long-run behavior, including the possibility of spatial mixing of multi-products in an intermediate segment of the region. Their model is modified in Okabe and Kume (1983) by deriving product demand functions from a utility function explicitly and by investigating a dynamic adjustment process analytically. It is shown that land use patterns tends to be unstable, and are likely to fluctuate over time. Obviously, this conclusion depends crucially on the assumption of static (myopic) price expectations, which can be found in almost all cobweb-type models including the ones mentioned above.

1.2.2. Long-run growth analysis

We are now in a position to review long-run growth models which incorporate spatial elements explicitly. Almost all these models are based on von Thünen's monocentric city model, and are dynamized by introducing population growth, demand growth, and/or transportation improvements.

Miyao (1977b, 1981) constructs supply-oriented models of urban production growth with population growth and transportation improvements. His first model is a typical neoclassical growth model with the exogenous growth of urban population and endogenous transportation improvements. In a monocentric city with only one industry having a constant-returns-to-scale production function and using land and labor as inputs, perfect competition leads to the condition of zero profit

$$C[r(x), w] = 1 - \tau - cx, \tag{1.78}$$

where C is the unit cost function, i.e., the minimum production cost per unit of output, depending on land rent $r(x)$ at x and the wage rate w. On the right-hand side of (1.78), the exogenously given product price is normalized as unity, τ is the rate of tax to finance transportation investment, and c is unit transport cost. (1.78) may be solved for r as

$$r(x) = r(1 - \tau - cx, w), \tag{1.79}$$

and the labor-land ratio at $x, n(x)$, can be written as

$$n(x) = n[r(x), w] = n[r(1 - \tau - cx, w), w]. \tag{1.80}$$

Assuming that a constant fraction g of land at each distance x from the central market is used for production $(0 < g \leqslant 1)$, the full employment condition is

$$2\pi g \int_0^{x_1} n(x)x\mathrm{d}x = N, \tag{1.81}$$

where x_1 is the urban boundary and N is the total population (labor force) in the city. The market rent condition that the overall rent function should be continuous at the urban boundary is expressed as

$$r(x_1) = r_0, \tag{1.82}$$

where r_0 is agricultural land rent, which is exogenously given. The system can determine the equilibrium values of w and x_1 as well as the equilibrium functional forms of $r(x)$ and $n(x)$, given N, c, and all the other parameter values.

In order to dynamize the system, derive $x_1 = [1 - \tau - C(r_0, w)]/c$ from (1.78) and (1.82). Letting $z \equiv cx$, we find from (1.80) and (1.81)

$$G(w) \equiv 2\pi g \int_0^{1 - \tau - C(r_0, w)} n[r(1 - \tau - z, w), w] z \mathrm{d}z = Nc^2. \tag{1.83}$$

Define

$$k \equiv 1/(Nc^2). \tag{1.84}$$

Then, it follows from (1.83) that w is stationary if and only if k is stationary over time, i.e., $0 = \hat{k} = -2\hat{c} - \hat{N}$. In other words, in order to maintain a stationary value of w over time, the rate of population growth $\hat{N}$ must be twice as high as the rate of decrease of unit transport cost $(-\hat{c})$. Here, N is assumed to be growing at an exogenously given rate,

$$\hat{N} = \mu > 0, \tag{1.85}$$

and the rate of decrease of unit transport cost is an increasing function of the amount of transportation investment per unit of land devoted to transportation,

$$-\hat{c} = f(S/J), \tag{1.86}$$

with $f'(\ ) > 0, f(0) = 0$, and $f(\infty) = \infty$, where S is total transportation investment which is evenly distributed over the land area used for transportation J so as to produce a uniform rate of reduction of c in the city. Since total transportation investment is equal to total tax revenue,

$$S = 2\pi g\tau \int_0^{x_1} f[n(x)]x\mathrm{d}x, \tag{1.87}$$

where $f(\ )$ is the output-land ratio expressed as a function of $n(x)$ at x. And

$$J = 2\pi\sigma \int_0^{x_1} x\mathrm{d}x = \pi\sigma(x_1)^2, \tag{1.88}$$

where σ is a constant fraction of land available for transportation. Combining (1.84)–(1.88), we obtain the fundamental dynamic equation,

$$\hat{k} = -2\hat{c} - \hat{N} = 2f(S/J) - \mu = H(k) - \mu, \tag{1.89}$$

where S/J turns out to be a sole function of k, that is, $S/J = s(k)$, and thus $2f[s(k)] \equiv H(k)$.

The existence, uniqueness, and global stability of a steady growth equilibrium with $\hat{k} = 0$ can be established, if the production function is Cobb–Douglas,

$$f(n) = n^a, \quad 0 < a < 1, \tag{1.90}$$

and the opportunity cost of land is zero,

$$r_0 = 0. \tag{1.91}$$

Furthermore, defining total net output Y as total gross output minus total tax payment and total transport cost,

$$Y \equiv 2\pi g \int_0^{x_1} (1 - \tau - cx) f[n(x)] x \, dx, \tag{1.92}$$

it is shown under the present assumptions, (1.90) and (1.91), that the steady growth equilibrium value of net output per capita Y/N is maximized when the tax rate is equal to the land elasticity of output, i.e.,

$$\tau = 1 - a. \tag{1.93}$$

Since the land elasticity of output, $1 - a$, is equal to the ratio of total land rent to total net output, this optimality result is quite analogous to the so-called "golden rule of accumulation" in the neoclassical theory of economic growth.

Miyao's second model (1981) assumes that unit transport cost is decreasing at an exogenously given rate

$$-\hat{c} = \eta > 0, \tag{1.94}$$

while the rate of net inflow of population to the city depends on the difference between the wage rate w in the city and the national wage rate $\bar{w}$, which is given exogenously,

$$\hat{N} = \mu(w - \bar{w}), \tag{1.95}$$

where $\mu'(\;) > 0, \mu(0) = 0$, and $\mu(\infty) = \infty$. Setting $\tau = 0$ in (1.83), we find $G(w) = 1/k$ or $w = G^{-1}(1/k)$. Then the fundamental dynamic equation becomes

$$\hat{k} = -2\hat{c} - \hat{N} = 2\eta - \mu[G^{-1}(1/k) - \bar{w}]. \tag{1.96}$$

Since the right-hand side of (1.96) is shown to be decreasing in k under some mild assumptions on $f(\;)$, the existence, uniqueness, and global stability of a steady growth equilibrium will be readily established.

Carlberg (1981) introduces capital input into a von Thünen-type growth model without assuming transportation improvements. He shows that among the cases of CES production functions, Cobb–Douglas is the only case where long-run growth is possible, if the amount of land is exogenously fixed and population is growing at a positive constant rate. In this case, however, population density will rise without limit. It is further shown that if the urban boundary is determined endogenously as in the Miyao model, no long-run growth may be possible even in the Cobb–Douglas case. The main difference between Carlberg's result and Miyao's stems from the fact that Carlberg does not assume a steady improvement in transportation over time, as Miyao does.

The spatial dynamic production models so far examined are neoclassical in nature and thus essentially supply-oriented. In the literature, however, there are some other spatial dynamic models, which may be regarded as demand-supply interactive. In fact, a large scale econometric model · of the demand-supply interactive type which deals with spatial structure and growth in a metropolitan area is constructed in Engle, Fisher, Harris, and Rothenberg (1972), which contains not only production, but also housing, government, etc. A submodel of the whole system is explained in Engle (1974), where the dynamics of the "Macro" subsystem is governed by the following three dynamic equations:

$$\hat{W} = \omega(u, \theta), \qquad \omega_1 < 0, \quad \omega_2 > 0, \tag{1.97}$$

$$\hat{K} = \kappa(v), \qquad \kappa' > 0, \tag{1.98}$$

$$\hat{M} = \mu(w, u), \qquad \mu_1 > 0, \quad \mu_2 < 0, \tag{1.99}$$

where W is the nominal wage rate, K is capital, M is population, u is the unemployment rate, θ is the expected rate of inflation, v is the rate of return on capital, and w is the real wage rate. These variables are for the metropolitan area in question and the corresponding values for the rest of the nation are given and constant. In addition, the equality of demand and supply is written as

$$D^1(p, c) + D^2(p, I, c) = Y(W, p, r, K), \tag{1.100}$$

where D^1 is export demand, D^2 is local demand, Y is output supply, p is the price of output, c is unit transport cost, I is disposable income, and r is land rent. On the right-hand side of (1.100), output depends on the employment of labor, land, and capital, and is expressed as a function of the factor prices, given K. This equation can be solved for p and Y as

$$p = p(W, r, c, I, K), \quad Y = Y(W, r, c, I, K). \tag{1.101}$$

And it is assumed that

$$r = r(I, c), \quad I = I(Y). \tag{1.102}$$

The degree of agglomeration economies enters the functions $\kappa(\ )$ in (1.98) and

$Y(\ )$ in (1.100). The model is not closed, since it is part of the larger system.

Based on Engle's model, particularly with (1.97)–(1.99), Miyao (1980, 1981) develops a von Thünen-type dynamic production model and examines its dynamic property rigorously. In his model, a firm which is located as distance x from the CBD, has the following Cobb–Douglas production function

$$Y(x)=L(x)^{\alpha}K(x)^{\beta}N(x)^{\gamma}, \quad \alpha, \beta, \gamma>0, \quad \alpha+\beta+\gamma=1, \tag{1.103}$$

Assuming that unit transport cost c is constant and the opportunity cost of land r_0 is zero, the following "aggregate production function" can be derived:

$$Y=AL^{\alpha}K^{\beta}N^{\gamma}, \quad A>0, \tag{1.104}$$

where K, N, and Y are the aggregate amounts of capital, labor, and output, respectively,

$$K=2\pi g \int_0^{x_1} \frac{K(x)}{L(x)} x\, dx, \quad N=2\pi g \int_0^{x_1} \frac{N(x)}{L(x)} x\, dx, \quad Y=2\pi g \int_0^{x_1} \frac{Y(x)}{L(x)} x\, dx, \tag{1.105}$$

and L is

$$L=2\pi g \int_0^{x_1} (1-cx/p)^{1/\alpha} x\, dx, \tag{1.106}$$

which might be called the "efficient stock of land", consisting of all individual pieces of land with their respective weights of efficiency, net of transport cost. This concept is analogous to the efficient stock of capital in the context of technical progress, studied in Solow (1960). It is further shown that

$$L=B(p/c)^2, \quad B>0, \tag{1.107}$$

That is, more land can be profitably utilized, as the price of output increases and/or unit transport cost decreases. In the presence of agglomeration economies, it is assumed that $A=Y^{\xi}(0\leqslant\xi<1)$ and thus (1.104) becomes

$$Y=AL^{\alpha/(1-\xi)}K^{\beta/(1-\xi)}N^{\gamma/(1-\xi)}. \tag{1.108}$$

Considering the case of no agglomeration economies, we find from (1.104) and (1.107) that

$$Y=C(p/c)^{2\alpha}K^{\beta}N^{\gamma}, \quad C>0, \tag{1.109}$$

where C is some positive constant.

Furthermore, the total demand for output is assumed to be

$$D=D_0 p^{-d} e^{ht}, \quad D_0, d, h>0, \tag{1.110}$$

which gives

$$\hat{D}=h-d\cdot\hat{p}. \tag{1.111}$$

For a steady growth equilibrium, we should have $D = Y$, and all the factors, L, K, and N, must grow at the same rate as D and Y. This, combined with (1.97)–(1.99) and (1.107), means that

$$h - d \cdot \hat{p} = \hat{L} = 2(\hat{p} - \hat{c}), \tag{1.112}$$

$$h - d \cdot \hat{p} = \hat{K} = \kappa(v), \tag{1.113}$$

$$h - d \cdot \hat{p} = \hat{N} = \hat{M} = \mu(w, u), \tag{1.114}$$

$$\hat{p} = \hat{W} = \omega(u, \hat{p}), \tag{1.115}$$

where it is assumed that the expected rate of inflation θ is equal to the actual rate $\hat{p}$, and the rate of change of unit transport cost is constant, $\hat{c} = \eta \gtrless 0$. Then, (1.112) determines $\hat{p}^*$, and thus (1.115) gives u^*. (1.113) and (1.114), therefore, determine v^* and w^*, respectively. The steady growth equilibrium is shown to be locally stable if

$$\omega_2 < 1 + \frac{2\alpha}{\gamma} + \frac{(\alpha + \beta)d}{\gamma}, \tag{1.116}$$

where $\omega_2 \equiv \partial\omega / \partial\hat{p}$. In the presence of agglomeration economies ($\xi > 0$), the local stability condition becomes

$$\omega_2 < 1 + \frac{2\alpha}{\gamma} + \frac{(1 - \xi)(\alpha + \beta)d}{\gamma}. \tag{1.117}$$

This is more likely to be met, if (1) nominal wage increases are less responsive to price increases so that ω_2 is smaller, (2) demand is more price elastic so that d is greater, or (3) the degree of agglomeration economies ξ is smaller. Although local stability is obtained under these conditions, global stability cannot be ensured in general, and the system tends to exhibit cyclical fluctuations over time.

This model may be regarded as an extension of the demand-supply interactive models reviewed in the previous section, not only in terms of spatial aspects, but also in terms of additional dynamic elements such as wage-price dynamics and capital movements. By assuming agglomeration economies, the model can capture the essential feature of the cumulative causation principle. In fact, not only the supply side, but also the demand side of the Miyao model are very similar to the typical cumulative causation model. For example, compare (1.111) with (1.60). The present model, as an extended demand-supply interactive model, seems to show a rich variety of dynamic properties in the long run, and is capable of producing both locally stable and globally unstable processes within the system.

Finally, some of the weaknesses which are shared by almost all the dynamic urban production models surveyed above should be pointed out. The first one is the lack of analysis of spatial interaction and land allocation between industrial and non-industrial activities in the city, the latter being represented by housing for consumers and workers. There are very few dynamic models which incorporate both production and housing in a spatial setting in the literature, as already mentioned at the outset. Another weakness is the almost complete neglect of the durability of structure and capital in the dynamic process of production. Correspondingly, producers' expectations about the future are either ignored or treated very naively. The almost complete lack of attention to these important dynamic factors in the existing production models seems even odd, when compared to rapid developments of dynamic urban *residential* models incorporating structural durability and expectations behavior in the last few years.

2. Dynamic urban residential models

Urban residential models which deal with household location and travel choice as well as housing production and consumption have been rapidly developed in the last decade or so. Many authors have constructed such residential models on the basis of von Thünen's spatial production model so as to take account of the spatial structure of residential cities. Most of the urban residential models, however, are essentially static in nature and focus only on the long-run equilibrium of urban structure.

Very recently, there have been a number of serious attempts to dynamize urban residential models by incorporating dynamic factors such as changes in population, income, transportation costs, opportunity costs of land, etc. With the emphasis on spatial structure, dynamic urban residential models are concerned primarily with the effects of those dynamic factors on the spatial patterns of urban growth, rather than the causes of growth themselves.

In the literature, two kinds of dynamic urban residential models can be clearly identified. The first kind is those dynamic models which draw directly on the static models of residential location, and do not assume the durability of housing structure at least explicitly. The second kind is those which explicitly assume housing durability in the dynamic context. This distinction is meaningful and important because of strikingly different results between those two kinds of models.

2.1. Residential models without housing durability

In this section we examine the type of urban residential models originally developed by Alonso (1964), Mills (1967), Muth (1969), and others. Those models are intended to analyze the long-run equilibrium patterns of residential location and urban structure, and do not explicitly take account of the durability of housing capital. First, we look at the dynamic stability analysis of the Alonso–Mills–Muth model, and then take up long-run growth models which are direct extensions of the static model without housing durability.

2.1.1. Dynamic stability analysis

Before discussing the dynamics of urban residential location, it is useful to review the structure of the static Alonso–Mills–Muth model with many household classes.

In a monocentric city, there are assumed to be a number of household classes with different utility functions, different incomes, and/or different transport cost functions, whereas each class consists of homogeneous households which are identical in terms of utility, income, and transport cost functions. In equilibrium, households are located in concentric rings (zones) around the CBD, and each zone is occupied by a single class of households. Both zones and classes are numbered in ascending order of distance from the CBD so that zone i corresponds to class i.

A household in class i, located at distance x from the CBD, maximizes its utility, which depends on a consumption good z_i and residential land (space) h_i,

$$U_i(x) = U_i[z_i(x), h_i(x)], \tag{2.1}$$

subject to its budget constraint

$$z_i(x) + r(x)h_i(x) = w_i - c_i(x), \tag{2.2}$$

where the price of the consumption good, being given exogenously, is normalized as unity, $r(x)$ is the market land rent at x, w_i is household income for class i, and $c_i(x)$ is transport (commuting) cost for class i; $c_i(x)$ is assumed to be a strictly increasing function of distance x. In equilibrium, all households in class i must achieve the same utility level, say u_i, which is independent of x. In terms of the indirect utility function V_i, this condition may be expressed as

$$V_i[r_i(x), w_i - c_i(x)] = u_i \quad (i = 1, \dots, m), \tag{2.3}$$

which defines class i's bid rent $r_i(x)$, that is, the maximum rent that households in class i are willing to pay for each location x, while maintaining the utility level u_i. For zone i to be occupied by class i, it is necessary to have

$$r(x) = r_i(x) \geqslant r_j(x) \quad \text{for all } j \quad \text{for } x_{i-1} \leqslant x \leqslant x_i, \tag{2.4}$$

where x_{i-1} and x_i are the inner and outer boundaries (radii) of zone i, respectively. This means that class i's bid rents become the prevailing market rents inside zone i.

Class i's bid rent at x is obtained by solving (2.3) for $r_i(x)$ as

$$r_i(x) = r_i[w_i - c_i(x), u_i] \quad \text{for} \quad x_{i-1} \leqslant x \leqslant x_i \quad (i = 1, \dots, m). \tag{2.5}$$

Then, the demand for land by a household in class i at x becomes

$$h_i(x) = h_i[r_i\{w_i - c_i(x), u_i\}, w_i - c_i(x)]$$
$$= h_i[w_i - c_i(x), u_i] \quad \text{for} \quad x_{i-1} \leqslant x \leqslant x_i \quad (i = 1, \ldots, m). \tag{2.6}$$

At each distance x from the CBD, a fraction g of the land area is assumed to be available for residential use, where $g(x) > 0$ for all x. Then, the condition that all households in class i should be housed in zone i can be written as

$$2\pi \int_{x_{i-1}}^{x_i} \frac{g(x)x}{h_i(x)} dx = N_i \quad (i = 1, \ldots, m), \tag{2.7}$$

where N_i is the total number of households in class i. Finally, the condition that the market rent function should be continuous at all boundaries is expressed as

$$r_i(x_i) = r_{i+1}(x_i) \quad (i = 1, \ldots, m-1), \quad r_m(x_m) = r_0, \tag{2.8}$$

where r_0 is the opportunity cost of land, e.g., agricultural land rent, which is given exogenously.

In the so-called "closed city" case, the total number of households in each class, N_i $(i = 1, \ldots, m)$, is exogenously given, whereas the utility level for each class, u_i $(i = 1, \ldots, m)$, is endogenously determined within the system (2.5)–(2.8). Wheaton (1974) obtains some comparative static results in the closed city model, where there is assumed to be only one class of households. Miyao (1975, 1981) and Hartwick, Schweizer, and Varaiya (1976a, 1976b) generalize Wheaton's results in the case of many household classes. These studies show that the residential city tends to expand outward, as N_i increases, w_i increases, or r_0 decreases. It is also proved that, assuming $c_i(x) = c_i x$, a decrease in c_i has qualitatively the same effect as an increase in w_i and flattens the rent gradient.

The dynamic stability property of the equilibrium in the closed city model is examined in Miyao (1975, 1981), where a dynamic adjustment process of boundary positions is introduced: A boundary between two classes will be adjusted gradually through time in such a way as to move outward *or* inward, according as the bid rent of the inner class is higher *or* lower than that of the outer class at the boundary. This adjustment process can be formally written as

$$\dot{x}_i = f_i[r_i(x_i) - r_{i+1}(x_i)] \quad (i = 1, \ldots, m-1),$$
$$\dot{x}_m = f_m[r_m(x_m) - r_0], \tag{2.9}$$

where the dot indicates differentiation with respect to time, and

$$f_i'(\ ) > 0, \quad f_i(0) = 0 \quad (i = 1, \ldots, m). \tag{2.10}$$

It is easy to see from (2.6) and (2.7) that u_i is a function of x_{i-1} and x_i,

$$u_i = u_i(x_{i-1}, x_i) \quad (i = 1, \ldots, m), \tag{2.11}$$

given N_i and w_i. Thus, in view of (2.5), the system (2.10) can be rewritten as

$$
\begin{aligned}
\dot{x}_i &= f_i[r_i\{w_i - c_i(x_i), u_i(x_{i-1}, x_i)\} \\
&\quad - f_{i+1}\{w_{i+1} - c_{i+1}(x_i), u_{i+1}(x_i, x_{i+1})\}] \quad (i=1,\ldots,m-1), \\
\dot{x}_m &= f_m[r_m\{w_m - c_m(x_m), u_m(x_{m-1}, x_m)\} - r_0].
\end{aligned}
\tag{2.12}
$$

It is shown that the system (2.12) is locally stable for any positive speeds of adjustment $f_i'(0) > 0$ $(i=1,\ldots,m)$, if at each boundary between two classes the inner class has a higher ratio of marginal transport cost to land per household than the outer class, i.e.,

$$
c_i'(x_i^*)/h_i(x_i^*) > c_{i+1}'(x_i^*)/h_{i+1}(x_i^*) \quad (i=1,\ldots,m),
\tag{2.13}
$$

and land is a non-Giffen good for all households, i.e.,

$$
\partial h_i[r_i(x), w_i - c_i(x)]/\partial r_i(x) < 0 \quad \text{for} \quad x_{i-1}^* \leqslant x \leqslant x_i^* \quad (i=1,\ldots,m),
\tag{2.14}
$$

where x_i^* is the equilibrium value of x_i $(i=1,\ldots,m)$.

In the "open city" case, the utility levels, u_i $(i=1,\ldots,m)$, are exogenous, and household class sizes, $N_i(i=1,\ldots,m)$, are endogenously determined by (2.5)–(2.8), just contrary to the closed city model. In his comparative static analysis of the open city, Wheaton (1974) shows that rents increase at all locations and the city expands, as income increases, unit transport cost decreases, the utility level decreases, or the opportunity cost of land decreases. Unlike the closed city case, there is no flattening of the rent gradient when income increases or unit transport cost decreases in the open city case. In the general case of m household classes, as examined in Miyao (1978, 1981), class i's bid rent function is $r_i(x) = r_i[w_i - c_i(x), u_i]$ and, therefore, changes in w_i, c_i, and u_i will only affect the bid rents of class i and the inner and outer boundaries of zone i, x_{i-1} and x_i, but not the bid rents of any other class or the position of any other boundary. By the same token, a decrease in r_0 will move x_m outward, but no other boundary will be affected.

Miyao (1979, 1981) offers a dynamic stability analysis by introducing a dynamic adjustment process of household movement into and out of the open city. The number of households in each class N_i is assumed to increase *or* decrease through time, due to in-migration or out-migration, as the utility level u_i attained by the households in class i within the city is higher *or* lower than a certain utility level $\bar{u}_i$, which those households can obtain outside the city:

$$
\dot{N}_i = f_i(u_i - \bar{u}_i) \quad (i=1,\ldots,m),
\tag{2.15}
$$

with $f_i'(\ ) > 0$ and $f_i(0) = 0$, where u_i is determined for given values of N_i's at each point in time, as in the closed city case,

$$u_i = u_i(N_1, \ldots, N_m) \quad (i=1, \ldots, m). \tag{2.16}$$

It is clear that the long-run equilibrium with $N_i = 0$ $(i=1, \ldots, m)$ will yield the equilibrium values of N_i's in the open city case. The system (2.15) is shown to be locally stable for any positive speeds of adjustment $f_i'(0) > 0$ $(i=1, \ldots, m)$, if both (2.13) and (2.14) are satisfied.

It should be noted that in the open city case the equilibrium may become unstable if certain types of externality are present. For example, Miyao (1978, 1981) assumes negative intergroup externality, that means that different classes of households dislike each other, an assumption which is adopted from the dynamic, but nonspatial models of Schelling (1969, 1971). In a simple case with two household classes having different incomes $(w_1 < w_2)$ and Cobb–Douglas utility functions

$$U_i = z_i^a h_i^b N_j^{-c_i}, \quad i \neq j \quad (i, j = 1, 2), \tag{2.17}$$

with a, b, and c_i being positive constants, the "interior" equilibrium with $N_1^* > 0$ and $N_2^* > 0$ is unstable, provided that the degree of negative externality is so high that

$$c_i \geq b \quad (i = 1, 2), \tag{2.18}$$

even though both conditions (2.13) and (2.14) are in fact satisfied in this model. Kanemoto (1980a,b) and Miyao, Shapiro, and Knapp (1980) also find instability results in their dynamic models with somewhat different types of negative externality.

2.1.2. Long-run growth analysis

We now turn to long-run growth models, which are directly based on the Alonso–Mills–Muth model. In those growth models, the main driving force behind urban dynamics is the growth of population and labor force in the city, coupled with other dynamic factors such as transportation improvements, income growth, etc. The purpose of the growth analysis is to examine under what conditions long-run urban growth can be sustained and what kind of long-run behavior the dynamic urban system will exhibit.

Miyao (1977c, 1981) develops a "neoclassical" model of urban residential growth with exogenous population growth and endogenous transportation improvements. First, assume a typical monocentric city with one homogeneous class of households which maximize their Cobb–Douglas utility function

$$U(x) = z(x)^a h(x)^b, \quad a, b > 0, \tag{2.19}$$

subject to

$$z(x)+r(x)h(x)=1-\tau-cx, \tag{2.20}$$

where the price of the consumption good and income are both normalized as unity, τ is the tax rate, and c is unit transport cost. Then, the rent function becomes

$$r(x)=A(1-\tau-cx)^{(a+b)/b_u-1/b}, \tag{2.21}$$

and the demand for land by a household becomes

$$h(x)=B(1-\tau-cx)^{-a/b}u^{-1/b}, \tag{2.22}$$

where A and B are positive constants, and u is the maximized level of utility. Assuming that $g(x)=g$, condition (2.7) may be written as

$$2\pi g\int_0^{x_1}\frac{x}{h(x)}\,\mathrm{d}x=Cu^{-1/b}\int_0^{x_1}x(1-\tau-cx)^{a/b}\,\mathrm{d}x=N, \tag{2.23}$$

where C is a positive constant, x_1 is the urban boundary, and N is the total number of households in the city. Finally, condition (2.8) can be expressed as

$$r(x_1)=A(1-\tau-cx_1)^{(a+b)/b}u^{-1/b}=r_0, \tag{2.24}$$

where r_0 is the opportunity cost of land. For simplicity, there is assumed to be enough vacant land around the city so that $r_0=0$, which gives $x_1=(1-\tau)/c$ from (2.24). This, together with (2.23), leads to

$$u=Dk^b(1-\tau)^{a+2b}, \tag{2.25}$$

where D is a positive constant, and

$$k\equiv 1/(Nc^2). \tag{2.26}$$

It follows from (2.25) and (2.26) that with a given value of τ, u is stationary if and only if k is stationary over time, i.e., $0=\hat{k}=-2\hat{c}-\hat{N}$. That is to say, the rate of growth of urban population $\hat{N}$ must be twice as high as the rate of decrease of unit transport cost $(-\hat{c})$ in order to obtain a steady growth equilibrium.

The existence, uniqueness and global stability of the steady growth equilibrium are proved by assuming that urban population is growing at a constant rate,

$$\hat{N}=\mu>0, \tag{2.27}$$

and that the rate of decrease of unit transport cost depends on the amount of transportation investment per unit of land devoted to transportation,

$$-\hat{c}=f(S/J),\quad\text{with }f'(\ )>0,\quad f(0)=0,\quad f(\infty)=\infty, \tag{2.28}$$

where S is total transportation investment, $S=\tau N$, and J is the total land area used for transportation:

$$J = 2\pi\sigma \int_0^{x_1} x\, dx = \pi\sigma(x_1)^2, \tag{2.29}$$

where σ is a constant fraction of land devoted to transportation at each x. Then, we find the following dynamic equation:

$$\hat{k} = -2\hat{c} - \hat{N} = 2f\left[\frac{\tau N}{\pi\sigma(x_1)^2}\right] - \mu = 2f\left[\frac{\tau}{\pi\sigma(1-\tau)^2 k}\right] - \mu, \tag{2.30}$$

from (2.26)–(2.29). The steady growth equilibrium value of k is obtained by setting $\hat{k}=0$ in (2.30), and the uniqueness and global stability of the steady growth equilibrium follow direct from (2.27), (2.28), and (2.30) in much the same way as in the one-sector neoclassical model of economic growth. It can be seen from (2.21) and (2.22) that in the steady growth equilibrium both rents $r(x)$ and densities $1/h(x)$ will become higher at all locations and their gradients become flatter over time.

Miyao's analysis shows that essentially the same results hold in the case of two household classes with different incomes, but idential Cobb–Douglas utility functions. In equilibrium the lower income class with $w_1 < 1$ occupies the inner ring of the city, whereas the higher income class with $w_2 = 1$ lives in the outer ring. Their bid rent functions are

$$r_1(x) = A[w_1(1-\tau)-cx]^{(a+b)/b}u_1^{-1/b},$$
$$r_2(x) = A(1-\tau-cx)^{(a+b)/b}u_2^{-1/b}, \tag{2.31}$$

where u_1 and u_2 are the maximized levels of utility for class 1 and class 2, respectively. And the boundary between the two classes, x_1, and the urban boundary, x_2, is determined by

$$r_1(x_1) = r_2(x_1), \quad r_2(x_2) = r_0 = 0. \tag{2.32}$$

Assuming that $\hat{N}_1 = \hat{N}_2 = \mu > 0$ and (2.28), and defining $k \equiv 1/[(w_1 N_1 + N_2)c^2]$, we have exactly the same dynamic equation as (2.30), which ensures the existence, uniqueness and global stability of a steady growth equilibrium in the case of two classes. It is also shown in the both one-class and two-class cases that the steady growth equilibrium level(s) of utility is maximized when the tax rate is equal to $b/(a+b)$. Since $b/(a+b)$ is equal to the ratio of total rent payment to net income, i.e., land share in net income, this optimality result is analogous to the so-called golden rule of accumulation in the neoclassical theory of economic growth.

While Miyao's model, assuming the exogenous growth of urban population, is based on the closed city model, a long-run growth analysis, of the open city model with in- and out-migration has also been presented in the literature. In an

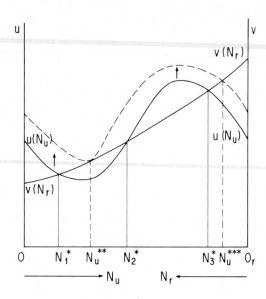

Figure 2.1.

attempt to explain sudden, explosive urban growth phenomena, Papageorgiou (1980) begins with the inverse relation between the urban population N_u and the level of utility u in the open city with one household class, and modifies it by introducing production activity in the residential city, following the nonspatial model of Casetti (1980). In the urban sector, production is assumed to exhibit increasing returns such that $dw/dN_u > 0$ for relatively small values of N_u, and decreasing returns, $dw/dN_u < 0$, for larger values of N_u. Given this property, du/dN_u is likely to be positive for some intermediate range of N_u, and $u(N_u)$ may be represented by the curve in Figure 2.1. On the other hand, the rural sector yields the level of utility v, which is negatively related to the rural population N_r. By assuming that the total population $N = N_u + N_r$ in the economy is constant and measuring N_u from the origin O_u to the right and N_r from O_r to the left in Figure 2.1, we find three equilibrium points, N_1^*, N_2^*, and N_3^*, where $u = v$ so that no further migration between the two sectors takes place. Papageorgiou argues that as income rises due to technological progress, the curve $u(N_u)$ tends to shifts up, and beyond a certain point the urban population will show a sudden, explosive increase from N_u^{**} to N_u^{***}.

In a more recent paper which is somewhat similar to Papageorgiou's, but is a little more spatially aggregated than his, Miyao (1983) incorporates the natural growth of population and the dynamic adjustment of the urban boundary in addition to migration between the urban and rural sectors. His general system consists of the following three dynamic equations:

$$\hat{N}_u = m(u-v)N_r/N_u + \mu_u(u), \tag{2.33}$$

$$\hat{N}_r = -m(u-v) + \mu_r(v), \tag{2.34}$$

$$\hat{L}_u = f(r_u - r_r), \tag{2.35}$$

where m, μ_u, μ_r, L_u, r_u, and r_r denote the rate of rural–urban migration in proportion to the rural population, the natural growth rate of the urban population, that of the rural population, the total amount of urban land (boundary), the land rent in the urban sector, and that in the rural sector, respectively. To close the system, the utility and price variables are expressed as functions of N_u, N_r, and L_u: the indirect utility function for the urban sector $u(r_u, I_u)$ gives the demand for urban land per household $h_u(r_u, I_u)$, where I_u is household income in the urban sector. Then, r_u is determined by the market clearance condition for urban land, $L_u = N_u h_u(r_u, I_u)$, which can be solved for r_u as $r_u(I_u, N_u/L_u)$. Similarly, $v(r_r, I_r)$, $h_r(r_r, I_r)$, and $r_r(I_r, N_r/L_r)$ can be obtained, where I_r is rural household income and L_r is the total amount of rural land. For simplicity, the total amount of land available in the economy is assumed to be exogenously fixed as L, so that $L_r = L - L_u$. Furthermore, I_u is an increasing function of N_u/L_u due to agglomeration economies in the urban sector, whereas I_r is a decreasing function of N_r/L_r because of the law of diminishing returns in agriculture.

Miyao considers two special cases; one with no adjustment of the boundary between the two sectors, and one with no natural population growth. In the former case with an initial value of N_u being sufficiently small, both the urban and rural sectors will grow in terms of population in the initial phase of economic development, and then the rural population will start to decline while the urban population will continue to grow. Eventually, both sectors will start to lose population. In the latter case with boundary adjustment, but no natural population growth, the city tends to show a cyclical movement in terms of population and land area, provided that the degree of urban agglomeration economies measured by the elasticity of I_u with respect to N_u/L_u is sufficiently high. If, on the other hand, the degree of urban agglomeration economies is relatively low, both the urban population and urban land area will asymptotically approach their long-run equilibrium values.

Based on the optimality analysis of Isard and Kanemoto (1976), Kanemoto (1980b) examines the optimal growth of a system of identical cities with both residential and production activities. As in the typical residential city mdoel, the utility of a household depends on a consumption good and residential space, and transport cost is a sole function of distance. In each city, production is subject to increasing returns with respect to population (labor force) so that per capita output can be written as

$$f(k, N) \quad \text{with} \quad f_k > 0, \quad f_N > 0, \tag{2.36}$$

where k is the capital-labor ratio, N is the total population in this city, and subscripts denote partial differentiation. The total population in the system of cities as a whole is

$$M = mN, \tag{2.37}$$

where m is the number of cities in the system. Assuming that M is growing at a constant rate, $\hat{M} = \mu$, and that households and capital are both perfectly mobile between cities, Kanemoto's optimization problem is to maximize the undiscounted sum of household utility (in fact, the undiscounted sum of the difference between the instantaneous utility level u and the optimal steady-state utility level u^*) over infinite time horizon, given a certain initial value of the capital-labor ratio:

$$k(0) = k_0. \tag{2.38}$$

The first stage of optimization is to choose the amount of the consumption good and residential space for each household, given c and N, where

$$c = f(k, N) - \dot{k} - \lambda k, \tag{2.39}$$

λ being the rate of capital depreciation. This yields the utility level u as a function of c and N; $u = U(c, N)$. Then, the second stage of optimization is to maximize

$$\int_0^\infty [U\{c(t), N(t)\} - u^*] dt, \tag{2.40}$$

subject to (2.37)–(2.39).

By solving this problem, Kanemoto shows that at the optimal steady state the number of cities increases at the same rate as overall population growth, while leaving the configuration of each city unchanged over time, and that the optimal path which solves the above problem must converge to the steady state. It is concluded that in the small neighborhood of the optimal steady state, population tends to increase in each city (that is, the growth rate of the number of cities approaches the growth rate of overall population *from below*), as the capital-labor ratio is increasing toward its steady-state level, provided that $f_{kN} \geqslant 0$, i.e., k and N are complementary in production, and $\partial[-U_N/U_c]/\partial c \geqslant 0$, i.e., the absolute value of the marginal rate of substitution between N and c increases with c, and that the former is large relative to the latter. If the former is small relative to the latter or the former is negative while the latter is nonnegative, it is optimal to have a declining population in each city as the capital-labor ratio increases in the small neighborhood of the steady state.

2.2. Dynamic models with housing durability

There have recently been more attempts to build residential growth models which take account of the durability of housing. It turns out that those models which assume housing durability show strikingly different properties from the typical Alonso–Mills–Muth model. In the literature we can distinguish between two types of growth models with housing durability according to their assumption on expectations, namely, myopic expectations models and perfect foresight models. Furthermore, some models are intended to be descriptive, while others are normative in nature. Since most of the perfect foresight models are closely related to normative optimality analysis, we take up those normative models and descriptive models with perfect foresight together, after overviewing myopic expectations models which are almost completely descriptive.

2.2.1. Myopic expectations models

In the theoretical literature on housing, the importance of durability has been pointed out by a number of authors, notably, Muth (1973) and Evans (1975). Empirically, housing durability has been regarded by Harrison and Kain (1974) as the main factor which can explain much of the cumulative growth process of American cities in the last several decades. Along the line of these studies, Anas (1976, 1978) sets up a spatial model of residential growth which assumes completely durable housing and myopic expectations. Based on these rather drastic assumptions, the Anas model presents an alternative view on urban growth with some important implications, which contrast sharply with the properties of the Alonso–Mills–Muth model. More specifically, Anas assumes that housing is completely durable physically, and the cost of housing demolition is so high that no replacement of existing housing capital can take place economically, whereas households (renters) are perfectly mobile with no moving cost incurred within the city. With regard to expectations, developers, land-owners, and households are all myopic in the sense that they expect current variables to remain unchanged indefinitely in the future. The history of the city is viewed as a sequence of new housing developments. At time t, population growth occurs in the city, and new construction takes place only at the urban fringe to accommodate the additional number of households. As a result, at time t the city consists of t rings of residential land and housing with the urban boundary x_t, where inside the city the ith ring was developed at time i with its outer boundary x_i ($i = 1, \ldots, t-1$).

First, consider the closed city case. There is assumed to be only one homogeneous class of households which maximize

$$U(x)_t = [z(x)_t]^a [h(x)_t]^b, \quad a, b > 0, \quad a + b = 1, \tag{2.41}$$

subject to

$$z(x)_t + p(x)_t h(x)_t - c(x)_t = w_t, \quad \text{for} \quad 0 < x \leqslant x_t, \tag{2.42}$$

where $p(x)_t$ is the price of housing at distance x from the CBD at time t, and $h(x)_t$ is the amount of housing consumed at distance x at time t. Because of the assumption of completely durable housing, we have $h(x)_t = h(x)_i$ for $x_{i-1} < x \leqslant x_i$ $(i = 1, \ldots, t-1)$. In equilibrium, the housing price gradient is negative *within ring t*,

$$\partial [p(x)_t]/\partial x = -c'(x)_t/h(x)_t \quad \text{for} \quad x_{t-1} < x \leqslant x_t, \tag{2.43}$$

but the maximized utility level at time t, u_t^*, is common for all households at all locations within the city,

$$U(x)_t = u_t^* \quad \text{for} \quad x_{i-1} < x \leqslant x_i \quad (i = 1, \ldots, t). \tag{2.44}$$

Housing is supplied competitively by developers who bid up land rents so as to maximize $r(x)_t = [p(x)_t h(x)_t - \rho_t K(x)_t - \omega_t N(x)_t]/L(x)_t$ for all x, where $L(x)_t$, $K(x)_t$, and $N(x)_t$ are the amounts of land, capital, and labor used to produce $h(x)_t$ units of housing at distance x at time t, $r(x)_t$ is the land rent at distance x at time t, and ρ_t and ω_t are the prices of capital and labor inputs at time t. By expressing $p(x)_t h(x)_t$ as a function of $h(x)_t$ and u_t^* from (2.41)–(2.44), we can formally state the problem of maximizing $r(x)_t$ as follows:

$$\max r(x)_t = [w_t - c(x)_t - (u_t^*)^{1/a}\{h(x)_t\}^{-b/a} - \rho_t K(x)_t$$
$$- \omega_t N(x)_t]/L(x)_t, \quad \text{for} \quad 0 < x \leqslant x_t, \tag{2.45}$$

with respect to $K(x)_t$, $N(x)_t$, and $L(x)_t$, subject to the production function for housing

$$h(x) = [K(x)_t]^\alpha [L(x)_t]^\beta [N(x)_t]^\gamma, \quad \alpha, \beta, \gamma > 0, \quad \alpha + \beta + \gamma = 1,$$
$$\text{for} \quad 0 < x \leqslant x_t, \tag{2.46}$$

and

$$K(x)_t = K(x)_i, \quad N(x)_t = N(x)_i, \quad L(x)_t = L(x)_i, \quad \text{for} \quad 0 < x \leqslant x_i \quad (i = 1, \ldots, t-1),$$
$$\rho_t = \rho_i, \quad \omega_t = \omega_i, \quad \text{for} \quad t > i, \quad \text{for} \quad x_{i-1} < x \leqslant x_i \quad (i = 1, \ldots, t-1), \tag{2.47}$$

where (2.47) follows from the assumption that durable inputs for housing production cannot be adjusted once housing is built and the suppliers of inputs continue to receive ρ_i and ω_i per unit of capital and labor as "annual dividends" for $t > i$. This maximization problem can be solved for $K(x)_t$, $N(x)_t$, $L(x)_t$, $h(x)_t$, and $r(x)_t$ as functions of u_t^*. Furthermore, in equilibrium the zero profit condition for housing,

$$p(x)_t h(x)_i - r(x)_t L(x)_i - \rho_i K(x)_i - \omega_i N(x)_i = 0, \quad \text{for} \quad x_{i-1} < x \leqslant x_i,$$
$$(i = 1, \ldots, t), \tag{2.48}$$

will yield $p(x)_t$ as a function of u_t^*. Finally, the utility level u_t^* and the urban boundary x_t at time t are determined by the following two conditions: the additional number of households $M_t - M_{t-1}$ must be accommodated in ring t,

$$M_t - M_{t-1} = 2\pi \int_{x_{t-1}}^{x_t} \frac{x}{L(x)_t} \, dx, \tag{2.49}$$

and the market rent function should be continuous at x_t,

$$r(x_t)_t = r_{0t}, \tag{2.50}$$

where r_{0t} is the agricultural land rent at time t.

Anas (1978) proves that in the closed city case, the sequence of boundary densities, $1/L(x_1)_1, \ldots, 1/L(x_t)_t$, is increasing with distance, and will be increasing faster, as r_{0t} is increasing, w_t is decreasing, or c_t is increasing over time, where c_t is unit transport cost: $c(x)_t = c_t x$. This follows from

$$1/L(x_t)_t = r_{0t}/[\beta b\{w_t - c(x_t)_t\}], \tag{2.51}$$

which is obtained by combining $p(x)_t h(x)_t = b[w_t - c(x)_t]$ from (2.41) and (2.42) and $r(x)_t L(x)_t = \beta p(x)_t h(x)_t$ from (2.46), and also considering (2.50). It is easy to see from (2.51) that sufficiently increasing income and/or decreasing unit transport cost can yield a declining sequence of boundary densities, and in that case the gradient of the boundary densities becomes steeper with a higher rate of income increase or transport cost decrease. All these results are sharply different from those of the Alonso–Mills–Muth model.

In the open city case where the utility level u_t^* is an exogenous parameter, the subsystem (2.41)–(2.48) can determine all the variables except the urban boundary, x_t, and the growth in population, $M_t - M_{t-1}$, which are determined by (2.49) and (2.50). It is shown that the maximization problem (2.45) gives

$$1/L(x_t)_t = C(u_t^*)^{-1}(r_{0t})^{1-\beta b}(\rho_t)^{-\alpha b}(\omega_t)^{-\gamma b}, \tag{2.52}$$

where C is a positive constant. This means that increases in r_{0t} or decreases in u_t^* will lead to increasing boundary densities, *provided that* the urban boundary is expanding over time. Since the boundary density in (2.52) does not depend on w_t or c_t, increasing income and/or decreasing transport cost may be assumed so as to ensure the boundary expansion. Changes in w_t and c_t by themselves, however, have no effect on boundary densities, contrary to the closed city case. Also note that changes in ρ_t and ω_t have an effect on boundary densities only in the open city case.

By taking time to be continuous, Anas further shows that in the both open and closed city cases with rising income ($\dot{w}_t > 0$) and rising utility ($\dot{u}_t^* > 0$), the land price and rent at any given x will first increase over time and subsequently decline if utility increases sufficiently. Thus, as illustrated in Figure 2.2, land prices and rents tend to rise initially in the inner segment of the city (from time t_1 to t_2), and

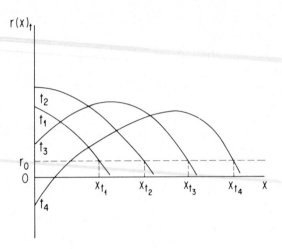

Figure 2.2.

then will fall (from t_2 to t_3). This leads to a negative rent gradient for the inner segment, and eventually negative rent levels at some locations (at time t_4). Suburbanization due to increasing income and rising welfare will decrease the demand for housing in the inner city area, and cause housing obsolescence and abondonment, unless households living in the inner city neighborhoods are subsidized by the government.

As pointed out above, the Anas model assumes that demolition is too costly to justify any redevelopment economically, once housing is built. In contrast, Brueckner (1980a, 1980b) adopts the assumption of zero demolition cost, while maintaining the myopic expectations assumption in his vintage model of residential growth. Brueckner's model supposes that housing services are produced according to the constant-returns-to-scale production function

$$h(x)_t = F[K(x)_t, L(x)_t], \tag{2.53}$$

at distance x from the CBD at time t, using capital K and land L as inputs; and housing is deteriorating physically at a constant rate λ, so that the amount of housing services offered at time t' by a house built at time t is $h(x)_i \, e^{-\lambda(t'-t)}$. Because of the assumption of constant returns to scale, competition leads to

$$[p(x)_t/(\lambda+\theta)]h(x)_t = V_t K(x)_t + \pi(x)_t L(x)_t, \tag{2.54}$$

where $p(x)_t$ is the price of housing services, θ is the interest rate, V_t is the price of capital, and $\pi(x)_t$ is the price of land. Since $h/L = F(K/L, 1) \equiv f(k)$, (2.54) can be rewritten as

$$[p(x)_t/(\lambda+\theta)] f[k(x)_t] - V_t k(x)_t = \pi(x)_t. \tag{2.55}$$

A condition under which housing redevelopment occurs is derived by comparing the expected profit from continuing to operate an existing building with that from demolishing the existing building and constructing a new one on the original land. Since the present value of the expected *revenue* from continuing to operate an old house built at time i per unit of land from time t on is

$$[p(x)_t^i/(\lambda + \theta)] f [k(x)_i] e^{-\lambda(t-i)}, \tag{2.56}$$

where $p(x)_t^i$ is the price of housing services offered at time t by a house built at time i, and the present value of the expected revenue from redevelopment, *net of new development costs*, at time t is

$$[p(x)_t/(\lambda + \theta)] f [k(x)_t] - V_t k(x)_t, \tag{2.57}$$

redevelopment occurs if (2.57) exceeds (2.56). First, note that whether redevelopment occurs or not, there is a sunk cost, $V_i k(x)_i + \pi(x)_i$, which was paid to purchase capital and land at time i, and which should be subtracted from both (2.56) and (2.57) in order to compute *profits* rather than revenues. Second, (2.57) is exactly equal to the left-hand side of (2.55). Thus, the above condition can be restated as follows: redevelopment takes place if the present value of the expected revenue from continuing to utilize an old building falls below the (resale) price of the original land. Third, owing to the assumption of zero demolition cost, housing abandonment will never occur, as redevelopment becomes profitable before land rents fall below zero.

Based on this analysis, Brueckner (1980a) takes up an open city model with one homogeneous class of households, and assumes Cobb–Douglas utility and production functions as well as constant rates of growth of utility, income, unit transport cost, the price of capital, and the price of agricultural land. It is proved, among other things, that the age of a building at demolition does not depend on the construction date or the location of the building and that the lifespan of a building is positively related to the rate of increase of the price of capital and is negatively related to the rate of housing deterioration. His numerical simulation produces generally declining structural and population densities with distance, and discontinuous decreases in these variables are observed when building ages increase discontinuously with distance due to redevelopment. In this model there seems to be a strong tendency toward redevelopment in the inner segment of the city, instead of having housing obsolescence and abandonment in the central city neighborhoods as suggested by the Anas model.

Along the line of Brueckner, Wheaton (1982a, 1983) develops a closed city model with one household class having a utility function which directly depends on the amounts of housing capital and residential land. Wheaton's closed city analysis more or less confirms the results of Brueckner's open city model by showing that redevelopment tends to yield substantially higher structural and population densities than those in the old surrounding areas, and it occurs normally at central locations in an outward manner. Only when both structural and population densities sharply decrease with distance, redevelopment can occur at peripheral locations. His simulation results indicate generally declining, but often discontinuous density functions with distance, similar to Brueckner's in the open city case. Furthermore, it is argued that population growth, either by itself or coupled with changes in unit transport cost, leads to redevelopment because existing population density becomes suboptimal, whereas growth with rising income tends to make the amount of capital in existing housing suboptimal and thus cause redevelopment in the closed city case.

The Brueckner–Wheaton model with one household class is extended by Brueckner (1980b) and Vousden (1980) so as to allow two household classes with different incomes, but with identical utility functions in the open city case. Brueckner, applying his previous model and assuming constant growth rates of utility, income, and unit transport cost, proves that initially the household class with the highest ratio of income to unit transport cost lives in the outer segment of the city and then the process of filtering of housing tends to occur around the boundary between the two classes. Filtering is shown to delay redevelopment. More specifically, according to his simulation results, the poorer class with lower growth rates of utility, income, and unit transport cost will bid away some housing units of the richer class around the boundary between the classes in the outward direction. In the next stage of urban growth, redevelopment will take place in the inner segment and also in some part of the outer segment except the blocks of housing which underwent filtering around the boundary. This leads to irregular and discontinuous density patterns with a sudden jump in density in the outer segment of the city. Eventually, the interaction of redevelopment and filtering yields spatial intermixing and leapfrogging in terms of household income, density, and building age structure, a result which contrasts quite sharply with the patterns of complete segregation and uniformly declining density found in the Alonso–Mills–Muth model with many household classes. This tendency toward the spatial intermixing of two income classes, especially in the outer segment of the city, is also pointed out by Vousden (1980), even though filtering may not occur at all in the case of constant utility over time.

2.2.2. Perfect foresight and normative models

Dismissing the assumption of myopic expectations as "unrealistic", a number of authors have attempted to develop urban residential models with durable housing under perfect foresight. Some such attempts are made in Arnott (1980) which assumes flexible dwelling size in the closed city case, and in Brueckner (1981) which takes account of housing demolition and redevelopment under stationary conditions in the open city case. Some of the features of these two analyses are adopted in the closed city model of Brueckner and Rabenau (1981) which investigates the effects of an exogenous population change that is fully anticipated by developers, and generates a variety of possible land use patterns including leap-frog sprawl and discontinuous density gradients.

These *descriptive* urban growth models assuming perfect foresight on the part of developers are further refined in Fujita (1982) which shows the possibility of positive density and rent gradients and in Wheaton (1982b, 1983) which proves that under competition urban land development can possibly take place from the outside inward, just the opposite to the typical development pattern, i.e., from the inside outward. To see how this reversed development pattern can occur, consider a simplified version of the Fujita–Wheaton model with a constant marginal transport cost. Following Wheaton's formulation, assume a homogeneous class of households maximizing the utility function

$$U(x)_t = U[z(x)_t, L(x)_t, K(x)_t], \tag{2.58}$$

subject to

$$z(x)_t + R(x)_t + cx = w_t, \tag{2.59}$$

where utility depends on a consumption good z, land L, and housing capital K, and R is the total rent for housing, i.e., a combination of L and K, at location x. Setting (2.58) equal to u_t and solving it for z, we find from (2.59) that

$$R(x)_t = w_t - cx - z[u_t, L(x)_t, K(x)_t] = R[w_t, x, u_t, L(x)_t, K(x)_t]. \tag{2.60}$$

Given that the τth period begins at $T_{\tau-1}$ and ends at $T_\tau(\tau = 1, \ldots, n)$, a developer who intends to develop a unit of land at the beginning of period t will choose L and K so as to maximize the present value of the net revenue per acre, $P(x; t)$, at each location x, that is,

$$\max_{L, K} P(x; t) = \sum_{\tau=1}^{t-1} D_\tau r_{0\tau} + \sum_{\tau=t}^{n} D_\tau \frac{R(w_\tau, x, u_\tau, L, K)}{L} - \frac{V_t K e^{-\theta T_{t-1}}}{L}, \tag{2.61}$$

where r_0 is agricultural rent, V is the cost of housing capital, θ is the rate of interest, and D_τ is the discount factor:

$$D_\tau \equiv (e^{-\theta T_{\tau-1}} - e^{-\theta T_\tau})/\theta \quad (\tau = 1, \ldots, n). \tag{2.62}$$

Furthermore, land is developed in the time period with the highest present value $P(x; \tau)$ at location x, and the set of locations $\mathscr{L}_t$ to be developed in period t can be expressed as

$$\mathscr{L}_t = \{x : P(x; t) \geqslant P(x; \tau) \text{ for all } \tau\} \quad (t = 1, \ldots, n). \tag{2.63}$$

Finally, the total amount of land developed in period t should be just sufficient to house the population growth during that period.

$$2\pi \int_{\mathscr{L}_t} \frac{x}{L(x)_t} \, dx = M_t - M_{t-1} \quad (t=1,\ldots,n), \tag{2.64}$$

which is essentially the same condition as (2.49).

Wheaton argues that development occurs from the outside in, if the "present value bid function" $P(x;t)$ becomes steeper over time, i.e.,

$$0 > \partial P(x;t)/\partial x > \partial P(x;t+1)/\partial x, \tag{2.65}$$

so that $P(x;t) < P(x;t+1)$ in the inner segment of the city and $P(x;t) > P(x;t+1)$ in the outer segment. Since

$$\frac{\partial P(x;t)}{\partial x} - \frac{\partial P(x;t+1)}{\partial x} = \left(\sum_{\tau=t+1}^{n} \frac{D_\tau c}{L_t} \right) \left[\frac{L_t}{L_{t+1}} - e^{\theta(T_t - T_{t-1})} \right], \tag{2.66}$$

the inequality in (2.65) holds if θ is sufficiently small and L_t/L_{t+1} is greater than one and sufficiently large. The latter condition means that the density of residential development $1/L_\tau$ is increasing sufficiently over time, and thus some inner segment of the city is initially left vacant for higher-density development in a later period.

In a somewhat different open city model, assuming only two time periods, Mills (1981) demonstrates that leap-frog development and discontinuous rent gradients may occur in the case of perfect foresight and that the assumption of uncertainty and heterogeneous expectations can yield a spatial intermixing of various kinds of land use (and possibly non-use) in addition to leap-frog development. Fujita (1983) summarizes all these descriptive models of residential growth with perfect foresight and further examines a generalized version of the Fujita–Wheaton model with many types of buildings and activities to show that competition under perfect foresight may lead to all sorts of sprawl-fashioned development such as leap-frog, mixed, and scattered development patterns.

On the other hand, these sprawl patterns can be also Pareto-optimal in an intertemporal sense, as shown in Ohls and Pines (1975), Pines (1976), and Fujita (1976a, 1976b, 1983), which assume the durability and adjustment costs of housing capital and investigate the optimal processes of residential growth and land development. Specifically, Fujita considers a monocentric city with many types of houses, indicated by subscript i, and many types of households, represented by subscript k, located in many concentric rings which are numbered in ascending order of commuting distance $(j=1,\ldots,J)$. Each type of housing can be characterized by its structure and its lot size. Let $H_{ij}(t)$ be the number of houses of type i located in ring j at time t, $I_{ij}(t)$ be the number of houses of type i newly constructed in ring j at time t, L_i be the lot size of a house of type i, $N_{ijk}(t)$ be the number of households of type k living in houses of type i in ring j at time t, $N_k(t)$ be the total number of households of type k, a_i be the amount of land per unit of housing of type i, A_j be the total land area in ring j, $B_i(t)$ be the cost of constructing a house of type i at time t, and R_{ijk} be the maximum (bid) rent that a household of type k can pay for a house of type i in ring j at time t for a given utility level u_k, that is,

$$R_{ijk}[u_k(t), t] = w_k(t) - c_{jk}(t) - z(u_k, i, t),$$

which is similar to (2.60). Then, the dynamic optimization problem is to maximize the present value of the net rent revenue from residential development in the city as a whole, i.e.,

$$\max \int_0^\infty e^{-\theta t} \left\{ \sum_i \sum_j \sum_k R_{ijk}[u_k(t), t] N_{ijk}(t) - \sum_i \sum_j B_i(t) I_{ij}(t) \right\}, \tag{2.67}$$

with respect to $I_{ij}(t)$ and $N_{ijk}(t)$, subject to:

$$\dot{H}_{ij}(t) = I_{ij}(t) \geq 0, \tag{2.68}$$

$$\sum_k N_{ijk}(t) \leq H_{ij}(t), \tag{2.69}$$

$$\sum_i \sum_j N_{ijk}(t) = N_k(t), \tag{2.70}$$

$$\sum_i a_i H_{ij}(t) \leq A_j, \tag{2.71}$$

$$H_{ij}(0) = H^0_{ij} \geq 0, \tag{2.72}$$

where a utility stream is arbitrarily specified as $u_k(t)$ for $0 < t < \infty$ for each k.

Fujita proves that any solution to the optimization problem (2.67) with an arbitrarily given utility stream is also a competitive market solution, where each developer has perfect foresight and maximizes the present value of the net revenue per unit of land for housing of type i in ring j:

$$P_{ij}(t) = \int_0^t e^{-\theta \tau} r_{\theta \tau} d\tau + \int_t^\infty e^{-\theta \tau} \frac{R_{ij}(\tau)}{L_i} d\tau - \frac{B_i(t) e^{-\theta t}}{L_i}, \tag{2.73}$$

which is a continuous-time version of (2.61); and each household of type k maximizes its utility

$$U_k(z_k, i, t), \text{ subject to } z_k + R_{ij}(t) + c_{jk}(t) = w_k(t) + S_k(t), \tag{2.74}$$

where $R_{ij}(t)$ is the market (total) rent for a house of type i in ring j at time t, and $S_k(t)$ is an appropriately chosen *income subsidy or tax* for each household of type k at time t. Conversely, for any given set of values of $S_k(t)$, there exists a certain utility stream $u_k(t)$ such that the optimization problem has a solution which coincides with the competitive solution for the given values of $S_k(t)$. In this sense, the set of optimal solutions is equivalent to the set of competitive solutions. It is further demonstrated that urban sprawl, i.e., leap-frog, mixed, and scattered development patterns, can be a solution to the optimization problem for some utility stream.

Somewhat similar optimality results are found in Ripper and Varaiya (1974) and Pines and Werczberger (1982) which employ a linear programming approach to dynamic urban land use, whereas Fujita's optimum control approach is adopted in Hockman and Pines (1980, 1982) to compare optimal and competitive development patterns under the assumption of flexible dwelling unit size. Due to this assumption, land rents and densities always decline with greater commuting distance in the Hockman–Pines model, in contrast to Fujita's result (1982, 1983) that there is a possibility of positive rent and density gradients in the case of completely durable housing. Optimal and competitive solutions involving urban renewal and upgrading are obtained in Akita and Fujita (1982), Fujita (1983), and Pines and Werczberger (1982), which again indicate a wide variety of equilibrium development patterns, including sprawl patterns, that are socially optimal.

3. Concluding remarks

After reviewing dynamic urban models, no one fails to be impressed with the speed at which progress has been made to incorporate many important dynamic elements in those models in the last several years. Less than two decades ago, what was available to deal with urban growth was just a handful of non-spatial production growth models, which could not shed much light on the dynamic process of metropolitan growth and suburbanization. Now there exist all kinds of dynamic urban models which take explicit account of both time and space with certain assumptions regarding durability and expectations. More implications are currently being drawn from those complex models so as to help understand the long-run process of urban growth and the effect of government policies in the dynamic context.

There seem to be several directions in which the existing models can be extended. First, as pointed out before, the gap between production and residential models must be filled. It appears that time is ripe for the development of a dynamic model of land use for both production and housing as well as transportation, where developers can play a significant role in realizing urban agglomeration economies which benefit producers, households, and landowners. As a first step, the assumption of the spaceless CBD with exogenously given household income should be dropped and the production-employment aspect must be endogenized in the existing residential growth models.

Second, aside from the obvious necessity to consider more reasonable assumptions regarding expectations, uncertainty, and adjustment costs for landowners and developers, those dynamic elements should be also utilized to generate a more realistic kind of household behavior than the assumption of freely mobile renters in the existing residential models. Especially, we need to address the problem of home ownership in the context of urban growth in order to understand the mechanism of suburbanization and the effect of housing policies on urban growth.

Third, most of the existing dynamic urban models deal with a single city which is either closed or open. Since a city is only part of a larger system and moves along with the rest of the system, the dynamic analysis of a single city should always be taken cautiously and be regarded as a first step toward a more general treatment of a city which interacts with the rest of the system. In order to obtain some ideas and intuition in that direction, it will be useful to examine regional growth theory and rural–urban migration theory which treat a city in a broader framework. Since these theories traditionally emphasize production and employment as the main driving force, their integration with urban residential models will help bridge the aforementioned gap between production and residential growth models.

References

Akita, T. and M. Fujita (1982) 'Spatial development processes with renewal in a growing city', *Environment and Planning A*, 14:205–223.
Alonso, W. (1964) *Location and land use*. Cambridge, Mass.: Harvard University Press.
Anas, A. (1976) 'Short-run dynamics in the spatial housing market', in: G.J. Papageorgiou, ed., *Mathematical land use theory*. Lexington, Mass.: D.C. Heath and Co., 261–275.
Anas, A. (1978) 'Dynaics of urban residential growth', *Journal of Urban Economics*, 5:66–87.
Anderson, R.J. (1970) 'A note on economic base studies and regional econometric forecasting models', *Journal of Regional Science*, 10:325–333.
Arnott, R.J. (1980) 'A simple urban growth model with durable housing', *Regional Science and urban Economics*, 10:53–76.
Arrow, K.J. and M. McManus (1958) 'A note on dynamic stability', *Econometrica*, 26:297–305.
Beckmann, M.J. (1972) 'Von Thunen Revisited: A neoclassical land use model', *Swedish Journal of Economics*, 74:1–7.
Bell, F.W. (1967) 'An econometric forecasting model for a region', *Journal of Regional Science*, 7:109–127.
Borts, G.H. (1971) 'Growth and capital movements among United States regions in the postwar period' in: J.F. Kain and J.R. Meyer, eds., *Essays in regional economics*. Cambridge, Mass.: Harvard University Press, 189–217.
Borts, G.H. and J.L. Stein (1964) *Economic growth in a free market*. New York: Columbia University Press.
Brueckner, J.K. (1980a) 'A vintage model of urban growth', *Journal of Urban Economics*, 8:389–402.
Brueckner, J.K. (1980b) 'Residential succession and land-use dynamics in a vintage model of urban housing', *Regional Science and Urban Economics*, 10:225–240.
Brueckner, J.K. (1981) 'A dynamic model of housing production', *Journal of Urban Economics*, 10:1–14.

Brueckner, J.K. and B.V. Rabenau (1981) 'Dynamics of land use for a closed city', *Regional Science and Urban Economics*, 11:1–17.

Carlberg, M. (1981) 'An economic growth model of the productive city', in: P. Nijkamp and P. Rietveld, eds., *Cities in transition: problems and policies*. Alphen aan den Rijn, The Netherlands: Sijthoff and Noordhoff, 271–293.

Casetti, E. (1980) 'Equilibrium population partitions between urban and agricultural occupations', *Geographical Analysis*, 12:47–54.

Conroy, M.E. (1975) *The challenge of urban economic development*. Lexington, Mass.: D.C. Heath.

Czamanski, S. (1964), 'A model of urban growth', *Papers of the Regional Science Association*, 13:177–200.

Czamanski, S. (1965), 'A method of forecasting metropolitan growth by means of distributed lags analysis', *Journal of Regional Science*, 6:35–49.

Day, R.H. and E.H. Tinney (1969) 'A dynamic von Thünen model', *Geographical Analysis*, 1:137–151.

Day, R.H. and P.E. Kennedy (1970) 'On a dynamic location model of production', *Journal of Regional Science*, 10:191–197.

Day, R.H., P.E. Kennedy and E.H. Tinney (1978) 'A cobweb version of the von Thünen model', in: R.H. Day and A. Cigno, eds., *Modelling economic change: The recursive programming approach*. Amsterdam: North-Holland, 217–231.

Dendrinos, D.S. (1982) 'On the dynamic stability of Interurban/regional labor and capital movements', *Journal of Regional Science*, 22:529–540.

Dixon, R. and A.P. Thirlwall (1975) 'A model of regional growth-rate differences on Kaldorian lines', *Oxford Economic Papers*, 27:201–214.

Engle, R.F., F.M. Fisher, J.R. Harris and J. Rothenberg (1972) 'An econometric simulation model of intra-metropolitan housing location: housing business, transportation and local government', *American Economic Review*, 62:87–97.

Engle, R.F. (1974) 'Issues in the specification of an econometric model of metropolitan growth', *Journal of Urban Economics*, 1:250–267.

Evans, A.W. (1975) 'Rent and housing in the theory of urban growth', *Journal of Regional Science*, 15, 113–125.

Friedman, J. and W. Alonso, ed. (1964) *Regional development and planning: a reader*. Cambridge, Mass.: MIT Press.

Fujita, M. (1976a) 'Spatial patterns of urban growth: optimum and market', *Journal of Urban Economics*, 3:209–241.

Fujita, M. (1976b) 'Toward a dynamic theory of urban land use', *Papers of the Regional Science Association*, 37:133–165.

Fujita, M. (1982) 'Spatial patterns of residential development', *Journal of Urban Economics*, 12:22–52.

Fujita, M. (1983) 'Urban spatial dynamics: A survey', *Sistemi Urbani*, 5.

Gerking, S.D. and A.M. Isserman (1981), 'Bifurcation and the time pattern of impacts in the economic base model', *Journal of Regional Science*, 21:451–467.

Glickman, N.J. (1971) 'An econometric forecasting model for the Philadelphia region', *Journal of Regional Science*, 11:15–32.

Greenwood, M.J. (1973) 'Urban economic growth and migration: their interaction', *Environment and Planning*, 5:91–112.

Hall, O.P. and J.A. Licari (1974) 'Building small region econometric models: extension of Glickman's structure to Los Angeles', *Journal of Regional Science*, 14:337–353.

Harrison, D. and J.F. Kain (1974) 'Cumulative urban growth and urban density functions', *Journal of Urban Economics*, 1:61–98.

Hartwick, J., U. Schweizer and P. Varaiya (1976a), 'Comparative statistics of a residential economy with several classes', in. G.J. Papageorgiou, ed., *Mathematical land use theory*. Lexington, Mass.: D.C. Heath, 55–78.

Hartwick, J., U. Schweizer and P. Varaiya (1976b) 'Comparative statics of a residential economy with several classes', *Journal of Economic Theory*, 13:396–413.

Harvey, A.S. (1974) 'A dualistic model of urban growth', *The Annals of Regional Science*, 8:58–69.

Hockman, O. and D. Pines (1980) 'Costs of adjustment and demolition costs in residential construction and their effects on urban growth', *Journal of Urban Economics*, 7:2–19.

Hockman, O. and D. Pines (1982) 'Costs of adjustment and the spatial pattern of a growing open city', *Econometrica*, 50:1371–1389.

Isard, W. and Y. Kanemoto (1976) 'Stages in space-time development', *Papers of the Regional Science Association*, 37:99–131.

Jacobs, J. (1970) *The economy of cities*. New York: Random House.

Kaldor, N. (1970). 'The case for regional policies', *Scottish Journal of Political Economy*, 17:337–348.

Kanemoto, Y. (1980a) 'Externality, migration, and urban crises', *Journal of Urban Economics*, 8:150–164.

Kanemoto, Y. (1980b) *Theories of urban externalities*. Amsterdam: North-Holland.

Klein, L.R. (1969) 'The specification of regional econometric models', *Papers of the Regional Science Association*, 23:105–115.

Lewis, W.C. and J.R. Prescott (1972) 'Urban-regional development and growth centers: an econometric study', *Journal of Regional Science*, 12:57–70.

Mazek, W.F. and J. Chang (1972) 'The chicken and egg fowl-up in migration: Comment', *Southern Economic Journal*, 39:133–139.

McNulty, J. (1977) 'A test of the time dimension in economic base analysis', *Land Economics*, 53:359–368.

Mills, E.S. (1967) 'An aggregative model of resource allocation in a metropolitan area', *American Economic Review*, 57:197–210.

Mills, E.S. (1972) *Studies in the structure of the urban economy*. Johns Hopkins Press, Baltimore.

Mills, D.E. (1981) 'Growth, speculation and sprawl in a monocentric city', *Journal of Urban Economics*, 10:201–226.

Miron, J.R. (1979) 'Migration and urban economic growth', *Regional Science and Urban Economics*, 9:159–183.

Miyao, T. (1975) 'Dynamics and comparative statics in the theory of residential location', *Journal of Economic Theory*, 11:133–146.

Miyao, (1977a) 'Some dynamic and comparative static properties of a spatial model of production', *Review of Economic Studies*, 44:321–327.

Miyao, T. (1977b) 'A long-run analysis of urban growth over space', *Canadian Journal of Economics*, 10:678–686.

Miyao, T. (1977c) 'The golden rule of urban transportation investment', *Journal of Urban Economics*, 4:448–458.

Miyao, T. (1978) 'Dynamic instability of a mixed city in the presence of neighborhood externalities', *American Economic Review*, 68:454–463.

Miyao, T. (1979) 'Dynamic stability of an open city with many household classes', *Journal of Urban Economics*, 6:292–298.

Miyao, T. (1980) 'Dynamics of metropolitan growth and unemployment', *Journal of Urban Economics*, 8:222–235.

Miyao, T. (1981) *Dynamic analysis of the urban economy*. New York: Academic Press.

Miyao, T. (1983) 'Rural and urban population changes and the stages of economic development: a unified approach', *Environment and Planning A*, 15:1161–1174.

Miyao, T., P. Shapiro and D. Knapp (1980) 'On the existence, uniqueness, and stability of spatial equilibrium in an open city with externalities', *Journal of Urban Economics*, 8:139–149.

Moody, H.T. and F.W. Puffer (1969) 'A gross regional product approach to regional model-building', *Western Economic Journal*, 7:391–402.

Moody, H.T. and F.W. Puffer (1970) 'The empirical verification of the urban base multiplier: traditional and adjustment process models', *Land Economics*, 46:91–98.

Muth, R.F. (1968) 'Differential growth among large U.S. cities', in: J.P. Quirk and A.M. Zarley, eds., *Papers in quantitative economics*. Lawrence: University Press of Kansas, 311–355.

Muth, R.F. (1969) *Cities and housing*. Chicago: University of Chicago Press.

Muth, R.F. (1971) 'Migration: chicken or egg?' *Southern Economic Journal*, 37:295–306.

Muth, R.F. (1972) 'The chicken or egg fowl-up in migration: reply', *Southern Economic Journal*, 39:139–142.

Muth, R.F. (1973) 'A vintage model of the housing stock', *Papers of the Regional Science Association*, 30:141–156.

Mydral, G. (1957) *Economic theory and under-developed regions*. London: Gerald Ducknorth.

Niedercorn, J.H. and J.F. Kain (1963) 'An econometric model of metropolitan development', *Papers and Proceedings of the Regional Science Association*, 11:123–143.

Niedercorn, J.H. (1963) 'An econometric model of metropolitan employment and population growth', RM-3758-RC, Santa Monica, RAND Corporation.

North, D.C. (1955) 'Location theory and regional economic growth', *Journal of Political Economy*, 63:243–258.

Ohls, J.C. and D. Pines (1975) 'Continuous urban development and economic efficiency', *Land Economics*, 51:224–234.

Okabe, A. and Y. Kume (1983) 'A dynamic von Thunen model with a demand function', *Journal of Urban Economics*, 14:355–369.

Okun, B. (1968) 'Interstate population migration and state income inequality: a simultaneous equation approach', *Economic Development and Cultural Change*, 16:297–313.

Paelinck, J. (1970) 'Dynamic urban growth models', *Papers of the Regional Science Association*, 24:25–37.

Papageorgiou, G.J. (1980) 'On sudden urban growth', *Environment and Planning A*, 12:1035–1050.

Pfouts, R.W., ed. (1960) *The techniques of urban economic analysis*. West Trenton, New Jersey: Chandler-Davis.

Pines, D. (1976) 'Dynamic aspects of land use patterns in a growing city', in: G.J. Papageorgiou, ed., *Mathematical land use theory*. Lexington, Mass.: D.C. Heath and Co., 229–243.

Pines, D. and E. Werczberger (1982) 'A linear programming model of the urban housing and land markets: static and dynamic aspects', *Regional Science and Urban Economics*, 12:211–233.

Rabenau, B.V. (1976) 'Optimal growth of a factory town', *Journal of Urban Economics*, 3:97–112.

Rabenau, B.V. (1979) 'Urban growth with agglomeration economies and diseconomies', *Geographia Polonica*, 42:77–90.

Rabenau, B.V. and D.A. Hanson (1979) 'The provision of public goods in a growing urban economy', *Regional Science and Urban Economics*, 9:1–20.

Richardson, H.W. (1971) *Urban economics*. Harmondsworth, England: Penguin.

Richardson, H.W. (1973) *Regional growth theory*. New York: John Wiley.

Richardson, H.W. (1978) 'The state of regional economics: a survey article', *International Regional Science Review*, 3:1–48.

Ripper, M. and P. Varaiya (1974) 'An optimizing model of urban development', *Environment and Planning A*, 6:149–168.

Romans, J.T. (1965) *Capital exports and growth among U.S. regions*. Middletown, Connecticut: Wesleyan University Press.

Schelling, T.C. (1969) 'Models of segregation', *American Economic Review*, 59:488–493.

Schelling, T.C. (1971) 'Dynamic models of segregation', *Journal of Mathematical Sociology*, 1:143–186.

Siebert, H. (1965) *Regional economic growth: theory and policy*. Scranton, Penn.: International Textbook.

Smith, D.M. (1974) 'Regional growth: interstate and intersectoral factor reallocation', *Review of Economics and Statistics*, 61:353–359.

Smith, D.M. (1975) 'Neoclassical growth models and regional growth in the U.S.', *Journal of Regional Science*, 15:165–181.

Solow, R.M. (1960) 'Investment and technical progress', in: K.J. Arrow, S. Karlin, and P. Suppes, eds., *Mathematical methods in the social sciences*. Stanford: Stanford University Press, 89–104.

Solow, R.M. (1974) 'On equilibrium models of urban location', in: M. Parkin, ed., *Essays in Modern Economics*. London: Longman Group, 2–16.

Thompson, W.R. (1965) *A preface to urban economics*. Baltimore: Johns Hopkins Press.

Todaro, M.P. (1969) 'A model of labor migration and urban unemployment in less developed countries', *American Economic Review*, 59:138–148.

Vousden, N. (1980) 'An open-city model with nonmalleable housing', *Journal of Urban Economics*, 7:248–277.

Wheaton, W.C. (1974) 'A comparative static analysis of urban spatial structure', *Journal of Urban Economics*, 9:223–237.

Wheaton, W.C. (1982a) 'Urban spatial development with durable but replaceable capital', *Journal of Urban Economics*, 12:53–67.

Wheaton, W.C. (1982b) 'Urban residential growth under perfect foresight', *Journal of Urban Economics*, 12:1–21.

Wheaton, W.C. (1983) 'Theories of urban growth and metropolitan spatial development', in J.V. Henderson, ed., *Research in Urban Economics, Vol. 3*. Greenwich, Conn.: JAI Press, 3–36.

Winger, A.R. (1969) 'Supply oriented urban economic models', *Journal of the American Institute of Planners*, 35:30–34.

Chapter 23

GENERAL EQUILIBRIUM MODELING
OF SYSTEMS OF CITIES

J. VERNON HENDERSON

Brown University

Introduction

This paper presents the economic properties of a system of cities which are embedded in a general equilibrium model of an economy. We develop the properties of the system first in a closed static economy. We examine: (i) how and why the economic functions and sizes of cities vary, (ii) how prices and wages vary across cities, (iii) what are the determinants of the size distribution of cities, (iv) what are the impacts of natural resources on the spatial allocation of resources and clustering of cities, and (v) what are the impacts of governmental policies on the system of cities and spatial configurations of resource usage. Then we open the economy to economic growth and international trade. We examine the impacts of economic growth, trade patterns and trade policies on a system of cities in an economy.

The goals of the paper are to provide an overview of the basic theoretical propositions about systems of cities which exist in the literature, to pose basic policy questions in a theoretical framework relevant to researchers interested in urban development, and to note the basic questions about a system of cities which remain unanswered. The theoretical framework is based on the work of Henderson (1972, 1974, 1982a, 1982b), Henderson and Ioannides (1981), Hochman (1977, 1981), Kanemoto (1978) and Upton (1981).

While a general equilibrium model of a system of cities has only been in the literature for about a decade, the model has important antecedents which have influenced its form and development; and some of its critical aspects have solid empirical backing. We start with a review of these antecedents, which give us the basic elements of a system of cities.

Handbook of Regional and Urban Economics, Volume II, Edited by E.S. Mills

1. Elements of a model of a system of cities

1.1. Background

The notion in theoretical work that economies consist of systems of cities emanates from central plan theory [Christaller (1966) and Beckmann (1958)] based on a Loschian (1954) framework of retailers having endogenously determined market areas and hence scale of production. Central place models are formulated on the notion that in traditional economies towns exist to serve an agricultural based population. Given that base, there is a hierarchy of cities and production patterns where cities export down the hierarchy to smaller cities and to the rural population. The models have a reduced form structure, without explicit for-mulation of demand and supply technology and without any consideration of the internal make-up of cities and the housing of the urban based population. Hence, there are no prices or clearing of markets in the model [Beckmann (1958)]. While we want to move away from an agriculturally based economy, to explicitly model supply and demand and the internal structure of cities, and to reformulate the notion of a hierarchy, this early literature establishes the notion of a system of cities.

What are the bases of cities which have primary functions other than retailing to rural areas and smaller towns; and how do we model their basic form? In a classic paper, Mills (1967) suggested that cities form in an economy because there are scale economies in industrial production which lead workers and firms to cluster together in large agglomerations, rather than dispersing more or less evenly over the geographic area of the economy (with or without an agricultural sector). Greater scale of economic activities in cities enhances productivity through "communications" among firms which enhance the speed of adoption of new technological innovations and of reaction to changing national and in-ternational market conditions, through labor market economies for workers and firms searching respectively for specific jobs and specific skill combinations, through greater opportunities for specialization in firm (and worker) activities, and through scale economies in provision of intermediate common inputs (docking facilities, warehousing, power, etc.). The scale economies are dependent on workers and firms working together in close spatial proximity in, for example, a Central Business District of a city. Finally, these scale economies apply to the production of goods which are exported from the city to other cities or economies.

At the same time, there are consumption and certain production diseconomies connected with people clustering together in urban areas, such as commuting cost increases in a monocentric city, and such disamenities as crime, pollution, and social conflict. In a monocentric city where almost all residents work in a Central

Business District, as city size expands, residents on average live further and further from the city center and have to commute greater and greater distances. The effect of these diseconomies will be to eventually offset production scale benefits as a city's size increases, limiting cities to various equilibrium sizes [Mills (1967) and Dixit (1973)].

Given cities exist and are limited in efficient sizes, how do they relate to each other? The basic notion here is that there are different types of cities, where each type specializes in the production of a different traded good. The fact that at least smaller and medium size cities are highly specialized in their production patterns is well established empirically [Alexandersson (1959), Bergsman, Greenston and Healy (1975), and Henderson (1986a)]. Note this fact contradicts the traditional notion that smaller and medium size cities are part of a hierarchy as modelled in central place theory. The question is why do cities specialize? Henderson (1972, 1974) argues that specialization occurs if there are no production benefits or positive externalities from locating two different industries in the same place. If they are located together, because workers in both industries are living and commuting in the same city, this raises the spatial area of the city and average commuting costs for a given degree of scale economy exploitation in any one industry. Separating the industries into different cities allows for a greater degree of scale economy exploitation in each industry relative to a given level of commuting costs and city spatial area.

This argument concerning scale economies is strengthened if scale economies are ones of localization, not urbanization. Localization economies are ones *internal* to each industry, where scale is measured by total employment (or output) in *that* industry in *that* urban area. Urbanization economies are external to the specific industry, and result from the level of all economic activity internal to a city, measured by, say, total city population. In this case, only the size of the city, not its industry composition, affects the extent of scale effects relevant to a particular industry.

If scale effects are ones of localization, then for a *given* city size and associated cost of living, scale effects and hence incomes are maximized by concentrating local export employment all in one industry, rather than dissipating the scale effects by spreading employment over many industries. However, if scale effects are ones of urbanization, then this specialization may not matter since it is the general level of economic activity rather than its industry specific concentration which enhances productivity.[1] There is now strong empirical evidence that indeed economies of scale for most manufacturing industries are ones of localization, not urbanization [Sveikauskas (1978) and Henderson (1986a)].

---

[1] Note specialization can occur if scale economies are only ones of urbanization, since goods with different degrees of urbanization economies have different city sizes which are most efficient for their worker residents.

The extent of specialization of cities is, of course, limited. There are a range of goods produced in almost all urban areas – general retailing, schooling, housing services, auto repairs, dry cleaning, etc. These services as well as some manufactured goods are nontraded simply because the transport costs of intercity trade are prohibitive. Specialization is also limited by the fact that some industries are strongly linked in production. The traditional linkages are physical input–output ones, although these may be weaker in a modern economy [Bergsman et al. (1975)]. There are also linkages through labor force, communications, and service input interactions among industries. Thus urban specialization in practice implies specialization in producing groups of goods, given a large nontraded good sector in each city.

In addition, there is the empirical evidence [Bergsman et al. (1975) and Henderson (1986a)] that, while the very largest metropolitan areas do exhibit some tendency towards specialization, some large part of their work force is found in a whole spectrum of industrial classifications, unlike smaller urban areas. That evidence may not be inconsistent with the notion of specialization in this paper. Given the above discussion, specialization occurs primarily at the level of a monocentric city contained in a single political jurisdiction, a description that could be given of a smaller urban area. However, a very large metropolitan area may contain several or many specialized industrial centers surrounded by the residences of their work force and governed independently in a jurisdictionally fragmented metropolitan area. In short, a large metropolitan area may contain a number of "cities" that could exist on their own, a notion that is developed later in the paper.

Given these notions that an economy consists of a system of cities of limited efficient sizes, where there are different types specialized in different activities, we can now turn to a formal model of a system of cities. Before examining the system, we must develop a model of a single city and then work up from there.

1.2. Model of a single city

In order to analyze the characteristics of a system of cities, the model of a single city must be chosen carefully. We will utilize a specific functional form model, without explicit spatial dimensions. There are three reasons for this choice of modelling strategy. A sophisticated spatial model of a single city is too cumbersome to develop the properties of a system of cities within a paper of acceptable length and exposition.[2] In fact, it generally takes a whole paper to develop the properties of a single city if a spatial model is used [e.g., Dixit (1973) or Wheaton

---

[2]An exception is the fixed lot size model in Henderson (1977, Chapter 5).

(1974)]. Moreover, that level of detail for a single city adds little or nothing to the analysis of the properties of a system of cities. Second specific functional forms are used in part, because for certain propositions closed form solutions are highly desirable. However, specific functional forms are also chosen over general functional forms because when general functional forms are used in this type of complex model with scale (dis)economies, in developing propositions through comparative statics, various output elasticities with respect to inputs are defined and propositions can only be proved with these elasticities treated as *global* constants [e.g., Hochman (1977)]. It is not clear it is an improvement to implicitly introduce specific functional forms at the point of proving propositions, relative to defining specific functional forms to begin with.

The model of a single city consists of three components – production sector, consumption sector, and the local government sector. We start with the production sector.

1.2.1. Production

Two final outputs are produced in each city. One is the traded good the city specializes in, which is produced with capital and labor under constant returns to scale at the firm level. Firms are subject to a Hicks' neutral shift factor, where increasing industry employment results in increased industry efficiency for all firms. Since such economies of scale are external to the firm, perfect competition and exhaustion of firm revenue by factor payments prevail [Chipman (1970)]; and we may deal with the industry production function

$$X = Ag(N)\hat{N}_0^{\alpha}\hat{K}_0^{1-\alpha}. \tag{1}$$

x, $\hat{N}_0$, and $\hat{K}_0$ are respectively industry output, labor inputs, and capital stock. $g(N)$ is the shift factor, where N is the number of city residents (who divide their time between X production and commuting). The specification of $g(N)$ presumes specialization in X production and would not prior to specialization include residents employed in and commuting to other industries, given we are assuming economies of scale are localization ones. The form of $g(N)$ will be presented below.

The second good produced in the city is a nontraded good, housing. Housing is produced with capital and "land" sites under constant returns to scale; and the industry production function is

$$H = Bl^{\beta}\hat{K}_1^{1-\beta}. \tag{2}$$

l are land sites produced with time, or labor, inputs subject to shift factors; or

$$l = (DN^{-\delta}\hat{K}_2^{\gamma})\hat{N}_2. \tag{3}$$

$\hat{N}_2$ represents total labor resources, or time by residents, devoted to commuting in the city for a *given number of residents* (N) and public capital inputs ($\hat{K}_2$). Thus $\hat{N}_2$ indicates the amount of land on the flat featureless plain "claimed" through commuting by a given number of residents. $N^{-\delta}$ represents a spatial complexity factor. If, say, both $\hat{N}_2$ and N double, land sites do not double because, in a spatial world, the new people located on the city edge must spend more time on average getting from their home site to work and back (in a monocentric model) and hence site production is less efficient. Proceeds from site sales ("rents") are exhausted by payments to $\hat{N}_2$ (i.e., rents are distributed within the city). For more on this "as if" model of a spatial world, see Henderson (1972, 1974).

$\hat{K}_2$ represents public investment in transport facilities (roads) which reduces commuting time needed to produce sites. Note that the introduction of a public sector providing public capital is critical to our understanding of cities. Almost half the space of a city is public capital (including roads and sidewalks). In a growth context, a city cannot form and grow until much of its non-malleable public capital has been laid out. In general (in)efficient operations of local governments in providing infrastructure critically affect the sizes of cities, as we will discuss later.

Profit-maximization behavior yields normal value of marginal product equals factor price equations for production of X, H, and l, given firms perceive input and output prices as fixed.[3] By substitution of these equations back into the production function we obtain unit cost functions for X and H, where w, r, p_l, p, and q are respectively the local wage rate, the national capital rental rate, the local price of sites, the local price of housing, and the national price of the traded good.

$$q = c_0 w^\alpha r^{1-\alpha} g(N)^{-1}, \tag{4}$$

$$p = c_1 p_l^\beta r^{1-\beta}, \tag{5}$$

where c_0 and c_1 are defined in footnote 4.[4] Throughout the paper to simplify notation, we redefine groups of parameters as new constants, c_i, in footnotes. (4) can be conveniently rearranged to express city wages as a function of city size and variables exogenous to a single city, traded good prices (q) and capital rentals (r).

$$w = c_0^{-1/\alpha} q^{1/\alpha} r^{(\alpha-1)/\alpha} g(N)^{1/\alpha}. \tag{4'}$$

In (4'), holding output and capital rental prices fixed, wages rise with city size given positive scale effects.

Finally, there are on the production side, full employment equations for the city where

$$\hat{N}_0 + \hat{N}_2 = N, \tag{6}$$

$$\hat{K}_0 + \hat{K}_1 + \hat{K}_2 = K. \tag{7}$$

---

[3]Note for l, this implies $w = p_l l / \hat{N}_2$.
[4]$c_0 \equiv A^{-1} \alpha^{-\alpha} (1-\alpha)^{\alpha-1}$ and $c_1 \equiv B^{-1} \beta^{-\beta} (1-\beta)^{\beta-1}$.

1.2.2. Consumption

Residents have utility functions of the form $U = E^1 x_1^{a_1} x_2^{a_2} \ldots x_n^{a_n} h^b$ where we define $f \equiv \sum_{j=1}^{n} a_j + b$. x_j are traded goods, one of which is produced by this type of city and exported and the others imported; and h is housing consumption. Individuals derive income from wage payments and pay equal per person taxes to finance public transport expenditures. Thus

$$y = w - r\hat{K}_2/N. \tag{8}$$

y is income, and $r\hat{K}_2/N$ are local taxes financing $\hat{K}_2$. In this presentation of the system of cities model we assume capital rentals are distributed to owners outside the cities or outside the country, so that they are not spent on urban housing. The algebraically more complicated case, where capital rentals are spent in cities is presented in Hochman (1977) and Henderson (1982b).

Given utility-maximizing behavior by urban residents, we can derive demand equations for x_j and h where for housing, for example, total city demand is

$$H = \frac{b}{f}(yN)p^{-1}, \quad f \equiv \sum_{j=1}^{n} a_j + b. \tag{9}$$

Substituting these demand equations into the utility function, we get the indirect utility function

$$U = E\left(\sum_{j=1}^{n} q_j^{-a_j}\right) y^f p^{-b}, \quad E \equiv E' \sum_{j=1}^{n} (a_j/f)^{a_j}. \tag{10}$$

1.2.3. The local government

A local government is introduced to determine the level of public investment $\hat{K}_2$. In the context of a competitive, costless political process, it is assumed competing potential and incumbent governments seek to maximize the welfare of fully informed voter-residents so as to be re-elected. Given the fixed rental price of capital in national markets, for any city population, the government chooses $\hat{K}_2$ to maximize U in (10).

1.2.4. Solution for a single city

To solve the model we make substitutions of marginal productivity conditions into the basic housing demand [(9)] equals housing supply [(2)] equation. These substitutions after rearrangement yield[5]

$$\hat{N}_2 = (\beta b/f)w^{-1}Ny, \tag{11}$$

---

[5] $c_2 \equiv D^{-\beta} c_1 c_0^{-\beta/\alpha}$.

$$p = c_2 q^{\beta/\alpha} r^{1-\beta/\alpha} N^{\delta\beta} \hat{K}_2^{-\beta\gamma} g(N)^{\beta/\alpha},$$ (12)

$$\hat{K}_1 = ((1-\beta)b/f)Nyr^{-1}.$$ (13)

Next we solve for $\hat{K}_2$ employed by the city. The city perceives r and q as exogenous [thus from (4') w varies only with N]. Into (10) we substitute $y = w - r\hat{K}_2/N$ from (8) and for p from (12). Maximizing U with respect to $\hat{K}_2$, for any N, and solving $(\partial U/\partial \hat{K}_2)/\hat{K}_2 = 0$ yields

$$\hat{K}_2 = (\gamma\beta b/f)yr^{-1}N.$$ (14)

Note that (11), (13) and (14) are industry or city demand functions for factors in different uses and they display the normal income, price, and scale properties of these functions. For example, in (14), public investment rises with income and city population and falls with opportunity cost.

Finally, we solve for city income, output, and utility levels substituting into (8) for $\hat{K}_2$ yields

$$y = (f/f + \gamma\beta b))w.$$ (15)

To solve for city output, we substitute in for $\hat{K}_0$, $\hat{N}_0$, y, and w to get[6]

$$X = c_3 g(N)^{1/\alpha}(r^{-1}q)^{(1-\alpha)/\alpha}.$$ (16)

Finally, substituting into (10) for y from (15), for w from (4'), for p from (12), and for $\hat{K}_2$ from (14) yields[7]

$$U = E_0 \left(\prod_{j=1}^{n} q_j^{-a_j} \right) [c_0^{-1} qr^{-1} g(N)]^{(f-b\beta(1-\gamma))/\alpha} r^{f-b} N^{\beta b(\gamma-\delta)}.$$ (17)

Note that the usual partial equilibrium properties of $dU/dq > 0$ and $\partial U/\partial r < 0$ hold (where from (20) below we must constrain $f - b\beta(1-\gamma) - \alpha(f-b) > 0$).

There are several equivalent ways to solve for city size. Henderson (1986b) proves that in a general equilibrium context, the only *stable* solution corresponds to one where, at the local level, $\partial U/\partial N = 0$. Alternatively this size may be obtained through the direct actions of economic agents, such as competitive land developers who may set up cities in a national economy. These developers earn temporary profits in inefficient solutions by setting up and selling lots in cities of more efficient sizes than current cities. Finally, $\partial U/\partial N = 0$ could be achieved by local governments limiting city size to this utility-maximizing level, through a set of zoning ordinances. Here we solve $\partial U/\partial N = 0$, under the assumption that a city faces fixed capital rental and traded good prices, or that it is one of many cities producing its export good and borrowing in capital markets.

---

[6] $c_3 \equiv c_0^{-/\alpha}\alpha^{-1}(f - b\beta(1-\gamma))(f+\gamma\beta b)^{-1}.$
[7] $E_0 \equiv E[f/(f+\gamma\beta b)]^{f+\gamma\beta b}[\beta^\beta B(1-\beta)^{1-\beta}D^\beta(\gamma\beta b/f)^{\gamma\beta}]^b.$

Before solving $\partial U/\partial N = 0$ for the efficient N, we must specify the nature of the external localization economies function $g(N)$. To do so, we borrow from the econometric literature on the nature of localization economies [Henderson (1986b)] and specify that

$$g(N) = e^{-\phi/N}. \tag{18}$$

This is a declining degree, or elasticity, of scale economy formulation where

$$\frac{dg(\cdot)}{dN} \cdot \frac{N}{g(\cdot)} = \phi/N > 0.$$

Apart from the fact that (18) is justified from empirical work, it is critical in the overall model to break the logarithmic linearity of the system of equations so as to get unique, non-infinitesimal and non-infinite, efficient city sizes. This can be done either by having the degree of scale economies peter out, so the agglomeration benefits of increasing city size die out, by having the degree of diseconomies in land site production escalate (i.e., increasing congestion) so urban costs of living escalate with city size increases [Henderson (1974)], or by having city size itself be an increasing disamenity in the utility function [Henderson (1982a,b)].

Substituting in (18) for $g(N)$ into (17) and solving $\partial U/\partial N = 0$ we get efficient city size is[8]

$$N = \frac{\phi}{\alpha}\left(\frac{f - b\beta(1-\gamma)}{\beta b(\delta - \gamma)}\right)$$

$$= \frac{\phi}{\alpha}(\psi), \quad \psi \equiv \frac{f - b\beta(1-\gamma)}{\beta b(\delta - \gamma)}. \tag{19}$$

Existence of positive city sizes and satisfaction of second order conditions together require $f - b\beta(1-\gamma)$, $\beta b(\delta - \gamma) > 0$, or $\psi > 0$. $(f - b\beta(1-\gamma))/(\beta b(\delta - \gamma))$ is a common parameter collection throughout the paper, so we redefine it as ψ. Note in (19), if consumers' taste parameter for housing b/f rises, if the land intensity of housing production β rises, or if spatial complexity parameter δ rises, efficient city sizes fall. All of these factors lead to greater increases in costs of living as a city's size expands. Either more land is utilized by consumers increasing commuting distances or commuting becomes more costly. Finally, if the productivity of infrastructure investments, γ, rises, efficient city sizes rise since costs of living rise more slowly. Other properties implicit in (19) will be noted later.

We have now solved for basic variables in terms of prices (r and q) facing cities.

---

[8]Note that in deriving $\partial U/\partial N = 0$, it is equivalent either to assume we are choosing the optimal N for any $\hat{K}_2$ and then substituting for $\hat{K}_2$ (if necessary) from (14) or to substitute in first for the optimal $\hat{K}_2$ as a function of r and N as we have done and then optimize.

For some purposes it is necessary to also solve for economic variables in terms of the aggregate capital-to-labor usage in a city. By substituting into the full employment equations we get

$$r = qA(1-\alpha)g(N)c_4^{-\alpha}k^{-a},$$ (20)

where k is the city's total capital-to-labor ratio, or usage, and

$$c_4 \equiv (1-\alpha)(f + \gamma\beta b)/(f - b\beta(1-\gamma) - \alpha(f-b)).$$

Note that $c_4 > 0$ requires that $f - b\beta(1-\gamma) - \alpha(f-b) > 0$. Since all other variables are functions of r, q, and N, they can be solved in terms of q, N, and k, by substituting in for r. We note[9]

$$w = [qA\alpha c_4^{1-\alpha}]g(N)k^{1-\alpha},$$

$$U_0 = E_1 \left(\prod_{j=1}^{n} q_j^{-a_j} \right) (qg(N))^{f-b} (c_4 k)^{f-b\beta(1-\gamma)-\alpha(f-b)} N^{-b\beta(\delta-\gamma)},$$ (17')

$$X = c_5 N k^{1-\alpha} g(N).$$ (16')

2. Basic properties of a system of cities

2.1. General equilibrium properties

Using the equations for a single city we can solve for the characteristics of equilibrium in a system composed of n types of cities. We do so looking at equilibrium in national markets given equilibrium conditions in individual cities. We assume capital and labor are perfectly mobile within the economy. At this point subscripting is introduced, where N_j, ϕ_j, α_j, w_j, q_j, etc. refer to values of parameters and variables for the jth type of city with the first type, where $q_1 = 1$ is chosen as the numeraire. The parameters of housing and site production and all utility functions are the same across cities. Only the production sector differs.

2.1.1. Variations in sizes across city types

First, re-examining the city size equation we see that

$$N_j = \frac{\phi_j}{\alpha_j}\psi$$ (19')

where ψ in (19) is common to all cities. Thus comparing different types of cities,

---

[9] $E_1 \equiv E_0 A^{f-b} \alpha^{(f-b\beta(1-\gamma))} (1-\alpha)^{-b+\beta b(1-\gamma)}$ and $c_5 \equiv Ac_4^{(1-\alpha)}(f-b\beta(1-\gamma))/(f+\gamma\beta b).$

N_j is a linear function of ϕ_j/α_j, where $\partial N/\partial\phi > 0$, $\partial N/\partial\alpha < 0$. City sizes increase with the degree of scale economies which indicate a city's ability to pay higher wages for a given capital rental. Sizes also increase with capital intensity in production, where increased capital intensity means that a city can support a given wage-capital rental ratio with less population and a lower cost of living. As $\phi/\alpha \to 0$, city size becomes negligible. We could think of goods with low levels of scale (ϕ) as being rural or agricultural products, where our "city" becomes a family farm or small village. That is, there is nothing in the model which limits the inclusion of an agricultural sector, defined as the smallest type of "city".

It is easy to see the difficulties in moving to general functional forms from specific functional forms by considering equation (19') and its derivation. ϕ and α are global parameters. In a general functional form context they should be parameters defined at the margin. Without knowing intra-marginal movements of ϕ and α, one could not conclude that $\partial N/\partial\phi > 0$ or $\partial N/\partial\alpha < 0$. Worse, without globally restricting ϕ and α, we cannot conclude that $U(\cdot)$ in (17) has a single maximum point with respect to N or that it has a maximum point at all. In short, without imposing a number of strong assumptions on the general functional form model one cannot proceed as we are doing. The assumptions in this paper about functional forms are made for this reason.

2.1.2. Variations in prices across city types

To solve for the other properties of a system of cities we impose equilibrium in national labor, capital, and output markets. For labor market equilibrium, between any pairs of cities, laborers must be equally well off so that they do not move. Therefore, $U_j = U_1$ and from (17) solving out of q_j we get

$$q_j^{1/\alpha_j}/q_1^{1/\alpha_1} \equiv q_j^{1/\alpha_j} = (Z_1/Z_j)^{r^{(\alpha_1-\alpha_j)/(\alpha_1\alpha_j)}}, \tag{21}$$

where

$$Z_i \equiv c_0^{-1/\alpha_i} g_i(N_i)^{1/\alpha_i} N_i^{-\psi}.$$

(21) can be used to solve for the variations in wages and costs of living across city types. We form the ratio w_j/w_1 using (4') and them substitute in (21) to get

$$w_j/w_1 = (N_j/N_1)^{1/\psi}. \tag{22}$$

For housing prices we form the ratio of p_j/p_1 from (12) after substituting in (14) for $\hat{K}_2$, and then substitute in (21) to get

$$p_j/p_1 = (N_j/N_1)^{1/\psi}. \tag{23}$$

Given $\psi > 0$, (22) and (23) unambiguously state that in comparing types of cities both wages and housing prices are *greater* as the size of cities rise across city types, for *equal utility levels* across cities. The point of course is intuitive. Wages and cost-of-living rise with city size because respectively scale economy benefit are greater and commuting distances and the corresponding housing costs are greater. To maintain equal utility across cities, in the absence of other considerations, they must each rise by the same percentage, as city size increases. The fact that wages and costs-of-living rise with city size is documented empirically in the numerous wage-amenity studies [e.g., Rosen (1978), Izraeli (1979), Getz and Huang (1978), Hoch (1977)].

2.1.3. Variations in capital usage

Hochman (1977) pointed out that it is important to note how capital usage varies across city types. From national capital market equilibrium, $r_j = r_1$. Equating r_j and r_1 in (20) and substituting in for c_4 from (20) and q_j from (21) yields

$$\frac{k_j}{k_1} = \left| \frac{\alpha_1(f - b\beta(1-\gamma)) - \alpha_j(f-b))}{\alpha_j(f-b\beta(1-\gamma)) - \alpha_1(f-b))} \right| \left(\frac{N_j^{1/\psi}}{N_1} \right). \tag{24}$$

By straight differentiation after substituting in (19') it can be shown that

$$\partial(k_j/k_1)/\partial\alpha_j < 0, \qquad \partial(k_j/k_1)/\partial\phi_j > 0 \quad \text{and} \quad dk_j/k_j = dk_1/k_1.$$

A city's capital usage increases as scale economies and capital intensity in export production increase. That is, for

$$\phi_j = \phi_1 [\alpha_j = \alpha_1], \ k_j > k_1 \quad \text{if} \quad \alpha_j < \alpha_1 [\phi_j > \phi_1].$$

However, neither $\alpha_j < \alpha_1$ nor $N_j > N_1$ necessarily imply $k_j > k_1$.

This distinction between the overall capital usage of a city (including capital usage in housing and social overhead capital) and capital intensity in production of the city's good is critical. Equally critical is the fact that, potentially, capital intensive goods could be produced in high labor usage cities. A sufficient condition for the type j city to have relatively high capital usage ($k_j > k_1$) is that both X_j be relatively capital intensive ($\alpha_j < \alpha_1$) and the jth type city be larger ($\phi_j/\alpha_j > \phi_1/\alpha_1$). However, even if $\alpha_j < \alpha_1$, k_1 can exceed k_j if $\phi_1/\alpha_1 > \phi_j/\alpha_j$ and 1 type cities are larger, hence have higher wage costs, and thus spend more per capita on capital in housing and public transportation. We will show later that if $k_1 > k_j$ when $\alpha_1 > \alpha_j$, the stability of equilibrium comes into question and economies will tend to completely specialize if they engage in international trade.

2.2. The numbers and size distribution of cities in a closed economy

To solve for the ratio of numbers of each type of city, denoted by m_j, we equate national demand and supply for each type of good. National supply is $m_j X_j$.

National demand, providing all people have the same logarithmic linear utility functions is $(a_j/f)Iq_j^{-1}$, where I is national income net of local taxes. Thus for any two types of cities

$$m_j X_j/(m_1 X_1)=(a_j/a_1)q_j^{-1}$$

or substituting in (16) for X_j and X_1 and then (21) for q_j

$$\frac{m_j}{m_1}=\frac{a_j}{a_1}\frac{\alpha_j}{\alpha_1}\left(\frac{N_j}{N_1}\right)^{-1-1/\psi}$$

$$=\frac{a_j}{a_1}\frac{\alpha_j}{\alpha_1}\left(\frac{\alpha_j/\phi_j}{\alpha_1/\phi_1}\right)^{-1-1/\psi} \tag{25}$$

m_j/m_1 increases as a_j/a_1 (relative demand for X_j) increases, and as α_j/α_1 increases or ϕ_j/ϕ_1 declines and hence N_j/N_1 declines from equation (19'). The later result simply indicates that the same relative amount of X_j would be produced in more but smaller cities.

From (19) and (25) it should be clear that the sizes and numbers of each type of city reflect underlying demand and supply conditions in the economy. *Moreover, any regularities in the patterns of cities and their size distribution imply very specific demand and supply conditions.* Location and regional specialists often assert two regularities in the size distribution of cities. It is instructive to note these and explore their implications in one illustrative context. The point is to illustrate the direct link between demand and supply patterns in national output and spatial patterns of cities.

The two asserted regularities are the geometric series rule and the rank size rule. For the former we first index our different types of cities so that $N_1>N_2>\cdots>N_n$. Given this ranking the rule is that the numbers of cities by size and type form a geometric series where, for some parameter θ,

$$m_j=m_1(\theta)^{j-1},\quad \theta>1.$$

The rank size rule states that if we rank all cities in the economy so the largest is ranked 1 and the sth largest s, and we multiply rank by population for each city, the multiple is the same number (equals the population of the largest city) for all cities in the economy. Since the rule applies to a continuum of cities, whereas a system of cities implies discrete groupings, the following interpretation is usually utilized [Beckmann 1958)] and is adapted to the present model. Suppose there are other, as yet, unspecified effects on city sizes so that cities of each type are distributed about the predicted population N_j in (19) when the predicted N_j is the population of the median city of that type, $N_{j\hat{m}}$. We examine the rank size rule as applied to these median cities of each type. The rank of city size $N_{j\hat{m}}$ is $R(N_{j\hat{m}})$, where $R(_{j\hat{m}})=\Sigma_{i=1}^{j} m_i-\frac{1}{2}m_j$. The rank size rule implies $R(N_{j\hat{m}})N_{j\hat{m}}=R(N_{i\hat{m}})N_{l\hat{m}}$ all i, j.

Suppose we impose both rules and assume that $1/\psi \to 0$ so that

$$m_j \approx m_1 \left(\frac{a_j}{a_1}\right) \left(\frac{\alpha_j}{\alpha_1}\right)^2 \frac{\phi_1}{\phi_j},$$

where $1/\psi = b\beta(\gamma-\delta)/(f-b\beta(1-\gamma))$ must be small if coefficients take expected values such as $b/f = 0.2$, $\beta = 0.1$ and $(\gamma-\delta) < 0.5$. Then combining rules we can show that

$$(\phi_j/\alpha_j) = (\phi_1/\alpha_1) \left| \frac{\theta-1}{\theta^j + \theta^{j-1} - 2} \right|$$

$$a_j \alpha_j = (a_1 \alpha_1) \left| \frac{1 - \theta^{-1}}{1 + \theta^{-1} - 2\theta^{-j}} \right| \tag{26}$$

ϕ_j/α_j and $a_j\alpha_j$ are decreasing fractions of respectively ϕ_1/α_1 and $a_1\alpha_1$ as we move down the hierarchy.

Given these rules, econometric information on a few parameters places strong restrictions on the values of other parameters. We illustrate this, drawing from empirical work done on Saskatchewan, Canada. Schaeffer's (1977) work on Saskatchewan suggests that α_j declines rapidly moving from, say, 0.95 to 0.80 to 0.43 as we move from the largest to the next largest to the smallest (7th ranked) centers, reflecting perhaps increasing capital intensity as we move from service to manufacturing to extract centers. Suppose $\phi_1 = 100$ which is consistent with Henderson (1986). Given these movements in α_j, given $(\phi/\alpha)_1 = 0.105$ and given θ would equal 2 from Berry (1968) for Saskatchewan, the first equation tells us the remaining values of ϕ_j's which by the seventh rank city is very small (0.24). The second equation implies that the a_j change very little, with the ratio of a_2/a_1 being 0.59 and of a_7/a_1 being 0.55. Thus given information only on the α_j's and ϕ_1 the empirical regularities in the size distribution of cities would tell us values of the remaining ϕ_j and all a_j/a_1. Note that the a_j's here are shares in the value of regional output, not local demand parameters per se, since Saskatchewan is an open, rather than closed, economy.

In summary, regardless of whether the particular parametric values we have used are accurate or not, empirical phenomena such as the rank size rule and the geometric series rule governing the numbers of each type of city convey information about how underlying demand and supply parameters must vary across types of cities. The size distribution of cities is not an accident of nature but is directly linked to the regional composition of output and production conditions.

2.3. The impact of government policies on the system of cities

Any government policy which affects the national composition of output will affect the size distribution of cities, as should be clear from the previous section.

In this section we examine examples of two policies which are often perceived as having strong spatial impacts.

2.3.1. Urban infrastructure subsidies

Suppose infrastructure investments, $\hat{K}_2$, in cities are subsidized by the national government from revenue raised by a national income tax. This alters the per person income equation, (8), so it becomes

$$y = w(1-t) - r(1-s)\hat{K}_2/N. \tag{8a}$$

t is the national income tax rate and s is matching rate, or the proportion of local public infrastructure costs the national government will pay. Following Henderson (1982a), where a similar model is utilized, this program affects the local demand for infrastructure investment and local utility levels, as well as other variables. Specifically, (14) and (17) now become

$$\hat{K}_2^* = \hat{K}_2(1-s)^{-1} \tag{14a}$$

$$U^* = U(1-t)^{f + \gamma\beta b}(1-s)^{-\gamma\beta b} \tag{14b}$$

where $\hat{K}_2$ and U are the non-tax expressions in (14) and (17) respectively. For unchanged factor prices, the subsidy causes the use of $\hat{K}_2$ to rise, while t and s have respectively a negative and positive impact on utility levels.

What is the impact overall on the system of cities of this subsidy? We distinguish three cases.

Uniform subsidy to all cities. If all cities face the same subsidy rate for infrastructure investment, in terms of the "urban system" the subsidy passes neutrally through the system, leaving city sizes and relative numbers of each type of city unaffected. Note in (17a) the subsidy does not affect the N terms in U critical for solving for equilibrium city size. Second, because each city faces the same subsidy rate, the impact on each city type is the same and their relative positions are unchanged. Of course, prices and the national allocation of capital between urban infrastructure and other uses will be adversely affected as with any distortion of this type.

Uniform subsidy to just one type of city. Suppose the national government decides to favor any location which specializes in the production of a good which it wants to favor, such as iron and steel or autos. So it offers a subsidy on infrastructure investments to only this type of city, say the jth type of city producing x_j, financed out of national income tax revenues. Note given U^* for j type cities remains as in (17a), the efficient sizes of j type cities are unchanged. However, the numbers of j type cities are affected. If we resolve for q_j in eq. (21)

now we get

$$q_j = (Z_1/Z_j)^{\alpha_j} \cdot r^{(\alpha_1 - \alpha_j)/\alpha_1}(1 - s_j)^{\alpha_j \gamma \beta b/(f - b\beta(1 - \gamma))},$$

indicating that the relative cost of producing the output of the favored type of city falls, which leads to an increase in the numbers of that type of city. With appropriate substitutions, we can solve

$$(m_j/m_1)^* = (m_j/m_1)(1 - s_j)^{- \gamma \beta b/(f - b\beta(1 - \gamma))}$$

where (m_j/m_1) is the equilibrium *pre*-subsidy ratio of j type cities and $(m_j/m_1)^*$ the higher equilibrium ratio after subsidization. Apart from distorting the use of $\hat{K}_2$ in j type cities, the impact of subsidizing infrastructure in j type cities would be the same as subsidizing x_j production per se. Note one implication is that any one j type city does not benefit in the long run from the subsidy, because the value of the subsidy is not capitalized into higher wages (or land rents). Through competition amongst cities to become j type cities to get the subsidy, its benefits are dissipated.

Subsidy to just one particular city. Suppose the national government offers the subsidy rate s to only one particular city of type j, and to no other cities. An example would be a country favoring a national capital region, or one particular urban area as a center of commerce. This subsidy is paid out of the national income tax, although it benefits only one small part of country. If U_j is the utility in any other j type city, from (17a), utility in the favored city $\hat{U}_j$ is

$$\hat{U}_j = U_j(1 - s)^{- \gamma \beta b}.$$

For other j type cities, in Figure 1, equilibrium city sizes are at N_j^* where $\partial U_j/\partial N_j = 0$. At that point, in equilibrium $U_j = U_e$, where U_e is the equilibrium

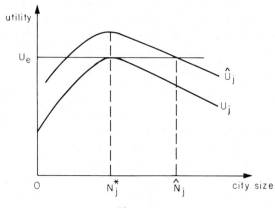

Figure 1.

utility level in national labor markets. However, in the favored city although $\partial \hat{U}_j / \partial N_j = 0$ at N_j^*, at N_j^* the $\hat{U}_j$ curve lies above U_j. With unrestricted entry the favored city will expand in size to $\hat{N}_j$ where $\hat{U}_j$ has declined to U_e. In that case, the impact of the subsidy is to attract people to this favored city, driving up costs-of-living relative to wages, until the potentially beneficial effect of the subsidy on this one city is dissipated through in-migration. This is a caricature of national capital regions in many countries, which are favored with special infrastructure investments.

A situation such as Figure 1 is ripe for restrictions on entry into the favored city. Suppose entry to the city can be costlessly regulated and that effective lump-sum residence fees can be charged. The residence or entry fees arise because if, say, city size is restricted to N_j^*, excluded residents would be willing to pay a premium equal to the monetized value of $\hat{U}(N_j^*) - U_e$ to live in the favored city. In a spatial model, entry could be regulated through zoning ordinances restricting the number of dwelling units. The premium would then be on the key to entry – obtaining a dwelling unit – and this premium could be a lump-sum rent surcharge above opportunity costs. That is, the benefits of living in the favored city would be capitalized into land prices, rather than dissipated by city expansion. In our nonspatial model the premium could equivalently be viewed as a direct residence fee imposed by the owner(s) of the site upon which the city is situated. These solutions are detailed in Henderson (1982a). In practice it is difficult to directly restrict city size with direct entry fees and/or effective restrictions on numbers of dwelling units. While land development may be officially restricted, it is hard to prohibit residents from crowding into existing developments or from "squatting" in illegal developments.

2.3.2. Minimum wage policies

In (22), we saw that nominal wages rise monotonically with city size. If we again index our city types so that $N_1 > N_2 > \cdots N_n$, then $w_1 > w_2 > \cdots > w_n$. A minimum wage law might be expected to set a floor on wages somewhere between w_1 and w_n. We assume effective minimum-wage policies are set and adjusted to meet some social or political criterion.

For example, in a closed economy, a national minimum-wage policy might effectively be implemented to fix all nominal wages at the level prevailing in some visible industry, say the k industry in city type k where $N_1 > \cdots > N_k > \cdots > N_n$. Turning to U defined in terms of w and r (see eqs. (4) and (17)), for all cities smaller than type k, if, for $i = k+1, \ldots, n$, w_i must equal w_k and given that r's are equalized across cities, then

$$N_i^{\beta b(\gamma - \delta)} = N_k^{\beta b(\gamma - \delta)}.$$

This implies

$$N_i = N_k, \quad i = k+1, \ldots, n.$$

The intuitive explanation is that the government has intervened on the production side in type i cities to equalize their wages to type k cities. Equilibrium of population allocation then requires that type i cities have the same consumption conditions as type k cities, which requires city sizes to be the same. Since type k cities are not regulated their sizes are unchanged and are determined by the condition $\partial U / \partial N_k = 0$. So it must be that sizes of cities $k+1$ through n increase to N_k. But then sizes of type i cities can no longer be determined by the condition $\partial U / \partial N_i = 0$. Figure 2 depicts the resulting situation in type i cities and assumes that entry to type i cities is not restricted.

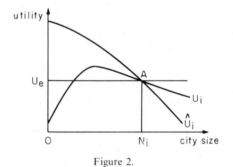

Figure 2.

U_i is utility for city type i that would exist if i cities paid unregulated competitive wages, given (new) equilibrium prices; and N_i^* is equilibrium city size. Regulated utility is $\hat{U}_i$. Given a fixed w, U_i declines continuously for $N_i \geq 0$ because consumption conditions deteriorate continuously. Equilibrium is at A where (1) utility in type i cities equals the opportunity value, (2) producers can pay the minimum wage (i.e., $\hat{U}_i = U_i$), and (3) $N_i = N_k$. $\hat{U}_i$ lies above U_i to the left of A since $w_i < w_i = w_k$; and $\hat{U}_i$ lies below U_i to the right of A since $w_i > w_i = w_k$.

What happens to the relative numbers of cities? For $j = 1, \ldots, k-1$, m_j / m_k is unchanged in eq. (25). For $i = k+1, \ldots, n$, things are different. We can derive eq. (25) through substitutions to the same result. Then in eq. (25) since $N_i = N_k$ for $i = k+1, \ldots, n$

$$\frac{m_i}{m_k} = \frac{a_i}{a_k} \frac{\alpha_i}{\alpha_k}.$$

Comparing this with the expression before the minimum wage which included a N_i, N_k term greater than one, we see that m_i / m_k declines given N_i has risen. This is not surprising.

2.4. Impact of natural resources on a system of cities

The analysis of the impact of natural resources on a system of cities is at a very preliminary stage in the literature. In this section we outline two of the basic ideas put forward so far. The first deals with competition amongst cities for urban sites with favorable amenity endowments. The second deals with modeling the spatial configurations of cities engaged in natural resource using production versus those engaged in footloose production. Neither model meets Beckmann's (1968) call for a general analysis of spatial configurations of primary, intermediate, and final production.

2.4.1. Urban site amenities

Geographic locations have different endowments of amenities which affect consumers and producers. Consumer amenities could be represented by a vector attributes, where through a functional relationship these attributes determine the value of the shift term, E, of the utility function. E could vary with an urban site's climate, access to outdoor recreation alternatives, access to drinking water, and so on. Similarly, producer amenities could affect the value of the shift term, A_j, for each type of city. Such amenities could include natural harbors, access to fresh water, climate, elevation, etc. and their impact on the shift term could differ according the type of good X_j being produced.

Upton (1981) has modeled this type of situation for a single type of city. In our framework, his analysis models equilibrium among all cities of one type, say the jth type. Assume all possible urban sites in the economy have different amenity vectors. Favorable vectors increase the values of E and A_j which from (17) increase potential utility for a given city size. Thus looking at the jth type of cities, given they will be on different quality sites, they will have different utility paths. In our model, each path will have a maximum point at the same N_j but cities on better quality sites will have higher paths (at each city size). Then just as in Figure 1 where cities had different heights to their utility paths because their infrastructure costs varied, with free entry cities with better amenity vectors and higher utility paths will be larger.

In relative terms, the benefits of better amenity vectors will be dissipated by cities on better sites expanding until their cost-of-living increases drive their utility levels down to that prevailing nationally. In absolute terms, citizens in an economy with better selection of urban sites should be better off than citizens in an economy with inferior sites. However, *within* either economy, utility levels cannot differ by urban site quality, given equilibrium in national labor markets.

Formally, modeling equilibrium when urban site qualities and city sizes of the same type differ in size is cumbersome [Upton (1981)]. However, it provides a basis for all cities in an economy being of somewhat different sizes even if they produce the same goods. In terms of the rank size analysis of Section 2.2, it is one way for cities of the same type to deviate in size about the median size city and in theory would permit the rank size rule to hold perfectly.

The next question concerns how to extend this analysis to multiple types of cities. On the production side, different types of production may weight amenities differently and thus different types of cities may have different preferred bundles and hence different willingness-to-pay for any particular bundle. In this context, city types should initially sort themselves out on some basis of production-appropriate amenities. However, we focus on amenities providing equal benefits to all types of cities, such as consumer amenities affecting the E shift factor in (17). Then comparing different types of cities, it seems reasonable that in equilibrium larger *types* of cities would occupy better sites, so that the m_1 cities of type 1 would occupy the best m_1 sites, type 2 cities the next best m_2 sites, and so on. Why is this a reasonable speculation? In the way we have formulated the problem, the factors affecting the E's are like public goods. Larger cities have more people to enjoy the public good benefits and thus are willing to pay more in total for amenities through, say, land rents in an explicit spatial model. Alternatively stated, larger cities have higher rent gradients and higher total urban rents. In competition they thus can pay more for sites of better quality and can bid them away from smaller types of cities.

2.4.2. Natural resources and spatial configurations of cities: The metropolitan area

The second way natural resources appear in a system of cities in the literature [Henderson (1982b)] is in an attempt to explain the phenomenon of metropolitan areas. The analysis so far relates to economies composed of cities that are essentially monocentric. Even today much of the urbanized population in most countries remain in cities that are primarily monocentric. In some countries, however, a significant portion of the urbanized population resides in large multinucleated metropolitan areas. We could interpret these areas as essentially being clusters of cities that would in other circumstances be spatially separate monocentric cities. Different types of cities could cluster together simply to reduce the transport costs of intercity trade among themselves. One limit on this clustering would be the need for cities to spatially disperse to utilize spatially dispersed resources.

To see the forces at work, we first consider the polar case opposite to the case where cities are all monocentric. Consider an economy composed only of metropolitan areas, where we treat metropolitan areas spatially as clusters of monocentric cities. A simple model that generates different size metropolitan areas and inter-metro area trade is as follows. Suppose some types of cities require the use of natural resources in production, while others do not. The natural resources locations are at various spots on the flat plain of the economy and the natural resources are very expensive to transport. Different types of cities using different types of resources would generally be separate spatially and would trade with each other across space.

In addition to natural resource using cities, there are a variety of other types of cities which are footloose. To reduce the costs of intercity trade these footloose cities cluster around the cities using site specific natural resources, to form multinucleated metropolitan areas composed of numerous different cities. Inter-metropolitan trade involves only natural resource products and metropolitan areas are self-sufficient in footloose products.

Specifically assume the footloose type of cities are indexed by t and there are h types of them, or $t = 1, \ldots, h$. For a natural resource city labelled i, the characteristics of its metropolitan area are as follows. Within the metropolitan area the demand (see (25)) for the good produced by the jth footloose city is

$$(a_j/f)(f/(f + \gamma \beta b))\left(w_i^* N_i^* + \sum_{t=1}^{h} w_t N_t m_t^* \right) q_j^{-1},$$

where m_t^* is the number of tth type footloose cities in the metropolitan area. The supply of the jth good (assuming no intra-metropolitan area transport costs of trade) is

$$m_j^* X_j = m_j^* [(f - b\beta(1-\gamma))(f + \gamma \beta b)^{-1}(1 - \alpha_j)^{(1-\alpha_j)/\alpha_j} A_j^{1/\alpha_j}] N_j r^{1 - 1/\alpha_j} q^{-1 + 1/\alpha_j} q_j (N_j)^{1/\alpha_j}$$

from (16). Equating demand and supply for the h footloose goods, substituting in for w from (4) and then for q_i/q_j and q_t/q_j from (21), and rearranging we end up with a set of h linear equations in h unknowns, m_t^*, which may be solved directly by applying Cramer's rule. The solutions take the form

$$m_j^* = \left(\frac{N_i}{N_j} \right)^{1 + 1/\psi} |J_j|/|J_0|$$

(27)

where $|J_j|$ and $|J_0|$ are parametrically defined.[10]

It is, of course, desirable that the m_j^* be large enough numbers to avoid lumpiness problems in solution, which can require that $N_i \gg N_j$ if $\alpha_j a_j/f$ is relatively small.

Metropolitan area population, from (27), is

$$N_{MA} = N_i + (N_i^{1 + 1/\psi}) \left[\sum_{t=1}^{h} \frac{|J_t| N_t^{-1/\psi}}{|J_0|} \right].$$

(28)

Thus in this system of metropolitan areas, area population is an increasing

---

[10]$|J_0|$ is the determinant of a matrix with diagonal elements $(f - b\beta(1-\gamma) - a_t \alpha_t)/(a_t \alpha_t)$ and off-diagonal elements all (-1). $|J_j|$ is that determinant when the jth column is replaced by a column with elements all equal to $(f - b\beta(1-\gamma) - a_i \alpha_i)/(a_i \alpha_i)$. The J_0 matrix is a dominant diagonal matrix and, given $(f - b\beta(1-\gamma) - a_i \alpha_i)/(a_i \alpha_i) > 0$ there is a unique solution with the $m_j^* > 0$ [McKenzie (1960)].

function (at an increasing rate) of the base natural resource city population (N_i). If an economy produces relatively few footloose products and, say, fills its consumption gaps through international imports, then N_{MA} can be shown to be unambiguously smaller than in an economy producing more of its consumption of footloose products or even exporting them. In (27) and (28) $|J_j|/|J_0|$ increases as the range of *produced* footloose goods rises. Thus, the numbers of existing types of footloose cities rise as well as the numbers of new types. Secondly as demand for the jth footloose good is satisfied less and less by international imports, the numbers of j (and all) type cities will rise in the metropolitan area. In short, the need for and extent of clustering will increase. Finally, we note that eq. (28) requires a re-analysis of the size distribution of cities when cities are defined as metropolitan areas. As in (25) the numbers of each type of metropolitan area are defined by the numbers of each type of natural resource cities consistent with national demand for those products.

In the paper we now have modeled two polar cases, one where urban areas are implicitly all monocentric and the other where they are all multinucleated. What is left is to mix the two cases. Unfortunately, to do so immediately introduces city size lumpiness problems, which makes formal analysis cumbersome. However, we can outline the basic ideas. A critical assumption in the metro area analysis is that each core natural resource city of each cluster has sufficient population to support a number of each type of footloose city.[11] However, some resources cities may be so small that they cannot support any footloose cities or only one or two of the smallest types. Moreover, some footloose cities may be so large and/or their national demand sufficiently small that the whole economy can only support one or two of that type of city. Then only one or two metropolitan areas would have that type of footloose production.

These considerations suggest the following pattern of urban areas. Small independent monocentric cities and small metropolitan areas (and farms) would import almost all footloose products and all natural resource products except the one they are specialized in. They would export their own natural resource product to all other types of cities and metropolitan areas. Larger metropolitan areas would be self-sufficient in all except a few footloose products and each self-sufficient in only one natural resource product. They would export some footloose production to independent monocentric cities and smaller metropolitan areas. They would each import from all other types of resource cities (whether independent or contained in metropolitan areas) and import their missing footloose products from the very largest metropolitan areas. These few very

---

[11]Suppose the core city can support $n + 1/z$ type j footloose cities of *efficient* size where n is an integer and $z > 1$. If n is "large" then we can split the $(1/z) N_j$ population among the n cities without significantly altering factor payments; and thus for illustrative purposes we can ignore these fractions. However, if n is "small" (e.g., 1 or 2), splitting $(1/z) N_j$ among n cities will significantly alter conditions.

largest areas would be self-sufficient in all footloose products and in only one natural resource product. They could export a whole range of footloose products to small metropolitan areas and independent monocentric cities, as well as exporting a few footloose products to medium to large size metropolitan areas.

3. Growth and international trade

At the national level in the basic systems of cities model there are constant returns to scale. If we double factor endowments we double the number of cities of each type leaving capital rentals and utility levels unchanged. Given this constant returns to scale feature the basic growth and trade theorems carry over directly and we now turn to these.

3.1. Growth

We start with the one-sector growth model. For a one-sector growth model, there is only one type of city. Thus only one X good is produced in the economy and we normalize its price at 1. National full employment of resources then requires that the k in each city equals the national capital-labor ratio.

Additions to the nation's capital stock are made through investment, where in physical terms units of X may be costlessly converted into units of K. Investment equals savings, where we adopt the standard neoclassical growth theory assumption that all and only capital income is saved (corresponding to the implicit assumption above that no capital rentals are spent on consumption goods in cities).

Differentiating the national k ratio and rearranging we get

$$\dot{k} = k(\dot{K}/\bar{K} - n).$$

$\dot{k} \equiv \mathrm{d}k/\mathrm{d}t$, $\dot{K} \equiv \mathrm{d}\bar{K}/\mathrm{d}t$ which is the growth in national capital stock, and $n \equiv (\mathrm{d}\bar{N}/\mathrm{d}t)/\bar{N}$, which is the exogenous rate of national population growth (plus, if one wants, an exogenous rate of depreciation on capital). $\dot{K}$ equals gross investment which equals savings which in turn by our assumptions equals $r\bar{K}$. Substituting in (26), yields the basic equation of motion

$$\frac{\dot{k}}{k} = A(1-\alpha)g(N)c_4^{-\alpha}k^{-\alpha} - n, \tag{29}$$

whose steady-state solution is given by

$$k^* = (n^{-1}A(1-\alpha)g(N)c_4^{-\alpha})^{1/\alpha}. \tag{30}$$

By textbook proofs [Burmeister and Dobell (1970)] existence and stability follow because α, $1-\alpha>0$ so that (for existence) as $k\to0$, $\dot{k}>0$ and as $k\to\infty$, $\dot{k}<0$. Uniqueness follows from the strict concavity of the $\dot{k}$ function ($d^2\dot{k}/dk^2<0$). The steady-state values of r and U are from (20) and (17′)[12]

$$r^*=n,\tag{31}$$

$$U^*=E_2g(N)^{f-b\beta(1-\gamma)/\alpha}N^{-b\beta(\delta-\gamma)}n^{-(f-b\beta(1'-\gamma)-\alpha(f-b))/\alpha}.\tag{32}$$

As always in this type of model, the steady-state return on capital equals the population growth rate, independent of the technological parameters of the model. Increases in n raise r^* but lower U^* ($c_4>0$ in (20) requires the exponent of n in (32) to be negative).

In a steady-state solution with no technological change, city size in (19) is constant. The number of cities m is thus $m=\bar{N}/N$, where $\bar{N}$ is current national population. Differentiating yields

$$\frac{\dot{m}}{m}=n.\tag{33}$$

This is the fundamental steady-state growth property of a system of cities. The economy grows by churning out new cities at the rate of national population growth.

If there is technological change which affects efficient city sizes, then economic growth may not involve an increase in the number of cities. For example, the "congestion" factor δ in the land supply function (eq. (3)) may decline with technological change. A decline in δ would lead to an increase in efficient city sizes from (19). If there is continuous technological change with δ declining continuously, a new steady-state is difficult to define. However, intermittent technological change with an approach path to a new steady-state is a straight forward exercise, where efficient city sizes increase instantaneously at the time of technological change. This leads to an instantaneous drop in the number of cities (needed to house the instantaneous population) and reconcentration of capital and labor in surviving cities. This change is followed again by expansion in numbers of cities as the population grows over time. Complications arise if, say, public urban infrastructure is immobile so capital cannot all flow out of unneeded cities. This result is abandoned towns and infrastructure which may be later reclaimed as the national population grows. These phenomena are analyzed in detail in Henderson and Ioannides (1981).

A two-sector growth model is a straightforward extension.

---

[12] $E_2\equiv E_0(A\alpha(1-\alpha)^{(1-\alpha)/\alpha})^{f-b\beta(1-\gamma)}$.

Two-sector growth model

In a two-sector growth model there are two types of cities – one type is specialized in the production of an export good and the other type in the production of the investment good. The investment good is X_1, which is produced in m_1 cities are priced at $q_1 = 1$. The consumption good is X_2, which is produced in m_2 cities and priced at q_2. By combining national full employment equations we get the relationship.

$$m_1/m_2 = (N_2/N_1)(k_2 - k)(k - k_1)^{-1},$$ (34)

where k is the economy capital-labor ratio. Now in examining the motion of the economy and evaluating $\dot{k} = k(\dot{K}/\bar{K} - n)$, we have $\dot{K} = m_1 X_1$ by assumption. Secondly, savings equal $r(m_1 K_1 + m_2 K_2)$. Thus, the equation of motion becomes

$$\dot{k} = k\left[rk^{-1}\left(\frac{m_1 N_1}{N} k_1 + \frac{m_2 N_2}{N} k_2 \right) - n \right].$$ (35)

To evaluate (39), we take the

$$\dot{K} = m_1 X_1 = r(m_1 N_1 k_1 + m_2 N_2 k_2)$$

equation and substitute in for X_1 from (16'), for r from (20), and $m_2 N_2$ from the full employment relationship (34) and solve out for k_1 and k_2 in terms of k. The result is substituted back into (34) to solve for m_1 and m_2. These results are substituted into (35) along with eq. (20) for r to get[13]

$$\dot{k} = c_8 k^{1-\alpha_1} - nk.$$ (36)

Therefore, in a steady state where $\dot{k} = 0$,

$$k^* = (c_8/n)^{1/\alpha_1}.$$ (37)

Examining the $\dot{k}/k$ and $d^2 \dot{k}/dk^2$ relationships, existence and uniqueness, as well as

---

[13]The results are

$k_1 = k(c_7 + c_6 - 1)/(c_6 c_7)$

$k_2 = k(c_7 + c_6 - 1)/c_6$

$m_1 = \dfrac{N}{N_1} c_7/(c_7 + c_6 - 1)$

$m_2 = \dfrac{N}{N_2} (c_6 - 1)/(c_7 + c_6 - 1)$

where

$c_6 \equiv (f - b\beta(1-\gamma))/(f - b\beta(1-\gamma) - \alpha_1(f - b))$,

$c_7 \equiv (\alpha_1/\alpha_2)(f - b\beta(1-\gamma) - \alpha_2(f-b))/(f - b\beta(1-\gamma) - \alpha_1(f-b))(N_2/N_1)^{1/\psi}$ and

$c_8 \equiv A_1(1-\alpha_1)g_1(N_1)(c_4(c_6 + c_7 - 1)/c_6 c_6)^{-\alpha_1}.$

stability follow immediately by standard proofs, given $1 - \alpha_1$, $\alpha_1 > 0$. By substituting into (25) and (22b) for r and U, we get the new steady-state values:[14]

$$r^* = n,$$
$$U^* = c_9(n)^{-(f - b\beta(1 - \gamma) - a_2\alpha_2)/\alpha_1}. \tag{38}$$

What happens to cities in steady-state equilibrium? From equations in footnote 13, m_1/m_2 is a parametrically defined constant. Therefore, from the full employment equation

$$\dot{m}_1/m_1 = \dot{m}_2/m_2 = n. \tag{39}$$

As in a one-sector model, growth occurs through growth in the numbers of cities, not through growth in city size. In a multisector model, the numbers of different types of cities grow at the same rate, the rate of national population growth.

3.2. International trade

In examining international trade theorems, the first task is to develop the conditions under which economies will completely specialize when engaged in international trade. For unspecialized economies we can then apply textbook versions of the factor price equalization, Rybczynski, and Stolper–Samuelson theorems to an economy composed of only two types of cities.

Stability and specialization

We assume an economy which could potentially produce two traded goods, X_1 and X_2, and have two types of cities; and we assume X_2 is relatively capital intensive, or that $\alpha_1 > \alpha_2$. A basic question is whether, when the economy engages in international trade, it will completely specialize in the production of only one traded good and hence have only one type of city. *A necessary condition for nonspecialization is that, given $\alpha_1 > \alpha_2$, $k_1 < k_2$. That is, the capital intensive good must be produced in the high capital usage city.* If the labor intensive good is produced in the high capital usage city, the economy will completely specialize in trade. This condition is similar to that in Neary (1978) which states that the good which is capital intensive in value terms must be capital intensive in physical terms for stability, or that in Jones (1968) for the Rybczynski and Stolper–Samuelson theorems to hold simultaneously which states that the good which is capital intensive at the margin must be capital intensive on average.

Stability of nonspecialization can be examined in a traditional framework or in

---

[14] $c_9 \equiv E_0 F_2^{a_2} F_1^{(f - b\beta(1 - \gamma) - a_2\alpha_2)/\alpha_1}$ where $F_i = \alpha_i^{\alpha_i}(1 - \alpha_i)^{(1 - \alpha_i)} A_i g_i(N_i) N_i^{-\alpha_i/\psi}$.

a more recent framework proposed by Neary (1978). Both yield the same conclusion but we follow Neary. Within each city competitive factor markets always clear to ensure local full employment of factors which in turn ensures national full employment. Within these local markets, firms' competition for factors ensures that unit production costs always rise to meet the world price level; competition for factors always eliminates profits. The stability question is whether from any initial trade equilibrium we will return to that equilibrium when the allocation of factors *between* types of cities is shocked so that $U_1 \neq U_2$ and $r_1 \neq r_2$. After the shock capital and labor move among types of cities in response to factor return differentials. Assuming resources are always fully employed, the adjustment equations are

$$d(N_1 m_1)/dt = d_1(U_1 - U_2) \quad \text{and} \quad d(K_1 m_1)/dt = d_2(r_1 - r_2).$$

Differentiating and substituting in the economy full employment equations and doing a Taylor series expansion of U_i and r_i about the initial equilibrium values of K_1^* and N_1^* (where potentially $U_1 = U_2$, $r_1 = r_2$), we end up with the equations $\dot{\pi} = A\pi$, where $\pi_k = K_1 - K_1^*$. Stability or convergence over time to the solution K_1^*, N_1^* requires the matrix A to have a dominant negative diagonal [McKenzie (1960)]. In our model, this requires $k_2 > k_1$ when $\alpha_1 > \alpha_2$, which is the condition for stability stated above.

In the discussion of trade theorems below which are applied to a non-specialized economy we assume $k_2 > k_1$, given $\alpha_1 > \alpha_2$. Earlier we showed that a sufficient but not necessary condition for this is $N_2 > N_1$. We should add that instability of nonspecialized trade equilibrium for $k_2 < k_1$ suggests that there may be problems with stability in autarky. In particular, Hicksian static "stability" conditions do not hold, as in Hochman (1977).

We now turn to the standard trade theorems – the Rybczynski, Stolper–Samuelson, and factor price equalization theorems. We prove the theorems in the context of our model, and discuss their implications for interpretation of urban phenomena.

The Rybczynski theorem states that when an open economy faces fixed terms of trade (TOT), if its national capital-to-labor ratio increases, the output of its capital intensive good rises relative to its labor intensive good (the theorem may also be stated in terms of absolutes). For an urban economy this means as relative capital abundance increases, the relative number of X_2 producing cities will increase. If these are larger cities this means that the ratio of large to small cities will increase in the economy.

Clearly this theorem has strong implications for the size distribution of cities in an economy. Relative increases in the abundance of one factor to another in an economy will lead to relative increases or decreases in the ratio of large to small cities and the degree of urban concentration in the economy.

To prove the theorem we investigate the change in $\hat{X}_1/\hat{X}_2 = (m_1 X_1)/(m_2 X_2)$ as

$\hat{k}$ increases. First, we note that N_1 and N_2 are fixed from eq. (19); and, from (20) and (21), if the TOT are fixed then so are r, k_1 and k_2. Therefore, from eq. (16'), X_1 and X_2 are fixed. Therefore, total outputs, $\hat{X}_1$ and $\hat{X}_2$, vary only as m_1 and m_2 vary, where $d(\hat{X}_1/\hat{X}_2)/d(m_1/m_2)>0$. To investigate the change in m_1 and m_2 we differentiate (34) (given k_1 and k_2 are fixed) to get

$$d(m_1/m_2)d\hat{k}|_{\hat{q}^2}=(N_2/N_1)\frac{(k_1-k_2)}{(\hat{k}-k_1)^2}<0 \quad \text{iff} \quad k_2>k_1.$$

Thus if $\hat{k}$ increases, if the type 2 city has relatively high capital usage, m_1/m_2 falls and thus the relative output of the high capital usage rises. Note, however, that the Rybczynski theorem is stated in terms of capital intensive goods, not high capital usage cities. But, for countries facing fixed TOT, nonspecialization in trade requires that high capital usage cities are ones producing capital intensive goods. Thus the Rybczynski theorem holds in our model.

The Stopler–Samuelson theorem states that for an open economy, if the relative price of a traded good increases, the return to the factor used intensively in producing that good will rise and return to the other factor will fall. From (21) and (17)

$$\partial r/\partial(q_2) \qquad \text{iff} \quad \alpha_1 > \alpha_2,$$
$$\partial U/\partial(q_2)<0 \quad \text{iff} \quad \alpha_1 > \alpha_2.$$

Unlike the Rybczynski theorem, which required assumptions about k_1 and k_2 imposed through stability requirements, this theorem holds without qualification.

Note if q_2 rises because of a trade policy (or otherwise), this policy has spatial impacts. Tariff policies which, for example, raise the relative price of X_2 will lead to an expansion in X_2 production. This will be accomplished by an increase in the number of cities devoted to X_2 production. If these happen to be larger cities, this will increase the ratio of large to small cities and the degree of urban concentration. Undoubtedly many countries today which are concerned because their populations are crowding into large cities are simultaneously pursuing trade and other national policies which are inadvertently encouraging this urban concentration.

Finally, there is the factor price equalization theorem. This theorem states that if traded good prices are equalized across countries, so are factor returns. In the version applicable to an urban economy, factor returns refer to capital rentals and utility levels, not wages, since wages are not even equalized within economies. If production technology and urban characteristics are identical between any two economies, factor price equalization for r follows directly from eq. (21) and for U follows from eq. (17) given equalized r's.

References

Alexandersson, G. (1959) *The industrial structure of American cities*. Lincoln: The University of Nebraska Press.

Beckmann, M.J. (1958) 'City hierarchies and distribution of city size', *Economic Development and Cultural Change*, 6:243–48.

Beckmann, M.J. (1968) *Location theory*. New York: Random House.

Bergsman, J., P. Greenston and R. Healy (1975) 'A classification of economic activities based on location patterns', *Journal of Urban Economics*, 2:1–28.

Berry, B. (1968) *Geography of market centers and retail distribution*. Englewood Cliffs: Prentice-Hall.

Burmeister, E. and R. Dobell (1970) *Mathematical theories of economic growth*. New York: The Macmillan Co.

Chipman, J.S. (1970) 'External diseconomies of scale and competitive equilibrium', *Quarterly Journal of Economics*, 84:347–85.

Christaller, W. (1966) *The central places of southern Germany*. Englewood Cliffs: Prentice-Hall.

Dixit, A. (1973) 'The optimum factory town', *Bell Journal of Economics and Management Science*, 4:637–654.

Getz, M. and Y. Huang (1978) 'Consumer revealed preference for environmental goods'. *Review of Economics and Statistics*, 449–458.

Henderson, J.V. (1972) 'The sizes and types of cities: a general equilibrium model', Unpublished Ph.D. dissertation, University of Chicago.

Henderson, J.V. (1974) 'The sizes and types of cities', *American Economic Review*, 64:640–656.

Henderson, J.V. (1982a) 'Systems of cities in closed and open economies', *Regional Science and Urban Economics*, 12:325–350.

Henderson, J.V. (1982b) 'The impact of government policies on urban concentration', *Journal of Urban Economics*, 12:280–303.

Henderson, J.V. (1986a) 'Efficiency of resources usage and city size', *Journal of Urban Economics*, 19:47–70.

Henderson, J.V. (1986b) *Economic theory and the cities*. New York: Academic Press.

Henderson, J.V. and Y. Ioannides (1981) 'Aspects of growth in a system of cities', *Journal of Urban Economics*, 10:117–139.

Hoch, I. (1977) 'Climates, wages, and quality of life', in: L. Wingo and A. Evans, eds., *Public economics and the quality of life*. Baltimore: Johns Hopkins Press, 28–65.

Hochman, O. (1977) 'A two factor three sector model of an economy with cities: a contribution to urban economics and international trade theories', mimeo.

Hochman, O. (1981) 'Land rents, optimal taxation, and local fiscal independence in an economy with local public goods', *Journal of Public Economics*, 59–85.

Izraeli, O. (1979) 'Externalities and intercity wage and price differentials', in: G. Tolley et al., *Urban growth policy in a market economy*. New York: Academic Press.

Jones, R. W. (1968) 'Variable returns to scale in general equilibrium', *International Economic Review*, 10:261–272.

Kanemoto, Y. (1978) 'Optimal growth of cities', Discussion Paper 78-02, University of British Columbia, mimeo.

Lösch, A. (1954) *The economics of location*. New Haven.

McKenzie, L.W. (1960) 'Matrices with dominant diagonals and economic theory', in: *Proceedings of a Symposium on Mathematical Methods in the Social Sciences*. Palo Alto, Calif.: Stanford University Press.

Mills, E.S. (1967) 'An aggregative model of resource allocation in a metropolitan area', *American Economic Review*, 57:197–210.

Neary, J.P. (1978) 'Dynamic stability and the theory of factor-market distortions', *American Economic Review*, 68:671–682.

Rosen, S. (1978) 'Wage-based indexes of urban quality of life', in: P. Mieszkowski and M. Straszheim. eds., *Current issues in urban economics*. Baltimore: Johns Hopkins Press.

Schaeffer, G.P. (1977) 'The urban hierarchy and urban area production function', *Urban Studies*, 14:315–326.
Sveikauskas, L. (1978) 'The productivity of cities', mimeo. 1–94.
Upton, C. (1981) 'An equilibrium model of city sizes', *Journal of Urban Economics*, 10:15–36.
Wheaton, W. (1974) 'A comparative static analysis of urban spatial structure', *Journal of Economic Theory*, 9:223–237.

PART 2

SPECIFIC URBAN MARKETS

Chapter 24

ECONOMIC THEORY AND HOUSING

RICHARD ARNOTT

Queen's University

Introduction

This survey will review the current state of the art in neoclassical microeconomic modelling of the housing sector in developed, mixed economies[1] as a basis for both describing its operation and identifying the appropriate role of government.

Housing has a set of intrinsic characteristics which make it significantly different from any other good. As a result, the operation of the housing market is significantly different from that of any other market. These points are elaborated in Section 1. Models of the housing market can conveniently be grouped into two classes. Those that treat the housing market as being competitive are surveyed in Sections 2 and 3. The rest attempt to capture some of the imperfections in the housing market, and are discussed in Section 4.

This survey has several related themes. First, the competitive theory of housing markets is reasonably sophisticated and well-developed. Second, there is no well-worked-out, imperfectly competitive or non-competitive theory of the housing market, only partial models. Third, it is hard to ascertain the adequacy of the competitive theory in explaining a particular housing market phenomenon or the effects of a particular housing policy because of the absence of well-articulated alternative models. Fourth, since the appropriate role of government in the housing sector depends crucially on the competitiveness of the market, which is hard to judge, existing theory provides little guidance concerning desirable government intervention. And fifth, though further development of the competitive theory of housing markets is needed, the highest priority item on the research agenda should be the development of imperfectly competitive and non-competitive theories of the housing market.

*The author would like to thank Steffen Ziss and Salman Wakil for assistance with the preparation of the survey. Very helpful comments on a previous draft from the following are gratefully acknowledged: Ralph Braid, Jan Brueckner, Masahisa Fujita, Lawrence Jones, Yoshitsugu Kanemoto, Edwin Mills, Edgar Olsen, David Pines, Lawrence Smith, Konrad Stahl, and Mahlon Straszheim.

[1]Thus, no attention is given to models of the housing sector for less developed or Eastern Bloc countries, nor to non-neoclassical models of the housing market.

Handbook of Regional and Urban Economics, Volume II, Edited by E.S. Mills
© *1987, Elsevier Science Publishers B.V.*

1. Housing: A singular and peculiar commodity[2]

Housing has a unique set of characteristics: *necessity* (housing satisfies a basic human need, shelter), *importance* (for most households, it is the single most important item of consumption), *durability* (housing is the most durable of major commodities[3]), *spatial fixity* (with only minor exceptions, a housing unit cannot be transported at reasonable cost), *indivisibility* (households typically do not mix fractions of housing units), *complexity and multi-dimensional heterogeneity* (a housing unit has a great number of characteristics), *thinness of the market* (housing units and households are sparse in characteristics space), *nonconvexities in production* (rehabilitation, demolition and reconstruction, and conversion involve discontinuous changes that are caused by production nonconvexities), *the importance of informational asymmetries* (e.g., potential occupants are not fully aware of each housing unit's characteristics, and landlord and tenant do not know each other's traits), *the importance of transactions costs* (search costs, moving costs, and transaction fees), and *the near-absence of relevant insurance and futures markets*.

Most goods contain some or all of these characteristics to some degree. But only in housing are they all so pronounced. These characteristics interact to cause the operation of the housing market to be significantly different from that of any other market. Some of the unusual features of the market will be discussed shortly. But before this is done, a terminological digression is necessary.

The usage of the terminology related to competition in the theoretical literature is not uniform. In this survey, *perfectly competitive* will be used in the sense of Arrow [Arrow and Hahn (1971)] and Debreu (1959).[4] The term *competitive* will be used to refer to economies that are perfectly competitive except for possible production nonconvexities and the possible indivisibility of housing.[5] An economy is said to be *imperfectly competitive* if all agents are price-takers, but market imperfections – asymmetric information, transactions costs, externalities,

[2]This section and the next draw heavily on Rothenberg (1978) and Stahl (1985) which provide excellent discussions of the peculiar characteristics of housing and the housing market.

[3]A frequently-cited statistic is that the number of housing units constructed annually typically constitutes only about 2% of the housing stock.

[4]Recall that in the Arrow–Debreu model of perfect competition, there are profit-maximizing, price-taking firms with independent, convex production sets, utility-maximizing, price-taking households with independent, convex, consumption sets, no transactions costs, symmetric information, and a complete set of state-contingent markets.

[5]In a perfectly competitive economy, a typical household would choose to consume housing at a variety of locations. This, however, is inconsistent with observation. Thus, competitive models of spatial housing markets adapt the Arrow–Debreu assumptions by requiring that each household consume housing at only one location.

etc. – are present.[6] Finally, a *non-competitive* economy is one in which there are some agents who are price setters.

Some economists refer to the set of institutions relating to the provision of housing services as the "housing sector" and separate the sector into the housing markets and non-market institutions. In this survey, the term "housing market" will be used in its popular sense as synonymous with "housing sector".

1.1. Housing supply

The most natural way to describe a housing unit is to exhaustively list its characteristics. Modelling the housing market, however, requires a relatively simple description of housing technology and demand. As a result, housing economists typically describe a housing unit in terms of one or several indexes of characteristics. At the extreme of aggregation, a housing unit can be described in terms of the number of units of housing service it provides as measured by, say, the rent it commands at a point in time. With an intermediate degree of aggregation, a housing unit may be described in terms of its location, floor area, and quality, and the structural density of the building in which it is located.

Viewing housing in this way, one may distinguish four housing production processes. The first is *construction* whereby land and capital are combined to produce the housing unit. The second is *maintenance* which entails the gradual application of capital to an existing unit with fixed floor area, location, and structural density, to slow the rate of quality deterioration. An improvement in quality is often called upgrading, and a deterioration, downgrading. The third, *rehabilitation*, is similar to maintenance except that it involves the sudden application of capital to produce a discontinuous increase in quality. The fourth is *conversion* which involves changing the size of units in a building with location and structural density fixed. With downward conversion, unit size is reduced, while with upward conversion, it is enlarged. Conversion almost always occurs discontinuously.The fact that changes in structural density, unit size, and quality may occur discontinuously indicates that there are nonconvexities in the technology of housing production.

Because of the thinness of the housing market, a household is unlikely to find any housing unit close to ideal and therefore has a strong incentive to modify the unit to suit its tastes. Relatedly, housing services are produced by combining the housing unit with personal furniture and accessories. Also, because of transaction

---

[6]The market is imperfect in the sense that it does not conform with the assumptions of the Arrow–Debreu model of perfect competition. The presence of market imperfections may, but do not necessarily, imply market inefficiency.

costs, routine maintenance is usually done more cheaply by the household itself. For all these reasons, household time and money are typically important inputs into the production of housing services.

Due to lags in construction and to the relatively small effect of annual construction on the total stock of housing, housing supply responds only partially to cyclical movements in demand. Rent therefore tends to move pro-cyclically. The amortized costs of construction, meanwhile, bear little systematic relation to the business cycle. Thus, the rate of housing construction is sensitive to the state of the macroeconomy and is in fact one of the most volatile components of the business cycle.

Because of the length of approval and construction lags, as well as the durability of housing, builder expectations play a critical role in the timing of construction. If these expectations are wide of the mark, the resultant excess demand or supply in the market for housing can cause local housing booms and busts.[7]

1.2. Housing demand

When a household rents or purchases a housing unit, it obtains not only the physical unit but also because of spatial fixity, a neighborhood, a set of public services, and tax obligations. It also acquires a set of legal rights and obligations, of which those related to security of tenure are particularly important.

The type of housing a household acquires is sensitive to its income and demographic characteristics,[8] and depends as well on relative prices, of course. The location of the unit is strongly influenced by household members' job locations. Furthermore, housing is such an important item of consumption that there is likely significant simultaneity between the household's three major sets of decisions – household composition (formation, dissolution, number of children, etc.), job choice, and housing consumption.

The flow of services from a good is normally obtained through its purchase. For the housing market, however, renting is typically as common as owning, and in many countries co-operative ownership is common. A household must therefore make a tenure choice decision.[9] Since almost all housing market policies are targetted either on renters or on a particular class of owners, it is

[7]Such booms and busts are often ascribed to speculative activity. Since speculation is so poorly understood, however, it is probably best to look first to market fundamentals for an explanation of a boom or a bust.

[8]In housing market theory, the number of households is typically treated as exogenous. Yet the number and type of households (through children leaving home, divorce and separation, choice in family size, elderly parents living apart from their children, etc.) is sensitive to economic conditions generally and is also influenced by housing policy. On this subject, see Smith et al. (1985).

[9]The mode of tenure is the form of contract under which a household occupies a housing unit.

important for sound policy analysis to have a good understanding of tenure choice.[10]

The market value of a housing unit is typically several times an occupant's income and the value of a nation's housing stock is a significant proportion of its total capital stock. The role of housing as an asset is therefore important. For the typical homeowner, his house is the major asset in his portfolio; as a consequence, both consumption and portfolio motives enter the housing purchase decision.

Because of the cost of moving and of search, and in the case of homeowners of buying and selling, households typically stay in a housing unit for several years. Thus, the household does not instantaneously adjust its housing unit choice as conditions change. An important implication of this is that few households will move immediately in response to the introduction of a new housing policy.

The nature of capital markets, which will be commented on shortly, also substantially affects housing demand.

1.3. Housing market exchange and operation

Many imperfections are evident in the way housing units are exchanged. First, due to the thinness of both households and housing units in characteristics space, as well as mobility costs on both sides of the market, both the suppliers and demanders of housing have some market power.

Second, while in a competitive market prices adjust instantaneously to clear markets, in the housing market there is a negative relationship between the level of demand and the vacancy rate. This implies that prices do not adjust instantaneously and that some other adjustment mechanism must be at work. Some of the explanations of housing market adjustment which treat vacancy rates are discussed in Section 4. All are based on imperfections in the housing market.

Third, the regulations affecting housing unit production, exchange and consumption (e.g. building codes, zoning, noise by-laws), as well as the variety and complexity of housing contracts, suggest that both asymmetries in information and externalities are significant.

Fourth, a peculiar set of capital market institutions have developed in each country vis-à-vis home purchase. In the Anglo–Saxon world, the principal borrowing instrument is the mortgage. Several characteristics of the mortgage instrument – the requirement that the house be used as collateral, and credit rationing[11] – provide strong evidence that housing capital markets are strongly

---

[10]Some aspects of tenure choice are discussed in section 4.

[11]With a perfect capital market, the prospective homebuyer could borrow as much as he wished at a risk-adjusted rate of interest, which would vary with the size of the loan. The imperfection of the market does not necessarily imply inefficiency.

imperfect. These capital market imperfections stem from asymmetries in information and transactions costs.[12]

Fifth, due to moving, search, advertising, and modification costs, only a small proportion of housing units are likely to be on the market at a given time.

There are also several noteworthy features with respect to the operation of the housing market. Because of the durability of housing, history matters – the effects of any policy or exogeneous change on the market will depend on the characteristics of the housing stock. Also, in housing markets in which the government is relatively laissez-faire, demand and supply typically interact in such a way that most low-income households occupy older, deteriorated housing that was previously occupied by the more prosperous.[13] Finally, government intervention in the housing market is pervasive, even in North America.[14] Not only is there typically a myriad of regulations, taxes, and subsidies that impinge on the market, but also in most European countries a significant proportion of housing units are allocated by administrative decision, and in some the presence of government is so pronounced that it is questionable whether one should even talk of a housing *market*.

1.4. The welfare economics of housing[15]

In perfectly competitive economies, equilibrium exists and is Pareto efficient (the first theorem of welfare economics). Furthermore, any Pareto optimum can be achieved as a competitive equilibrium with appropriate lump-sum redistribution (the second theorem of welfare economics). In such economies, therefore, there is

[12] Because the lender is unable to identify the riskiness of the borrower, adverse selection problems [see Diamond and Rothschild (1978)] arise. Since the lender is unable to properly monitor the actions of the borrower that affect the probability of default, there are also problems of moral hazard [again see readings in Diamond and Rothschild (1978)].

[13] The term "filtering" is used to refer either to the phenomenon whereby a residential building is occupied by households of increasingly low relative income as it ages, or to the change in quality of a residential building as it ages. According to the second definition, downward filtering is equivalent to downgrading and upward filtering to upgrading. Typically, but not always, most housing units constructed are of high to medium quality and of large to medium size, and are modified as they age for use by lower-income households via downward conversion and filtering.

[14] For reasons of space, there is no discussion of housing policy per se.

[15] For a survey of welfare economics up to 1970, see Arrow and Scitovsky (1969). This survey covers the basic welfare theorems and classical imperfections such as technological externalities. There is no good survey of welfare economics with non-classical imperfections – asymmetric information, transactions costs, incomplete markets, etc. However, Arnott and Stiglitz (1986a, b), which treat welfare economics when moral hazard is present, provide a flavor of how non-classical imperfections affect the welfare properties economies. The general result is that, in the presence of non-classical imperfections, competitive equilibrium (if it exists) is essentially never constrained (i.e. subject to the information technology) efficient, and the potential scope for welfare-improving government intervention is very large. Other pertinent articles are contained in Diamond and Rotschild (1978).

no efficiency argument for government intervention, and the efficient way to achieve equity, if consumer sovereignty is respected, is to redistribute in lump-sum fashion.

In imperfectly competitive and non-competitive economies, the appropriate role of government depends on the nature of the imperfections. The presence of an imperfection does not necessarily imply that government intervention is justified. For instance, moving costs are an imperfection (i.e. inconsistent with the assumptions of the Arrow–Debreu model) but by themselves create no inefficiency. Somewhat more subtly, the technology which gives rise to an imperfection may restrict the effectiveness of government intervention. As an example, an externality may not be internalized, even when property rights are well-defined, because of the costs of determining how much compensation should be paid to the various injured parties; but for the same reason, the costs of government intervention may exceed the benefits. Nevertheless, the presence of imperfections does expand the scope of possibly justifiable government intervention. Many of the efficiency arguments, such as the restriction of monopoly power, should be familiar. The equity argument is perhaps less so: Ideally, if consumer sovereignty is respected, equity should be achieved via lump-sum redistribution. If the redistribution is to be lump-sum, it must be based on intrinsic or exogenous characteristics of individuals that reflect need. But such characteristics are typically unobservable, as a result of which redistribution must be based on characteristics over which the individual has control (e.g., income). Redistribution in these circumstances necessarily has efficiency effects, and the optimal form of redistribution may entail government intervention in many markets, including the housing market.[16] Thus, the appropriate form and scope of government intervention in the housing market depends on the nature and magnitude of imperfections in the market, as well as the technology of government intervention.

1.5. Modelling the housing market

Perhaps the main issue in housing market theory at present is in what circumstances the housing market should be modelled as competitive. The majority view, at least among North American economists, has been that while in some contexts (e.g., analyzing the effects of macroeconomic policy on vacancy rates) imperfections in the housing market cannot be ignored, in most contexts, the housing market acts essentially as a competitive market because it has a large number of buyers and sellers. A more pragmatic defence for treating the housing

---

[16]This theme is developed in Atkinson and Stiglitz (1980), for example.

market as competitive is that the only well-developed models of housing are competitive, and for want of better, it is necessary to work with the tools at hand. In recent years, however, there has been increasing dissatisfaction with these defenses. First, at least a significant minority of housing policy economists have assumed the housing market to be competitive in arguing against government intervention. It is one thing to adopt the competitive assumption as expedient in positive analysis, and quite another to use it as a basis for policy prescription. Second, significant progress has been made in the last two decades (the literatures on asymmetric information, search theory and game theory) in modelling non-competitive and imperfectly competitive markets. There is hope that application of this work to the housing market may lead to well-articulated imperfectly competitive or non-competitive models of the housing market. To decide on the range of applicability of competitive models of the housing market, it will be necessary to refine such models, develop credible imperfectly competitive and non-competitive models, and compare their performances empirically.

2. The housing market as the market for housing services

Up to the early 1960s, the dominant form of housing market analysis was Marshallian. The housing market was viewed as the market for housing services, with equilibrium being determined by a Walrasian interaction of demand and supply. The analysis was diagrammatic and discursive rather than algebraic. It is easy now to dismiss this work as primitive. Yet to view the housing market as a competitive market for housing services was an impressive feat of simplification. Furthermore, this mode of analysis is still predominant in policy discussion, and, in the hands of a skilled practitioner with a good understanding of the operation of the market, can be quite effective and illuminating.

As an example, consider the application of this mode of analysis to the study of the effects of a rent subsidy of s. Suppose that prior to the rent subsidy, the housing market is in long-run equilibrium with the price of housing services equal to the long-run supply price, $\bar{p}$ (minimum long-run average cost). Equilibrium quantity is q^b, and the pre-subsidy demand curve D^b. Now the (unanticipated) subsidy is introduced. The immediate effect is to shift up the demand curve from D^b to D^a. Because of construction lags and the durability of structures, the instantaneous supply curve is vertical. In response to the increased demand, there is an immediate price rise from $\bar{p}$ to p_0. Suppliers gradually respond (the supply curve rotating around $(q^b, \bar{p})$ from S_0 to S_1 to S_∞) to the price rise, causing the supply curve to become increasingly elastic. Eventually, the price falls back to $\bar{p}$ and the quantity of housing services provided by the market increases to q^a_∞. The analysis could be made more sophisticated: If moving costs were treated, housing consumers would respond sluggishly to the price rise and as time proceeds

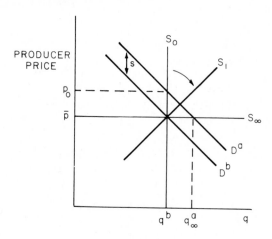

Figure 1. Marshallian analysis of a rent subsidy.

housing demand would become more elastic. Also, the housing market could be separated into submarkets and the interaction between the submarkets treated. Furthermore, the demand and supply elasticities over time could be estimated, and the time path of the equilibrium price and quantity of housing services forecast.

In *Cities and Housing*, a modern classic, Muth formalized and extended the Marshallian analysis. He analyzed only the stationary state. The housing producer at a particular location chooses the capital–land ratio, k, to maximize profits. The quantity of housing services provided when k units of capital are applied to a unit area of land is $Q(k)$, where $Q' > 0$ and $Q'' < 0$ (primes denote derivatives). Muth terms Q the housing production function. Where the rents on land at this location, capital and housing services are R, ρ_k, and p respectively, the housing producer's problem, in the absence of government, is to maximize profits per unit area of land, i.e.

$$\max_k p\, Q(k) - \rho_k k - R. \tag{1}$$

The first-order condition is

$$pQ' - \rho_k = 0; \tag{2}$$

capital should be applied to land up to the point where marginal revenue equals marginal cost. Competition among housing producers drives profits to zero, and hence land rents are $R = p(Q - Q'k)$. Since the elasticity of substitution between capital and land in housing production is $\sigma = -(Q - Q'k)/(Q''k^2)$, differentiation of (2) gives

$$\frac{p}{k}\frac{dk}{dp}=\frac{R\sigma}{\rho_k k};$$ (3)

the elasticity of the capital–land ratio with respect to housing rent equals the ratio of land to capital factor share times the elasticity of substitution.

Muth also examined the effect of accessibility on housing rent and housing services per unit area of land (housing density). To illustrate this, suppose that households are identical, but, because they live at different locations, differ in the amount they have to pay for transport costs, f. Competition will result in households having equal utilities. Where $\bar{V}$ is the equilibrium utility level, V the indirect utility function, and Y exogenous household income, this condition can be expressed as

$$V(p(f), Y-f)=\bar{V}.$$ (4)

From (4), it follows that

$$-h\frac{dp}{df}=1,$$ (5)

where h is household consumption of housing, which states that housing rent adjusts so that a unit increase in transport cost is just offset by a unit fall in the rent paid for a housing unit. The following illustrative comparative static results can readily be obtained:

$$\frac{dQ}{df}=Q'\frac{dp}{df}\frac{dk}{dp}<0, \qquad \frac{dR}{df}=-pQ''k\frac{dp}{df}\frac{dk}{dp}<0,$$ (6a, b)

$$\frac{d(\rho_k k/R)}{df}=(\sigma-1)\rho_k k\frac{dR}{df}\gtreqless 0 \quad \text{as} \quad \sigma\lesseqgtr 1, \quad \text{and,}$$ (6c)

$$\frac{dh}{df}=\left(\frac{\partial h}{\partial p_{\ddot{u}}}\right)\frac{dp}{df}.$$ (6d)

At less accessible locations: (a) the capital–land ratio is lower; (b) land rent is reduced; (c) the land share in housing is larger/smaller according to whether the elasticity of substitution between land and capital in housing production is greater/less than one; and (d) housing consumption is higher/lower according to whether the compensated elasticity of demand for housing is greater/less than one.[17]

[17]Another noteworthy result is that, under reasonable conditions, the population density gradient (population vs accessibility) can be shown to be bowed-in towards the origin. This has provided the theoretical basis for the estimation of urban density gradients.

A few comments are in order. First, as mentioned previously, the Muth model described a long-run stationary state. It has never been successfully modified to treat adjustment dynamics. Relatedly, it does not provide an explicit treatment of housing durability. Second, much of the empirical work on housing markets has gone into estimating the parameters of the Muth model. Since however, actual housing markets are unlikely to be close to a long-run stationary state, the parameters estimated are likely to be biased. Third, the Muthian production function is really a composite function, capturing not only the relationship between construction costs and structural density (floor-area ratio), but also households' tastes vis-a-vis structural density [see Grieson (1974)].

One can criticize the Muthian model for its excessive simplicity, but it was the first formal, general equilibrium model of the housing market, and almost all the subsequent mainstream housing market theory has evolved from it.

3. More sophisticated models of competitive housing markets

During the seventies, there was rapid, sustained, and systematic progress in modelling competitive housing markets. There were essentially three separate lines of development that are now being integrated. First, residential location theory or the "new urban economics" provided a formal and workable general equilibrium model with differentiated space. Second, non-stationary, spatial, durable housing market models were developed. And third, Sweeney (1974a, b) constructed an aspatial, stationary-state, general equilibrium model of durable housing with endogenous maintenance and quality. The full and successful integration of these models would solve for the non-stationary, dynamic general equilibrium of an economy in which there is differentiated space and durable housing with endogenous quality and maintenance. Serious empirical estimation and policy implementation of these models is only beginning.

3.1. Residential location theory or the new urban economics

In the late sixties and early seventies, the new urban economics was founded. Important early contributions were Mills (1967, 1972), Beckmann (1969), Solow and Vickrey (1971), Solow (1972), Mirrlees (1972), and Wheaton (1974). All drew on the seminal work of Alonso (1964) and Muth (1969) which incorporates material from earlier papers, e.g. Muth (1961).

Consider the following very simple model. There is a fixed number of identical households, N, each of which derives utility, u, from lot size, T, and a numeraire good, C. Different households live on annular lots at different distances from the central business district (CBD) a point in space at which all non-residential activity takes place. Each day each household commutes to and from the CBD to work and shop, and commuting costs depend only on radial distance. Beyond the circular residential area is farmland for which farmers bid r_A per unit area. The city's income from production, I, is exogenous, and there is external ownership of land.

There are several ways to solve for competitive equilibrium. A constructive method will prove insightful. In competitive equilibrium, the identical households receive the same utility and income. Furthermore, each household's consumption bundle is characterized by the tangency of its budget line and an indifference curve. Conjecture that the equilibrium utility level is u^0. Take the first household and locate it at the city center. Calculate this household's budget line in T–C space, which is tangent to u^0 and intercepts the C-axis at I/N. From this, one obtains both lot size and rent at the city center. Take the second household and place it just beyond the first household's lot. Since the first household's lot size is known, the transport costs incurred by the second household can be computed, and hence its income net of transport costs. Calculate the second household's budget line, lot size, and rent. Continue adding households in this manner until rent equals r_A. Beyond this location, land goes to farmers because they bid more for it than households. If the number of households fitted into the city via this procedure, $\tilde{N}$, exceeds (is less than) N, and if lot size is a normal good, then the equilibrium utility level is higher (lower) than u^0. Repeat the above procedure with a $u^1 > (<)u^0$. Proceed until $N = \tilde{N}$.

The above model is termed the basic, semi-closed monocentric city model. The fully-closed city model also has a fixed population, but land ownership is internal to the city so that there is no rent leakage. In an open city model, meanwhile, there is a variable population but a fixed utility level – households migrate into and out of the city costlessly until the utility levels in the city and the rest of the world are equalized.

In the Arrow–Debreu model, land at different locations is treated as a set of differentiated commodities. With identical households and convexity of preferences, each household would consume an equal share of land at each settled location. In a circular monocentric city, this would entail each household consuming a pie-slice of land. In the model described above, however, each household consumes land at only one location; this implies a nonconvexity in the household consumption set. Thus, models in residential location theory are, according to the distinction made earlier, competitive rather than perfectly competitive. As a consequence, the standard existence and optimality proofs for the Arrow–Debreu model do not apply. However, Mirrlees (1972) and Fujita (1976b, 1985) inter alios have proved existence and optimality for several residential location models, and it is generally accepted that in the absence of externalities, existence and optimality obtain.[18]

The monocentric city model has been extended in numerous directions, to include multiple household groups [e.g., Hartwick, Schweizer and Varaiya (1976) business land use [e.g., Mills (1967)], pollution [e.g., Henderson (1977)], multiple centers [e.g., Fujita and Ogawa (1982)], transport congestion [e.g., Kanemoto (1980)], etc.

Muthian-type housing can be readily incorporated into the monocentric city model. One may employ the same constructive method as above, except that for each household, solve for *housing* rent and *housing* consumption, and then use (2) and $R = pQ(k) - \rho_k k$ to obtain the associated land rent and lot size.[19] Structural density decreases monotonically as distance from the city center increases. The procedure is similar with multiple household groups.

3.2. Non-stationary durable housing models

In the mid-seventies, several researchers expressed dissatisfaction with the stationary nature of the Muthian model [e.g., Harrison and Kain (1974)]. They argued that a satisfactory theory of urban spatial structure must take into account the city's past spatial development – history matters – and perhaps builders' expectations of the future as well, and also that the spatial structure of a growing city with durable housing capital may be substantially different from that of a stationary city.

Fujita (1976b), Anas (1978), and Arnott (1980), among others, started work on non-stationary, durable housing models. In these models, it was assumed on the supply side that housing, once constructed, is indestructible and externally immutable (the shell of the building cannot be altered). Also, depreciation and maintenance were ignored or treated as exogenous. The models differed, however, in their treatment of conversion (internal malleability) and expectations. Arnott (1980), for example, assumed that apartment size can be altered costlessly and that builders have perfect foresight, while Anas (1978) assumed that apartment size is fixed over the life of a building and that builders have static expectations. For the sake of exposition, Arnott and Lewis' (1979) treatment of the supply side is discussed.[20]

---

[18]The difficulties in establishing a general existence proof are considered by most to be of a technical nature.

[19]Alternatively, one can treat households as constructing their own housing. Where $h = TQ(k)$ is the housing production function and $u(c, h)$ is the utility function expressed in terms of other goods and housing, one may define $\tilde{u}(\tilde{c}, T) = u(c, TQ(k))$ where $\tilde{c} = c + p_k k$, which specifies utility in terms of land and a composite good comprising other goods and housing capital.

[20]A more complete review of urban spatial dynamics is provided in Fujita (1983).

Consider a landlord-builder who has to decide when to build and at what capital–land ratio, knowing the future time-path of housing rents. Let t denote time, T the date of construction, p_k the purchase price of capital (as distinct from ρ_k, the rental price of capital), and L current land value, with p and Q defined as before. For simplification, it is assumed that the interest rate, r, and the price of capital are constant over time. Then the landlord's profit-maximization problem is

$$\max_{T,k} \int_T^\infty p(t)Q(k)\,\mathrm{e}^{-rt}\,\mathrm{d}t - p_k k\,\mathrm{e}^{-rT} - L. \tag{7}$$

The first-order conditions are[21]

$$T: (-p(T)Q(k)+rp_k k)\,\mathrm{e}^{-rT}=0, \quad \text{and} \tag{8a}$$

$$k: \int_T^\infty p(t)Q'\,\mathrm{e}^{-rt}\,\mathrm{d}t - p_k\,\mathrm{e}^{-rT}=0. \tag{8b}$$

(8a) states that development should take place when the benefits from postponing development (the interest saved on construction costs) equal the costs (the rent foregone). (8b) indicates that the increase in the discounted revenue from adding a unit of capital should just cover the cost. Land value is bid up to the point where the present value of profit is zero when the profit-maximizing development decisions are made.

Combine (8a) and (8b) to give

$$\frac{Q'(k(T))k(T)}{Q(k(T))}=\frac{r-\bar{g}(T)}{r}, \tag{8c}$$

where $\bar{g}(T)$ is the average future growth rate of rents at time T and is implicitly defined by the equation

$$\int_T^\infty p(t)\,\mathrm{e}^{-rt}\,\mathrm{d}t = \int_T^\infty p(T)\,\mathrm{e}^{-(r-\bar{g}(T))t}\,\mathrm{d}t. \tag{9}$$

(8c) implies that (conditional on development at the profit-maximizing time) as long as $\sigma s_k < 1$, where s_k is capital's share in housing ($Q'k/Q$), profit-maximizing structural density is directly proportional to the average future growth rate of rents.

Now embed this model of the housing producer's decision into a monocentric city, where x is distance from the city center. Rewrite (8a) and (8b) with distance from the center of the city included, and differentiate the resulting expressions

---

[21] The second-order conditions reduce to $g > r(s_k)(1 - s_k)\sigma$ where $g \equiv (\partial p/\partial T)/p$ and s_k is capital's share in housing production.

with respect to x. One obtains

$$\text{sgn}\left(\frac{\mathrm{d}T}{\mathrm{d}x}\right) = \text{sgn}\left(\left(\frac{\partial\Phi/\partial x}{\Phi}\right)\left(\frac{p}{\partial p/\partial x}\right)\sigma s_k - 1\right), \quad \text{and} \tag{10a}$$

$$\text{sgn}\left(\frac{\mathrm{d}k}{\mathrm{d}x}\right) = \text{sgn}\left(\frac{\partial p}{\partial T}\frac{\partial\Phi}{\partial x} - \frac{\partial p}{\partial x}\frac{\partial\Phi}{\partial T}\right), \tag{10b}$$

where

$$\Phi(T, x) \equiv \int_T^\infty p(t, x)\,e^{-r(t-T)}\,\mathrm{d}t = \frac{p(T, x)}{r - \bar{g}(T, x)}, \tag{10c}$$

is the discounted rent from a unit of housing at location x at time T, and $\bar{g}(T, x)$ is defined by (9) with the dependence on x explicit.

To illustrate these results, consider a few scenarios. First, suppose that transport costs and utility change in such a way that rents grow exponentially at a constant rate everywhere in the city throughout time. It follows from (8c) that structural density will be the same at all locations. From (10a), meanwhile, $\text{sgn}(\mathrm{d}T/\mathrm{d}x) = \text{sgn}(1 - \sigma s_k)$. In accordance with the results of almost all empirical studies [reviewed in McDonald (1981)] it is assumed that $\sigma < 1$, in which case $\mathrm{d}T/\mathrm{d}x > 0$. Thus, the city expands outwards at a constant structural density.

Second, suppose that rent grows at the same exponential rate at all locations at each point in time, but that the rate may vary over time. From (10b), $\text{sgn}(\mathrm{d}k/\mathrm{d}x) = \text{sgn}(\partial\bar{g}/\partial T)$, while from (10a), $\text{sgn}(\mathrm{d}T/\mathrm{d}x) = \text{sgn}(1 - \sigma s_k)$. The city expands outwards with structural density depending on the average future growth rate of rents. Thus, one explanation for the stylized fact that housing density tends to fall away from the center is that the growth rate of housing rents tends to fall as a city matures.

Finally, suppose that rents grow at a constant exponential rate over time at each location in a city, but at different rates at different locations. Then, from (10b),

$$\text{sgn}\left(\frac{\mathrm{d}k}{\mathrm{d}x}\right) = \text{sgn}\left(\frac{\partial\bar{g}}{\partial x}\right),$$

while from (10a),

$$\text{sgn}\left(\frac{\mathrm{d}T}{\mathrm{d}x}\right) = \text{sgn}\left(1 - \left(1 + \left(\frac{\partial\bar{g}/\partial x}{r - \bar{g}}\right)\left(\frac{p}{\partial p/\partial x}\right)\sigma s_k\right)\right).$$

It follows that if $\partial\bar{g}/\partial x$ is negative and sufficiently large in absolute value, the city will first develop at low density in the suburbs and then grow inwards at higher density. The reason for this is that with a higher growth rate for rents downtown,

it may become profitable to leave the land there vacant for a period and
construct later at a higher density. This possibility provides one explanation for
leap-frog development [Ohls and Pines (1975)].

In the above discussion only the supply side of the market was treated. On the
demand side of all the models in this branch of the literature, households
maximize utility subject to a contemporaneous budget constraint. Putting together the demand and supply sides in an economy with commuting costs to a
single center generates a non-stationary, monocentric city with durable housing
in which the spatial structure of the city depends in a complex way on consumer
tastes, housing technology, and the time paths of income, the price of capital,
population, the interest rate, and transport costs as a function of distance.

Non-stationary durable housing models have shown that the durability of
housing can significantly affect the spatial structure of a city. Not only do these
models permit a richer set of spatial structures than does the Muth model, but
also the economic determinants of spatial structures are quite different. The set of
papers by Fujita (1976a,b, 1982, 1985) on this class of models merit special
mention for their high quality and systematic development.

The next stage of development was the treatment of demolition and reconstruction [Brueckner (1980, 1981)]. At any site, there may be a sequence of
buildings. Index the buildings on the site by i, with $i=1$ denoting the first
building, etc. If $D(k)$ is the cost of demolition per unit area of land at time t for a
building with capital-land ratio k, then the modified landlord-builder's problem is

$$\max_{\{T_i, k_i\}} \sum_i \left\{ \int_{T_i}^{T_{i+1}} p(t)Q(k_i)e^{-rt}dt - p_k k_i e^{-rT_i} - D(k_i)e^{-rT_{i+1}} \right\}.$$

The first-order conditions are similar to (8a) and (8b). But in deciding on T_i for
$i \neq 1$, the builder will take into account the costs of demolishing the current
building on the site and the rent foregone from it. In deciding on k_i, he will take
into account the lifetime of the building and future demolition costs. When this
treatment of the builder's problem is embedded in a general equilibrium spatial
model, one obtains a succession of waves of development. Since the waves can
move inwards or be discontinuous because of leap-frogging, however, the spatial
structure that evolves can be very complex.

3.3. The Sweeney model

The life cycle of a house and the phenomenon of filtering (see fn. 12) had been
discussed previously in the literature [e.g., Grigsby (1963)] but Sweeney (1974a,
b) was the first to model the process. He viewed the housing stock as a com-

modity hierarchy of products differentiated by quality, $\{S_i\}$, where S_i is the number of units of housing at the ith quality level, with $i = 1, \ldots, n$ and $i = 1$ corresponding to the lowest quality level. Demand is described by the functions $D_i(p)$ where D_i is the number of units of housing of quality i demanded and $p = [p_1, \ldots, p_n]$ the vector of housing rents. Temporary equilibrium is characterized by the equations

$$p \geq 0, \quad \text{and} \quad D_i(p) \leq S_i \quad \text{and} \quad (D_i(p) - S_i)p_i = 0 \quad \text{for all } i. \tag{11}$$

The housing stock dynamics are expressed as follows for each i:

$$\dot{S}_i = -\frac{S_i}{x_i} + \frac{S_{i+1}}{x_{i+1}} + E_i, \tag{12}$$

where x_i is the average tenure time at the ith level, E_i the rate of construction at the ith level, and $\dot{S}_i$ the time derivative of S_i. Note that (12) assumes that housing is doomed to deteriorate in quality over time. The tenure time of a unit of housing at the ith level depends on the amount spent on maintenance per unit of time; thus, $x_i = x_i(m_i)$, with $x_i' > 0$, where m_i is maintenance expenditures on a unit of housing of quality i. Total construction costs at quality i per unit of time, meanwhile, are given by $C_i = \gamma_i(E_i)$ with $\gamma_i' > 0$ and $\gamma_i'' > 0$.[22]

The stationary state equilibrium in which p and $\{S_i\}$ are constant over time can now be derived.[23] Consider a landlord who owns a unit of housing that has just entered quality level i. With competition, the market value of the unit, V_i, equals the maximum present value of profit that can be obtained from it. Without loss of generality, we may view the landlord as selling the unit when it has just entered quality level $i - 1$ (with $V_0 = 0$). Then

$$V_i = \max\left(0, \max_{m_i}\left(\int_0^{x_i(m_i)} (p_i - m_i)e^{-rt}\, dt + V_{i-1}e^{-rx_i(m_i)}\right)\right). \tag{13}$$

From (13), the profit-maximizing maintenance level, provided it is positive, is given by

$$((p_i - m_i) - rV_{i-1})e^{-rx_i}x_i' - \left(\frac{1 - e^{-rx_i}}{r}\right) = 0. \tag{14}$$

If m_i is increased by one dollar, discounted maintenance expenses rise by $((1 - e^{-rx_i})/r) + m_i e^{-rx_i}x_i'$ and discounted rental revenues by $p_i e^{-rx_i}x_i'$, while the discounted sales price falls by $rV_{i-1}e^{-rx_i}x_i'$. From (13) and (14), one obtains $m_i(p)$ and $V_i(p)$.

---

[22] Sweeney also treated the case where $C_i = k_i E_i$, k_i a constant.
[23] Since Sweeney's model is non-spatial, housing units are abandoned rather than demolished.

At each quality level, the rate of construction is determined by the condition that marginal cost, γ_i', equal marginal revenue, V_i, which gives $E_i = E_i(p)$.

Stationary-state equilibrium can then be characterized by a p and $\{S_i\}$ satisfying (11) and (12) with $\dot{S} = 0$, where $x_i(p)$ and $E_i(p)$ are solved as indicated above. Imposing certain conditions on the aggregate demand function, Sweeney was able to prove the existence of a stationary-state equilibrium, and under other assumptions derive various comparative static results.

In providing microfoundations for the aggregate demand function, Sweeney assumed that each household consumes a single unit of housing.

Sweeney's papers were important for several reasons. He formalized a new and more sophisticated way of conceptualizing the housing market which highlights quality differentiation of the housing stock and clearly distinguishes between construction and maintenance as elements of the housing production technology. He also provided a clear and elegant description of the economic determinants of change in the quality composition of the housing stock. Furthermore, while he did not explicitly do so, his model can accommodate a treatment of the demand side of the market which allows households to choose both the quality and size of a housing unit. Thus, using his model, the policy analyst can derive a richer set of predictions concerning the effects of a policy or exogenous change than is possible using the Muth model.

Three weaknesses of Sweeney's model are that it is aspatial, specifies the maintenance technology in such a way that housing units are doomed to deteriorate, and treats housing quality as discrete, which, while appropriate for empirical application, obscures some of the economics. All weaknesses have been addressed in subsequent work. Arnott, Davidson, and Pines (1983, 1986) provide a richer and more general treatment of the supply side of the housing market in stationary state, extending Sweeney's model to include space and a maintenance technology in which upgrading and rehabilitation are possible. Braid (1981, 1984) has reformulated the Sweeney model treating quality as continuous. One advantage of this is that, in the place of (14), one obtains the more transparent condition that expenditure on maintenance should be made until last dollar increases the value of the building by one dollar.

These critical comments notwithstanding, Sweeney's papers deserve high praise, not only because they were seminal but also because they were of exceptionally high quality, in terms of technique, exposition, and economic reasoning. These papers along with Fujita's are the best and most significant papers on the economic theory of housing written during the seventies.

3.4. The eighties – synthesizing the developments of the seventies

The pace of research on competitive models of the housing market in the eighties has been slack. But some progress has been made in integrating the various lines of development of the seventies.

Arnott, Davidson, and Pines (1983, 1986) (ADP) provided a description of the supply side of the housing market in stationary state that is similar to Sweeney's, but they incorporate space, treat quality as continuous, and provide a more general specification of the maintenance technology. On his site, the landlord-builder may construct either a single, infinite-lived building, or a sequence of buildings described by a periodic cycle of construction, downgrading, and demolition. More specifically, he chooses construction quality (q_0), lifespan (τ- possibly infinite), terminal quality (q_τ), structural density (μ), and maintenance over the life of the building ($m(t)$ where t is building age) to maximize the present value of profits. Where $p(q)$ is housing rent per unit of floor space of quality q, L is land value, and $K(q_0, \mu)$ are construction costs, discounted profits are

$$\Pi = \left\{ \int_0^\tau \mu(p(q(t)) - m(t)) e^{-rt} \, dt - K(q_0, \mu) \right\} (1 - e^{-r\tau})^{-1} - L. \tag{15}$$

When the building is infinite-lived, $\tau = \infty$ and $(1 - e^{-r\tau})^{-1} = 1$. And when there is an infinite sequence of finite-lived buildings, $(1 - e^{-r\tau})^{-1}$ gives the ratio of discounted net revenue from the sequence of buildings to those from the first building.[24] The maintenance technology is characterized by the function

$$\dot{q} = g(q, m). \tag{16}$$

This specification of the technology permits upgrading or downgrading, but is restrictive in assuming that a building's rate of deterioration does not depend on its age per se.[25]

Subject to reasonable restrictions on the construction and maintenance technologies, ADP provide a complete characterization of the solution and a rich set of comparative static results. It is shown that a single, infinite-lived building provides greater profits than a sequence of buildings when construction costs are high relative to maintenance, and that the sequence of buildings is more profitable when construction costs are relatively low. Structural density typically increases as housing rents and land values increase, but this need not always occur.

Arnott, Braid, Davidson, and Pines (1986) (ABDP) embedded the above supply model in a stationary general equilibrium, monocentric city model. On the demand side, they improved on Sweeney in permitting a household to choose both the quality and floor area of the housing unit, but treated only a single

---

[24] $1 + e^{-rt} + e^{-2rt} + e^{-3rt} \cdots = (1 - e^{rt})^{-1}$

[25] A rehabilitation technology may also be introduced, $R(q, \bar{q}; \mu)$ which describes the cost per unit area of floor space in a building of structural density μ of rehabilitation from quality $\underline{q}$ to quality $\bar{q}$.

household group. Under somewhat restrictive conditions, they proved existence[26] and obtained a set of comparative static results which indicate that, while structural density typically falls as distance from the city center increases, the spatial structure of the housing stock by quality and unit size depends in a complex way on the construction and maintenance technologies and the characteristics of demand.

Complete integration of the three strands of literature described earlier will require extending the model of ABDP to treat a continuum of differentiated households and a non-stationary economic environment. These extensions will be mathematically, though not conceptually, difficult. In the absence of analytical solutions to these extensions, computer simulation may prove useful.[27]

3.5. Other models and concluding comments

Different models are appropriate for different purposes. Providing a detailed description of the housing technology, which accounts for production nonconvexities, is certainly valuable in some contexts. But to a policy maker interested in broad trends over time and space, such detail is not only unnecessary, since aggregation tends to smooth nonconvexities,[28] but also distracting. Hochman and Pines (1982) constructed a model circumventing the discontinuities which arise from demolition and reconstruction by assuming that housing density can be adjusted up or down continuously, subject to convex adjustment costs.[29] The model is spatial and non-stationary, but does not treat quality differences.

Relatedly, it may prove useful, in some contexts, to provide different descriptions of the commodity housing. Housing has many characteristics. Aggregation over these characteristics to obtain a summary description of the commodity inevitably entails some "aggregation loss", and how this aggregation loss is minimized depends on context. In ABDP, a building is described in terms of its quality, location, and structural density, and tastes for housing are defined

---

[26]In all the competitive housing models without externalities constructed to date, competitive equilibrium exists and is efficient. The natural conjecture is that the same will be true of more complex and realistic models. Uniqueness of equilibrium has not been addressed.

Practically no work has been done in investigating the existence and properties of competitive equilibrium in an economy with housing in which there are externalities. [Stahl (1980), however, has investigated the landlord-builder's problem in a Sweeney-type model in which there are externalities.] The general literature on externalities prompts the conjecture that externalities may cause either non-existence or a multiplicity of competitive equilibria.

[27]Arnott (1985) is in the process of constructing such a simulation model.

[28]That is, if one had only aggregate information on the housing stock, one could probably rationalize it on the assumption of a convex housing production technology.

[29]It is interesting to note that continuous upwards adjustment of structural density is common in cities in the Middle East.

over quality and floor area. This aggregation was chosen in the light of policy concerns and household tastes in developed Western countries. In other situations, however, different aggregations might be preferable. For example, in a less developed country, the availability of basic amenities – heat, running water, sanitary facilities – might be of more concern than quality. In any event, construction of housing models which describe housing in terms of a different set of aggregate characteristics may prove insightful.

Whatever set of aggregate characteristics housing is described in terms of, empirical implementation will require the construction of aggregate characteristic indexes from the set of basic housing characteristics. Since aggregation inevitably entails aggregation loss, the question naturally arises as to whether it might not be useful to model housing in terms of its basic characteristics. This is the approach taken in the hedonic price literature. The basic theory was developed by Rosen (1974), and it has been extensively applied in empirical work on housing [see Follain and Jimenez (1985) for a review of the literature]. Let $z = (z_i, \ldots, z_n)$ be a vector of housing characteristics and $p(z)$ be the hedonic price function – the market price for a given bundle of basic characteristics. On the demand side, the household is viewed as choosing a bundle of basic characteristics, i.e. $\max_{x, z} u(x, z; \alpha)$ subject to $y = x + p(z)$, where x is a composite of nonhousing goods, y is household income, and α is a taste parameter. On the supply side, firms produce bundles of basic characteristics to maximize profits, i.e. $\max_z = p(z) - c(z; \beta)$ where $c(z; \beta)$ is the cost of producing z given factor prices β. The interaction of supply and demand generates the market-clearing hedonic price function.

Since any practical housing market theory must be expressed in terms of basic housing characteristics or aggregate housing characteristics, which are indexes formed from basic housing characteristics, reliable estimation of hedonic price functions and of the underlying supply and demand parameters is essential for any sound, quantitative analysis of the housing market. Hedonic theories of the housing market, which describe housing in terms of only its basic characteristics, are therefore valuable in providing a sound theoretical basis for empirical estimation. They are not, however, particularly useful for conceptual analysis. First, the detail required in the description of housing tends to obscure basic insights. For example, while in some contexts, it might be of interest to know how a particular housing policy will affect the equilibrium number of two-car garages by households with particular financial and demographic characteristics, such information would usually be distracting. Second, description of the technology for the production of housing characteristics which treats durability and "joint clayness" (that certain characteristics, once bundled, can only be unbundled at very high cost) is very difficult. For this reason, hedonic price theories of housing are most useful in providing a conceptual basis for the determination of a temporary equilibrium in which supply is fixed.

To sum up: In recent years, considerable progress has been made in modelling competitive housing markets. A central issue has been the level of aggregation at which to model the housing market. Early models examined the market for housing services, possibly with submarkets differentiated by location, and housing and tenure types. These models were criticized as being too crude to address many housing policy concerns. One reaction was to disaggregate as much as possible and to treat the housing market as a set of markets for housing characteristics. Doing so provides a useful theoretical basis for empirical work, but a distractingly detailed description of the market. One of the main trends of theoretical housing research over the past fifteen years has been to develop models in between these two extremes of aggregation.

Another major issue has been the treatment of housing durability. Earlier models ignored durability or treated it crudely, distinguishing between the market for housing stock and the market for housing services, a flow. Current models, meanwhile, are explicitly dynamic and treat construction, demolition, rehabilitation, and maintenance. Relatedly, earlier models, by neglecting dynamics and durability, failed to satisfactorily treat the dynamic spatial evolution of the housing stock. In recent models, not only does history matter, but also the current spatial form of the housing market depends on expectations concerning the future. Finally, with the elaboration of the new urban economics, models of the housing market can be incorporated into general equilibrium spatial models of the city, thereby permitting formal treatment of the interlinkages between housing, transportation, pollution, firm location, etc.

We are now close to having an analytical model of competitive housing markets that is dynamic and non-stationary, in which space is differentiated, households choose unit size and quality, and landlord-builders, through construction, demolition, rehabilitation, and maintenance, choose the structural density and quality of their housing over time. There are still several problems to be solved[30] and further refinements to be made.[31] Nevertheless, it is fair to say

---

[30]In the corresponding stationary-state model, existence of equilibrium where there is a continuum of differentiated consumers and a continuum of differentiated locations has yet to be proved. Since, however, standard proofs can be used to demonstrate existence with an arbitrarily large but finite number of differentiated consumers and locations, this problem appears to be mathematical rather than economic. Relatedly, efficiency of competitive equilibrium has yet to be proved. Since, however, there are no readily identifiable externalities, the conjecture is that competitive equilibrium is efficient. Uniqueness has not yet been investigated, but in view of the nonconvexity of the production technology, the possibility of multiple equilibria appears likely.

Extension to a non-stationary environment will prove mathematically difficult, but is unlikely to be conceptually troublesome.

[31]Further refinements to be made include: (i) further disaggregation in the description of the commodity housing; for example, various theorists have suggested that it may be useful to treat durability as another aggregate housing characteristic; (ii) allowing the maintenance technology to be dependent on building age; and (iii) providing households with lifetime rather than single-period budget constraints.

that our conceptual understanding of the operation of a competitive housing market is good. Furthermore, it is now possible to construct simulation models of a competitive housing market that are arbitrarily complex.[32]

In what respects actual housing markets act as the competitive theory suggests is another matter. As mentioned earlier, to ascertain this it will be necessary to develop alternative models and then to test them against the competitive models. Remarkably there has been virtually no econometric estimation of the competitive housing models developed over the last fifteen years. While there has been considerable empirical housing market research, much of it of high quality, over that period, most of it has estimated either parameters of the Muth model, or models of the housing market that incorporate imperfectly competitive or non-competitive features, such as moving costs, vacancy rates, and tenure choice, in a largely ad hoc fashion. Now that housing theorists are turning to modelling imperfectly competitive and non-competitive models of the housing market, one hopes that theoretical and empirical research on housing markets will again move forward together, as occurred successfully in Muth's work.

4. Modelling some imperfectly competitive and non-competitive aspects of the housing market

Over the past fifteen years, general theorists have devoted a lot of attention to the behavior of imperfectly competitive and non-competitive economies (in which the assumptions of the Arrow–Debroeu model are relaxed). There have been three principal overlapping lines of development – asymmetric information, search theory, and strategic behavior. This work is slowly being incorporated into models of housing markets, but much remains to be done.

The discussion that follows is selective.

4.1. Vacancy rates

Similarities between the vacancy rate in housing markets and the unemployment rate in labor markets have frequently been noted, but only recently have theories of unemployment been adapted to treat housing vacancies.

The analogy between the housing vacancy rate and the unemployment rate cannot be perfect since in the housing market, vacancies are a manifestation of the excess supply of a commodity, while unemployment entails the excess supply of an input. Furthermore, in the labor market, job vacancies and unemployment

---

[32]Computational costs impose a practical constraint on the feasible complexity.

occur together, while in the housing market, there are vacancies but no one without housing. Yet much of the work that has been done on the microfoundations of unemployment can be modified fairly straightforwardly to treat vacancy rates in the housing market.

Search theory [see Mortensen (1984) and McCall (1982) for an overview of the literature] provides the basis for one important strand of unemployment theory [see Diamond and Yellin (1985) for a recent example]. Just as workers search for a higher-paying job or one that better matches their tastes and abilities, so households search for more suitable housing at a lower price. Because search is costly, landlords face downward-sloping demand curves. In consequence, they will set price, p, above marginal cost, c. Freedom of entry and exit, meanwhile, will drive profits to zero. Thus, $p(1-v)=c$, where v is the vacancy rate.[33]

The stylized facts concerning vacancy rates are not well-documented [but see Rosen and Smith (1983)], yet it appears to be the case that vacancy rates are lower the larger the housing market and are counter-cyclical. The former stylized fact is consistent with search-based theories – the smaller the housing market, the thinner is it likely to be, and consequently the less elastic the demand facing each landlord. The latter stylized fact is harder to explain. In good times, households have the disposable income to upgrade their housing and to pay moving costs, while in bad times, because of moving costs, households are apt to stay put rather than move to cheaper housing. Thus, there is likely to be considerably more turnover in the rental housing market in periods of prosperity. For a given vacancy rate, therefore, there will be more households searching over the same number of vacant units in good times than in bad, an effect which by itself results in the landlord facing less elastic demand by searchers in good times and generates pro-cyclicity of the vacancy rate. There are other effects, which presumably more than offset this one. Most important is probably the demand elasticity of sitting tenants. In bad times, sitting tenants, because they can ill afford to move, are almost captive, while in good times they are mobile. Thus, the overall demand (sitting plus prospective tenants) facing a landlord may well be less elastic in troughs than in peaks. It has also been suggested that landlord and tenant enter into a long-term implicit contract, whereby the less risk-averse landlord provides his tenants with insurance against cyclical fluctuations in demand by setting rents below their instantaneous profit-maximizing levels in upturns and above in downturns[34] [see Azariadis and Stiglitz (1983) for a review of the implicit contracts literature which analyzes the analogous phenomenon in

[33]Guasch and Marshall (1985) provide a search-based model of vacancy rates.

[34]The quantitative significance of this effect in North America is questionable because mobility rates are so high (the average rental household moves on average every two or three years) but it may be important in Europe where mobility rates tend to be significantly lower.

the context of labor markets]. Finally, it should be noted that rent controls, of one form or another, are a significant determinant of vacancy rates in a large proportion of Western housing markets.

4.2. Tenure choice and the asset demand for housing

In a perfectly competitive economy, a household's consumption and portfolio composition decisions are separable. It makes no difference to a household whether it owns or rents, since through the purchase of other assets it can achieve the same set of state-contingent consumption possibilities under both tenure modes. When the assumptions of the Arrow–Debreu model are relaxed, however, this separability may no longer obtain.

Henderson and Ioannides (1983) have developed an interesting imperfectly competitive model of tenure choice, in which the interaction of two imperfections determines the tenure mode chosen. The first of these is that a typical renter takes less care of his unit than is efficient because the increase in value from better care accrues to the landlord.[35] The second imperfection is that asset markets are thin, so that a household is unable to diversify away the risk associated with homeownership. If housing is a relatively risky asset, then ceteris paribus one will observe more risk-averse households renting and less risk-averse households owning.[36]

This model is insightful, but neglects a number of other determinants of tenure choice that have been identified:

1. Owners face greater transaction costs associated with moving than renters. Thus, households that are more likely to move are more likely to rent.
2. Capital market imperfections are significant. In an empirical analysis, Jones (1985) found that most households become owner-occupiers when they can afford the downpayment and meet the debt service provisions for a house satisfying their consumption demand. Artle and Varaiya (1978) and Brueckner (1985) have developed models of tenure choice based on this stylized fact.
3. Households differ in their ability to modify units to suit their tastes; ceteris paribus handier people will own and less handy people rent [Weiss (1978)].
4. Households also differ in the care they choose to take; if landlords are unable to monitor care, then a careful household will have an incentive to own since the market rent will be set to provide a landlord with the market

---

[35]It is assumed that the landlord can monitor a tenant's level of care only imperfectly.

[36]Eldor, Pines, and Schwartz (1985) point out that, depending on the covariance of the return from housing with other assets and labor income, the purchase of housing may *reduce* portfolio risk.

rate of return given the average level of care of renters [Henderson and Ioannides (1983)].

5. Owning offers greater security of tenure.
6. Government policy may encourage homeownership. The deductibility of mortgage interest and property tax payments, and the non-taxation of imputed rent and capital gains on housing, in computing income tax payable, encourages homeownership by the rich, since with progressivity the value of the deductions rises with income.

4.3. Mobility costs

Several papers have examined mobility costs in the housing market [Weinberg, Friedman, and Mayo (1981), Hanushek and Quigley (1979), and Venti and Wise (1984)]. All focused on the effect that, because of mobility costs, households do not instantaneously adjust their housing unit choice. This has significant implications for the process of adjustment of the housing market to exogenous and policy changes. Mobility costs also influence the search technology,[37] and, as noted earlier, affect the nature of vacancy rate adjustment.

4.4. Imperfect capital markets

It has already been noted that imperfections in capital markets affect the household's tenure choice and housing consumption decisions. They also influence builder's supply decisions. General theorists have only recently started analyzing the form of capital markets [Gale and Hellwig (1984)]. As a result, capital market imperfections have typically been treated in an ad hoc fashion. In the context of housing, the capital market imperfections facing renters have been captured by assuming that they are subject to a period-by-period, rather than an intertemporal, budget constraint. Homeowners or prospective homeowners, meanwhile, are assumed to maximize utility, subject to being able to borrow only via a mortgage contract, the form of which is taken as exogenous.[38]

[37]Because of mobility costs, a household does not search continuously through time. Instead, it makes a decision to initiate search when it is sufficiently dissatisfied with its current housing that it anticipates the gains from search to exceed mobility costs (or, more precisely, the optimal time to initiate search occurs when the expected marginal benefit of postponing initiating search (which includes the expected benefit of postponing moving costs) equals the expected marginal costs].

[38]It has previously been noted that this procedure was followed in Artle and Varaiya (1978) and Brueckner (1986). There is also a body of literature on the effects of the mortgage tilt (that mortgage payments are constant in nominal rather than real terms, or more generally are imperfectly adjusted to changes in the inflation rate) – see Arvan and Brueckner (1985).

While there has been little explicit theoretical modelling of imperfectly competitive housing markets, a number of empirically-based housing simulation models have been developed which incorporate imperfect features of the market [Anas (1982, 1983) Anas et al. (1984), DeLeeuw and Struyk (1977), Engle et al. (1972). Forrester (1969), Ingram et al. (1971), Kain et al. (1976), Lowry (1964), Kain and Apgar (1985), Behrig and Goldrain (1985), and Wegener (1985)]. The strength of such models is in positive analysis – their ability to forecast. Their weaknesses stem from the ad hoc nature of many of the assumptions concerning individual behavior and market adjustment, and their complexity. Because of their complexity and their lack of strong theoretical foundations, it is often difficult to understand the simulation results. Also, due to their lack of a common theoretical base, it is hard to compare the models. Finally, since there are features of the models which are not solidly-based on individual maximizing behavior, they are poor tools for welfare analysis. Such models will become more useful as their theoretical bases are strengthened.

As was argued earlier, the highest priority item on the research agenda in the economic thery of housing markets is the development of imperfectly competitive and non-competitive models of the housing market. This is essential for the analysis of appropriate government intervention in the housing market. It is also necessary in order to reverse the unfortunate divergence between theoretical and empirical work that has occurred during the last decade.

References

Alonso, W. (1964) *Location and land use*. Cambridge, Mass.: Harvard University Press.

Anas, A. (1978) 'Dynamics of urban residential growth', *Journal of Urban Economics*, 5:66–87.

Anas, A. (1982) *Residential location markets and urban transportation: economic theory, econometrics, and policy analysis with discrete choice models*. New York: Academic Press.

Anas, A. (1983) 'The Chicago area transportation land use analysis system', mimeo.

Anas, A., et al., (1984) 'The Swedish housing market: structure, policy issues, and modelling, The Council on Urban and Regional Planning', The Technological Institute, Northwestern University, working paper.

Arnott, R. (1980) 'A simple urban growth model with durable housing', *Regional Science and Urban Economics*, 10:53–76.

Arnott, R. (1985) 'HOPSIM: a housing policy simulation model', mimeo.

Arnott, R., R. Braid, R. Davidson and D. Pines (1986) 'A general equilibrium spatial model of housing quality and quantity', mimeo.

Arnott, R., R. Davidson and D. Pines (1983) 'Housing quality, maintenance and rehabilitation', *Review of Economic Studies*, 50:467–494.

Arnott, R., R. Davidson and D. Pines (1986) 'The spatial aspects of housing quality, quantity, and maintenance', *Journal of Urban Economics*, 19:190–217.

Arnott, R. and F. Lewis (1979) 'The transition of land to urban use', *Journal of Political Economy*, 87:161–169.

Arnott, R. and J.E. Stiglitz (1986b) 'The welfare economics of moral hazard', Institute for Economic Research, Queen's University, Discussion Paper 635.

Arnott, R. and J.E. Stiglitz (1986a) 'Moral hazard and optimal commodity taxation', *Journal of Public Economics*, 29:1–24.

Arrow, K. and T. Scitovsky (1969) *Readings in welfare economics*. Homewood, Ill.: Richard D. Irwin.

Arrow, K. and F. Hahn (1971) *General competitive analysis*. Amsterdam: North-Holland.

Artle, R. and P. Varaiya (1978) 'Life cycle consumption and ownership', *Journal of Economic Theory*, 18:35–58.

Arvan, L. and J. Brueckner (1985) 'Risk sharing in the adjustable-rate loan market: are existing contracts efficient?', *Office of Real Estate Research*, no. 22. Champaign-Urbana: University of Illinois.

Atkinson, A. and J. Stiglitz (1980) *Lectures on public economics*. New York: McGraw-Hill.

Azariadis, C. and J. Stiglitz (1983) 'Implicit contracts and fixed price equilibria', *Quarterly Journal of Economics*, 98:1–22.

Beckmann, M. (1969) 'On the distribution of urban rent and residential density', *Journal of Economic Theory*, 1:60–67.

Behrig, K. and G. Goldrian (1985) 'The Ifo housing market model', in: K. Stahl, ed., *Microeconomic models of housing markets*. Berlin: Springer-Verlag.

Braid, R. (1981) 'The short-run comparative statics of a rental housing market', *Journal of Urban Economics*, 10:280–310.

Braid, R. (1984) 'The effects of government housing policies in a vintage filtering model', *Journal of Urban Economics*, 16:272–296.

Brueckner, J. (1980) 'A vintage model of urban growth', *Journal of Urban Economics*, 8:389–402.

Brueckner, J. (1981) 'A dynamic model of housing production', *Journal of Urban Economics*, 10:1–14.

Brueckner, J. (1986) 'The down payment constraint and housing tenure choice: a simplified exposition', *Regional Science and Urban Economics*, forthcoming.

Debreu, G. (1959) *Theory of value: an axiomatic analysis of economic equilibrium*. New Haven: Yale University Press.

DeLeeuw, F. and R. Struyk (1977) 'Analyzing housing policies with the Urban Institute model', in: G.K. Ingram, ed., *Residential location and urban housing markets*. Cambridge, Mass.: Ballinger.

Diamond, P. and M. Rothschild (1978) *Uncertainty in economics*. New York: Academic Press.

Diamond, P. and J. Yellin (1985) 'Pricing and distribution of money holdings in a search economy', Department of Economics, M.I.T., working paper 370.

Eldor, R., D. Pines and A. Schwartz (1985) 'The determinants of the household demand for hedging instruments', The Foerder Institute for Economic Research, Tel-Aviv University, working paper no. 1–85.

Engle, R., F. Fisher, J. Harris and J. Rothenberg (1972) 'An econometric simulation of intra-metropolitan housing location: housing, business, transportation, and local government', *American Economic Review*, 62:87–97.

Follain, J. and E. Jimenez (1985) 'Estimating the demand for housing characteristics', *Regional Science and Urban Economics*, 15:77–109.

Forrester, J.W. (1969) *Urban dynamics*. Cambridge, Mass.: M.I.T. Press.

Fujita, M. (1976a) 'Toward a dynamic theory of land use', *Papers of the Regional Science Association*, 37:133–165.

Fujita, M. (1976b) 'Spatial patterns of urban growth: optimum and market', *Journal of Urban Economics*, 3:209–224.

Fujita, M. (1982) 'Spatial patterns of residential development', *Journal of Urban Economics*, 12:22–52.

Fujita, M. (1983) 'Urban spatial dynamics: a review', *Sistemi Urbani*, 3:411–475.

Fujita, M. (1985) 'Existence and uniqueness of equilibrium and optimal land use: boundary rent curve approach', *Regional Science and Urban Economics*, 15:295–324.

Fujita, M. and H. Ogawa (1982) 'Multiple equilibria and structural transition of non-monocentric urban configurations', *Regional Science and Urban Economics*, 12:161–196.

Gale, D. and M. Hellwig (1984) 'Incentive-compatible debt contracts: the one-period problem', *London School of Economics* discussion paper no. 84–97.

Grieson, R.E. (1974) 'The economics of property taxes and land values: the elasticity of supply of structures', *Journal of Urban Economics*, 1:367–381.

Grigsby, W. (1963) *Housing markets and public policy*. Philadelphia, Pa.: University of Pennsylvania Press.

Guasch, J. and R. Marshall (1985) 'Age of rental units and vacancy characteristics', *Regional Science and Urban Economics*, 15:403–419.

Hanushek, E. and J. Quigley (1979) 'The dynamics of the housing market: a stock adjustment model of housing consumption', *Journal of Urban Economics*, 6:90–111.

Harrison, D. and J.F. Kain (1974) 'Cumulative urban growth and urban density functions', *Journal of Urban Economics*, 1:68–98.

Hartwick, J., U. Schweizer and P. Varaiya (1976) 'Comparative statics of a residential economy with several classes', *Journal of Economic Theory*, 13:396–413.

Henderson, J.V. (1977) 'Externalities in a spatial context', *Journal of Public Economics*, 7:89–110.

Henderson, J.V. and Y. Ioannides (1983) 'A model of housing tenure choice', *American Economic Review*, 73:98–113.

Hochman, O. and D. Pines (1982) 'Costs of adjustment and the spatial pattern of a growing, open city', *Econometrica*, 50:1371–1392.

Ingram, G., J. Kain and T. Ginn (1971) *The Detroit prototype of the NBER simulation model*. New York: National Bureau of Economic Research.

Jones, L. (1985) 'Wealth and housing', Faculty of Commerce, University of British Columbia, mimeo.

Kain, J., W. Apgar and T. Ginn (1976) 'Simulation of the market effects of housing allowances', vol. 1: description of the NBER urban simulation model, mimeo.

Kain, J. and W. Apgar (1985) 'The Harvard urban development simulation model', in: K. Stahl, ed., *Microeconomic models of housing markets*. (Berlin: Springer-Verlag).

Kanemoto, Y. (1980) *Theories of urban externalities*. Amsterdam: North-Holland.

Lowry, I.S. (1964) 'A model of metropolis', RM-4035-RC, Rand Corporation.

McCall, J.J. (1982) *The economics of information and uncertainty*. Chicago: The University of Chicago Press.

McDonald, J. (1981) 'Capital-land distribution in urban housing: a survey of empirical estimates', *Journal of Urban Economics*, 9:190–211.

Mills, E.S. (1967) 'An aggregative model of resource allocation in a metropolitan area', *American Economic Review*, 57:197–211.

Mills, E.S. (1972) *Studies in the structure of the urban economy*. Baltimore: Johns Hopkins University Press.

Mirrlees, J.A. (1972) 'The optimum town', *Swedish Journal of Economics*, 74:114–135.

Mortensen, D. (1984) 'Job search and labor market analysis', Northwestern University, Center for Mathematical Studies in Economics and Management Science, mimeo.

Muth, R. (1961) 'Economic change and rural-urban land conversion', *Econometrica*, 29:1–23.

Muth, R.F. (1969) *Cities and housing*. Chicago: The University of Chicago Press.

Ohls, J. and D. Pines (1975) 'Discontinuous urban development and economic efficiency', *Land Economics*, 51:224–234.

J. Quigley (1979) 'What have we learned about urban housing markets', in: P. Mieszkowski and M. Straszheim, eds., *Current issues in urban economics*. Baltimore: Johns Hopkins.

Rosen, K. and L. Smith (1983) 'The price adjustment process for rental housing and the natural vacancy rate', *American Economic Review*, 73:779–786.

Rosen, S. (1974) 'Hedonic prices and implicit markets', *Journal of Political Economy*, 82:35–55.

Rothenberg, J. (1978) 'Urban housing markets and housing policy', in: J. Bernstein and W.G. Mellon, eds., *Selected readings in quantitative urban analysis*. Oxford: Pergamon Press.

Smith, L., et al., (1985) 'The demand for housing, household headship rates, and household formation', *Urban Studies*, 21:407–414.

Solow, R. (1972) 'Congestion, density and the use of land in transportation', *Swedish Journal of Economics*, 74:161–173.

Solow, R. and W. Vickrey (1971) 'Land use in a long, narrow city', *Journal of Economic Theory*, 3:430–447.

Stahl, K. (1980) 'Externalities and housing unit maintenance', University of Dortmund Working Papers in Economic Theory and Urban Economics, 800.

Stahl, K. (1985) 'Microeconomic analysis of housing markets', in: K. Stahl, ed., *Microeconomics models of housing market*. Berlin: Springer-Verlag.

Sweeney, J. L. (1974a) 'Quality, commodity hierarchies and housing markets', *Econometrica*, 42:147–167.

Sweeney, J.L. (1974b) 'A commodity hierarchy model of the rental housing market', *Journal of Urban Economics*, 1:288–323.

Sweeney, J.L. (1974c) 'Modelling housing markets: commodity hierarchies in a spatial setting', *Stanford Journal of International Studies*, 9:167–197.

Venti, S. and D. Wise (1984) 'Moving and housing expenditure: transportation costs and disequilibrium', *Journal of Public Economics*, 23: 207–243.

Wegener, M. (1985) 'The Dortmund housing market model: a Monte Carlo simulation of a regional housing market', in: K. Stahl, ed., *Microeconomic models of housing markets*. Berlin: Springer-Verlag.

Weinberg, D., J. Friedman and S. Mayo (1981) 'Intraurban residential mobility: the role of transactions costs, market imperfections, and household disequilibrium', *Journal of Urban Economics*, 9:332–348.

Weiss, Y. (1978) 'Capital gains, discriminatory taxes, and the choice between renting and owning a house', *Journal of Public Economics*, 10:45–55.

Wheaton, W. (1974) 'A comparative static analysis of urban spatial structure', *Journal of Economic Theory*, 9:223–237.

Wheaton, W., (1979) 'Monocentric models of urban land use, contributions and criticisms', in: P. Mieszkowski and M. Straszheim, eds., *Current Issues in Urban Economics*. Baltimore: Johns Hopkins.

Chapter 25

THE DEMAND AND SUPPLY OF HOUSING SERVICE: A CRITICAL SURVEY OF THE EMPIRICAL LITERATURE

EDGAR O. OLSEN*

University of Virginia

1. Introduction

Spurred in large part by expenditures on data collection and research under the Experimental Housing Allowance Program and the Annual Housing Survey, the past decade has witnessed an enormous increase in the quantity of empirical research in housing economics. As a result, it was not possible to survey the entire literature within the constraints on time and length appropriate for this volume. This paper focuses on the demand and supply of housing service, which is a composite of all attributes of housing valued by consumers. Although this is an important part of the literature, it certainly does not account for the majority of studies. There are many studies on the demand and supply of housing stock [Muth (1960), McDonald (1981)], the demand and supply of particular attributes or bundles of attributes [King (1976), Straszheim (this volume), Follain and Jimenez (1985), Kain and Quigley (1975), Bartik and Smith (this volume)], the consequences of racial consciousness [Yinger (1979)], and the effects of government programs [Olsen (1983), Rosen (1986), Weicher (1979)]. However, the demand and supply of housing service are the foundations upon which work on the other topics is built.

2. The demand for housing service

There is a massive literature on the demand for housing service. The recent literature has been largely devoted to estimating relationships more consistent

*I thank Chuck Manski for allowing me to audit his superbly taught graduate sequence in econometrics at the University of Wisconsin and Jim Berkovec and Wake Epps for their advice on many of the econometric issues that arose during the writing of this paper. Since their words of wisdom may have lost something in the translation, they should not be blamed for errors contained herein. I also thank Richard Arnott, Alan Caniglia, Claire Hammond, and Gregor MacDonald for detailed comments on an earlier draft.

Handbook of Regional and Urban Economics, Volume II, Edited by E.S. Mills

with deterministic models, such as the Muth–Mills model of the spatial variation in housing prices within urban areas, and aspects of reality, such as the income tax treatment of homeownership in the United States, that have been in existence for many years.[1] As a result of the improved specifications of the equations estimated and the availability of more and better data, the range of estimates of the income elasticity of demand for housing service has been reduced and the central tendency has shifted somewhat, and similarly for the price elasticity. In recent years almost all estimates of these elasticities have been less than one in absolute value. Since the results of the bulk of the major studies are contained in several survey articles, this section will focus on methodological developments.[2]

Before proceeding it is desirable to recognize that differences in estimates of the income and price elasticities do not all result from shortcomings in methodology. First, different households have different tastes and hence different demand functions. So even if all households had a demand function of the same form, different samples from the same population would yield different estimates. Second, there is no reason to believe that the population mean values of the parameters are the same in different times and places. Therefore, even highly accurate estimates of these population means could be quite different for different populations. Third, it is undoubtedly the case that each household's price and income elasticities of demand are functions of prices and income. When demand functions that are not linear in the logarithms of the variables are estimated, elasticities are typically calculated at the sample means of the explanatory variables. So even if the estimated demand functions were identical, the reported elasticities could be quite different.[3] These considerations suggest that divergences in previous estimates do not provide a compelling argument for additional estimates of income and price elasticities of demand. A more compelling justification is a divergence between the relationships that have been estimated and well-known aspects of reality or strongly held theoretical presumptions. It is to this matter that we now turn.

---

[1] Recent developments in economic theory such as rational expectations have had little influence as yet.

[2] See DeLeeuw's review (1971) of some of the more influential studies of the 1960's. Mayo's survey (1981) of the literature of the 1970's, and Mayo and Malpezzi's review (1985) of the evidence on housing demand in developing countries.

[3] Results reported by Hanushek and Quigley (1979, p. 100) and Goodman and Kawai (1984, pp. 1053–1055) illustrate the potential importance of this consideration. Hanushek and Quigley find that the permanent income elasticities of housing demand are twice as large in Pittsburgh and Phoenix when evaluated at the SMSA median rather than the sample mean values of the variables involved. Goodman and Kawai estimate separate linear demand functions for owners and renters. When income and price elasticities are calculated at the within-group means of the variables, differences in elasticities between tenure types are on the order of fifty percent. When they are evaluated at the mean income of either owners or renters, the differences disappear. Another reason for differences in estimated elasticities is that the demand function is often assumed to be log-linear and estimated using samples with different joint distributions of prices and income. This misspecification of functional form will lead to systematic differences in parameter estimates for different sample distributions of the explanatory variables.

Since almost all contributors to the empirical literature on housing demand stress the importance of using a measure of permanent rather than current income, this section begins with the specification of a simple model of intertemporal choice and the derivation of its implications for explaining current housing expenditure. It is shown that highly restrictive assumptions must be added to a general intertemporal model to justify the estimated demand functions that appear in the published literature. Accepting these restrictive assumptions for the sake of argument, we then consider the problems that have attracted the most attention, namely the measurement of expected current income and current housing prices and problems associated with the use of aggregate data. Before leaving the simple world of linear budget constraints, two unpublished attempts to estimate intertemporal indifference maps are described. Many recent contributions to the empirical literature on housing demand are attempts to account for various sources of nonlinearities in budget constraints and unobserved differences in tastes. The final subsection of this section deals with three sources of nonlinearities: a housing allowance program, moving costs, and the income tax treatment of homeownership.

2.1. A simple model of intertemporal choice

In deciding on current housing consumption, indeed, current consumption of any good, it is reasonable to believe that individuals take account of their expectations about future incomes and prices. In explaining variations in housing expenditure, almost all contributors to the recent literature claim to be using a measure of permanent rather than current income. Unfortunately, the measures used in studies based on household data are really proxies for expected income in the current period, for example, last period's actual income, the mean income for the past few years, and predicted income based on a regression of current income on household characteristics. Future incomes and prices are ignored in almost all cases.[4] The shortcomings of existing studies which result from these omissions will be discussed taking a standard model of intertemporal choice as the appropriate model. It will be shown that almost all housing demand equations are misspecified relative to this model.[5]

A standard model of intertemporal choice assumes that an individual maximizes a utility function defined over the quantities of all goods in all time periods during which the individual expects to be alive, subject to the constraint that the

---

[4] A few authors justify the inclusion of demographic variables such as the age and education of the head of the household in the demand function on these grounds.

[5] For equations consistent with this model, see Hammond (1982) and Caniglia (1983). Many others are consistent with the model under highly restrictive assumptions about the intertemporal utility function or budget constraint.

present value of future expenditure is equal to wealth including the present value of future labor income.

For ease of exposition, many simplifying assumptions will be made at the outset. The following will be maintained throughout this section. First, the individual has no doubt concerning future incomes and prices and how long he will live. The individual's expectations may not be realized, but he does not recognize this possibility when making decisions concerning current consumption. Second, labor income and the quantities of services provided by governments are not subject to individual choice. Third, all private goods can be divided into two composite commodities called housing service and other goods. Fourth, each consumer has a Stone–Geary indifference map of the form

$$U_i = \prod_{t=1}^{l_i} (H_{it} - \eta_i)^{\gamma_i/l_i} (X_{it} - \theta_i)^{(1-\gamma_i)/l_i}, \tag{1}$$

where U_i is a utility index for the ith person, l_i his life expectancy, H_{it} his housing consumption and X_{it} consumption of other goods in time period t, and γ_i, η_i, and θ_i are his parameters.[6] This specification is sufficiently general to illustrate the shortcomings of the overwhelming majority of demand functions that have been estimated. This is not to say that these demand functions are special cases of the demand functions corresponding to this indifference map but rather that the shortcomings discussed are largely independent of the choice of functional form. Notice that the parameters are assumed to be the same in every time period for a particular individual but are allowed to be different for different individuals. Fifth, observed housing expenditure in the current period for each member of the population is assumed to be equal to optimal expenditure plus an unobserved random variable with mean zero. This allows for the possibility that a person with given tastes would make different choices if confronted repeatedly with the same budget space.

Initially we will make some additional simplifying assumptions that will be relaxed later. First, assume that the option of owner occupancy is not available. All households are renters. Second, assume that the vector of parameters $(\gamma_i, \eta_i, \theta_i)$ is the same for all households. That is, $(\gamma_i, \eta_i, \theta_i) = (\gamma, \eta, \theta)$ for all i. Third, assume that the taxes used to finance government services are lump-sum. Fourth, assume that the ith person's budget constraint is

$$\sum_{t=1}^{l_i} (P_{it}^h H_{it} + P_{it}^x X_{it}) = \sum_{t=1}^{l_i} Y_{it} + \mathrm{NHW}_i \equiv W_i, \tag{2}$$

where P_{it}^h, P_{it}^x, and Y_{it} are the present values of expected prices and after-tax, non-

---

[6] More generally, the ith person's indifference map is of the form

$$U_i = f_i(H_{i1}, \dots, H_{il_i}, X_{i1}, \dots, X_{il_i}).$$

interest incomes and NHW_i and W_i are non-human and total wealth at the beginning of the current period. Fifth, assume that the sample is a random sample from the population of interest.

2.2. Implications of the model for explaining current housing expenditure

Under the preceding assumptions, the observed housing expenditure of the ith household in the sample in the first period will be

$$P_{i1}^h H_{i1} = P_{i1}^h \eta + (\gamma/l_i) \left\{ W_i - \sum_{t=1}^{l_i} (P_{it}^h \eta + P_{it}^x \theta) \right\} + u_i, \tag{3}$$

where the u_i are independent, identically distributed random variables with mean zero.[7] (3) can be rewritten as

$$P_{i1}^h H_{i1} = (\gamma/l_i) W_i + \{1 - (\gamma/l_i)\} \eta P_{i1}^h - (\gamma/l_i) \theta P_{i1}^x$$
$$- (\gamma/l_i) \sum_{t=2}^{l_i} (P_{it}^h \eta + P_{it}^x \theta) + u_i. \tag{4}$$

The estimated demand functions that appear in the published literature differ from (4) in a number of important respects.[8] Most obviously, expected future prices and wealth are rarely included. Various proxies for wealth are used, but these almost always ignore expected future incomes. A less obvious deficiency of the estimated demand functions is their failure to account for life expectancy. From eq. (4) we can see immediately that the effect of a particular change in wealth (or an expected price) on housing consumption in the current period depends on life expectancy. On reflection, it should be clear that this will be true for almost all indifference maps. A person with a short expected life will spend more of a given increase in wealth on current housing consumption than will a person with a long expected life.

One way to view the demand functions that have been estimated is as correctly specified functions under assumptions even more restrictive than the preceding. For example, suppose that we assume that the budget constraints facing the ith person are

$$P_{it}^h H_{it} + P_{it}^x X_{it} = Y_{it}, \quad t = 1, 2, \ldots, l_i, \tag{5}$$

---

[7]More generally,

$$P_{i1}^h H_{i1} = h_i(P_{i1}^h, \ldots, P_{il_i}^h, P_{i1}^x, \ldots, P_{il_i}^x, W_i, l_i) + u_i.$$

[8]Hammond's and Caniglia's unpublished dissertations do contain estimates of stochastic relationships similar to this equation.

instead of (2). That is, lending and borrowing are impossible. In this case, housing expenditure in the first period will be

$$P^h_{i1} H_{i1} = \gamma Y_{i1} + (1 - \gamma)\eta P^h_{i1} - \gamma \theta P^x_{i1} + u_i, \tag{6}$$

which is to say that current housing expenditure depends only on current expected income and prices. It should be noted that this result is crucially dependent upon the intertemporal separability of the assumed utility function. In the absence of intertemporal separability, the indifference map defined over the current consumption bundle will shift in response to changes in expected future incomes and prices because these changes will lead to changes in desired future consumption bundles.

This equation, which is similar to those that have been estimated, can be derived under alternative assumptions. For example, retain the original assumption concerning the budget constraint (namely, (2)) but add the following assumptions. First, the person begins his life as an independent decisionmaker without any non-human wealth. Second, he expects prices and income to increase at a rate equal to the interest rate, and his expectations have been fulfilled up to the present period. These assumptions imply that $Y_{it} = Y_{i1}$, $P^h_{it} = P^h_{i1}$, $P^x_{it} = P^x_{i1}$ for all t and $\text{NHW}_i = 0$ at the beginning of the person's working life. Substituting these expressions into (3) yields (6). This equation combined with a similar equation for expenditure on other goods imply that total spending during the first period will be equal to total labor income. Hence, non-human wealth at the beginning of the second period will be zero, and the outcome is the same in each succeeding period. The optimal consumption bundle does not change over time.[9]

2.3. Measures of income used in estimating housing expenditure functions

Almost all of the improvements in the estimation of housing demand functions in recent years can be viewed as attempts to better estimate a stochastic relationship such as (6). Therefore, in most of the remainder of this section, this will be taken as the correctly specified model. That is, we will make the highly restrictive

---

[9]More generally, if the person's utility function is of the form

$$U = \sum_{t=1}^{l} (1/(1+\tau))^{t-1} u(H_t, X_t),$$

his rate of time preference τ is equal to the real rate of interest, and he begins without any non-human wealth and expects prices and labor income to increase at the same constant rate, then his consumption bundle will be the same in each period. As a result, total expenditure in each period will be equal to labor income in that period, and the quantity of each good demanded in a period can be written as a function of that period's prices and labor income. I wish to thank Richard Arnott for bringing this more general result to my attention.

assumptions that lead to (6). For ease of exposition, it will be assumed in this subsection that all households face the same vector of prices. Unless otherwise noted, a hat above a parameter indicates its OLS estimator, which is by far the most widely used estimator in the literature.

The simplest equation that has been estimated is of the form

$$P_{i1}^h H_{i1} = \alpha_0 + \alpha_1 Y_{i1}^0 + u_i. \tag{7}$$

where Y_{i1}^0 is observed income in the current period. If the observed income is that expected when the consumption decision is made and if prices are the same for all consumers, then $\hat{\alpha}_1$ is an unbiased estimator of γ in (6) and $\hat{\alpha}_0$ an unbiased estimator of $(1-\gamma)\eta P_1^h - \gamma\theta P_1^x.$[10] The parameters η and θ are not identified.

One of the earliest contributions to the methodology for estimating housing demand functions was the recognition that observed income may differ from the income that was expected when the decision concerning current housing consumption was made due, for example, to unemployment or divorce [Muth (1960); Reid (1962)]. The deviation between observed and expected income might be appropriately viewed as a random draw from a distribution with mean zero for each individual. That is, $Y_{i1}^0 = Y_{i1} + v_i$, where $E(v_i|Y_{i1})=0$. In this case, we have a familiar errors-in-variables problem. OLS estimators are inconsistent and the asymptotic expectation of $\hat{\alpha}_1$ is less than α_1. Almost all studies that estimate an equation such as (7) using, alternatively, current income and a measure of expected income find that the coefficient of the latter is greater than that of the former.[11]

Twenty to twenty-five years ago the typical approach to this problem was to use total consumption expenditure as a proxy for expected current or permanent income.[12] If we ignore the relationship between the error term and observed explanatory variables, this approach is easily justified. Under the assumption of intertemporal separability, current housing expenditure can be written as a function of current total consumption and prices. For example, in the model leading up to (3),

$$P_{i1}^x X_{i1} = P_{i1}^x \theta + [(1-\gamma)/l_i]\left\{ W_i - \sum_{t=1}^{l_i} (P_{it}^h \eta + P_{it}^x \theta) \right\} + v_i, \tag{8}$$

and hence total consumption in the first period is

$$C_{i1} = P_{i1}^h \eta + P_{i1}^x \theta + (1/l_i)\left\{ W_i - \sum_{t=1}^{l_i} (P_{it}^h \eta + P_{it}^x \theta) \right\} + \varepsilon_i, \tag{9}$$

---

[10]In this case, $Y_{i1}^0 = Y_{i1}$. Recall that Y_{1i} is a random variable only because its value depends upon the identity of the household draw on the ith draw by random sampling and that the Y_{i1} are independent of the u_i.

[11]See, for example, Polinsky and Ellwood (1979, pp. 202–203) and Mayo (1981, pp. 97–98).

[12]See, for example, Houthakker (1957), Muth (1960), and Reid (1962).

where

$$\varepsilon_i = u_i + v_i. \tag{9}$$

Substitution of eq. (9) into eq. (3) leads to

$$P_{i1}^h H_{i1} = \gamma C_{i1} + (1 - \gamma)\eta P_{i1}^h - \gamma \theta P_{i1}^x + \omega_i, \tag{10}$$

where $\omega_i = u_i - \gamma(u_i + v_i)$. If there is no variation in prices, it is convenient to rewrite eq. (10) as

$$P_{i1}^h H_{i1} = \alpha_0 + \alpha_1 C_{i1} + \omega_i. \tag{11}$$

Unfortunately, ω_i in (11) may be correlated with ε_i in (9) and so C_{i1} may be correlated with ω_i.[13] As a result, OLS estimators may be inconsistent. The merit of this approach to estimating the parameters of the demand function depends in part on the extent of the correlation between C_{i1} and ω_i in (11) compared with that between Y_{i1}^0 and u_i in (7).

Other proxies for expected income in the current period have been more common in recent years primarily because the major sources of data such as the Annual Housing Survey and the Experimental Housing Allowance Program do not contain information on total consumption.

A widely used proxy is the household's mean real income over some period ending in, or centering around, the current period.[14] Under the assumptions that real income is expected to be constant over time and that observed real income in each period is equal to expected real income plus the value of a random variable with mean zero, this estimator of expected income in the current period in unbiased and has a smaller variance than the observed income in this period. If real income is expected to increase by a constant amount each period, the unbiasedness of the estimator of expected current income requires that the incomes used to calculate the mean be centered around the current period.[15] Therefore, under certain assumptions, using mean rather than current income will ameliorate the errors-in-variables problem associated with deviations between expected and observed current income. Mean income is not, however, a good proxy for permanent income or wealth because it takes no account of differences in life expectancy or in the time profiles of expected income.

Another proxy for current expected income that has been used is predicted income based on a regression of current observed income on household characteristics such as age, education, sex, and race.[16] The assumptions under which the

---

[13] The sign of the correlation depends on the relative magnitudes of the parameter γ, the covariance between u_i and v_i, and the variances of these two random variables.

[14] See, for example, Carliner (1973), Friedman and Weinberg (1981), and Goodman and Kawai (1982).

[15] This does not appear to be widely recognized. Other time paths of expected income call for other estimators of this period's expected income.

[16] See, for example, Struyk (1976, Chapter 4 and appendix C) and Goodman and Kawai (1982).

estimators have desirable properties can be easily stated. If we continue to make either set of assumptions that led to (6) and the assumption of no price variation, this equation can be written

$$P_{i1}^h H_{i1} = \alpha_0 + \gamma Y_{i1} + u_i, \tag{12}$$

where Y_{i1} is the unobserved expected income of the ith household to enter the sample and Y_{i1} and u_i are uncorrelated. Observed current income is assumed to be equal to expected income plus a random draw from a distribution with mean zero. That is,

$$Y_{i1}^0 = Y_{i1} + v_i, \tag{13}$$

where $E(v_i|Y_{i1}) = 0$. Finally, expected income in the current period is assumed to depend on observed characteristics of the individual and an error term that reflects unobserved characteristics. Specifically,

$$Y_{i1} = \delta_0 + \sum_{k=1}^{m} \delta_k Z_{ki} + w_i. \tag{14}$$

The usual approach to estimating the parameters of interest, namely α_0 and γ in (12), is to substitute (14) into (13), to estimate the parameters of this equation by OLS, to use these estimates to predict Y_{i1} for each observation, to rewrite (12) so that $\hat{Y}_{1i}$ is the observed explanatory variable, and to estimate this equation by OLS. If the $E(w_i|Z_{1i}, \ldots, Z_{mi}) = 0$ in eq. (14), $\hat{\alpha}_0$ and $\hat{\gamma}$ are consistent estimators. However, in the literature devoted to explaining differences in earnings, the possibility of a significant correlation between the error term and included explanatory variables is frequently mentioned. For example, measures of ability are rarely included and are believed to be correlated with included variables such as years of schooling.[17] If w_i is correlated with the Z_{ki}, then $\hat{\alpha}_0$ and $\hat{\gamma}$ will be inconsistent estimators. Even if w_i is uncorrelated with the Z_{ki}, this approach is not necessarily superior to using actual income as a proxy for expected income. If the variance of v_i is small and the variance of w_i is large, the inconsistency of the OLS estimators of the regression of housing expenditure on actual income will be more than offset by their smaller variance.[18]

Finally, instrumental variables have been used to reduce the inconsistency resulting from using actual income as a proxy for expected income in estimating housing expenditure equations.[19] Across a population, the correlation between last period's actual income and this period's expected income is likely to be high

---

[17]Griliches and Mason (1972) and Chamberlain (1977) have found that this particular correlation is small and leads to little bias.

[18]The fit of earnings functions based on micro data is generally poor, and reflection suggests that individuals can predict their income during the coming year with considerable accuracy. Public and private insurance protects individuals from income loss due to many important, unpredictable events.

[19]See, for example, Lee (1968) and Lee and Kong (1977).

and the correlation between last period's actual income and the difference between this period's expected and actual income is likely to be low. For this reason, it is reasonable to use last period's actual income as an instrument in estimating the relationship between mean housing expenditure and expected income when actual income is used as a proxy for expected income.

2.4. Treatment of prices in estimating housing expenditure functions

There have been numerous estimates of the relationship between housing expenditure and income based on household data because information on these magnitudes is abundant. Price indices for housing and other goods are often not included among the explanatory variables either because it is assumed that there is no variation in prices in the population or because such indices are unavailable and expensive to produce.[20]

The assumption of no price variation is often made when the data refer to a single urban area. Unfortunately, this assumption is contrary to an implication of the simplest model of the determination of housing prices within an urban area.[21] This model implies that the price per unit of housing service will be lower farther from the central business district because land prices are lower and the prices of other inputs used to produce housing are the same. More complicated models lead to more complicated variations in land price with location but only by happenstance will housing prices be the same everywhere.

If prices paid by different households in the same urban area are different but uncorrelated with household income, the failure to include prices in the equation to be estimated will make it impossible to estimate all of the parameters of the indifference map but will not lead to inconsistent estimates of the parameters estimated. Unfortunately, the aforementioned model leads us to expect a correlation between income and housing price. If tastes are assumed to be identical, the sign of the correlation depends on income and price elasticities of demand for housing service. Under realistic assumptions about these elasticities, the correlation between income and housing price will be negative. Although theoretical reasoning suggests a correlation between income and housing price, it has nothing to say about the magnitude of this correlation and, hence, about the magnitude of the bias in estimating the parameters of demand functions that results from the failure to include housing price in the equation. Available evidence [Polinsky and Ellwood (1979, p. 204); Mayo and Malpezzi (1985, p. 33)] suggests that the bias is small.[22]

[20]The difficulty in producing good housing price indices is that dwellings differ in many ways.
[21]See, for example, Mills (1980, Chapter 5).
[22]Two explanations come immediately to mind. First, the simple model does not take account of many important determinants of housing price. Second, the estimated housing prices used to obtain this result may be bad proxies for true prices.

When data on households living in different urban areas is used to estimate housing demand functions, it is common to assume that households living in the same urban area face the same set of prices and to use price indices across urban areas based on the U.S. Bureau of Labor Statistics's budgets for an urban family of four persons.[23] One problem with this procedure was discussed in the preceding paragraph. Here too the available evidence [Polinsky and Ellwood, (1979, p. 204)] suggests that the resulting bias is small.

Despite Polinsky and Ellwood's findings, it is premature to dismiss the desirability of attempting to calculate the prices facing individual consumers even when data on households living in different urban areas is used. Additional studies are needed to confirm their conclusions. Furthermore, when data for only a single urban area is available, information on the prices facing individual consumers is usually necessary to identify the parameters of the utility function.[24]

Several methods for calculating the price per unit of housing service associated with a particular dwelling unit have been developed.

The method originated by Muth (1971) and refined by Polinsky and Ellwood (1979) can be used when data on the price per unit and quantity of land are available. The method involves combining this data with information on the selling price of the dwelling and a residential construction cost index (e.g., the Boeckh index) to estimate a production function with two inputs – land and a composite of all other inputs. To make the method tractable, the production function is assumed to be linear homogeneous.[25] Given the estimated production function, average cost can be written as a function of the input price indices. The housing price index is obtained by evaluating this function at the input prices associated with each dwelling.

Two drawbacks of this method are worth noting. First, it implicitly assumes that the market is in long-run equilibrium. Otherwise, price would not be equal to average cost. Second, the price obtained is the price per unit of housing stock rather than the price per unit of housing service. Housing service is produced with housing stock and other inputs. It is difficult to imagine a plausible set of assumptions under which the price of service is proportional to the price of stock.[26] Despite these drawbacks, this has clearly been an important contribution to the methodology for estimating housing demand functions.

---

[23]In recent years, the BLS housing price index has been increasingly supplanted by an index produced by researchers at the Urban Institute using data from the Annual Housing Survey. See, for example, Malpezzi, Ozanne, and Thibodeau (1980) and Follain, Ozanne, and Alburger (1979).

[24]For some simple indifference maps, more readily available data can be used under somewhat plausible assumptions. See, for example, Olsen and Barton (1983, pp. 309–312).

[25]More specifically, a CES form is usually assumed.

[26]If the production function is linear homogeneous and if the price of housing stock is proportional to the price of operating inputs, then this would be the case. However, it is not plausible to believe that the prices of non-land inputs used to build a structure are independent of its location but that the prices of inputs used to maintain it are more expensive at locations where land is more expensive.

Another approach to calculating the prices facing different consumers in a single housing market is to assume that the price per unit of housing service received by sellers is the same everywhere (or is uncorrelated with income and other explanatory variables in the demand function) and to use data on differences in per-unit taxes and subsidies for housing facing consumers to construct a housing price index [Friedman and Weinberg (1981)]. This method is not widely applicable because few government housing programs simply rotate budget constraints or shift them in a parallel fashion [Olsen (1971, pp. 168–169); Olsen (1972, pp. 1083–84); Kraft and Olsen (1977, pp. 52–53); Olsen (1983, pp. 208–209); Reeder (1985, pp. 352–354)].[27] However, under the Experimental Housing Allowance Program, a small percentage of low-income households in Pittsburgh and Phoenix were offered a subsidy equal to a fixed fraction of their housing expenditure. Different households selected at random were offered different fractions and hence faced different housing prices. The advantage of this data for estimating housing demand is that the sample variability in the price of housing service relative to other goods is much larger than in other data bases, and so it is possible to make much more accurate estimates of the indifference map parameters.

Before leaving our discussion of the treatment of housing price in the estimation of housing demand functions, it is worth noting that measurement error in this variable has received much less attention than the measurement error associated with deviations between current expected and observed income even though it is likely to be much more important.

2.5. Problems with using aggregate data to estimate housing expenditure functions

Up to this point, we have discussed estimation based on data for households. Many estimates of demand functions are based on aggregate data because this type of data is less expensive to obtain.[28] We turn now to the special problems associated with its use.

If the mean values of the variables are the means for random samples from the population of interest and if the means are the appropriate means given the assumed functional form of the regression equation, then aggregation does not result in any bias in OLS estimators. For example, if the housing expenditure of the ith household selected at random from some population is a linear function of

---

[27]Indeed, as a result of government programs, virtually everyone in the United States has a highly nonlinear budget frontier, contrary to an assumption underlying almost all estimated behavioral relationships in economics.

[28]At some cost the underlying household data could usually have been obtained, but in many cases the cost would have been substantial.

current income and prices plus an error term that can be viewed as a random draw from some distribution and if the first n_1 observations are assigned to group 1, the second n_2 to group 2, and so on, then the OLS estimators of a regression of mean housing expenditure on mean income and prices are unbiased estimators of the parameters of the household regression. The assumptions underlying this result, however, are usually not satisfied for demand functions that have been estimated with aggregate data.

Some studies assume functions linear in the logarithms of the variables and use data on the logarithms of the means of these variables to estimate its parameters. Data on the means of the logarithms of the variables are not used because they are not readily available. Polinsky and Ellwood's evidence (1979) suggests that the bias resulting from this misspecification alone is small.

The more troubling deviation from the preceding assumptions is that the means refer to sets of households that cannot be regarded as random samples from some population. Instead they refer to households who have chosen to live in particular geographical areas.

Some studies rely on data on the mean values of variables for different census tracts in an urban area. Since housing within a census tract is relatively homogeneous compared with housing throughout the urban area, this is an instance of endogenous sampling.[29] The consequence for the properties of the estimators is easily illustrated. Assume that all households in an urban area face the same prices. Assume that desired current housing expenditure of each household depends only on expected current income. Assume that there is no difference between desired and observed current housing expenditure R or between expected and observed current income Y for any household. However, suppose that there are differences in taste among households so that different households with the same income may spend different amounts on housing and that the distribution of the taste parameters is the same at every income level. For illustrative purposes, assume that the same number of households in the urban area have rent-income combinations indicated by the points A through I in Figure 1. The height of the solid line is the $E(R|Y)$, and suppose that we want to estimate its parameters. If the urban area is divided into 5 geographical areas where the rent of all units in the ith area is R_i (e.g., area 2 contains households with rent-income combinations B and F) and if we use data on the mean rent and income in these areas to estimate a linear relationship, the OLS estimate of the slope will be greater than γ and the estimate of the intercept will be less than α as indicated by the dashed line in Figure 1.

Using data on 200 households living in Chicago, Smith and Campbell (1978) have obtained results that suggest the bias could be large. When they group

---

[29]On the general topic of endogenous sampling, see Hausman and Wise (1981).

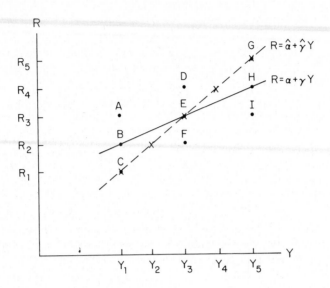

Figure 1. Bias resulting from use of census data.

households according to the magnitude of housing expenditure and regress the logarithm of mean housing expenditure on the logarithm of mean income, they get estimates of the income elasticity of demand twice as large as when the means are for groups of the same size obtained by random assignment. Notice that both regressions suffer from the first type of aggregation bias mentioned above, namely using the logarithm of means rather than the means of the logarithms of the variables. Furthermore, since the observations are not grouped by census tract, this study does not estimate the magnitude of the bias attributable to the use of census tract means.

Another type of bias emerges when OLS is used to estimate a demand function based on the mean values of variables in different urban areas, namely the usual simultaneous-equations bias. If one household happens to spend more than its utility-maximizing amount on housing and less on other goods, this will have a miniscule effect on market demands and hence market prices. That is, the correlation between the error term and prices in an equation such as (7) is close to zero and so can be ignored. The correlation between the mean of the error terms of all consumers in the market and price is much greater and should not be ignored. One solution to the bias created by this correlation is to estimate a simultaneous-equations model. This approach has rarely been taken in housing economics. At the very least, it would seem desirable to follow DeLeeuw's lead

(1971, pp. 7–9) and obtain the reverse least-squares estimates of the parameters.[30] Under plausible assumptions, if the direct least-squares estimate of the slope coefficient of interest has the sign expected for a demand function, then this coefficient lies between the probability limits of its direct and reverse least-squares estimators [Leamer (1981)].

Up to this point, we have considered only disadvantages of using aggregate data. It has been claimed that aggregation across households has an advantage, namely that it reduces the bias associated with using current observed income as a proxy for current expected income. The intuition is that within a group positive and negative deviations of observed from expected income cancel with the result that the variance in the mean of the deviations is less than the variation in the deviations. The problem with this argument is that the extent of the inconsistency of the OLS estimator (that is, the difference between the parameter and the probability limit of its OLS estimator) also depends on the variance of expected income. Indeed, under the usual assumptions, it depends on the ratio of this variance to the variance in the measurement error [Johnston (1972, p. 282)]. If households are assigned randomly to groups, then the ratio of these variances will be the same for group means as for household data.

2.6. Recent attempts to estimate intertemporal indifference maps

It has not been until quite recently that anyone has attempted to estimate an intertemporal model of the sort described at the beginning of this section. Hammond (1982) and Caniglia (1983) assume that each household maximizes an intertemporal utility function defined over housing service and other goods in each period, subject to a budget constraint that restricts the present value of future consumption to be equal to wealth. Their assumptions imply that a household's current housing expenditure depends on its wealth, expected prices, interest rates, life expectancy, and all of the parameters of the utility function. Current housing expenditure is observed, but the explanatory variables must be predicted before the parameters can be estimated. Hammond and Caniglia devote considerable effort to the prediction of unobserved past and expected future non-interest income. Their primary sources of data are the Annual Housing Survey (Hammond) and the Panel Study of Income Dynamics (Caniglia). Using data for households in these samples, they regress income on household characteristics such as the years of schooling, age, and sex of the head of the household. This equation, together with an estimate of the expected rate of growth in real income

---

[30]The reverse least-squares estimates of the parameters are the least-squares estimates of the parameters when the demand function is rewritten so that price is the dependent variable.

and (in the case of Caniglia's study) observed income over a three-year period, are used to predict each household's expected non-interest income in each year of its expected working life. It is assumed that each household starts and ends its working life with no non-human capital. The preceding predictions and assumptions make it possible to express wealth at the observed stage of the life cycle in terms of the utility function parameters and predicted values of the other explanatory variables. Predictions of these other variables are made under extremely simple assumptions. For example, it is assumed that relative prices are expected to remain the same over time, and BLS and (in the case of Hammond) Urban Institute cross-sectional price indices are used. Nonlinear least-squares estimates of the parameters of the indifference map are obtained separately for households with similar observed characteristics using observed current income and predicted values of the other variables. Although the assumptions underlying these estimates are quite restrictive, they are not more restrictive than the assumptions needed to justify previous research. They are only more explicit and thereby make clear directions for future improvements in the methodology for estimating housing demand functions.

 2.7. Relaxing the assumptions of the simple model: Heterogeneous tastes and nonlinear budget frontiers

Many recent contributions can be viewed as attempts to account for realistic deviations from some of the assumptions made at the beginning of this section, especially unobserved differences in tastes and various sources of nonlinearities in budget constraints.

Researchers who wish to account for differences in taste typically assume that all households in the population of interest have an indifference map with the same functional form. The parameters of the indifference map, or equivalently, the parameters of the corresponding system of behavioral equations, are allowed to be different for different households. It is extremely rare to have enough data on particular households to estimate their indifference-map parameters, and in any event, this is not usually of interest. What are desired are parameter estimates for a typical household. If (1) all households face linear budget constraints, (2) the behavioral equations are sufficiently simple functions of the taste parameters, and (3) the data are generated by random sampling from the population of interest, then consistent estimates of the mean taste parameters can be easily obtained.[31] Suppose, for example, that we alter the assumptions underlying (6) to allow for

---

[31] If households have different tastes and the data are not generated by random sampling, then it is difficult to see how anything of interest can be estimated based on a single observation for each household.

differences in tastes and that the data are generated by simple random sampling from some population. To account for taste differences, we attach the subscript i to each parameter. This yields

$$P_{i1}^h H_{i1} = \gamma_i Y_{i1} + (1 - \gamma_i)\eta_i P_{i1}^h - \gamma_i \theta_i P_{i1}^x + u_i. \tag{15}$$

Since the identity of the household selected on the ith draw will be different in different samples, all variables in (15) are random variables. We can write each indifference-map parameter as the sum of its population mean and the household's deviation from this mean, specifically, $\gamma_i = \gamma + g_i$, $\eta_i = \eta + e_i$, and $\theta_i = \theta + t_i$. After rearranging terms, this yields

$$P_{i1}^h H_{i1} = \gamma Y_{i1} + (1 - \gamma)\eta P_{i1}^h - \gamma \theta P_{i1}^x + \delta_i, \tag{16}$$

where

$$\delta_i = g_i Y_{i1} + [(1 - \gamma)e_i - g_i(\eta + e_i)]P_{i1}^h - [\gamma t_i + g_i(\theta + t_i)]P_{i1}^x + u_i.$$

If the random variables g_i, u_i, e_i, and t_i are mutually independent and each is independent of the random vector $(Y_{i1}, P_{i1}^h, P_{i1}^x)$, $E(\delta_i|Y_{i1}, P_{i1}^h, P_{i1}^x) = 0$ and OLS estimators of the mean taste parameters γ, η, and θ are consistent. So, if budget constraints are linear, accounting for unobserved differences in tastes is easy.

An important recent development in applied microeconomics is the recognition that no one faces anything vaguely resembling a linear budget constraint and that

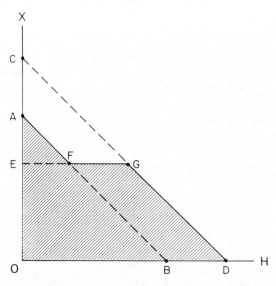

Figure 2. Budget space under housing allowance program.

all previously estimated behavioral equations are misspecified on this account. This has led to the development of econometric methods for estimating the parameters of the indifference maps of households facing such budget constraints, or equivalently, the parameters of their output demand and input supply functions [Burtless and Hausman (1978); Hausman (1981); Moffitt and Nicholson (1982)].

Government programs account for many nonlinearities in budget frontiers. In the earliest attempt to account for this phenomenon in housing economics, Hausman and Wise (1980) estimate the mean parameters of a housing expenditure function using data on households eligible for a minimum-rent type of housing allowance. Under this program, each family is eligible to receive a cash payment provided that it spends at least a specified amount on housing. Since it is not illegal to pay higher than the market price for housing, the minimum-rent requirement places an upper limit on expenditure on, and hence the quantity of, other goods. Since the minimum rent exceeded the payment to each household in the housing allowance program considered by Hausman and Wise, the maximum expenditure on non-housing goods is less than income for each participant.

Ignoring the possibility of illegal behavior, the budget space of an eligible household will have the general shape of the shaded area in Figure 2.[32] The quantities of housing services H and other goods X are measured along the horizontal and vertical axes, respectively. In the absence of any subsidy, the household's budget frontier is the line segment AB. If the household were given an unrestricted cash grant, its budget frontier would be the line segment CD. The minimum-rent requirement limits consumption of non-housing goods to an amount no greater than OE if the household participates in the program. Since participation is voluntary, an eligible household may choose consumption bundles in the triangle OAB. If it does participate, it can choose bundles in the quadrilateral $OEGD$. Since the household can do either, its budget space is the shaded area.[33]

A tempting approach to estimating the mean parameters of a housing demand function for a population facing such budget spaces (based on data for a random sample from this population) is to ignore observations on households that choose the kink point G, pretend that households that choose a bundle on AF face the linear budget constraint AB and that those that choose a bundle on GD face the

---

[32] In this case, illegal behavior might take several forms. The landlord might be bribed to certify falsely that the tenant has paid the minimum rent. Alternatively, the tenant might pay the minimum rent and receive a rebate for his landlord.

[33] In light of this description of the budget constraint, the title of Hausman and Wise's article may seem puzzling. This title probably occurred to them because they measure housing consumption along the vertical axis and consumption of other goods along the horizontal axis. Maximum consumption of housing service is a discontinuous function of consumption of non-housing goods. However, the key feature of the budget constraint with which they deal is not the discontinuity of the budget frontier but rather the non-convexity of the budget space.

linear budget constraint *CD*, specify a demand function that is linear in its parameters, and use OLS to estimate these parameters. This approach has two serious problems. First, ignoring observations at the kink point *G* will probably lead to selection bias. Imagine, for example, that all households in the population are maximizing their well-being subject to the budget constraint depicted in Figure 2 and that they choose either the kink point *G* or a point along *GD*. Obviously, the households that choose *G* have the weakest taste for housing and, hence, the mean housing consumption of other households conditional on income and prices is greater than the mean housing consumption of all households. Second, even if no household's utility maximizing bundle occurs at a kink point, this is an unsatisfactory approach because OLS estimators will be inconsistent. Among households with the same budget frontier *AFGD*, those with the weakest taste for housing and hence the smallest error terms will select a bundle on *AF*, while those with the strongest taste for housing and largest error terms will select a bundle on *GD*. Therefore, the error term in the housing demand equation would be correlated with income.

Hausman and Wise account for unobserved differences in taste and failure to maximize by deriving and estimating a likelihood function conditional on observed determinants of taste and *all* of the parameters of the budget space. Under plausible assumptions about error terms, their estimators are consistent.

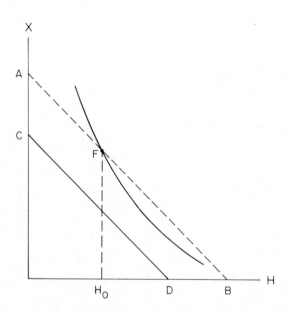

Figure 3. Budget space accounting for moving costs.

They also show how to use their results to predict the outcomes of minimum-rent housing allowances with parameters different from those used in the EHAP

Moving costs are another source of nonlinearity in the budget constraint facing a household. For the moment, ignore intertemporal considerations. That is, imagine that the consumer expects the current period to be his last. In Figure 3, the quantities of housing services H and other goods X are measured along the axes. Imagine that the household occupies a dwelling that will provide H_0 units of housing service in the current period. It is usually assumed that the household has a linear budget frontier such as the dashed line AB.[34] However, when moving costs are taken into account, it is clear that this is not the case. A simple view of the consequence of moving cost for the consumer's budget frontier is that his options are to stay put, which enables him to have the bundle F, or to move, which enables him to have bundles on the line CD. If units of the composite of other goods are defined so that its price is one, AC is the out-of-pocket cost of moving.[35] If this were the consumer's budget frontier and if the consumer's preferences were as indicated in Figure 3, he would choose the bundle F at which the marginal rate of commodity substitution between housing service and other goods is not equal to the ratio of market prices.

Since the decision to move affects future consumption possibilities, an intertemporal model is necessary to properly account for moving costs. Despite Muth's seminal work (1974), the typical approach to this problem in the literature is quite different. Demand functions are estimated using data on recent movers only, on the argument that they have chosen consumption bundles such that marginal rates of substitution are equal to relative prices.[36] In the presence of moving costs, it should be clear that choosing such a consumption bundle will almost always be inconsistent with intertemporal utility maximization, even for someone who has just moved. To see this, assume that a household cannot control the flow of service from its dwelling and that, for all dwellings, the landlord's profit-maximizing policy is to allow the unit to deteriorate continuously. Suppose that a household's intertemporal preferences are such that if

---

[34]This assumes that the price per unit of housing service is the same for dwellings providing different quantities. That is, at any point in time units that provide twice as much housing service rent for twice as much. Clearly, this need not be the case in the housing market except in long-run equilibrium. For example, the fixed total amount of housing service available in the market period cannot be distributed among consumers in any way. There may be no price per unit of housing service at which the vector of quantities demanded corresponds exactly to the vector of quantities provided by existing units. In this case, the equilibrium price per unit of housing service will be different for dwellings providing different quantities. This source of nonlinearity in budget frontiers has received little attention in the literature, possibly due to its intractability.

[35]For simplicity, psychological costs will be ignored, which is not to say that they are unimportant.

[36]It is often said that recent movers are more nearly in equilibrium, though this is probably not what is meant. Presumably, all households are trying to maximize their well-being subject to the constraints that they face, and there is no reason to believe that recent movers are more successful.

moving were costless and the intertemporal budget constraint were linear, it would choose an increasing time path of housing consumption.[37] Finally, assume that with costly moving it is not optimal for the household to move in every period. Under these assumptions, a household that has just moved will not choose a consumption bundle at which marginal rates of substitution are equal to relative prices.

Several recent studies [Weinberg, Friedman, and Mayo (1981); Venti and Wise (1984)] have investigated the effect of moving costs on a household's short-run response to changes in its circumstances.[38] Although these studies are not based on a well-developed intertemporal model of consumer choice, they provide fairly persuasive evidence that moving costs, especially of a nonmonetary nature, are important. Specifically, if moving costs were zero, the short-run response in housing consumption to changes in a household's budget space would be much greater, at least within the range of changes in budget spaces brought about by the Experimental Housing Allowance Program which provided the data for these studies.

Up to this point in the analysis, we have assumed that all households are renters. There are many studies devoted entirely to explaining tenure choice [Li (1977); Boehm (1981)]. Here we focus on the implications of tenure choice and the income tax treatment of homeownership in the United States for estimating housing demand functions.

It is important to be clear at the outset concerning what we seek to estimate. Regardless of whether a person is an owner at a particular time, that person is assumed to have a demand function for owner-occupied housing. This function tells us the quantity of housing service that the person would demand if forced to be an owner. For simplicity, everyone is assumed to have a function of the same form, but not necessarily with the same parameters. One objective is to estimate the population means of these parameters. Similar remarks apply to the demand for rental housing service.

The overwhelming majority of studies of housing demand simply use data on households who have chosen a particular tenure to estimate the corresponding population demand function. Lee and Trost (1978) show that OLS estimators of the parameters of these relationships are inconsistent estimators of the parameters of interest under plausible assumptions. Specifically, assume that the available data are for a random sample from the population of renters and

---

[37]This is consistent with Caniglia's finding (1983, pp. 60–61).

[38]The paper by Venti and Wise contains an exemplary discussion of the nature of the error terms involved (see, for example, page 213) and of how to estimate indifference-map parameters when households face discontinuous budget spaces. Although the indifference map estimated has the undesirable property that it shifts with every change in the budget space, this shortcoming can be easily remedied and may have had little effect on their results.

owners. Assume also that the rental demand function of the ith household in the sample is of the form

$$H_i^r = h^r(Y_i, P_i^r, P_i^x; \beta^r) + u_i^r, \tag{17}$$

where H_i^r is its demand for rental housing service; Y_i its expected current income; P_i^r and P_i^x are expected current prices of rental housing service and other goods, respectively; β^r is a vector of mean parameters for the entire population; and the u_i^r are independent, identically distributed random variables with $E(u_i^r|Y_i, P_i^r, P_x^i) = 0$. This equation applies to all members of the sample not just to those who happen to be renters at some point in time. Indeed, among all renters in the population with the same income and facing the same prices, the mean of the error term is not necessarily zero. So if random sampling is limited to those households, $E(u_i^r|Y_i, P_i^r, P_i^x) \neq 0$ necessarily. Similarly, the owner demand function of the ith household in the sample is of the form

$$H_i^0 = h^0(Y_i, P_i^0, P_i^x; \beta^0) + u_i^0, \tag{18}$$

where the symbols are defined in obvious ways and $E(u_i^0|Y_i, P_i^0, P_i^x) = 0$. To complete the model, it is assumed that the ith household in the sample will be a renter if and only if

$$T(Y_i, P_i^r, P_i^0, P_i^x; \gamma) > \tau_i, \tag{19}$$

where γ is a vector of mean parameters for the population and the τ_i are independent, identically distributed random variables with

$$E(\tau_i|Y_i, P_i^r, P_i^0, P_i^x) = 0.^{39}$$

Obviously, the household will be an owner if the inequality is reversed.

If the renter subsample is used to estimate (17) and the owner sample to estimate (18), the consistency of the OLS estimators of β^r and β^0 hinges on the relationship between the unobserved random variables in (17)–(19) conditional on the values of the observed random variables Y_i, P_i^r, P_i^0, and P_i^x. The joint distribution of u_i^r, u_i^0, and τ_i conditional on Y_i, P_i^r, P_i^0, and P_i^x is assumed to be the same for all vectors of values of the observed random variables and for all observations.[40] If τ_i is independent of u_i^r and u_i^0, then OLS estimators of β^r and β^0 are consistent. However, it is more reasonable to believe that these random variables are correlated and hence that OLS estimators are inconsistent.

These results are easy to understand. Suppose that τ_i is independent of u_i^r and that initially all households are renters. OLS estimators of the parameters of (17)

---

[39] The housing demand functions h^r and h^0 and the function T could have additional arguments, but this is inessential for our purposes.

[40] It is worth noting that this assumption will almost always be violated if (17)–(19) are derived from explicit utility functions allowing for differences in taste. Each of the error terms will typically depend in part on income and prices.

based on a random sample of renters will be consistent. Now suppose that the price of owner-occupied housing falls so that some households want to own. According to inequality (19), households with the largest τ_i will become owners. Conditional on any set of values for Y_i, P_i^r, and P_i^0, these households will have values of u^r with the same distribution as the distribution for renters before the change. Therefore, among the remaining renters, it will still be the case that $E(u_i^r|Y_i, P_i^r, P_i^0)=0$ and OLS estimators of the parameters of (17) based on a random sample of the remaining renters will be consistent. If τ_i is not independent of u_i^r, it is not necessarily the case that the conditional expectation of the error term is equal to zero for all values of the observed explanatory variables.

Lee and Trost do not give any reason to expect that u_i^r and τ_i are correlated. However, it is easy to construct an argument. It is reasonable to believe that u_i^r and u_i^0 are positively correlated because households with a stronger than average taste for rental housing will have a stronger than average taste for owner-occupied housing. If the price per unit of housing service in the owner-occupied sector falls and other prices stay the same, then we expect households with the strongest taste for housing to shift from the rental to the owner sector. Therefore, the mean housing consumption of renters with the same income Y_i and prices P_i^r and P_i^x would decline at some initial values of these exogenous variables and possibly stay the same at others. So OLS estimators of components of β^r in (17) based on a random sample of renters will not be consistent.

The hypothesis that the error term in the tenure choice equation is uncorrelated with the error term in a housing consumption equation has been tested in a number of studies. Rosen (1979, p. 15) is unable to reject this hypothesis. Lee and Trost (1978, p. 376) reject it but find that the correlation leads to little bias in OLS estimators of the parameters of the housing consumption equations. Gillingham and Hagemann (1983, p. 31) conclude that "ignoring the effect of tenure choice would give a seriously biased estimate of the impact of a change in price and/or income on the demand for housing for at least some household types and income levels".

Not only do these studies yield different conclusions but they have serious shortcomings. For example, the equations explaining housing consumption and tenure choice should be, but are not, derivable from the same utility function.[41]

[41] In his study of the choice among the owner-occupied, unsubsidized rental, and subsidized rental sectors in the United Kingdom, King (1980) solves this problem. However, his study shares some of the deficiencies of the others. For example, he assumes that each participant in a government program can choose any quantity of housing service desired at a price equal to the producer price multiplied by the ratio of subsidized to market rent. Previous research suggests that this may be a very poor approximation of reality. For instance, Olsen (1972, p. 1091) estimated that the ratio of controlled to market rent in New York City in 1965 was 0.71 but that occupants of rent-controlled units consumed 4 percent *less* housing service that they would have consumed in the absence of rent control. If the long-run price elasticity of demand was only 0.60, we would expect an increase of 17 percent under King's assumption.

Lee and Trost (p. 370) use price indices that are inappropriate for work with cross-sectional data. Finally, none of the studies accounts for the nonlinearity in budget constraints resulting from the income tax treatment of homeownership. So at present it is possible to believe that the correlations between the error terms in the tenure choice and each housing expenditure equation are negligible and hence that little is lost by using only data for households that have made a particular tenure choice to estimate the parameters of (17) or (18). For simplicity, this will be assumed in the remainder of this section.

It is widely believed that the special treatment of homeownership under the federal income tax has had an important effect on the proportion of households that are owners in the United States and the housing consumption of these households. Nevertheless, most estimates of housing demand functions based on data for owner-occupants completely ignore these provisions or fail to account for major features such as the nonlinearity in the budget constraint resulting from the progressivity of the tax or the differential effect of these provisions on the prices of various inputs used to provide housing services in the owner sector.

Under the federal income tax, investment in owner-occupied housing is treated more favorably than most other investments. In order to treat investment in owner-occupied housing similarly to investment in rental housing, owners would declare as income the difference between the market rent of their home and their expenses such as mortgage interest, property taxes, depreciation, and maintenance. Under the federal income tax, owner-occupants do not include the market rent of their home as income but are allowed to deduct mortgage interest and property taxes. As a result, their income is understated by the excess of market rent over non-deductible expenses such as depreciation and maintenance. Alternatively, we could say that income is understated by the sum of net market rent, mortgage interest, and property taxes. These income tax provisions not only make homeownership more attractive relative to renting but also make housing more attractive relative to other goods for homeowners.[42]

The individual income tax also provides subsidies to investment in rental housing primarily by permitting deductions for depreciation in excess of true depreciation, but these subsidies are relatively small. In fiscal year 1981, the income tax provided subsidies to owner-occupants amounting to substantially more than $33 billion compared with about $2 billion to renters [U.S. Executive Office of the President (1981, p. 236)].[43] (About 65 percent of households in the United States are homeowners.)

The effect of the progressive income tax combined with these itemized de-

----

[42]The net effect of all taxes on housing consumption is less clear because some taxes (e.g., the property tax) may weigh more heavily on the housing sector than on other sectors.

[43]The subsidy to owner-occupants is underestimated because it does not include the tax saving due to the failure to include net market rent in taxable income.

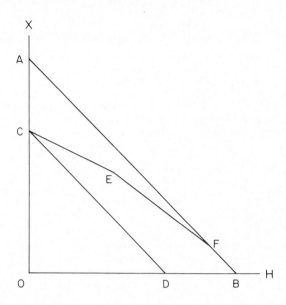

Figure 4. Budget space accounting for provisions of progressive income tax.

ductions on a consumer's budget constraint conditional on homeownership can be easily depicted under certain simplifying assumptions. First, assume that the consumer faces no other taxes or subsidies. Second, ignore the effects of this tax on producer prices. Third, assume that the consumer cares about three things – housing service, other goods, and leisure. Figure 4 depicts a cross-section of the budget frontier corresponding to a certain quantity of leisure L'. In this diagram, the quantity of housing service is measured along the horizontal axis and expenditure on other goods along the vertical axis. In the absence of the income tax, this consumer would have budget constraint AB if he chose the quantity of leisure L'. Assume that without the special treatment of homeownership this person would be in the second tax bracket, pay a tax AC, and face the budget constraint CD. The income tax provisions reduce the prices of some, but not all, inputs used to produce housing service for owner-occupants. These reductions are greater for people in higher marginal tax brackets [MacRae and Turner (1981)]. Therefore, the price per unit of housing service is lower the higher the marginal tax bracket. As the person whose conditional budget constraint is depicted in Figure 4 increases his consumption of housing service from zero up to some point, his taxable income falls but he remains in the same marginal tax bracket and so faces the same price per unit of housing service. Beyond that point (E in Figure 4), his deductions are large enough so that his taxable income is in the next marginal tax bracket, and if his housing consumption is sufficiently large,

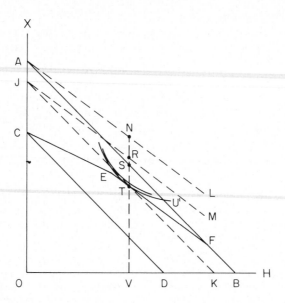

Figure 5. Misspecification of budget space under a progressive income tax.

he will pay no income tax. Therefore, the income tax provisions for homeownership result in the conditional budget constraint *CEFB*.

Figure 5 depicts the treatment of the income tax provisions in the literature
devoted to estimating the demand function for owner-occupied housing service.
The budget constraints *AB*, *CD* and *CEFB* have the same interpretation as in
Figure 4. In particular, *CEFB* is the household's budget constraint in the
presence of these provisions. Consumption bundle *T* on indifference curve *U'* is
the household's most preferred point on this budget constraint. Some authors
[e.g., Lee and Trost (1978)] have ignored the income tax provisions. They have
proceeded as if the household's budget constraint is *AB* and its preferred
consumption bundle is *S*. Others [e.g., Gillingham and Hagemann (1983)] have
accounted only for the effect of the income tax on the marginal price per unit of
housing service, that is, they have proceeded as if the household's budget
constraint is *AL* and its preferred consumption bundle is *N*. Still others [e.g.,
Polinsky and Ellwood (1979)] have adjusted income for the tax paid, *ST*, but have
not adjusted the price. These authors have proceeded as if *T* is the preferred point
on budget constraint *JK*. Other studies [e.g., Rosen (1979)] have used after-tax
income and the correct marginal price, which is to say that they have proceeded
as if the budget constraint is *JM* and the preferred consumption bundle is *R*.
Only the study by MacRae and Turner (1981) is based on the budget constraint
CEFB. In addition this study correctly accounts for the differential effect of the
income tax provisions on the prices of various inputs used to provide housing
service in the owner sector.

MacRae and Turner attempt to estimate the parameters of a housing demand function, derived from an explicit utility function, by the method of least squares. The demand function is obtained by maximizing the utility function subject to a *linear* budget constraint. The incomes and prices used to estimate this function are based on the presumption that if a household chooses a consumption bundle within one of the line segments that form the nonlinear budget frontier, the household would select the same bundle were its budget constraint to be the line containing this segment and extending to the axes. This is the same presumption underlying the approach rejected by Hausman and Wise (1980) in their study based on data from the Experimental Housing Allowance Program. If the chosen consumption bundle is the utility-maximizing bundle for all households, then the presumption is clearly correct but OLS estimators will be inconsistent for the aforementioned reasons.[44] Deleting households that choose kink points such as E and F will almost surely lead to selection bias and the error term in the regression will be correlated with the explanatory variables Y/P^x and P^h/P^x. The latter problem is easy to understand by reference to Figure 4. Among households with the same budget constraint $CEFB$, those with the strongest taste for housing and hence the largest values of the error term in the housing demand equation will tend to choose consumption bundles on the segment FB. Relatively large values of Y/P^x and P^h/P^x will be used for these households, namely OA and OA/OB. Those with the weakest taste for housing and hence the smallest values of the error term will tend to choose bundles on CE. Relatively small values of Y/P^x and P^h/P^x will be used for these households, namely OC and the slope of the segment CE. Although MacRae and Turner (p. 348) argue that the resulting bias in OLS estimators will not be excessive, there will be little basis for this judgement until the Hausman–Wise approach is used.

3. The supply of housing service

Empirical studies of the supply of housing service are as scarce as studies of its demand are abundant. Indeed, there are not enough studies of any parameter to make it worthwhile to discuss the central tendency of the estimates.[45] One reason for this difference is the scarcity of data, especially on individual providers of housing service.[46] Use of the more readily available aggregate market data requires the development and estimation of a model of the workings of the

---

[44]If we allow for failure to maximize, the presumption is not necessarily correct. Understanding why is not important for present purposes.

[45]There are numerous estimates of the elasticity of substitution between land and non-land inputs in the production of housing *stock* [McDonald (1981)], but this is outside the scope of this paper.

[46]Data from the Experimental Housing Allowance Program will help to fill this gap. See, for example, Rydell (1982).

relevant output and input markets, which was not necessary in order to estimate demand functions with household data. Since the cost of studying supply has been large, it is not surprising that the number of studies is small.

Before proceeding with a discussion of the major studies, let me mention several general shortcomings of this literature. First, many decisions that affect the supply of housing service in the current period also affect its supply in future periods, for example, painting the house. Therefore, expectations about future prices and technology should be important determinants of current supply decisions. Such expectations are consistently ignored in the empirical literature. Second, stochastic assumptions are rarely stated, let alone justified, and so it is difficult to make judgements concerning the properties of the estimators used.

3.1. Production functions

In 1964 Muth developed a simple model of the interactions between a competitive output market and competitive markets for the inputs used to produce this output. In this model industry output is allowed to affect the prices of the inputs. That is, the input supply curves facing the industry are not necessarily completely elastic. One of the equations involved is a production function. The assumptions of this model imply a number of relationships between output and input prices and quantities, which are determined within the model, and income per family, which is determined outside of the model. In one of the few attempts to estimate a production function for housing service, Muth (1973) treats housing service as a good produced with real estate and current inputs.[47] He estimates the parameters of this production function indirectly by estimating one of the aforementioned relationships, namely a relationship between expenditures on real estate, on the one hand, and mean household income and indices of the prices of real estate and current inputs, on the other. The parameters of the production function can be written as functions of the parameters of this relationship, and Muth estimates the former by estimating the latter and substituting the results into the functions relating the two sets of parameters. One problem with this approach is that the error term in the stochastic relationship explaining real estate expenditure is likely to be correlated with several of the explanatory variables, namely the input prices. If, for example, the demand for housing

[47] See also Ingram and Oron (1977) and Neels (1981). The primary contribution of the former is conceptual because the data used have serious deficiencies. The empirical estimates are based on a non-random sample of 29 apartment buildings in Boston. During about half of the years to which the data refer, the units were subject to rent control and no serious attempt was made to model its effect. Furthermore, a reasonable index of the quantity of housing service was used as an index of the quantity of one of the inputs involved in the production of this good due to the absence of a better alternative.

service in a metropolitan area is higher than average for unexplained reasons, then the demands for the inputs used to produce housing service and hence the prices of these inputs might be higher on this account. In this event, OLS estimators will be inconsistent.

3.2. Supply functions

The empirical literature on the estimation of supply functions has focused on long-run functions perhaps because there are infinitely many short-runs and there is no reason to believe that any two markets (or the same market at two points in time) have the same short-run supply curve.[48] However, even long-run supply curves need not be the same in different markets because the vector of input prices associated with each level of output may be different due, for example, to differences in price elasticities of input supplies facing the housing sector in different places.[49] Since this difficulty is ignored in the empirical literature, the discussion in this Section will focus on other issues.

   In the most frequently cited article, DeLeeuw and Ekanem (1971) used cross-sectional data on median household income, the number of households, and indices of output and input prices in 38 metropolitan areas to estimate a reduced-form relationship explaining an index of the price per unit of housing service. The equation estimated is derived from a demand and long-run supply function under the assumption that all markets were approximately in long-run equilibrium.[50] Unfortunately, their specification of the long-run supply function is inconsistent with standard economic theory and hence the results cannot be interpreted.[51] In theory, since all managers are assumed to be equally knowledgeable about the technology for producing the good, the long-run equilibrium supply price is the minimum long-run average cost of production of any firm potentially in the market. This minimum average cost can be written as a function of input prices and the parameters of the production function. DeLeeuw and Ekanem wrote the long-run equilibrium supply price of housing service as a function of the quantity

[48]For each firm there are infinitely many short-runs defined by the firm's total fixed cost and the maximum quantities of various inputs that the firm can use at zero marginal cost. Furthermore, at any point in time different firms can be in different short-runs. Estimation of short-run supply curves would appear to require data on these magnitudes for individual firms or the belief that these variables are uncorrelated with included explanatory variables.

[49]I thank Richard Arnott for bringing this point to my attention.

[50]DeLeeuw and Ekanem (p. 812) did include the vacancy rate in some regressions to attempt to capture deviations from long-run equilibrium, but its coefficient was never statistically significant and its inclusion had little effect on the other coefficients.

[51]This specification error appears to have gone unnoticed in the literature and, indeed, has been repeated several times [Grieson (1973); Ozanne and Struyk (1978); Follain (1979)]. I might add that I was a discussant for DeLeeuw and Ekanem's paper prior to its publication and failed to see the problem.

of this good as well as input prices. If the function relating supply price to input prices is correctly specified, theory tells us that the coefficient of quantity in their relationship is zero regardless of whether the long-run supply curve is upward sloping or completely elastic. Therefore, the estimated coefficient of the quantity of housing service tells us nothing about the elasticity of the long-run supply curve for this good. A properly specified relationship explaining long-run supply price will contain either the quantity of the good or input prices, but not both. Since DeLeeuw and Ekanem were interested in how the long-run supply price varies with output when input prices adjust as they do, they should not have included input prices in the equation to be estimated.

In the most ambitious study of housing supply to date, Rydell (1982) estimates the price elasticity of supply from various sources in the long-run and the path of adjustment in price and quantity towards their long-run equilibrium values in response to an increase in demand. He notes that the supply response to a change in demand can consist of changes in the number and the identity of existing units occupied, in the flow of services from these units, and in the housing stock. The latter may involve increased development on land initially devoted to residential use or an expansion of the residential area. Not surprisingly, Rydell finds that the initial supply response is dominated by occupancy changes. The magnitude of this response depends on the initial state of the market. If the initial vacancy rate is 4 percent, a 3 percent increase in demand will lead to 0.96 percent increase in the quantity of services consumed and a 4.07 percent increase in price. If the initial vacancy rate is 10 percent, the same increase in demand will lead to a 1.87 percent increase in quantity and a 2.26 percent increase in price.[52] Surprisingly, Rydell finds that repairs to existing units are not an important part of the supply response at any point on the path of adjustment to the new long-run equilibrium. If true, this may be because few increases in aggregate demand for housing service involve increases at all quality levels. The data used by Rydell are from the Housing Allowance Supply Experiment which increased the demand for units meeting certain housing standards and decreased the demand for other units. This should be expected to induce decreased maintenance on some units [Olsen (1969, pp. 619–621)]. Rydell estimates that, within three years, changes in the inventory of housing account for the bulk of the supply response to a change in demand. The estimated long-run price elasticity of supply of housing service is 11.5. Rydell attributes 58 percent of this responsiveness to increased housing stock in the initial residential area, 40 percent to increased housing stock outside the original residential area, and 2 percent to upgrading of the initial stock.

Although this study is an important contribution to our understanding of the supply of housing service, it has a number of shortcomings. First, the model

---

[52]These estimates depend in part on his assumption about the demand function, namely that the price elasticity of demand is 0.5. This is well within the range of previous estimates.

underlying the estimation of the inventory and occupancy elasticities is a simultaneous-equations model, and one of the explanatory variables in the equation estimated is an endogenous variable. Therefore, it is reasonable to believe that Rydell's OLS estimators are inconsistent under plausible assumptions about error terms. (He makes no explicit assumptions about error terms.) Second, Rydell uses the number of housing units in a metropolitan area as an index of the flow of housing service that these units would provide if they were all occupied, He asserts (p. 39) that the two are highly correlated but offers no evidence to support this assertion. Third, the model involves the concept of a long-run equilibrium vacancy rate but does not explain its determination. Fourth, the distinction between the price elasticity of supply from repairs and from developing existing residential land more intensively is unclear. Obviously, repair is one way of using existing residential land more intensively and expenditures on repairs are included under improvements in estimating the latter elasticity (p. 33). Furthermore, estimates of these two elasticities are based on logically inconsistent assumptions. In estimating the repair elasticity, a Leontief production function is assumed [Rydell and Neels (1982, p. 12)]. In estimating the elasticity from using existing residential land more intensively, variable input proportions are assumed [Rydell (1982, pp. 31–33)].

In light of the problems with all existing estimates, we should be modest in making claims about the magnitudes of supply elasticities.

4. Conclusions

Let me conclude with some suggestions for future research. First, it is abundantly clear that the marginal benefit from studying housing supply is much greater than the marginal benefit from studying housing demand. Since data from EHAP has greatly reduced the relative cost of learning about supply behavior, it is desirable that this topic receive relatively more attention. Second, it is clear that almost all existing contributions to this literature suffer from known specification errors. Therefore, it would be highly desirable to have more studies such as Polinsky and Ellwood (1979) which use high quality data to produce estimates of the parameters of interest that avoid all currently recognized specification errors and then to compare these with estimates based on the same data but on models involving various combinations of specification errors. The results of such studies will enable us to adjust previous estimates of parameters for specification bias and thereby form a more accurate impression concerning what the literature has to say about these parameters. Third, the estimates in the literature are based on the usually implicit assumption that neither buyers nor sellers of housing service have market power. Although the overwhelming majority of economists may consider this assumption to be close to the truth, I suspect that the majority of the population believe landlords earn excessive profits and that many misguided government programs such as rent control stem from this perception. Much is to be gained by disspelling this misperception, if indeed it is a misperception. Yet almost none of the empirical literature addresses the issue, in part because no well-developed noncompetitive model exists.

In addition to these suggestions concerning topics for future research, the preceding survey makes clear several opportunities for improving the methodology. First, it is desirable to model explicitly intertemporal budget constraints and objective functions, preferably in a way which accounts for uncertainty. Relationships that have been estimated cannot be justified except under highly restrictive assumptions about intertemporal matters. Second, nonlinearities in budget constraints are pervasive and important. For example, if a person saves, he receives one interest rate. If he borrows he pays a higher one. The interest rate on a second mortgage is normally higher than that on a first mortgage. More attention should be devoted to accurately describing budget constraints and to the econometric problems associated with nonlinear constraints.

References

Boehm, T.P. (1981) 'Tenure choice and expected mobility: a synthesis', *Journal of Urban Economics*, 10:375–389.

Burtless, G. and J. Hausman (1978) 'The effect of taxation on labor supply: evaluating the Gary income maintenance experiment', *Journal of Political Economy*, 86:1103–1130.

Caniglia, A.S. (1983) 'Intertemporal effects and the analysis of public housing programs', Ph.D. dissertation, University of Virginia.

Carliner, G. (1973) 'Income elasticity of housing demand', *Review of Economics and Statistics*, 55:528–532.

Chamberlain, G. (1977) '*Education, income, and ability revisited*', *Journal of Econometrics*, 5:241–257.

DeLeeuw, F. (1971) 'The demand for housing: A review of cross-section evidence', *Review of Economics and Statistics*, 53:1–10.

DeLeeuw, F. and N.F. Ekanem (1971) 'The supply of rental housing', *American Economic Review*, 61:806–817.

Follain, J.R. (1979) 'The price elasticity of the long-run supply of new housing construction', *Land Economics*, 55:190–199.

Follain, J.R. and L. Ozanne with V.M. Alburger (1979) *Place to place indexes of the price of housing*. Washington, D.C.: Urban Institute.

Follain, J.R. and E. Jimenez (1985) 'Estimating the demand for housing characteristics: A survey and critique', *Regional Science and Urban Economics*, 15:77–107.

Friedman, J. and D.H. Weinberg (1981) 'The demand for rental housing: evidence from the housing allowance demand experiment', *Journal of Urban Economics*, 9:311–331.

Gillingham, R. and R. Hagemann (1983) 'Cross-sectional estimation of a simultaneous model of tenure choice and housing services demand', *Journal of Urban Economics*, 14:16–39.

Goodman, A.C. and M. Kawai (1982) 'Permanent income, hedonic prices, and demand for housing: new evidence', *Journal of Urban Economics*, 12:214–237.

Goodman, A.C. and M. Kawai (1984) 'Replicative evidence on the demand for owner-occupied and rental housing', *Southern Economic Journal*, 50:1036–1057.

Grieson, R.E. (1973) 'The supply of rental housing: comment', *American Economic Review*, 63:433–436.

Griliches, Z. and W.M. Mason (1972) 'Education, income, and ability', *Journal of Political Economy*, 80:S74–S103.

Chapter 26

URBAN TRANSPORTATION

MICHAEL E. BEESLEY
The London Business School

MICHAEL A. KEMP
Charles River Associates, Incorporated

1. Introduction

1.1. Evolving policy concerns

As in other fields, what interests transport economists tends to follow what interests policymakers. Predominant in the policy concerns of the early 1960s were whether mass transit should be substituted for car travel, how to deal with the increase of congestion on urban roads, and the possible impact of these on urban development. Europeans had the extra incentive that the characteristic American response to growth in automobile use – building urban freeways – perhaps might, at their lower car ownership levels, be avoided. Public policy discouraged what was referred to as "urban sprawl" – that is to say, falling urban densities. It heeded the warnings provided by those who showed that low urban densities were a complement to growing automobile ownership [Meyer, Kain, and Wohl (1965)].

Among economists, there was an emerging consensus on what was necessary: if established policies precluded substantial changes in the relative prices of modes, evaluate alternative investments in urban infrastracture by means of social cost/benefit analysis. In the case of urban rail, for example, this was expected to show substantial justification through relieving roads of congestion, among other benefits. But such second-best solutions were, to economists, less preferable than repairing market failure by road pricing. Hence the interest shown in such studies as that of the Victoria Line [Foster and Beesley (1963)] and, at the same time, in the practicalities of road pricing. The first serious study of the latter was the U.K. Smeed Committee Report [U.K. Ministry of Transport (1964)], which built on previous theoretical work by Vickrey (1963), Walters (1961), and others.

Handbook of Regional and Urban Economics, Volume II, Edited by E.S. Mills
© *1987, Elsevier Science Publishers B.V.*

Twenty years later, the technical fascination with evaluating investments or other policy changes persists, and some recent urban transportation texts devote much space to marginal social cost pricing [Glaister (1981), Heilbrun (1981)]. Policy concerns have moved on, however, partly because of a recognition that rather too much was expected of both heavy transit investments and road pricing. The considerable public investment in mass transit modes, particularly notable in U.S. cities, has made little impact on car ownership or use. Also, transit investments have had limited urban development impacts, absent other reinforcing policies [Knight and Trygg (1977)]. Increasingly, Western cities have encountered and accommodated citizens' resistance to new investment in urban roads. But rationing congestion by price – long recognized as technically feasible, and given a technological fillip in the meantime by microelectronic developments – has been adopted to date in no developed country, and in one developing country only, namely Singapore (though intentions and ambitions to do so are still reported, particularly in other Asian cities). The reasons for this are chiefly a failure to realize the rapidly worsening congestion foreseen in the early 1960s [Meyer and Gomez–Ibanez (1981)], and rooted political objection to what was perceived as a new, intrusive form of tax.

In the early 1960s, however, most of the actual planning in urban transport – which originally centered on the question of justifying road investments, and then moved towards the incorporation of other modes – proceeded without much influence by professional economists. In particular, large scale urban travel modeling was conducted principally by engineers. Since then, economists' interest in the area has grown. As we discuss (in Section 2), much of this work has been directed at exploring the ways of reconciling established practical procedures with economic principles. But in the U.S. and the U.K. in particular, more immediate policy issues have also claimed increasing attention from economists.

1.2. Industry conduct and performance

A natural concomitant of these influences towards inaction on infrastructure and the use of pricing to ration use has been a deepening interest in sustaining public passenger transport, and a concern for industry conduct and performance. A major spur to this has been the continuing long-term decline of most urban public transport passenger modes. Both in Western Europe and the U.S., the instinct for preservation of the urban status quo emerged in the 1970s in the form of government subsidy for conventional (that is, incumbent) passenger modes on an unprecedented scale. For example, in the early 1980s in the U.K., one of the European countries least dedicated to public transport subsidies, the countrywide average public subventures from all sources was about 30% of total costs, heavily weighted towards urban areas. In the United States, subsidies comprised between 55% and 60% of industrywide operating revenues. The trend towards subsidization in those two countries may be meeting or have met its peak; the recession of the early 1980s prompted retrenchment. But heavy subsidization is still a major component of policy in most Western countries.

The 1960s had a conventional economic wisdom about subsidy also: that it should be paid for specific services, in a manner consistent with contriving competitive bids for the service. As things turned out, subsidy was paid to incumbents, principally to operators of conventional large bus and rail mass transit systems. Over the 1960s and 1970s the protection these enjoyed from entry remained practically universal in the Western world.

The growing external support for incumbent operators quickened interest in different ways to apply subsidy efficiently – that is, in accord with the subsidy-givers' objectives, and at lowest cost. An important stimulus has also been the suspicion that subsidy leaks into costs. The hypothesis is that the subsidy system itself begets rents to suppliers to public operators, more particularly to the major cost element, labor. Hence, there has been a growth in interest in devising rules satisfying simultaneously the perceived management needs of both parties to the subsidy transactions – the givers (the governments) and the receivers (the incumbent operators).

This interest in incumbents' operations coincided with a revised interest in the possible role in urban transport of new and expanded rival public transport modes. In all Western economies for a long time (and in the U.S. since the 1920s), the markets have been protected from entry by regulatory hurdles. Entry into mass transit provision has been most closely regulated. At the other end of the vehicle size spectrum, taxis and similar operations have been regulated by quantity, with rare exceptions for particular cities such as London and Washington. A set of complementary factors has mounted a challenge to the rationale of regulation, more particularly in the U.S. and U.K.

First was the example offered by deregulation in other transport fields. Prominent among these have been the airline, intercity bus, and rail deregulation in the U.S. in the late 1970s and early 1980s. In the U.K., the harbinger was quantity deregulation of the road freight industry in 1969, following the freeing of rail freight from rate control, carrier obligations, and exempting long-distance rail passenger operation from fares control. A contributory factor was a spreading realization of the great variety and relevance of urban transport provision in developing countries. Most developing countries have some formal regulation of urban transport, but in many the rules are ineffective, and in others, deliberately liberal. Developed countries' increasing polarization of passenger road vehicle supply – towards automobile-like offerings at one end, and to ever larger buses at the other (larger because of changes to supposedly more favorable capital/labor ratios) – have looked increasingly open to question. As in all highly-regulated situations, avoidance of regulations was also evident, emerging as a proliferation of integrated passenger-carrying operations by, for example, public health authorities, human service agencies, and so on. Textbooks of the early 1980s duly began to reflect these concerns. For example, Glaister (1981) includes a chapter on "regulation, taxation, and subsidy"; Nash (1982), one on "competition, regulation, and integration in public transport".

1.3. Summary

The predominant concern of transport economists interested in urban issues in the early 1960s was of justifying investment in alternative modes and of dealing directly with congestion through pricing − in other words, in applying the principles of welfare economics to what seemed obvious candidates. Although this interest persists, by the early 1980s attention has shifted to matters more in the province of the industrial economist − questions of incumbency, entry of new firms, and the application of rules for management action. The leading impetus in this change has been shifts in the policy and in the interests of policymakers, presumably reflecting in part their perceptions of public concerns and opinion. But there has also been a supply-side shift in what the analysts have themselves felt able to offer. It is their changing responses which form our main theme.

At the beginning of the 1960s, by far the greatest efforts were applied to urban transport modeling and forecasting, searching for prescriptions for the urban area as a whole. We review developments in urban transport analysis and modeling efforts. The most intensive work has been devised to illuminate investment decisions. This comprises the characterization of demand, of supply, of equilibration, and consequent evaluation. We then consider developments in the economics of particular modes: approaches to describing competitive equilibria, and the related questions of emergence of competitive contractual arrangements. The third section of the chapter reviews the tools for decisionmaking in urban transport, issues bearing on the management of subsidy, the improvement of modal performance, and the requisites for effective regulation.

2. Analysis of urban transportation demand and supply behavior

The investigation and analysis of consumer and supplier decisionmaking in urban transportation is complicated by the large number of dimensions in which choices may be made, and the complex physical and behavioral linkages between many of these variables. Travelers may choose the locations of their activities, and the routes, times, and modes of traveling between those locations. Their choices are influenced not only by the price and income variables that would enter a neoclassical demand function; they are affected importantly by the service quality offered by available routes or modes, particularly travel times, scheduling and physical convenience, reliability, and so on. Moreover, that service quality is itself the result of demand and supply interactions. For instance, a congested highway or a crowded bus offers lower average speeds and comfort levels than at times and places where demand is lighter.

Suppliers, too, decide not only how much capacity to provide but also when, where, and how to provide it. Their objective functions have grown increasingly multifarious as government involvement in urban transportation – both re-gulatory and financial – has expanded.

2.1. "Urban transportation planning" study methods

Attempts to understand urban travel behavior have been driven substantially by pragmatic planning concerns. In surveying the historical development of urban transportation analysis, an obvious start is with the methodology of the urban transportation planning (UTP) studies conducted in substantially all major cities of the western developed countries – and in many cities in developing countries – since the late 1950s. The resources expended in these studies have clearly outweighed all other urban transportation analysis activities.

The initial focus of the UTP studies was on the highway investment decision, and although the objectives and procedures evolved somewhat during the 1960s and early 1970s in response to the changing concerns of policymakers, their primary purpose – infrastructure planning – and the basic architecture of the methods remained unchanged. These methods have been described and discussed extensively in the textbooks,[1] and only a short review is warranted here.

Figure 1 illustrates the basic schematic structure of the UTP study procedures. A similar schema has sometimes been adopted in studies of intercity passenger and freight transportation.[2] The various consumer choices are treated sequen-tially in four major submodels, labeled *A* through *D* in the figure. For the most part, these submodels are descriptive rather than analytic, which limits faith in their forecasting ability.

Because of the degree of geographical detail required in the forecasts of traffic flows, the estimation of the models is highly data-intensive, and hence expensive. In a medium-sized metropolitan area, for example, a home-interview survey is required to obtain one-day travel patterns for all residents of between 10,000 and 20,000 sample households; there will be a one-day usage survey for several

---

[1] See, for example, Wohl and Martin (1967); Domencich and McFadden (1975); Stopher and Meyburg (1975); Manheim (1979).

[2] Meyer and Straszheim (1971, Chapter 7).

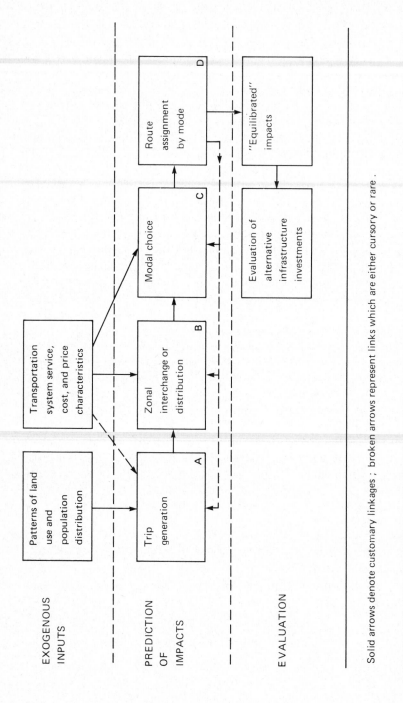

Figure 1. Schematic representation of the UTP model structure.

Solid arrows denote customary linkages ; broken arrows represent links which are either cursory or rare .

thousand commercial vehicles and taxis; observations will be made of traffic volumes across several "screenlines"; and data will be collected on peak and off-peak travel times on all major links of the highway and transit networks. Detailed land use data are also required. In large part because of these costly data needs, new full-scale UTP studies have been rare since the early 1970s.

The area under study is divided into a number of small "traffic zones", typically several hundred. The *trip generation* submodel relates the number of person trips generated in each zone for a specific major purpose (typically, home-based work trips, home-based nonwork trips, and non-home-based trips) to variables describing the socioeconomic characteristics of zonal residents. Linear multiple regression methods are frequently used to estimate the submodel, using either zonal averages (with attendant ecological correlation problems[3]) or, more rarely, observations for individual sample households. Service attributes of the transportation system have not generally been included in the pool of candidate independent variables, so that trip generation is assumed to be inelastic with respect to service quality, despite abundant empirical evidence that this is not true. Often, similar regression equations are also estimated for the numbers of trips, by purpose category, *attracted to* each traffic zone, using such variables as employment data or retail floor space as predictors.

In the second component of the UTP model, the *trip distribution* submodel, the volumes of person trips between each pair of origin and destination traffic zones are predicted, again stratified by purpose category. Usual inputs are the zonal trip production (and often attraction) volumes estimated by the previous step, together with a very limited characterization of the service offered by the transportation system between the two zones.

The functional specification used most commonly in this component is the so-called gravity model.[4] In UTP applications, the trips from zone i to zone j are deemed to be the product of the total trips produced in zone i, the total trips attracted to zone j (or some proxy for trip attractions), and an inverse function of the transportation service quality between the two zones. Linear constraints ensure that the resultant interzonal trip matrix sums correctly to whatever marginal totals are given, and iterative estimation procedures may be used to reach internal consistency.

The most common representation of service quality has been the shortest-route highway travel time from i to j, as determined from network analysis, raised to a power determined empirically by goodness-of-fit considerations. In some instances, a product of travel time and out-of-pocket money cost, each with their own exponent, has been used. In the United Kingdom, the sum of the out-of-pocket costs and the monetarized average value of the travel time – dubbed the "generalized cost" – has often been employed.

---

[3] Fleet and Robertson (1968).
[4] Isard (1960) reviews the genre.

The gravity model formulation for spatial interactions developed since the 1930s by heuristic analogy with the algebraic expression of Newton's law of gravitation. In relatively complicated gravity model specifications, the large number of free parameters affords high levels of fit to the data, but provides challenges with regard to estimation procedures. The model has slim theoretical justification, although Wilson (1967) has used the mathematics of statistical mechanics – which deals with the aggregate behavior of molecules, each moving randomly – to show that certain categories of gravity model should provide good representations of the aggregate behavior of travelers, under the assumption that the total regional expenditure on transportation (time and money costs considered together) is constant. Niedercorn and Bechdolt (1969) and Golob and Beckman (1971) have derived gravity model-type specifications from economic theory, given assumptions about the utility function.

The third major component of the UTP scheme is the *modal split* submodel, which allocates the trips for each zonal pair between the available means of travel. Most commonly, only two modes have been considered: private automobile (or other private vehicle), and public transit. There has, perhaps, been greater variation in procedures here than for the two preceding submodels, but the most common approach has been to relate transit's share of trips to ratios or differences between the times and/or costs of the two modes. The socioeconomic characteristics of the origin zone might be incorporated directly, or used for stratification. The relationships have been developed using regression techniques, or sometimes simply by judgment.

In the *route assignment* submodel, the person trips from zone i to zone j, for a specific purpose category and by a specific mode, are assigned throughout a simplified representation of the physical highway or transit network. For private automobile travel, person trips must first be converted to vehicle trips using average vehicle occupancy information. The sophistication of the route assignment component of the UTP model increased considerably over the 1950s and 1960s. In the current suite of UTP programs developed by the U.S. Government, automobile trips are assigned to alternative highway routes in a probabilistic manner considering their implied travel times. Capacity constraints, based on empirically-determined generic speed/traffic volume relationships for highway links of different types, are embedded in an iterative procedure designed to equilibrate the vehicle flows and speeds on each network link. *Transit* network assignment is a similar but often simpler procedure. The service characteristics implied by the equilibrium link speeds may be fed back to earlier submodels which incorporate level-of-service variables, but this has been done comparatively rarely.

For the economist, submodels *A* through *C* together constitute the *demand* component of the UTP approach. Only the first element, the trip generation model, influences the total level of demand, typically independently of the prices and travel times for the available travel options. The succeeding elements are basically share models, allocating this total demand successively among destinations, modes, and routes. The choice of the time of day for travel is not treated explicitly; separate forecasts are usually made for 24-hour and peak-hour travel flows, assuming zero cross-elasticities between peak and off-peak travel.

Supply behavior is not modeled explicitly. Major infrastructure investments to be evaluated are determined exogenously and are characterized as network inputs to the UTP model. Traffic management policies or decisions about the supply of highway-based transit services can be reflected only very imperfectly, although some improvements were made during the 1970s.

The speed/flow relationships for highway network links are not directly analogous to a neoclassical supply function; rather, they are "performance functions" which show how the travel speed is affected by the level of supply. *Equilibration* in the UTP model is achieved by internal iteration of traffic volumes and speeds within the route assignment submodel, and (much more rarely) by feeding back speed/travel time through one or more of the earlier submodels.

UTP study methods have been criticized extensively for their high cost, and for their lack of policy sensitivity as well as for their technical deficiencies.[5] The major technical problems are the lack of defensible behavioral theories underlying several of the submodels; the neglect of some causal relationships felt to be important (such as the influence of service quality on the level of tripmaking); conceptual and empirical inconsistencies between related variables in the submodels; and the strong behavioral assumptions implicit in the sequential structure. Also, the assumptions and relationships used in the forecasting model have often been inconsistent with those used to compute traveler benefits in the later evaluation phase of the UTP studies.

2.2. Choice structures

Awareness of these problems in the mid-1960s spurred interest in improvements, most noticeably in the treatment of demand. It was suggested that more recourse to economics, and to utility theory in particular, presented the most promising way forward.[6] Two strands of work influenced the thinking. First, so-called "direct demand models" – estimating the volumes of trips by mode between each pair of zones in a single equation – had been successfully developed for intercity passenger demand forecasting.[7] Some of this work, influenced by the ideas of

---

[5] Manheim (1979, Chapter 11) surveys the criticisms.
[6] Kraft and Wohl (1967).
[7] Kraft (1963); Quandt and Baumol (1966).

Lancaster (1966), characterized modal choices by their hedonic service attributes rather than by variables specific to a particular technology. This is particularly useful for attempting to forecast demand for a new mode, with a combination of attributes different from any existing choice. Charles River Associates (1967, 1968) first estimated a direct demand model for an urban area.

The second influence was the development of probabilistic models of individual modal choice,[8] in which the individual's probability of choosing one of two modal alternatives (given that a trip was to be made) was related stochastically to key price and service attributes of the two options. The probability function was linear, logit, or probit in form, and was frequently estimated using discriminant analysis techniques. The work was similar to, and built upon, early efforts to infer travelers' marginal valuations of travel time for work trips from time and money tradeoffs observed in binary choice situations.[9]

From these foundations has developed a now voluminous literature on urban travel demand analysis and forecasting, including many empirical applications.[10] Space permits only a limited review of key features and issues. Concern over the problems created by the sequential choice assumptions of the UTP methods focused substantial attention on the analysis of sequential and simultaneous choice structures. The large number of dimensions of choice for urban tripmaking – frequency, time of day, destination, mode, and route, compounded with the longer-term decisions about how many vehicles to own and where to locate – makes it unlikely that the traveler is reconsidering all of the dimensions and available options simultaneously each time he takes a trip. Moreover, representing all of these dimensions adequately in a single demand function is usually impractical, unless the behavior under study is constrained in some way.

It is generally necessary, therefore, to specify a sequential procedure, founded on assumptions about the hierarchy of choices, with the hierarchy usually defined in terms of the length of time over which a particular decision is known or assumed to be reappraised. Manheim (1973) and Ben–Akiva (1974) show that internal consistency between a simultaneous choice demand function (desired for theoretical reasons) and an equivalent set of nested sequential choice equations (used because of pragmatic estimation considerations) requires that
- the conditional equations of the sequential model must be share equations;
- the joint probability, simultaneous form must equal the product of the parts of the sequential form for all values of the independent variables (and conversely, the parts of the sequential form must equal the marginal and conditional probabilities implied by the simultaneous form); and

---

[8] Warner (1962) and Quarmby (1967) were among the first in this field.
[9] Beesley (1965); Lisco (1967).
[10] Good surveys are provided by Brand (1973), Lerman (1983), and Horowitz (1983). The textbooks by Manheim (1979) and Hensher and Johnson (1981) also cover this field.

– the sequential equations must be linked through composite level of service variables (sometimes referred to as an "inclusive price"), defined in such a way as to ensure consistency.

The inclusive price is essentially a weighted average of the service characteristics offered by choices treated lower down (that is, later) in the sequential structure. For example, in a destination choice equation each alternative destination's inclusive price represents an average expectation of the costs (in time, money, and so on) of travelling to that destination, derived from the characteristics of the alternative modes and the probabilities of using each of them. The specification of the inclusive prices should reflect tradeoffs between key variables known or assumed to influence decisions made later in the sequence.

2.3. Random-utility demand models

The most notable developments in the analysis of demand have centered around the use of so-called discrete-choice random-utility models. These propose that an individual consumer's preferences between available alternatives can be described with a utility function that is separable into two additive components:
– a deterministic component, accounting for the systematic effects of observed attributes of both the consumer and the choice options; and
– a random component, representing the effects of unobserved attributes, measurement deficiencies, and mis-specification of the deterministic component.

The individual is assumed to choose the alternative with the greatest utility. The model predicts the probability that a randomly-selected consumer with particular characteristics will choose a specific option; this is the same as the chance that the utility of the option exceeds that of any other alternative.

An analytical expression of the choice probabilities obviously requires some assumptions about the probability distributions of the random variables. In the form most frequently applied (for reasons of analytical and computational tractability), the probability distributions of the stochastic components have been assumed to be such[11] as to derive a multinomial logit form[12] for the choice probability, namely

$$P_i = \exp[V(z_{ki})] \Big/ \sum_i \exp[V(z_{ki})]$$

---

[11] The appropriate assumption is that the random variables are independently and identically distributed with a Gumbel Type I distribution.

[12] Luce (1959).

where P_i is the probability of the individual's choosing option i; V is the deterministic component of the utility function; and z_{ki} is a vector of attributes k of option i (probably including tripmaker attributes). If the random variables are distributed multinomially normal, which is probably a more obvious assumption to make, the corresponding choice probability function is the multinomial *probit* form, but cumbersomeness in estimation has inhibited the use of this model.

As well as assuming the probability distributions of the random elements, it is also necessary to specify the functional form of the deterministic component, $V(z_{ki})$. Again, computational tractability has determined common practice: V is typically assumed to be linear in the parameters (although not necessarily linear in the influencing variables, z_{ki}). Variables categorizing the individual decision-makers may enter explicitly into the utility function, or they may be used for stratification purposes. Estimation of the multinomial logit model is usually by maximum-likelihood methods, although occasionally analysts have adduced particular reasons for employing least squares or maximum score estimation techniques.

Aggregation has been a particularly thorny problem with these individual choice models. First, there may be aggregation biases in the estimation of the model because of lack of detail in the available data set. Secondly, practical investment and service planning applications generally require geographically specific estimates of aggregate travel demand ("trip tables") to equilibrate with supply characteristics, whereas the random utility models forecast the probability that specific individuals will opt for each of a set of choices. Naive methods of aggregating individual behavior – usually employing zonal average values of the influencing variables in the utility function with the hope of generating a zonal probability, with or without stratification of the population – may, because of the non-linear nature of the probability functions, produce potentially large forecasting errors.[13] Numerical procedures for aggregating probabilities can be applied to the full population ("total enumeration") – often infeasible, or at the least a costly and cumbersome approach – or more usually, to a representative sample. Even the latter method is computationally difficult and expensive. An analytical procedure is available for aggregating the probit model, but this advantage is offset by the computational complexity of multinomial probit estimation. However, with careful stratification or sample enumeration techniques, most analysts now believe that aggregation errors can be kept below the levels of other sources of error, and attention recently has shifted away from the aggregation problem.

The logit model possesses the property that the relative probability of an individual's choosing one alternative over a specified second alternative is

---

[13]Koppelman (1976).

independent of any other alternatives that may be available. This *"independence of irrelevant alternatives"* *(IIA) property* has advantages in constraining the problem without introducing bias when dealing with a very large choice set, and in applying the model to predict choices from a modified set. However, the IIA property also means that one has to be careful to ensure that the options included in the choice set are truly independent of each other; it is easy to generate simple examples which illustrate that the inclusion of alternatives for which the probabilities of choice are intercorrelated can produce highly erroneous predictions. Much attention has been paid to devising tests of violations of the IIA assumption and other assumptions of the multinomial logit form. The problem can often be overcome by "nesting" logit models in a sequential choice structure, such that the IIA assumption is not violated at any level of nesting.

Another focus of interest has been the *geographical transferability* of random utility choice models. Since the unit of observation for such models is the individual traveler, and variables describing geographical aggregates (traffic zones, say) are not included, and since the models often may include a wide representation of factors potentially influencing traveler choice, the hope of robust geographical transferability has often been expressed. However, what limited testing of this has been carried out has not been encouraging. Relatedly, tests of the ability of the models to predict the demand for new options (ones not included in the estimation choice set), based on their service characteristics, have also produced disappointing results. Some work has been done to explore possible methods of "tuning" estimated random utility models to new areas or new options without full-scale recalibration [Koppelman and Wilmot (1982)].

A final topic worthy of mention in a brief summary is the *data requirements* of these demand models. Because every individual observation is employed in model estimation, rather than the average values for aggregates, much smaller samples can be used to provide equivalent levels of precision than were typical of, say, the UTP studies. More detailed information is required for each observation, however. Some work has focused on sampling strategies that simplify or reduce the cost of data collection. In particular, the use of "choice-based samples" – for which by design the observations are stratified on the choice variable as is the case with surveys of car drivers or transit patrons – and their implications for estimation have been explored. Because of the relatively large number of influencing variables, random utility models have been found to be particularly sensitive to errors in measurements, and this is especially a problem with level-of-service variables, most notably when these are derived from network models.

2.4. Summary

So the outcomes from the considerable attention paid to improved methods of travel demand analysis throughout the 1970s have been mixed. Urban transportation applications have spurred a rich vein of new econometric analysis with potentially much wider topical applicability, yet difficulties have been experienced in translating the academicians' work into practical planning tools. The strengths of the random utility models are *flexibility* – a very broad range of consumer choices and tradeoffs have been explored using the same general set of methods – and *efficiency*, particularly in terms of data quantity (but not quality) requirements. The ability to derive simplified techniques, suitable for computation with a hand calculator or microcomputer, is also noteworthy. On the negative side, the demonstrated sensitivity to measurement errors and errors in specification is problematic. The potential benefits which might be expected because random utility models are "more behaviorally-based" than aggregate models – specifically geographical transferability and more trustworthy predictions of the demand for new alternatives – have generally not been realized. The problem remains of relating the output of the models to the requirements of transport operators for robust statements about revenues and costs.

3. Decision taking in urban transit

As noted in Section 1, policy concerns have shifted from the output of urban transport planning processes to what *operators* do. Economists' concerns have reacted accordingly. Work useful for aiding decisions about changes in supply in urban areas has arisen in several ways. In part, this has been an extension of traditional approaches; in part it was a direct reaction to particular problems faced by operators. We deal with the former first.

3.1. Demand and supply analysis

Apart from improving urban travel demand analysis with the disaggregate random utility models, there have been some econometric analyses based on time series of aggregate demand for specific facilities or services, most notably of public transport patronage. Some of this work – that most oriented to short-term ridership or revenue forecasting – has used Box–Jenkins types of models.[14] Other analysts have used regression methods, with a greater interest in exploring structural demand and supply relationships. The two most ambitious studies of this type are those by Gaudry (1975) and Kemp (1981a), who specified simultaneous equations models of transit ridership and estimated them from monthly time-series data for Montreal in the former case, and pooled time-series/cross sectional data (by bus route) for San Diego in the latter.

---

[14] For example, Harmatuck (1975); McLeod, Everest, and Paulley (1980); Nihan and Holmesland (1980); and Wang (1984).

Two types of summary statistics, deduced from the empirical analysis of urban travel demand, enter into policy deliberations. These are, first, the direct and cross-elasticities of demand with respect to prices and other influencing variables, and second, the implied marginal valuations of travel times (or of other major influences). Such values provide major dimensions for decisions about the services to be provided – for instance, their fares or their service quality, including frequency and speed. Although for detailed planning and policymaking purposes, elasticity estimates are rarely of value when divorced from the demand model from which they have been abstracted, and may lead to erroneous conclusions, in practice the robustness of certain key elasticity values reduces the risks of problems.[15] Surveys of relevant evidence have been produced for the price elasticities of transportation fuels [Charles River Associates (1976)], and for the price sensitivity of urban travel and the implications for possible pricing policies [Pucher and Rothenberg (1976)]. The most comprehensive body of elasticity evidence has been assembled for the various factors affecting public transit patronage, both for the United States [Mayworm, Lago, and McEnroe (1980)] and for a wider group of developed countries [Bly and Webster, eds. (1980)].

The elasticity surveys permit some broad generalizations:
- Virtually all estimates of market direct and cross-elasticities with respect to money price for all aspects of urban travel demand (gasoline consumption, toll road usage, parking demand, transit patronage, etc.) are inelastic at customary price levels.
- There is typically a greater sensitivity of demand to travel times than to money prices, at least for work journeys. The time spent in getting to and from the vehicle(s) or in transfering between vehicles (so-called "access times") generally appears to affect demand more than time spent traveling in the vehicle(s) ("linehaul time").
- Most U.S. and U.K. estimates of the short-run price elasticity of gasoline demand for private cars lie in the narrow range between -0.2 and -0.3. Estimates of the sensitivity to price over the longer run are more diverse, ranging from -0.3 to -1.4.
- Estimates of short-run transit fare elasticities typically vary within the range -0.1 to -0.7, with most estimates clustering between -0.2 and -0.5. The elasticities are numerically small when the purpose of travel is a relatively "strong" one or when alternative means of travel are unavailable or highly priced. Thus, fare elasticities are low (numerically) for work-related journeys, peak-hour services, and services in dense central city areas. Patronage is most sensitive to price at off-peak times, for short journeys, in relatively affluent markets, and at times and places without traffic congestion. Transit demand is

---

[15]Kemp (1981b).

often more sensitive to automobile price changes than to transit fare changes.
– The regularity observed in "systemwide" or "total market" elasticity estimates
  may mask much greater heterogeniety in demand behavior among various
  market segments.

The empirical evidence on consumer valuations of travel time savings has been
reviewed comprehensively by Hensher (1976) and earlier by Harrison and
Quarmby (1969). As a broad rule of thumb, travel time changes for trips to and
from work appear to be valued at roughly a third to a half of the wage rate,
although a great deal of heterogeneity has been observed in values for different
types of trips and tripmakers. The use of values of time in project evaluation often
ignores such complexities, and employs the dubious assumption that the average
consumer's total valuation of a travel time change is linearly related to the
magnitude of the change, even for very small time changes. Such difficulties have
not prevented widespread use of average time values in justifying investments. A
further use of time values, in the assessment of service characteristics such as
bus frequency and size, is reported later.

Urban transportation supply analysis has been mostly concerned to investigate
how the performance of the system (including external impacts on nonusers and
the environment) relates to capital and labor inputs, to system management and
regulatory policies, and to the level of demand; and to investigate cost
relationships.

Much of this work has drawn on physics and engineering (for example, fluid
flow analogs, or the production of automotive emissions), on operations research
(for example, queuing theory and network analysis), and on mathematical
programming and simulation modeling. The contribution of the economics
discipline *per se* has been comparatively small, particularly in the development of
performance functions. The most notable contributions have been in the development of analytical frameworks drawing on econometric simultaneous equations
techniques,[16] in the investigation of cost structures (particularly for public
transport investments and operations), and in the application of economic
principles for private and public policy analysis.

The work on costs has had several important strands.[17] One, notable for the
contention which has arisen surrounding its relevance to public investment
policies, is the examination of the capital and operating costs for various modal
alternatives in hypothetical urban corridors of varying travel demand densities.
This work, following Meyer, Kain, and Wohl (1965), typically employs simple,
average assumptions about supply and demand, and develops analytical cost
functions using engineering data, with a view to comparing the long-run average
costs at various levels of aggregate demand. In comparisons between high quality

---

[16] For example, Florian and Gaudry (1980) and Morlok (1980).
[17] The literature on urban bus costs has been surveyed by McGillivray, Kemp and Beesley (1980).

bus and rapid rail services with approximately equal service characteristics, these analyses have generally shown the bus option to be cheaper than rapid rail except at densities so high as to be relatively rare in corridors currently without rail services. While these conclusions have been strongly contested on a number of grounds,[18] they have helped engender a skepticism among most transport economists of the appropriateness of new rapid rail investments in medium-density U.S. cities, a viewpoint that has been reflected in the majority of urban economics textbooks and has been reinforced by the operating experience of new systems in San Francisco, Washington DC, Miami, and other cities.[19]

The second strand of work on costs has been the investigation of scale economies in various types of urban transportation enterprise. The consensus of the work on urban bus services in developed countries suggests that economies of scale are very elusive – unless, following Mohring (1972), one includes the implicit value of traveler time as a component of the total economic costs of travel. We discuss this work later, along with several other types of work on transit costs.

3.2. Efficiency in public transport

Most western cities, besides (and at least in part because of) close regulation, have been subject to increasing concentration of public transport organizations. Creation of over-arching authorities charged with "planning" and providing urban transport services has become very common. In the last ten years or so, there have arisen two further important areas for policy decisions, namely testing the efficiency of current services, and providing performance variables for guiding management decisions in public transport organizations. Moreover, the new organizations have usually been the means for transmitting public subsidy to transport users. Greater use of public funds has generated interest in rules for their efficient allocation, whether for arguing the scale of (or change in) total subsidy, or for suggesting how organizations can develop internal rules for allocation. Contributions here have been based mainly on the U.K. experience.

Public transport operators' main reaction to adverse market conditions and rising real costs was, in the 1970s as in the 1960s, to attempt to increase efficiency in production. Because of a high proportion of labor costs, an increase in labor productivity has been seen as particularly important. A typical reaction in Europe, for example, was increased standardization of equipment – including buses (also promoted by the federal government in the U.S.A.) – and substitution of one-person operation (OPO) for two-person operation. Nash and Brown

[18]See, for example, Vuchic (1975).
[19]The "rail vs bus" debate is summarized in more detail by Kemp and Cheslow (1976).

(1972) estimated a cost-saving of 15% among municipal operators from conversion to OPO in the late 1960s, a result broadly confirmed on later data (1968–
74) for similar U.K. operations by Boyd (1981a).

But strong criticism of this kind of adaptation emerged. First, standardization
of bus sizes was, in effect, argued to have centered on too large a bus.
Jansson (1980), taking up Mohring's (1972) argument that passengers' travel
(including waiting) time should enter the reckoning, analyzed the "square root
formula" for optimal frequency of service. In this, bus costs for a given bus size
are traded against user costs in a variety of likely urban service conditions. It
emerges that for a fixed bus size, frequency of service should be about proportional to the square root of the number of passengers carried on a route, not
(as might be supposed) proportionate to total passengers. An economy of resource
use with increasing service is implied, a form of economy of industry size. Where
choice of bus size is allowed, bus sizes should be "much smaller in general",
particularly on thin (that is, low passenger flow) routes, than most commonly
adopted. Most Western cities have most service offered in buses with over 45
seats.

In Jansson's analysis, passenger demand is assumed to be independent of the
quality of service or fare paid; there is a given flow per unit time. Passengers' time
is valued as part of a cost-minimization exercise, in which the chief arguments are
their waiting times (which reduce with increased service and smaller buses), and
bus operator costs which rise with better service. Representation of passenger
time in equivalent cash terms, as required by such models, has of course been
helped by the work on values of time noted earlier. Walters (1979a), using similar
methods, came to much the same conclusion: bus sizes are typically too big.

Secondly, OPO was attacked on two main grounds. It was argued to encourage the movement to larger, and more elaborate, costly buses in order to
increase labor productivity further. More important, it reduced service quality
by slowing up service. Boyd (1981b), following up the data set on U.K.
municipal operators (Boyd, 1981a), showed that its introduction led with a
lag to falls in demand, causing average revenue losses of 11%. This work also
criticized fare policies. To ease drivers' operation, OPO was accompanied by a
decrease in fare differentiation, one example of which was flat fares.

Limited fare differentiation policies in both the U.S. (with a long history of flat
fares) and the U.K. have come under attack from several quarters. In the U.K., it
was customary pre-OPO to taper the fare with distance, such that successive
distance increments were priced progressively less. Turvey (1975) found these
illogical when the short-run marginal costs of frustrating or crowding of the
journeys of other passengers are considered. Another way of reducing the
marginal fares facing passengers was by issuing transit passes or travel cards.
These give passengers access to all routes on a system, perhaps with constraints
on use at crowded times. They became frequent in the 1970s. The effect of these

passes was, of course, to dissociate the decision for particular trips from a particular cash outlay for the trip. White (1981a) estimated that by the late 1970s more than half of the transit trips in Western Europe and up to 20% in the U.K. were undertaken by these forms of payments. These concessions certainly produced a greater quantity of passenger miles, but have recently come under attack for the corollary of lower revenue yields, unsurprising in view of the known values of price elasticities quoted earlier [Doxsey (1984)].

3.3. Market entry

Walters (1979b), examining the experience of Kuala Lumpur, showed large consumer and (net) producer gains from a policy change which allowed 400 privately-owned minibuses to operate alongside larger, municipal buses. The hypothesis that the minibuses, because of higher costs per vehicle mile, were suitable only for "thin" routes was found to be incorrect. They prospered most on heavily used routes, thus according with Jansson's view. White (1981b) argued that Walters' results underestimate minibus costs, and that there have been considerable diversions of passengers from conventional buses. Both of these were later argued by Walters (1981) not to have a substantial effect on his inferences. Both authors agreed that present constraints on the choice of bus sizes by conventional operators (self-imposed or not) strongly and adversely influenced their market positions.

That there is often a large supply gap in the market between taxi and conventional bus operation has been underlined by work on so-called paratransit service forms [Kirby et al. (1975)]. In recent years, there has been much interest in both the U.S. and the U.K. in experiments with demand-responsive innovations (shared-ride cabs to provide dial-a-ride services or to feed conventional bus services, for example), subscription bus services, jitneys, and the promotion of ride-sharing for commutation. Moreover, a great deal of evidence about the variety of vehicle sizes and types of service offered in relatively freely entered cities in developing countries has also been assembled, which is taken to indict the suppression of choice in the typical Western urban areas [Roth and Wynne (1982)].

The question of the sustainability of entry has been tackled by Viton. He explored the possibility of profitable bus service by present public operators [Viton (1980)], using a simulation approach similar in spirit to that of Jansson (1980) but presenting conditions typical of those found in the San Francisco Bay area in the late 1970s. Operator performance was modeled by representing the number of routes provided, bus frequency, and fares. Competitors face similar cost conditions, deemed to be unaffected by change in competition. Consumer choice was represented by a discrete choice, utility-maximizing consumer facing choices between cars and conventional buses. Viewing the operator as a duo-polist, setting profit-maximizing fares and quantities of service against car competition, certain services are indeed shown to be sustainable. Entry is most likely with high quality services at up to three times conventional fares. This is consistent with several cases of successful, unsubsidized private operation that have been observed in U.S. urban markets [Morlok and Viton (1980)].

Further work on the same model [Viton (1982)] addressed the question of sustainability of a single private entrant faced with a possibly subsidized oper-ator. Subsidized operation does, as expected, deter entry, but if admitted the entrant would often be profitable. In order to offset welfare losses sustained by the consumers who prefer low quality, public operation, a lump sum profit tax would have to be given to the public operator to replace lost subsidy. Were this done, the welfare gain would be unambiguous. Where there are two duopolist providers (for example, rapid rail and bus), similar conclusions were found to apply. When products are differentiated by rival transit operators, both can be viable in direct competition. In the San Francisco Bay area this implies con-siderable change to rapid rail services– shorter trains, and higher service frequen-cies, for example. The case of multiple competitors, further market differentia-tion, and in consequence, the conditions in which incumbent operators could sustain themselves in the face of unrestricted entry, have yet to be explored.

3.4. Subsidy, and costs of operation

A further line of work has considered the relation between subsidy provision to operators and the effect on their unit costs. This work was stimulated in part by the rapid growth in subsidy to transit operators in the 1970s. By 1980 in the United States, bus, rail rapid transit, and commuter rail properties on average each had an operating subsidy per passenger greater than the average fare paid [Pucher, Markstedt, and Hirschman (1983)]. In the United Kingdom in the early 1980s, some 30% of total costs of urban bus operations were represented by subsidy. Table 1 lists estimates, by the U.K. Department of Transport, of countrywide bus operating subsidies for a selection of Western countries.

Despite obvious problems of causality, there is considerable agreement with the conclusion of Pucher and his coworkers that transit subsidies have probably exacerbated cost increases. By comparing cross-sections of 77 and 135 U.S. properties in 1979 and 1980, respectively, they found in general that the larger the subsidy the higher the unit costs. A similar finding is that of Bly, Webster, and Pounds (1980), who tackled the problem of identifying subsidy effects in a transnational comparison of 18 Western countries. They concluded, from analysis of time series data from 1965 to 1977, that an extra 10% of subsidy raises wage costs by about 2 to 3% and reduces productivity (Kms. operated per employee) by

Table 1
Subsidy levels in Western countries (buses and coaches, countrywide).

	% subsidy	Year
Australia	45.1	1981
Belgium	73.0	1982
Canada	51.1	1982
Finland	14.2	1982
France	57.6	1976
Great Britain	26.0	1982
Greece (Athens only)	20.5	1977
Ireland	11.3	1977
Italy	70.3	1981
Netherlands	78.6	1981
New Zealand	40.0	1979
Norway	21.6	1981
Spain	12.8	1976
Sweden	55.9	1980
Switzerland	28.3	1982
U.S.A.	62.1	1982

Source: U.K. Department of Transport.

a similar amount. Cost increases indeed followed subsidy increases, and not vice-versa. The main beneficiaries, chiefly because of their importance in the cost structure, have probably been members of labor unions, as Pucher et al. note.

3.5. Management rules

In parallel with these rising concerns about the effect and uses of subsidy have been questions of the criteria by which the public operator manages the operation, a natural concomitant of the growth of externally provided subsidy. This external source was superimposed on the traditional method of providing subsidy in bus companies, namely the internal transfer from "profitable" to "unprofitable" services. To preserve this "cross-subsidy" arrangement was, indeed, an important objective of promoting amalgamations among bus companies, conversions to public ownership, and the establishment of unitary transport authorities in urban areas.

Wide professional interest in rules for allocating a given subsidy within the organization arose after London Transport announced its adherence to the objective of maximizing passenger miles, subject to a budget constraint, in 1975. Nash (1978), Glaister and Collings (1978), and Bos (1978) developed the argument, which recognizes that there is a hierarchical ordering in public subsidy. A government grants subsidy; its scale depends on criteria which will include public transport "needs" as a necessary, but by no means sufficient, condition. (Other government commitments also enter the decision at this level, of course.) The public transport operator then receives what to him is an arbitrary budget, but one whose size can be influenced to varying degrees by his performance. Thus, the operator's practical need is to have a decision rule to which lower level managers with separate responsibilities can refer. The internal managerial pressures are for a relatively simple criterion for action, something that will replace an alternative decentralized rule such as the open market might provide. The arguments in the implied welfare function of the subsidy user must be acceptable to, or at least negotiable with, the subsidy giver.

The commentators on London Transport's objective have shown that a rule such as passenger mile maximization subject to a budget constraint can lead to strong divergences from optimal price and service outcomes, if simply applied without qualification. In the calculations, the principal arguments in the welfare function are cash outlays, time spent by customers, and the resource costs of provision. The simple rule will, for example, tend to exploit inelastic demands in order to increase output on services where demand is elastic. Weighting systems can be incorporated to correct for these perverse effects. One obvious example would be an inverse elasticity rule applied to services, perhaps modified by some marginal social evaluation of the income of the users [Glaister (1981)]. However, there is also a traditional argument in favor of externally derived weights which would contain additional arguments. They might, for example, reflect congestion or pollution. These may or may not be correlated with passengers' use of public transport.[20]

Because the *external* weights are quite likely to diverge from the *internal*, more complications are added. Hence, though a "naive" passenger maximization rule is almost certainly preferable to alternative "naive" rules like passenger vehicle maximization, it must lose its managerial appeal of simplicity to become a plausible representation of likely social preferences. Frankena (1983) notes the need to specify simultaneously the subsidized operator's objective, demand, and cost functions in judging whether subsidy is efficient.

Could the proponents of the "naive" passenger measure nevertheless argue for the application of the rule as a practical way to improve on the present position, recognizing that it will have to be complicated or abandoned later? Such is, after all, the fate of most "practical" management rules-of-thumb, useful more for their impact than for their suitability for permanent adoption. For this to be so, present practice must be so out of line with potential that the rule at least points

---

[20]For example, with high traffic flows congestion will probably be decreased if customers are diverted from other road vehicles to buses. With lower flows the reverse may be true. Public transport itself can add to congestion.

in the right direction for change. That this indeed may be so was shown by Beesley, Gist, and Glaister (1983). The authors studied a selection of London Transport services, bus and underground, to test whether the effects of applying a naive rule such as passenger mile maximization would indicate substantial improvement from the status quo. Consumers', producers', and external gains and losses of road congestion were measured. The range of marginal social net benefits available to equivalent changes in policy variables (fares or service levels) across the services was remarkable, indicating that considerable social gains could be obtained by internal reallocation of resources.

3.6. Summary

To summarize, public transport has been found wanting in many dimensions of performance. On some of these dimensions, the internal ones of choice of equipment and managerial decision rules, operators can initiate change relatively easily. On others, such as reduction of factor costs via improving labor productivity, little unilateral action is possible. Testing of markets and reversal of fares and service policies are difficult to accomplish without simultaneous and substantial supply side changes. A natural question to ask is whether deregulation of urban transport and/or transfer of public properties to private owners would improve welfare. In practical terms, these questions are asked for bus operations rather than urban rail. That this is sensible is apparently supported on the one hand by the consensus that bus operations show few if any economies of scale, and on the other hand, by the scarcely-challenged proposition that urban rail operations do.

In fact, the issues concern not long-run costs so much as the predicted effect on parties involved in the change. The work cited earlier makes it most unlikely that unequivocal assurances can be made that losses to some parties will not ensue from a change. Moreover, since incumbents start from a position of a strong concentration of relevant information, and have not been revealed in the past to be willing to promote changes in regulation and ownership, the burden of persuasion that changes should be made is a difficult one. Nevertheless, in the U.K. at least, recent and quite drastic proposals for deregulation and transfer to private ownership have been made by the Government (U.K. Department of Transport, 1984), and are planned for implementation in October 1986.

4. New directions for urban transport analysis

We have seen how the current problems facing transport policymakers at urban-wide and operational levels have influenced analysis in the last twenty years. The advice of twenty years ago was largely ignored. Skepticism about the pay-off to urban rail investment has not prevented the emergence of new rapid rail systems in major U.S. cities and elsewhere. Strongly supported alternatives, like bus-oriented infrastructure investments have, by and large, failed to appear. As noted earlier, rationing road congestion by price has only one significant exponent so far, Singapore. We have also seen that these failures of persuasion did not prevent technical interest in investment planning from developing, notably in the UTP field. Rather, the scope of the transport economist broadened. It seems at least possible that the pattern of policy interest will move further from analysis useful for urban-wide planning towards the opening up of urban transport markets.

This will often involve a substitution of private for the public ownership which is characteristic of many Western urban transport operations, and the dismantling of the regulatory framework that has typically concentrated on discouraging entry to the public operators' markets.

Several studies of ownership issues have been made, in the vein of comparing public with private ownership with respect to profits and costs in broadly similar urban conditions. Pashigian (1976) showed that in the United States, "socialization occurred first in cities where users had greater political strength", and that, over a sample of 40 systems for 1960 and 1970, regulation had the effect of lowering profit margins more for public than for private operators. But over time "the regulatory agencies have been captured not by the transit firms but by the riders". Where private and public bus operators coexist in the same market, subject to similar regulative prices but not on entry, private operation appears to have substantially lower costs.

A change from public to private ownership may not, in the long run, be necessary to realize the costs savings. Deregulation of entry barriers, allied to lack of scale economies, may suffice. Incumbent public operators, with no inherent advantages in the scale of organization, would necessarily shrink. The benefit of flexible part-time labor and its use, reported from a simulation model of labor work rules by Chomitz and Lave (1981) as potentially available in existing U.S. properties, particularly in the peaks, would then be available to all operators. Relaxation of other work rules would be even more significant for costs. Such restrictions are also unlikely to survive deregulation and free entry. Nevertheless, the transition period from the currently highly protected industry to free entry is a period of very great prospective concern to decisionmakers. It might well be deemed necessary to transfer present incumbents' ownership rights to private operators in order to combat the initial market power that they would yield. Such a change has been suggested in the U.K. government policy statement on buses.

Much of the work just reviewed seeks to establish a framework in which urban transport pricing and service decisions can be appraised, representing the consumer interest by postulating a value of his travel time. As reported earlier, the volumes or rates of tripmaking are often treated as givens in these models. But formal demonstration of propositions to substitute different varieties of modes require a further description of consumer behavior, notably reaction to the different service levels provided and the prices offered at a given service level. Demand has two main arguments, price (or fare charged) and service quality. Service quality, in turn, is determined most importantly by the supply quantities forthcoming. Supply has to be remunerated in the revenues received. Revenue, of course, depends on fares charged (plus a subsidy, if available to the operator). Hence, there arises a need simultaneously to specify demand and supply conditions, and to describe how the market will realize equilibrium. In the body of work just described, this problem, though recognized explicitly or implicitly, is tackled in effect by truncating the demand side characterization – that is, by the assumption of fixed passenger quantities of flows.

Truncation of demand – avoiding the question of a mode's aggregate market size – while useful to show possibilities of substitution, does not permit statements to be made about the output and prices which one expects to be established in competition between modes, or sustainable output for a given mode. Hence, resolving questions involving judgments about intervention in markets through regulation (or more usually in practice, deregulation) or by subsidy require further specification. Some recent work has tackled this for particular modes. Beesley and Glaister (1983) consider the case of the cruising taxi market characteristic of large towns, in effect taking up the well-known problem posed for students by Milton Friedman of the effect of a regulated fare charge by Chicago. Contributions to this literature have been many and are reviewed in the paper. The authors found that essential points of difficulty in characterizing the market satisfactorily are (i) the interaction of service levels with supply, as just described, and (ii) economies of system size (that is, non-proportional increments of inputs for increasing service levels). Conditions for both local equilibria, such as might be associated with constraints on supply, and global equilibria, associated with freely competitive conditions, are defined.

The implications of this investigation for founding policies on conventional (comparative-static) welfare arguments are found to be daunting. Intervention via subsidy in a competitive taxi industry is certainly found to be justifiable in principle, largely because of the economies of system size. But the prediction of the interaction of demand and supply for application to problems of constraints on supply (for example, restrictions on vehicle numbers or fares) requires far more information than can be reasonably expected of regulators. There seems no reason to suppose that other modes are essentially different from taxis in these respects. In general, the more modes are allowed – jitneys plying the same routes as conventional buses, for instance – the more complex is the required description of market equilibria. The inference is that arguments for intervention or deregulation may well necessarily put more weight on non-static comparisons or effects. These include the impact of deregulation on innovation, the reactions of incumbents, and the effects on changing established labor contracts, and on terms of entry. In short, the argument must embrace views of the dynamics of market structure.

Finally, if indeed the trend of policy interests is becoming more sympathetic to freeing markets, there seems a case for paying renewed attention to the general pricing frameworks, specifically for the use of roads. And so our survey has come full-circle. Twenty years ago, the most sophisticated part of the urban transport economist's equipment was, arguably, that concerning road pricing in congested areas. Here, it seemed, was a clear case for equating price with marginal social cost, where the cost largely arises from the actions of road users themselves. It seemed readily extendible to other externalities: pollution and noise are correlated with traffic density and would be reduced by applying congestion taxes. The proliferation of prices required for different places, times of day, and vehicles was realized, but shown to be possible to apply even with the electronic techniques and costs of the late 1960s [Beesley (1973, Chapter 9)]. Proxies for a fully-fledged system have been worked out (such as the central area licences used in Singapore), and their relation to other rationing devices such as parking restrictions and the fully-fledged systems has been shown [Thomson (1974); Greater London Council (1974)].

Work in developing the insights into road pricing continues. Gomez–Ibanez and Fauth (1980) considered potential constraint measures for Boston, Massachusetts. They compared parking charges, applying tolls to freeways, and two forms of area licenses, one for local streets and the other for all streets. Parking and local area charges proved most beneficial, in terms of user cash and times saved, and was substantial ($20 m. a year, at 1975 prices). At the same time, Howitt (1980) explained political and institutional resistance in Boston and other U.S. cities in terms of the difficulty of organizing support for not-easily-perceived benefits and costs, as compared to easily-mounted opposition, boundary problems, interagency rivalry,. and risky commitment of resources.

Further technical contributions have been made by Tzedakis (1980), who analyzed a hitherto-unexplained congestion dimension – the hindrance of faster by slower vehicles. He finds that congestion costs are sensitive to speeds of slow and fast vehicles, and because of limitations on overtaking, to the length of road. Else (1981) demonstrated that prices based on discrete time intervals would be incorrect; they must depend on how traffic builds up and disperses. This would imply that a form of spot pricing is preferable, thus indicating the use of electronic metering rather than prices based on licensed entry to congested areas.

Thus, in spite of warnings such as those by Forsyth (1977) about the many ambiguities facing transport economists in making predictions about the effect of their pricing recommendations on urban areas, interest in road congestion pricing continues to develop. Now that policymakers are more often turning towards the lifting of market controls to encourage a large variety in road use, the pricing tool may not remain neglected. It is a tool, moreover, whose real cost must be falling quite dramatically alongside that of the information technology devices.

References

Beesley, M.E. (1965) 'The value of time spent in travelling: some new evidence', *Economica*, 32:174–185.

Beesley, M.E. (1973) *Urban transport: studies in economic policy*. London, U.K.: Butterworths.

Beesley, M.E. and S. Glaister (1983) 'Information for regulating: the case of taxis', *Economic Journal*, 93:594–615.

Beesley, M.E., P. Gist and S. Glaister (1983) 'Cost benefit analysis and London's transport policies', *Progress in Planning*, 19:169–269.

Ben Akiva, E.M. (1974) 'Structure of passenger travel demand models', *Transportation Research Record*, 526:26–42. Washington, D.C.: National Research Council, Transportation Research Board.

Bly, P.H. and F.V. Webster, eds., (1980) *The demand for public transport, Report of the International Collaborative Study of the Factors Affecting Public Transport Patronage*. Crowthorne, U.K.: U.K. Transport and Road Research Laboratory.

Bly, P.H., F.V. Webster and S. Pounds (1980) 'Subsidisation of urban public transport', Supplementary Report 541. Crowthorne, U.K.: U.K. Transport and Road Research Laboratory.

Bos, D. (1978) 'Distributional effects of maximisation of passenger miles', *Journal of Transport Economics and Policy*, 12:322–329.

Boyd, C.W. (1981a) 'Cost savings from one man operation of buses: a re evaluation', *Journal of Transport Economics and Policy*, 15:59–66.

Boyd, C.W. (1981b) 'The impact of reduced service quality on demand for bus travel: the case of one-man operation', *Journal of Transport Economics and Policy*, 15:167–177.

Brand, D. (1973) 'Travel demand forecasting: some foundations and a review', in: *Urban travel demand forecasting*. Special Report 143:239–282. Washington, D.C.: National Research Council, Transportation Research Board.

Charles River Associates, Inc. (1967) *A model of urban passenger travel demand in the San Francisco metropolitan area*. Cambridge, Mass.: Charles River Associates, Inc.

Charles River Associates, Inc. (1968) *An evaluation of free transit service*. Cambridge, Mass.: Charles River Associates, Inc.

Charles River Associates, Inc. (1976) *Price elasticities of demand for transportation fuels*. Cambridge, Mass.: Charles River Associates, Inc.

Chomitz, K.M. and C.A. Lave (1981) *Part-time labor, work rules, and transit costs*. Washington, D.C.: U.S. Department of Transportation, Urban Mass Transportation Administration.

Domencich, T.A. and D. McFadden (1975) *Urban travel demand: a behavioral analysis*. Amsterdam: North Holland.

Doxsey, L.B. (1984) 'Demand for unlimited use transit passes', *Journal of Transport Economics and Policy*, 14:53–80.

Else, P.K. (1981) 'A reformulation of the theory of optimal congestion taxes', *Journal of Transport Economics and Policy*, 15:217–232.

Fleet, C.R. and S.R. Robertson (1968) 'Trip generation in the transportation planning process', *Highway Research Record*, 240:11–31. Washington D.C.: National Research Council, Highway Research Board.

Florian, M. and M. Gaudry (1980) 'A conceptual framework for the supply side in transportation systems', *Transportation Research B*, 14B:1–8.

Forsyth, P.J. (1977) 'The pricing of urban transport: some implications of recent theory', in: D.A. Hensher, ed., *Urban transport economics*. Cambridge, U.K.: Cambridge University Press, 20–43.

Foster, C.D. and M.E. Beesley (1963) 'Estimating the social benefit of constructing an underground railway in London', *Journal of the Royal Statistical Society, Series A*, 126:46–92.

Frankena, M.W. (1983) 'Public transport objectives and subsidy formulas', *Journal of Transport Economics and Policy*, 17:67–76.

Gaudry, M. (1975) 'An aggregate time-series analysis of urban transit demand: the Montreal case', *Transportation Research*, 9:249–258.

Glaister, S. (1981) *Fundamentals of transport economics*. New York, N.Y.: St. Martin's Press.

Glaister, S. and J.J. Collings (1978) 'Maximisation of passenger miles in theory and practice', *Journal of Transport Economics and Policy*, 12:304–321.

Golob, T.F. and M.J. Beckmann (1971) 'A utility model for travel forecasting', *Transportation Science*, 5:79–90.

Gomez-Ibanez, J.A., and G.R. Fauth (1980) 'Downtown auto restraint policies: the costs and benefits for Boston', *Journal of Transport Economics and Policy*, 14:133–153.

Greater London Council (1974) *Supplementary licensing*. London, U.K.: Greater London Council.

Harmatuck, D.J. (1975) 'The effects of a service interruption on bus ridership levels in a middle-sized community', *Transportation Research*, 9:43–54.

Harrison, A.J. and D.A. Quarmby (1969) *Theoretical and practical research on an estimation of time-saving*. Report on Sixth Round Table on Transport Economics. Paris (France): European Conference, of Ministers of Transports.

Heilbrun, J. (1981) *Urban economics and public policy*. Second Edition. New York, N.Y.: St. Martin's Press.

Hensher, D.A. (1976) 'Review of studies leading to existing values of travel time', *Transportation research record*, 587:30–41. Washington D.C.: National Research Council, Transportation Research Board.

Hensher, D.A. and L.W. Johnson (1981) *Applied discrete-choice modelling*. London, U.K.: Croom Helm.

Horowitz, J.L. (1983) 'Evaluation of discrete-choice random-utility models as practical tools of transportation systems analysis', in: *Travel analysis methods for the 1980s*. Special Report 201:127–136. Washington, D.C.: National Research Council, Transportation Research Board.

Howitt, A.M. (1980) 'Downtown auto restraint policies: adopting and implementing urban transport innovations', *Journal of Transport Economics and Policy*, 14:155–167.

Isard, W. (1960) *Methods of regional analysis*. Cambridge, Mass.: The MIT Press.

Jansson, J.O. (1980) 'A simple bus line model for optimisation of service frequency and bus size', *Journal of Transport Economics and Policy*, 14:53–80.

Kemp, M.A. (1981a) 'A simultaneous equations analysis of route demand and supply, and its application to the San Diego bus system', Research Paper 1470–2. Washington, D.C.: The Urban Institute.

Kemp, M.A. (1981b) 'Planning for fare changes: a guide to developing, interpreting, and using fare elasticity information for transit planners', Research Paper 1428–05. Washington, D.C.: The Urban Institute.

Kemp, M.A. and M.D. Cheslow (1976) 'Transportation', in: W. Gorham and N. Glazer, eds., *The urban predicament*, 281–356. Washington, D.C.: The Urban Institute.

Kirby, R.F., K.U. Bhatt, M.A. Kemp, R.G. McGillivray and M. Wohl (1975) *Para-transit: neglected options for urban mobility*. Washington, D.C.: The Urban Institute.

Knight, R.L. and L. Trygg (1977) *Land use impacts of rapid transit: implications of recent experience*. Washington, D.C.: U.S. Department of Transportation.

Koppelman, F.S. (1976) 'Guidelines for aggregate travel prediction using disaggregate choice models', *Transportation Research Record*, 610:15–24. Washington, D.C.: National Research Council, Transportation Research Board.

Koppelman, F.S. and C.G. Wilmot (1982) 'Transferability analysis of disaggregate choice models', *Transportation Research Record*, 895:18–24. Washington, D.C.: National Research Council, Transportation Research Board.

Kraft, G. (1963) *Demand for intercity passenger travel in the Washington-Boston corridor. Part V.* Boston, Mass.: Systems Analysis and Research Corporation.

Kraft, G. and M. Wohl (1967) 'New directions for passenger demand analysis and forecasting', *Transportation Research*, 1:205–230.

Lancaster, K.J. (1966) 'A new approach to consumer theory', *Journal of Political Economy*, 84:132–157.

Lerman, S.R. (1983) 'Mathematical models of travel demand: a state-of-the-art review', in: *Travel analysis methods for the 1980s*. Special Report 201:114–127. Washington, D.C.: National Research Council, Transportation Research Board.

Lisco, T.E. (1967) 'The value of commuters' travel time: a study in urban transportation', University of Chicago Ph.D. thesis. Ann Arbor Mich.: University Microfilms.

Luce, R.D. (1959) *Individual choice behavior*. New York, N.Y.: Wiley.

Manheim, M.L. (1973) 'Practical implications of some fundamental properties of travel-demand models', *Highway Research Record*, 422:21–38. Washington, D.C.: National Research Council, Highway Research Board.

Manheim, M.L. (1979) *Fundamentals of transportation systems analysis, Vol. 1: basic concepts*. Cambridge, Mass.: The MIT Press.

Mayworm, P., A.M. Lago and J.M. McEnroe (1980) *Patronage impacts of changes in transit fares and services*. Washington, D.C.: U.S. Department of Transportation, Urban Mass Transportation Administration.

McGillivray, R.G., M.A. Kemp and M.E. Beesley (1980) 'Urban bus transit costing', Research Paper 1200-72-1. Washington, D.C.: The Urban Institute.

McLeod, G., J.T. Everest and N.J. Paulley (1980) 'Analysis of rail and air passenger flows between London and Glasgow using Box-Jenkins methods', Supplementary Report 524. Crowthorne, U.K.: U.K. Transport and Road Research Laboratory.

Meyer, J.R. and J.A. Gomez-Ibanez (1981) *Autos, transit, and cities*. Cambridge, Mass.: Harvard University Press.

Meyer, J.R. and M.R. Straszheim (1971) *Techniques of transport planning. Vol. 1: pricing and project evaluation*. Washington, D.C.: The Brookings Institution.

Meyer, J.R., J.F. Kain and M. Wohl (1965) *The urban transportation-problem*. Cambridge, Mass.: Harvard University Press.

Mohring, H. (1972) 'Optimization and scale economies in urban bus transportation', *American Economic Review*, 62:591–604.

Morlok, E.K. (1980) 'Types of transportation supply functions and their applications', *Transportation Research B*, 14B: 9–27.

Morlok, E.K. and P.A. Viton (1980) 'Self-sustaining public transportation services', *Transport Policy and Decision Making*, 1:169–194.

Nash, C.A. (1978) 'Management objectives in bus transport', *Journal of Transport Economics and Policy*, 12:70–85.

Nash, C.A. (1982) *Economics of public transport*. London, U.K.: Longman.

Nash, C.A. and R.H. Brown (1972) 'Cost savings from one-man operation of buses', *Journal of Transport Economics and Policy*, 6:281–284.

Niedercorn, J.H. and B.V. Bechdolt, Jr. (1969) 'An economic derivation of the "gravity law" of spatial interaction', *Journal of Regional Science*, 9:273–282.

Nihan, N.L. and K.O. Holmesland (1980) 'Use of the Box and Jenkins time series technique in traffic forecasting', *Transportation*, 9:125–143.

Pashigian, B.P. (1976) 'Consequences and causes of public ownership of urban transit facilities', *Journal of Political Economy*, 84:1239–1259.

Pucher, J., A. Markstedt and I. Hirschman (1983) 'Impacts of subsidies on the costs of urban public transport', *Journal of Transport Economics and Policy*, 17:155–176.

Pucher, J. and J. Rothenberg (1976) *Pricing in urban transportation: a survey of empirical evidence on the elasticity of travel demand*. Cambridge, Mass.: Massachusetts Institute of Technology.

Quandt, R.E. and W.J. Baumol (1966) 'The demand for abstract transport modes: theory and measurement', *Journal of Regional Science*, 6:13–26.

Quarmby, D.A. (1967) 'Choice of travel mode for the journey to work: some findings', *Journal of Transport Economics and Policy*, 1:273–314.

Roth, G. and G.G. Wynne (1982) *Free enterprise urban transportation*. New Brunswick N.J.: Transaction Books.

Stopher, P.R. and A.H. Meyburg (1975) *Urban transportation modeling and planning*. Lexington, Mass.: D.C. Heath & Company.

Thomson, J.M. (1974) *Modern transport economics*. Harmondsworth, U.K.: Penguin Books.

Turvey, R. (1975) 'A simple analysis of optimal fares on scheduled transport services', *Economic Journal*, 85:1–9.

Tzedakis, A. (1980) 'Different vehicle speeds and congestion costs', *Journal of Transport Economics and Policy*, 14:81–103.

U.K. Department of Transport (1984) *Buses*. Cmnd. 9300. London, U.K.: Her Majesty's Stationery Office.

U.K. Ministry of Transport (1964) *Road pricing: the economic and technical possibilities*. London, U.K.: Her Majesty's Stationery Office.

Vickrey, W.S. (1963) 'Pricing in urban and suburban public transport', *American Economic Review*, 53:452–489.

Viton, P.A. (1980) 'The possibility of profitable bus service', *Journal of Transport Economics and Policy*, 14:185–203.

Viton, P.A. (1982) 'Privately-provided urban transport services – entry deterrence and welfare', *Journal of Transport Economies and Policy*, 16:85–94.

Vuchic, V.R. (1975) 'Comperative analysis and selection of transit modes', *Transportation Research Record*, 559:51–62. Washington D.C.: National Research Council, Transportation Research Board.

Walters, A.A. (1961) 'The theory and measurement of private and social cost of highway congestion', *Econometrica*, 29:676–699.

Walters, A.A. (1979a) 'Costs and scale of bus services', Staff Working Paper 325. Washington, D.C.: The World Bank.

Walters, A.A. (1979b) 'The benefits of minibuses: the case of Kuala Lumpur', *Journal of Transport Economics and Policy*, 13:320–334.

Walters, A.A. (1981). 'The benefits of minibuses – a rejoinder', *Journal of Transport Economics and Policy*, 15:79–80.

Warner, S.L. (1962) *Stochastic choice of mode in urban travel: a study in binary choice*. Evanston, Ill.: Northwestern University Press.

Wang, G.H.K. and D. Skinner (1984) 'The impact of fare and gasoline price changes on monthly transit ridership: empirical evidence from seven U.S. transit authorities', *Transportation Research B*, 18B:29–41.

White, P.R. (1981a) '"Travelcard" tickets in urban public transport', *Journal of Transport Economics and Policy*, 15:17–34.

White, P.R. (1981b) 'The benefits of minibuses – a comment', *Journal of Transport Economics and Policy*, 15:77–79.

Wilson, A.G. (1967) 'A statistical theory of spatial distribution models', *Transportation Research*, 1:253–269.

Wohl, M. and B.V. Martin (1967) *Traffic system analysis for engineers and planners*. New York, N.Y.: McGraw Hill Book Company.

Chapter 27

URBAN PUBLIC FACILITY LOCATION

CHARLES REVELLE

The Johns Hopkins University

1. Introduction

The siting of facilities is a subject which has sparked interest in an amazingly long list of disciplines. Among the disciplines from which significant location research has sprung are economics, geography, regional science, regional planning, operations research/optimization, applied mathematics, industrial engineering, management science, electrical engineering, transportation engineering, and environmental engineering. The long list of disciplines reflects the pervasiveness of the location question in the various sectors of the private and public economy.

With so many disciplines contributing to the development of this field, it is difficult to survey the literature in a comprehensive way. While efforts are made in this direction, no claim is made for the comprehensiveness of this survey. Instead, an attempt is made to select those papers and emphases with an element of centrality relative to the question of urban public facility location. In addition to centrality, most of the research efforts considered here are related to one another. That is, synthesis of research themes is also an aim of this work.

The papers and concerns taken up in this chapter will be discussed from a distinct point of view, namely, "Can the concept or model be applied to locational decision making?" This is relatively broad, but still allows us to eliminate the most theoretical works. Theory, therefore, is likely to be emphasized only where it can impact on decisions; that is, where data and/or conditions make it possible to apply the theory.

This emphasis on application may be disquieting to some individuals. The emphasis on models for which adequate data already exist or may easily be obtained may be a deficiency of this survey – or it may be its strength. The use of the numerous objectives considered here as opposed to a single economic efficiency objective may also be viewed as a weakness, but the use of many objectives may also be a strength. Certainly, the author recognizes that economic efficiency is a critically important objective. It may even be the *most* important

Handbook of Regional and Urban Economics, Volume II, Edited by E.S. Mills
© *1987, Elsevier Science Publishers B.V.*

objective. Nonetheless, many models and many researchers do not consider the economic efficiency objective at all.

One has to ask why so many researchers in so many disciplines have not utilized a concept so widely accepted as a conceptual base for public policy decisions, since facility siting decisions are surely examples of public policy in the making.

Fundamentally, the economic efficiency objective is de-emphasized here because either the data needed for its use have not been obtained or could be obtained only at enormous cost or even if obtained would be highly suspect. We are talking here about such parameters as the value of medical service, the value of travel time by trip purpose, the economic damage to structures per minute of delay by fire equipment, the value of human life, and similar quantities. While there are those who are bold enough to assert knowledge of these parameters, this author is more cautious. He is willing to begin to estimate the implied values of such parameters only *after* decisions are made on numbers of facilities and the positions of those facilities.

Even then, publicly proclaimed estimates of these parameters, derived from decisions already made, strike fear into decision makers, both appointed and elected, who might use these models. Decision makers would rather focus on measures of goodness that are less controversial than, for instance, the value of lives saved by a pattern of ambulance deployment. Examples of such measures will be discussed in the context of the specific model applications that are discussed.

With the economic efficiency objective placed to one side for the moment, surrogate objectives must be suggested if facilities are to be sited in a rational fashion. The surrogate objectives, by and large, focus on accessibility. To a certain degree, they are trivial objectives; that is, it is fairly easy to conceptualize these objectives. Though these objectives are relatively easy to conceptualize, the model frameworks within which these objectives are implemented are not necessarily simple. The framework of implementation is almost always an optimization or mathematical programming problem, although solution may be accomplished by a heuristic procedure rather than by an algorithm which is guaranteed to find the mathematical optimum. The organization of most of this chapter will correspond to the several objectives and conceptual frameworks that have so far been explored for facility siting in the public sector.

In the following section, we focus on objectives; then specific application areas will be considered and models appropriate to these areas will be developed. Throughout, the assumption is made that demands and facilities are located on a network rather than existing at points in an undifferentiated space. Accordingly, a distance matrix is assumed to exist which contains the shortest time or distance between all required pairs of points.

2. Objectives for urban public facility location

The objectives that we use for public facility location most often focus on access. These objectives are almost intuitively obvious and yet are valuable measures because they conform to the notions and ideas of many people, including decision makers.

The first formulation in both sequence of development and in terms of its theoretical importance is the *p*-median problem, so named by Hakimi (1964, 1965). Although Hakimi was interested in the location of switching centers in a communications network, researchers quickly recognized that the formulation was applicable to the problem of siting central facilities to which people might come for service. The possibility of service radiating from the facilities to points of demand was also recognized. The problem with people travelling to facilities may be stated as:

Locate *p* facilities on a network with discrete demands so that the average travel time of all users is a minimum. Every user is assumed to travel to his nearest facility.

We can assume that the set of eligible sites for facilities is precisely the set of demand points and junctions of the underlying network without a loss of generality, a fact asserted and proved by Hakimi (1964, 1965). This problem can be stated as a zero-one programming problem as follows:

$$\min Z = \sum_{i=1}^{n} \sum_{j=1}^{n} a_i d_{ij} x_{ij},$$

subject to

$$\sum_{j=1}^{n} x_{ij} = 1, \qquad i = 1, 2, \ldots, n,$$

$$x_{ij} - x_{jj} \leq 0, \qquad i, j = 1, 2, \ldots, n, \quad i \neq j,$$

$$\sum_{j=1}^{n} x_{jj} = p,$$

$$x_{ij} = (0, 1), \quad i, j = 1, 2, \ldots, n,$$

where

a_i = relevant population at demand node i;
d_{ij} = shortest distance, node i to node j;
n = number of nodes;

$p =$ number of facilities;

$$x_{ij} = \begin{cases} 1 \text{ if node } i \text{ assigns to a facility at } j, \\ 0 \text{ otherwise; and} \end{cases}$$

$$x_{jj} = \begin{cases} 1 \text{ if a facility opens at node } j, \\ 0 \text{ otherwise.} \end{cases}$$

The objective minimizes total population miles; the average distance would be obtained by dividing the total population miles by the sum of all people who travelled. Numerous solution procedures have been advanced for this problem statement and a listing through about 1977 is found in ReVelle et al. (1977). Probably the most accessible solution procedure is to solve this problem as a continuous linear program. Surprisingly, the frequency of termination with all zero-one variables seems to be on the order of 95%. Since that time several additional works have appeared on this subject; these include papers by Narula et al. (1977), ReVelle et al. (1979), Boffey (1978) and Galvao (1978). The work of Narula, et al., in particular seems to offer promise of the ability to handle relatively larger p-median problems than have been solved in the past. Problems of 100 to 200 nodes have been handled by linear programming and its variants as well as by heuristic procedures.

Our interest here, however, is primarily with problem statement as opposed to solution procedure, although we do not deny the importance of the latter. Even so simple a problem as this can be viewed as a problem in two objectives, in this case, the minimum average travel burden and the minimum number of facilities. Trade-off curves which place these two objectives in opposition can easily be constructed.

What is the economic implication of minimizing average distance or minimizing its equivalent, total people miles subject to a constraint on the number of facilities? First, it should be pointed out that the explicit constraint on number of facilities suggests that the investment available for establishing and operating facilities is probably less than the socially optimal level of investment. If it were not, we should be maximizing the difference between the value of service and the sum of the costs of obtaining it. If all obtain the service, the value of service obtained would be a known constant, and we would then minimize the sum of access cost and the cost of establishing/providing the service. The number of facilities would be chosen from the results of the analysis. Where an explicit limit is placed on the number of facilities or on the investment in facilities, and if we assume that the service is zero priced, we have only the access cost to minimize. To see this, we let:

$v =$ value of service to an individual (assumed the same throughout the system), and

$c =$ cost per minute or mile of travel (including lost opportunities as well as out-of-pocket expenses).

Then an objective of maximizing value to the region would be

$$\max Z = v \sum_{i=1}^{n} a_i - c \sum_{j=1}^{n} \sum_{i=1}^{n} a_i d_{ij} x_{ij},$$

which is equivalent to

$$\min Z = c \sum_{j=1}^{n} \sum_{i=1}^{n} a_i d_{ij} x_{ij}.$$

This latter form suggests that minimizing the objective of total population miles maximizes the value of the service to the region given the budget constraint reflected in the choice of p facilities.

There is another way to view the p-median, and that is in a multi-objective sense in which a solution choice is made from the tradeoff curve of access (population-miles) versus number of facilities. Implied in any particular choice of a number of facilities is that the reduction of access cost from adding one facility is lower in value than the cost of that facility. If we are talking about going from eight up to nine facilities and reject the addition, we have implied that

$$f > c(Z_8 - Z_9)$$

where

    f = the cost of a facility;
    Z_8 = people-miles achieved by eight facilities; and
    Z_9 = people-miles achieved by nine facilities.

Thus, c, the cost of travel might be imputed to be

$$c < f/(Z_8 - Z_9).$$

Similarly, we can derive the implied fact that the cost of travel is bounded from below:

$$c > f/(Z_7 - Z_8).$$

While we can as economists make these arguments on the economic interpretation of choices, in fact, a decision maker operating in the real world is unlikely to admit to or even want to hear such implications. The decision maker is unlikely to wish to be held to a value of travel-time because s/he knows that the cost of travel differs across economic categories and may even be a function of, rather than independent of, distance. And there is some value in the decision makers point of view just as there is value in ours.

The p-median problem when applied to the siting of facilities carries with it an implicit burden of assumptions about the cost structure of operation, construction, and maintenance. This implicit structure is best seen in the formulation of a related and more general model which we refer to as the Investment

Constrained Facility Location Problem, a formulation due to Rojeski and ReVelle (1970). Whereas the *p*-median problem constrains the *number* of central facilities, this formulation restricts the investment in facilities. In other words, a pool of funds has been allocated to establish an unknown number of facilities for a particular region.

Let the cost of the *j*th facility be given by

$$L_j = b_j + c_j S_j,$$

where

S_j = the size to which the *j*th facility is built,

$c_j = \sum_{i=1}^{n} a_i x_{ij}$ = the number of people who will use the facility,

f_j = the fixed cost incurred if the facility is built at *j*, and

b_j = the cost per unit of population served at *j*.

The parameters a_i and the variables x_{ij} are as defined earlier. Since the fixed cost occurs only if *j* is assigned to itself, the previous equation can be written

$$L_j = f_j x_{jj} + b_j \sum_{i=1}^{n} a_i x_{ij},$$

The total cost is

$$TC = \sum_{j=1}^{n} L_j = \sum_{j=1}^{n} f_j x_{jj} + \sum_{j=1}^{n} b_j \sum_{i=1}^{n} a_i x_{ij}.$$

A generalized constraint on investment, *M*, takes the form

$$\sum_{j=1}^{n} f_j x_{jj} + \sum_{j=1}^{n} b_j \sum_{i=1}^{n} a_i x_{ij} \leq M.$$

If the cost b_j were the same for all *j*, the constraint would become simply

$$\sum_{j=1}^{n} f_j x_{jj} + b \sum_{j=1}^{n} \sum_{i=1}^{n} a_i x_{ij} \leq M.$$

However,

$$\sum_{j=1}^{n} \sum_{i=1}^{n} a_i x_{ij} = \sum_{i=1}^{n} a_i,$$

so that the second term is a constant. This yields a constraint only on fixed cost,

$$\sum_{j=1}^{n} f_j x_{jj} \leq M - b \sum_{i=1}^{n} a_i.$$

Now if the f_j were the same for all j, the constraint would become

$$\sum_{j=1}^{n} x_{jj} \leq \frac{M - b \sum_{i=1}^{n} a_i}{f}.$$

And the number of central facilities, p, is then defined

$$p = \left[\frac{M - b \sum_{i=1}^{n} a_i}{f} \right],$$

where [ ] denotes "the integer part of".

The specification of p facilities then rests on the assumptions:

(1) that all fixed costs are equal and regionally invariant, and

(2) all expansion or service costs are equal and regionally invariant.

Alternatively, the number of facilities might frequently be arrived at in the political arena rather than chosen by an analytical method. As an example, the choice might represent a compromise between the legislative and executive branches of government or be given to an agency as a constraint within which to work. Such choices on the number of facilities are commonly made.

Returning to the investment constraint, we can structure the location problem as follows,

$$\min Z = \sum_{j=1}^{n} \sum_{i=1}^{n} a_i d_{ij} x_{ij},$$

subject to

$$\sum_{j=1}^{n} x_{ij} = 1, \quad i = 1, 2, \ldots, n, \tag{1}$$

$$x_{jj} \geq x_{ij}, \qquad i, j = 1, 2, \ldots, n,$$
$$i \neq j, \tag{2}$$

$$\sum_{j=1}^{n} f_j x_{jj} + \sum_{j=1}^{n} b_j \sum_{i=1}^{n} a_i x_{ij} \leq M, \tag{3}$$

$$x_{ij} = (0, 1), \quad i = 1, 2, \ldots, n,$$
$$j = 1, 2, \ldots, n, \tag{4}$$

where all variables and parameters are as previously defined.

This formulation as it stands has two flaws. First, unless an integer programming code is employed, the solution will not, in general, consist of all zero-one variables when solved as a continuous linear program. Further, the application of an integer programming code to this problem as structured is likely to be prohibitively expensive. For this reason, Rojeski and ReVelle used the Method of Resources Variation to produce integer solutions. The method generated pairs of integer solutions at slightly different levels of investment in facilities, but was cumbersome in that at least three linear programming problems were required for each pair of points and because hand calculations were necessary to decide which new problems to run. Solution difficulty then was the first flaw. The second flaw had to do with assignment of demand areas to facilities which were not their closest facility. We correct for this second flaw momentarily. For now, we focus on a new solution method for the Investment Constrained Facility Location Problem.

While the Method of Resource Variation as applied to this problem is reported in the literature (Rojeski and ReVelle), the multi-objective generating method has not previously been applied to this problem. This method is drawn from the growing literature of multi objective programming [see Cohon (1978)]. To apply the method, we interpret the problem as a formulation with two objectives. These objectives are

(1) the minimization of average distance, and

(2) the minimization of investment.

In more formal terms, the statement of objectives is

$$\min Z_1 = \sum_{j=1}^{n} \sum_{i=1}^{n} a_i d_{ij} x_{ij},$$

$$Z_2 = \sum_{j=1}^{n} f_j x_{jj} + \sum_{j=1}^{n} b_j \sum_{i=1}^{n} a_i x_{ij},$$

subject to the same constraints as before less any restrictions on number of facilities or investment in facilities.

Using the weighting method of multi-objective programming, we can restate the objectives in a single set of terms as follows:

$$\min Z = w Z_1 + (1-w) Z_2,$$

where

$w = $ a weight between zero and one.

Expanding this objective, we obtain

$$\min Z = \sum_{j=1}^{n} \sum_{i=1}^{n} w a_i d_{ij} x_{ij} + \sum_{j=1}^{n} (1-w) f_j x_{jj}$$

$$+ \sum_{j=1}^{n} \sum_{i=1}^{n} (1-w) b_j a_i x_{ij},$$

which can be simplified to

$$\min Z = \sum_{j=1}^{n} \sum_{i=1}^{n} c_{ij} x_{ij} + \sum_{j=1}^{n} h_j x_{jj},$$

where

$$c_{ij} = w a_i d_{ij} + (1-w) b_j a_i, \quad \text{and}$$
$$h_j = (1-w) f_j.$$

If this objective is minimized using continuous linear programming subject to the constraints indicated, the result can confidently be expected to be all zero-one with a frequency in excess of 95%. This is because the objective and constraints are precisely in the form of the well-known plant location problem due to Balinski (1965), which Morris (1978) has shown by experiment to terminate with all zero-one variables in over 95% of randomly generated test problems. Experience has shown the post-simplex application of Branch and Bound resolves the few fractional solutions with relative ease.

With the problem resolved in integers it is a simple matter to vary the weight w between zero and one and produce solutions with various pairs of investment and average distance. As the weight on average distance is increased, the value of average distance decreases and the investment required increases. Ranging the weight w then is a simple technique for producing the tradeoff curve between average distance and investment, far simpler than the Method of Resource Variation, referred to earlier. This methodology for producing a tradeoff curve will be suggested later for other similar location problems in which costs vary across the network.

A second flaw was referred to in the investment constrained formulation, namely that some demand areas may be assigned in the optimal solution to facilities which are not their closest. If assignment is by fiat, this anomaly presents no difficulty, but if people behave rationally and minimize distance, then the result does not conform to consumer behavior. To appreciate the cause of this difficulty in the formulation, it suffices to look at the multi-objective formulation just structured which, we observed, is precisely in the form of the plant location problem. It is well known that in an optimal solution to the plant location problem demand areas can receive their shipments from plants which are not physically closest; this is because cost is minimized when a demand area is served by the plant whose sum of processing/manufacturing cost plus transport cost to the demand area is least – and this may not be the closest plant. The same sort of process is at work in the present problem of average distance versus investment.

If it is assumed that people are not assigned by fiat but choose their closest facility, then it becomes necessary to correct the assignments of those areas assigned to non-closest facilities. Rojeski and ReVelle suggested a constraint of the following form to force assignments to closest open facilities. Let us say that in a particular optimal solution demand area i currently assigns to a facility at h which is not its closest and that the facility at j is its closest. Then we rerun the mathematical program with the constraint

$$x_{ij} \geq x_{jj} - \sum_{k \in N_{ij}} x_{kk},$$

where N_{ij} is the set of sites k that are closer to i than j is. In words, this constraint says that unless a site k which is closer to i than j is in the solution, the demand area i must assign to j. It is recommended that these constraints are added only as necessary, viz., when an assignment is observed to a non-closest facility.

This completes the discussion of the Investment Constrained Facility Location Problem which we pointed out is a generalization of the p-median problem in which facility costs, both fixed and variable, are different across the network. The shape of the tradeoff curve between average distance and investment is illustrated in the Figure 1 where the dotted lines and shaded areas indicate that some points interior to the tradeoff curve may not have been generated by the weighting method.

There are other ways in which the p-median formulation and its generalized form can be viewed as a multiple objective problem, but we postpone these for a more general discussion which will include other model types. Nonetheless, one additional objective applied to p-median leads to both new insights and new models.

That objective, or consideration, is the maximum time or distance which can separate a user from his nearest facility. That objective was first included in the p-

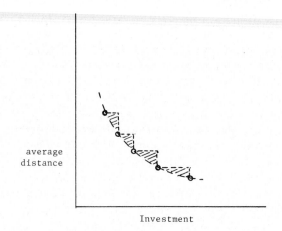

Figure 1.   Average distance travelled as a function of investment.

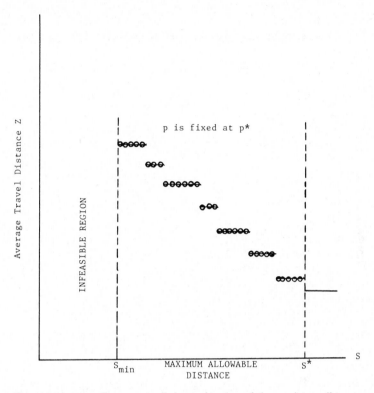

Figure 2. Average distance travelled as a function of the maximum distance.

median model by Toregas et al. (1971) who showed the form of the tradeoff between the average travel distance and the maximum travel distance. In the graph above (Figure 2), a version of which originally appeared in Toregas et al., S is the maximum distance between any user and his nearest facility. At values of S greater than S^* one observes no effects on the solution to the p-median problem. Once the maximum distance is reduced to values less than S^* the average travel burden will increase as the maximum distance is further decremented. At values of maximum distance below S_{min} no feasible arrangement of p facilities can be found which meets the maximum distance requirement. It is of interest that not all of the points on this tradeoff curve are meaningful in the multi-objective sense since some of the points are inferior or dominated. Only the left-most corner point of each flat line is non-inferior since other members of the line give larger values of S for the same average distance.

The addition of a maximum distance constraint produces both a multi-objective view of the p-median problem and a new formulation as well. The point

S_{min} on the graph represents the smallest value of maximum distance that can be achieved by p facilities. No spatial pattern exists that can make the p facilities cover all points of demand within a maximum distance less than s_{min}; viz, the number of facilities is insufficient. Suppose a decision maker has specified a value of S less than S_{min}. What number of facilities is sufficient to cover all points of demand within S? This leads directly to the statement of the location set covering problem as posed by Toregas, et al. (1971).

Find the minimum number of facilities and their locations so that each point of demand will have a facility within S time units.

In mathematics, this problem may be stated simply as:

$$\min Z = \sum_{j=1}^{n} x_j,$$

subject to

$$\sum_{j \in N_i} x_j \geq 1, \qquad i = 1, 2, \ldots, n,$$

$$x_j = (0, 1), \qquad j = 1, 2, \ldots, n,$$

where

n = number of nodes;

d_{ij} = shortest distance, node i to node j;

S = maximum allowable distance that may separate node i from its nearest facility; and

$N_i = \{j | d_{ij} \leq S\}$.

Again, the assumption here is that demand nodes and facility sites are coincident, but the sites and demand nodes could be disjoint or overlap as required by the problem setting. Several methods, including linear programming, have been suggested to solve this zero-one problem [see Toregas et al. (1971) and Toregas and ReVelle (1973)]. Problems with thousands of nodes should be possible to solve with modern computers.

One can solve the location set covering problem for successive values of S and investigate how the number of facilities is influenced by the maximum distance. The multiple objective tradeoff curve so obtained is illustrated in Figure 3. The curve, as anticipated, exhibits an increase in the number of facilities as the maximum distance is reduced; since this is an integer program that increase occurs in discrete jumps. For many values of S, however, the required number of facilities remains the same as for larger values. For instance, for distances between S_B and S_A, three facilities are required. Reducing the maximum distance within

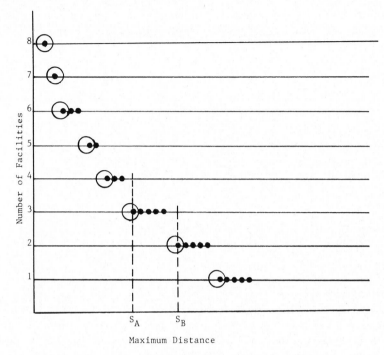

Figure 3. Number of facilities as a function of maximum distance.

this interval has no effect on the number of facilities, although the spatial pattern of facilities may be altered to meet the tighter distance requirement. The solution at S_A represents the smallest maximum distance for which three facilities are still adequate. Indeed, the arrangement of facilities at S_A is the solution to a different problem, that of minimizing the maximum distance that separates any demand point from its nearest facility given that three facilities can be sited. This is a discrete solution space version of the problem which Hakimi named the *p*-center problem (1964, 1965); by discrete solution space is meant that eligible sites are specified in advance. This solution procedure for the *p*-center problem was suggested by Christofides and Viola (1971) and by Minieka (1970).

In general, each of the left-most corner points (circled on the graph) represents a solution to the minimum maximum distance problem or *p*-center problem. All solutions to the right of these corner points on the same flat portion of the curve are dominated by (are inferior to) the left-most point — in that the left corner point utilizes the same number of facilities but achieves a superior and smaller value of maximum distance.

The location set covering problem carries with it an implicit economic assump-

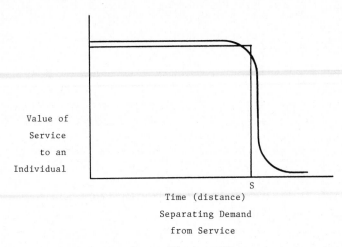

Figure 4. Value of service as a function of distance to service.

tion about the value of service to an individual. The shape of the curve of value of service as a function of the time (or distance) that separates a user and its nearest server is illustrated in Figure 4. The shape suggests that across a broad range of times the value is not sensitive to the precise elapsed time, but that beyond about S a striking loss in value occurs, so that it is essential to have all population served within this time. Further, it is implied that the value of the service is so large as compared to the cost of the facilities that the number of facilities required is not at issue.

Berlin (1972) and Daskin and Stern (1981) both recognized the "looseness" in the location set covering formulation and the p-center formulation. That is, both recognized that the existence of multiple alternate optima to these problems allowed the optimization of secondary objectives. Both attacked the location set covering problem in essentially the same way – as a multi-objective problem. The two objectives used were the minimum number of facilities and the maximum of redundant coverage. By redundant coverage is meant the number of coverers within the maximum distance in excess of the single coverer that is required as a result of the basic coverage constraint. Berlin formulated the problem in the following way:

$$\max Z = \sum_{i=1}^{n} \sum_{j \in N_i} x_j = \sum_{j=1}^{n} C_j x_j,$$

subject to

$$\sum_{j \in N_i} x_j \geq 1, \quad i = 1, 2, \ldots, n,$$

$$\sum_{j=1}^{n} x_j = p,$$

$$x_j = 0, 1, \quad j = 1, 2, \ldots, n,$$

where p is the least number of facilities needed to cover all nodes within the distance standard and C_j is the number of demand areas covered by facility j. The problem may be solved as a relaxed linear program with Branch and Bound utilized as necessary. The objective counts the total number of times that each and every demand point is covered. Although this quantity is not redundant coverage, it differs from redundant coverage by the constant n. That is, n, the number of demand points, is the total number of coverages actually required. Coverers in excess of n are considered redundant. Maximizing the total number of times that demand points are covered then maximizes redundant coverage. One can parameterize on p to determine the tradeoff between redundant coverage and the number of facilities.

Daskin and Stern's formulation explicitly counts redundant coverers:

$$\max Z = \sum_{i=1}^{n} S_i .$$

subject to

$$\sum_{j \in N_i} x_j - S_i \geq 1, \quad i = 1, 2, \ldots, n,$$

$$\sum_{j=1}^{n} x_j = p,$$

$$x_j = 0, 1, \quad j = 1, 2, \ldots, n,$$

$$S_i \geq 0, \quad i = 1, 2, \ldots, n,$$

where p is as defined above and S_i is the number of coverers in excess of one available to cover demand i. By varying p one can tradeoff the maximum of redundant coverage against the minimum number of facilities. Solution of this problem via relaxed LP and the cut constraint suggested by Toregas et al. is reported. No theoretical difference exists between the two Berlin and Daskin and Stern formulations.

Plane and Hendricks (1977) also recognized that multiple alternate optima exist to the location set covering problem. In their application, many firefighting facilities were already in place and it was important for them to use as many of the existing facilities as possible. Thus, they chose as an objective, in addition to the minimization of total number of facilities, the maximization of the sites chosen where facilities were already in place. Their formulation, adapted to the form shown for Berlin and for Daskin and Stern, is:

$$\max \sum_{j \in J_o} x_j$$

subject to

$$\sum_{j \in N_i} x_j \geq 1, \quad i = 1, 2, \ldots, n,$$

$$\sum_{j=1}^{n} x_j = p,$$

$$x_j = 0, 1, \quad j = 1, 2, \ldots, n,$$

where p is, again, the least number of facilities necessary for unitary coverage and J_0 is the set of sites at which facilities already exist. By varying p, one can trade the number of sites chosen at existing facilities against the total number of facilities allowed.

Both Berlin and Daskin and Stern, although they focused on redundant coverage, were not able to distinguish between the value, for example, of providing second coverage versus the value of providing fifth coverage of a demand. Not only do these formulations fall short in adequately counting the value of coverage; in addition, a demand zone, even though low in demand, could come out to be highly favored in coverage, if it were within the distance standard of many potential facilities. Thus, it is important to both count actual demand or frequency and to distinguish between the sequential coverages of an area.

To correct these defects, at least in a partial way, Hogan and ReVelle (1983) showed how to maximize the *population* covered *twice* subject to the constraint that all demand areas are covered at least once.[1] Their formulation is:

$$\max Z = \sum_{i=1}^{n} a_i u_i$$

subject to

$$\sum_{j \in N_i} x_j - u_i \geq 1, \quad i = 1, 2, \ldots, n,$$

$$\sum_{j=1}^{n} x_j = p,$$

$$x_j = 0, 1, \quad j = 1, 2, \ldots, n,$$

$$u_i = 0, 1, \quad i = 1, 2, \ldots, n,$$

[1]The problem is strongly related to the maximal covering location problem which will be introduced shortly.

where a_i is the population at i, or the demand frequency at i. The variable u_i denotes whether or not demand area i is covered a second time. The number of facilities is initially constrained to be equal to the least number of facilities for first coverage, but can be varied to allow exploration of the tradeoff between number of facilities and the population which is doubly covered. Such a tradeoff curve would begin at some positive value of double coverage because almost any placement of facilities causes some double coverage. The problem can be solved as a relaxed linear programming problem with u_i constrained to be less than or equal to one.

We are not constrained to use as the distance standard for double coverage the same value as was used for first coverage. A larger value of the distance standard makes some sense of measurement of double coverage. Using R as that larger distance, we can define

$$H_i = \{j | d_{ij} \leq R\},$$

where

$$R > S.$$

Then the formulation for maximizing double coverage within R, given required single coverage within S, becomes:

$$\max Z = \sum_{i=1}^{n} a_i u_i$$

subject to

$$\sum_{j \in H_i} x_j - u_i \geq 1, \qquad i = 1, 2, \ldots, n,$$

$$\sum_{j \in N_i} x_j \geq 1, \qquad i = 1, 2, \ldots, n,$$

$$\sum_{j=1}^{n} x_j = p,$$

$$x_j = 0, 1, \qquad j = 1, 2, \ldots, n,$$

$$u_i = 0, 1, \qquad i = 1, 2, \ldots, n,$$

where, again, relaxed *LP* is recommended for solution with the individual u_i constrained less than or equal to one. Other modifications of the Location Set Covering Problem, such as to count triple and subsequent coverage, are possible.

Though the location set covering problem was initially appealing, the required coverage of *all* points of demand has been recognized as being a very restrictive condition – in that a larger number of facilities might be needed than the budget allowed. As an example, ten facilities might be required for all demand points to be covered within 30 minutes and yet the funds exist for only seven facilities to be constructed. The logical question is how well the seven that can be afforded can be deployed; a measure of effectiveness is needed. The maximal covering location problem, formulated and solved by Church and ReVelle (1974) offers a measure of effectiveness. That problem can be stated as:

> Allocate p facilities to positions on the network so that the greatest possible total population can be covered (service can be reached) within a stated time or distance standard.

In mathematical terms, the problem is:

$$\max Z = \sum_{i=1}^{n} a_i y_i$$

subject to

$$y_i \leq \sum_{j \in N_i} x_j, \qquad i = 1, 2, \ldots, n,$$

$$\sum_{j=1}^{n} x_j = p,$$

where the only new definition is

> $y_i = 1$ if point i is covered within S; 0 otherwise.

All other terms are as defined earlier. Again, this particular formulation assumes coincidence of demand points and potential facility sites, an assumption easy to relax or alter. Solution of this problem has been accomplished both by heuristics and by relaxed linear programming. For solution by relaxed linear programming, it is necessary to append a constraint that bounds each y_i at an upper limit of one. Problems with a thousand or more demand nodes should be possible to solve using linear programming.

Just as the p-median problem is implicitly a multi-objective problem in travel burden and number of facilities, so, too, is the maximal covering location problem. The tradeoff between population covered within a stated distance and the number of facilities allocated to the network is shown in Figure 5. This curve exhibits the expected concave shape in which the marginal increment of population coverage declines with each additional facility sited. From the graph it can be seen that covering all the demand points requires 12 facilities (a solution to the location set covering problem); these 12 facilities represent 50 percent more facilities than the number needed (eight) to cover 90 percent of the population. The information for choices by the decision maker is clearly laid out.

The same l-shaped value function that was implicitly assumed to underlie the location set covering problem also underlays the maximal covering location problem. Now, however, the economic value of service is more nearly compar

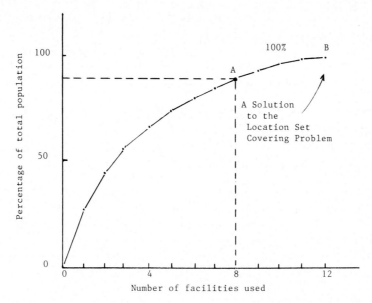

Figure 5. Coverage as a function of number of facilities.

able with the cost of the facilities. If one visualizes point A on Figure 5 as the solution chosen, then the following economic argument can be made about the value of service.

Let v = value of service to an individual (the height of the horizontal line in Figure 4);
  f = the cost of a facility; and
  Z_k = the population covered by k optimally located facilities.

Suppose an eight-facility solution is chosen; it is implied that the cost of an additional facility equals or exceeds the value added by the ninth facility, i.e.

$$f > v(Z_9 - Z_8).$$

This suggests that the value of service is bounded by

$$v < f/(Z_9 - Z_8),$$

and in a similar fashion we can derive

$$v > f/(Z_8 - Z_7),$$

which is a very similar form to the value imputation derived from the p-median, the only difference being in the units of the objective function, Z.

It is in the context of the maximal covering location problem that the need for a multiple objective examination of alternatives becomes most apparent. We will illustrate by example the importance of a multiobjective approach to the maximal covering problem.

The population coverage we spoke of implied that the population was always in the same locale, day and night, in all seasons, and year after year. Of course, it is not. Work and education take people from their dwellings day and night, placing them in commerce, factories, and schools for substantial portions of their time. Populations may change during the year due to tourist movements in or out and the movements of migratory labor. Indeed, patterns of migration are constantly transforming the spatial structures of cities and regions.

Thus in Figure 6a, we display a tradeoff curve derived from hypothetical data which illustrates how well the facilities that optimize one objective (Z_1, the day-time population) achieve another coverage objective (Z_2, the night-time population). This tradeoff curve was derived by optimizing the weighted objective function $w Z_1 + (1-w) Z_2$ subject to the usual constraints and by ranging the weight between 0 and 1. As the weight on the two kinds of populations is ranged in value, coverage emphasis gradually shifts from one objective to the other. Two properties especially of the solutions on the tradeoff curve require explanation.

One property is that the solution points are only those on the outer hull of the bicriterion space – even though points may exist in the gaps between these hull points which are noninferior. The weighting method of generating alternatives was used to produce these hull points because the problem is a zero-one programming problem which is solved by a method which does not admit the addition of constraints. (Constraints on other objectives are likely to produce fractional solutions.) The weighting method is unable to produce points in the gaps because these points lie interior to the hull and hence will never be contacted by the outward moving plane of the two-objective function. These interior points may be found by cuts of a special sort.

A second interesting property is the regularity of the problem's decision space. The graph (Figure 6b) beneath the tradeoff curve depicts the incremental changes in the facility sites that are chosen as the weights on the two objectives are changed. The nodes that are listed in both the far right and far left columns and indicated by a light horizontal line are nodes at which a facility was located in at least one of the solutions on the tradeoff curve. Underneath each labelled solution in Figure 6a, the three facilities which are opened in the solution are indicated. Solid lines show the movement in the pattern of facility positions that occurred as the objective weights were varied. It is of interest that adjacent points on the tradeoff curve (6a) differ in the position of only a single facility (6b). Significantly, one facility does not alter its position throughout the entire range of the two objectives. We have said that the set of facilities whose position remains constant through the range of objectives belongs to the "core". Such "core" facilities seem to be logical candidates to include in a recommendation no matter the decision

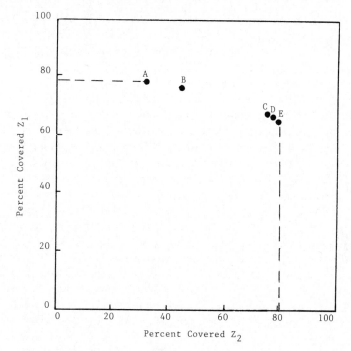

Figure 6a.

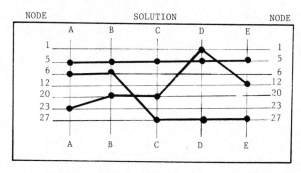

Figure 6b.

Figure 6. Tradeoff curve and solutions for two conflicting maximal coverage objectives.

maker's position on the relative importance of the objectives. If all objectives have been appropriately enumerated, there can be no disagreement about facilities in the core.

One can analyze the tradeoff between serving day and night populations in the p-median as well as in the maximal covering problem. The twin objectives in the case of day and night are (1) minimize average travel time of the day-time populations to their nearest facility and (2) minimize average travel time of the night-time populations to their nearest facility. If the travel is to or from emergency facilities, one could consider the day and night frequencies of emergencies that occur in each demand zone.

Other objectives can be and were identified for the maximal covering model in a study of the Baltimore Fire Service [see Schilling et al. (1979)]. In the United States, fire protection location decisions respond to two separate sets of criteria. One criterion comes from the consuming public; people demand that facilities should be sited in order to be near people and to save lives. Another criterion is provided by the fire insurance companies who settle insurance claims when structures are damaged by fire. The greater the value of the property lost, the greater the payout of the insurance. The fire insurance companies are, therefore, interested in the protection of property. Unfortunately, the only fire protection location standards in the United States are those developed by the insurance companies. These standards are stated in terms of an area's nearness to fire suppression and rescue equipment. According to the standards, high value districts require closer coverage than residential areas; populations are not considered. City fire departments are graded by the insurance companies on how well they meet the criteria for nearness to high value property and to residential districts.

These two criteria, protecting people and protecting property, yielded a number of new objectives in the Baltimore fire study:

Maximize population covered within a distance standard;

Maximize the value of property covered within a distance standard; and

Maximize the area covered within a distance standard.

The degree to which one would wish to cover people rather than property might be influenced by the fire frequency in a given locale. A high fire frequency in a given area would suggest a greater need for coverage than a comparable area of low fire frequency. Thus, in addition to the three objectives above, we formulated three more objectives:

Maximize fire frequency covered within a distance standard;

Maximize coverage of people at risk (fire frequency times population) within a distance standard; and

Maximize coverage of property value at risk (fire frequency times property value) within a distance standard.

Siting patterns for fire equipment were analyzed and compared using these six criteria. Although the simplest tradeoff curves would display population coverage versus property value coverage, proper comparison of patterns should involve all the objectives of the decision process.

To compare siting patterns under multiple objectives, we developed a method

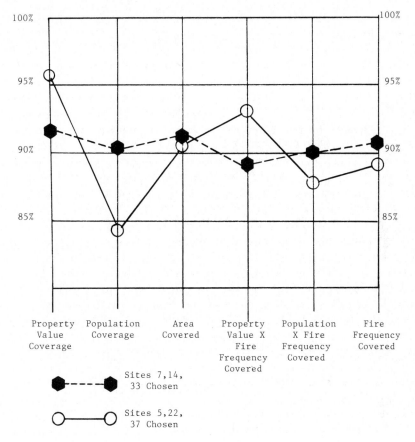

Figure 7. A value path display of two location alternatives.

to display simultaneously the six objective values achieved by a given pattern of equipment deployment. This display technique is called Value Paths [see Schilling et al. (1983)] for the lines which trace out the levels of achievement of a particular alternative.

A Value Path display utilizes a set of equally spaced vertical lines of the same height. Each vertical line represents an objective, and the intersection of the value path with the vertical line reflects the achievement for that particular objective. The lines may have physical units or may be in percentage terms, the top of the line representing 100 percent attainment or the maximum possible level of achievement of that objective. A typical value path for a location configuration is shown in Figure 7. Sometimes it is possible to discard a value path because it can be shown that the path is dominated by some other path (by some other solution or set of locations).

Still another objective was identified in the Baltimore fire study. The operating rule of the Department was that the closest non-busy company (brigade) would be assigned to a call. This policy can and did cause some companies to work significantly harder than others. Workload was thus added as a seventh criterion in the study. Workload location models have been reported on by Weaver and Church (1980), and by Siler (1977), both papers addressing the workload of ambulances rather than fire equipment.

These three models, the *p*-median, the location set covering, and the maximal covering problem, are all related. The location set covering can be derived conceptually from tightening maximum distance constraints on the *p*-median; the maximal covering problem can be derived from the location set covering problem by the recognition that resource limitations exist on the expenditures for coverage of demand points. These three models have another feature in common; they all use some or all of the same basic data: (1) population or demand and its location and (2) shortest distances or time between demand points and facilities. In addition, Church and ReVelle (1976) have shown that the maximal covering model is a special case from a data standpoint of the *p*-median model. That derivation follows.

The maximal covering location problem may be converted to a minimization problem by defining a new variable equal to the complement of y_i:

$$\bar{y}_i = 1 - y_i = \begin{cases} 1 & \text{if demand } i \text{ is uncovered,} \\ 0 & \text{otherwise.} \end{cases}$$

When we replace y_i by $(1 - \bar{y}_i)$, the problem becomes:

$$\min \sum_{i=1}^{n} a_i \bar{y}_i$$

subject to

$$\sum_{j \in N_i} x_j + \bar{y}_i \geq 1, \qquad \forall i,$$

$$\sum_{j=1}^{n} x_j = p,$$

$$(x_j, \bar{y}_i = 0, 1), \qquad \forall i, j.$$

This problem can be solved as a relaxed *LP* without the upper bound on $\bar{y}_i$ that was needed for y_i.

The minimization form offers us still another view of the problem. Recall that the objective of the *p*-median problem was the minimization of average distance which was written as

$$\min \sum_{i=1}^{n} \sum_{j=1}^{n} a_i d_{ij} x_{ij}.$$

Of course, the constraints described earlier for the p-median still apply. Now, the coefficients of the objective function can be recast in the following way:

$$(a_i d_{ij})' = \begin{cases} a_i, & d_{ij} > S, \\ 0, & d_{ij} \leq S, \end{cases}$$

so that solution of the p-median with this transformed data solves the maximal covering location problem. See Church and ReVelle (1976).

The maximum covering model and the backup coverage model are intimately linked in structure. Daskin (1983) makes this point most forcefully when he generalizes the backup coverage model in maximal covering form. His Maximum Expected Covering Model accounts for the probabilities of servers being busy. The model is strongly related in concept to that of Hogan and ReVelle but counts coverage extended to first, second, third and all subsequent levels of coverage.

Daskin begins with the assumption that the probability of a server being busy is the same for all servers and can be estimated. Let q be the probability that any server is busy when a call for its services arrives. Then, given p facilities on the network, the Maximum Expected Covering Problem can be written:

$$\max \sum_{i=1}^{n} \sum_{k=1}^{m} (q)^{k-1}(1-q)a_i y_{ik}$$

subject to

$$\sum_{k=1}^{m} y_{ik} - \sum_{j \in N_i} x_j \leq 0, \qquad \forall i,$$

$$\sum_{j=1}^{n} x_j = p,$$

$$y_{ij}, x_j = 0, 1, \quad \forall i, j.$$

The term $(q^{k-1})(1-q)$ is the probability that a server is available to provide the kth level of coverage. The variable y_{ik} is $(0, 1)$; it is one if node i is covered for the kth time. That is, it is one if the number of servers within S of node i is k. Because $(q^{k-1})(1-q)$ decreases as k gets larger, y_{ik+1} will not enter a basis unless y_{ik} does first, since the value of covering node i for the $(k+1)$st time is less than the value of covering it for the kth time. That is, each successive coverage of node i provides a smaller increment of value to the objective. A particular node still remains attractive to cover by virtue of its weight a_i, but coverages after the first are successively lower in value. In this new model the variable x_j may take on values of $0, 1, 2$, etc; that is, several servers may be positioned at the same site if this increases the expected level of coverage. Of course, node i cannot be covered a greater number of times than the number of eligible facility sites in N_i.

2.1. Dynamic and future-oriented location models

The p-median problem, the location set covering problem, and the maximal covering location problem can and have all been extended to problems in which demand and supply change in time, and in which future demands are an explicit consideration. These problems are less easy to state because it is not immediately clear whether goals are to be optimized at the end of or throughout some time horizon.

Initially, the simplest model, the location set covering problem, was examined [ReVelle et al. (1976)] in three possible ways. We define J_T as the set of facility sites j available for siting at T, the end of the horizon. In addition, it is assumed that no demand area phases out and no facility site becomes ineligible as time progresses.

The first of the three models assumes that full information on future periods exists today in terms of both demand areas and facility sites. Sites can be chosen today for the optimal strategy from among positions that will bring full benefits only later in the horizon. The optimal solution to this "known growth" model would come from solution of a single location set covering problem with all demand points, present and future in place, and all sites eligible to house facilities. Let K_F be the set of sites chosen from solution of this clairvoyant model. Not all members of K_F need to be built initially. In fact, the choice of which facilities to build initially and in each of the subsequent periods would be determined by solution of additional location set covering problems. In these additional problems the available sites are chosen out of K_F not J_T. In addition, some sites would already be occupied in periods after the first period. The demand points to be covered in each period's problem would be those extant at the time and not previously covered. Such a clairvoyant model clearly should require fewer facilities than in a model less sure of the future.

Although these conclusions were keyed to the context of the location set covering problem, the analysis can easily be extended to the p-median problem and the maximal covering location problem. In the p-median problem, solution of the "known growth" scenario produces a set of facilities (again call it K_F) which minimize average distance at the end of the horizon. For each period before the last, the solution of a p-median problem on the extant demand and supply points would site a stated number of new facilities at sites chosen out of K_F that were not already occupied by virtue of being chosen from solutions to earlier period problems. In the last period, the total of sites occupied from previous solutions and positioned in the last period would be equal to the number of facilities allocated at the end of the horizon. In a similar fashion the "known growth" scenario can be extended to the maximal covering location problem. That is, the problem formulation would use the optimal end-of-horizon set of facility sites as the eligible sites from which to draw in each period's maximal covering problem rather than the entire set of initially eligible sites.

In the second of the three time domain location set covering models, referred to as "Restricted Availability of Sites", all future demand points are known, as well as all the sites which are eligible to have facilities throughout the horizon. Now, however, some sites may not be available until the demand in their sector is sufficient to justify the existence of those facilities. Again, the location set covering problem is solved at the end of the horizon to determine a set of facilities K_F from which to draw in each period's planning problem. The restriction that some of the facility sites in K_F cannot be utilized at the optimal moment would generally cause more facilities to be required than in the first of these models. Extensions to the p-median problem and maximal covering problem are relatively straight-forward. In the p-median problem, we expect the average distance to be larger (worse) in each period than in the model where the future is known with certainty. In the maximal covering problem, the population covered will probably be less (worse) period by period than in the comparable model in which the future is clear.

In the third of the three models, the future is unknown until just before it occurs. That is, the location set covering problem is solved in the first period. The facilities sited remain in their place in the second period's problem in which new facilities are added to accommodate the additional demand that has materialized. The process of facility addition to meet newly occurring demand is repeated period by period to the end of the horizon. Of course, this lack of information about future demand results, in general, in more facilities required in the final solution than in either of the preceding models. In the p-median problem, this lack of information on demand results in a final higher average distance than in the preceding models. In the maximal covering problem, it results in a lesser population finally covered.

These three structures in no sense constitute a comprehensive examination of the time–domain problem. The assumption of a facility remaining in place through-out the horizon may in some cases be too restrictive. For instance, although expensive structures such as fire houses or hospitals are unlikely to be phased out within a planning horizon, other facilities such as ambulances may be more mobile. In the U.S. since ambulances are usually positioned in a subset of a city's existing fire houses, it is entirely possible physically that an ambulance could be redeployed each year to meet emerging demands. The political ramifications of moving an ambulance, from the author's personal experience, must still be carefully examined. Nonetheless, Chrissis et al. (1982) have considered the location set covering problem in which facilities may be phased in or phased out as demands change in time. They use x_{jt} as a zero-one variable indicating whether a facility exists at site j in time t. Using the difference between two non-negative variables, they define new variables which indicate whether a facility is phased in or out in the second of two consecutive time periods; viz:

$$x_{jt} - x_{jt-1} = y_{jt}^+ - y_{jt}^-,$$

where $y_{jt}^+ = 1$ indicates that a facility is at j in t, but was not in $t-1$, and $y_{jt}^- = 1$ indicates that a facility is not at j in t even though it was at j in $t-1$. If a facility is at j in t and also in $t-1$, the two variables take on values of zero – as they do also where no facility is at j in either t or $t-1$. The variables behave in this desirable way because positive costs are associated with phasing in or phasing out a facility in the objective function. Of course, these new constraints are used in addition to the basic covering constraints. The authors provide computational experience on this problem as a linear integer programming problem amended by branch and bound. They also convert the problem to a non-linear programming problem and utilize an approximation procedure for the modified problem. Solution of the linear integer program, though the slower of the two procedures, confirmed that their approximation procedure did find optimal zero-one solutions on the test problems at hand.

Gunawardane (1982) examines the location set covering problem from a somewhat similar perspective as ReVelle, et al. He notes that by selecting the appropriate alternate optimum to the set covering problem that the building of some facilities can be delayed in time, an attractive option in the public sector. His formulation of the dynamic location set covering problem is:

$$\min Z = \sum_{j=1}^{n} \sum_{t=1}^{T} (T-t)x_{jt}$$

subject to

$$\sum_{j \in N_i} \sum_{t=1}^{t_i} x_{jt} \geq 1, \qquad \forall i \in I,$$

$$x_{jt} = (0, 1), \qquad \forall j, t,$$

where t_i = the period in which demand i first arises.

The basic constraints require the coverage of each demand point i only as it occurs by the siting of a facility within N_i in some period before demand i has arisen or in the period it arises. This formulation is likely to provide a superior pattern of time phasing as compared to the first dynamic model discussed, delaying facilities until they are absolutely necessary – because the objective is equivalent to minimizing the number of time periods in which facilities exist. In fact, time phasing is a direct output of the model. Again, relaxed linear programming produced all zero-one solutions. Gunawardane also pursues the phase-out issue, as Chrissis, et al. did, using the difference between two non-negative variables.

The maximal covering location problem is likewise approached as a dynamic problem by Gunawardane. He seeks to

$$\max Z = \sum_{i=1}^{n} \sum_{t=1}^{T} a_{it} y_{it}$$

subject to

$$y_{it} \leq \sum_{j \in N_i} x_{jt}, \quad \forall i = 1, 2, \ldots, n, \quad t = 1, 2, \ldots, T,$$

$$x_{jt} \leq x_{j,t-1}, \quad j \in J_1, \quad t = 2, 3, \ldots, T,$$

$$x_{jt} \geq x_{j,t-1}, \quad j \in J - J_1, \quad t = 2, 3, \ldots, T,$$

$$\sum_{j=1}^{n} x_{jt} \leq p_t, \quad t = 1, 2, \ldots, T,$$

$$x_{jt}, y_{it} = 0, 1, \quad \forall j, \forall i, \forall t,$$

where

$y_{it} = (1, 0)$; 1 if demand area i covered in period t;
$x_{jt} = (1, 0)$; 1 if a facility at j during period t;
$a_{it} =$ population at i during t;
$J_1 =$ the set of facilities open at the beginning; and
$J =$ the set of all facility sites.

This model requires that facilities once opened within the span of this planning horizon remain open through the horizon *and* that once the facilities which were open initially are closed, they remain closed through the remainder of the planning horizon. Gunawardane solved a number of this problem type as relaxed linear programs with y_{it} upper bounded at one and found 0–1 solutions in all cases.

A clear dilemma is posed by this last problem formulation as Gunawardane has implicitly assumed that a unit of certain population covered today is equivalent to a unit of uncertain population covered at some time in the future. No interest based discounting or discounting based on prediction uncertainty is included. To a certain extent, this lapse is forgivable since the most Gunawardane could have done is to have included a time-indexed factor, f_t, in the coverage objective. In a subsequent model such a factor was introduced with units of monetary benefits per unit of coverage in time period t, but how f_t might be determined would be an investigation in itself and probably one with a doubtful outcome. Nonetheless, the twin discounting issues should somehow be addressed.

A multi-objective programming approach to dealing with the time domain maximal covering location problem and the discounting issues is provided by Schilling (1980). Schilling structures the simplest version of the problem thusly:

$$\max \left\{ \begin{array}{l} Z_1 = \sum_{i=1}^{n} a1_i y_i \\ \\ Z_2 = \sum_{i=1}^{n} a2_i y_i, \end{array} \right\}$$

subject to

$$y_i \leq \sum_{j \in N_i} x_j, \quad i = 1, 2, \ldots, n,$$

$$\sum_{j=1}^{n} x_j = p,$$

$$x_j, y_i = 0, 1, \quad \forall i, \forall j,$$

where

$a1_i$ = the population at i in the present period, and
$a2_i$ = the projected population at i in a subsequent planning period.

All other variables and parameters are as defined previously.

The multi-objective approach admits of no single answer, but rather a tradeoff between objectives, in this case a tradeoff between coverage in the present and coverage at the future time. When present coverage alone is maximized, future coverage is likely to suffer. When future coverage alone is maximized, the pattern of facility siting will result in a degradation of present coverage. We can conceive of maximizing one objective, say present coverage, and constraining future coverage to be above some lower bound. Solving this problem with successively increased values of the lower bound produces lower values of present coverage and the required tradeoff between present and future coverage.

This curve of pareto-optimal solutions (one coverage can be increased only at the expense of decrementing the other), would, in fact, have to be produced by the weighting method of multi-objective programming. The constraint method described above could only be utilized if an efficient integer programming code existed – which is not the case.

The weighting method of multi-objective programming, in contrast, produces a new problem in precisely the same form as the original maximal covering problem, to wit:

$$\max Z_{\text{combined}} = w \sum_{i=1}^{n} a1_i y_i + (1-w) \sum_{i=1}^{n} a2_i y_i \quad \text{or}$$

$$Z_{\text{combined}} = \sum_{i=1}^{n} \{wa1_i + (1-w)a2_i\} y_i,$$

subject to the same constraints as before where $0 \le w \le 1$. When $w=1$, present coverage is maximized; when $w=0$, future coverage is maximized. As w is ranged from 0 to 1, points on the non-inferior curve of present versus future coverage are traced out. The fact that the new problem produced by the weighting approach has the same form as the original problem means that relaxed linear programming supplemented by an occasional post-simplex branch and bound will be sufficient to produce integer solutions. Each point on the tradeoff curve indicates a present and a future coverage and corresponds to a particular facility siting pattern (see Figure 6 for a representative shape.)

Now this tradeoff curve is meant to replace an analyst's estimate of the value of future coverage. When a decision maker picks some point on the tradeoff curve, the implication is that degrading present coverage further than its current value to obtain more of coverage of an uncertain future is simply not worth the sacrifice. No precise value of the worth of future coverage is implied, but a range of possible values could produce such a decision. By transferring to the decision maker the necessity of weighing the relative value of future coverage, one sidesteps the conceptually thorny problem of how to apply a discounting based both on interest rates and prediction uncertainties.

Now $a1_i$ and $a2_i$ need not represent present and future populations in demand area i. They could represent populations at i in two different and perhaps equally likely futures. In such a case, the multi-objective program could be used to determine the tradeoff between coverage of two plausible futures. A given pattern of facility sites might do well in population coverage in one future growth scenario and relatively less well in the other. What is desired is a pattern that does relatively well in both futures and is Pareto-optimal.

The notion of alternate futures lead Schilling and his colleagues at Johns Hopkins to formulate a more robust approach to siting in the face of uncertain futures. Referred to as "Options Analysis," Schilling (1982) describes a procedure to isolate strategies which do well in several future scenarios. Schilling's novel work is reformulated here along slightly different lines in order to emphasize the role of multi-objectives.

If a strategy could be found which performed well across all possible futures, the decision maker would have a policy that could be safely followed for perhaps a length of time – without fear that he will be far wrong no matter what the future brings.

To present the model we first need to "normalize" the two futures to put them in comparable terms. To do this, we convert the $a1_i$ and $a2_i$ from population numbers to population fractions by dividing by $\sum_{i=1}^{n} a1_i$ in the former case and by $\sum_{i=1}^{n} a2_i$ in the latter. We now construct in Figure 8 a tradeoff curve in which

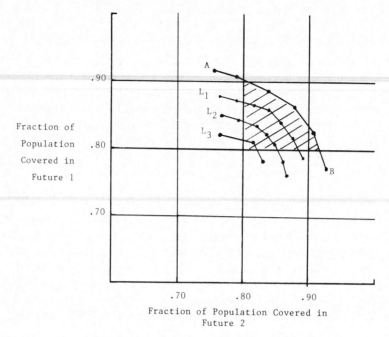

Figure 8. Population covered in two futures.

the objectives are the population fractions. In this hypothetical curve we note that it appears likely that there are a number of possible solutions which maintain population fraction greater than 0.80 in both futures. These solutions fall in the shaded cone indicated in Figure 8.

Within this cone, we seek a solution with the maximum number of facilities in common with the solutions at A and B. This problem may be stated as an integer programming problem – which is difficult to solve – which we then modify to a problem form that can be solved relatively simply. The integer programming problem with p facilities available for both futures is:

$$\max \sum_{j=1}^{n} u_j,$$

subject to

$$y1_i \leq \sum_{j \in N_i} x1_j, \quad i \in I_1,$$

$$y2_i \leq \sum_{j \in N_i} x2_j, \quad i \in I_2,$$

$$\sum_{i=1}^{n} a1_i y1_i \geq 0.80,$$

$$\sum_{i=1}^{n} a2_i y2_i \geq 0.80,$$

$$u_j \leq x1_j, \qquad j = 1, 2, \ldots, n,$$

$$u_j \leq x2_j, \qquad j = 1, 2, \ldots, n,$$

$$\sum_{j=1}^{n} x1_j = p,$$

$$\sum_{j=1}^{n} x2_j = p,$$

$$x1_j, x2_j, y1_i, y2_i, u_j = (0, 1) \quad \forall i, j,$$

where

I_1 = the set of demands in future 1;
I_2 = the set of demands in future 2;
$x1_j = 1, 0$; it is 1 if a facility sited at j for future 1 coverage;
$x2_j = 1, 0$; it is 1 if a facility sited at j for future 2 coverage;
$y1_i = 1, 0$; it is 1 if i is covered in future 1;
$y2_i = 1, 0$; it is 1 if i is covered in future 2;
$u_j = 1, 0$; it should be 1 if facilities are sited at j in both futures.

Because of this problem's structure, the relaxed *LP* is unlikely to terminate with all zero-ones. However, we can recast the problem as a multi-objective maximal covering problem, and maximize the two coverage objectives subject to a constraint on the number of facilities in common to both facility plans. That is:

$$\max Z_1 = \sum_{i=1}^{n} a1_i y1_i$$

$$Z_2 = \sum_{i=1}^{n} a2_i y2_i$$

subject to

$$y1_i \leq \sum_{j \in N_i} x1_j, \quad i \in I_1,$$

$$y2_i \leq \sum_{j \in N_i} x2_j, \quad i \in I_2,$$

$$u_j \leq x1_j, \quad \forall_j,$$

$$u_j \leq x2_j, \quad \forall_j,$$

$$\sum_{j=1}^{n} u_j = m,$$

$$\sum_{j=1}^{n} x1_j = p,$$

$$\sum_{j=1}^{n} x2_j = p,$$

where m is the number of facilities in common to both plans.

Experience with multi-objective maximal covering problems similar in structure to this one suggests that if the weighting method is utilized, solutions will be all zero-one with high frequency. Using the weighting method, we would create the following objective:

$$\max Z = w \sum_{i=1}^{n} a1_i \, y1_i + (1-w) \sum_{i=1}^{n} a2_i \, y2_i.$$

By ranging the weight from zero to one, the tradeoff curve between objectives will be traced out subject to the constraint that m_1 facilities are common to both plans. In Figure 8 above, this is shown as line L_1. If the objective weights are again ranged subject to a constraint on m_2 facilities in common, the line L_2 is traced out. In a similar fashion Line L_3 is traced out for m_3 facilities in common. Line L_4 corresponding to m_4 facilities in common is likewise traced out, but its coverage values do not intersect the cone. Hence, no solution exists which provides m_4 facilities in common and which achieves at least 80% coverage in both futures. The points on L_1, L_2 and L_3 in the cone are all candidates for the solution which achieves at least 80% coverage, but the points are distinguished from one another by the number of facilities they have in common with the two facility plans. In general, the higher the coverage curve, the fewer number of facilities are held in common. If 80% coverage in both futures is really sufficient, the point on L_3 and associated facility plan would likely be chosen because it provides the largest number of facilities in common.

The location set covering version of the problem is easier to state.

$$\max \sum_{j=1}^{n} u_j$$

$$\sum_{j \in N_i} x1_j \geq 1, \qquad \forall i \in I_1,$$

$$\sum_{j \in N_i} x2_j \geq 1, \qquad \forall i \in I_2,$$

$$u_j \leq x1_j, \qquad j = 1, 2, \ldots, n,$$

$$u_j \leq x2_j, \qquad j = 1, 2, \ldots, n,$$

$$\sum_{j=1}^{n} x1_j = p,$$

$$\sum_{j=1}^{n} x2_j = p.$$

This problem version merely maximizes the facilities in common that fully cover both future demand sets, given that a sufficient number of facilities is available for complete coverage in both scenarios.

2.2. Simultaneous siting of services and facilities

Schilling et al. (1979) solve a set of location problems which arose in a study of the Baltimore City Fire Protection System – in which the location of fire stations, engine (pumpers) brigades and truck (ladder) brigades were all free to vary. Also, the distance standards for coverage by engine brigades was different than the distance standard for coverage by truck brigades. These standards were issued by the Insurance Services Organization, an arm of the insurance industry. The basic conceptual problem that Schilling et al., confront is the simultaneous allocation of both facilities and equipment.

In their model, predetermined numbers of facilities (stations) and speciality equipment (engine brigades and truck brigades) are to be allocated. A demand point is "covered" only if engine and truck brigades are both within their prescribed distance standards. That is, a fixed number of facilities is to be located; these facilities are to be allocated equipment of several sorts in limited quantities and the best possible performance level is sought.

The problem can be cast in the context of a maximal covering model as follows:

$$\max Z = \sum_{i=1}^{n} a_i y_i,$$

subject to

$$\sum_{j \in N_i^E} x_j^E \geq y_i \quad \text{for all } i \in I,$$

$$\sum_{j \in N_i^T} x_j^T \geq y_i \quad \text{for all } i \in I,$$

$$\sum_{j \in J} x_j^E = p^E,$$

$$\sum_{j \in J} x_j^T = p^T,$$

$$\sum_{j \in J} z_j = p^z,$$

$$x_j^E \le z_j, \quad \forall j,$$

$$x_j^T \le z_j, \quad \forall j,$$

$$y_i, x_j^E, x_j^T, z_j = 0, 1, \quad \forall i, \forall j,$$

where

S^E = the distance standard for engine brigades;

S^T = the distance standard for truck brigades;

$N_i^E = \{j | d_{ji} \le S^E\}$ = sites which could provide *engine* brigade coverage for node i;

$N_i^T = \{j | d_{ji} \le S^T\}$ = the sites which could provide *truck* brigade coverage for node i;

$x_j^E = (1, 0)$; it is one if an engine brigade is sited at j;

$x_j^T = (1, 0)$; it is one if a truck brigade is sited at j;

p^E = the number of engine companies allocated;

p^T = the number of truck companies allocated;

$y_i = (1, 0)$; it is one if demand area i is covered;

$z_j = (1, 0)$; it is one if a facility (or station house) is located at j;

p^z = the number of facilities (station houses) to be allocated.

The first two constraints define the condition for coverage, namely the simultaneous presence of both engine brigades and truck brigades within their applicable distance standards. The next three constraints limit the number of engines, trucks, and stations. The sixth and seventh constraints enforce the presence of a station prior to the allocation of an engine or truck brigade. The model, which has been named the FLEET model for Facility Location Equipment Emplacement Technique, can be extended to many kinds of equipment, not just two.

The model assumes a clean slate; i.e., that no facilities, or equipment are yet in place. This condition is easy to modify – variables can be set equal to one by the addition of constraints or the variables can be replaced by one in the constraint set. One extreme case is that existing stations are the only eligible sites and equipment is to be redistributed in these stations to improve coverage.

An interesting situation is one in which the conversion of equipment is allowed. Conversion of fire equipment requires only the cost of a new fire engine or new fire truck. The crew that operates the equipment is already employed, so that the major expenditure is already ongoing. In this case, the two constraints on the number of engine brigades and on the number of truck brigades would be merged to the following single constraint

$$\sum_{j \in J} x_j^E + \sum_{j \in J} x_j^T = p^E + p^T,$$

which merely limits the total number of crews without specifying limits on each type. Optimal proportions of each kind of special equipment would thus be obtained.

FLEET problems have been solved using relaxed linear programming. In the examples reported in the literature, all integer solutions resulted, but such an outcome in all cases would be an unreasonable expectation. Fractional solutions, however, should be resolvable using branch and bound – based on experience with the maximal covering location problem.

2.3. The utilization objective and location models

Another category of model has been considered whose basic objective has a far different character than the models discussed so far. These models place utilization in the objective and note that utilization of facilities from a particular demand area is not a characteristic simply of the demand but also of the level of transportation effort that must be expended to get people from the demand point to the nearest facility.

Teitz (1968) was the first to focus on the utilization issue for publicly-owned facilities, although he did not suggest a methodology to solve the elegant problem he posed. Teitz asked what the most appropriate location design would be to maximize the utilization of services given a limited budget, first, for the investment in facilities and, second, for the provision of service. His objective presumed that a knowledge of consumer behaviour was already at hand. Teitz, also, suggested that the monetary constraint should include not only the annualized investment costs which other models explicitly or implicitly assume but also the operating costs of the system which are, in turn, a function of the level of utilization. This later assumption sets his location paradigm apart from many other views of facility systems.

In Teitz' model a single service is distributed out of N facilities which are of identical scale (size) S. The service is zero-priced to all who expend the effort to reach to a facility. The total number of users per unit of time, Q, (say, users per annum) is given in terms of the variables, scale S and number of facilities N; viz:

$$Q = Q(S, N).$$

The system cost is composed of operating costs and capital costs. Let

$C_o(Q)$ = annual operating costs as a function of utilization and
$C_c(S, N)$ = annualized capital costs and annual maintenance expenditures as a function of the scale and number of facilities.

Operating costs are, in turn, a function of S and N by substitution:

$$C_o(Q) = C_o(Q(SN)).$$

Total annual system cost is:

$$C_T = C_o(Q(S, N)) + C_c(S, N),$$

which is constrained to be less than an annual budget B.

The full problem statement is:

$$\max Q(S, N) \text{ subject to } C_o(Q(S, N)) + C_c(S, N) \leq B.$$

This is the essence of the Teitz model.

Although it was not translated into spatial decisions by Teitz, ReVelle and Church (1977) showed how the p-median model could be applied to the specific problem posed by Teitz. That is, they showed how the p-median format could be used incrementally to arrive at both the decisions on location and on the scale of facilities that Teitz suggested were the crux of the problem. Details of the methodology are omitted for lack of space in this brief review.

In the location problem of Holmes, Williams and Brown (1972), a utilization function is suggested for the number who travel from each demand node as function of the distance to the closest facility. The utilization function for node i depends on the distance to the nearest facility:

$$u_{ij} = \begin{cases} a_i\left(1 - \dfrac{d_{ij}}{S}\right), & d_{ij} < S, \\ 0, & d_{ij} \geq S, \end{cases}$$

where

u_{ij} = the number of individuals from i who will utilize a facility at j if that j is their closest facility;

a_i = the number of individuals from i who will utilize the facility if it is placed at i;

d_{ij} = the distance (shortest) from i to its nearest facility j; and

S = a threshold distance beyond which utilization from any demand point falls to zero.

The formula for u_{ij} insures that u_{ij} falls to zero when the distance to the nearest facility is S. This maximum utilization model can be structured in a p-median type format, using the notation introduced there.

$$\max Z = \sum_{i=1}^{n} \sum_{j=1}^{n} u_{ij} x_{ij},$$

subject to

$$\sum_{j=1}^{n} x_{ij} = 1, \qquad i = 1, 2, \ldots, n,$$

$$\sum_{j=1}^{n} x_{jj} = p,$$

$$x_{jj} - x_{ij} \geq 0, \qquad i, j = 1, 2, \ldots, n; \quad i \neq j,$$

$$x_{ij} = 0, 1.$$

Although there are slight differences between the model shown here and that of Holmes et al., the results of application will be the same. In particular, since we defined utilization as 0 beyond S, assignments of a node beyond S can occur at zero cost. In contrast, Holmes et al. allowed no assignment to be made ($\Sigma_{j=1}^{n} x_{ij} \leq 1$) if the distance were greater than S because u_{ij} was allowed to be negative beyond S.

If sufficient facilities are available so that all demands will have a facility *within* S, no utilization will fall to zero. ReVelle, et al., (1975) show that this special situation gives rise to equivalence between the maximum utilization and minimum average distance formulation of the p-median problem. The objective using the utilization function is to maximize:

$$Z = \sum_{i=1}^{n} \sum_{j=1}^{n} a_i \left(1 - \frac{d_{ij}}{S}\right) x_{ij} \quad \text{or} \quad \sum_{i=1}^{n} a_i \sum_{j=1}^{n} x_{ij} - \left(\frac{1}{S}\right) \sum_{i=1}^{n} \sum_{j=1}^{n} a_i d_{ij} x_{ij}.$$

Since $\Sigma_{j=1}^{n} x_{ij} = 1$, the first term of the above expression may be stated as

$$\sum_{i=1}^{n} a_i \sum_{j=1}^{n} x_{ij} = \sum_{i=1}^{n} a_i,$$

which is a constant and hence is non-optimizable. It is sufficient then to:

$$\max Z = -\sum_{i=1}^{n} \sum_{j=1}^{n} a_i d_{ij} x_{ij},$$

or equivalently to:

$$\min Z = \sum_{i=1}^{n} \sum_{j=1}^{n} a_i d_{ij} x_{ij}.$$

That is, for this special case of linearly declining utilization and identical threshold distances for all nodes, maximum utilization is achieved by minimizing average distance.

2.4. Maximizing social welfare

One model takes a frankly economic approach to the siting of urban public facilities. The model due to Wagner and Falkson (1975) attempts to site facilities in such a way as to maximize social welfare, where social welfare is represented by the sum of consumers' surplus and producers' surplus. Maximizing this quantity is appropriate if (1) the marginal utility of income is constant; (2) the existing distribution of income is optimal; and (3) there are no strong externalities in production or consumption.

Consumers' surplus, the net gain to the users of the facility system, is the difference between the value of the service and the price at which the service is provided summed over all consumers. In turn, the price of providing the service is the sum of the transportation cost and the factory price of the service. Producers' surplus is the difference between the factory price of the service and the cost of providing the service.

Two models are provided by Wagner and Falkson to reflect two possible organizational situations. Both utilize the same objective, that of efficiency as reflected by the sum of consumers' and producers' surplus. The first model assumes a "public fiat" environment in which users can be directed to service at or by a particular facility. The second model presumes that consumers will be free to choose the facility from which to obtain their services. To begin with, we develop the "public fiat" model and then append the constraints necessary to the second situation, the "serve-all-comers" environment.

The notation is largely the same as that used in the p-median problem, and the assumption of facilities restricted to demand nodes is also retained. The "willingness-to-pay" for a unit of service of a consumer at i is taken as V_i and is assumed to be the same for all consumers at the ith node.

Consumers' surplus for a consumer at i served from a facility at j is given by

$$CS_{ij} = V_i - c_{ij} - P_j^s,$$

where c_{ij} is the cost of either a consumer going from i to j or the service moving from j to i, and P_j^s is the factory price at j. The total consumers' surplus over all users of the facility system is

$$CS = \sum_{j=1}^{n} \sum_{i=1}^{n} (V_i - c_{ij} - P_j^s) a_i x_{ij},$$

where a_i is the population at demand node i and x_{ij} is a $(0, 1)$ variable indicating assignment.

Producers' surplus is captured by the following expression:

$$PS = \sum_{j=1}^{n} \sum_{i=1}^{n} (P_j^s - e_j) a_i x_{ij} - \sum_{j=1}^{n} f_j y_j,$$

where e_j is the expansion cost at j; f_j is the fixed cost to open the facility at j and y_j is a $(0, 1)$ variable denoting whether a facility is sited at j.

The sum of consumers' and producers' surplus results in the efficiency objective to be maximized; to wit,

$$\max Z = \sum_{j=1}^{n} \sum_{i=1}^{n} (V_i - e_j - c_{ij}) a_i x_{ij} - \sum_{j=1}^{n} f_j y_j.$$

The above objective is optimized subject to the following constraints:

$$\sum_{j=1}^{n} x_{ij} \leq 1, \quad i = 1, \ldots, n,$$

$$y_j \geq x_i, \quad j = 1, \ldots, n,$$

where all variables are required to be $(0, 1)$. Assignments for which $(V_i - e_j - c_{ij})$ are negative will not be made as they would reduce the value of the objective. As a consequence, the corresponding assignment variables, x_{ij}, can be eliminated from consideration. Note, too, that a demand node need not be serviced if the facilities that are sited result in all values of $(V_i - e_j - c_{ij})$ being negative for a particular demand node i.

Because some facilities have lower expansion costs than others it is possible to have demand nodes assigned to facilities which are not physically their closest. Presumably consumers would attempt to behave rationally and would wish to utilize their closest facility resulting in different costs than calculated by the model. The "public fiat" model presumes, however, that consumers can be assigned to a particular facility thus insuring that calculated costs would be incurred costs.

The "Serve-all-Comers" model, in contrast, allows/assumes that consumers do use their nearest facility. Only minor modifications to the "public fiat" model are needed. First, constraints that force assignment to the closest facility are added. Such constraints were described earlier in the discussion of the model of Rojeski and ReVelle, but Wagner and Falkson have derived another form of constraint which enforces this condition. These closest facility constraints, however, should force a demand node to assign to the open facility for which $(V_i - c_{ij} - P_j^s)$ is a maximum (and positive).

Second, it is noted that the people at demand node i *will* present themselves for service at some j if

$$\max_{\text{open } j} (V_i - c_{ij} - P_j^s) > 0.$$

Since the model would, in fact, not assign demand node i if $V_i - e_j - c_{ij} < 0$ for all open j, a constraint must be added to ensure that demand node i will be assigned if its population does present itself for service. Wagner and Falkson use for this purpose

$$\sum_{j=1}^{n} x_{ij} \geq y_j,$$

for all (i,j) pairs such that $(V_i - c_{ij} - P_j^s) > 0$.

2.5. Applications

The applications of locational technologies to urban problems have focussed primarily on emergency systems such as ambulance deployment and fire protection. Covering models in their various forms have received predominant attention. Applications have tended to follow the direction of development of new models.

Beginning in the middle 1970s, Public Technology Incorporated (PTI), an offshoot of the International City Managers Association, began to apply the location set covering problem (LSCP) and its variants to the siting of fire stations. Numerous U.S. cities applied the location package to test the adequacy of their fire protection plans. Often their use consisted of checking how well a particular set of fire station sites performed in providing city-wide coverage – as opposed to actually siting facilities using the model. Some 75 cities were claimed as users of the PTI package for fire station location. In 1977, PTI modified the packages for use in parks and recreation siting and ambulance deployment. Their use of the concept of a distance standard was a seminal application. Plane and Hendricks (1977) report application of the LSCP is the siting of fire stations in Denver, Colorado. Their variant of the LSCP is described earlier in the paper.

The maximal covering location problem (MCLP) developed in 1973 by Church and ReVelle, found application in 1978 in an analysis of the ambulance system of Austin, Texas. Eaton and co-workers [see Eaton et al. (1985)] used the MCLP to site 12 ambulances, providing both basic and advanced life support; a total of 146 possible sites were eligible as bases for the ambulances. The city aimed to achieve 95% population coverage within five minutes travel time of an ambulance. Austin, by implementing a solution suggested by the study, saved $3.4 million in construction cost. Another $1.2 million in operating costs is claimed as additional savings each year.

The FLEET model of Schilling et al. was applied in Baltimore in 1976–77. In this application, both equipment and fire houses were on the table for relocation. Areas of the city with excessive coverage were identified in the study and superfluous units in one section of the city were relocated to other areas. Use of multiple objectives such as population coverage, property coverage, fire coverage, etc., contributed to a ready acceptance of the study results.

The notion of backup coverage, developed by Berlin, Daskin and Stern, and Hogan and ReVelle was applied in Santo Domingo, Dominican Republic by Eaton et al. Eaton's study, remarkably carried out in a non-computerized environment, counted backup coverage as total coverage in excess of first coverage and weighted the backup coverage by section of the city with the population in that section. A number of components of the study were in the process of being implemented in 1984.

The most recent application of these models occurred in Bangkok, Thailand where Fujiwara et al. utilized Daskin's expected covering model to suggest positions for ambulance vehicles. Current coverage levels, they found, can be achieved with only 15 of the original 21 ambulances. Whether their results were implemented is not known.

References

Balinski, M. (1965) 'Integer programming, methods, uses and computation', *Management Science*, 12:253.

Berlin, G.N. (1972) 'Facility location and vehicle allocation for provision of an emergency service', Ph.D. dissertation, The Johns Hopkins University.

Boffey, B. (1978) 'On finding *p* medians', International Symposium on Locational Decisions, Banff, Alberta, Canada.

Chrissis, J.W., R.P., Davis and D.M. Miller (1982) 'The dynamic set covering problem', *Applied Mathematics Modelling*, vol. 6.

Christofides, N. and P. Viola (1971) 'The optimum location of multi-centers on a graph', *Operational Research Quarterly*, 22:145.

Church, R. and C. ReVelle (1974) 'The maximal covering location problem', *Papers of the Regional Science Association*.

Church, R. and C. ReVelle (1976) 'Theoretical and computational links between the p-median, location set covering, and the maximal covering location problem', *Geographical Analysis*, 8:406.

Cohon, J. (1978) *Multiobjective programming and planning*. New York: Academic Press.

Daskin, M. and E. Stern (1981) 'A multi-objective set covering model for EMS vehicle deployment', *Transportation Science*, 15:137.

Daskin, M. (1983) 'A maximum expected covering location model: formulation, properties and heuristic solution', *Transportation Science*, 17:48.

Eaton, D., M. Hector, U. Sanchez, R. Lantigua, and J. Morgan (1986) 'Determining ambulance deployment in the Santo Domingo, Dominican Republic', *Journal of the Operational Research Society*, 37:113.

Eaton, D., M. Daskin, D. Simmons, B. Bulloch, and G. Jansma (1985) 'Determining emergency medical service vehicle deployment in Austin, Texas', *Interfaces*, 15:96.

Fujiwara, O., T. Makjamroen and K. Gupta (1986) 'Ambulance deployment analysis: a case study of Bangkok', *European Journal of Operations Research*.

Galvao, R. (1978) 'A dual bounded algorithm for the *p*-median', International Symposium on Locational Decisions, Banff, Alberta, Canada.

Gunawardane, G. (1982) 'Dynamic versions of set covering type public facility location problems', *European Journal of Operational Research*.

Hakimi, S. (1964) 'Optimum locations of switching centers and the absolute centers and medians of a graph', *Operations Research*, 12:450.

Hakimi, S. (1965) 'Optimum distribution of switching centers in a communications network and some related graph theoretic problems', *Operations Research*, 13:462.

Hogan, K. and C. ReVelle (1983) 'Backup coverage concepts in the location of emergency services', *Modelling and Simulation*, 14:1423.

Holmes, J., F. Williams, and L. Brown (1972) 'Facility location under a maximum travel restriction: an example using day care facilities', *Geographical Analysis*, 4:258.

Minieka, E. (1970) 'The M-centre problem', *SIAM Review*, 12:138.

Morris, J. (1978) 'On the extent to which certain fixed-charge depot location problems can be solved by LP', *Journal of the Operational Research Society*, 29:71–76.

Narula, S., U. Ogbu and H. Samuelson (1977) 'An algorithm for the p-median problem', *Operations Research*, 28:709.

Plane, D. and T. Hendricks (1977) 'Mathematical programming and the location of fire companies for the denver fire department', *Operations Research*, 25:563.

ReVelle, C. and R. Church, (1977) 'A spatial model for the location construct of Teitz', *Papers of the Regional Science Association*, 39.

ReVelle, C., D. Bigman, D. Schilling, J. Cohon and R. Church (1977) 'Facility location: a review of context-free and EMS models', *Health Services Research*.

ReVelle, C., R. Church and D. Schilling (1975) 'A note on the location model of Holmes, Williams and Brown', *Geographical Analysis*, 7:457.

ReVelle, C., K. Rosing and H. Rosing-Vogelaar (1979) 'The p-median and its linear programming relaxation: an approach to large problems', *Operational Research*.

ReVelle, C., C. Toregas and L. Falkson (1976) 'Applications of the location set covering pro blem', *Geographical Analysis*, January.

Rojeski, P. and C. ReVelle (1970) 'Central facilities location under an investment constraint', *Geographical Analysis*, 2:343.

Schilling, D. (1980) 'Dynamic location modelling for public sector facilities: a multi-criteria approach', *Decision Sciences*, 11.

Schilling, D. (1982) 'Strategic facility planning: the analysis of options', *Decision Sciences*, 13:1.

Schilling, D., D. Elzinga, J. Cohon, R. Church and C. ReVelle (1979) 'The TEAM/FLEET models for simultaneous facility and equipment siting', *Transportation Science*, 13:167.

Schilling, D., C. ReVelle, J. Cohon and D. Elzinga (1980) 'Some models for fire protection locational decisions', *European Journal of Operations Research*, 5:1.

Schilling, D., C. ReVelle and J. Cohon (1983) 'An approach to the display and analysis of multi-objective problems', *Socio-Economic Planning Sciences*, 17:57.

Siler, K.F. (1977) 'Level load retrieval time: a new criterion for EMS facility sites', *Health Services Research*, 12:416–426.

Teitz, M. (1968) 'Toward a theory of urban public facility location', *Papers of the Regional Science Association*, 21:35.

Toregas, C. and C. ReVelle (1973) 'Binary logic solutions to a class of location problems', *Geographical Analysis*, 5:145.

Toregas, C., R. Swain, C. ReVelle and L. Bergman (1971) 'The location of emergency service facilities', *Operations Research*, 19:1363.

Wagner, J. and L. Falkson (1975) 'The optimal model location of public facilities with price-sensitive demand', *Geographical Analysis*, 7:69.

Weaver, D. and R. Church (1980) 'A multi-criteria approach to ambulance location', *Modelling and Simulation*, 11.

Chapter 28

RURAL–URBAN MIGRATION IN DEVELOPING COUNTRIES

DIPAK MAZUMDAR

University of Toronto
The World Bank*

Introduction

Migration is a response of individuals to better opportunities, and should in principle increase economic welfare unambiguously. The problem connected with rural–urban migration could then be of two different types: (1) private response to migration could be due to non-economic factors ("city lights", etc.); excessive because of gambling instincts; or a desperate act after being pushed out from traditional rural activities due to population growth; (2) social returns to migration may be less than private returns because the distribution of non-labor factors between rural and urban location (which involve labor migration) is less than optimum; or because the distributional consequences of migration are not necessarily equalizing.

This essay has been written to bring the available evidence to focus on some of these issues. It is unrealistic to assume that definite answers can be given when the literature, although substantial, covers only a fraction of prevalent rural–urban migration streams. The purpose is the limited one of discussing a sample of the research which has tried to tackle these questions.

Section 1 gives an overview of the scale of rural–urban migration in LDCs, and considers the hypothesis of over-urbanization. Section 2 is a selective review of the literature on the determinants of migration, with particular emphasis on the relative importance of economic and non-economic factors. Section 3 takes a closer look at the discussion of urban labor markets in the literature and the

---

*The World Bank does not accept responsibility for the views expressed herein which are those of the author(s) and should not be attributed to the World Bank or to its affiliated organizations. The findings, interpretations, and conclusions are the results of research supported by the Bank; they do not necessarily represent official policy of the Bank. The designations employed, the presentation of the material, and any maps used in this document are solely for the convenience of the reader and do not imply the expression of any opinion whatsoever on the part of the World Bank or its affiliates concerning the legal status of any country, territory, city, area, or of its authorities, or concerning the delimitations of its boundaries, or national affiliation.

Handbook of Regional and Urban Economics, Volume II, Edited by E.S. Mills
© *1987, Elsevier Science Publishers B.V.*

various views as to how the process of migration is shaped by labor market segmentation in the urban economy. Finally, Section 4 looks at some of the more important aspects of the "social efficiency" of rural–urban migration: from the point of view of achieving more equal distribution of earnings between households (or regions); and of the distribution of non-labor resources between rural and urban areas.

1. The scale of urbanization and migration

1.1. General overview

Table 1 gives the percentage of urban population in different regions of the world, and the annual percentage rates of growth in rural and urban areas over the last three decades. It is clear that the rate of urbanization is proceeding apace everywhere. But the differential rate of growth of urban and rural population in 1950–80 has not been all that different in low income Asia than among industrialized countries. On the other hand, the differential growth rates seem to be definitely higher for some parts of the middle income countries, particularly for

Table 1
Rural and urban population in different regions

Country group	Percentage urban population, 1980	Average annual 1950–80	Percentage growth
		Urban	Rural
All developing countries	28.7	3.4	1.7
Excluding China	35.4	3.8	1.7
Low Income	—	—	—
Asia	19.5	4.4	2.0
China[a]	13.2	2.5	1.8
India	23.3	3.2	1.8
Africa	19.2	7.0	2.5
Middle Income	—	—	—
East Asia Pacific	31.9	4.1	1.8
Middle East and North Africa	46.8	4.4	1.6
Sub-Saharan Africa	49.4	3.1	1.0
Latin America and Caribbean	65.3	4.1	0.8
Southern Europe	47.1	3.8	0.5
Industrial Countries[b]	77.0	1.8	−0.7

Source: World Development Report (1984, Table 4.3, p. 66).
[a]Government estimate for 1979.
[b]Excludes East European market economies.

Latin America and the Caribbean where the level of urbanization achieved by 1980 is very high and coming close to the level of industrialized countries.

Not all of the differential rates of urban growth can, of course, be attributed to migration from rural areas. "Natural population increase is estimated to account for 60 percent of the rise in urban population according to a U.N. sample of twenty-nine developing countries. Perhaps another 8–15 percent is attributable to the reclassification of rural to urban status".[1] As a country urbanizes, natural increase within the city becomes an increasingly important cause of urban growth simply because of the sheer size of the urban to rural population. Thus internal migration has been seen to play a decreasing role over time in several Latin American cities as regions even though the rate of urban growth has been high.[2]

The impact of rural–urban migration on economic growth, and on the pressure of population on land, depend not just on the rate of urban growth which is fuelled by migration, but crucially on the proportion of the rural population which is affected by city-wide migration. It is not often realized that rural–urban migration in many LDCs is a small part of all internal migration. The data for India for the period of migration between 1966 and 1970 are given in Table 2 and show clearly that the predominant type of movement is short distance rural-to-rural movement. The perspective is important in any discussion of rural–urban migration in LDCs. Jolly (1971) estimated that *gross* rural–urban migration (i.e. not correcting for return migration) in the 1950's was only 3 percent of rural population in South Asia, 6 percent in South East Asia and 7 percent in Africa.

Two points should, however, be mentioned regarding the impact of the scale of migration on the rural economy pulling in opposing directions. Large cities often establish "lines of migration" such that fairly small rural areas supply a disprop-

Table 2

Male migration by migration category, India 1966–70

Distance category	Percentage of total male migration	Percentage distribution				
		Rural to rural	Rural to urban	Urban to urban	Urban to rural	Total
Within district	60.8	65.5	18.7	7.5	8.3	100.0
Inter district	32.1	33.3	26.6	29.6	10.5	100.0
Inter state	7.1	24.2	31.6	34.4	9.8	100.0

Source: S. Dhar (1980), adapted from Tables 2.6 and 2.7.

[1] World Development Report (1984, p. 97).
[2] Cf. Bryan Roberts (1978, p. 105).

ortionate amount of migrants to the city in question, and when such lines of migration are established tend to last over prolonged periods.[3]

On the other hand, a point which overemphasizes the consequence of rural–urban migration is the prevalence of temporary migration. A feature of the city-ward migration in many LDCs is that a substantial proportion of migrants are temporary. They are generally lumped together with the more permanent migrants in Census returns. But the absence of migrants from rural areas for a limited period is likely to have quite different effects than more permanent movements. In general, the overall urban migration figures will overestimate the impact on rural economies. Further aspects of temporary migration are discussed in Section 3.

1.2. The over-urbanization thesis

In spite of the scepticism expressed in the last few paragraphs about the allegedly massive scale of rural–rural migration, it has been suggested that LDCs have been experiencing a rate or urbanization much more pronounced than the developed countries during their early stages of growth. The thesis of over-urbanization has been sometimes explicitly stated in the literature, and even if it is not formally spelled out it seems always to be lurking behind the scene in discussions of city-ward migration.

The hypothesis of overurbanization draws its support from two presumptions: factors tending to "push" people out of rural areas, and factors "pulling" people towards the cities. Among the first are the expectations that the pressure of population has nearly exhausted both the external and internal margins of cultivation, pushing people hopelessly towards cities for some kind of meagre living. The "pull" factors emphasize city lights and the rural–urban wage gap. The latter in particular has been highlighted in models of city-ward migration associated with the names of Harris and Todaro. Migrants are attracted to the towns, not because they are assured of an increase in wages, but because they gamble on being absorbed in high wage employment. They are willing to be openly unemployed or accept very low earnings in the urban labor market for a period of time in the expectation of achieving a high lifetime income.

We will look into the research on determinants of migration in more depth in the later sections. At this point it might be useful to summarize the results of some work which has tried to answer the question: are LDCs of today urbanizing faster than developed countries did during their earlier periods of growth?

---

[3]An example is the predominance of the district of Ratnagiri, a narrow coastal district in Maharashtra, which has been responsible for something like 20–25 percent of all the migration in to Bombay City. The pattern has persisted for nearly a century.

The relationship between urbanization and per capita income has been a topic of lasting interest to researchers who have looked at the levels of urbanization on an international cross-section basis or over time. The hypothesis is that the functional form connecting the two is logistic given by an equation of the type:

$$U^{-1} = a + b e^{g(y)} \tag{1}$$

where u is the percent of population urbanized; g is a function of y, the per capita GNP; e is the base of natural logarithms; and a and b are parameters to be estimated.

The key characteristics of the logistic function is that the urban share responds slowly to economic development at low levels of per capita income, then accelerates, but again slows down at higher levels.

Mills and Becker (1986) have recently estimated a variant of (1) with a large international data set spanning the years 1960 to 1980.

Apart from using several versions of per capita GNP Mills and Becker included two other explanatory variables in their regression model.

(1) The share of agricultural employment (A). It was argued that "economic base theory shows that since industrial output is mostly sold outside the urban area in which it is produced, it influences but is not influenced by the population of the urban area. That makes it a desirable independent variable in our regressions." At the same time an unknown part of services production is consumed outside the urban area (e.g. agriculture education extension and research services.) There is thus a case for including the share of manufacturing and service industries together among the explanatory variables. Alternatively, we could use the share of agricultural employment: this is equivalent to including the sum of manufacturing and services employment since the three categories sum to unity.[4]

(2) If the hypothesis that developing countries were urbanizing faster than is justified by their pace of economic development were true, then time should be correlated with urbanization. Mills and Becker therefore added time to the set of explanatory variables to test the overurbanization hypothesis.

After some experimentation Mills and Becker found that the best estimate of the logistic equation performed as well as the simpler parabolic form of the functional relationship between urban share and per capita GNP. An example of

---

[4]"It is by no means true that inclusion of agriculture's share makes the relationship with the urban shares definitional. In both developed and developing countries, large amounts of non-agricultural employment are located in rural areas" [Becker and Mills (1986, Chapter 3)].

their set of best equations is the following:

$$U_{it} = 73.0286 - 0.7157 A_{it} + 13.3706 Y_{it} - 6.6886 Y_{it}^2 + 1.0338 t$$
$$\qquad\qquad\quad (15.19) \qquad (1.67) \qquad (1.58) \qquad (1.30)$$
$$R^2 = 0.799$$

$N = 105$ consisting of various countries i and years t. (t values are given in parentheses.)

A and Y were correlated (about -0.35 in the sample), so that only one tended to be significant in the same regression. Addition of A^2 added little to the regressions, but the deletion of Y^2 made most regressions somewhat less satisfactory.

It is seen from the co-efficient of t in the equation that urbanization increases as time passes, but the significance level of the co-efficient of t is not high and the value is also small. The urban share increases only one percentage point per decade as a result of the passage of time. "The conclusion is that urbanization occurs independently of economic development to only a negligible extent."[5]

The predictions from the above equation for urban shares in different groups of countries are compared to the actuals in Table 3.

Table 3
Predicted and actual values of U, 1980

	Country type		
	Average low income	Average middle income	Average industrial
Actual	17	50	77
Predicted	24.6	46.1	77.5

Source: Mills and Becker (1986, Table 5, Chapter 3).

The predicted urban share is not as close to the actual value for low-income countries as for the average industrial country. But the interesting point is that the actual urban share for the low income countries is lower than what would be expected on the basis of the experience of the industrial countries.[6] From the evidence of this and other equations, Mills and Becker concluded that there is nothing in these estimated models to suggest that present day developing countries are urbanizing too much or at a higher rate.

[5] Mills and Becker (1986, p. 20).
[6] For a similar result – not employing econometric technique – see Preston (1969).

2. The determinants of rural–urban migration

The determinants of rural–urban migration can be approached through either a micro- or a macro-migration function. The former makes use of data on personal characteristics of individuals who have migrated from rural to urban areas. Macro-migration functions, on the other hand, look for explanation of inter-area migration flows using as independent variable characteristics of the areas involved in the migration process – on the implicit assumption that such characteristics represent the "average" for the migrants involved in the place-to-place movement.

Clearly the data on personal characteristics of individual migrants would be the superior body of material to use in migration functions. But their widespread use is not possible because they have to depend on survey data ideally collected both at the rural and urban ends. Some studies have made use of less than ideal data, utilizing survey data either in the rural areas [e.g. Hay (1980)] or in the urban areas [Banerjee (1981)].

Macro-migration functions are much more common and have achieved some interesting results in a number of countries.[7] The starting point of these functions is the well-known gravity model. Based somewhat dubiously on nineteenth century physics, it hypothesizes that the gross migration flow between two areas is directly proportional to the size of the two regions and inversely proportional to the distance between them [Zipf (1946)]. This formulation leads to a double logarithmic equation which can be estimated:

$$M_{ij} = \log K + a_i \quad \text{by} \quad P_i + a_2 \log P_j - a_3 \log D_{ij}, \qquad (2)$$

where

M_{ij} is gross migration from area i to area j, (generally normalized by dividing the gross flow by the area of origin population);
P_i, P_j are the population of i and j respectively;
D_{ij} is the distance between i and j;
and K is a constant.

Although some attempts have been made to give behavioral content to this mechanical model[8] generally it is expanded to include economic variables. These have included income (or wages) in the origin and destination areas; employment rates (or variants to give an index of labor market tightness); as well as some "push" factors.

---

[7] These models often seek to explain several different migration flows of which rural–urban is only a part. However, some studies have specifically distinguished rural–urban flows, e.g. Barnham and Sabot; Fields; Bannerjee and Kanbur.

[8] See for example, Niedercorn and Bechdolt (1969).

If these economic variables are added to the gravity model in multiplicative forms representing ratios of variables in destination and origin areas, we get an expanded double logarithmic equation in which M_{ij} of eq. (2) is in logarithms, and there are terms added to the right hand side giving economic characteristics of areas i and j. More recent work has used as a starting point the idea that the "migration decision is indirectly a choice between a finite number of mutually exclusive discrete alternatives. As such it is amenable to analysis by the poly-tomous logistic model."[9] The application of this model to migration decisions leads also to the formulation of a double logarithmic migration function [see Schultz (1982) and Fields (1982)]. Schultz, however, suggests that "the gravity model is still insufficient, for it does not make use of the information contained in the relative frequency of non-migration as does the logit model. ... In the limit as the unit of time diminishes over which migration is measured, differences between the two specifications of the migration model might be expected to diminish."[10]

Our interest in this essay is, however, not strictly methodological. Rather we would like to see from the numerous studies available what are the more robust results which comes through as determinants of migration flows.

2.1. Distance

This is probably the most pervasive of all explanatory variables. Most migration functions produce a significant negative co-efficient for distance between the areas of origin and destination, when included with other economic variables. In fact in one particular study in Colombia in the first run of the migration function with distance, wage and employment variables, the only consistently significant point which came through was the strong deterrent effect of distance for gross, lifetime as well as recent migration rates [Fields (1982)].[11] This result is as true of developed as of developing country studies.

Observers have often expressed surprise at the strength of the variable because the economic cost of transportation is generally estimated to be quite small. Lansing and Mueller (1967) concluded that about 500 moves studied between 1961 and 1963 in the United States cost less than $50. Levy and Wadyeki in Colombia found that direct costs were a mere fraction of the added income required to induce a migrant to move longer distances. After all, the gains from migration extend into the lifetime of the migrant (see below). From what we

---

[9]Fields (1982, p. 542).

[10]Schultz (1982, p. 576).

[11]Readers may like to note that lifetime migration refers to a person living in area j and born in area i. If area i is unspecified we can talk about gross migration – the rate of migration is then derived by dividing by the population of j.

know about the hierarchy of wage structures in urban areas ranked by size, it is extremely unlikely that in any economy the potential economic gain from migration will not be increased by travelling further distance for a large majority of migrants.

Psychic costs and availability of information about labor markets have been maintained as the most likely factors involved in the deterrent effect of distance. The latter derives support from the evidence that negative co-efficient of distance is in most studies found to be less for more educated migrants whose information network is presumably wider. In Schultz' Venezuelan study, for example, the elasticity of migration with respect to distance fell from -1.59 for those with no education to -0.656 for those with some higher education.[12] These results are very similar for the United States [cf. Schwartz (1973)].

The importance of distance as an explanatory variable has implications for an aspect of migration literature dealing with stage migration. Ever since Ravenstein (1889) and Redford (1926) noted the pattern of rural areas supplying migrants to smaller towns during the English Industrial Revolution, and the latter supplying larger towns and so on, studies in the United States as well as in developing countries have emphasized the role of "stages" in the migration process. Research in Chile, Colombia and Mexico has shown that most migrants came from areas close to the existing centers [Singer (1973); Herrick (1965); Morse (1971)].

Several authors have, however, noted that stage migration is likely to be the prevalent pattern if there is a well-developed hierarchy in terms of size of urban centers. When large primate cities play a significant role in the distribution of the urban population short-distance migration may not be the dominant form of rural–urban movements. Large cities typically develop their individual "catchment areas" from which migrants are drawn – and these areas are not necessarily concentrically distributed in terms of distance. If then most migration functions find distance as a strong explanatory variable in place-to-place migration, it implies that migration to primate cities does *not* dominate migration flows in many LDCs. Nevertheless, migration to large cities is an important type of movement, and the characteristics could be different from aggregate rural–urban or place-to-place migration. Some of the problems associated with migration to primate cities are further discussed in Section 3.

2.2. Population

We have seen above that population in both places of origin and destination is singled out in the gravity model along with distance. The behavioral assumption behind this premise is obscure. In any event, accounting for *past* (lifetime)

---

[12]Schultz (1982), Table 2, eq. 1.

migration in terms of *current* population, as many estimated models have done, introduces serious biases in an econometric sense. "Since migrants are counted in current destination populations and excluded from current origin populations, a positive and negative correlation (bias) is definitely introduced" [Schultz (1982, p. 568)]. To correct for this bias Schultz redefines population size variables ex ante, as the number of persons born in the region. With these modifications, population size in the destination area can be interpreted to be proxies for (a) the absolute level of economic opportunities, and (b) the presence of contacts to help assimilation. Population density, in the area of origin, on the other hand, can be expected to influence migration through its effect on transportation costs, the marginal product of labor, etc. With these modifications Schultz found in his Venezuelan Study the gravity effect of destination native born population size was quite robust, the elasticity of migration with respect to this variable increasing from 0.2 for the unschooled to 0.9 with some secondary schooling. The degree of urbanization in the destination region was not part of the explanation because it was separately introduced and significant. However, the interpretation of the result still remains ambiguous because we are summarizing the experience of several generations of both migrants and native born population of the destination region.

It might be more appropriate to use the contact (family and friends) variable more directly by introducing the stock of past migrants (i.e. prior to the period covered by the dependent variable M_{ij}). Studies which have done this invariably come with a significant co-efficient of the expected positive sign for this variable.[13] In fact, Greenwood argues that because in the usual estimation of a migration function the explanatory variables influence migration partly through their past effect on the distribution of migrants, the inclusion of the past migrant stock variable would reduce the parameter estimates of the other variables. He verifies this hypothesis for the United States, for the individual States as well as the country as a whole. In particular, the "true" (current) direct effects of distance are considerably reduced.

Although the past migration patterns determine the present patterns significantly, this argument cannot be carried to its logical conclusion, as otherwise we will see ever increasing concentration of population. Eventually areas of large population (or in-migration) must start repelling migrants, at least relatively to other areas. Such dynamic effects or changes over time cannot be captured by cross-section migration function studies. However, the important point brought out by the discussion here is that the cumulative nature of migration flows does work against redistributive effects of population transfer over considerable periods of time in most countries. (This point is discussed further in the last section.)

[13] Examples are Anand (1971) for India; Greenwood (1969, 1970, and 1972) for the U.S.A.; Levy and Wadycki (1973 for several countries) and Banerjee and Kanbur (1981) for India.

2.3. Economic variables

We can now turn to more strictly economic variables, of which three sets have been most widely considered: (i) income or wages in the destination and origin areas; (ii) employment conditions in the respective labor markets; and (iii) factors affecting the position of the supply curve of labor in the area of origin like population growth relative to the availability of land.

A word of caution should be mentioned at the very outset about several of the migration studies. More often than not migration over a long period (typically lifetime or since the last census date) is sought to be explained by economic variables which refer to present conditions. Data limitations do not allow much choice: focusing the study on recent migrants is more correct but limits the scope of the work.

2.3.1. Relative income

Almost all migration research in developed and developing countries comes to a strong conclusion that the net effect of migration is to increase the income of migrants on average, and that gross migration flows are very sensitive to income differences. Some studies have found it useful to compare the income performance of migrants from a given locality and of individuals with similar (human capital) characteristics who have remained behind. In the United States most work has come out with a net profit for migrants, although sometimes it is found that migrants have to take an earnings cut for up to five years before registering further earnings growth.[14] The overall conclusion of such studies in developing countries is no different.[15]

While the conclusion on net positive return from migration is an important one, the performance of different types of migrants in the urban labor market – and in different parts of it – is also a topic of great interest. It is discussed in the next section.

Turning to the role of income variables in migration functions, the influence of the destination wage on the rate of migration is generally significant and quantitatively quite substantial. Sabot, for example, finds that ceteris paribus the wage elasticity of the migration rate was 2.0 for urban wages in Tanzania.[16]

An important point which has emerged from this class of studies should now be emphasized. This is the observed asymmetry between destination and origin conditions. Most migration functions have found, both in the U.S. and in developing countries, that destination wage is much more important in determining the migration rate than the wage at the place of origin. One explanation

---

[14]See Greenwood (1975) for a summary of the U.S. literature.
[15]For a summary of evidence from Taiwan, Kenya and Brazil see Yap (1975, p. 27).
[16]Sabot (1979, p. 122). Results from four studies are compared in Yap.

might be that personal characteristics dominate the decision of the population on whether or not to migrate, whereas income levels at the destination influence the places to which the migrants are most likely to go. Another hypothesis is based on the idea that capital market imperfections significantly affect mobility. While low origin income means low opportunity cost of migration it also implies limited ability to finance migration. The latter may dominate the migration decision up to a point. The two effects working against each other make the origin income variable weak.

Banerjee and Kanbur (1981) used this idea to derive a function of net benefit from rural–urban migration which is non-linear in relation to rural income. Their estimate of inter-state rural–urban migration rates[17] in India in 1961 yields a significant positive co-efficient for rural income and a negative co-efficient for the square of this term. The hypothesis of a non-monotonic relationship between migration propensity and rural income was further supported by the result that an index of poverty in the origin (rural) area which was also included in the model has a significant *negative* co-efficient. This "runs counter to the idea of rural push necessarily leading to more migration. Rather, poverty appears to hinder out-migration in the Indian case, perhaps because the ability to finance migration expenditures is lowest for the poorest of the poor."[18]

2.3.2. Employment conditions

Labor market conditions are only partly expressed through the wage or income levels. The ease of entry or the possibility of holding on to a desirable job depends on the tightness of the market which can be approximated by some measure of unemployment or the employment rate. This point has been particularly emphasized in the Harris–Todaro class of models in which rural–urban migrants respond to expected wage given as the product of the probability of securing an urban job and the (higher) urban wage. The Harris–Todaro framework, of course, is cast in a dual labor market framework *within* the urban economy in which the high wage refers to the maintained wage in the formal sector. This aspect of the problem is considered in the next section. In migration studies, however, a single average urban wage is often used along with employment conditions as explanatory variables.

The results are mixed. In the United States several studies have found the unemployment rate as an insignificant variable in migration function or sometimes of the wrong sign.[19] It has been suggested that this may be partly because unemployment tends to be highest among the least mobile groups in the

---

[17]Male migration in the year prior to the Census only.
[18]Banerjee and Kanbur (1981, p. 21).
[19]See the references given in Greenwood (1975, footnote 10, p. 403).

labor force (e.g. the very young and the old, or the least educated). Among LDC studies Barnham and Sabot (1977) found that in Tanzania the expected wage (as adjusted for the probability of being employed) explained a larger proportion of the variance. Schultz found that in Venezuela (1982) the employment rate at origin was never significant and destination employment conditions were significant only for the secondary and higher-educated groups. For the latter, however, the elasticity of migration with respect to employment was greater than that with respect to wages. In his study of Colombia, Fields (1982) found that strong correlation between average income and employment rate in the regions considered destroyed the performance of the model where both variables were included, but the destination income was highly significant except for the least educated when employment probabilities were excluded from the regression.

2.3.3. Push factors

We have already noted that the role of low origin income as a push factor is dubious. But other push factors have in some studies yielded significant results. Arnold and Cochrane (1980) found that in Thailand the greater the proportion of land farmed in a *changwat*, the greater the outflow of migration. In the India study Banerjee and Kanbur (1981) got the result that ceteris paribus the more unequal is the distribution of land the higher is the rate of migration. In the Venezuelan work Schultz (1982) concluded: "the measure of population growth or shift in labor supply is strongly associated with migration.... The only peculiarity in these findings is the unanticipated effect of origin population growth upon the migration of the unschooled. In this case, the tendency is for the least-educated group to be unwilling or unable to migrate out of regions that exhibit more rapid rates of population increase".[20] This last point provides further support for the hypothesis that the least educated are less sensitive to economic variables affecting mobility – a point which has wider implications for the redistributive effects of migration discussed in Section 4.

2.4. Limitations of migration functions

In concluding this section it might be pertinent to draw attention to methodological criticisms which purists can and do make about the usual type of migration functions estimated to throw light on the determinants of migration. The major criticism is that in a reduced form migration equation – even when we are using survey data – we can only observe the earnings of the immigrant at his

---

[20]Schultz (1982), p. 585.

point of residence. This level of earnings is compared to his unobserved earnings at the earlier location (his area of origin). We assume that the latter can be inferred by relating his "characteristics" to the characteristics and earnings of those currently found at the other location. But in fact the migration decision partitions the population into those who expect to gain by moving and those who expect to gain by staying. Thus to the extent that the migrants' and non-migrants' earnings are affected by this process of "selection" (apart from the effect of observed characteristics) the comparison of earnings related to migration is biased.

Recent advances in statistical analysis of selected samples have enabled systems of structural equations to be estimated which describe an individual's propensity to migrate along with the wage structures of the migration and non-migration regimes. In principle, consistent estimates of these equations can be used to predict the unbiased wage gains to migration. Not enough empirical work has been done along these lines to show clearly if this extra effort can produce proportionately larger pay-off in terms of more dependable results. One exercise by DaVanzo and Hosdt using data from the Panel Study of Income Dynamics in the U.S. did not reveal much selectivity bias on wage rates in the year following the migration decision, although the authors suggested that the picture might change when additional wage gains in subsequent years were considered.

The last point brings out the importance of the analysis of longitudinal data in evaluating the determinants of migration. Migration produces changes over a prolonged period in a person's life, even if we confine ourselves to strictly economic changes. It is unlikely that decisions are ever taken on the basis of a point-in-time comparison as the cross section migration functions would, strictly speaking, imply. But the difficulty and expense of collecting longitudinal data sets have stood in the way of recurring empirical work on life-cycle effects of migration. It should be noted that, as in other fields of economics, inference about lifetime effects from cross section material can sometimes be misleading. For example, a common finding that migrant workers often earn less than native born workers with similar characteristics during the first few years after migration, but more thereafter, may be a reflection of the "vintage effect" showing that less and less enterprising migrants joint the stream as the migration process gets under way.[21]

Changes over time in relative incomes of areas affected by migration streams also seem to be of the essence of the question: is migration aiding the process of equalizing returns to factors of production in an economy? Migration studies in many countries have found that large income differences are observed between

---

[21] Other aspects of the lifetime effects of migration on earnings are stressed in Stark and Bloom (1985).

areas (for similar sex–age–education groups) even when labor mobility has been known to be high. For example, Fields (1982) concluded at the end of his Colombia study:[22] "The large income differentials suggest that wage flexibility has not come close to equilibrating labor markets spatially". This observation may well be consistent with several points which have been suggested in the literature of the determinants of migration reviewed above – the importance of "push" factors, distance, contact with past migrants – which weaken the response purely in terms of wage differentials. But we would like an observation like Fields' to be supported further with evidence on the time-trend of interregional income differentials.

3. The urban labor market and migration

The starting point of a discussion of the non-homogeneous nature of urban labor markets which has particular significance to rural–urban migration is the Harris–Todaro model (1970). It is hypothesized that migration is not able to achieve equalization of wages between the urban and rural areas because of the maintenance of elevated wages in the urban formal sector through government wage policies, trade union action or a mixture of the two. Rather migrants equate expected wages (i.e. actual wages discounted by the probability of employment) in the urban areas to the alternative rural income. More migrants are attracted to town than job availability warrants producing a positive unemployment at any point of time – which is a function of the rural–urban wage gap. The model was soon modified to include the "informal" sector of the urban economy on the assumption that entry was easy in this sector and the pattern of work was such that it did not impede the search for a job in the formal sector [cf. Mazumdar (1975); Fields (1975)]. The implication of this class of models was that with flexible earnings in the informal sector, their average level would be lower not only than formal sector wages but also lower than average rural wages. The migrant's loss of income while he waited in the informal sector, was a kind of investment for the possibility of securing a high wage formal sector job.[23]

In this formulation migrants as individual utility maximizers do not lose but social costs are positive both because marginal productivity of labor is low in the informal urban sector and because costs of urban infrastructure are high due to "excessive" migration.

These models require empirical support in two major areas: (i) the process of

---

[22]Fields (1982, p. 558).

[23]Mazumdar also examined the model in a dynamic setting and arrived at the conclusion that if the basic premises of the model were correct it will lead to a widening disparity over time in the earnings in the formal and informal sector.

wage determination in the urban formal sector; and (ii) the stylization of the informal sector as one of transition for migrants on th‧ way to employment in the formal sector. Research – some predating the Harris–Todaro proposal – has cast doubt on the assumptions in both areas. We will consider the two topics in turn.

3.1. Wage determination in the formal sector

Wage differentials between the formal sector, and at least some parts of the informal sector have been noticed in many economies. The problem is always one of comparing the levels of earnings of workers of equivalent skill. But if for instance, we compare wages of workers in large firms with those in the small-scale sector, there is generally a pronounced size-related differential after controlling for the human capital attributes of the workers.[24] It is not however, immediately obvious that such differentials can be largely attributed to institutional factors. For one thing, even within the "factory" sector which is covered by wage and labor legislation, large differentials are observed related to the size of factories. Secondly, wage levels in the large scale industrial sector have been relatively high well before the era of trade unions and government intervention in the labor market – which is very much a post World War II phenomenon in most LDCs.[25]

The starting point of an analysis of the wage differential between the large and small sector of the labor market in LDCs must be the recognition of a basic feature of rural–urban migration in these economies – the distinction between individual migrants who come to the urban areas without breaking their ties with the rural economy, and family migrants who give up rural residence and activities in a much more permanent way.[26] The supply price of the latter will be necessarily at a higher level because of several reasons; the nature of peasant farm systems which make the opportunity cost of the absence of a single individual from the farm for a limited period much smaller than that of a permanent shift; the lower earner-dependent ratio of the family in towns where women and children have less scope for market activity; the substantially higher differential cost of living in town for a family than an individual (housing cost and cost of protection against old age, unemployment, etc.). Given this difference in the supply prices of individual and family migrant, if demand for labor in the urban market were undifferentiated, little family migration will take place as long as the operation of the agricultural economy allowed for a plentiful supply of individual migrants.

[24] See for example my study of wages in Bombay City [Mazumdar (1983a)]. Male workers in the largest factories earned 2.3 times the wages of casual workers in the city after controlling for age, education, etc.
[25] Cf. Mazumdar (1973).
[26] For a fuller discussion see Mazumdar (1983a).

This was indeed the experience of a large part of the African urban or non-agricultural sector for a long time before the end of the colonial era. In some LDCs, however, the employers in emerging modern industry saw the value of the higher efficiency of stable labor committed to industrial work.[27] Wage levels were set at a high enough level to attract stable family migrants. Thus we find the emergence of a modern sector with wage levels that were perceptibly higher than the earnings of labor in those activities in which individual unstable migrants dominated. The latter did not offer the same incentive for wage increase because of a weaker link between stability and efficiency.[28]

Once a labor force which is potentially stable in relation to urban residence is formed, further forces may operate at the individual firm level to lower turnover rates even more to reduce inter-firm mobility. The reasons for creating firm-specific labor force are many. The literature has particularly mentioned the wage-efficiency theory and the internal labor market phenomenon. Individual employers find it profitable to increase wages as long as worker efficiency responds proportionately more. With incomplete information about the individual productivity of many workers this result cannot be achieved through piece work or wage discrimination systems. There is no general market for "superior" labor. Rather, each firm is faced with an inelastic supply of potentially productive workers who will be responsive to the incentives of high wages. Up to a point an increase in wage will increase the proportion of such workers in the enterprise and lead to a more than proportionate increase in labor efficiency.[29]

Another point which is related to the incentive effects of a high wage policy is that with a firm-specific labor force the employer–employee relationship takes on the character of an implicit contract with the understanding that employers would not pass on short-term fluctuations in demand by cutting wages in return for the workers attaining a certain level of sustained productivity. Profit sharing is also a part of this type of relationship. Internal labor market models stress the organizational aspect of labor management. The characteristic of such markets is that jobs within the enterprise are arranged in lines of progression. New workers are recruited principally to fill jobs at the bottom of the ladder, while vacancies in higher levels are filled as much as possible through promotion. Apart from encouraging loyalty to the organization, this policy is expected to reduce costs related to training and screening of workers for jobs requiring specific skills. Internal labor markets are fully developed in large organizations. The prediction of this model is that the experience-earnings profile of workers in such units will be much sharper than in other types of firms.

---

[27]The African research looking into the economics of migratory labor is rich in the evidence of higher productivity of stable labor. A study in Durban (University of Natal, 1945) showed that labor productivity of state labor could be as much as three times that of migrant labor.

[28]Cf. Mazumdar (1973).

[29]Cf. Maleanson (1981).

There are thus powerful economic forces which tend to establish the wage level in the formal sector at a relatively high level. Of course, once an exclusive body of firm specific labor force has been formed the workers in these firms might get unionized – and most likely participate in collective bargaining. But it is often the case that unionism is a consequence rather than the cause of the creation of the high wage sector, and historical studies would in many cases reveal that the net effect of unions per se on wage levels in the formal sector is small.

If this view of wage determination is correct then the implications for rural– urban migration are rather different from those of the Harris–Todaro model. For one thing, the problem of large wage differentials within the urban labor force is more one of distribution of income than of creating "distortions" or inefficiency in a neo-classical sense. If high wages are formed by economic forces, the difference in efficiency wages (and labor costs) is much less than observed wage differentials between different sectors of the urban labor market. Secondly, the rate of turnover of the stabilized labor force in the formal sector is generally quite low. Further, increases in output in this sector can be expected to come as much through increases in labor productivity (and wages) as through growth in employment. The net effect is that the probability of getting a formal sector job would generally be quite low for many migrants when the total number of vacancies is small relative to the potential supply of migrants. It follows that the dominance of the effect of the expected formal sector wage on the decision to migrate is probably exaggerated. Finally, the selection of new recruits through a lottery type of mechanism in the formal sector is probably an inappropriate description when implicit contracts and internal labor markets play a dominant role in the management decisions in this sector. We now turn to a more detailed discussion of the mechanism of recruitment of formal sector workers.

3.2. Recruitment of new workers and inter-sector mobility

The Harris–Todaro models view the informal sector as staging posts of workers on the way to the formal sector. A question immediately arises about the lumping together of a variety of economic activities under the blanket term of the "informal sector". At least three different segments of the labor market have to be distinguished within the latter. There are the casual workers who are hired on a day-to-day contract in construction, transportation, service trades and even some types of large scale industry. Secondly, there are more regular workers employed in the small-scale units outside the factory sector. Thirdly, there are the self-employed who are a very heterogeneous group ranging all the way from shoeshine boys to owners of small businesses earning substantially more than formal sector workers of low skill.

Taking the last group first, empirical surveys have consistently shown that only a small percentage of the self-employed have low earnings as the Harris–Todaro model would have us believe [cf. Mazumdar (1976)]. Nor are they necessarily recent migrants. Field workers have generally tended to reject the free entry characterization of the self-employed sector as a whole. There are significant constraints for a worker to be established in this sector – whether due to capital requirements or locational advantages – and a large proportion of this group accordingly are older, longer-term urban residents.[30] Some studies have made the point that the self-employed sector is a net receiver of workers from the formal sector as the latter seek to invest their savings from relatively high wages to found their own shops or businesses.[31]

Turning now to the casual workers and wage employees in small units, the evidence might at first sight support the Harris–Todaro characteristics of labor market processes. Not only are wages substantially lower in these sectors than in the formal sector, but they also seem to be the repository of young workers and recent migrants. In a large survey in Bombay City in 1972–1973 the percentage distribution of the sample in the three sectors by duration of residence in the City was found to be as in Table 4.

Table 4
Percentage distribution of sample by duration of residence

Sector	Migrants: years of residence						Natives
	1	1–2	3–5	6–10	11–20	20+	
Casual	4.9	14.8	21.2	10.7	12.4	5.1	20.9
Small-scale	4.5	8.6	16.3	17.0	19.3	14.0	20.3
Factory	0.1	0.8	4.3	10.3	30.4	32.6	22.3

Source: Mazumdar (1983b, Table 5, p. 185).

This pattern is consistent with the hypothesis that recent migrants first enter the casual and small-scale sector, but then "graduate" to the factory sector. But the clear verification of the hypothesis can only come from evidence about the extent of graduation in the market. Our data showed that the proportion of factory workers at the time of the survey whose first jobs were in other urban wage sectors was only 25 percent. These figures, of course, represent the average experience of a large number of workers over varying periods of time. In his study of migration into Delhi, Biswajit Banerjee compared the proportion of new migrants who had entered the informal sector in a particular year but had moved to the formal sector within a 12-month period with the proportion of new arrivals

---

[30] For some examples, see Amin (1974); Bienefield (1974); House (1978); Oberai (1977); Sabot (1979).

[31] Mazumdar (1981) on Malaysia and Balan et al. (1973) on Monterray, Mexico.

who had found jobs in the formal sector directly. His figures showed that in 1967 new arrivals were at least four to six times more likely to get formal sector employment than those who had entered the informal sector in 1966.[32]

The Asian evidence points strongly to the conclusion that the market for recruitment to formal sector jobs is located much more in rural areas than in the urban informal sector, as implied by the graduation hypothesis. The reasons for this are partly on the supply and partly on the demand side of the labor market. On the supply side the sustained impact of return migration and low wages on the potential efficiency of a worker seeking entry into the formal sector is significant. On the demand side, the value attached by employers to social cohesion of a firm specific labor force leads them to depend on existing employees or their plant level supervisors to introduce new applicants for vacancies. Studies in India and Africa have repeatedly noted the importance of kinship ties in the recruitment process so that we end up with what Poppola noted in his study of Ahmedabad Factories, a "de facto closed shop system".[33]

If this view of the recruitment process is correct, then the idea of the informed sector as a stepping stone to formal sector jobs is not empirically valid. The large proportion of recent migrants in the informal wage sector observed, for example, in Table 1 can be reconciled with this conclusion if we recognize the importance of short-term migrants in this sector. Many of these migrants, as explained earlier, are willing to work for low wages for short periods of time and return to the rural areas. Evidence has been cited elsewhere about the importance of return migration in the Bombay labor market.[34]

3.3. Inter country differences

The importance of temporary and permanent migrants in the formulation of wage differentials in the urban economy differs from country to country. In particular, short-term male migration to the towns seems very much to be an African and Asian phenomenon. In Latin America rural urban migration is widely recognized to be of a permanent type, though one study in Colombia has noted that "returness (from urban to rural areas) numbers a quarter to 40 percent of those who had ever left the towns and villages for longer than a season".[35] Urban labor market structures seem to offer greater scope for female

---

[32] Banerjee (1983, p. 414).

[33] Poppola (1977, p. 153).

[34] Cf. Mazumdar (1983b, pp. 187–9). According to the demographic calculations cited, in the decade between the two censuses of 1961 and 1971 roughly half the gross influx of population into Bombay City was offset through out-migration. The peak rate of out-migration was not among the older post-retirement age groups, but in the 30–35 group.

[35] Alan B. Simmons (1970) quoted in Joan Nelson (1976, p. 731).

employment in Latin America (partially in domestic service) than they do in Asia or Africa. Thus the observed sex ratio in towns is somewhat unbalanced in favor of females in Latin American cities while many Asian and African cities show a masculine character.[36] This difference may have given the impression that there is a major difference in the incidence of temporary migrants as between the three continents. But although research on this topic is incomplete there can be no doubt that conditions for return migration are much less favorable in Latin America and the difference has much to do with the migrants' retention of claims to land rights. Nelson writes: "In much of Africa and South Asia, a man who owns or shares rights to land is likely to leave his wife at home when he goes away to work, while a landless man is more likely to bring his wife with him to the city. In a loosely structured rural society such as characterizes much of Latin America, even migrants who owned land would normally hesitate to leave their wives and children unprotected and unsupervised for extended periods".[37]

Urban labor markets which are heavily influenced by temporary migration will tend to show a large wage difference between the formal and informal sector than would be the case otherwise. The prevalence of such migration increases the downward pressure on wages in the informal sector. But even in the absence of this factor significant wage differences between the two sectors can and do exist because the formation of well-developed internal markets results in high wages in some types of units. With permanent migrants dominating both the formal and informal sectors, workers in the high wage units are as likely to be recruited directly from rural areas through contacts and kinship ties. Thus the distributive implications with or without temporary migration will differ in degree, and not in kind. The next section looks at the redistributive effects of rural–urban migration in a wider context.

4. Migration and redistribution of income

Migration of all types – including rural–urban migration – can be expected to be a powerful force in the redistribution of labor to areas where economic opportunities are better and should be a factor tending to favor equalization of incomes. The fact that most migration studies reveal a significant responsiveness to destination wages (or incomes), as noted in Section 1, lends support to the view that labor is better off economically through migration. (This is also borne out by individual studies of migrants as against non-migrants.) But private gains through migration do not necessarily imply a more equal distribution of income either across regions or households. This Section raises some issues which

---

[36] Comparative figures are given in Nelson (1976, Table 1, p. 727).

[37] Nelson, op. cit., p. 738.

have been noticed in the migration literature on its wider redistributional consequences.

The optimistic view about the redistribution effects of migration derives support from the observed role of high man–land ratio on migration streams. Push factors associated with density of population was seen to be significant in some of the macro migration functions discussed in Section 2. Non-economic micro studies have also established "that where land is scarce, man/land ratios correlate significantly and positively with various measures of migration in Polynesia [Walsh and Trlin (1973)], Turkey [Ministry of Village Affairs (1965–1968)], Chile [Shaw (1974)], Andean America as a whole [Preston (1969)] and Pakistan [Rochin (1972)]".[38]

But we have noted in Section 2 that powerful "non-equilibrating" forces are provided by the nature of the migration process. The importance of contacts and friends in the area of destination is fundamental to the cumulative process which leads to the result that poor (or densely populated villages) are not systematically and smoothly brought into the catchment areas of growing towns. Smaller towns would typically draw migrants from nearby areas (the deterrent "distance" effect, Section 2), while large cities develop their own lines of migration which tend to be stable over time.

A second important point is that although poor villages with great inequality may be disproportionately large suppliers of migrants, it does not follow that the poorest in such (or other) villages provide the bulk of the migration stream. The importance of availability of finance for supporting migration has been stressed in cost-benefit models (Banerjee and Kanbur). In their study of 40 North India villages Connell and others (1976) found that only 5 percent of the working migrants came from households with agricultural labor as a primary occupation, though these households accounted for 19 percent of these in the villages. A study of the same material revealed that at the farm level there were only two clear positive associations between man/land ratios and emigration and six clear negative associations.[39] As Banerjee and Kanbur have argued, after controlling for age, sex and education, the curve relating propensity to migrate and household income is likely to be of the inverted U-shaped type. The poorest would seldom dominate the migration stream.

There is also an important difference between migration to the high wage urban formal sector, and other less stable types of migration to the casual or small-scale sectors. As discussed in the last section the latter is dominated by temporary migrants. Even when the intention of such migrants might be to look for a higher permanent income stream, the prospect for achieving this status is small given the typical recruitment process in formal sector firms. The fact that

---

[38] M. Lipton (1982, p. 201). The references are also documented in ibid. 222–228.
[39] Das Gupta and Lashley (1975) quoted by M. Lipton (1982, p. 201).

kinship ties of existing employees dominate the selection of new entrants in the formal sector direct from the rural areas has the strong implication that traditional hierarchical systems in rural labor markets, e.g. caste relationships in India, would be carried over into the urban labor market. Thus John Harris (1982) in his study of the Coimbatore labor market in South India found that the dominant agricultural castes of the region were most strongly represented in the regular work force of large engineering firms, whereas general casual labor in the town was dominated by members of the scheduled castes (who also contribute the bulk of landless agricultural labor). Lipton concluded that the two different types of rural–urban migration *increases* inequality in the rural community. "Pull migration allows the better-off to advance as a group, while push migration (though individually usually better than the alternative) weakens the poor and sets some of their potential leaders roaming the countryside without a base."[40]

More traditional demographic factors in migration selectivity – which have been well known in the literature – also work in a way which increases private gain but worsens rural inequality. These selectivity factors refer particularly to age and education.

Age: In all countries migration is concentrated in the 15–30 age group, with a substantial portion in the 15–24 sub-group. The economic explanation – that lifetime income gains are larger for the young – has been stressed for a long time (e.g. Sjaastad). Since the proportion of outmigration from this age group is seldom very large in any single rural community, probably the adverse effect on rural productivity and growth is not by itself very significant. But when it is combined with the fact that a substantial number of these young people come from middle income families, and that such migrants are likely to be the more permanently absent, it has implications for the rural society. These migrants have the potentiality of leadership in an economic as well as political sense, and their absence removes the possibility of the most likely challenge for village gerontocracy.

Education: We turn next to education selectivity in rural–urban migration. Although in terms of sheer numbers migrants are not dominated by higher educational groups (reflecting the education distribution in the rural areas of LDCs), evidence from most countries shows that the propensity to migrate is generally higher for the more educated. This is not merely due to the age selectivity noted earlier, and the fact that the young tend to be more educated. Controlling for age, migration rates increase with education.[41] In Colombia for example, the migration rate was seen to increase monotonically with education, and was four times as high for those with higher education as for those with

---

[40]Lipton (1982, p. 196).
[41]For example, Barnum and Sabot, Table 1, p. 17 and Caldwell, Table 3.5, p. 65 for Tanzania and Ghana respectively.

none.[42] Macro studies in most countries report the result that the higher the school enrollments or average level of educational attainment in the area of origin, the higher the rate of migration from the origin to the other areas.[43]

The higher migration rate of the educated may be due to a combination of three factors with varying importance: (i) wage differentials – regional or rural–urban – may be larger for the more educated; (ii) the responsiveness of individuals to wage incentives may be larger for the educated; and (iii) the role of growth of new vacancies may increase with education relatively more in the urban labor market. Of these factors there is considerable evidence to support the last two, but the small amount of research which has been done on the first point does not support the hypothesis. Fields (1982) in his study of Colombia distinguished twelve zones identified by rural and urban areas. He concluded: "Though the absolute gains are much greater for those with more education, the percentage gains in making a move are quire similar for various education groups".[44] The same study, however, found that the better educated groups exhibited more responsiveness to differences in income as shown by the higher co-efficients of origin and destination income in the macro migration function.[45] Similar results were obtained by Schultz (1982) in Venezuela who concluded that "the unmeasured benefits of urban over rural areas appear to increase with education".[46]

While the educated probably do show more incentive for private gain in an entrepreneurial sense, their higher propensity to migrate is also related to the higher growth rate of jobs requiring educational qualifications in the urban economy. In our discussion of the Harris–Todaro class of models in Section 3 we tended to discount the importance attached in these models to employment probability when we considered the urban formal sector as a whole. However, if we concentrate on the subset of the educated the emphasis on employment is probably much more realistic. In fact, Schultz in his work on macro migration functions in Venezuela worked with separate regressions for different education groups and found that destination employment conditions were statistically significant only for the secondary and higher educated groups.

The location of a large part of the market for educated labor in the urban economy is a feature of recent economic development of LDCs. This concentration is encouraged by the content of school courses. As Caldwell wrote

[42] Fields (1982, p. 553).
[43] Greenwood (1971) on India, Huntington (1974) on Kenya, and Levy and Wadycki (1972) on Venezuela.
[44] Fields (1982, p. 554).
[45] Fields (1982, p. 556).
[46] Schultz (1982, p. 584).

about Ghana: "Almost inevitably that which has been taught has hardly ever been about traditional society and has never sought to encourage a firmer establishment in that society. Rather it has been about a foreign way of life, most closely approximated in the towns, or about aspects of society only found in the modernized sector of the economy which is identified to a considerably degree with the towns."[47] A third factor which is responsible for encouraging the employment of the educated in town is what has come to be known in the literature as "bumping". As the supply of the educated increases (and to some extent the quality falls in any given grade) there is a tendency for employers to raise the educational requirements of job categories. Thus those with secondary schooling tend to be hired for jobs previously filled by primary school graduates and the latter in turn replace those with little or no schooling. Education upgrading is, of course, a feature of the public sector in which credentialism plays an important role in hiring rules. But evidence is widespread about similar processes occuring in large private sector firms.

The higher rate of demand relative to supply of educated job seekers is then a factor of importance in the education selectivity of rural–urban migrants. The point is reinforced if we recognize that formalized selection for vacancies, e.g. through employment exchanges, is much more common for educated labor. Thus physical presence in the urban labor market for job search a la Harris–Todaro makes more sense for the educated.

This does not mean that informal contacts and kinship ties are not important for the more educated rural–urban migrants. The point is that the importance of this factor is revealed as much in the preparation and financing of job search as in the direct recruitment to the high wage sector. Both these factors in the migration process lead to unequalizing distribution. The cost of acquiring education for migration is high as is the cost of waiting in the que when necessary. Successful migrants who have been able to get on to a higher income curve are more able to bear these costs and also to reduce the costs of acquiring information of succeeding migrants. The resultant chain migration favors richer families and richer villages.

The distribution of non-labor factors and rural–urban migration

So far in this section we have been discussing the question: given the distribution of resources between rural and urban areas, does the response of labor migration take place in a way which tends to equalize the distribution of earnings? Yet

[47] Caldwell (1969, p. 61).

policies affecting the share of investment going to the urban sector could be of primary importance in the determination of the distribution of income in the economy. The non-equalizing aspects of internal labor migration which has been discussed above could be of the "order of smalls". The point is of sufficient importance to be spelt out in detail.[48]

It may be useful to think in terms of the distribution of three factors of production between the rural and urban sectors: (1) private capital; (2) public capital; and (3) labor. The distribution of public capital probably in most LDCs play an automous role, and the marginal rates of return to capital as well as labor are determined by the way public capital is allocated to urban as against rural areas. Even if the distribution of labor and private capital equalizes their individual marginal rates of return in the two sectors, it will be far-fetched to assume that public capital is allocated in a way that achieves Pareto efficiency. First, much public investment in infrastructure or in sectors like education or health does not necessarily have a clearly recognized rate of return. Secondly, and perhaps more importantly, the "efficiency" of public investment, can hardly be divorced from the welfare of specified classes in society whose interests such investment tends to promote, and hence cannot be meaningfully disentangled from income distribution considerations. For example, the welfare of the middle or urban classes in many LDCs may be served most efficiently by concentrating public investment in urban areas, whereas policies designed to promote the well-being of the mass of low income people might be better served by a more widely dispersed, rural oriented pattern of public investment. Thus the distribution of public capital could be adjudged to be biased to urban areas in some views of the income distribution goals which one wants to pursue, and not on others.

The major conclusion on rural–urban labor migration processes which emerges from this argument is that excessive migration to urban areas is not the only, and probably not the major concern of those who have sought to focus attention on the problem of "overurbanization" in LDCs. The urban bias of public investment from the point of view of perpetuation of unequal distribution of income in the economy would seem to be the main thrust of the attack.[49] It follows that the responsiveness of rural–urban migration to this exogenous distribution of public capital could, indeed, be a factor mitigating nonequalizing growth. Rural–urban migration, at least, enables *some* of the low earning population in the countryside to participate to *some extent* in the lopsided economic development which the urban bias of investment creates. The fact that the migration process does not always proceed in a way which is ideal from the point of view of reducing

---

[48]The discussion here has benefitted much from a reading of the paper by Berry (1986). The reader is recommended to consult this paper for a more detailed argument.

[49]Cf. Lipton (1977).

earnings disparities between groups of workers is, at most, a small offsetting factor. To cite another example, the well-known trek of single female migrants to cities in Latin America is a factor of major importance in raising the incomes of poor working women, given the initial creation of high incomes for middle class urban families. Even if the single migrants did not come from the lowest income groups in the countryside their participation in the urban labor market could be judged to be a factor improving the distribution of income in the economy as a whole.

Thus in the discussions of the question of the social efficiency of rural–urban migration, taking into account its distributional consequences, the attention shifts to the general equilibrium of the economy as a whole involving the sectoral distribution of capital as well as labor. Unfortunately, empirical research on the causes and consequences of the rural–urban distribution of capital is still at the stage of infancy.

5. Summary

There has been widespread concern among policy makers about the pace of urbanization in LDCs in the last few decades. Excessive rural–urban migration has been singled out as one of the major economic and social problems of developing economies. This paper has reviewed some of the empirical work on the determinants and consequences of internal migration which might illuminate particular points n this concern.

An overall view of rural–urban migration in LDCs given in Section 1 makes the point that the evidence does *not* show that these economies are urbanizing at a rate which is much higher than the rate at which today's developed countries had urbanized during their process of growth. This, of course, does not mean that the problems posed by urban growth (the need for infrastructure investment, urban services, etc.) are not more acute in today's LDCs. The absolute numbers implied are so much higher even though the relative rates of growth are not very different by historical standards.

The first question to ask about the welfare consequences of migration is: does the evidence show that private gains to migration exceed the costs, as economic theory would predict? Ideally one requires longitudinal studies of migrants at their destination and compare their lifetime pattern of earnings with that of similar individuals or households who continued to be resident in the area of origin. However, longitudinal data sets are costly and time-consuming to collect. The literature on migration has, therefore, relied heavily on cross section determinants of migration flows at a point of time. A sample of this literature is surveyed in Section 2. The evidence presented from various countries provides overwhelming support for the conclusion that, both in developed and less developed economies, economic motivations are important in the way migrants distribute themselves between different receiving areas. Almost all migration research in developed and developing countries come to a strong conclusion that the net effect of migration is to increase the income of migrants on average, and that gross migration flows are very sensitive to income differences. But even at this rather inexact level of studying the determinants of migration some factors emerge consistently from the work on migration functions which suggest why migration flows might not be equilibrating. These factors include the important effect of distance as a deterrent, and the existence of family and friends in the area of destination (contributed partly by previous migration flows) as a significant element helping migration. Employment conditions in the destination are sometimes – but not always – significant as the expected wage hypothesis would predict. An important point which emerges from these studies is the assymetry between destination and origin conditions – most economic variables having a much weaker influence on the outflow of migrants from their area or origin. A relevant factor here is the cost of migration (taken in conjunction with capital market imperfection) so that, other things being equal, poverty hinders out-migration.

An important area of concern in rural–urban migration – relating both to its magnitude and its social efficiency – is the working on urban labor markets. A popular hypothesis in the LDC context has been suggested by the Harris–Todaro class of models which postulates a two-tier urban labor market – the wages in the "formal" sector being held at a high level by institutional factors, while the "informal" sector characterized by free entry has competitive determination of wages. Secondly, the hypothesis proposes, migrants to the urban labor market aspire to a job in the high wage formal sector, but their probability of getting such a job depends on their spending a period of time in the low wage informal sector from which labor to the formal sector is recruited. Section 3 uses this hypothesis as a starting point to summarize the empirical findings from research on urban labor markets, some pre-dating the Harris–Todaro proposal. The evidence casts doubt on the generality of both the points put forward by the Harris–Todaro model.

First, while the existence of a substantial wage gap between different sectors of the urban labor market – particularly between large factories and small establishment or casual labor – has been established for many LDCs, the importance of institutional, rather than economic reasons for maintaining such differentials is far from self-evident. Significant wage differentials are observed within the organized sector subject to labor legislation and other institutional factors, and there is evidence of wages being established at a relatively high level in the factory sector well before the coming of trade unions or government intervention in wage determination. Alternative hypotheses about the establishment and maintenance of high wages in the formal sector are reviewed in Section 3. The higher productivity of stable labor and the higher supply price of such labor moving to the towns with their families (relative to the low opportunity cost of the floating mass of lone migrants) provide the basic economic reason for high wages in the sectors in which the stability–productivity link is strong. If, indeed, economic factors are more important in explaining high urban wages in some sectors, differences in efficiency wage of labor will be much less than observed differences in wages per worker. Thus the concern with allocative inefficiency is seen to be exaggerated. Rather the problem is one of distribution of earnings within the urban labor market.

The Harris–Todaro suggestion about the possibility of "over-migration" in response to the expectation of a high formal sector wage is further undermined when we consider the empirical fact that family and kinship ties of existing factory workers exert overwhelming influence on the recruitment of new workers to the high wage sector. Several studies have shown that direct recruitment from rural areas rather than "graduation" from the informal urban sector is the dominant mode of hiring in the formal sector.

The thesis of misallocation and overmigration is thus discounted in this essay. But the problem of unequal distribution of income among migrants which the "segmented" urban labor market creates is a real one. This is particularly so because the formation of a stable labor force in the formal urban sector leads to further increases in wages above the supply price of stable family migrants via the internal labor market mechanism (as well unionism). Secondly, the kinship based method of recruitment may favor prosperous (or influential) rural groups to have access to the high wage sector, while the poorer sections of the rural households continue to provide the bulk of temporary migrants, dividing their time between the urban informal and rural labor markets at low levels of earnings.

This point is only a part of the wider consideration of the distribution effects of rural–urban migration. Our discussion in Section 4 draws attention to some important factors causing unequalizing distribution of earnings in the process of labor migration. Such are the cumulative nature of the process of migration which leads to the persistence of lines of migration between particular regions; the deterrent effect of distance, age and education selectivity; the imperfection of capital markets which favor the not-so-poor families in their ability to finance rural–urban migration. But Section 4 concludes with the observation that the lopsided distribution of co-operant factors particularly public capital may be – in many economies – the primary source of worsening of both inter- and intra-sectoral distribution of income. The quantitative importance of this factor may be substantially more than the problem associated with non-equalizing labor migration processes. Unfortunately detailed empirical research on this important issue is practically non-existent.

References

Amin, S. (ed.) (1974) *Modern migration in Western Africa*, Studies presented at the Eleventh African Seminar, Dakar, April 1972. Published for the International African Institute by Oxford University Press.

Anand, S. (1971) 'Rural–urban migration in India: an econometric study', Harvard University, mimeo.

Arnold, F. and S. Cochrane (1980) 'Economic motivation versus city lights: testing hypotheses about interchangwat migration in Thailand', *World Bank Staff Working Paper*, 416.

Balan, J., H.L. Browning and E. Jelin (1973) *Meir in a developing society: geographic and social mobility in Monterrey, Mexico*. Austin, Texas: University of Texas Press.

Banerjee, B. (1983) 'The role of the informal sector in the migration process: a test of probabilistic migration models and labor market segmentation for India', *Oxford Economic Papers*, 35:399–422.

Banerjee, B. and S.M. Kanbur (1981) 'On the specification and estimation of rural–urban migration functions', *Oxford Bulletin of Economics and Statistics*, 43:7–28.

Barnham, H. and R.H. Sabot, (1977) 'Education, employment possibilities and rural–urban migration in Tanzania', *Oxford Bulletin of Economics and Statistics*, 39.

Berry, A. (1986) 'The relative efficiency of the rural–urban migration process in Latin America, compared to those in Africa and Asia', Working Paper C9, Development Studies Program, University of Toronto.

Bienefield, M.A., (1974) 'The self employed of urban Tanzania', Discussion Paper no. 54, Institute of Development Studies, University of Sussex.

Caldwell, J.C. (1969) *African rural–urban migration: the movement to Ghana's towns*.

Connell, J., B. Das Gupta, R. Lashley and M. Lipton (1976) *Migration from Rural Areas*. Delhi.

Das Gupta, B. and R. Lashley (1975) 'Migration from villages: an Indian case study', *Economic and Political Weekly*.

Dhar, S. (1980) 'An analysis of internal migration in India', unpublished Ph.D. thesis, Yale University.

Fields, G.S. (1975) 'Rural–urban migration, urban unemployment and underemployment, and job search activity in LDC's', *Journal of Development Economics*, 2:165–87.

Fields, G.S. (1982) 'Place-to-place migration in Colombia', *Economic Development and Cultural Change*, 30:539–558.

Greenwood, M.J. (1969) 'An analysis of the determinants of geographic labor mobility in the United States', *Review of Economics and Statistics*, 51:189–94.

Greenwood, M.J. (1970) 'Lagged response in the decision to migrate', *Journal of Regional Science*, 10:375–84.

Greenwood, M.J. (1971) 'An analysis of the determinants of internal labor mobility in India', *Annals of Regional Science*, 5:137–51.

Greenwood, M.J. (1972) 'Lagged response in the decision to migrate: a reply', *Journal of Regional Science*, 12:311–24.

Greenwood, M.J. (1974) 'Education and the decision to migrate: an econometric analysis of migration in Venezuela', *Econometrica*, 42:377–88.

Greenwood, M.J. (1975) 'Research on internal migration in the United States: a survey', *Journal of Economic Literature*, 13:397–433.

Harris, J.R. and M.P. Todaro (1970) 'Migration, unemployment and development', *American Economic Review*, 60:126–42.

Harris, J. (1982) 'Small scale production of labor markets in Coimbatore', *Economic and Political Weekly*, June: 993–1002.

Hay, Michael J. (1980) 'A structural equation model of migration in Tunisia', *Economic Development and Cultural Change*, 27:345–58.

Herrick, B.H. (1965) *Urban migration and economic development in Chile*. Cambridge, Mass.

House, W.J. (1978) 'Nairobi's informal sector: a reservoir of dynamic entrepreneurs or a residual pool of surplus labor', Working Paper No. 347, Institute for Development Studies.

Huntington, H. (1974) 'An empirical study of ethnic linkages in Kenyan rural–urban migration', Unpublished Ph.D. Dissertation, SUNY/Binghampton.

Jolly, R. (1971) Rural–urban migration: dimension, causes, issues and policies.

Lansing, J.B. and E. Mueller, eds. (1967) 'The geographic mobility of labor', Ann Arbor, Survey

Research Center, Institute for Social Research, University of Michigan.

Levy, M. and W. Wadycki, (1974) 'The influence of family and friends on geographic labor mobility: an international comparison', *Review of Economics and Statistics*, 55:198–203.

Levy, M. and W. Wadycki (1974) 'What is the opportunity cost of moving? Reconsideration of the effects of distance on migration', *Economic Development and Cultural Change*, 22:198–214.

Lipton, M. (1977) *Why poor people stay poor: urban bias in world development*. Cambridge, Mass.: Harvard University Press.

Lipton, M. (1982) 'Migration from rural areas of poor countries: the impact on rural productivity and income distribution', in: R. R. Sabot, ed. *Migration and the labor market in developing countries*, Boulder, Colorado.

Maleanson, J.J. (1981) 'Unemployment and the efficiency wage hypothesis', *Economic Journal*, 91:844–66.

Mazumdar, D. (1973) 'Labor supply in early industrialization: the case of the bombay textile industry', *Economic History Review*, Second Series, 26:477–496.

Mazumdar, D. (1975) 'The theory of urban underemployment in less developed countries', *World Bank Staff Paper*, no. 198.

Mazumdar, D. (1976) 'Urban informal sector', *World Development*, 4:655–79.

Mazumdar, D. (1981) *The urban labor market and income distribution: a study of Malaysia*. Oxford.

Mazumdar, D. (1983a) 'Segmented labor markets in LDC's', *American Economic Review*, 73:254–259.

Mazumdar, D. (1983b) 'The rural–urban wage gap, migration and the working of urban labor markets: an interpretation based on a study of the workers of Bombay city', *Indian Economic Review*, 83:169–198.

Mills, E. and C. Becker (1986) *Studies in Indian urban development*. New York: Oxford University Press.

Ministry of Village Affairs (1965–68) *Kuy Eranter Etudierine Gore*, Vols. 1–26. Ankara.

Morse, R.M. (1971) 'Trends and issues in Latin American urban research, 1965–70, Part III', *Latin American Research Review*, 6:19–75.

Nelson, J.M. (1976) 'Sojourners versus new urbanites: causes and consequences of temporary versus permanent cityward migration in development countries', *Economic Development and Cultural Change*, 24:721–57.

Niedercorn, J.H. and B.V. Bechdolt, (1969) 'An economic derivation of the gravity law of spatial interaction', *Journal of Regional Science*, 9:273–82.

Oberai, A.S. (1977) 'Migration, unemployment and urban labor market: a case study of the Sudan', *International Labor Review*, 115:211–23.

Poppola, T.S. (1977) 'Mobility and wage structure in an urban labour market: a study of Ahmedabad (India)', in: S. Karmappan, ed., *Studies of urban labour market behaviour in developing countries*. Geneva: International Institute for Labour Studies.

Preston, S.H. (1969) 'Urban growth in developing countries: a demographic reappraisal', *Population and Development Review*, 5:195–215.

Ravenstein, E.G. (1889) 'The laws of migration', *Journal of the Royal Statistical Society*, Part I, 48, June 1885, 167–227; and Part II, 52:241–301.

Redford, A. (1926) *Labour migration in England, 1800–1850*. Manchester.

Roberts, B. (1978) *Cities of peasants: the political economy of urbanization in the third world*. London.

Rochin, R.I. (1972) 'Inter-relationships between farm environment, off-farm migration and rates of adoption', Ph.D. dissertation, Purdue University, Lafayette.

Sabot, R.H. (1979) *Economic development and urban migration: Tanzania 1900–1971*. Oxford.

Schultz, T.P. (1982) 'Lifetime migration with educational strata in Venezuela', *Economic Development and Cultural Change*, 30:559–583.

Schwartz, A. (1973) 'Interpreting the effect of distance on migration', *Journal of Political Economy*, 81:1153–69.

Shaw, R.R. (1974) 'Land tenure and rural exodus in Latin America', *Economic Development and Cultural Change* 23.

Simmons, A.B. (1970) 'The emergence of planning orientation in a modernizing community: migration, adaptation and family planning in highland Colombia', Cornell University Latin American Studies Program, Dissertation Series no. 15.

Singer, P. (1973) *Economia politica da urbanizacao*. Sao Paulo: Editora Brasiliense.

Sjaastad, L. (1962) 'The costs and returns of human migration', *Journal of Political Economy*, 70:80–93.

Stark, O. and D.E. Bloom (1985) 'The new economics of labor migration', *American Economic Review*, 75:173–78.

Walsh, A.C. and A.D. Trlin (1973) 'Ninean migration', *Journal of Polynesian Sociology* 32, 1.

World Bank, (1984) *World Development Report*, Oxford University Press.

Yap, L. (1975) 'Internal migration in less developed countries: a survey of the literature', *World Bank Staff Working Paper*, 215.

Zipf, G.K. (1946) 'The $P_1 P_2/D$ hypothesis: on the intercity movement of persons', *American Sociological Review*, 11:677–86.

PART 3

URBAN GOVERNMENT BEHAVIOR AND ISSUES

Chapter 29

THEORETICAL ANALYSIS OF LOCAL PUBLIC ECONOMICS

DAVID E. WILDASIN*

Indiana University

1. Introduction

Local public economics, even theoretical local public economics, is a diverse, large, and growing field. It is an area in which ongoing policy debates continually present important new topics for economic analysis, both theoretical and empirical. Theoretical work in the area has contributed much to the understanding of policy issues, and has motivated many empirical studies. Empirical analysis, in turn, has frequently presented findings that challenge existing theoretical models and prompt the development of new ones. Together, these factors make the field an intellectually stimulating one.

They also make it somewhat difficult to survey. Indeed, any short survey must inevitably be rather selective in its coverage. The objective of the present essay is to provide a coherent and reasonably integrated view of major issues and recent developments in theoretical local public economics. In doing so, it must leave aside explicit consideration of most policy and empirical problems.

From the theoretical perspective, the fundamental goal of local public economics must be to understand how local governments affect resource allocation. In reality, of course, they do this in many ways, and it is difficult to study them all simultaneously. Conceptual clarity requires a separation of major issues which can then be examined, and better understood, in comparative isolation from one another. In broadest terms, this survey is organized around three major problems, corresponding roughly to Sections 2, 3, and 4. The first concerns the

*I am grateful to Edwin Mills for editorial advice and to J. Wilson for helpful discussions. I also acknowledge the advice and assistance of a number of other individuals who provided comments on an earlier somewhat more lengthy and comprehensive survey of the field of urban public finance, Wildasin (1986a), or who provided me with access to published and unpublished work. These individuals include R. Arnott, E. Berglas, J. Brueckner, D. Epple, E. Gramlich, J.V. Henderson, P. Hobson, R. Inman, Y. Kanemoto, P. Mieszkowski, W. Oates, D. Pines, T. Romer, D. Rubinfeld, U. Schweizer, J. Sonstelie, D. Starrett, T. N. Tideman, J. Wilson, J. Yinger, and G. Zodrow. Their help was invaluable for the earlier project, and equally deserves acknowledgement here.

Handbook of Regional and Urban Economics, Volume II, Edited by E.S. Mills
© *1987, Elsevier Science Publishers B.V.*

distribution of households across jurisdictions. The second involves the allocation of non-human resources within and across jurisdictions. The third concerns the allocation of resources through the institution of the local public sector itself.

More specifically: Section 2 examines how local government tax, expenditure, and zoning policies affect the locational choices of mobile households, and asks whether and under what conditions these policies result in efficient or inefficient equilibria. The issue of optimal jurisdiction size, or of the optimal number of jurisdictions, is also discussed in Section II.

Section 3 considers first the incidence and allocative effects of property and land taxation. In much (although not all) of the literature, the discussion of these issues focuses on interjurisdictional capital flows and abstracts from mobility of households. Section 3 also discusses the phenomena of tax exporting, tax competition, and, more generally, the determination of optimal local tax structure.

Section 4 focuses on the local government as a decisionmaking unit that makes important resource allocation decisions, particularly regarding the level of provision of local public goods. Median voter models of local public expenditure determination are discussed first. We then consider the effects of local taxes and public good provision on property values. This finally permits a more integrated treatment of household locational choice, property market equilibrium, and local government decisionmaking.

One advantage of this approach to research in urban public finance is that it highlights the contrasting institutional mechanisms through which resource allocation decisions are made. Roughly speaking, Sections 2 and 3 are concerned with the impact of local government policies on market-determined variables such as equilibrium prices, locational assignments, etc. Analyses of questions of this type, though they may be complex in detail and may involve many unusual features, are conceptually in a class of problems familiar to all students of public finance, that is, the class of problems that treats government policies, or changes in government policies, as exogenous to the system being modeled. The object of the analysis in problems of this type is to understand how the exogenous variables influence the endogenous ones, that is, how parametric changes in government policy affect market equilibrium and, more generally, the entire state of the economic system. Sometimes these questions are posed in a strictly positive spirit, as when one seeks to determine how taxes affect equilibrium factor prices, and sometimes they arise in normative analyses, as when one seeks to evaluate the welfare effects of incremental policy changes or to find an optimal policy.

By contrast, Section 4 is much more concerned with modeling the determination of local public policies themselves. That is, rather than treating public policies as exogenous variables, they become endogenous variables in models that attempt to represent both economic and political behavior. This, of course, is a highly ambitious objective, more ambitious than simply analyzing the response of the market to exogenous local government policies. There is a wide variety of models of local government behavior appearing in the literature, often with quite different assumptions about who the relevant decisionmakers are (voters, landowners, bureaucrats), their objectives (obtaining desired levels of public services, raising property values, increasing the size of the local budget), and the constraints under which they operate (they may be mobile or immobile, perfectly competitive or not, perfectly informed or not), etc. This diversity reflects the fact that the institutional structure, i.e. the local political process, through which decisions are made is at least superficially quite different from the usual market environment to which economic theory is ordinarily applied.

While it is hoped that this approach to theoretical local public economics is a useful one, it is unfortunately impossible to do justice to the entire subject in the limited space of this survey. A number of important issues cannot be discussed here in depth, and many can only be mentioned in passing. Interested readers may find it useful to peruse recent volumes edited by Thisse and Zoller (1984) and Zodrow (1984), and a survey by Rubinfeld (forthcoming). In particular, the former volume contains a substantial review of the local public finance literature by Pestieau (1984). Wildasin (1986a) provides a survey that is organized roughly along the same lines as the present one, but that covers many additional topics and goes into details that had to be omitted here for brevity's sake. Ultimately, of course, one must go to the original literature for a thorough understanding of the subject.

2. Locational assignment of households

The most interesting problems in local public economics are those in which the openness of the individual jurisdictions plays a major role. (When localities are treated as closed, each is like an independent country on a small scale, and the usual principles of closed-economy public finance apply without modification.) Openness can take the form of commodity and non-human factor flows across jurisdictional boundaries, of population flows, or, in general, of both. Relatively few studies in the literature deal with the general case. Rather, models which feature commodity trade often assume that the population of each jurisdiction is fixed, while models which emphasize locational choice often assume that only one commodity can flow across boundaries, and only then to distribute land rents and profits to non-resident owners of land and/or firms. Both strategies of analysis can of course be quite appropriate, but one should bear in mind that each suppresses certain issues that might be important for some purposes. This section focuses on models in which mobility of households plays the central role. It begins, in Section 2.1, with a simple economy in which there is a fixed set of jurisdictions, each providing some public services, and within which households may reside. The first task is to analyze the efficient assignment of households to jurisdictions. Then, after defining an equilibrium assignment of households, we explore the conditions under which an equilibrium will be efficient. It turns out that the efficiency of equilibria depends critically on the structure of local taxes: equilibria can be efficient if taxes are set appropriately, but if not, they provide incentives for inefficient locational choices.

Section 2.2 discusses the determination of the optimal number of jurisdictions, or, equivalently, of optimal city size. The optimal number of jurisdictions can be derived from a welfare maximization problem, and the resulting characterization has an interesting interpretation in terms of the "Henry George Theorem." This problem is closely related to the problems of optimal city size and of locational efficiency, since the number of households per jurisdiction varies inversely with the number of jurisdictions, and the results bear a close resemblance to those of Section 2.1.

2.1. Locational efficiency

In an economic system containing multiple jurisdictions, such as cities, states, provinces, school districts, etc., several conditions must be met for a fully efficient allocation of resources to be achieved. As is true for closed economies, markets for goods and factors must function efficiently within each jurisdiction. Moreover, each jurisdiction's government must provide efficient levels of public services to its residents. Possible breakdowns in these types of efficiency are discussed in subsequent sections. But in a system of open jurisdictions, among which households may move, there is a further dimension of efficient resource allocation to be considered, and upon which we now focus. That is, households must be distributed across jurisdictions in an efficient way.

In order to address this question, it is useful to present a simple model. Let us assume a fixed set of $M \geq 2$ jurisdictions, indexed by a subscript i. Each contains a fixed amount of homogeneous land T_i.[1] Suppose that there is a fixed total population of N individuals in the entire economy, each of whom must locate in one and only one jurisdiction. Each household supplies one unit of homogeneous labor, which is used, along with land, in a production process which produces a

---

[1] Homogeneity of land is a common simplifying assumption in the literature. Some analyses incorporate heterogeneity in the form of differential accessibility of various parcels to a central employment location, as in the standard monocentric city model of urban economics. (See, e.g. Straszheim's contribution to this volume for a discussion of such models.) For the most part, the results discussed in this survey do not depend critically on the homogeneity of land, in the sense that they carry over directly, or in recognizable extensions, to the heterogenous case. For some discussion of urban public finance issues in the monocentric city context, see, e.g. Kanemoto (1980) and Henderson (1985a).

single homogeneous product, used as a numeraire good. Let $F_i(n_i, T_i)$ be a well-behaved constant returns to scale production function for locality i, showing the amount of output produced as a function of local population, n_i, and local land.

Each jurisdiction provides a single public good or service z_i which is consumed only by residents. To produce z_i units of this local public good requires $C_i(n_i, z_i)$ units of numeraire. Note that C_i may depend on the size of population being served: if $C_{in} \triangleq \partial C_i / \partial n_i > 0$, we say that the local public good is subject to *congestion* or *crowding*, or is an *impure* local public good. If $C_{in} = 0$, the local public good is *uncongested* or *pure*. In the special case where C_i is proportional to n_i, i.e. $C_i(n_i, z_i) = n_i c_i(z_i)$, we shall say that the local public good is *quasi-private* or that it exhibits *constant per capita costs*.

To clarify these concepts, consider the case of elementary and secondary education. The level of education is measured, in the present notation, by z_i. z_i might correspond to the mean score on a standardized achievement test. (In a more sophisticated model, z_i might be a vector of attributes of the educational system, including variables such as percentage of dropouts, percentage of students going on to college, quality of athletic or other extra-curricular programs, or any other features of the system that are important to residents.) Note that z_i is the amount or quantity of education made available to or consumed by each resident, though z_i might be measured by what would be called, in ordinary parlance, the "quality" of education. The number of students educated, represented in this model by the number of resident's in the locality, n_i, does not measure the amount or quantity of education but simply the size of the population being served. $C_{iz} = \partial C_i / \partial z_i$ is the marginal cost of education in the sense that it is the marginal cost of increasing the level of education delivered to a fixed population. This corresponds to what would be called the marginal cost of a public good in a typical closed-economy public finance model. $C_{in} > 0$, in the present context, means that additional resources are required if one is to expand the population being provided with a given level of education. For example, C_{in} might represent the cost of obtaining the extra teachers, buildings, etc. that are required to maintain mean achievement scores in the face of an expanded student population. To say that $C_{in} > 0$ is equivalent to saying that an increase in n_i would cause z_i to fall, if the jurisdiction keeps the amount of resources spent on education fixed as population rises. This justifies the use of the terms "congestion" or "crowding" when referring to goods for which $C_{in} > 0$: an increase in population, with expenditure held fixed, causes a deterioration of public services.[2] C_{in} has also been called the marginal cost of a local public good, though of course

---

[2] An equivalent way of representing the technology of local public good provision, sometimes encountered in the literature, is to write $z_i = g(n_i, C_i)$ where C_i represents expenditures for, or the level of inputs used in, the provision of the local public good. In this case, $\partial g / \partial n_i < 0$ would imply congestion.

it is conceptually quite distinct from C_{iz}. The two will always be unambiguously distinguished here.[3]

We have now specified the technologies for private and public good provision, and it remains to discuss the preference side of the model. For simplicity, assume that all consumers derive utility only from consumption of the numeraire good and the local public good. Furthermore, assume that all households have identical preferences, and that they are treated identically within each jurisdiction. The utility of a household in locality i, therefore, is a function of its consumption x_i of the numeraire and of z_i, denoted by $u(x_i, z_i)$.

The technological constraints on the economy require that total production of the numeraire good be equal to its consumption by consumers plus its use as a public input, and that the total population of the economy be located in some jurisdiction. Hence, a feasible allocation of resources, which is completely described by vectors (n_i), (x_i), and (z_i), must satisfy

$$\sum_i [F_i(n_i, T_i) - n_i x_i - C_i(n_i, z_i)] = 0 , \tag{1.1}$$

$$N - \sum_i n_i = 0. \tag{1.2}$$

How does one characterize an efficient allocation of resources for this economy? One way to proceed would be to maximize the utility of residents in one jurisdiction, say 1, subject to the constraint that households in other jurisdictions receive at least an exogenously-prescribed level of utility. Equivalently, one could set up a social welfare maximization problem with the utilities of residents in different jurisdictions as arguments. As shown in the theory of the optimal monocentric city [see Mirrlees (1972) and Wildasin (1986b)] and in more general contexts as well [Stiglitz (1982), Chang and Wildasin (1986)], quite familiar social welfare criteria, such as utilitarianism, can result in optimal allocations in which identical individuals are given different utilities. Such optima cannot generally be sustained as equilibria in systems which allow free mobility of households, however, since migratory flows will arbitrage away any utility differentials among jurisdictions. Therefore, it is appropriate to impose equal utilities as a constraint at the outset, and to ask what allocation of resources will maximize the common

---

[3] Empirical work indicates that most local public services exhibit a high degree of crowding or impurity. Indeed, quasi-privateness seems typical. Oates (1986) points out, however, that more populous localities may find it optimal to offer a wider range of relatively pure or uncongestible services than do less populous ones. This could give rise empirically to an *apparent* quasi-privateness, or at least to an overestimate of the degree of congestion of local public services. This argument illustrates the important fact that quantification of the level of local public services is very difficult in practice.

level of utility for all households. Thus, we consider the problem[4]

$$\max_{<(x_i),(n_i)>} u_1(x_1,z_1),$$

subject to (1.1), (1.2), and

$$u_i(x_i,z_i)=u_1(x_1,z_1) \quad i=2,\ldots,M. \tag{1.3}$$

Note that (z_i) is not included in the list of instruments for this problem. This is to emphasize the fact that the results to be derived below do not depend on the optimality or otherwise of the levels of public good provision in the economy.

Associating Lagrange multipliers μ, π, and λ_i with the constraints (1.1), (1.2), and (1.3), respectively, one finds the first-order conditions

$$u_{11}\left(1-\sum_{i\neq1}\lambda_i\right)-\mu=0, \tag{2.1}$$

$$\lambda_i u_{i1}-\mu=0 \quad i=2,\ldots,M, \tag{2.2}$$

$$\mu(F_{in}-x_i-C_{in})-\pi=0 \quad i=1,\ldots,M, \tag{2.3}$$

for $x_1,x_i(i\neq1)$, and n_i, resp., where n_i is treated as a continuous variable. Here $u_{i1}\overset{\Delta}{=}\partial u_i/\partial x_i$ and $F_{in}\overset{\Delta}{=}\partial F_i/\partial n_i$. The most important of these conditions is (2.3), which implies that

$$F_{in}-x_i-C_{in}=F_{jn}-x_j-C_{jn}, \tag{3}$$

for all jurisdictions i, j.

Consider the interpretation of (3) in the special case where there are no public goods in the economy. Then (1.3) implies $x_i=x_j$ and (3) just reduces to $F_{in}=F_{jn}$. As expected intuitively, efficiency is achieved in the pure private goods economy when total output is maximized, which occurs when the marginal product of labor is equalized everywhere.

Next consider the special case where there are local public goods, but they are purely public, i.e. $C_{in}=C_{jn}=0$. Then, by (1.3), x_i-x_j (which may be positive or negative) is the compensating differential in private good consumption that keeps utility constant in the face of whatever differential exists in public good provision, z_j-z_i. If $z_j>z_i$, then $x_i>x_j$, and it is socially more costly to assign households to locality i rather than j. Nonetheless, it may be efficient to do so, provided that workers in i are sufficiently more productive. At an optimum, (3) implies that the productivity differential $F_{in}-F_{jn}$ just balances the compensating differential x_i-x_j arising from unequal levels of public service provision.

[4] In formulating this problem, it is assumed for simplicity that $n_i>0$, for all i, at an optimum. This assumption could be violated if there are strong scale economies in private or public good production. See Stiglitz (1977) and Schweizer (1985) for some discussion of this problem. For the sake of simplified exposition, this survey will implicitly assume smoothness, interior solutions, etc. wherever convenient.

Finally, in the general case, the same principles continue to apply, except that one must take into account the marginal congestion costs C_{in}, C_{jn} that households impose when assigned to one locality or the other. The net benefit from assigning a household to a jurisdiction is reduced by this amount.

While this model is very simple, its basic message holds in more general settings [see Wildasin (1986a)]. A version of (3) holds in models where there are many types of households, possibly exhibiting interpersonal crowding tastes or distastes, and with multiple types of private consumption goods, including possibly residential land. The essential efficiency condition is that, for each household type, the value of incremental output obtained by adding one more household to a locality, net of the value of the household's private good consumption and any marginal congestion or crowding costs, must be equated across jurisdictions.

It is worth emphasizing that efficiency condition (3) holds irrespective of the values of the z_i's. One can easily amend the above optimization problem by including the z_i's as instruments, in which case the first-order conditions for the z_i's and x_i's can be manipulated to show that

$$n_i u_{i2}/u_{i1} = C_{iz},$$ (4)

must hold for all i – which is just the standard Samuelsonian condition for efficient public expenditure. This extension is of interest for two reasons. First, observe that it does not alter the derivation of equation (3) which, by itself, is therefore a necessary but not sufficient condition for full efficiency of resource allocation.[5] Since (3) describes the efficient distribution of population, conditional on public good provision, let us say that the economy has achieved *locational efficiency* when it is satisfied. Second, it is useful to observe that (4) characterizes the efficient z_i's regardless of their congestibility features. Thus, (4) applies to both pure and impure local public goods, including quasi-private ones.

Now let us define a competitive equilibrium for this simple economy. Suppose first that each jurisdiction is required to use taxes on land rents or head taxes residents to finance its purchases of inputs for exogenously specified levels of public good provision. It is assumed that jurisdictions use only uniform taxes, and can tax all land rents generated within their borders, no matter what the residence of the owner may be, but cannot tax land rents from other jurisdictions accruing to their residents. In other words, land rents are taxed at source. (Other cases are considered below.) Households own their labor and are also endowed with ownership of all of the land in the economy. Firms hire land and labor in

---

[5]Obviously, the optimal (n_i) vector that satisfies (3) will depend on the (z_i) vector. That is, the efficient population distribution certainly depends on the levels of local public good provision. What should be stressed, however, is the fact that the *form* of the locational efficiency condition is independent of (z_i).

competitive markets and maximize profits. Furthermore, assume that all households have equal endowments of land and labor – in particular, each owns a share T_i/N of the land in locality i. Finally, assume that households are freely mobile, and make utility-maximizing locational choices, believing that their individual decisions will leave all factor prices and tax rates unchanged.

Under these assumptions, the gross wage and land rent for labor and land will be

$$w_i = F_{in} \quad \text{all } i,$$ (5.1)

$$r_i = F_{it} \quad \text{all } i,$$ (5.2)

where $F_{it} = \partial F_i/\partial T_i$. Let τ_{in} and τ_{ir} be the head tax and ad valorem land tax rates in locality i. Then the budget constraint for a household locating in jurisdiction i is

$$x_i = w_i + \sum_j (1 - \tau_{jr}) r_j T_j/N - \tau_{in} \quad \text{all } i,$$ (5.3)

while the balanced-budget constraint for the government in jurisdiction i is

$$n_i \tau_{in} + \tau_{ir} r_j T_j = C_i(n_i, z_i).$$ (5.4)

Eq. (5.3) states that households use their net income to obtain the numeraire private good, and that net income consists of wages plus net land rents minus the head tax. Given constant returns to scale and competitive production, no pure profits remain to be distributed to owners of firms. Constraint (5.4) requires that the own-source revenue for locality i equal its requirement for the provision of the level z_i of the public good, given the population n_i. A vector $(w_i, r_i, \tau_{in}, \tau_{ir})$ of factor prices and tax rates satisfying (5), and also satisfying (1.3), will be called a *competitive equilibrium* for this economy. Condition (1.3) embodies the free mobility of households: in a competitive equilibrium, all utility differentials are competed away. Note that conditions (5) and Euler's theorem imply (1.1): this is Walras' law for this economy, and it guarantees that the economy-wide resource constraint for the numeraire good will be met.

The stage is now set for an examination of the conditions under which a competitive equilibrium may be efficient. Specifically, one must determine whether or not the locational efficiency condition (3) is satisfied in a competitive equilibrium. (It is obvious that the public expenditure efficiency condition (4) need not be met, since the (z_i) vector has been fixed arbitrarily.) The answer to this question varies, depending on the assumptions made about local tax structure and about the congestibility of local public goods. In the literature, many different assumptions have been made, and conclusions differ accordingly.

Some readers might wonder why efficiency cannot always be achieved, given that head taxes are allowable instruments in this model. It might therefore be best to begin with the case where all localities use only head taxes to finance their expenditures.

Proposition 1.

Under a regime of pure head taxation, a competitive equilibrium will be locationally efficient if local public goods are quasi-private, and possibly in other cases as well. Efficiency is not generally achieved under head taxation, however.

To see how this result is established, use the household budget constraint (5.3) and the factor pricing equation (5.1) to show that

$$F_{in} - x_i - \tau_{in} = F_{jn} - x_j - \tau_{jn} \quad \text{all } i, j. \tag{6}$$

Comparing this to the locational efficiency condition (3), it is clear that an equilibrium will be efficient if and only if

$$C_{in} - C_{jn} = \tau_{in} - \tau_{jn} \quad \text{all } i, j. \tag{7}$$

When head taxes are the only revenue source, (7) holds if local public goods are quasi-private because the government budget constraint (5.4) with head taxation implies $\tau_{in} = C_i / n_i$. Since $C_i = n_i c_i(z_i)$ in the quasi-private case,

$$\tau_{in} = C_i / n_i = c_i(z_i) = C_{in}$$

which guarantees (7). More generally, (7) could hold under pure head taxation whenever the per capita cost of local public goods is at a minimum with respect to population size, since this again implies $C_i / n_i = C_{in}$.

Despite these "positive" results on the efficiency of equilibrium, there are obviously situations where equilibria will not be efficient. To take one example, suppose local public goods are purely public, but that the levels of the z_i's are such that the per capita costs of local public goods are unequal. Then $\tau_{in} \neq \tau_{jn}$ for some i and j, while the left-hand-side of (7) is zero ($C_{in} = C_{jn} = 0$). Efficiency breaks down in this case. Thus, several authors, including Buchanan and Goetz (1972), Flatters et al. (1974), and Bewley (1981), who explicitly or implicitly restrict attention to the case where only head taxes can be used to finance local public goods, conclude that efficiency is achievable only under special conditions, such as when local public goods are quasi-private.

Why do head taxes not guarantee locational efficiency in economies with local public goods? The answer is simply that they are not neutral when levied at the local level in an economy with mobile households: households can successfully avoid the head taxes imposed in any one locality by moving to another. In the quasi-private case, non-neutral taxes are needed for efficiency because migrant households impose congestion externalities on jurisdictions that they enter, and a location-contingent tax serves to internalize this externality. In the quasi-private case, sole reliance on a head tax is sufficient for the efficiency of a competitive equalibrium because the tax that internalizes the congestion externality ($\tau_{in} = C_{in}$) also happens to balance the local budget ($\tau_{in} = C_i/n_i$). In general, however, a head tax alone cannot simultaneously achieve both of these conditions. An additional instrument, provided in the present model by the tax on land rents, is needed. In fact, it is easy to see, by comparing (3), (5.4), and (7), that

Proposition 2.

In general, locational efficiency can be achieved by setting $\tau_{in} = C_{in}$, all i, and by then setting τ_{ir} so as to satisfy (5.4) for all i.

Results of this type appear in Helpman et al. (1976), Hochman (1981, 1982a, 1982b), Wildasin (1980) and elsewhere.

To illustrate the application of Proposition 2, if local public goods are purely public, a pure land rent tax will suffice to insure locational efficiency [Negishi (1972), Wildasin (1977)], while, as noted above, inefficiency will typically result in this case under head taxation. By contrast, pure land rent taxation with congestible public goods is generally incompatible with locational efficiency [Bucovetsky (1981)]. These results accord with the intuition developed above: when there are no congestion effects to internalize, it is efficient to rely solely on land rent taxation. Recall that we have assumed all land rent taxes accrue to the jurisdiction in which the rents are generated. Thus, a household's land rent tax is not location-contingent, and is therefore neutral with respect to locational choices.

So far we have discussed the efficiency implications of local taxation only within the context of a very simple model with very limited tax instruments. The basic principles, however, generalize: congestion effects must be internalized to achieve locational efficiency, which can be done not only with head taxes but with other residence-contingent taxes. In practice, wage income taxes, sales taxes, and property taxes (the part of property taxes that falls on mobile residential capital) might all serve this purpose, although each of these is also likely to distort certain other margins of decisionmaking. For example, a wage income tax might discourage the supply of labor, in additon to discouraging entry into a jurisdiction. Similarly, a tax on residential housing can discourage housing consumption, as well as serve to internalize congestion costs. In view of the prominent role of the property tax in the financing of local public services, this case is empirically important. Hamilton (1975, 1983) has argued, however [see also Mills and Oates, (1975) and Mills, (1979)], that localities can use zoning constraints to prevent property taxes from distorting housing consumption decisions. Optimal zoning would replicate the economic effects of true head taxes. Zodrow and Mieszkowski (1983) question whether zoning can function in the ideal way that is required for locational efficiency. This seems to be an empirical question. Note, however, that zoning need not be perfect in order for the property tax to approximate a system of head taxation.

In any case, many taxes could potentially play the role of the head tax in our simple model. Taxes on capital income (including land rents) could serve this function if such income is taxed in the income recipient's jurisdiction of residence. This is how some capital income is in fact treated under state individual income taxes in the U.S.: states tax the dividend, profit, and rental income accruing to their residents regardless of source. By contrast, a state corporation income tax taxes capital income at its source and would be locationally neutral from the viewpoint of the households that own the corporation – that is, the state corporation income tax is not contingent on the location of the owners.[6] Redistributive transfers administered at the local level provide important examples of location–contingent negative taxes. Since they provide an artificial incentive for households to enter a locality, they are generally incompatible with locational efficiency.

Finally, land rent taxation in our simple model represents any sort of tax that is neutral with respect to household locational choice. For example, equivalent results obtain in models where land is used for residential housing purposes rather than as a factor of production in the non-residential sector of the economy. Also, taxes on other natural resources (oil, coal, etc.) would be locationally neutral, and while these taxes may not be important for many cities or other small jurisdictions, they certainly are important for larger jurisdictions such as some U.S. states or Canadian provinces. The urban property tax itself is of course partly assessed against the value of land, and so to some extent exemplifies the land tax in the model. Furthermore, the stock of urban residential and business capital is quite durable. For sufficiently short time frames, one might also regard this part of the tax as functioning like the land tax in our model.[7]

2.2. Optimal jurisdiction size

The discussion thus far has been restricted to the analysis of the distribution of a fixed population among a fixed set of jurisdictions. This framework is not particularly well-suited for an investigation of the optimal size of a jurisdiction, since the average jurisdiction size is exogenously fixed.

---

[6]See Boadway and Flatters (1982) and Boadway and Wildasin (1984, Chapter 15) for more discussion of the distinction between source-based and residence-based taxation.

[7]This view, of course, conflicts with the long run view, noted above, in which residential capital migrates along with households. The differing role of the property tax in the short and long run points out an important limitation of the foregoing analysis, namely its static nature. An explicitly dynamic model of household migration with durable residential capital would present an important advance over existing studies.

Let us therefore consider a different type of economy, one in which the number of localities can vary. There are two ways that one can imagine doing this. First, one might suppose that the total endowment of land available to the set of all localities is fixed, and that the only question is how to partition the fixed land to form jurisdictions. Second, one might suppose that land is available, either for free or at a cost, for the creation of new jurisdictions. We can analyze both cases briefly.

In the first, let T be the total amount of land to be allocated among M jurisdictions. Since heterogeneity of households complicates matters somewhat, the assumption is maintained that all households are identical. Also assume that all jurisdictions have access to identical technologies for production of private and public goods.

If each jurisdiction is constrained to provide an exogeneously-specified level $\bar{z}$ of the local public good, the utility of each household will depend only on the common level $\bar{x}$ of private good consumed. Given constant returns to scale in private good production, total output of the numeraire private good, which is the sum across all M identical jurisdictions of their individual outputs, is given by $MF(N/M, T/M) = F(N, T)$, where F is the common production function for all localities. Note that this is independent of M. To maximize $\bar{x}$, therefore, M should be chosen to minimize the total cost, across all jurisdictions, of providing $\bar{z}$. That is, M should be chosen to

$$\min_{\langle M \rangle} MC(N/M, \bar{z}), \tag{8}$$

where C is the cost function for the local public good faced by all jurisdictions. If M is sufficiently large that it can be treated as a continuous variable, the solution to (8) will be characterized by

$$\frac{C}{N/M} = C_n, \tag{9}$$

i.e. equality of average and marginal cost of public goods with respect to population. Of course, this is simply the rule for least-cost provision of public goods. If there are no congestion effects ($C_n = 0$) or if congestion effects are sufficiently small, the optimal M is 1. If the local public good is quasi-private, the optimal M is indeterminate.

Now suppose that new land is available at a cost per unit of r. Again suppose each jurisdiction must provide $\bar{z}$ units of the local public good. Then the problem, assuming that land must be paid for from the production of the numeraire good, is to

$$\max_{\langle M \rangle} \bar{x} = N^{-1} [MF(N/M, T) - MC(N/M, \bar{z}) - rMT], \tag{10}$$

where T, the amount of land per locality, is now taken as fixed. The first-order condition for this problem, again treating M as continuously variable, yields (after some rearrangement)

$$\bar{x} = \frac{F - C - rT}{N/M} = F_n - C_n,$$ (11)

or, by Euler's theorem,

$$(F_t - r)T = C - C_n \frac{N}{M}.$$ (12)

To interpret (11), think of the determination of M as equivalent to the determination of population size for each jurisdiction, N/M. Adding one more household to a representative jurisdiction raises $\bar{x}$, and thus welfare, if the household adds more to the net production of numeraire than it consumes. An entrant adds F_n of output, but imposes congestion costs of C_n. (11) shows that the net marginal production of an additional household is just balanced against its consumption of $\bar{x}$. See, e.g., Schweizer (1983a,b) for further analysis along these lines.

To understand (12), consider first the case where the local public good is purely public, so that $C_n = 0$, and where r, the cost of land, is zero as well. Then (12) states that the imputed rent on land in each locality is equated to expenditure on the local public good. Since this optimum could be sustained (once the optimal number of jurisdictions was somehow established) by each jurisdiction taxing away all land rents and using no other taxes, this result has been called the "Henry George Theorem", and it appears, along with much further discussion, in Flatters et al. (1974), Stiglitz (1977), Arnott (1979), Arnott and Stiglitz (1979), and Berglas (1982), among others.

When $r > 0$, the interpretation is modified slightly: the cost of pure local public goods would be covered by a 100 percent tax on differential land rents, that is, land rents in excess of the opportunity cost. When local public goods are impure, so that $C_n > 0$, a head tax would be needed to internalize the congestion externality, according to our earlier discussion of locational efficiency. If this tax is imposed, $C - C_n(N/M)$ would represent the additional costs of local public good provision that would have to be met by land taxation. (12) shows that when the number of jurisdictions is optimal, this remaining land tax would just exhaust (differential) land rents. In the special case of a quasi-private local public good, the right-hand-side of (12) is zero, so that $F_t = r$ when M is optimized. In particular, $M \to \infty$ when $r = 0$: in this case, the optimal policy is to endow each household with its own jurisdiction, since there are no scale economies in local public good provision.

In this discussion of the determination of the number of jurisdictions, we have focused on the normative problem of finding an optimum. As noted above, once an optimum number of jurisdictions has been achieved, the attainment of an efficient allocation reduces to the problem of achieving locational efficiency. This explains the close similarity between the locational efficiency results, summarized in Proposition 2, and the Henry George Theorem in its general form (i.e., with allowance for impure local public goods). For an arbitrary M, we know that head taxes that internalize congestion costs, together with land taxes that provide any needed additional revenue, insure locational efficiency. The Henry George Theorem tells us, in addition, that these land taxes will precisely exhaust (differential) land rents, when M is chosen optimally.

The positive or public choice question of how M is or might be chosen has not yet been addressed. It is not difficult, however, to imagine how this might be done, at least if each jurisdiction is somehow institutionally committed to using (or finds it optimal to choose) efficient taxes. Suppose that M were not optimal, e.g., suppose $F_t T - [C - C_n(N/M)] > rT$. By the Henry George Theorem, this means that land rents net of land taxes would be greater on any T units of land that were taken from their alternative use, at rent r, and used to form a new jurisdiction providing $\bar{z}$ units of the local public good. If one imagines an institutional framework such that landowners can set up new jurisdictions if desired, it follows that $F_t T - [C - C_n(N/M)] > rT$ cannot persist in equilibrium: new jurisdictions would "enter", causing M to rise, N/M to fall, and F_t to fall. If $C - C_n(N/M)$ rises with M (which will occur if C is convex in its first argument) or at least falls more slowly than $F_t T$, entry will compete away the excess net land rents. Conversely, $F_t T - [C - C_n(N/M)] < rT$ cannot hold in equilibrium: exit will cause M to fall. In equilibrium, the Henry George Theorem is satisfied, and an optimal M is achieved.

Models of this sort, in which land developers control the formation of jurisdictions, appear, for example, in Stiglitz (1983a,b). In clubs models such as Berglas and Pines (1981), entry and exit of profit maximizing club owners causes an efficient number of clubs to obtain in equilibrium. It is a notable fact that these models provide an example of an institutional framework within which self-interested behavior leads to efficient formation of jurisdictions. Whether or not such a model might have explanatory power as a positive theory of jurisdiction formation is unknown at present. It would not be far-fetched, however, to hypothesize that land rent differentials trigger political behavior that results in outcomes similar to those predicted by the developer model. Such positive theories warrant further investigation, both theoretical and empirical. Section 4 discusses local public choice models in greater depth.

3. Local taxation with mobile commodities: Incidence and efficiency analysis

Section 2 has examined in some detail how local tax policy can affect the locational choices of households, and the implications of such policies for efficient resource allocation. It has abstracted, however, from any interjurisdictional commodity flows other than the migration (or, given the static nature of the model, one might better say "assignment") of households, plus a flow of numeraire that compensates non-resident landowners for the use of their land. By contrast, this section deals with problems of local public finance in which trade in goods and/or factors plays a much more significant role. It begins with a review of recent research on property taxation, especially concerning the incidence of the property tax. Interjurisdictional mobility of capital figures prominently in this discussion. Land taxation is considered in Section 3.2. Other tax issues, including tax exporting and tax competition, are treated in Section 3.3. The flow of goods and factors across jurisdictional boundaries is critically important here as well. Section 3.4 briefly considers the incentives for excessive or inadequate local spending that are created by tax exporting and tax competition.

3.1. Property taxation

The incidence and allocative effects of property taxation are issues that can be considered from varying perspectives. In particular, one can analyze the effect of a property tax change in a single locality, or one can consider the impact of an entire system of property taxes imposed simultaneously by many localities. Also, when studying the tax imposed by a single locality, one can restrict attention to its impact within the locality or one can consider its effect on the general equilibrium of the whole economy. As a matter of fact, each of these perspectives can be useful for different purposes. One must bear in mind the question to be investigated, however, in order to avoid confusion.

Let us begin by considering the effect of an increase in the rate of property taxation in a single small jurisdiction. Here, "small" means that the jurisdiction faces demands and supplies for goods and factors, on the external market, that are very highly elastic. Suppose in particular that this is true of the supply of (homogeneous) capital: capital is freely mobile across jurisdictions, and net capital returns in all locations are equalized in long-run equilibrium. If the share of capital in each locality is small, and the demand elasticity for capital in individual jurisdictions is moderately large, the supply of capital to each locality will be highly elastic, even if the supply of capital to the economy as a whole is highly inelastic.

Now suppose that property taxes are assessed on the value of residential and/or commercial and industrial real property. Conceptually, the value of a parcel of property depends both on the land and on the structure on the parcel, and therefore the property tax is often considered to be like two taxes administered simultaneously: a tax on land value, and a tax on capital. In the static framework within which discussions of property tax incidence have usually taken place, the part of the tax assessed against land is borne by landowners, in the form of a reduction in net land rents.[8] The incidence of the part that falls on capital has been the subject of more analysis.

A common approach is to suppose that the tax rate on capital can be varied independently of that on land, at least hypothetically, and to conduct a comparative static analysis of the effect of a change in this tax rate. The essential features of such an analysis are easily understood. Let t_i be the ad valorem tax rate on capital in locality i, K_i and T_i the amount of capital and land in the jurisdiction, r_i the gross rental value of land, and ρ the net return to capital. T_i is exogenously fixed, but K_i is variable, and is assumed to adjust so as to provide a net return equal to that obtained on external markets, ρ. The individual jurisdiction is assumed to be small relative to the capital market so that ρ is exogenous. Suppose that land and capital are used by perfectly competitive profit maximizing firms, operating under conditions of constant returns to scale, to produce a single output. This good might be residential housing or some other non-traded good, or it might be an exported commodity. Let $D_i(p_i)$ be the demand for this good as a function of its price. For non-traded goods, the elasticity of demand $\varepsilon_i \overset{\Delta}{=} \mathrm{d} \log D_i/\mathrm{d} \log p_i$ is presumed to be considerably less than infinite. This may also be true for traded goods if the jurisdiction's producers, though individually small, are collectively large relative to the external market.

In equilibrium, gross land rents equal the value of output less gross outlays on capital, while the price of the output is equal to its unit cost of production, $\gamma_i(\rho[1+t_i], r_i)$. Hence

$$r_i T_i = p_i D_i(p_i) - \rho(1+t_i)K_i, \tag{13.1}$$

$$p_i = \gamma_i(\rho[1+t_i], r_i). \tag{13.2}$$

Let an asterisk denote a proportionate change in a variable (e.g., $p_i^* = \mathrm{d}p_i/p_i$, $t_i^* = \mathrm{d}t_i/(1+t_i)$) and let f_{iT} and f_{iK} denote the gross value shares of land and capital (i.e., $f_{iT} \overset{\Delta}{=} r_i T_i/p_i D_i$, and similarly for f_{iK}). Then differentiation of the system (13) yields

$$r_i^* f_{iT} = (1+\varepsilon_i)p_i^* - f_{iK}(K_i^* + t_i^*), \tag{14.1}$$

$$p_i^* = f_{iK} t_i^* + f_{iT} r_i^*, \tag{14.2}$$

using well-known properties of the unit cost function. Since $T_i^* = 0$, one has $K_i^* = \sigma_i(r_i^* - t_i^*)$, where σ_i is the elasticity of substitution between land and capital.

---

[8]The usual sorts of caveats must be imposed for this result to follow. See, e.g. Mieszkowski (1969) or McLure (1975) for general discussions of tax incidence. As can be seen from these articles, or from Feldstein (1977), the presumption that land taxes are not shifted depends on several simplifying assumptions: the general equilibrium relative price changes brought about by reduced consumption by landowners and increased spending by government are ignored, as are possible changes in landowners' supplies of other factors of production. Other questions that arise in an intertemporal setting are discussed below.

Thus eliminating K_i^* from (14.1), and using (14.2) to eliminate p_i^*, one obtains

$$(f_{iK}\sigma_i - f_{iT}\varepsilon_i)r_i^* = (\varepsilon_i + \sigma_i)f_{iK}t_i^*. \tag{15.1}$$

Solving for r_i^* and substituting back into (14.2) finally yields

$$p_i^* = \frac{f_{iK}\sigma_i}{f_{iK}\sigma_i - f_{iT}\varepsilon_i}t_i^*. \tag{15.2}$$

To see the implications of these results for tax incidence, note first that ε_i and σ_i are crucial parameters. The intuitive role that they play in (15.1) is as follows: an increase in the tax rate causes an increase in the cost of capital to the firms in the locality. This induces substitution of land for capital, as firms respond to the change in the relative factor prices, to an extent that depends on σ_i. The greater is this substitution effect, the larger is the bidding up of the price of the fixed supply of land. On the other hand, an increase in the cost of capital causes an increase in the cost of production, which reduces output to an extent that depends on the demand elasticity ε_i. This tends to reduce the demand for land and puts downward pressure on r_i. As (15.1) reveals, these effects are exactly in balance when $\sigma_i = |\varepsilon_i|$, for then $r_i^* = 0$. In this case, as shown by either (14.2) or (15.2), the effect of the tax is to raise the output price by $f_{iK}t_i^*$. The burden of the tax is therefore shifted from capital to consumers. If we consider a tax on residential housing, consumers may be tenants, and the conclusion is then that the tax is shifted from landlords to tenants. Similar conclusions apply if the output corresponds to other non-traded goods. If the output is a traded good, then one concludes in this case (where $\sigma + \varepsilon = 0$) that the tax on capital is *exported*, or, more accurately, that its burden is split between resident and non-resident consumers in proportion to their consumption shares of total output.

If σ_i is smaller than $|\varepsilon_i|$, (15.1) shows that $r_i^* < 0$, because the output effect dominates the substitution effect. If $\sigma_i = 0$, no substitution is possible. Since T_i is fixed, total output and hence the output price cannot change, as confirmed by (15.2). Hence, as (15.1) or (14.2) shows, r_i must fall enough to keep the unit cost of production constant in the face of an increase in the cost of capital. In this case, none of the tax is shifted to consumers, hence there can be no tax exporting if the output is a traded good, and the burden of the tax on capital is shifted to landowners. If, to take the other extreme, σ_i is very large ($\sigma_i \to \infty$), the substitution effect dominates the output effect and $r_i^* = t_i^*$, as shown by (15.1). By (14.2) or (15.2), it then follows that $p_i^* = t_i^*$, that is, the tax actually makes landowners better off at the expense of consumers, who bear more than the full burden of the tax.

Now consider the role of the demand elasticity, ε_i. It, of course, determines the size of the output effect. If $\varepsilon_i = 0$, this effect cannot operate and all the conclusions of the $\sigma_i \to \infty$ case emerge again. If instead $\varepsilon_i \to -\infty$, the output effect dominates, $p_i^* = 0$, and r_i falls to offset the rise in the gross cost of capital.

In the literature, various models have appeared that produce results of the type just described. Aaron (1975), in summarizing the traditional or "old view" of property tax incidence, presents a partial equilibrium argument under which the part of the property tax assessed on capital is passed forward to tenants or consumers of other goods in the form of higher housing or other output prices. Since this partial equilibrium view abstracts from the effects of the "structures" part of the property tax on the return to land, it probably is best understood as corresponding to the case $\sigma_i + \varepsilon_i = 0$, in which $r_i^* = 0$. Aaron also discusses the fact, however, that capital flows in response to changes in a jurisdiction's property tax rate will change factor proportions and therefore may change factor prices. Aaron notes, for example, that a tax increase can cause a capital outflow, a corresponding reduction in the capital/land ratio, and hence a fall in land rents. In terms of the model just developed, this corresponds to the case where $\sigma_i < |\varepsilon_i|$.

The relationship between output and substitution effects identified above underlies the results of a number of other studies. In some work [e.g., LeRoy (1976)], the analysis is conducted within the context of a monocentric city model with explicit spatial structure. Other investigators consider a variable supply of land [Hobson (forthcoming)] or vary the structure of the model in other ways, for example by distinguishing between housing and non-housing production. Studies of this latter type, such as Sonstelie (1979) or Lin (1985), have examined the effects of differential taxation of capital across uses. For additional analyses of property tax incidence in settings comparable to the above, see Grieson (1974) and Haurin (1980). Mieszkowski (1972) discusses some of the complications involved in moving to the case of more than one immobile factor. Arnott and MacKinnon (1977) and Sullivan (1984) present computable general equilibrium models in which the effects of property taxation can be simulated. It should be noted that in most of this literature, the limiting case $\varepsilon_i \to -\infty$ is often implicitly or explicitly assumed for traded goods, which means that exporting of the property tax, in the form of higher output prices, is precluded. In the case where the tax is imposed on residential housing or some other non-traded good, of course, tax exporting is ruled out by the structure of the model. Section 3.3 below considers tax exporting in more detail.

So far, we have focused on the effects of property tax changes in a single jurisdiction. From the viewpoint of tax incidence, at least for small jurisdictions, it might appear that the *only* effects of such a tax change, aside from the case where the jurisdiction exports a commodity for which it has a significant market share, are those which occur within the taxing jurisdiction – i.e., effects which show up in the prices of non-traded goods (e.g., land). An interesting demonstration that this is not the case is provided by Bradford (1978) and Mieszkowski and Zodrow (1984b), who cite Brown (1924) as an antecedent. These authors emphasize that a complete incidence analysis of a tax change in an individual locality must consider the effects of the tax not only within the locality but outside of it as well. At first sight one might think that the rest of the economy is affected so slightly by a tax change in one small jurisdiction that these effects can be ignored. A simple example, however, will demonstrate that this is not so.

Using the notation developed earlier in this section, let ρ, t_i, and K_i be the net return to capital, the tax rate on capital, and the amount of capital in locality i. Suppose for the moment that each locality produces a single traded good, the price of which is taken as exogenous at $p_i = \bar{p}$, and that $\phi_i(K_i)$ is the output of this good as a function of the amount of capital in the jurisdiction. Imagine that ϕ_i is derived from an underlying constant-returns to scale function of K_i and T_i, so that ϕ_i can be assumed strictly concave in K_i alone. Finally, to make the exposition as simple as possible, assume that the land endowment and technology of all localities are identical, that all tax rates are initially identical ($t_i = \bar{t}$, all $i = 1, \ldots, M$), and that the total stock of capital in the economy is fixed at $\bar{K}$. In equilibrium, net returns on capital are equalized, so that

$$\bar{p}\phi_i'(K_i) = (1 + t_i)\rho \quad \text{all } i, \tag{16.1}$$

and all capital is employed, so that

$$\bar{K} - \sum_i K_i = 0. \tag{16.2}$$

This provides a system of $M + 1$ equations which determine equilibrium values of the K_i's and ρ, given the t_i's as parameters. More precisely, (16.1) can be used to solve for each K_i in terms of $(1 + t_i)\rho$, such that

$$K_i' \triangleq \frac{\mathrm{d} K_i([1 + t_i]\rho)}{\mathrm{d}([1 + t_i]\rho)} = \frac{1}{\bar{p}\phi_i''} < 0. \tag{17}$$

Substitution of the $K_i(\cdot)$ functions into (16.2) allows one to solve for ρ in terms of the t_i's.

Now suppose one jurisdiction i raises its tax rate. From (16.2) we obtain

$$\frac{\partial \rho}{\partial t_i} = \frac{-\rho K_i'}{\Sigma_j (1 + t_j) K_j'} = -\frac{\rho}{1 + \bar{t}} \frac{1}{M}, \tag{18}$$

using the simplifying assumption that all jurisdictions are identical.

As (18) shows, a tax increase by one small jurisdiction (i.e., in the case where M is large) will have a small effect on the equilibrium net return to capital. Indeed, this justifies the perception, from the viewpoint of any one locality, that ρ is exogenously fixed. However, note that the total reduction in the net return to the economy as a whole is

$$\frac{\partial \rho}{\partial t_i} \bar{K} = \frac{\rho}{1 + \bar{t}} \frac{\bar{K}}{M} \frac{\rho}{1 - \bar{t}} K_i. \tag{19}$$

The amount of incremental tax revenue collected in locality i is

$$\frac{dt_i \rho K_i}{dt_i} \simeq \rho K_i + t_i \rho K_i'. \tag{20}$$

If $\bar{t} = 0$, i.e., if we start from a zero-tax initial situation, (19) and (20) imply that the tax in locality i reduces net capital income in the economy as a whole by exactly the amount of the tax collected in i. Although the amount of tax burden shifted from locality i to capital owners in the economy as a whole is small compared to the total return to capital in the entire economy, it is *not* small relative to the amount of tax collected in the taxing jurisdiction.

Now recall the discussion which showed that when the output price facing an individual locality is fixed ($\varepsilon_i \to -\infty$), the imposition of an incremental tax on capital causes a reduction in total land rents. In fact, if $t_i = 0$ initially, (14.2) implies that the reduction in land rents is equal to the amount of incremental tax revenue collected. There seems to be a paradox here: on the one hand, the tax is fully shifted to landowners in the taxing jurisdiction, and on the other hand it is fully shifted to capital in the economy as a whole. The resolution of the paradox rests on a recognition that it is the flow of capital from the taxing locality to the rest of the economy that depresses (slightly) the economy-wide net return to capital. It lowers the net return to capital because the capital/land ratio outside the taxing jurisdiction is (slightly) increased. But this change in factor intensity also means that the return to land in the rest of the economy is increasing, and one can show (in the simple case of identical jurisdictions) that the total loss of net land rents in the taxing jurisdiction is equal to the total gain in net land rents in the remaining jurisdictions. This resolves the paradox, since the tax burden that shows up twice – once in depressed local land rents and once in a lower economy-wide return to capital – is offset (once) by the increase in land rents outside the taxing locality.

While the case of initially zero tax rates is easier to analyze ($\bar{t} = 0$), the conclusions do not change very much when $\bar{t} > 0$. Here, the taxing jurisdiction receives less incremental tax revenue from an increase in the tax rate because of the loss of tax revenue on capital leaving the locality, as reflected in the $t_i \rho K_i'$ term in (20). The capital flow increases tax revenue by $-\bar{t}\rho K_i'$ in the rest of the economy, however. One could therefore characterize the general case where $\bar{t} > 0$ as follows: the increase in one locality's tax on capital causes an economy-wide reduction in the net return to capital equal to the product of the incremental tax per unit of capital and the amount of capital initially located in the taxing jurisdiction. In addition, there are transfers from taxpayers and landowners in the taxing jurisdiction to taxpayers and landowners in the rest of the economy.

Finally, allowing p_i to vary, as for instance in the case where one is analyzing the residential property tax, changes the results slightly once again. The increase in the price of housing in the taxing jurisdiction would partially offset the reduction in local land rents. There would also be a reduction in the price of housing in other localities.

All of the foregoing discussion has been simplified by the assumption that all localities are identical in terms of technologies, fixed resource endowments, and initial tax rates. The conclusions of the analysis will certainly differ if this assumption is relaxed. (Note that differential tax rates will introduce excess burden complications that are discussed further below.) Presumably the conclusions would be essentially unchanged for small departures from this restrictive assumption, however. (Simulations might be used to verify this conjecture. Also, there is scope here for additional theoretical work.)

We have now analyzed two types of property tax incidence problems: we have explored, first, what happens in an individual locality when its tax rate changes, and second, what happens in a *system* of localities when an individual locality changes its tax rate. Mieszkowski (1972) and subsequently Aaron (1975) and others have investigated a third question: what is the effect of property taxes imposed by *all* localities in a system of local governments? The analysis of the impact of a system of local property taxes is one of the main features of what has come to be called the "new view" of property tax incidence.

The simplest world in which to evaluate the incidence of a system of local property taxes is one in which a fixed stock of capital is allocated among a set of jurisdictions. In this world, a simultaneous increase in the property tax rate in all jurisdictions is identical to a general capital tax (ignoring the tax on land for simplicity). Given the fixed supply of total capital, together with the other usual simplifying assumptions of tax incidence analysis, this tax will be borne entirely by capital, and will not be shifted to other factors or to consumers of housing or other goods. As Aaron (1975) emphasizes, this result has far-reaching implications when compared to the "old view", according to which the property tax would be passed forward into housing or other output prices and would be regressively or, at best, proportionally distributed with respect to income. Since capital income and/or wealth is distributed more unequally than total income, the new view suggests, in contrast, that the property tax is progressive in its incidence. Of course, it must be kept in mind that this conclusion is conditional on the assumption of a fixed supply of capital. If one examines capital taxation in a growing economy in which the capital stock depends on the savings behavior of households, incidence analysis might lead to quite different conclusions.[9]

Proponents of the new view of property tax incidence recognize, of course, that property tax rates in practice vary considerably, both across jurisdictions and

---

[9]It is not possible to consider here the general question of the incidence of capital income taxation, since this would involve an examination of a large part of the literature of public finance of the past decade or so. For discussion of the issues involved in dynamic tax incidence analysis and some references to the literature, see Atkinson and Stiglitz (1980), Boadway and Wildasin (1984), and Kotlikoff (1984).

across sectors (e.g., residential vs. non-residential capital). The intuition behind the new view would suggest that a system of non-uniform property taxation could be regarded as a system of uniform taxation at some average rate, together with a system of jurisdiction- or sector-specific tax differentials. "On average" the tax would be borne by capital, while the differentials would be shifted through mechanisms like those analyzed above in our discussion of taxation in individual jurisdictions. As Courant (1977) shows, however, the concept of an average tax rate is elusive. In general, there is no uniform tax rate that would produce the same total revenue and simultaneously lower the net return to capital by the same amount as a given system of non-uniform taxation. For a given tax revenue, the net return to capital under a uniform tax would depend on the precise production technologies in the various localities, and could be either higher or lower than an equal-revenue non-uniform system. Despite this difficulty with the concept of the "average" tax rate, however, the essential new view conclusion – that the system of property taxation depresses the net return to capital, rather than leaving the net return unaffected as traditional analysis would have it – remains unchanged.

Let us now turn to a discussion of the allocative effects of property taxation. Except possibly in a dynamic setting, as discussed in Section 3.2, it is generally agreed that the part of the property tax that is assessed against land is neutral and by itself does not distort any decisionmaking margin. The part of the tax that falls on capital, by contrast, may obviously be non-neutral, as discussed formally in Brueckner (forthcoming).

A conventional argument is that this part of the tax generates an efficiency loss by increasing the gross price of capital for a small open jurisdiction that faces a perfectly elastic capital supply. To present this argument diagrammatically, let MP_1 and MP_2 in Figure 1 be marginal product of capital schedules for a single small jurisdiction 1 and an aggregate of all other jurisdictions, denoted by 2, resp. Suppose $\bar{K}$ is the fixed supply of capital to the economy as a whole, and let K_1, the amount of capital allocated to locality 1, be measured in the positive direction along the horizontal axis. Then the difference between $\bar{K}$ and K_1 represents the amount of capital in jurisdiction 2. To capture the notion that 1 is small, MP_2 is shown as horizontal, at least in the relevant range, although this is not crucial for the analysis. Suppose each jurisdiction is imposing a tax on capital at ad valorem rates $t_1 = t_2 = \bar{t}$. The net return to capital is fixed at $\rho = MP_2/(1 + t_2)$. The equilibrium amount of capital is K_1^e. If locality 1 were now to eliminate its property tax, it would experience a capital inflow that would result in a new equilibrium at $K_1 = K_1'$. From the viewpoint of locality 1, the tax at rate t_1 discourages "development" and produces an excess burden of abc.

It is immediately apparent, however, that this analysis is incomplete and misleading, because the initial equilibrium, with equal tax rates and $K_1 = K_1^e$, is clearly efficient. (The marginal product of capital is equalized across jurisdic-

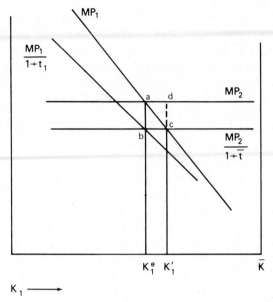

Figure 1.

tions.) Hence, the elimination of the tax in locality 1, instead of enhancing the efficiency of resource allocation, actually creates a distortion resulting in a loss of output to the economy as a whole equal to *acd*. The explanation for the apparent contradiction is easily found, of course: in a second best situation, given that $t_2 = \bar{t}$, an equal tax in locality 1 offsets the non-neutrality of the property tax in jurisdiction 2. The apparent excess burden in locality 1 of *abc* is more than offset by an increase in tax revenue to locality 2 equal to *abcd*, resulting from the flow of capital of $K'_1 - K^e_1$ to locality 2 and yielding a net benefit of *acd*. Thus, a policy that may be welfare improving for an individual jurisdiction need not be socially welfare-enhancing.[10] [See Gordon (1983), Wilson (1985a) and Wildasin (forthcoming).]

It is important to analyze the allocative effects of property taxes in a framework that takes not only the interjurisdictional mobility of capital into account, but the intersectoral mobility of capital as well. In the U.S. and in other countries, effective tax rates on capital vary widely across industries and types of capital. One important source of intersectoral variation in tax rates is the taxation of income from capital in the business sector of the economy via the corporate and personal income taxes. Such taxes do not fall on the returns to capital in the

---

[10] In an economy in which the capital stock is not exogenously fixed, the property tax might also distort the efficiency of resource allocation through its impact on savings behavior. The general problem of the distortionary impact of capital taxation is beyond the scope of this survey, but see the references of the preceding footnote for an introduction to the issues.

residential sector of the economy, especially capital invested in owner-occupied housing. In such a system, the residential property tax may reduce the variations in effective tax rates across categories of capital, and therefore may improve the efficiency of resource allocation. Hobson (1985) and Thirsk (1982) discuss this issue, and Devarajan et al. (1980) and Hamilton and Whalley (1985) present simulations which illustrate the potential efficiency gains from property taxation in models with other capital taxes.

The preceding discussion has been comparatively silent on the implications of household mobility for the analysis of the incidence and efficiency effects of property taxation. Indeed, in much of the property tax literature, interjurisdictional mobility is implicitly or explicitly restricted to capital, with households appearing, if at all, in a composite immobile factor of production (often called land). In all of the formal analysis presented up to this point, for example, one might have supposed that each jurisdiction consists simply of a single immobile household, or a group of identical immobile households. While this convenient simplifying assumption is often very useful, it may also be misleading.

For example, the work of Hamilton (1983) and others, mentioned in Section 2, suggests that zoning and household mobility must be taken into account in the analysis of property taxation. In a world of ideal zoning, capital would not flow freely, independently of population, so as to equalize net returns everywhere. The deadweight loss from property tax distortions would be obviated in such a system. Mieszkowski and Zodrow (1983, 1984a,b) contend that ideal zoning will not likely be achieved. As long as zoning policies leave some scope for the escape of capital from taxation, there will be the possibility of inefficient interjurisdictional or intersectoral allocations of capital. Nonetheless, these views are not necessarily mutually exclusive. A priori, one might suppose that, in practice, property taxes have some of the effects attributed to them in fiscal zoning models (i.e., they may influence locational choices by households somewhat like head taxes) and also some of the effects suggested by the "new view" literature (i.e., they act somewhat like taxes on mobile capital). Perhaps a theoretical synthesis of the two approaches is necessary.

Another illustration of the potential inadequacy of ignoring household mobility in the analysis of property taxation is provided by Wilson (1984). Wilson considers the effect of an increase in a single locality's property tax, when that locality is part of a system of jurisdictions among which utility-maximizing households and capital can migrate freely. Each jurisdiction uses land, labor, and capital to produce a non-traded good such as residential housing. Wilson shows, however, that the mobility of households may make the elasticity of demand for the non-traded good infinitely elastic, even when each individual consumer has a finite demand elasticity. The upshot is that the expected incidence result in this case, that is, that the property tax is shifted forward to consumers of the non-traded good (e.g., residential housing), can be overturned. This result confirms, once again, that analysis of the property tax can be quite sensitive to the assumed mobility or immobility of households. See Brueckner (1981) and Hobson (forthcoming) for further investigation of property taxation with mobile households.

3.2. Land taxation

A simple partial equilibrium analysis of the effects of a tax on land is revealing. Given that "land" is interpreted as unimproved land, and given that one confines the analysis to a jurisdiction with exogenously fixed boundaries, land will be perfectly inelastically supplied. A land tax should therefore be neutral, with no shifting and no efficiency loss. This is the conventional view of land taxation, and, especially because of its neutrality feature, it has appealed to many students of urban public finance [e.g., Vickrey (1970)]. These standard conclusions on both the incidence and efficiency of land taxation have been challenged, however. Interestingly, in both cases, questions have arisen when land taxation is evaluated in an intertemporal setting.

In analyzing the incidence of a tax on land rents, Feldstein (1977) considers a simple two-period overlapping generations model in which households are not linked across generations by bequests or other transfers. Feldstein finds that the land rent tax induces households to hold larger amounts of capital, so that the net return to capital is depressed and the productivity (and thus gross factor prices) of other factors, including land, is increased. The land tax can thereby be shifted to capital. Calvo et al. (1979) however, point out that this result changes when one assumes rational bequest behavior. In this case, land taxes are fully capitalized into land values, and bequests are changed so as to leave the real intertemporal equilibrium of the economy undisturbed. Fane (1984) observes that Feldstein's original conclusion results from an implicit intergenerational transfer caused by land taxation: land values fall to reflect the taxes that landowners will pay throughout the future, and this makes the current generation worse off at the expense of future generations. Intergenerational altruism can nullify the effect of this transfer, as the Calvo et al. analysis demonstrates. But the effect can also be nullified, for example, by having the government give bonds to landowners at the time the land tax is imposed, to be financed by future land rent tax collections. Such bonds would have a present value equal to the present value of these taxes, i.e., equal to the capitalized loss in land values that the taxes generate. Such bonds would therefore leave the net worth of landowners, and the real equilibrium of the economy, unchanged – even in the absence of private bequests motivated by intergenerational altruism.

The neutrality of land value taxation has been studied by several authors, including Bentick (1979) and Mills (1981), who conclude that neutrality breaks down in a dynamic economy. A simple way to appreciate the essence of the non-neutrality argument is as follows. Consider first the simple special case of a parcel of land that can be developed in a way that will yield a constant return of R per year in perpetuity. If returns are discounted at rate r, and the market value of the property is taxed at rate t, then its market value V must satisfy

$$V = \frac{R - tV}{r} = \frac{R}{r + t}. \tag{21}$$

Comparing V with and without a tax on land value (i.e., with $t > 0$ vs. $t = 0$), it is clear that the effect of land value taxation on land value is identical to that of an increase in the discount rate. Although the valuation formula analogous to (21) becomes more complex in the more general case where the return to land R or the discount rate r may vary over time, it is still true that an increase in the rate of land value taxation is similar to an increase in the discount rate. On the basis of this observation, Bentick (1979) and Mills (1981) argue that land value taxation promotes excessively rapid development of land: uses of land with low immediate returns and high deferred returns appear relatively less attractive in the presence of such taxes than projects that yield higher returns in the present or immediate future. As emphasized in Wildasin (1982), this non-neutrality can be traced to the fact that the market value of a parcel differs over time according to its use, so that land value tax liabilities are not use-independent. Nonetheless, neutral land taxation is still achievable, even in an intertemporal setting. A per unit tax on land, for example, would be independent of the use to which land is put, and would be neutral. A tax on some "standard value" of land, again independent of use, would similarly be neutral.

3.3. More complex structures of local taxation, production and trade

The property tax is a mainstay of local taxation in the U.S. and many other countries. At least as a first approximation, it is often useful and appropriate to assume that this is the only tax instrument available to localities. One should recognize, however, that this is only an approximation. Some local governments, both in the U.S. and elsewhere, use sales or income taxes. Many use fees or special assessments to finance utilities or certain types of improvements. At the state or provincial level, one finds substantial use of taxes on both individual and corporate income, sales, property, minerals and other natural resources, wealth, and other bases. Furthermore, the property tax itself may not be such a simple instrument as it might first appear. For example, effective property tax rates can vary across classes of property, such as commercial, light industrial, heavy industrial, single family residential, multi-family residential, agricultural, etc. In particular, the ratio of assessed to market value often differs from one category of property to another. Variations in assessment practice might be the result of explicit decisions to assess some kinds of property more heavily than others, or they might arise in a more implicit – or even inadvertent – fashion.

Not only can localities have more complex tax structures than is captured by simple models of uniform property taxation. The local economy itself might contain several industries, among which there could be factor or intermediate good flows, and there could be in general a complex pattern of interjurisdictional trade. This, too, is important for understanding the effects of local taxation.

A number of studies have examined the incidence and welfare effects of local taxation in models which incorporate some of these added features. For example, McLure (1969, 1970, 1971), Homma (1977), and Gerking and Mutti (1981) examine tax incidence in an economy with open regions which may produce more than one good and which trade goods and factors. In models of this type, results often depend on the general equilibrium adjustment of factor markets, as industries expand or contract in response to tax changes. As expected from other work on tax incidence in the Harberger (1962) tradition, these analyses show that factor intensities and ease of factor substitution are frequently important determinants of tax incidence.

An intriguing possibility that occurs in open economy tax incidence analysis is that taxes may be shifted to households that do not reside in the taxing jurisdiction, a phenomenon known as tax exporting. As mentioned earlier, one of the ways that tax exporting can occur is through the effect of local taxes on the output prices of traded goods. Equally, it can occur through a lowering of input prices for traded factors. Most of the discussion in the literature has focused on the case where the taxing jurisdiction has a "significant" effect on the price of a traded commodity, i.e., where the jurisdiction is not "small" and, in the language of international trade theory, can affect the terms of trade. For example, it has been suggested [see, e.g., McLure (1983) and Mieszkowski and Toder (1983)] that severance taxes on natural resources, such as coal produced in several western states in the U.S. (which collectively produce a large share of certain types of coal), might reduce output and drive up the price paid by (largely) non-resident consumers for these resources or derived products. As another example, many localities impose taxes on hotels or restaurant meals, presumably because these tend to fall especially on non-residents. It might even be argued that such local taxes as the property tax are shifted to non-residents. As indicated in the analysis in Section 3.1 above, this can occur if the output price faced by firms in the locality is not parametrically given. If local firms produce differentiated traded goods, they may have some monopoly power even if they are small in some sense. (Formal modeling along these lines would be quite useful.) For studies that analyze tax exporting in terms of the effect of local taxes on traded goods prices, see, e.g., McLure (1964, 1967, 1981).

There may be other important tax exporting mechanisms open to localities, in addition to exploitation of monopoly or monopsony power. In the U.S., state and local government taxes are presently (1985) deductible expenses under the federal individual income tax. This means that a portion (depending on the taxpayers' marginal tax rates) of state and local taxes assessed on households that itemize their deductions are shifted, via the federal income tax, to all federal taxpayers. (There is some controversy about the removal of this feature of the tax law.) Some of the implications of state and local tax deductibility are examined by Zimmerman (1983), Gramlich (1985), and Inman (1985).

Finally, our earlier discussion of property tax incidence has shown that even when an individual jurisdiction takes external output and factor prices as fixed, it does not necessarily follow that local taxes, e.g., on capital, are borne only by residents. Since a property tax imposed by one small locality can be borne by capital in the economy as a whole, it could be argued that taxes can be exported even by small, open jurisdictions. Recall, however, that the property tax imposed by a single locality will also change land values and/or non-traded goods prices, and that these effects tend to reverse the shifting of the burden from the locality to outsiders.

How might a locality optimally exploit its ability to export taxes? More generally, what is an optimal tax structure for an individual jurisdiction, with or without the ability to influence the terms of trade? These questions are investigated in Arnott and Grieson (1981), who examine an individual jurisdiction inhabited by a single immobile household (or many identical immobile households). Many of the results obtained by Arnott and Grieson are recognizable as a blend of results from the theory of optimal tariffs, on the one hand, and the theory of optimal taxation on the other. They show that the optimal tax structure can be characterized in terms of a modified inverse elasticity formula.[11] This formula shows that when the jurisdiction is small in the market for a particular traded good, the optimal tax on that good is zero. In cases where the locality can affect the terms of trade, one obtains the usual optimal tariff rule, slightly modified if the household in the taxing jurisdiction itself consumes the traded good. In short, the intuition behind the concept of tax exporting is formally vindicated, and turns out to be essentially equivalent to the terms of trade effect of a tariff. For non-traded goods, the Arnott–Grieson analysis yields results quite like those obtained in the standard theory of closed-economy optimal taxation.

3.4. Behavioral models of local taxation and expenditure

In general, it is difficult to model local government policy determination, since political decisionmaking processes are not well understood. Tractable and useful models can be constructed, however, on the hypothesis that each jurisdiction

---

[11]This formula can be derived under certain simplifying assumptions, including an absence of cross-price effects. See the original paper for details.

contains a single immobile household (or many such) and that local policies are chosen to maximize welfare for this household.[12]

It is natural to ask, in this setting, whether or not equilibrium local policies are socially efficient. In general, the answer is no. Tax exporting possibilities, for example, might induce a locality to use a distortionary tax on traded goods in place of a non-distortionary tax on local land, in an effort to shift the burden of local taxes to non-residents. Tax exporting may also lower the cost of local public goods to the jurisdiction, and induce inefficiently high levels of local public expenditure, as argued, e.g., by McLure (1967), Oates (1972), or Zimmerman (1983). It should be noted that the degree of distortion of local public spending depends on the entire structure of local taxation, however, and not just on the presence or absence of tax exporting, as discussed by Mieszkowski and Toder (1983) and Wildasin (1984b).

There may also be incentives for inefficient local policy when localities are not able to influence the terms of trade. First, as noted above, a tax on mobile capital may generate a welfare loss from the perspective of a single jurisdiction, even if the tax is non-distortionary from the perspective of the entire economy. This may induce a locality to distort its tax structure away from socially efficient taxes, toward more distortionary ones. Second, this may induce localities to keep tax rates, and thus local public spending, too low – a phenomenon often called tax competition, and analyzed by Zodrow and Mieszkowski (1986), Wilson (1986), Wildasin (forthcoming) and others. More generally, as shown by Wilson (1985b), the taxation of mobile capital in an economy with interjurisdictional trade in commodities might result in too little public good provision in some localities and too much in others.

Finally, it is worth noting that in systems where the number of jurisdictions is small, the possibility exists of strategy interaction in the determination of local public policy. Analysis of local government behavior in a small-number setting appears in Kolstad and Wolak (1983) and Mintz and Tulkens (1984).

4. Local public expenditure theory

A distinguishing characteristic of research in local public economics has been the sustained effort, in both theoretical and empirical work, to develop predictive models of local public expenditure.

Models of this sort – which we shall refer to here as *public choice* models, although this term should be interpreted very broadly in the present context –

---

[12]By contrast, welfare analysis with many households, particularly mobile ones, is more problematic. See, e.g. Starrett (1980), Boadway (1982), and Gordon (1983) for analysis of local policy with mobile households.

arise with much greater frequency in local public finance than in the analysis of public policy at the level of the central government. There are at least three reasons why this is the case.

First, local governments are numerous. This stimulates formal modeling of local government behavior in two ways. On the one hand, they provide ample observations for cross-sectional empirical analysis. At the central government level, empirical analysis is generally restricted to time series or to international cross-sections. The former is problematic because the institutional framework of government policymaking is always evolving and is subject to many unique historical events, while the latter presents equally difficult problems arising from the unique institutional structures found in different countries. On the other hand, because of the sheer number of local governments, analysts who seek to explain local policy determination are almost forced to develop abstract models which can be implemented in a more or less formal way. One must model local governments at "arm's length", as it were, simply because no one can imagine telling detailed stories about unique historical and institutional developments for hundreds or thousands of individual localities.

Second, there are many policy questions which hinge in a crucial way on the behavior of local governments. For example, note that around $\frac{1}{3}$ of the funding for local government expenditure in the U.S. comes from higher level (state and federal) governments. In some other countries the proportion is even higher. (See Prud'homme, this volume.) It is clear that transfers of this magnitude must have enormous effects on local tax and expenditure policy. These effects could vary widely, however, depending on the behavioral response of the recipient governments. Thus, in order to deal with very practical problems of grant policy design and reform, an analyst immediately confronts the problem of predicting the response of a large system of local governments to parametric changes in their environment. This clearly necessitates model building in which the policies of local governments are endogenous variables. The need for a behavioral theory of local governments arises in many other contexts as well. To take a further example of great current interest in the U.S., such a theory is essential for a satisfactory analysis of the effect of the proposed elimination of federal income tax deductibility of state and local taxes.

Third, models of local government behavior have been developed partly as a result of the inherent intellectual dynamics of the field. In particular, Tiebout's famous 1956 paper has provided a powerful stimulus in this direction. The Tiebout article was a direct response to Samuelson's classic 1954 and 1955 papers on public expenditure theory, in which it was claimed that there exists no market or other mechanism that would provide proper incentives for the efficient provision of public goods. Tiebout argued, instead, that when households can freely choose the jurisdictions in which they will reside, there will be a kind of market for local public goods which will provide the proper institutional framework for the attainment of efficient resource allocation. In view of the apparently powerful arguments adduced by Samuelson, this is a most provocative conclusion. Although the Tiebout paper attracted relatively little attention for a decade or more after its publication, it has motivated a great deal of more recent work. Much of this work, unlike the original Tiebout paper itself, has been primarily concerned with modeling the determination of local policy, since it is clear that a fully efficient allocation of resources cannot be achieved under arbitrary specifications of exogenously fixed local taxes and public expenditures, whether households are freely mobile or not.

This section discusses several approaches to the problem of modeling local fiscal policy determination. Like most of the literature, determination of local public spending is the focus of attention, with tax structure assuming a very simple form (e.g. a uniform head tax or land tax). While this is a useful and convenient modeling strategy, it does suppress most of the issues treated in Section 3 of this review. An important problem for future research is to develop models which better enable one to investigate simultaneous determination of tax and expenditure policy, especially in an environment with mobile households.

4.1. Voting models in a non-spatial environment

A great deal of empirical analysis of local public expenditure has been based on the Bowen (1943) – Black (1948) model of voting for a fixed population of voters. That model, it will be recalled, shows that a simple majority voting equilibrium exists when the alternatives to be decided upon can be ordered in such a way that every voter's preferences over the alternatives satisfy the single-peakedness property. In this case, the equilibrium will be the median preferred alternative. The individual with the median preferred alternative is called the *median voter*.

Median voter models have been applied in the local public finance context by assuming that each locality provides a single public good, the quantity of which varies directly with local public expenditure, and that the tax system in each jurisdiction assigns resident households fixed (or other well-behaved) shares of the cost of the local public good. If one assumes in addition that households cannot exit public facilities in order to use private alternatives (e.g., if one cannot send one's children to private rather than public schools), households with well-behaved underlying preferences over consumption of private and public goods will have single-peaked preferences for local public spending.[13] One can then

---

[13]See Stiglitz (1974) for a demonstration that single-peakedness can fail when private education is available as a substitute for public education. The essential intuition is that if the quantity of public education is very low, households choose private education and prefer still smaller levels of public education (which imposes costs but no benefits). If the quantity of public education is somewhat higher, one may withdraw from the private system. Then still higher levels of public education would be desired. The result is a U-shaped preference curve at low levels of public education.

regress local spending against the median voter's income and tax price, or proxies thereof, in order to obtain estimates of price and income elasticities of demand. To control for congestion effects, local population is often included as an explanatory variable. Studies of this sort include Barr and Davis (1966), Barlow (1970), Borcherding and Deacon (1972), Bergstrom and Goodman (1973), and Inman (1978).[14] A potential difficulty with this approach is that it is not easy to identify the median voter, and therefore to determine that voter's income or tax share. Bergstrom and Goodman prove a fundamental theorem that provides conditions under which income and price elasticities will be correctly estimated when expenditure is regressed against median income, and the median income household's tax share, a result that greatly facilitates empirical implementation of the median voter model.

The median voter model has been criticized, revised, and extended in many ways. One might object, for example, to the assumption that each locality provides a single public good. The single-peakedness condition generally does not obtain when issues are multidimensional, as shown, e.g. in Plott (1967) and Kramer (1973).

One might also criticize the empirical implementation of the model because it does not allow one specifically to test whether or not the equilibrium outcome is actually equal to the ideal point of the median voter [Romer and Rosenthal (1979a)]. Rather, this is a maintained hypothesis on the basis of which the relevant demand parameters can be estimated. Indeed, Borcherding et al. (1977), Courant et al. (1979), Romer and Rosenthal (1978, 1979), Gramlich (1982), and others have developed theoretical and empirical models in which public spending is determined in part by the influence of self-interested bureaucrats. The channels of bureaucratic influence range from manipulation of the agenda put before the electorate, to turning out to vote in higher proportions than other segments of the population.[15] Generally, it is assumed that bureaucrats prefer larger budgets to smaller ones, and, of course, the implication of models built around this assumption is that equilibrium budgets will be higher than the median voter (or the median voter within the set of non-bureaucratic voters) would prefer.

The median voter model has been important for empirical work partly because it relates observed equilibrium outcomes of the political process to the underlying preference structure of voters. In empirical work based on the median voter model, the jurisdiction is the unit of observation. An alternative approach, developed by Bergstrom et al. (1982) and Gramlich and Rubinfeld (1982), is based

---

[14]For critical reviews of the literature, see Inman (1979) and Rubinfeld (forthcoming).

[15]As stressed by Ledyard (1984), it is important to develop a theory of rational turnout for elections. The problem is that the expected payoff from voting is very small when large numbers of individuals vote, and it is not clear why rational individuals would incur the costs involved in going to vote. Ledyard develops a model of rational voters and analyzes the amount of voting observed in equilibrium and the behavior of candidates seeking election in such a world.

on surveys of individual voter preferences. While surveys might be unreliable guides of how individuals would actually vote, these authors find that the price and income elasticities estimated from the survey data are similar to those obtained from the median voter literature. The survey data, therefore, seem compatible with actual voting behavior as revealed in median voter models. Models estimated from voter surveys, however, have the added advantage that they allow one to determine the effect of many individual characteristics (age, race, occupation, religion, sex, etc.) on the demand for local public spending. This information is not easily inferred from median voter models.

Conventional median voter models ignore the possibility of household mobility. Mobility can be important for several reasons. First, as indicated by Goldstein and Pauly (1981), if mobility leads to clustering of individuals in communities of similar tastes, estimates of the income elasticity of demand for local public goods, derived from cross-section regressions, will be biased. Second, consider the basic problem of existence of equilibrium: how can one be certain that there exists a level of public good provision for each locality (together with a tax system for financing it) and an assignment of households to localities such that (i) the local public policy in each locality is a political equilibrium, given the assignment of households to jurisdictions, and (ii) no household has an incentive to relocate to another jurisdiction, given the public policies of each jurisdiction? The detailed investigation of this problem, of course, requires a specification of the tax system by which local public goods are financed, of the political process by which decisions are made, and of the economic environment which forms the background for the political process, and which is affected by local public policies. One simple example of such a specification is provided by Westhoff (1977), who assumes that localities use proportional wealth taxes to finance their spending on pure local public goods, that public expenditure decisions are determined by simple majority voting, and that there is only one homogeneous private good, not locationally fixed, in the private sector of the economy. With this structure and some additional assumptions, Westhoff proves existence of an equilibrium, but notes [see also Westhoff (1979)] that equilibria may not be stable.

Recall from Propositions 1 and 2 that equilibrium assignments of households to jurisdictions are generally inefficient if head or wealth taxes are used to finance pure local public goods. This means that even when equilibria exist in a model such as Westhoff's, they will be locationally inefficient. However, one might suspect that this need not be the case if spatially fixed commodities are included in the model. Furthermore, locationally-fixed commodities (land, durable structures) are empirically important in actual local tax structures. These considerations motivate interest in models which simultaneously accommodate household mobility, land or other property, and a public choice mechanism for determining local public policy. Enriching the economic environment by including spatially fixed goods complicates the modeling of the political

process, however. In particular, it is now necessary to take into account the possibility that local policy can affect equilibrium prices for some commodities, particularly residential property, and that anticipation of this effect might influence
voting behavior. Therefore, before turning to more complex voting models, it is
important to discuss the phenomenon of tax and expenditure capitalization.

4.2. Tax and expenditure capitalization

Standard asset valuation principles dictate that anticipated tax payments tend to
reduce the price of land or other forms of property that are subject to local taxes.
However, an increase in local taxes that is accompanied by an increase in local
public good provision need not depress the value of a parcel of property.
Intuitively, if rental or ownership of property is used as an exclusion device for
local public goods, and if the level of local public good provision is "too" low, a
simultaneous increase in public spending and taxes will make property more
attractive on balance, and its price should rise. If the level of public good provision is
"too" high, presumably the effect of extra taxes would outwiegh that incremental
public spending, and an increase in public good provision would then lower property
values. Would property values be left unchanged by a small increment of local public
spending and taxes when the level of public good provision is "just right"?

Thorough theoretical and empirical analysis of these issues has been stimulated by
a seminal paper by Oates (1969). To illustrate the principles involved, consider a
simple model. Suppose each of M jurisdictions provides a pure local public good, at
level z_i, and that each uses a per unit tax on land, at rate τ_{ir}, to finance the cost of this
public good. Assume that each jurisdiction has an identical cost function $C(z_i)$ for the
local public good, and contains an identical amount T of perfectly divisible and
homogeneous land. Suppose that land is used for residential purposes by households,
and that the utility of each household is a function of its consumption of an all-purpose
private (numeraire) good, land, and the local public good. To keep the notation and
analysis simple, although this is not critical for the results, assume that all households
have identical preferences and endowments. In equilibrium, then, all n_i households in
a given locality will have identical consumption bundles, (x_i, t_i, z_i), of all-purpose
good, land, and the public good, and will achieve the utility level $u(x_i, t_i, z_i)$.

Let r_i be the net-of-tax price of land in i, let N be the total population of
households, and let $\bar{x}$ be the (common) endowment of all-purpose good held by
each household. Then the budget constraint facing each consumer residing in
locality i is

$$x_i + r_i(1 + \tau_{ir})t_i = \bar{x} + \sum_j r_j T_i/N \overset{\Delta}{=} \bar{w}, \tag{22}$$

say, given that each household has identical land endowments. If every locality
chooses its ad valorem land tax rate τ_{ir} to balance its budget, so that

$\tau_{ir} r_i = = C(z_i)$, this constraint becomes

$$x_i + (r_i + C[z_i]/T)t_i = \bar{w}, \tag{23}$$

which means that the maximized utility of a household living in i is given by the indirect utility function $v(r_i + C(z_i)/T, \bar{w}, z_i) \overset{\Delta}{=} v_i$, say.

Finally, suppose that households are costlessly mobile. Then, in equilibrium, the vectors (r_i) and (n_i) and a scalar $\bar{v}$ must satisfy the following conditions:

$$v_i = \bar{v} \quad \text{all } i \text{ (locational equilibrium)}, \tag{24.1}$$

$$-n_i \frac{v_{ir}}{v_{iw}} = T \quad \text{all } i \text{ (land market equilibrium)}, \tag{24.2}$$

where $\bar{v}$ represents the equilibrium utility level for all households and where v_{ir}, v_{iw} are derivatives of v_i w.r.t. $r_i + C(z_i)/T$ and w, resp. (Thus, $-v_{ir}/v_{iw} = t_i$, the demand for land in locality i.)

In the large literature on capitalization, two basic positive sorts of results have been derived. Both require that the number of localities be large. First, if M is sufficiently large, a small change in z_i should have a very small effect on $\bar{v}$. Suppose then that one uses (24.1) to solve for r_i implicitly in terms of z_i, holding $\bar{v}$ fixed. Then, using well-known properties of the indirect utility function, one obtains

$$t_i \frac{dr_i}{dz_i} = MRS_i - C'(z_i)\frac{t_i}{T}, \tag{25.1}$$

where $MRS_i = (\partial u/\partial z_i)/(\partial u/\partial x_i)$, evaluated, of course, at equilibrium values. Note first that this result potentially allows one to observe MRS_i: dr_i/dz_i, $C'(z_i)$, and the other terms in (25.1) are all observable in principle. Thus, in an important sense, households' preferences for local public goods are revealed in an economy of the type specified. Furthermore, multiplying (25.1) through by n_i and using the equilibrium condition (24.2), one has

$$T\frac{dr_i}{dz_i} = n_i MRS_i - C'(z_i), \tag{25.2}$$

that is, an increase in z_i will raise r_i if the sum of the marginal benefits of the local public good exceeds its cost. The reverse will be true if the marginal cost is greater than the marginal benefit. The Samuelsonian condition is met when $dr_i/dz_i = 0$.

A second kind of result on capitalization obtains when there are many localities, and their levels of public good provision are sufficiently close to one another to approximate a continuum of choice for households deciding where to live. In this case, if $r(z_i)$ denotes the equilibrium land price in a locality providing z_i units of the local public good, and if one assumes that the function r is differentiable, a condition for utility–maximizing locational choice by households is that $dv(\cdot)/dz_i = 0$, which reduces to (25.1) and again implies (25.2). Note the difference in the conceptual basis for this result: here, the z_i's are supposed to be fixed, and (25.1) is derived from utility–maximizing behavior by consumers. In the preceding derivation, (25.1) was obtained from a comparative statics exercise in which the level of an individual z_i changes. In the latter case, the fact that the marginal benefits and costs of local public goods are reflected in the change in equilibrium land prices might be summarized by saying that *comparative statics* capitalization effects occur. In the former case, where marginal benefits and costs are reflected in the structure of equilibrium land prices that obtain in a given equilibrium, we might say that *cross-sectional* capitalization obtains. At least in this model, it appears that the conditions for cross-sectional capitalization are more stringent than those for comparative statics capitalization.

Cross-sectional capitalization is particularly interesting because it invites empirical testing: one could imagine regressing observed r_i's on z_i's in order to check whether the Samuelsonian condition for efficient local public spending is satisfied. Of course, a "large" number of localities, or an approximation thereof, appears necessary (in general) for the derivation of both cross-sectional and comparative statics capitalization results, and it has been demonstrated in the literature that these results in fact break down when this assumption is relaxed. For examples of theoretical and empirical work on capitalization, consult Brueckner (1979, 1982, 1983), Edel and Sclar (1974), Hamilton (1976), Kanemoto (1980), Pauly (1976), Pines (1984, forthcoming), Sonstelie and Portney (1978, 1980a,b), Starrett (1981), and Wildasin (1979, 1984a).

4.3. Public choice in an economy with capitalization effects

Voting models of public expenditure determination, like the median voter model discussed in Section 4.1, have traditionally assumed that individual votes are determined by a comparison of the marginal benefit of the public good with its marginal tax-price, that is, the individual's share of the marginal cost of the public good as determined by the tax system. However, in an economy where households are mobile, and where equilibrium prices change in response to changes in public policy, this conception of voting behavior can be seriously inaccurate.

Consider, for example, a model like that of Section 4.2 above: identical households are costlessly mobile among a set of jurisdictions that, for simplicity, are assumed to differ only in their levels of public good provision and taxation. To generalize the model somewhat, let the local public good cost function be

$C(n_i, z_i)$, allowing possibly for congestion effects, and suppose each locality i can use both a head tax, at rate τ_{in}, and a land tax, at ad valorem rate τ_{ir}, to finance its spending. Finally, let us temporarily change the model by specifying that all land endowments are concentrated in the hands of absentee landowners who only consume the all-purpose private good and who therefore seek only to maximize their wealth. The other households in the economy are as specified earlier: each has a direct and indirect utility function u and v, and a private good endowment of $\bar{x}$. Of course, since these households are now assumed to own no land, and since head taxes are allowed, the budget constraint for a household located in jurisdiction i is slightly changed. It now reads

$$x_i + r_i(1 + \tau_{ir})t_i = \bar{x} - \tau_{in} \overset{\Delta}{=} w_i. \tag{26.1}$$

The direct utility function $u(x_i, t_i, z_i)$ is as before, and the indirect utility function is $v_i \overset{\Delta}{=} v(r_i[1 + \tau_{ir}], w_i, z_i)$. Households are assumed to be costlessly mobile, so that (24.1) holds in equilibrium. The government budget constraint for locality i is

$$\tau_{ir} r_i T + n_i \tau_{in} = C(n_i, z_i). \tag{26.2}$$

Using (26.2), we can express τ_{ir} in terms of τ_{in}, z_i, and n_i.

Finally, suppose that the number of localities is "large", i.e., that $\bar{v}$ in (24.1) is taken as exogenously fixed from the perspective of any single jurisdiction. Imagine that each locality has initially given policies $(\tau_{in}, \tau_{ir}, z_i)$, and that an initial equilibrium exists which satisfies (24) and (26.2). Now consider how one might model the determination of local policy. One possibility is to let the households initially residing in the jurisdiction constitute an electorate that votes on tax and expenditure policy. A problem immediately arises with this approach, however: by assumption, local policy cannot affect $\bar{v}$, the equilibrium utility level of the mobile households. Therefore, they should all be *indifferent* about $(\tau_{in}, \tau_{ir}, z_i)$. Any equilibrium in a voting model with such an electorate would be indeterminate.

Landowners, on the other hand, are affected in a significant way by local policy, and would therefore have an incentive to participate in the local political process. Note that (24.1) allows one to solve for the equilibrium net land rent r_i in terms of τ_{in}, τ_{ir}, and z_i. One can then use (24.2) to solve for the equilibrium n_i as a function of the same variables. Finally, use the government budget constraint to solve for τ_{ir} in terms of τ_{in} and z_i. Then, after straightforward manipulations, one finds

$$T \frac{\partial r_i}{\partial \tau_{in}} = (\tau_{in} - C_{in}) \frac{\partial n_i}{\partial \tau_{in}}, \tag{27.1}$$

and

$$T\frac{\partial r_i}{\partial z_i} = n_i MRS_i - C_{iz} + (\tau_{in} - C_{in})\frac{\partial n_i}{\partial z_i},$$ (27.2)

where C_{in} and C_{iz} are partial derivatives of C, evaluated at (n_i, z_i).[16]

The left-hand sides of (27) represent the change in equilibrium land values associated with changes in the local policy variables. In general, land values will not be invariant to local tax and expenditure policy, and it follows that landowners will not be indifferent about these policies.

Thus, allowance for costless mobility of households has a rather drastic effect on the analysis of the local public choice process. In this simple model, far from comparing marginal benefits and tax-prices in deciding how to vote, the consumers of local public services − the residents of each jurisdiction − actually become totally indifferent to local policy. Instead, landowners become the natural agents around which to build a model of local government decisionmaking.[17] Models of this type appear in Berglas and Pines (1981), Henderson (1980, 1985), Epple et al. (1985) and elsewhere. It is easy to see, from (27), that an equilibrium of local policies in such a model can be efficient. A land-value-maximizing policy would require setting $\partial r_i/\partial \tau_{in} = \partial r_i/\partial z_i = 0$, which, by (27.1), means that head taxes would internalize congestion effects, and, by (27.2), it then follows that the Samuelsonian condition for local public spending would be met. Overall efficiency − both efficient locational choice by households, and efficient local public spending − would thus be achieved in equilibrium. Of course, if instead jurisdictions are assumed not to have full flexibility in their choice of policy instruments, the equilibrium may not be efficient. Suppose, for example, that local public goods are congested and that localities, for some reason, are able only to use land taxation to finance local public goods. Then (27.2) reveals that z_i will be used indirectly to control entry into the locality. Expenditure efficiency will not, therefore, be achieved − a typical illustration of the problem of second best.

This simple model assumes an unrealistically sharp distinction between landowners and residents. In practice, one observes that many residents − especially in certain types of localities, such as suburbs of major cities − are homeowners. That is, they both own property in a jurisdiction, and consume public services there. This complicates the analysis of the political process considerably, although it does not necessarily invalidate the conclusion that an equilibrium can be efficient. To see the nature of this complexity, note first that it introduces an inherent heterogeneity of endowments among the households in the economy: households that own land or other property in one locality are essentially different from those owning land in another locality, because land in different

---

[16] For similar derivations, see Wildasin (1983).
[17] Alternatives to this approach appear in Epple et al., (1984) and Yinger (1982).

localities can trade at different prices. One must therefore move beyond the simple model of a single class of mobile households.[18] Second, when households can own property, the assumption of wealth-maximizing behavior by voter-residents may be hard to justify. If the resident-property owners in a locality also receive utility from the consumption of local public services, as one would naturally assume, they will presumably recognize that their decisions about local public good provision influence both the value of their property and their consumption opportunities. If a particular locality provides $\bar{z}$ units of a public service, if all other localities provide quite different levels of the local public good, and if the existing residents of the locality strongly prefer $\bar{z}$ or a similar level of the local public good, then the fact that $\bar{z}$ does not maximize property values does not necessarily imply that residents will vote for a different level of provision. It can still be argued, however [Wildasin (1979, 1984a)] that wealth maximization decisions can be separated from consumption decisions when the conditions for cross-sectional capitalization obtain, and that in this case rational voter-residents will prefer policies that lead to efficient outcomes.

Under less idealized circumstances, political equilibria need not have these efficiency properties. Henderson (1980, 1985b), for example, considers local policy determination in a two-period model. Suppose that a jurisdiction initially contains no residents, that local public goods are subject to congestion, and that property taxation along with fiscal zoning is used, in lieu of ideal head taxes, to internalize congestion externalities. Profit maximizing landowners might allow a certain amount of land to be developed in the first period, imposing zoning constraints that insure that each resident household bears its marginal congestion cost. Suppose, however, that not all land is developed in the first period. Then, in the second period, suppose that additional households are allowed to enter the locality. If landowners (i.e., owners of still-undeveloped land) contrive to control the political process, they will have an incentive to reduce second-period zoning requirements. In doing so, they can effect a transfer from first-period to second-period residents via the property tax: property tax payments by second-period residents will be lower than their marginal congestion costs, and property taxes paid by initial residents will be correspondingly higher. This transfer makes the locality more attractive to potential second-period residents, which allows developers to sell land for second-period development at a higher price. First-period residents, of course, would oppose this policy, and in fact have an incentive to increase zoning requirements. One can imagine models in which one or the other of these conflicting interests might dominate the other, so it is not clear whether or not one should expect over- or under-development in the second period. Also,

---

[18]This is not to insist that the equilibria with landowning households will necessarily involve utility differentials. Nonetheless, the prospect of obtaining higher wealth and utility than agents owning land in other jurisdictions will enter into the decisionmaking calculus of the landowners in any one locality.

if developers (and residents) can make binding first-period commitments about second-period policy, the problem of dynamically inconsistent policy and associated inefficiencies may be obviated. See Epple et al. (1985) for further analysis along these lines.

Finally, consider the implications of relaxation of the assumption of costless mobility of households. In the models of Henderson and Epple et al., households, once assigned to a jurisdiction, become completely immobile. More generally, one might suppose that households are able to relocate, but only at a cost. This case, covering the middle ground between complete immobility and perfect mobility, is presumably one of considerable empirical relevance. Preliminary analysis by Wildasin and Wilson (in preparation) indicates that it opens up a number of possibilities that do not arise in either of the conventional polar cases. For instance, suppose local government policies are controlled by landowners who seek to maximize land values in an economy with overlapping generations of finite-lived households. Suppose that households live for two periods, and that in the first period of life they are freely mobile. They choose a locality in which to reside so as to maximize expected lifetime utility. However, in the second period of life, they can only relocate at a cost. This cost is randomly distributed across households. In order to attract young households, jurisdictions must offer competitive tax and expenditure packages. Landowners also have an incentive to exploit their old residents by offering less favorable tax-expenditure policies, but their ability to do so is limited by the partial mobility of these households. If long-term (explicit or implicit) contracts or precommitments are possible, it will be profitable for landowners to trade away the opportunity to take advantage of their older residents, and a first-best efficient equilibrium will be achieved. If such contracts are not possible, however, landowners will exploit a monopsony relationship with their older residents, and, in equilibrium, some of these residents will find it optimal to relocate. Since migration is costly and (in this particular model) socially wasteful, it follows that the equilibrium will be inefficient. In fact, it can be shown that first-best efficient equilibria would be attained in either of the polar cases of costless mobility or complete immobility, but that the equilibria in intermediate cases of imperfect or costly mobility are generally ex ante Pareto inferior to these first-best equilibria. In particular, landowners are neither better off nor worse off in the presence of imperfect mobility, but the other households in the system have lower expected utilities.

Since this model is special in some respects, it is difficult to know how robust its conclusions are. It is simple, however, and basic qualitative conclusions drawn from it are unlikely to be reversed merely by adding realistic complications to the model. It suggests that the more realistic intermediate case of costly mobility may not be well approximated by the standard polar cases of free mobility or complete immobility. Presumably, further analysis of models with imperfect mobility will uncover other results that differ from those that depend on the standard idealizations, such as many of those described earlier in this section.[19]

4.4. Conclusion

The above discussion has identified several fruitful approaches to the analysis of local public choice, and has summarized some of the key findings that have been obtained in the literature. Obviously this literature has yielded many important insights into the process of local government decisionmaking. At the same time, local government behavior is clearly quite complex and it cannot be claimed that a satisfactory understanding of the local political process has yet been achieved. While the local public choice models that we have reviewed all bear some resemblance to observed institutional realities, they differ widely in terms of the aspects of reality that they emphasize, and the simplifications and abstractions that they make. This is to be expected in a field in which a standard theoretical framework has not been definitively established. There is clearly much scope for additional work.

In closing, it might be worthwhile emphasizing that theoretical work in local public choice, or in local public finance in general, has great potential relevance to many practical policy issues. Put somewhat differently, there are many policy problems that cannot be dealt with satisfactorily without appeal to some empirically-validated theoretical model. Consider, for example, that in the U.S. alone, the past decade and a half has seen bursts of popular attention focused on the fiscal problems of central cities, school finance reform, revenue sharing, state and local government indebtedness, public infrastructure, tax limitation movements, disentanglement of federal, state, and local responsibilities for income redistribution and health care, and federal income tax deductibility of state and local taxes. In each of these cases, an understanding of the behavior of local governments – whether they spend too much or too little, how they might respond to changes in transfers from higher level governments, how they make intertemporal resource allocation decisions – is central to the correct specification of policy. Practical policy issues such as these demand adequate theoretical and empirical models. In the long run, such practical problems can be expected to exert powerful influence over the development of theoretical local public economics.

---

[19]Indeed, mobility costs have played a central role in some analyses of state and local government redistribution. If one assumes that the recipient population consists of identical freely mobile individuals, the elasticity of the recipient population in any one locality with respect to that locality's level of redistribution can be very high, perhaps infinite. Jurisdictions facing such high elasticities would not find it optimal to engage in significant redistribution. Therefore, models which attempt to explain the significant redistribution that is actually carried out by lower-level governments have often assumed costly mobility. See, e.g. Gramlich (1985) and Brown and Oates (1985).

References

Aaron, H.J. (1975) *Who pays the property tax?* Washington, D.C.: Brookings.

Arnott, R.J. (1979) 'Optimal city size in a spatial economy', *Journal of Urban Economics*, 6:65–89.

Arnott, R.J. and R.E. Grieson (1981) 'Optimal fiscal policy for a state or local government', *Journal of Urban Economics*, 9:23–48.

Arnott, R.J. and J.G. MacKinnon (1977) 'The effects of the property tax: a general equilibrium simulation', *Journal of Urban Economics*, 4:389–407.

Arnott, R.J. and J.E. Stiglitz (1979) 'Aggregate land rents, expenditure on public goods, and optimal city size', *Quarterly Journal of Economics*, 93:471–500.

Atkinson, A.B. and J.E. Stiglitz (1980) *Lectures on public economics.* New York: McGraw-Hill.

Barlow, R. (1970) 'Efficiency aspects of local school finance', *Journal of Political Economy*, 78:1028–1040.

Barr, J.L. and O.A. Davis (1966) 'An elementary political and economic theory of the expenditures of local governments', *Southern Economic Journal.* 22:149–165.

Beck, J.H. (1983) 'Tax competition, uniform assessment, and the benefit principle', *Journal of Urban Economics*, 13:127–146.

Bentick, B.L. (1979) 'The impact of taxation and valuation practices on the timing and efficiency of land use', *Journal of Political Economy*, 87:859–868.

Berglas, E. (1982) 'User charges, local public services, and taxation of land rents', *Public Finance*, 37:178–188.

Berglas, E. and D. Pines (1981) 'Clubs, local public goods, and transportation models: a synthesis', *Journal of Public Economics*, 15:141–162.

Bergstrom, T.C. and R.P. Goodman (1973) 'Private demands for public goods', *American Economic Review*, 63:280–296.

Bergstrom, T.C., D.L. Rubinfeld and P. Shapiro (1982) 'Micro-based estimates of demand functions for local school expenditures', *Econometrica*, 50:1183–1205.

Bewley, T.F. (1981) 'A critique of Tiebout's theory of local public expenditures', *Econometrica*, 49:713–740.

Black, D. (1948) 'On the rationale of group decision-making', *Journal of Political Economy*, 56:23–34.

Boadway, R. (1982) 'On the method of taxation and the provision of local public goods: comment', *American Economic Review*, 72:846–851.

Boadway, R. and F. Flatters (1982) *Equalization in a federal state.* Ottawa: Economic Council of Canada.

Boadway, R.W. and D.E. Wildasin (1984) *Public sector economics*, 2nd edition. Boston: Little, Brown.

Borcherding, T.E., W.C. Bush and R.M. Spann (1977) 'The effects on public spending of the divisibility of public outputs in consumption, bureaucratic power, and the size of the tax-sharing group', in: T.E. Borcherding, ed., *Budgets and bureaucrats.* Durham: Duke University Press. 211–228.

Borcherding, T.E. and R.T. Deacon (1972) 'The demand for the services of non-federal governments', *American Economic Review*, 62:891–901.

Bowen, H.R. (1943) 'The interpretation of voting in the allocation of economic resources', *Quarterly Journal of Economics*, 58:27–48.

Bradford, D.F. (1978) 'Factor prices may be constant but factor returns are not', *Economics Letters*, 1:199–203.

Brown, C.C. and W.E. Oates (1985) 'Assistance to the poor in a federal system', unpublished.

Brown, H.G. (1924) *The economics of taxation.* New York: Holt and Co.

Brueckner, J.K. (1979) 'Property values, local public expenditure, and economic efficiency', *Journal of Public Economics*, 11:223–246.

Brueckner, J.K. (1981) 'Labor mobility and the incidence of the residential property tax', *Journal of Urban Economics*, 10:173–182.

Brueckner, J.K. (1982) 'A test for allocative efficiency in the local public sector', *Journal of Public Economics*, 19:311–331.

Brueckner, J.K. (1983) 'Property value maximization and public sector efficiency', *Journal of Urban Economics*, 14:1–16.

Brueckner, J.K. (forthcoming) 'A modern analysis of the effects of site value taxation', *National Tax Journal*.

Buchanan, J.M. and C.J. Goetz (1972) 'Efficiency limits of fiscal mobility: an assessment of the Tiebout model', *Journal of Public Economics*, 1:25–43.

Bucovetsky, S. (1981) 'Optimal jurisdictional fragmentation and mobility', *Journal of Public Economics*, 16:171–192.

Calvo, G.A., L.J. Kotlikoff and C.A. Rodriguez (1979) 'The incidence of a tax on pure rent: a new (?) reason for an old answer', *Journal of Political Economy*, 87:869–874.

Chang, F.R. and D.E. Wildasin (1986) 'Randomization of commodity taxes: an expenditure minimization approach', *Journal of Public Economics*, 31:329–345.

Courant, P.N. (1977) 'A general equilibrium model of heterogeneous local property taxes', *Journal of Public Economics*, 8:313–328.

Courant, P.N., E.M. Gramlich and D.L. Rubinfeld (1979) 'Public employee market power and the level of government spending', *American Economic Review*, 69:806–817.

Devarajan, S., D. Fullerton and R.A. Musgrave (1980) 'Estimating the distribution of tax burdens: a comparison of different approaches', *Journal of Public Economics*, 13:155–182.

Edel, M. and E. Sclar (1974) 'Taxes, spending, and property values: supply adjustment in a Tiebout-Oates model', *Journal of Political Economy*, 82:941–954.

Epple, D., R. Filimon, and T. Romer (1984) 'Equilibrium among local jurisdictions: toward an integrated treatment of voting and residential choice', *Journal of Public Economics*, 24:281–308.

Epple, D., T. Romer and R. Filimon (1985) 'Community development with endogenous land use controls', GSIA W.P. 28-84-85, Carnegie-Mellon University.

Fane, G. (1984) 'The incidence of a tax on pure rent: the old reason for the old answer', *Journal of Political Economy*, 92:329–333.

Feldstein, M. (1977) 'The surprising incidence of a tax on pure rent: a new answer to an old question', *Journal of Political Economy*, 85:349–360.

Flatters, F., V. Henderson, and P. Mieszkowski (1974) 'Public goods, efficiency and regional fiscal equalization', *Journal of Public Economics*, 3:99–112.

Gerking, S.D. and J.H. Mutti (1981) 'Possibilities for the exportation of production taxes: a general equilibrium analysis', *Journal of Public Economics*, 16:233–252.

Goldstein, G.S. and M.V. Pauly (1981) 'Tiebout bias on the demand for local public goods', *Journal of Public Economics*, 16:131–144.

Gordon, R.H. (1983) 'An optimal taxation approach to fiscal federalism'. *Quarterly Journal of Economics*, 98:567–586.

Gramlich, E.M. (1982) 'Models of excessive government spending: do the facts support the theories'? in: *Public finance and public employment*, Proceedings of the 36th Congress of the International Institute of Public Finance, Detroit: Wayne State University Press. 289–308.

Gramlich, E.M. and D.L. Rubinfeld (1982) 'Micro estimates of public spending demand functions and tests of the Tiebout and median voter hypothesis'. *Journal of Political Economy*, 90:536–560.

Gramlich, E.M. (1985) 'Reforming U.S. fiscal federalism arrangments', in: J.M. Quigley and D.L. Rubinfeld, eds., *American domestic priorities*. Berkeley: University of California Press. 34–69.

Grieson, R.E. (1974) 'The economies of property taxes and land values: the elasticity of supply of structures', *Journal of Urban Economics*, 1:367–381.

Hamilton, B. and J. Whalley (1985) 'Tax treatment of housing in a dynamic sequenced general equilibrium model', *Journal of Public Economics*, 27:157–176.

Hamilton, B.W. (1975) 'Zoning and property taxation in a system of local governments', *Urban Studies*, 12:205–211.

Hamilton, B.W. (1976) 'The effects of property taxes and local public spending on property values: a theoretical comment', *Journal of Political Economy*, 84:647–650.

Hamilton, B.W. (1983) 'A review: is the property tax a benefit tax?' in: G.R. Zodrow, ed., *Local provisions of public services: the Tiebout model after twenty-five years*. New York: Academic Press. 85–108.

Harberger, A.C. (1962) 'The incidence of the coporation income tax', *The Journal of Political Economy*, 70:215–240.

Haurin, D.R. (1980) 'The effect of property taxes on urban areas', *Journal of Urban Economics*, 7:384–396.

Helpman, E., D. Pines, and E. Borukhov (1976) 'The interaction between local government and urban residential location: Comment', *The American Economic Review*, 66:961–967.

Henderson, J.V. (1980) 'Community development: the effects of growth and uncertainty', *The American Economic Review*, 70:894–910.

Henderson, J.V. (1985a) *Economic theory and the cities*, 2nd. ed. New York: Academic Press.

Henderson, J.V. (1985b) 'the Tiebout model: bring back the entrepreneurs', *Journal of Political Economy*, 93:248–264.

Hobson, P. (forthcoming) 'The incidence of heterogeneous residential property taxes', *Journal of Public Economics*.

Hobson, P. (1985) 'The property tax: a survey', unpublished.

Hochman, O. (1981) 'Land rents, optimal taxation and local fiscal independence in an economy with local public goods', *Journal of Public Economics*, 15:59–85.

Hochman, O. (1982a) 'Congestable local public goods in an urban setting', *Journal of Urban Economics*, 11:290–310.

Hochman, O. (1982b) 'Clubs in an urban setting', *Journal of Urban Economics*, 12:85–101.

Homma, M. (1977) 'On the theory of interregional tax incidence', *Regional Science and Urban Economics*, 7:377–392.

Inman, R.P. (1978) 'Testing political economy's "as if" proposition; is the median voter really decisive'? *Public Choice*, 33:45–65.

Inman, R.P. (1979) 'The fiscal performance of local governments: an interpretative review', in: P. Mieszkowski and M. Straszheim, eds., *Current issues in urban economics*. Baltimore: Johns Hopkins University Press. 270–321.

Inman, R.P. (1985) 'Does deductibility influence local taxation?' unpublished.

Kanemoto, Y. (1980) *Theories of urban externalities*. Amsterdam: North-Holland.

Kolstad, C.D. and F.A. Wolak, Jr. (1983) 'Competition in interregional taxation: the case of western coal', *Journal of Political Economy*, 91:443–460.

Kotlikoff, L.J. (1984) 'Taxation and savings: a neoclassical perspective', *Journal of Economic Literature*, 22:1576–1629.

Kramer, G. (1973) 'On a class of equilibrium conditions for majority rule', *Econometrica*, 41:285–297.

Ledyard, J. (1984) 'The pure theory of large two-candidate elections', *Public Choice*, 44:7–41.

LeRoy, S.F. (1976) 'Urban land rent and the incidence of property taxes', *Journal of Urban Economics*, 3:167–179.

Lin, C. (1985) 'A general equilibrium analysis of property tax incidence', unpublished.

McLure, C.E., Jr. (1964) 'Commodity tax incidence in open economies', *National Tax Journal*, 17:187–204.

McLure, C.E. (1967) 'The interstate exporting of state and local taxes: estimates for 1962', *National Tax Journal*, 20:49–77.

McLure, C.E. (1969) 'The inter-regional incidence of general regional taxes', *Public Finance/Finances Publiques*, 24:457–483.

McLure, C.E. (1970) 'Taxarion, substitution, and industrial location', *Journal of Political Economy*, 78:112–132.

McLure, C.E. (1971) 'The theory of tax incidence with imperfect factor mobility', *Finanzarchiv*, 30:24–48.

McLure, C.E. (1975) 'General equilibrium incidence analysis: the harberger model after ten years', *Journal of Public Economics*, 4:125–161.

McLure, C.E. (1981) 'Market dominance and the exporting of state taxes', *National Tax Journal*, 34:483–486.

McLure, C.E., Jr. (1983) 'Tax exporting and the commerce clause', in: C.E. McLure, Jr. and P. Mieszkowski, eds., *Fiscal federalism and the taxation of natural resources*. Lexington: Lexington Books. 169–192.

Mieszkowski, P.M. (1969) 'Tax incidence theory: the effect of taxes on the distribution of income', *Journal of Economic Literature*, 7:1103–1124.

Mieszkowski, P.M. (1972) 'The property tax: an excise tax or a profits tax?' *Journal of Public Economics*, 1:73–96.

Mieszkowski, P.M. and E. Toder (1983) 'Taxation of energy resources', in: C. McLure and P. Mieszkowski, eds., *Fiscal federalism and the taxation of natural resources*. Lexington: Heath. 65–92.

Mieszkowski, P.M. and G.R. Zodrow (1984a) 'The new view of the property tax: a reformulation', NBER Working Paper no. 1481.

Mieszkowski, P.M. and G.R. Zodrow (1984b) 'The incidence of the local property tax: a re-evaluation', NBER Working Paper no. 1485.

Mills, D.E. (1981) 'The non-neutrality of land taxation', *National Tax Journal*, 34:125–130.

Mills, E.S. and W.E. Oates, eds. (1975) *Fiscal zoning and land use controls*. Lexington: Lexington Books.

Mills, E.S. (1979) 'Economic analysis of urban land-use controls', in: P. Mieszkowski and M. Straszheim, eds., *Current issues in urban economics*. Baltimore: Johns Hopkins University Press. 511–541.

Mintz, J. and H. Tulkens (1984) 'Commodity tax competition between member states of a federation: equilibrium and efficiency', CORE Discussion Paper no. 8427.

Mirrlees, J.A. (1972) 'The optimum town', *Swedish Journal of Economics*, 74:114–135.

Negishi, T. (1972) 'Public expenditure determined by boting with one's feet and fiscal profitability', *Swedish Journal of Economics*, 74:452–458.

Oates, W.E. (1969) 'The effects of property taxes and local public spending on property values: an empirical study of tax capitalization and the Tiebout hypothesis', *Journal of Political Economy*, 77:957–971.

Oates, W.E. (1972) *Fiscal federalism*. New York: Harcourt Brace Jovanovich.

Oates, W.E. (1986) 'On the measurement of congestion in the provision of local public goods', Sloan W.P. University of Maryland 23–85.

Pauly, M.V. (1976) 'A model of local government expenditure and tax capitalization', *Journal of Public Economics*, 6:231–242.

Pestieau, P. (1984) 'Fiscal mobility and local public goods: a survey of the theoretical and empirical studies of the Tiebout model', in: J.F. Thisse and H.G. Zoller, eds., *Locational analysis of public facilities*. Amsterdam: North-Holland, 11–41.

Pines, D. (1984) 'On the capitalization of land improvement projects', *Economics Letters*, 15:377–384.

Pines, D. (forthcoming) 'Profit maximizing developers and the optimal provision of local public goods in a closed system of a few cities', *La Revue Economique*.

Plott, C.R. (1967) 'Equilibrium and majority rule', *American Economic Review*, 57:787–806.

Romer, T. and H. Rosenthal (1978) 'Political resource allocation, controlled agendas, and the status quo', *Public Choice*, 33:27–43.

Romer, T. and H. Rosenthal (1979a) 'The elusive median voter', *Journal of Public Economics*, 12:143–170.

Romer, T. and H. Rosenthal (1979b) 'Bureaucrats vs Voters: on the political economy of resource allocation by direct democracy', *Quarterly Journal of Economics*, 93:563–588.

Rubinfeld, D.L. (forthcoming) 'The economics of the local public sector', in: Auerbach and M. Feldstein, eds., *Handbook of public economics*.

Samuelson, P.A. (1954) 'The pure theory of public expenditure', *Review of Economics and Statistics*, 36:387–389.

Samuelson, P.A. (1955) 'Diagrammatic exposition of a theory of public expenditure', *Review of Economics and Statistics*, 37:350–356.

Schweizer, U. (1983a) 'Edgeworth and the Henry George theorem: how to finance local public projects', in: J.F. Thisse and H.G. Zoller, eds., *Locational analysis of public facilities*. Amsterdam: North-Holland, 79–93.

Schweizer, U. (1983b) 'Efficient exchange with a variable number of consumers', *Econometrica*, 51:575–584.

Schweizer, U. (1985) 'Theory of city system structure', *Regional Science and Urban Economics*, 15:159–180.

Sonstelie, J.C. (1979) 'The incidence of a classified property tax', *Journal of Public Economics*, 12:75–86.

Sonstelie, C. and P.R. Portney (1978) 'Profit maximizing communities and the theory of local public expenditure', *Journal of Urban Economics*, 5:263–277.

Sonstelie, J.C. and P.R. Portney (1980a) 'Gross rents and market values: testing the implications of

Tiebout's hypothesis', *Journal of Urban Economics*, 7:102–118.

Sonstelie, J.C. and P.R. Portney (1980b) 'Take the money and run: a theory of voting in local referenda', *Journal of Urban Economics*, 8:187–195.

Starrett, D.A. (1980) 'On the method of taxation and the provision of local public goods', *American Economic Review*, 70:380–392.

Starrett, D.A. (1981) 'Land value capitalization in local public finance', *Journal of Political Economy*, 89:306–327.

Stiglitz, J.E. (1974) 'The demand for education in public and private school systems', *Journal of Public Economics*, 3:349–385.

Stiglitz, J.E. (1977) 'The theory of local public goods', in: M. Feldstein and R.P. Inman, eds., *The economies of public services*. London: Macmillan. 274–333.

Stiglitz, J.E. (1982) 'Utilitarianism and horizontal equity: the case for random taxation', *Journal of Public Economics*, 18:1–34.

Stiglitz, J.E. (1983a) 'Public goods in open economies with heterogeneous individuals', in: J.F. Thisse and H.G. Zoller, eds., *Locational analysis of public facilities*. Amsterdam: North-Holland. 55–78.

Stiglitz, J.E. (1983b) 'The theory of local public goods twenty-five years after Tiebout: a perspective', in: G.R. Zodrow, ed., *Local provisions of public services: the Tiebout model after twenty-five years*. New York: Academic Press. 17–54.

Sullivan, A.M. (1984) 'The general equilibrium effects of the Industrial property tax: incidence and excess burden', *Regional Science and Urban Economics*, 14:547–564.

Thirsk, W.R. (1982) 'Political sensitivity vs economic sensibility: a tale of two property taxes', in: W. Thirsk and J. Whalley, eds., *Tax policy options in the 1980s*. Canadian Tax Foundation. 348–401.

Thisse, J.F. and H.G. Zoller eds. (1984) *Locational analysis of public facilities*. Amsterdam: North-Holland.

Tiebout, C.M. (1956) 'A pure theory of local expenditures', *Journal of Political Economy*, 64:416–424.

Vickrey, W. (1970) 'Defining land value for tax purposes', in: D.M. Holland, ed., *The assessment of land value*. Madison: University of Wisconsin Press. 25–36.

Westhoff, F. (1977) 'Existence of equilibria in economies with a local public good', *Journal of Economic Theory*, 14:84–112.

Westhoff, F. (1979) 'Policy inferences from community choice models: a caution', *Journal of Urban Economics*, 6:535–549.

Wildasin, D.E. (1977) 'Public expenditures determined by voting with one's feet and public choice', *Scandinavian Journals of Economics*, 79:889–898.

Wildasin, D.E. (1979) 'Local public goods, property values, and local public choice', *Journal of Urban Economics*, 6:521–534.

Wildasin, D.E. (1980) 'Locational efficiency in a federal system', *Regional Science and Urban Economics*, 10:453–471.

Wildasin, D.E. (1982) 'More on the neutrality of land taxation', *National Tax Journal*, 35:105–115.

Wildasin, D.E. (1983) 'The Welfare effects of intergovernmental grants in an economy with independent jurisdictions', *Journal of Urban Economics*, 13:147–164.

Wildasin, D.E. (1984a) 'Tiebout-Lindahl equilibrium', unpublished.

Wildasin, D.E. (1984b) 'Tax exporting and the marginal cost of public expenditure', unpublished.

Wildasin, D.E. (1986a) *Urban public finance*. New York: Harwood Academic Publishers.

Wildasin, D.E. (1986b) 'Spatial variation of the marginal utility of income and unequal treatment of equals', *Journal of Urban Economics*, 19:125–129.

Wildasin, D.E. (forthcoming) 'Interjurisdictional capital mobility: fiscal externality and a corrective subsidy', *Journal of Urban Economics*.

Wildasin, D. and J. Wilson (in preparation), 'Imperfect labor mobility in models of local government behavior'.

Wilson, J.D. (1984) 'The excise tax effects of the property tax', *Journal of Public Economics*, 24:309–330.

Wilson, J.D. (1985a) 'Optimal property taxation in the presence of inter-regional capital mobility', *Journal of Urban Economics*, 18:73:89.

Wilson, J.D. (1985b) 'Property tax competition in the presence of inter-regional trade and capital mobility', unpublished.

Wilson, J.D. (1986) 'A theory of inter-regional tax competition', *Journal of Urban Economics*, 19:296–315.

Yinger, J. (1982) 'Capitalization and the theory of local public finance', *Journal of Political Economy*, 90:917–943.

Zimmerman, D. (1983) 'Resource misallocation from interstate tax exportation: estimates of excess spending and welfare loss in a median voter framework', *National Tax Journal*, 36:183–202.

Zodrow, G.R. and P. Mieszkowski (1983) 'The incidence of the property tax: the benefit view vs the new view', in: G.R. Zodrow, ed., *Local provision of public services: the Tiebout model after twenty-five years*. New York: Academic Press. 109–130.

Zodrow, G.R. ed. (1984) *Local provision of public services: the Tiebout model after twenty-five years*. New York: Academic Press.

Zodrow, G.R. and P. Mieszkowski (1986) 'Pigou, property taxation and the under-provision of local public goods', *Journal of Urban Economics*, 19:356–370.

Chapter 30

FINANCING URBAN PUBLIC SERVICES

RÉMY PRUD'HOMME

University of Paris XII

1. Introduction

Local, intermediate and national governments can, should, and do intervene in urban areas in three different manners. First, they impose constraints on households and enterprises, by telling them what not to do and, to a lesser extent, what to do: most land use laws and many environmental regulations are examples of this mode of intervention. Second, by means of taxes and subsidies, governments modify relative prices and consequently the behaviour of households and enterprises. Finally, governments intervene in urban areas by providing goods and services that would not, or not adequately, be provided by private markets. Such goods and services are often referred to as urban public services.

All urban public services are produced and delivered at a cost. This cost must be met. To put it otherwise, urban public services must be financed. This can be done in a number of ways that this chapter will attempt to explore and compare.

The issue is complicated, however, by the fact that urban public services are delivered by different entities: local, regional, central governments, but also ad hoc authorities (such as water boards, or school districts), semi-public bodies (such as sociétés d'économie mixte in France) and private enterprises strictly – or not so strictly – controlled by governments (such as utilities). The choice of who should be responsible for a particular service and of how the service should be financed are interrelated.

What is at stake in the choice of a financing system for one or several urban public services? Three dimensions, or implications, have to be taken into account.

The first, and most obvious, is financial: funds must be raised to meet the costs of the service that is provided. The choice of a particular type of tax, or of a user charge, has to be made in view of the elasticity of the revenue source relative to costs or to income. All other things equal, financing modes that will support the service in the long run will be preferred.

A second implication of a financing system is redistributive. The costs of urban public services must eventually be borne by someone: by the user, or by the taxpayer, by people from the urban area or by people from the whole country, by

Handbook of Regional and Urban Economics, Volume II, Edited by E.S. Mills
© *1987, Elsevier Science Publishers B.V.*

people who benefit from the service or by people who don't, by the present
generation or by future generations, etc. The financing systems utilized translate
costs into burdens. Of particular importance is the question of wether the costs
borne by each individual (or family) are proportional, progressive, or regressive
relative to the income of the individual (or family).

A third implication is allocative. Every financing system influences the allocation of resources. The very existence of a user charge will tend to decrease and
to limit the demand for the service charged. The structure of the charge system
will also influence the demand for the service charged: thus, for instance, peak
pricing for transportation, water, or electricity (i.e. higher pricing at peak hours)
will tend to even out demand over time, and by way of consequence the structure
of supply over time. Financing systems which offer the service free of charge, and
rely upon taxes, will also affect resource allocation, because taxes are rarely, if
ever, neutral from that point of view; thus, for instance, a system that relies on
property taxes will tend to hamper improvements in the quality of housing
(which would lead to tax increases).

What makes it difficult to select a "good" financing system is that it expected to
be good on these three grounds. One would like it to to yield enough money, to
redistribute income from rich to poor, and to induce substitutions and behaviours that will reduce costs and save resources. More often than not,
unfortunately, those objectives are contradictory.

The general tendency is to sacrifice resource allocation (which is the implication that is most difficult to visualize) to income redistribution, and income
redistribution (which is not always easy to analyze either) to financial need. There
is no reason why it should be so. As a matter of fact, the order of importance
should be just the opposite. Resource allocation considerations are essential
because they determine the available output of society. Income distribution
implications are also of prime importance; but it is not sure that pricing devices
offer the best way to redistribute income. Purely financial implications are of
course important; but they are hardly an objective in themselves. In practice,
what matters is to realize that any financing mechanism has implications in those
three areas, and that trade-offs and compromises must be made.

It is with this in mind that the various modes of financing must be examined.
Section 2 will present an overview of existing methods. The following sections will
discuss the role of user charges (Section 3), of taxes (Section 4), of grants (Section
5), and of loans (Section 6). A final section will attempt to conclude.

2. Overview

The various entities providing urban public services have five main sources of
income: (i) user charges, (ii) local government taxes, (iii) central government taxes,
(iv) loans, and (v) property and entrepreneurial income. It is not easy to assess
their present relative importance.

A mere description of the patterns of financing of public services in a given city or urban area would require a complete identification of the various entities responsible for each service, an analysis of the relationships (such as grants and subsidies) between those entities, and a study of how each entity finances its net expenditures. Only then would it be possible to find out what share of the cost is borne by local users, by local taxpayers, by national taxpayers, by future taxpayers, etc. Figure 1 offers a simplified graphic presentation of the money flows involved.

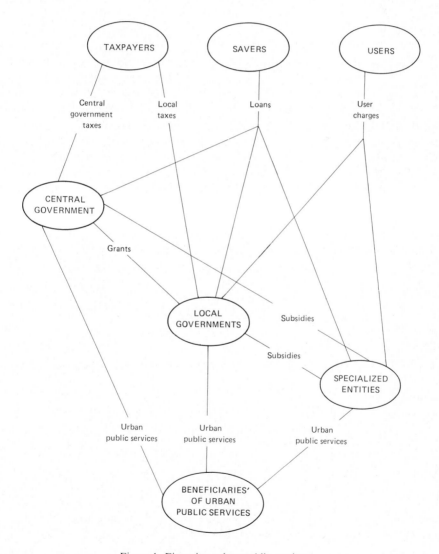

Figure 1. Financing urban public services.

When one wants to go from the descriptive stage to the normative stage, similar distinctions are equally useful and important. Clearly, the modes of financing most appropriate for a local government might well be completely irrelevant for a regulated utility.

Most available data relate to the way in which local governments finance their expenditures on urban public services, and in many cases discussions of the financing of urban public services tend to become discussions of the financing of local governments. It is true that, in many countries, local governments are responsible for the bulk of urban public services. But there are great differences between countries in this area: education, for instance, probably the costliest urban public service, which is provided by local governments in the U.S.A., is provided by the central government in France. Table 1 indicates the importance of local governments expenditures relative to total government expenditures, and to GNP, for a few developed countries. It shows large differences between countries, that cannot be fully explained by differences in the levels of urban public services offered in these countries. The distinction between local governments and urban public services should therefore be emphasized. Confusing the two concepts is dangerous: it reduces the range of policy options and leaves aside many useful possibilities for improvements and modifications. "Goods and services provided by local governments" is a poor and misleading proxy for "urban public services", although it is a proxy one is often forced to use for lack of better data.

Table 1

Importance of local governments expenditures, selected countries, 1982

	Relative to total public expenditures (%)	Relative to GDP (%)
Canada		
Local level	17	10
Province level	25	14
Denmark (1981)	45	35
France	15	8
Germany		
Local level	17	9
Lander level	25	14
Italy (1975)	18	10
Spain (1981)	8	3
Sweden	38	30
United Kingdom	24	13
U.S.A.		
Local level	19	9
State level	21	10

Sources: IMF, *Government Finance Statistics Yearbook* for local governments expenditures, and OECD for GDP.

Table 2

Revenues of local governments by source, selected countries, 1982

	Taxes (%)	Subsidies (%)	Other (%)	Total (%)
Canada				
Local level	37.9	47.9	14.2	100
State level	68.3	18.7	13.0	100
Denmark	39.4	52.7	8.4	100
France	41.3	44.1	14.5	100
Germany				
Local level	32.7	29.5	37.7	100
State level	69.2	17.8	13.0	100
Italy (1975)	11.2	81.5	6.2	100
Spain (1981)	42.7	30.7	26.5	100
Sweden	55.8	24.1	20.1	100
United Kingdom	31.8	43.0	25.1	100
U.S.A.				
Local level	37.8	40.9	21.3	100
State level	55.6	22.3	22.1	100

Source: IMF, *Government Finance Statistics Yearbook.*

Available data shown in Table 2 suggest that local taxes are the most important source of financing. But it is important to note that transfers from central or regional governments are nearly as important; in several countries, such as the U.K., France, Denmark, and above all the Netherlands, they are by now more important than local taxes; and in addition, such transfers are in many countries increasing more rapidly than local taxation. Charges would seem to rank third in importance.

Table 2 depicts the revenue sources of local governments, not of all entities providing urban public services. If specialized entities such as public transportation corporations, water distribution agencies, electricity and telephone utilities, were included, the importance of user charges would certainly be increased. The reason is that these entities cannot finance urban public services by means of taxation; they might benefit from transfers and grants from central or regional governments, and from local governments (which confuses the picture, as noted above), but they have to rely primarily upon charges. Also, if the urban public services directly provided by central governments were also taken into account, the share of central government taxation would increase, greatly in some countries.

For most countries therefore, depending upon what services are included in the analysis, it is likely that user charges are the most important source of financing of urban public services. Central government taxation would probably come next, followed by local taxation. What seems clear, at any rate, is the relative unimportance of loans and local government property income. It is unfortunately impossible to put figures on these flows. It is a fortiori impossible to compare financing structures over space or over time. It is clear, however, that the traditional presentation, according to which urban public services are provided by local governments and financed by local taxes, is a misleading simplification.

The general pattern of financing urban public services seems to be the following. First, for those services that are easy to sell at a price, user charges are utilized. Other services are supplied by local governments and financed by local taxes. But local taxation cannot, in most countries, cope with the growth of expenditures on such services. Local governments then turn to borrowing. But the possibilities of borrowing are quickly exhausted. Local governments must therefore, be and are financed by transfers from other levels of government, and/or urban public services are directly provided by central or regional governments. These various modes will be examined in turn.

3. User charges

A user charge is a price paid in exchange for a service provided by a political entity, or by an enterprise controlled by a political entity. It is always service-specific. Households and enterprises are free not to pay the charge, in which case they do not consume the service. A public bus ticket is a good example of a user charge. By this definition, pollution charges are not user charges. They are taxes assessed upon the amount of pollution discharged. Polluters do not pay for a depollution service they would be free not to get. They pay for a diseconomy they inflict upon society, a diseconomy that will – or will not – be corrected by the political entity that collects the charge. It is true that polluters can avoid the tax by reducing their discharges; but the same is true of any tax: we can all avoid our income taxes by reducing our income.

A number of urban public services can be financed, in whole or in part, by user charges. This is the case of the services that are or can be consumed privately, such as water provision, electricity provision, telephone, public transportation, most cultural performances (theatre, concerts, operas, etc.), refuse collection, water disposal, most health and education services. Those who are not willing to pay can be excluded from the consumption of such services.

Not all urban services are of that nature. It is technically impossible to prevent someone from benefiting from street cleaning, or from pollution abatement, or from street lighting, or from the deterrent effect of police protection. Such services cannot be financed by means of user charges.

The border line between the two types of services, however, is not always easy to draw, and can be moved by technological innovations. Thus, for instance, it was for many years considered impossible to charge for private automobile circulation and parking; it is by now recognized that it is easy to charge parking fees, and that it is possible to charge circulation fees (by requiring owners of automobiles using certain streets to purchase special stickers allowing them to use these streets, or by means of electronic devices). Even fire protection could – technologically speaking – be sold: only those houses or factories for which a fee has been paid would be protected; as a matter of fact, such a system was used in the U.S.A. in the 19th century, and one can still see in some cities, such as Baltimore, the copper plates that were fixed on houses to indicate that the owners had subscribed to fire protection. All things considered, many, perhaps most, urban public services could be priced.

It does not mean that they are, or that they should be. Table 3 gives, for some countries and some services, figures on the percentage of user charges in relation to current expenditures, that illustrate the importance of user charges in selected countries. Charging seems quite common for a number of environmental services. It is, for example, widespread in the case of sewerage: charges, based on the amount of water consumed, and levied to cover at least operating expenditures, are common in many cities.

Table 3
Importance of user charge revenues for selected urban public services, selected countries, mid-seventies

	U.K.	U.S.A.	Denmark	New Zealand	Belgium	Ireland	South Australia
Water supply	84			9		43	
Sewerage			144	17	7	25	84
Refuse	7		86		40	4	8
Swimming pools	26					32	
Libraries	6			16			
Parks	8						
Sports and recreation	15	16	16	43		13	
Cemetries	35				89		

Source: OECD.

The fact that, for a given service, the reliance on charges varies greatly from country to country suggests that political reasons, not technical constraints, account for the relative importance of user charges. In other words, it would be technically feasible to rely much more on charges. But would it be advisable? To answer this question, one must examine charges from the three viewpoints mentioned in the introduction.

(1) From an allocation of resources viewpoint, charges are often quite good. This is somewhat paradoxical. In principle, a good or service should be provided by a public entity only when it cannot be provided by the market: when it is a public good, when there are externalities associated with it, when it is a natural

monolopy, or when its production function is such that marginal costs are constantly lower than average costs. And in all these cases, financing by prices is either impossible or inappropriate. In practice, however, many urban public services do not fall into these categories and can be financed by user charges. For other urban public services, the fact that they should not be entirely and solely financed by user charges does not mean that they should not be partly financed in this fashion. It is therefore legitimate to examine how resource allocation could be improved by the used of charges.

User charges provide the entity entrusted with the supply of the service with interesting information on the demand for this service. The usefulness of the service for the public is at least equal to the amount of money paid for it by the public. If the marginal cost of production of the service is below the price that is charged, there is a clear indication that more should be provided, and that the additional resources devoted to this additional production will not be wasted – a certainty that can never be reached in the case of a service offered free of charge.

In addition, there are cases in which services provided at a price will induce cost-saving behaviours. Faced with the alternative of paying and consuming a given service, or not paying it and not consuming it, households and enterprises will look for substitutes that are cheaper for them – and, in general, for society as a whole. Water disposal provides an example of such resource-saving behaviours; let us take the case of an individual house or of a factory located quite far from the sewer system; if the owner is charged the cost of extending the sewer up to his house or factory, he may well find that some individual solution (such as a sceptic tank, that we shall assume to be as efficient as the sewer system) is cheaper, and select it; in this case, the charge will ensure that a given level of service is achieved at a lower resource cost.

Finally, for those services which are subject to congestion – and there are many such services in urban areas – charges will improve the utility derived from their consumption. The most obvious and familiar example here is street parking. Parking fees induce behaviours and substitutions that are beneficial for society. Similarly, peak pricing in public transportation induces or rather would induce, because it hardly exists, desirable changes in transportation choices: those who can travel off peak hours would be inclinded to do so, those who cannot would exert a pressure on their employers to have their working hours changed and/or select their home and work place in order to minimize peak hour travel.

(2) From a financial viewpoint, charges also have clear merits. They are the shortest way from the consumer of the service to the producer of the service; the consumer sees what he pays for, and the producer is induced to decrease cost. User charges are a strong incentive to efficiency.

(3) From a redistribution of income view point, charges are often said to fare less well. They cannot be used to redistribute income from rich to poor. But they do not redistribute income from poor to rich either, and this cannot be said of all services delivered free of charge [Le Grand (1982)].

These services are in effect financed by the local or central tax systems, which is not always very progressive; and they are consumed by whoever wants to consume them, or whoever can consume them. There are cases where the quantity of service consumed is in practice a function of income. This may happen because the consumption of the service required time, or education, or other expenditures that are only available to the rich, as in the case of arts museum or of marinas. It may happen because the supply of the service is unequally distributed over space and therefore over households. The example of water in the cities of some developing countries is particularly striking in this respect; water is often highly subsidized, for "social" reasons; as a result, the entities supplying water are poor and cannot provide water in every part of the city; they tend to provide it in the richest parts of the city; the poor end up buying the water they need on the private market at prices many times higher than the price paid by the rich for the water they use to water their lawns. In all such cases, gratuitousness or subsidies means regressiveness.

This shows that the distinction often made between free public services that are said to be progressive, and priced public services that are said to be regressive, is rather misleading.

Priced public services, however, can be priced in many different manners. In practice, the merits and demerits of a user charge as a means of financing a given urban public service depend very much upon the structure of the charge. Four families of prices can be considered.

(1) Average cost pricing has the advantages of simplicity and of budget balancing. But it does not always induce efficiency. And it does not contribute to income redistribution.

(2) Marginal cost pricing is prefered by economists, because it improves the allocation of resources. But it has a number of drawbacks. It is difficult to sell to politicians and to the general public: the idea that bus fares should be higher at peak hours, or even higher for longer trips, for instance, are not easily accepted; this is partly because there are genuine distributional difficulties involved, and partly because many decision makers tend to underestimate or to ignore the impacts of prices upon supply and demand.

A second difficulty, in practice, is that there are hundreds of marginal costs for certain services. The marginal cost of many urban public services is time and space specific (unlike the cost of most ordinary goods). The cost of supplying one unit of electricity, for instance, varies with the hour of the day, the month of the year, the location of the consumer, and the quantities he gets; and there are two units to consider: the maximum power the consumer has subscribed to (measured in kW), and the electricity he actually consumes (measured in kWh). The same can be said of the marginal cost of supplying a kilometer of bus trip or a liter of water. And the differences between these various costs are not minor differences that could easily be ignored; they can be enormous. One could argue that these differences have to be reflected by differences in prices. This is perfectly correct.

Prices that vary with time and space must be encouraged, if the allocative efficiency of prices is to be achieved. But there are limits to the complexity of a charge system. Too complex a system would be difficult and costly to administer (although the progress of electronics is lowering such costs rapidly). Too complex a system would be of no avail; the message embodied in charge diffentials would be blurred, and not understood by the users.

Thirdly, when marginal costs are constantly below average costs, marginal cost pricing means operating at a deficit. There are several solutions to this problem. In some cases, a distinction can and must be drawn between short-term marginal costs (that are below average costs), and long term marginal costs (that aren't); it is then advisable to charge according to long-term, also called "development", marginal costs. In other cases, a combination of user charges at marginal costs and of a deficit financed by taxes will be an excellent way of financing an urban public service. The real issue then would be: how will the subsidy be figured out, so as not to reduce the incentive of the entity that produces the service to cut production costs. In yet other cases, charges proportional to marginal costs, but sufficiently high to wipe out the deficit, will be preferred.

(3) Binomial charges are a third family of charges. The user pays a fixed sum, just to have the right to use the service, plus a variable sum, which is a function of the quantity he consumes. This is common in the case of electricity and of telephone; it is also used to a lesser extent in the cases of water and of steam. It could be utilized in many other cases.

Binomial charges have many advantages. They can reconcile marginal cost pricing (which can be applied to the variable charge) and total cost recovery. They reflect the nature of the "service" provided by a number of urban public services: the possibility to use it on the one hand, the actual use we make of it on the other hand. The potential use may be as important as the actual use. A public transportation system, for instance, is valuable for people who always use their own automobiles. Not only because in many large cities they could hardly use their automobiles if other people were not using public transportation – a well known case of externality, which is made clear by public transportation strikes. But more significantly perhaps, because automobile users know that they might one day need to use the public transportation system. The very existence of this system is like an insurance. There is no reason why this insurance should be provided free of charge. The lump sum of a binomial charge can be seen as an insurance premium. The same is true of hospital facilities for those whose health is good, or of electric heating for those who sun-heat their homes.

(4) Discriminatory charges, i.e. charges that vary with the user, can also be utilized. They are common in the case of water. Water sold for industrial usage is in some cities not sold at the same price as water sold for domestic usage. In some places, water sold in small quantities (supposed to be for the poor) is charged less than water sold in large quantities (presumed to be bought by the

rich); the price schedule is progressive. There are two justifications for discriminatory charges. One is economic, or rather, financial: if the price elasticities of the demand of different users are different, then different prices will yield more revenues for an entity in a monopoly position. This is a rather weak justification. Maximizing revenues is not or should not be the goal of an entity that provides an urban public service. Monopolies are never perfect and those who are overcharged will find alternatives that may turn out to be more costly to society.

The other reason behind discriminatory charges is redistributional. Discriminatory charges always imply income transfers. Such transfers might be desirable. Cross-subsidization of that sort is usually more effective than general subisidies; a subsidy to a good or to a service benefits users in proportion to their consumption of the good or service; if and when the rich consume more than the poor, they are subsidized more than the poor; the reverse is true with discriminatory charges properly designed. A careful analysis of the transfers embodied in the discriminatory scheme, however, is needed. Higher water prices for enterprises (relative to households) for instance, is probably regressive; the cost of water is passed into the prices of the products manufactured with water, and borne by the purchasers of these products – who may well be the poor.

User charges, therefore, are not a panacea for the financing of urban public services. They cannot be utilized for all services. When they can, the actual design of the charge is delicate. But user charges have many attractive features, and can be recommended as a "good" mode of financing. This is increasingly being recognized in practice, and their role in the financing of urban public services has been – and will continue to be – increasing.

4. Local taxes

Many urban public services are provided by local governments which get a large share (a big third, in many countries) of their income by means of taxation. The structure of local tax systems varies greatly from country to country, as indicated in Table 4. Anglo-Saxon countries rely primarily on property taxes, or more precisely on taxes assessed on the value of land and buildings: such taxes account for 100% of local taxes in the U.K. and in Ireland, for very high figures in Australia and in Canada, and for about three-fourths in the U.S.A. Scandinavian countries prefer taxes on income and profits, which are also important in Belgium. Many countries, including at the State level the U.S.A., Canada and Australia, impose taxes on consumption that are either general (on the sale of all items, with some exceptions) or specific (on the sale of designated goods or services). The basic problem is that those three types of taxes all have serious deficiencies.

Table 4
Structure of state and local governments tax receipts, selected OECD countries, 1981

	Taxes on income or profit (%)	Property taxes (%)	Taxes on consumption or use (%)	Other (%)
Belgium	59	—	19	21
Canada				
State	—	27	39	35(a)
Local	—	96	4	—
Denmark	89	10	—	1
France	18	29	6	47(c)
Germany				
State	47(b)	5	33	—
Local	79(b)	15	1	5
Italy	35	1	15	49
Japan	28	22	19	31
Netherlands	—	67	23	10
Spain	42	11	27	19
U.K.	—	100	—	—
U.S.A.				
State	37	4	59	—
Local	6	76	18	—

Source: OECD, Revenue Statistics of OECD Countries, 1965–1982
Notes: (a) Payroll tax; (b) State and local share of a national income tax; (c) Taxe professionelle or patente: it is a tax paid by enterprises and based partly on property and partly on payroll.

(1) Property taxes, as local taxes, raise three main issues: an issue of yield, an issue of equity, and an issue of impact.

Property taxes are said to lack buoyancy. This is not because the tax base does not increase as fast as national income: as a matter of fact, it does, and the urban land component of the tax base, which incorporates a growing rent element, normally increases faster than income. This is because assessed values tend to lag behind market values. Revisions of tax assessments are costly and cumbersome. They are rarely if ever undertaken every year, but only every 4–10 years. Instead, some crude index of the increase in market values is used to update the tax base yearly. But in order to be politically acceptable this index usually reflects the smallest increases in property values, thereby undervaluing many if not most properties.

This theory is not entirely borne out be the figures given in Table 5. They show that during the seventies, at least in the developed countries, local property taxes maintained their yields relative to GNP. In many cases, a relative decline in assessed values was compensated by an increase in tax rates. What is true, however, is that the yield of property taxes, during that decade, did not increase as fast as the yield of other tax revenues, that increased faster than GNP. As a

Table 5
Property taxes in selected countries, yields, 1970–79

	Property taxes/GNP (in %)		Property taxes/ Total tax revenues (in %)	
	1970	1979	1970	1979
Australia (a)	1.21	1.19	5.06	3.99
Denmark	1.28	1.24	3.18	2.82
France (b)	0.94	1.14	2.66	2.75
Germany (c)	0.36	0.37	1.08	1.45
Ireland	3.16	1.16	10.13	3.47
Spain (d)	0.24	0.13	1.40	0.53
U.K.	3.22	3.30	8.59	9.51
U.S.A.	3.66	3.60	11.99	9.29

Source: OECD (1983) Tables A1 and A2, pp. 208–209
Notes: (a) Local property tax; (b) Foncier bâti plus foncier non bâti (land taxes), plus taxe d'habitation (residence tax); (c) Grundsteuer (land tax); (d) Urban land tax.

result, the share of property taxes relative to total tax revenues (of all levels of governments) declined in many countries.

Property taxes also raise issues of equity. For many years, particularly in the U.S.A. and in the U.K., property taxes were seen as regressive. Taxes on industrial or commercial buildings, it was argued, are shifted to the consumers of industrial products or to the purchasers of goods; they are in effect consumption taxes, and as such are regressive, since the poor consume a larger amount of their income than the rich. Taxes on houses which are owner occupied are borne by the owners; the share of income devoted to housing is a declining function of income (the income elasticity of the demand for housing is below 1); therefore the share of income paid in taxes diminishes when income increases – which is the very definition of regressiveness. Furthermore, in some countries, such as the U.S.A., local property taxes are deductible from the income suject to income tax; in other words, they are partly borne by the federal government; but the share of the tax that is thus borne by the federal government increases with income (it is equal to the marginal tax rate), which decreases the burden of the property tax borne by the rich, and adds to the regressiveness of the tax. Taxes on rented houses are passed on to the tenants in the form of higher rents, and also tend to be regressive for that reason. Table 6 provides support for this view.

This traditional view (that remains the dominant view in political circles in most countries) has been criticized in recent years. First, it has been noted that, in many countries, such as the U.K. or France, low income families get tax deductions and tax rebates, that significantly reduce the amount of property tax they pay. The Layfield Committee made a distinction between the "gross" rates, as property taxes are called in the U.K., that are regressive, and the "net" (of tax

Table 6

Burden of various taxes for a hypothetical family of four, for various family income groups, U.S.A., 1972.

	Federal personal income tax	Social security taxes	Local property taxes	Local personal income tax	General sales taxes	Taxes
⁻5,000	3.0	5.2	4.6	0.5	1.8	15.1
7,500	6.2	5.2	3.6	1.1	1.6	17.1
10,000	8.4	4.7	3.5	1.1	1.4	17.1
20,000	13.3	2.3	3.1	2.3	1.1	22.2
25,000	15.1	1.9	2.9	2.7	0.9	23.5
50,000	23.2	0.9	2.5	3.7	0.7	31.0

Source: Advisory Commission on Intergovernmental Relations, *Federal State-Local Finances: Significant Features of Fiscal Federalism*, Washington Government Printing Office, 1974, table 38, p. 53.

rebates) rates that showed rates to be progressive in the bottom of the income distribution, proportional in the middle, and regressive in the higher half of the income distribution.

Then, there is a land element in the tax base. Land is in fixed supply and its price is determined by the demand curve for land. The property tax on land cannot be shifted forward in higher land prices. It is borne by the owners of land, not be the users of land. As a matter of fact, it is capitalized at the time of the introduction of the tax, or when tax rates are increased, in the form of lower land prices. But since land is predominantly owned by high income groups, the burden of the tax on the land component of the property tax is predominantly borne by high income groups. This tends to make the tax progressive rather than regressive.

This line of thought has been extended to the non-land elements of the tax base. Buildings as well as land are but one form of capital. If and when some forms of capital are more taxed than other, then capital owners will move their capital from highly taxed forms to other, thereby equalizing the after tax returns on all forms of capital. This general equilibrium analysis suggests that the burden of the property tax is borne by owners of capital in general. Since capital, just as land, is disproportionately owned by high income groups, these groups bear the burden of the property tax, which is finally more progressive than regressive.

This is illustrated by the figures of Table 7, prepared for the U.S.A. by Pechman and Okner (1974). It contrasts the incidence of the property tax according to two "views". The traditional view assumes that the share of the tax based on land is borne by land owners and that the share of the tax on buildings is borne as a function of housing consumption expenditures. The new view assumes that the tax is borne by all capital owners. These different assumptions lead to different conclusions. According to the traditional view, the property tax

Table 7
Property tax in relation to income, U.S.A., 1966

Family income (a) (in 1000$)	Tax income traditional view (%)	Tax income new view (%)
0–3	6.5	2.5
3–5	4.8	2.7
5–10	3.6	2.0
10–15	3.2	1.7
15–20	3.2	2.0
20–25	3.1	2.6
25–30	3.1	3.7
30–50	3.0	4.5
50–100	2.8	6.2
100–500	2.4	8.2
500–1000	1.7	9.6
Over 1000	0.8	10.1
Average	3.0	3.4

Source: Pechman and Okner (1974, p. 59).
Note: (a) Includes salaries, property income, transfers, capital gains, and imputed income for owner-occupied houses.

is definitely regressive; according to the new view, it is regressive over the four first income groups, and progressive thereafter.

A third issue raised by property taxes is their impact upon spatial segregation. Property taxes exacerbate intergovernmental disparities. The higher the average income in a local government area, the higher the tax base at the disposal of this local government. For a given tax rate, high income areas will have much higher tax revenues than low income areas. It is precisely those areas that are in the greatest need of tax revenues that will have the least. They will react by raising their tax rates. But this will induce the few rich that remained in the area, as well as activities, to move away. This will in turn reduce the tax base, and might lead to a further increase in tax rates. These communities are caught in a vicious circle. Far from reducing differences between communities, property taxation increases them; it leads to spatial segregation.

(2) Personal or corporate income taxes are not much better than property taxes. It is true that they are, or can be made to be, responsive to income: they are a good source of revenue from a financial viewpoint. It is also true that they are usually progressive, as shown in Table 6 for the U.S.A. But they exacerbate intergovernmental disparities just as property taxes do.

They place local government in front of an impossible dilemma: either they impose low tax rates, and the rich leave because they find the level of public services too low, or else they impose high tax rates, and the rich leave also because they find their tax burden too heavy. Local income taxes, at least in the case of fragmented urban areas, are therefore also segregationist.

In addition, local income taxes raise a problem of relationship with national income taxes, which are usually a major (often the major) element of national tax systems. If there is no relationship, i.e. if local governments can and do fix the rates of local income taxes as they please, then the freedom of national governments to ulitize income taxation as a policy tool for anticyclical or structural purposes will be limited. But if there is a relationship, it is the freedom of local governments that will be limited. One should note, in this respect, that shared income taxes like the German income tax are not really local taxes, contrary to what is suggested by the figures published by international organizations and quoted in Table 4. When local governments control neither the base nor the rate of a tax, that tax is not a local tax. It is a national tax raised by the central government, coupled with a subsidy granted by the central government to the local governments.

(3) Sales tax (always at the local level) can also be criticized. First, they are usually regressive; Table 6 certainly supports this view. Then, they discriminate between local governments: some areas, where many sales take place, will get much more revenues than other areas, where the needs may be as great or greater. Finally, they are usually difficult to assess and collect.

Some mechanism limiting local governments' expenditures is necessary. Is local taxation such a mechanism? In theory, it makes it possible for a local government to increase expenditures provided it increases tax burdens. And one can think of a Tiebout world in which there are local governments with high expenditures and high tax rates, as opposed to local governments with low expenditures and low tax rates.

Unfortunately, the conclusion that seems to emerge from the analysis of the various types of taxes is that there are no good local taxes. The main reason for this is that all tax bases are mobile between local governments. The costs of moving properties or incomes (which are the costs of changing the location of one's home, or the location of one's workplace if income is taxed where it is earned) or sales (which are the costs of changing the location of one's shopping places) are real. But they are not very high, and might become lower than differences in tax burdens between various local governments. This induces moves from high-rate to low-rate local governments, and frustrates any attempts at raising tax revenues. It is therefore doubtful that local taxation be an appropriate mechanism to limit and control local governments expenditures.

This is borne out by the experience of most countries. First, none of the many and diverse local tax systems that exist seems really satisfactory. "Local tax reform" has been on the agenda in many, if not most, countries. Countries relying upon property taxes are wondering whether they should not introduce income taxes; in the U.K., for instance, a number of Royal Commissions have been looking for "alternatives to the Rates". Countries relying upon income taxes are considering the merits of property taxation. The French taxe professionelle, which is a mixture of a tax on wages and on industrial and commercial property is constantly being modified. The only good local tax is the one that is in force elsewhere: the grass always looks greener in the neighbour's meadows.

Then, none of these tax systems is sufficient to provide the revenues needed by local governments. Local taxation only accounts for a minority – and declining – share of the income of local governments, and for an even smaller share of the money needed to finance urban public services.

5. Grants and subsidies

The development of grants and subsidies from central governments to local governments as a means of financing urban public services has occured in many countries over the last decades. This development was particularly striking in the U.S.A., in France, in the U.K. As shown in Table 2, grants now account for more than 40% of local governments' revenues in a number of countries, such as Denmark, France, the Netherlands, the U.K., and Japan. The figures given underestimate the importance of grants in some countries, such as Germany and Austria, where "shared taxes" are counted as local taxes, but should rather be seen as grants. In those countries, local (and also regiona) governments share with the Federal government the proceeds of various taxes, such as the personal income tax. As mentioned above this can be analyzed as money raised by the Federal government, and distributed to local (and regional) governments – which is the definition of a grant – according to a particular formula.

It could also be noted that the role played by regional governments often confuses the picture. In many countries, particularly but not exclusively in federal countries, regional governments act as intermediaries between central (or federal) governments and local governments, with transfer payments going from central to regional and to local as well as from regional to local governments. But the general trend is quite clear, and is for a growing importance of grants in local, and to a lesser extend regional, governments' resources.

This trend is easy to explain. Most of the criticisms addressed to local taxation do not apply to national or (to a lesser extent) to regional taxation. It is relatively easy to design "good" national tax systems, that is systems that are reasonably progressive, income-elastic, and nearly neutral vis-à-vis resource allocation. As a matter of fact, it has proved possible over the last two decades, in most countries, to significantly raise central government tax revenues without dramatic economic or political difficulties. In short, the money that is needed at the local level can more easily be raised at the central than at the local level. This is why, in most countries, this money has increasingly been raised by central governments and distributed as grants to local governments.

There are two types of grants: (i) block grants, or unconditional grants (also

called general grants), which are given to local governments with no strings
attached and can therefore be allocated by local authorities to whichever urban
public service they choose, and (ii) specific, or conditional grants, which are given
to local governments for the provisions of specific urban public services selected
by central governments.

Matching grants, which are subsidies given to local governments in proportion
to their expenditures, can be a form of block grants when they are given in
proportion to total expenditures, but they are more often a form of specific
grants, because they are usually given in proportion to expenditures for specific
purposes.

Specific grants can be more or less specific. They can be granted for a given
project (a school of a certain type) or for a given sector (education). In the former
case, the strings are very tight, and the local community has a choice of taking the
project as the central government wants it, or of not taking it. In the latter case,
the strings are looser, and the local authority retains some discretion in the use of
the subsidy it gets.

The differential impact of general and specific grants is shown on Figures 2a
and 2b, which represent a local government equipped with a family of indifference
curves between goods, good i and good j, which can be seen as all other goods,
and faced with a budget constraint AB. In the absence of any grant, the local
government will locate in M, and consume, or rather produce, a quantity $I1$ of
good i, and a quantity $J1$ of good j. What is the impact of a block grant? It moves
the budget constraint from AB to CD. Our local government locates in N, and
consumes $I2$ good i and $J2$ good j. It increases its consumption of both good i
and j. It also increases its satisfaction, since we are now on indifference curve $L2$
instead of indifference curve $L1$. Now, what is the impact of a specific grant
designed to favour the consumption of good i? This grant will lower the price
(cost of production) of good i, and therefore move the budget constraint from AB
to AD'. The local government will then locate in N', and consume a quantity $I1'$
of good i. The specific grant will increase the production of i, which was its
purpose. It will also increase the satisfaction derived by the local government
from its new choice. But the impact of the grant upon the production of other
goods cannot be predicted straightforwardly. It will depend upon the shape of the
indifference curve or, to put it otherwise, upon the income and the price
elasticities of the demand for i and j. The price effect of the subsidy will tend to
decrease the production of j; but the income effect will tend to increase it. In some
cases, as in the case depicted by Figure 1b, the net effect will be an absolute
decrease in the production of good j.

This analysis does not provide any answer to an important question: do grants
reduce local taxes or more generally local revenues? A one dollar grant certainly
increases local expenditures, but by how much? One could argue that matching
grants will increase local expenditures by more than one dollar, because local

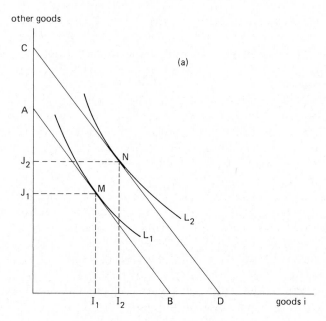

Figure 2a. Impact of a block grant.

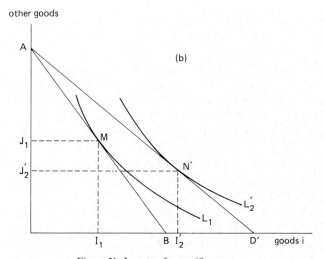

Figure 2b. Impact of a specific grant.

governments are grants maximizers and willing to spend more of their own funds in order to get "free" grants. One can also argue that grants will increase local expenditures by less than one dollar, and that part of the grants will serve to lower the tax burden. Much will depend upon the criteria according to which subsidies are granted.

A number of empirical studies, in the U.S.A., have attempted to throw light on this issue. Gramlich (1977) reviews a score of such studies. They are rather inconclusive. The elasticity of expenditures to grants received varies greatly according to the studies. More recent work by Gramlich–Galper (1973) and Jackson (1972) suggests that this elasticity is well below one, which would mean that a substantial portion of the grants results in lower local taxes.

General as well as specific grants have advantages as well as disadvantages. The main feature of specific grants is that they make it possible for central governments to influence the choices of local governments.

This can be seen as an advantage. One can argue that a number of urban public services, although delivered at the local level, fall within the responsability of central governments. The people live in a nation as well as in a local community. Central governments have a right, and even a duty, to develop "national policies" in the field of urban public services. They may find it necessary, for instance, to ensure that every citizen, irrespective of where he happens to live in the nation, can avail himself of a minimal level of education, health or waste disposal. Specific grants are a tool for the implementation of such "national policies".

This possibility given to central governments to influence the choice of local government can also be seen as a disadvantage, and is usually seen as such by local governments. It can be said that locally-elected politicians know what their constituents need and want better than central government civil servants. Specific grants will prevent local inhabitants from having the mix of services they want and which is, by definition, the one that would maximize their satisfaction.

Specific grants, then, make it possible for national governments to influence local governments, not to substitute them. It is often thought that urban public services should be either provided by central, regional, or local government; and indeed much of the discussion about fiscal federalism deals with the question of who should do what? As a matter of fact, for a number of services, the answer is that several levels of government should be involved, for different, but equally legitimate, reasons. Education, for instance should be – and in practice is – provided jointly by the three levels of government. The real question is not so much: who should do what?, but rather: how could the various levels of government cooperate? Specific grants are one answer to such a question.

On the other hand, specific grants tend to be difficult to administer. Central government officials cannot be adequately informed of all the details concerning the many specific projects they help finance. It is extremely difficult for them to choose amongst similar projects, put forward by different cities and competing for limited funds. This is why specific grants are in some cases associated with political patronage.

Block grants, by contrast, deprive central governments of a tool to carry national sectoral policies, but do not constrain the choices of local governments. In theory at least, block grants are more convenient than specific grants as an anticyclical instrument: the central government, which is responsible for macro-economic equilibria, can manipulate the total amount of subsidy in order to increase or decrease overall demand.

The key issue with block grants lies in the distribution formula. Usually, the total amount of grant is determined and then divided amongst local governments. Three criteria could be used: a criteria of resources, of costs, and of needs.

(1) Block grants can attempt to compensate differences in resources. Whatever the tax base, some local governments have more of it than others, on a per capita basis. It is fair to compensate for such differences, and many countries try and do it. Compensation may be partial or total. It would be total if the same tax rates were to bring the same amount of revenues in every local government. Total compensation, however, may not be desirable, for two reasons.

Total, guaranteed, compensation would suppress the interest of local governments for their tax bases. This would not be good. Local governments should have an incentive to attract people and industries. This is particularly true where differences in tax bases reflect differences in social costs, as is the case when industrial properties, that might be polluting or noisy or ugly, are included in the tax base. In such cases, local taxation provides a useful (although very imperfect) mechanism for internalizing externalities. In France, for instance, it would be very difficult to locate nuclear power plants or even waste treatment plants, if it were not for the increase in "taxe professionelle" they provide to the local governments that accept them.

Total compensation would determine not only what each community will get, but also the total amount of the subsidy. The amount that would be required to bring all local governments to the level of the richest local government is a function of some hypothetical tax rate. Let $B_1, B_2, \ldots, B_i, \ldots, B_n$, be the per capita tax base and $P_1, P_2, \ldots, P_i, \ldots P_n$, the population, of local governments, $1, 2, \ldots i,, \ldots n$, with $B_1 < B_2 \cdots < B_i < \cdots B_n$. Total compensation implies a tax rate r. The grant S_i to local government i will be:

$$S_i = r \cdot P_i(B_n - B_i)$$

The total amount of the subsidy, S, will be:

$$S = r \sum_i P_i(B_n - B_i)$$

and will be a function of r, P_i and B_i. For a given total subsidy S^0, it is always possible to find a rate that will compensate totally for differences in tax bases:

$$r = S^0 \Big/ \sum_i P_i(B_n - B_i)$$

But with a rate thus defined the total compensation is rather partial. It seems that only partial compensations are possible. The share that is compensated therefore remains a political decision.

The use of compensating criteria raises in practice another difficulty. For tax bases to be utilized in an allocation formula, they must be assessed in a similar manner throughout the country. Differences to be compensated are effective differences, not evaluated differences. This means that tax bases must be assessed by the central government, not by the local governments themselves.

A final problem is raised by non-tax resources of local governments. Should they be included in the allocation formula? The answer is not easy, because non-tax resources are very diverse. Some, such as "natural" resources like the proceeds from the sale of community timber, should probably be included, and reduce the amount of subsidy received. Other, that are the result of a quasi industrial activity, should rather be excluded.

(2) Should block grants compensate differences in costs? The cost of producing a unit of a given urban public service (e.g. the service provided by an hospital bed, or the collection and disposal of the domestic waste of a standard household) vary from community to community. It varies for several reasons. One is that there are often economies of scale in the production of urban public services. One other reason is that the efficiency of local governments may differ. A third is that labor and land costs are not the same in all communities. Should such differences in costs be compensated?

Many people would say yes, for the sake of equity. People living in a high cost area need urban public services as much (and often more) than people living in low cost areas. Is it not unfair that they would get less for the same tax effort? One can argue that relative production costs should be used as a criteria for the allocation of grants.

This criterion, or a similar one, is actually used in several countries. In the Netherlands, for instance, the main criteria, that governs about 80% of the block grant to local governments, is population; however, the subsidy allocated to each local government is not proportional to its population, but progressive; each community receives a per capita subsidy that increases with its size: in 1978, rural communities received 325 guilders per capita, whereas small (i.e. 20,000 to 50,000 inhabitants) cities received 400 guilders, and Amsterdam 780 guilders. It can also be noted that matching grants, in which the central government pays a given share of the costs incurred by each local government include an implicit cost equalization criterion.

There are, however, some reasons to believe that cost differences should not be compensated. From an allocation of resources viewpoint, it is never good to compensate cost differences. These differences often reflect differences in scarcities. They provide valuable informations, that should not be ignored or suppressed. Land, for instance, is scarcer in large cities than in small cities, and should be used more sparingly in the production of urban public services. Then, from a practical viewpoint, costs differences would be a criteria extremely difficult to implement. Costs differences are poorly known, and difficult to know. From an equity view point, finally, one should note that costs differences are probably associated with resources differences: high costs areas are likely to be also high resources areas. Inasmuch as resources inequality are only partially compensated, one can argue that resources differentials do in effect compensate costs differentials.

(3) Block grants should compensate differences in "needs". Economists are not very fond of the concept of needs, are prefer the notion of demand that describes preferences under a budget constraint. Yet, it seems clear that the quantity of urban public service that will provide a given level of satisfaction in and for a local government, on a per capita basis, will vary with the characteristics of each local government. It is, in particular, a function of:

– the physical structure of the community: large (in acres) local governments will have more roads to maintain, and "old" local governments more historic buildings to preserve;
– the demographic structure of the community: those communities where there are more children, for instance, will have to spend more on education;
– the social structure of the population: communities where the share of unemployed, of poor, of disabled, etc. is higher, will have higher social expenditures;
– the demographic evolution of the population: it is likely that communities where population increases rapidly, or decline, have higher per capita expenditures;
– the functions performed by the community: those places, like resorts, spas, large cities, where there are many non-residents have to spend more per resident.

Even if the concept of need is rather elusive, it describes a reality. The sentence: "all local government are not equal in terms of needs" has a meaning. The compensation of these inequalities can be an objective of a grants policy, and therefore offers a criterion for the allocation of grants.

This criterion, however, raises two issues. One is practical: it is very difficult to assess properly these "needs" of local governments. In the U.K., until a 1981 reform, regression analysis was used, that tried to explain the amount spent by a local government by means of a number of characteristics of this local government (such as area, number of children, etc.). For a given local government, with its characteristics known, it would be possible to determine its "normal" level of expenditures, or to put it otherwise, to determine its needs. A similar, but cruder method is used in Denmark. The total amount of the block grant is divided into 9 or 10 parts of unequal importance; each part is alloted to local governments according to a specific criterion: the number of children aged 0–6 years, the number of hospital beds, the number of kilometers of roads, etc. None of these methods is wholly satisfactory. They raise as many technical and political problems as they solve.

There is a second, more theoretical, issue associated with needs-based formulae. The needs that call for compensation are either of local interest, or of national interest. If they are of local interest – which is for instance, the case of local roads – there is no reason for the central government to intervene. If they are of national interest – which is for instance the case of historic monuments – there is a justification for the central government to intervene; but there is no reason for this intervention to take the form of a block grant; it should rather take the form of a specific grant, or be directly undertaken by the central government. Local governments can hardly argue: we want subsidies *because* of this particular need, but we don't want a subsidy *for* that need.

One could add that some needs criteria are not unambiguous. The amount of existing social capital, for instance, can be seen as a negative or as a positive criteria. One can argue that the more roads there are in a local government jurisdiction, the more money it needs, in order to maintain them; but one can also argue that the less roads there are, the more money is needed, in order to build enough roads.

One advantage of grants, and particularly of block grants, is that they make it possible for central governments to implement national *spatial* policies. The central government, if it so wishes, can contribute to the development of certain areas – broad geographic regions, backward areas, core cities, small-sized cities, etc. – by granting more subsidies to those areas than to other areas (all other things equal), thereby improving the level of urban public services, thus attracting people and activities into such areas.

It should also be noted that, even when distribution formulae do not favour explicit less-developed areas, grants systems tend to redistribute income from rich areas to poor areas. Let us assume that grants are a function of population only. Grants are financed by the general budget, i.e. by taxation. Even a proportional tax system would mean that inhabitants of rich areas contribute more than inhabitants of poor areas to the budget. Since they all receive the same amount of money, this means that inhabitants of rich areas subsidize inhabitants of poor areas. This would of course be truer with a progressive tax system.

Both specific and block grants are, in certain countries, limited to the financing of investment expenditures, of "infrastructures". The reasons for this limitation are that central governments are reluctant to commit themselves for long periods of time by accepting to subsidize current expenditures, and also that investment expenditures are considered more "strategic" than operating expenditures. This was the case in France for many types of grants. The European Economic Community, with its regional fund, is only allowed to subsidize infrastructures. This limitation is not without danger. Subsidies restricted to investments reduce the cost of capital relative to that of labour. As a result, they induce local governments to select capital-intensive (and labour-saving) technologies. In the field of waste disposal, for instance, this favours incinerators rather than dumps, as can be seen from the high ratio of incinerators to dumps to be found in France. At times of unemployment and of capital shortages, more neutral types of grants would probably be wiser.

Subsidies have become an important mode of financing urban public services. The real issue is not wether they should continue to be so (there is every reason to believe that they will), but rather to find out in more detail what their impacts are, what forms they should take, and how they should be allocated between local governments.

6. Loans

Borrowing is widely utilized as a means of financing urban public services. Conversely, local governments account for a large share of the public debt; in France, for instance, throughout the seventies, the debt of local governments was constantly higher than that of the central government.

The main reason is of course the key role of investments in urban public service provision. This role is so great that there is a tendency to confuse the service with the capital investment that is used to produce it, and to refer to "sewers" rather than to water disposal, or to "roads" rather than to transportation. The capital intensive nature of many urban public services justifies the use of borrowing: interests and loan repayment will be paid for by those who will actually benefit from the investment.

A second reason is that borrowing (unlike taxation) can be, and is, utilized by all entities responsible for urban service provision: utilities, agencies, local governments, etc.

A third reason is that those entities often have no other alternative sources of financing. Most of their tax and grant income is eaten up by operating expenditures. As they consist largely of wages and salaries, operating expenditures tend to rise faster than revenues and entities producing public services find it increasingly difficult to create surpluses out of their current accounts.

Finally, inflation is an incentive to borrowing. Interest and repayments are usually determined in nominal terms, and their real weight tend to decrease as time passes. Real rates of interest are therefore very low and can even be negative, as has been the case in France for all the years(except one) of the 1970–80 period.

Countries differ markedly in the relative importance of private and public lending institutions.

In some countries, local governments borrow primarily from public or semi-public institutions. In France, for instance, the powerful Caisse des Dépots et

Consignations and its affiliates account for more than four-fifths (81% for the 1976–82 period) of total lending to local governments; more than half of the remainder comes from Crédit Agricole and Crédit Mutuel, which are more like public institutions than commercial banks. The interest rates offered by these public lending institutions are usually significantly lower than market rates, and this sort of lending includes a kind of hidden, yet huge, public subsidy. This subsidy is distributed to local governments according to the amount of money that they borrow. The soundness of this apportionment criterion is questionable.

In other countries, such as the U.S.A., local governments, as well as other agencies, borrow from the market. They issue bonds, which compete with bonds issued by industrial and commercial enterprises. This competition is not entirely free, however, because local government bonds, or more precisely interest earned on them, are usually tax exempt. This – which can also be analyzed as a hidden and huge subsidy, distributed according to a questionable criterion – enables local government bonds to be attractive at below market rates. This reliance on the financial market gives local governments more freedom from central government controls, but also gives them much less certainty. The market, which is controlled by a limited number of powerful commercial banks, as is the case in the U.S.A., can suddenly deny local governments the borrowing they expect, or give it at high interest rates, because market conditions make it more profitable to lend to private investors.

In most countries, there exist a mix of public and private lending sources. But it is interesting to note that the evolution seems to be towards greater reliance on private sources, i.e. on the financial market. This has clearly been the trend in the U.K., with the Public Works Loan Board beginning as the sole source of loans, then becoming a major, and finally being a minor source of loans. And in France, the role of private lending institutions, which used to be negligible, is now increasing. Large cities find it easier to borrow, but small cities have in many countries (U.K., Netherlands, Germany, France) grouped together to float bonds which are afterwards distributed between cities.

Local borrowing is in most countries controlled by central governments. This is because local government borrowing and the amount of expenditures it finances are important elements of overall demand, that central governments want to control as part of their macro-economic policies; and also perhaps because it is thought that local governments should be protected from the temptation of borrowing too much. This control is not indirect, by means of interest rates, but rather direct, by means of ceilings, or of a priori approvals. But it is effective. A recent econometric study [Derycke and Gilbert (1985)] for France suggests that macro economic policies are powerful determinants of local borrowing.

A basic issue of debt management relates to the amount and structure of the debt. Many countries have debt ceilings for local governments, which are either constitutional or regulatory. But, even if they are below their ceiling, local governments may choose not to increase their debt. By so doing, they limit their interest payments.

The structure of a debt is often as or more important than its amount. Short term bonds should not be ruled out. Their interest rates are usually lower, and they can help even out discrepancies between intermittent tax resources and continuous expenditures. But too great a reliance on short term bonds is dangerous, as has been seen in the case of New York City.

7. Conclusion

The main conclusion that seems to emerge from this discussion if that urban public services cannot be financed entirely by local taxes. Local taxation, wether it is based on property, on income or on sales, does not attenuate existing disparities between local communities, but rather exacerbates them; it is therefore basically inequitable in its consequences; in addition, the need for funds increases faster than the proceeds of most local taxes, and it is becoming politically very difficult to raise tax rates; in one sense, one can say that there are no good local taxes.

The role that can be played by loans is, of necessity, limited. The financing of urban public services must therefore be met by user charges and central government grants. User charges probably have a bright future. It is technically possible to adapt user charges to a broad range of urban public service, such as water, waste disposal, transportation, recreation, etc. Obviously, there are some problems associated with user charges, the main one being that, in some cases (but certainly not in all) they could be inequitable; in such cases, direct subsidies to low income people, or differenciated prices, could be necessary. But charges have a number of merits: they can help internalize externalities, and induce the "producers" of urban public services to behave like private enterprises, i.e. to satisfy the customers and to minimize the costs of producing the services.

The increased role of central governments grants – which has been dramatic over the last two decades in many countries – is the other necessary development. It is a departure from the Tietbout model in which each local community offered a package of services and taxes, and in which the citizens would choose between the many packages offered by voting with their feet. The advantage of the model was that it incorporated a sort of automatic regulatory mechanism: those who wanted more services had to pay more taxes. The development of grants is breaking this precious link. Local governments will ask for more grants, without restraint. It will make the task of central governments more difficult: political mechanisms will be substituted for automatic mechanisms.

Urban public services must be financed. Yet, none of the modes of financing is satisfactory. Trade-offs between the shortcomings of the various modes have to be made, and are made. The optimal system is necessarily multi-modal, and complex, and evolving.

References

Bennet R.J. (1982) *Central grants to local governments. The political and economic impact of the rate support grant in England and Wales.* Cambridge: Cambridge University Press.

Brown, C.V. and P.M. Jackson (1982) *Public sector economics.* Oxford: Martin Robertson.

Brueckner, J.K. (1981) 'Labor mobility and the incidence of the residential property tax', *Journal of Urban Economics*, 10:173–182.

Derycke, P.H. and G. Gilbert (1985) 'Un modèle de comportement financier des communes françaises', *Revenue d'Economie Régionale et Urbaine*, 617–638.

Foster, C., R. Jackman, and M. Perlman, *Local government finance in a unitary state.* London: George Allen and Unwin.

Gramlich, E.M. (1977) 'Intergovernmental grants. A review of the empirical literature', in: W.E. Oates, ed, *The political economy of fiscal federalism.* Toronto: D.C. Heath & Co Lexington Books. 219–240.

Gramlich, E.M. and H. Galper,, (1973) 'State and local fiscal behavior and federal grants policy', *Brookings Papers on Economic Activity*, 15–58.

Haurin, D.R. (1981) 'Local income taxation in an urban area', *Journal of Urban Economics*, 10:323–337.

Jackson, J. (1972) 'Politics and the budgetary process', *Social Science Research*, 35–60.

Layfield, (1976) *Report of the committee of inquiry into local government finance*, Chairman Frank Layfield (Cmnd 6453). London: HMSO.

Le Grand, J. (1982) *The strategy of equality.* London: George Allen and Unwin.

LeRoy, S.F. (1976) 'Urban land rent and the incidence of property taxes', *Journal of Urban Economics*, 3:167–179.

Netzer, R. (1966) *Economics of the property tax.* Washington, D.C.: The Brookings Institution.

O.E.C.D. (1983) *Taxes on immovable property*, Paris: O.E.C.D.

Pechman, J. and B. Ochner (1974) *Who bears the tax burden.* Washington, D.C.: The Brookings Institution.

Polinsky, A. and D.L. Rubinfeld (1978) 'The long-run effects of a residential property tax and local public services', *Journal of Urban Economics*, 5:241–262.

Prud'homme, R. (1979) 'La répartition des subventions globales: réflexions à partir de l'expérience de la France, de la Grande-Bretagne, du Danemark et des Pays-Bas', *Revue d'Economie Régionale et Urbaine*, 151–173.

Slack, E. (1980) 'Local fiscal response to intergovernmental transfers', *Review of Economics and Statistics*, 62:364–370.

Starrett, D.A. (1980) 'On the method of taxation and the provision of local public goods', *American Economic Review*, 70:380–392.

Tiebout, C.M. (1956) 'A pure theory of local public expenditures', *Journal of Political Economy*, 64:416–424.

Chapter 31

URBAN AMENITIES AND PUBLIC POLICY

TIMOTHY J. BARTIK and V. KERRY SMITH*

Vanderbilt University

1. Introduction

Our textbooks routinely describe consumption in terms that to the uninitiated must resemble a glorified conversion process – money into satisfaction. Commodities are the intermediaries in this process. While this paradigm has been greatly refined in the nearly two centuries since Bentham, the most important recent contribution to consumption analysis is based on the recognition of the sterility of this "conversion process" view. These developments have been especially important to the modeling of individuals' residential location choices because communities are not alike, and the ways in which they differ are not easily accommodated in the traditional framework.

For example, how often have we heard a community described as a nice place to raise children; or this city, town, or neighborhood has charm or character? What are households consuming when they choose an attractive setting in which to live or work? They are consuming amenities. While in some of the past literature this term has been used to describe location specific goods, services, or characteristics that yield pleasure, we shall use it for location specific characteristics with either positive or negative contributions.

Amenities can be classified using many dimensions, such as geographic scale, degree of permanence, and the extent to which they are physically tangible. For example, one can describe the amenities of a region of the United States or, more narrowly, discuss those for an individual city, neighborhood, or even a single

*This research was partially supported by the United States Environmental Protection Agency under Cooperative Agreement No. CR 811075. It has not been subjected to the Agency's peer and administrative review and therefore does not necessarily reflect the views of the Agency, and no official endorsement should be inferred.

Thanks are due to Maureen Cropper, Irving Hoch, Ted McConnell, and Raymond Palmquist for suggestions on this research at an early stage of its development and to Edwin Mills and William Strange for comments on an earlier draft. In addition, we thank Jennifer Roback, Allan Goodman, Donald Jud, David Grether, Larry Ozanne, and Bruce Bender for providing some background information on the data used in their hedonic studies, even though we were unable to fully incorporate all this information in the paper.

Handbook of Regional and Urban Economics, Volume II, Edited by E.S. Mills
© *1987, Elsevier Science Publishers B.V.*

Table 1
Expenditures and amenity levels for twenty largest cities

| City | Amenity related expenditures (per capita) | | | | Measured air quality[d] | | | Perceived neighborhood amenities % reporting undesirable[e] | | Violent crime rate[f] |
	Education[a]	Police[b]	Air quality[c]	Water quality[c]	TSP	SO_2	Ozone	Neighborhood conditions	Neighborhood services	
New York	420.31	107.91	0.58	36.62	52	34	10.7	89.3	40.8	2.22
Chicago	441.45	121.72	0.84	17.80	69	34	6.9	79.8	41.9	0.85
Los Angeles	499.62	125.66	0.01	11.67	105	32	64.8	57.6	46.8	1.74
Philadelphia	378.12	100.12	1.01	88.91	53	51	8.2	82.6	39.2	1.04
Houston	253.96	75.04	0.91	63.85	76	—	26.8	84.3	39.0	—
Detroit	441.38	148.35	—	134.77	75	30	7.1	66.4	55.4	1.94
Dallas	294.86	72.65	0.21	58.83	61	—	1.1	50.7	39.1	1.36
San Diego	346.09	60.84	—	41.85	73	7	8.1	82.8	55.9	0.73
Phoenix	419.76	87.51	—	49.49	—	—	1.1	54.3	54.8	—
Baltimore	319.11	103.80	0.50	43.39	59	—	10.7	54.3	54.8	2.22
San Antonio	126.11	47.17	0.23	40.59	52	—	0.0	92.0	48.0	0.57
Indianapolis	192.99	58.26	0.62	119.34	67	—	2.1	89.9	48.0	0.98
San Francisco	237.02	105.00	—	177.89	51	7	2.5	85.7	43.2	1.74
Memphis	286.95	74.78	—	45.35	69	—	—	42.4	41.7	1.08
Washington, D.C.	437.84	179.16	0.84	139.36	52	38	17.0	58.0	53.1	2.28
Milwaukee	453.58	95.22	—	68.48	60	53	9.1	86.5	50.4	3.42
San Jose	—	58.67	—	32.25	—	—	—	—	—	4.12
Cleveland	405.00	123.19	2.63	106.65	73	56	22.7	89.3	37.8	12.43
Columbus	—	79.49	—	72.43	50	—	4.1	90.2	45.7	5.26
Boston	464.98	125.87	0.12	43.15	53	35	6.0	67.1	50.2	14.07

aThese estimates are for primary and secondary educational expenses from the *Digest of Educational Statistics*, 1982, for the 1979–80 operating year.

bThese estimates are taken from the *County and City Data Book* for 1983 and are for 1981 expenses.

cThese estimates are based on the total dollar expenditures by each city for fiscal year 1980 and are taken from the *State and Local Government Special Studies, No.103: Environmental Quality Control.*

dThese figures are taken from an unpublished summary of the indicator values for five pollutants in 102 urbanized areas prepared by the Environmental Protection Agency for 1978. The reported data have been checked with state records to assure consistency between federal and state measures of air quality.

TSP refers to total suspended particulates and is measured for the urban monitoring sites with complete data by the annual geometric mean averaged across all sites in micrograms per cubic meter.

SO_2 refers to sulfur dioxide and is measured for the continuous urban monitoring sites with sufficient hourly data by the annual arithmetic mean averaged across sites in micrograms per cubic meter.

Ozone is measured for the urban monitoring sites with sufficient seasonal data. In this case, we report the estimated annual exceedances at sites with sufficient data averaged over the sites.

eThese data are derived from the *Annual Housing Survey* for owner occupied housing units, and report the percent reporting undesirable neighborhood conditions and percent reporting inadequate neighborhood services. They are for varying years – 1977: Boston, Detroit, Dallas, Memphis, Washington, D.C., Baltimore, Los Angeles, and Phoenix; 1976: New York, Houston, Indianapolis, and Cleveland; 1975: Chicago, Philadelphia, San Diego, San Antonio, San Francisco, Milwaukee, and Columbus.

fThese data are the FBI total violent crimes per 100 population for 1981 as reported in the *Statistical Abstract of the U.S.* and the *County and City Data Book.*

block. Amenities also differ greatly in how rapidly they change. Finally, some amenities are closely related to physically measurable phenomena, while others are quite subjective and difficult to define. For example, the air quality of a location can be objectively measured, while the "charm" of a historic neighborhood cannot.

Amenities should be central to any realistic description of consumption, but our empirical ability to quantify their importance remains limited. Over a decade ago, Nordhaus and Tobin (1973) boldly stated that the negative urban amenities were about 5% of GNP. By contrast, some three years later in a review article on environmental economics, Fisher and Peterson (1976) described such efforts as pioneering but to be taken with a grain of salt.

Both before and after the Nordhaus–Tobin study, numerous micro-economic studies have attempted to show the importance of amenities. Models based on property values and wages have enjoyed sufficient success to have spawned substantial theoretical literature on the appropriate methods for measuring and interpreting the effects of amenities on market prices.

Before describing this work, we provide indirect evidence of the importance of urban amenities and discuss the potential role for public policy in their provision. Table 1 summarizes per capita expenditures on activities that are often associated with urban amenities – education, police, and air and water pollution abatement programs, as well as measures of the violent crime rate and air quality for 20 of the largest cities in the United States. In addition, based on the *Annual Housing Survey*, we report a summary of households' perceptions of amenities. While indirect and (in the case of the last set of variables) subjective, these data do indicate that it is reasonable to assume there are substantial differences in location specific amenities. For example, per capita expenditures for education ranged from 25% to more than 100% of the per capita annual spending for national defense across these cities, while per capita spending for pollution abatement (air and water at the city level) ranged from 2% to 36% of per capita defense spending.

As these data indicate, the public sector provides urban amenities. Education expenditures are an example. Of course, in many cases what is controlled by the public sector may bear only an indirect relation to the amenities that are valued by households.

Other amenities arise from private actions and the public sector attempts through regulation or other measures to affect what is available. Air and water quality cannot be produced by the public sector. Nonetheless, by limiting the emissions of pollutants into the atmosphere and water courses, the public sector influences their supply. In other cases, the mechanism is less clearcut. An amenity may be the result of a long process; a charming neighborhood, or quaint college town are not necessarily created through the conscious actions of either private economic agents or the public sector. Often they are accidents of history.

Nonetheless, local policies such as zoning, housing codes, and community development programs can influence the prospects for these amenities to arise and may maintain or destroy those that already exist.

It must be acknowledged that economic research on the relationships between policy and amenity supply, and between amenity supply and household satisfaction, cannot as yet provide precise estimates for policymakers. Nonetheless, both theory and empirical results have confirmed the importance of urban amenities to households. Moreover, in some cases, the models have begun to play a role in the evaluation of policy alternatives. This is especially true for air and water pollution policies.

Our review considers first the economic modeling of households' decisions concerning amenities, and these models' implications for using observed behavior to evaluate the importance of amenities. We believe the hedonic property value and wage models provide the appropriate frameworks for analyzing amenities. Consequently, we have focused most of our attention on these models.

Three related questions concerning hedonic models will be discussed. The first is the appropriate interpretation of estimated equilibrium relationships between housing prices (or wages) and amenities. The second is the use of these models to estimate a household's valuation of changes in amenities. The third is the use of hedonic price models to measure the benefits of policies that improve amenities. While these models are our primary focus, we also comment on the use of discrete choice and residential mobility models as alternative approaches for describing the influence of amenities on behavior.

We also discuss what we know based on intra- and inter-urban analyses of the effects of amenities on housing values and wages. In this discussion we have attempted to summarize the points of consistency in available empirical studies and the areas where further research is needed. We conclude this overview with a discussion of the research agenda implied by the work to date.

2. Modeling household selections of amenities

The theoretical roots of the hedonic framework, which provides the basis for a structural analysis of implicit markets for amenities or other qualitative features of commodities, can be found in Adam Smith's equalizing differences explanation for differing wages by occupation. Early contributions to hedonic theory were made by Court (1941), Houthakker (1952), Griliches (1961), Roy (1950), and Tinbergen (1956). However, Rosen's (1974) pathbreaking essay was the first to provide a unified treatment of the modeling of implicit markets. His careful description of the role of individuals' utility and firms' profit functions in determining the equilibrium rates of exchange for heterogeneous goods provided the logical basis for defining the relationship between the hedonic price function and economic agents' behavior.

A hedonic price function describes the relationship between the equilibrium price of a heterogeneous commodity and its characteristics. It results from a strategy adopted to model an individual's demands for a particular kind of heterogeneous good in which there are many different types of the same basic commodity, and the individual generally consumes only one of these types. Conventional models of this choice process would require that the outcome be described as a boundary solution (rather than an interior) for all but one good in each class. The hedonic model abstracts from the commodities for such cases and focuses on the characteristics of these commodities. With this reformulation an individual is viewed as considering all members of the set in terms of the characteristics each contains. Moreover, his decisions are assumed to be constrained by an exogenous price function. This function is the constraint (together with income) to this choice process.

The hedonic price function results from a market equilibrium. That is, it matches diverse demanders and suppliers with differentiated "types" of the commodity so that demand equals supply for all types, and none of the participating agents wishes to change his demand or supply decision. When it is reasonable to assume that individual economic agents (both households and firms) cannot influence the prices they face, then the hedonic price function is a double envelope – the highest bids of the households for goods with varying bundles of characteristics and the lowest offering prices of firms (or suppliers) making them available.[1] Equilibrium requires that each type of agent is paying (or receiving) his respective marginal willingness to pay (or marginal reservation price) for the last unit of each attribute of the commodity desired.

This is an interesting equilibrium concept that has caused much confusion in the hedonic literature and we return to it later. For now, however, our key point is that the hedonic framework is basically a modeling strategy. The hedonic approach includes both implicit restrictions on individual preferences and a characterization of the nature of the markets for the heterogeneous commodities.

2.1. Household choice in an intra-city framework

We begin with a simple hedonic model of residential location within a city. Section 2.6 below will discuss inter-city location decisions for which hedonic market for both housing and labor will be important. Households as demanders

---

[1] In the case of housing, the suppliers are likely to be composed of firms and households, with the latter offering resale of homes and the former new housing units. For households the offer function is presumably influenced by the cost conditions for new housing of comparable attributes as well as by what might be termed the household's perceived valuation or reservation price for the unit.

and firms (or landlords) as suppliers of housing are both assumed to be price takers. Moreover, in the intra-city framework, the household's employment decisions are treated as independent of (or predetermined to) their selection of a type of housing, including with it a residential location and its implied set of site-specific amenities.[2] Thus a formal model of the process we outlined above would describe the household as selecting a housing type, z, to maximize utility subject to the available budget and existing set of prices for the housing types, represented using the hedonic price function as in (1).

$$\max_{z,x} U(z, x; D) \text{ subject to } p(z) + x < y. \tag{1}$$

The vector, z, completely describes a house's characteristics, including amenities, $p(\cdot)$ is the hedonic price function for housing in the city, y is income, x is a non-housing commodity (with a price of unity), and D is a vector of household characteristics that describe the reasons for differences in preferences across individuals. The housing supplier chooses a z and number of units to offer, M, to maximize profits in the problem

$$\max_{z,M} M(p(z)) - C(M, z; S), \tag{2}$$

where $C(\cdot)$ is the cost function and S is a vector of supplier attributes that describes the reasons for all differences in supplier cost functions. It could include factor prices, variables measuring differences in firms' technologies, and other variables reflecting behavioral influences or constraints.

As we noted earlier, the existence of the hedonic price function is what assures that the equilibrium matching of what is demanded in relation to that offered will arise. Thus, the price function is that transformation of characteristics to dollars which assures that the distribution of bundles demanded (based on the distribution of D across households) will correspond to the distribution offered (based on the underlying distribution of S across firms). Analytical solutions to this problem have been possible in a few special cases. Tinbergen (1956) appears to have been the first to offer an analytical solution for this matching although in a labor market hedonic model rather than a housing model. Epple (1987) has reformulated the Tinbergen framework for the general hedonic model. Epple demonstrated that with consumers' preferences described by a quadratic utility function with one set of parameters in common across individuals and another set following a multivariate normal, together with housing characteristics assumed to be exogenously distributed as multivariate normal, then the equilibrium

---

[2] There have been limited attempts to undertake hedonic housing models across cities. Butler (1977) and Linneman (1977) report analyses based on micro-economic data. By contrast, Smith and Deyak (1975) undertook an analysis with city-wide averages of housing prices using census information.

hedonic price function would be a quadratic.[3] Cropper, Deck, McConnell, and Phipps (1985) assume linear utility function with parameters distributed uniformly across individuals, and housing characteristics exogenously distributed according to the uniform distribution. This specification also results in a quadratic hedonic. Aside from such special cases, analytical solutions have been intractable. This is unfortunate from the perspective of economic analysis. If the hedonic function could be explicitly derived as a function of demand and supplier parameters and the distribution of product characteristics, one might hope to be able to reverse this process, and derive a description of demander and supplier parameters from the estimated hedonic function.

Rosen avoided the problem of deriving an explicit analytical form for the hedonic price function by assuming the existence of a continuous function to describe the equilibrium price set. He focused on the role of this equilibrium relationship in revealing a household's marginal willingness to pay and a supplier's marginal offer prices for specific attributes of the housing bundle. That is, the marginal conditions from household and supplier maximization problems require that for each bundle of characteristics, z^a, the marginal price of each attribute from the equilibrium hedonic price function will be equal to the marginal willingness to pay (or marginal bid) and to the marginal offer price for the member of each of the respective groups selecting and offering that bundle, as in (3) below.[4]

$$\frac{\partial U/\partial z_j}{\partial U/\partial x} = \frac{\partial P}{\partial z_j}(z^a) = \frac{\partial C/\partial z_j}{M} \ . \tag{3}$$

Each element in (3) is a function. Conventional descriptions of this result have

---

[3] The basic form of the utility function used in this derivation was

$$U = \tfrac{1}{2}(z-a)^T \theta(z-a) + x \ ,$$

with θ a positive definite diagonal matrix common to all households. The a parameters are assumed to follow independent normals as were the characteristics available. The resulting hedonic price equation would then be given as:

$$P(z) = \psi^T z + \tfrac{1}{2} z^T A z \ ,$$

with $\psi = \theta(\tau - \Sigma^{1/2}\Omega^{1/2}\phi)$
$A = \theta(I - \Sigma^{1/2}\Omega^{1/2}) \ ,$

where τ = mean vector of the a parameters, Σ = diagonal covariance matrix for the a parameters, ϕ = mean vector for the attributes, Ω = diagonal covariance matrix for the attributes.

[4] Equilibrium condition (3) can easily be confusing. It looks as if the individual demander and supplier are somehow interacting to determine the marginal price schedule, just as aggregate demand and supply for ordinary commodities determines equilibrium prices. This analogy is misleading. Although the actions of all demanders and suppliers determine the hedonic price function, each individual agent faces an exogenous price schedule. No demand/supply simultaneity on the individual level is implied. Nonetheless, there are many econometric complications in estimating demand and supply parameters, as we discuss further on in the paper.

Hamer, Andrew M., and Linn, Johannes F., "Urbanization in
the Developing World: Patterns, Issues, and Policies,"
Chap. 32 in Edwin S. Mills, ed., Handbook of Regional and
Urban Economics, Amsterdam: North-Holland, 1987. Vol. 2, pp.
1255-84.

Hamer, Andrew M., and Linn, Johannes F., "Urbanization in
the Developing World: Patterns, Issues, and Policies,"
Chap. 32 in Edwin S. Mills, ed., Handbook of Regional and
Urban Economics, Amsterdam: North-Holland, 1987. Vol. 2, pp.
1255-84.

Hamer, Andrew M., and Linn, Johannes F., "Urbanization in
the Developing World: Patterns, Issues, and Policies,"
Chap. 32 in Edwin S. Mills, ed., Handbook of Regional and
Urban Economics, Amsterdam: North-Holland, 1987. Vol. 2, pp.
1255-84.

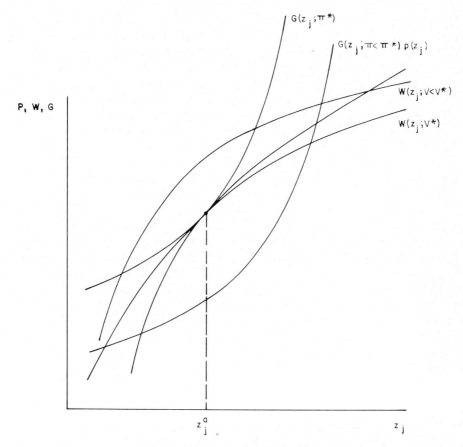

Figure 1. The relationship between market prices, bid prices, offer prices, and characteristic z_j, holding other characteristics constant at their optimal level.

used a diagram illustrating in two dimensions a cross-section of the $n+1$ dimensional equality implied by the equilibrium matching. Figure 1 reproduces this format using the bid (W) and offer (G) functions.[5]

The diagram shows bid curves and offer curves (i.e. the bid and offer functions holding utility and profit constant, respectively). In this illustration utility in-

---

[5] Both the bid and offer functions have been extensively used in the hedonic literature. The bid function is defined as the function $W(z; v, D)$ that solves $U(z, y - W; D) = v$, where v is some utility level. The bid function is a type of transformation of the utility function. Intuitively, the bid function gives the household's willingness to pay at some utility level for different housing types.

The offer function is defined as the function $G(z, \pi, s)$ that solves $GM - C(z, M; s) = \pi$. Intuitively, the offer function gives the price at which the supplier is willing to provide different housing types.

creases as an individual moves to lower bid curves in the diagram, because lower curves imply lower prices for the same housing bundle. Profits increase as a supplier moves to higher offer curves, because higher offer curves imply higher prices for the same housing bundle. The individual seeks to move to the lowest possible bid curve subject to the constraint of the price function. Similarly, a supplier seeks the highest possible offer curve subject to the same constraint. The particular demander and supplier shown in the diagram reach a maximum at a point z^a where bid, hedonic price, and offer curves are tangent.

2.2. Reversing the logic: The hedonic price function, preferences, and costs

One important use of the hedonic framework has been to retrieve the marginal willingness to pay and marginal offer functions from the equilibrium price function. This process has not proved to be as direct (or simple) as Rosen's original description seemed to imply. Figure 2 illustrates some of these difficulties.

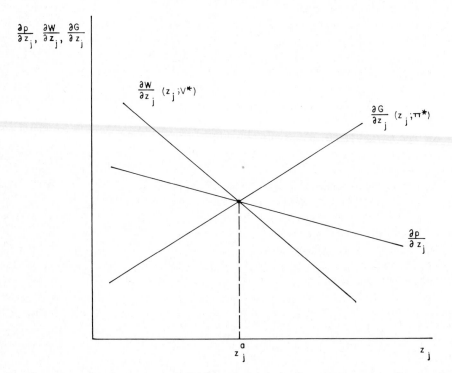

Figure 2. The marginal price, marginal bid, and marginal offer curves corresponding to the optimum in Figure 1.

The hedonic model's description of an equilibrium, together with our assumed ability to specify and estimate the price function leading to the equilibrium, implies we can retrieve information on points of intersection of the marginal bid, marginal offer, and marginal price functions for each attribute. For each z_i only the marginal price function is known, since it is the partial derivative of the hedonic price function. The assumption of an equilibrium, as given by (3), merely suggests that there exists a feasible matching at the given attribute vector.

The problems posed by this simultaneous equality are quite different from the simultaneity problem that is conventionally discussed in demand and supply models (and implicitly alluded to in Rosen's discussion). There is not a simultaneity between some individual's marginal bid and another's marginal offer function. Both households and firms are price-takers. However, both face a nonlinear price function. The implication of this feature is that when this information is used to estimate an individual's marginal bid function (or a firm's marginal offer function), the relevant identification problem involves distinguishing the marginal bid function from the marginal price function. Furthermore, when the hedonic price function is not linear, marginal prices of characteristics as well as quantities of characteristics are endogenously chosen by the household.

Most policy interest focuses on these marginal bid functions. Therefore, we will discuss the problems posed by using the equilibrium information to estimate them. The issues posed by recovering the marginal bid function can be organized as responses to four specific questions:

(1) How should the marginal bid function be specified so that it is capable of being estimated?
(2) What is the appropriate interpretation of a marginal bid function, given the non-linearity of the hedonic price function?
(3) How can the marginal bid function be identified and what assumptions or data (e.g. multimarket data) are required for this identification?
(4) What role can the resulting marginal bid function estimates play in the evaluation of the benefits of amenity improvements?

With respect to the first question of specification, we note an important misspecification in many applied hedonic studies. Rosen's original marginal bid function expressed marginal bids as a function of product characteristics and utility. To remove the unobservable utility level, Rosen and others have substituted income for utility in empirical estimation. This is incorrect because utility, viewed as an indirect function, depends also on the entire hedonic function. Including the entire function turns the marginal bid function into a functional.

A practical alternative is to substitute the arguments of direct utility into the marginal bid function. More specifically, if V represents the realized level of utility,

(4) describes the process analytically:

$$\frac{\partial W}{\partial z_j} = f(z, V, D) = f(z, U(z, x), D) = f(z, x, D) \, . \tag{4}$$

The marginal bid in this formulation depends on the chosen housing bundle, the level of non-housing expenditures, and demand shifters. This version of the marginal bid function may be termed an uncompensated marginal bid function, while Rosen's theoretical marginal bid function (holding utility constant) can be termed a compensated marginal bid function. This distinction is somewhat analogous to the distinction between ordinary Marshallian and Hicksian demand functions, although this analogy should not be carried too far.

While some researchers have attempted to invert the system of equations implied by (4), this is not always possible. There is nothing implausible with having the same marginal willingness to pay correspond to more than one vector of quantities. Indeed, given that the units in which amenities and other housing characteristics measured are often arbitrary, it may be difficult for the researcher to have any intuition about how marginal bids will vary with the quantities of housing characteristics. Furthermore, placing marginal prices on the right hand side of the equation does not eliminate the basic econometric problem that households endogenously choose both quantities and marginal prices. Inverting (4) would make the hedonic demand equations look more like ordinary demand equations. But this can be misleading.

The key difficulties of interpretation implied by our second question are created by the non-linearity of the hedonic price function, and the resulting non-constancy of the marginal prices for characteristics. One consequence is that hedonic demand parameters cannot be used for as many purposes as those of an ordinary demand function. More specifically, the hedonic demand parameters cannot be used for prediction, since both quantities and marginal prices are endogenous. Unlike the ordinary demand case, marginal prices do not describe the budget constraint facing the household, and thus the estimated relationship cannot be used to predict household responses to budget constraint shifts.[6] Equally important, as alluded to before, non-linearity implies that few a priori constraints can be placed on estimated demand parameters. For example, there is no presumption that there is a negative relationship between the quantity of a characteristic and the marginal bid for that characteristic. This is true even for the compensated marginal bid function. The second-order conditions for the

---

[6]While Palmquist (1985) has suggested that the budget constraint can be treated in a linearized form, this result relates to a neighborhood of the utility maximizing change. To use it requires knowledge of the optimal selection. Prediction implies estimating how an exogenous change will affect behavior. In general, in such cases we can expect that the linearized marginal prices will change. This approach offers no basis beyond the hedonic for measuring them. It is therefore subject to the same potential limitations.

individual's maximization problem simply require that the chosen bid function be "more concave" than the hedonic price function. This implies that the compensated marginal bid function must have a more negative slope than the marginal hedonic price function. But because of non-linearity, it is quite possible for the marginal price function for some characteristic to have a positive slope.

The best way to view a marginal bid function is as a description of a portion of household preferences. Under some conditions, the system of marginal bid equations may be integrable to recover a full description of the household's utility function. Even if this is impossible, a particular marginal bid equation may still be useful in estimating benefits of public policies, as we discuss further below.

The third question, of identification of marginal bid equations, has been widely debated in the literature. Before considering it, we should be specific in our definition of identification. We will consider identification of the marginal bid function as synonymous with the ability to obtain consistent estimates of its parameters. The econometric problem with consistent estimation of the marginal bid equation is that the quantities on the right hand side are endogenous.

Given this definition of identification, one plausible method of consistent estimation involves the use of instrumental variables. The problem involves assuring that the structure of the model distinguishes the marginal bid and the marginal price functions *and* finding appropriate instruments. Rosen's original article suggested that individual supplier characteristics would be appropriate instruments for the marginal bid equation. However, Rosen's supplier characteristics will generally be inappropriate instruments because they will be correlated with unobserved tastes that form part of the residual in the marginal bid function [Bartik (1987), Epple (1987), Diamond and Smith (1982)]. Because different types of suppliers provide different bundle-types, individuals with different tastes, by choosing their desired bundles, tend systematically to match with those types of suppliers making such bundles. For example, individuals with a greater taste for a freshly painted housing unit are more likely to choose units provided by a supplier who happens to be a professional house painter. The use of a variable for profession of the housing supplier as an instrument therefore yields biased estimates. Several researchers have proposed as instruments dummy variables for the hedonic price function of the observation (Bartik, Brown, Diamond and Smith, Mendelsohn, Palmquist). Such instruments require multi-market data. For example, in housing studies one might use as instruments dummy variables for the metropolitan area or time period of the observation, on the assumption that the hedonic price function for housing exogenously varies from city to city and over time. These types of instruments are appropriate only if unobserved tastes do not vary on average from one hedonic price function to another.

Given the difficulties of acquiring multi-market data, several researchers have explored the conditions under which identification is possible with data for only one market. In principle, single market identification can be accomplished with the use of additional information – in the form of functional restrictions on the marginal bid and price equations. These restrictions can be as simple as postulating a different functional form for the marginal bid (or marginal offer) and the marginal price functions or assuming some characteristic enters the marginal price function but not the marginal bid function. This allows characteristics or higher-order terms that are excluded from the marginal bid function to be used as instruments. This approach has often been accepted too quickly as the resolution of the problem, without an adequate justification for its maintained assumptions [see Linneman (1981), Harrison and Rubinfeld (1978) as examples]. As Diamond and Smith (1982) observed in considering it:

> "Such a procedure will yield estimates, as it provides the additional constraint needed for identification of the demand equation. However, the estimates will be as arbitrary as the assumptions underlying them".[7]

A stronger criticism of this approach has been made in Bartik (1985). Excluded characteristics will be endogenously chosen by households. If an excluded characteristic shifts the marginal price function for some characteristic, z_j, then households with stronger tastes for z_j tend to choose levels of the excluded characteristic that imply lower prices for z_j. Even if the characteristic is appropriately excluded from the marginal bid function for z_j, it is correlated with tastes for z_j in the residual, and hence is an inappropriate instrument. Researchers may, of course, decide to assume that unobserved tastes are negligible, but this assumption in practice can be questioned.

Similar criticisms can be made of Mendelsohn's (1985) non-instrumental variable approach to single-market identification. Mendelsohn argues that single market identification is possible by recognizing the relationship between non-linearities in the marginal price, marginal bid, and marginal offer functions. Taken together with the role of demand and supply shift variables that permit the analyst to observe the range of individual responses to these marginal prices, he argues we can in some cases recover estimates of the structural parameters. Unfortunately, this argument ignores the role of unobservable household traits in influencing site selection decisions. If, for example, there are unobservable variables influencing the marginal bid function then we do not have sufficient information to recover the structural parameters [Bartik (forthcoming), McConnell and Phipps (1985)].

The identification problem becomes even more complex when one recognizes

---

[7]Diamond and Smith (1982) p. 15. Of course, in general terms, this argument should not be surprising. All tests of hypotheses involve additional maintained hypotheses as McCloskey (1983) has so aptly described in his essay on the rhetoric of economics. What Diamond and Smith seem to be emphasizing is the completely arbitrary nature of the treatment of this problem in many past hedonic applications.

the potential for multiple sources of error in the hedonic model in addition to unobserved tastes. Site characteristics may be measured only by proxy variables, or may be unobservable. The same holds true for demander and supplier characteristics. These issues are important because the sources of error can affect our ability to construct instruments for variables that are jointly determined through the equilibrium or for those likely to be correlated with components of the errors from the factors contributing to the matching [see Epple (1987)].

Even if the issues associated with identification can be resolved, the best which can be expected from benefit estimates derived from a marginal bid function (i.e. the answer to our fourth question) is the equivalent of an extremely restricted partial equilibrium measure of an individual's willingness to pay. For example, suppose the air quality in an area improves. If moving costs or other adjustment costs prevent individuals from changing locations in response to this improvement (i.e. we effectively hold all prices and quantities constant for the individual), then the marginal bid function for air quality can be easily used to analyze the costs of a non-marginal improvement in air quality. The marginal bid function for air quality shows how the household's marginal valuation of air quality changes as air quality improves. By integrating between the before and after levels of air quality, an estimate of an individual's total valuation of the improvement in air quality can be derived. Given exogenous information on the change in rents associated with the air quality change, the total valuation can then be compared with the changes in rent in the area to determine the net effects on the individual of the improvement.[8] If one only wants to determine the net efficiency benefits of the improvement, the rent changes can be ignored because they only represent transfers between demanders and suppliers. But these simple benefit losses become incorrect if household relocation and the associated complete adjustment is allowed.

2.3. Measuring benefits of amenity improvements: Alternative approaches using property values

As mentioned above, the usual measure of the benefits of an amenity improvement, the willingness to pay of the original households choosing the improved sites, will in general be incorrect because households will adjust to the new pattern of amenities. However, this measure can be regarded as an underestimate of the true efficiency benefits, because household and other market adjustments must increase efficiency [Bartik (1985); Scotchmer (1985)]. Alternatively, the

---

[8] It is not the case that the hedonic price function can be used to predict the new equilibrium price set after the change in air quality.

household valuation measure can be seen as a short-run measure of the benefits of amenity improvements, before households have a chance to adjust. This may seem inconsistent with the basic hedonic model, which assumes household and landlord adjustment to the equilibrium hedonic price function. However, it is not, since it is certainly possible to assume the presence of significant adjustment costs, so that households and firms observed in a hedonic cross-section have on average achieved their long-run equilibrium position.

There are other methods of using property values to measure the benefits of exogenous amenity improvements. First, one may examine the relationship between amenity improvements and ex post changes in property values [Rothenberg (1967), Strotz (1968), Lind (1973), Pines and Weiss (1976), Starrett (1981)]. For example, Pines and Weiss develop a relationship linking benefits to changes in property values in both improved and unimproved areas. The problem with this approach is that it is difficult to measure these amenity-induced changes in property values. Before the improvement takes place, the property value changes will be difficult to predict. The original hedonic can not be used for prediction, because the hedonic will change for any larger amenity improvement. After the improvement takes place, property value changes will take place, but it would be extremely difficult to ascertain what changes are due to the amenity improvements and what changes are due to other forces.

This approach is empirically feasible if the improvements take place in a geographic area that is small relative to the market [Polinsky and Shavell (1976), Freeman (1974b)]. In this case, the original hedonic will not change because of the improvements. As a result, consumers do not change utility because of the improvements, all benefits accrue to landowners in the improved area in increased property values and these benefits can be measured using the original hedonic. If household moving costs are added to this type of model, the benefit measures are a hybrid of the property value measure and the original household's valuation measure [Greer and White (1981), Bartik (1986)]. For improved sites whose original occupants are forced to move, the property value measure must be adjusted downwards by some estimate of household moving costs. For improved sites whose original occupants stay, the household valuation measure will be an appropriate measure of efficiency benefits.

A second approach is to look only at marginal changes in amenities, although these changes may take place over a large spatial area. The benefits of some pattern of marginal amenity improvements have been shown to equal the sum of the marginal willingness to pay for the amenity improvement of the original occupant of each improved site [Freeman (1974b), Small (1975), Pines and Weiss (1976)]. This marginal willingness to pay can, of course, be calculated with knowledge only of the hedonic function, as the marginal willingness to pay will equal the hedonic marginal price of the amenity. The intuition behind this result is that adjustments by households and landlords to the new pattern of amenities can be ignored because of the envelope theorem.

The most general case is non-marginal amenity improvements that take place over a large spatial area, and change the hedonic price function in some fashion. As mentioned before, the household valuation measure provides a lower bound to efficiency benefits in this case. It can also be shown that the rent changes predicted by the original hedonic function, while not an accurate prediction of actual rent changes, will provide an upper bound to efficiency benefits [Bartik (1985), Kanemoto (1985)].[9] It is difficult to provide an intuitive rationale for this result. One approach is to consider the true benefits of some pattern of non-marginal amenity improvements as the integral of infinite series of marginal amenity improvements. At each small marginal step, the benefits are equal to the sum over all improved sites of the marginal price of the amenity, as discussed above. As amenities improve, the hedonic price function continuously changes in some fashion. Algebraically, this measure of true efficiency benefits can be written as:

$$\text{True Efficiency Benefits} = \sum_{j=1}^{N} \int_{k_0}^{k_1} \frac{\partial p^k}{\partial A_j} [A_j(k), \mathbf{Z}] \mathrm{d}k \tag{5}$$

where $j = 1, \ldots, N$ denotes the N improved sites, $A_j(k)$ describes how amenities at site j change as a function of a constructed variable k, and the k superscript on p indicates that the hedonic price function changes as the amenity improvements occur. The upper bound described here would simply eliminate the k superscript on p in (5) and calculate marginal price changes using the original hedonic. Intuitively, one would think that amenity improvements would tend to lower marginal amenity prices, and thus the (5) measure of true efficiency benefits is less than the rent increases predicted by the original hedonic.

Ideally, one would like to develop exact measures of benefits due to amenity improvements for the general cases, rather than upper or lower bounds or measures that only apply to special cases. As (5) suggests, such exact, general measures are possible if we can predict the equilibrium hedonic price function for alternative distributions of amenities. Such predictions require either analytical solutions or general equilibrium simulation models of the hedonic market. With such simulation models, the integration procedure implied by (5) is unnecessary because the model can simply calculate the household utility and supplier profit changes that would occur due to non-marginal amenity improvements.

---

[9]The result stated in the text is an oversimplification of the result in Bartik (1985) or Kanemoto (1985). The original hedonic is an upper bound only if the effects of amenity improvements on supplier costs and the supplier adjustment to the amenity improvements are small. These assumptions will often seem reasonable. What will always be an upper bound is the property value changes predicted by a hedonic property value function that only includes amenities, with housing characteristics allowed to be endogenously chosen by suppliers.

2.4. Discrete choice models, residential mobility models, and the valuation of amenities

The hedonic framework assumes each economic agent is unable to influence the outcome. Individuals are described *as if* they took this equilibrium function as given and therefore had their choices constrained by it. Most of the hedonic models have used these assumptions to focus on the household's marginal decisions on characteristics. An alternative conception of the process would treat household decisions within a discrete choice framework. There are two versions of this model that are relevant to amenity choice and valuation: the bid-rent model and the residential location model.

In the bid-rent model, individuals are assumed to establish bids for all housing units, based on a constrained utility maximization framework. Units are occupied by the household with the highest bid for that unit. Assuming each individual's preferences can be characterized in a random utility framework (with the errors assumed to follow independent Weibull distributions), this formulation implies a multinomial logit model will describe the probability that a particular individual is the highest bidder for a housing unit [Ellickson (1981)]. Moreover, since we observe both the choice and the selling price, Lerman and Kern (1983) have demonstrated how the model can be used to recover an estimate of an individual's willingness to pay for housing attributes. Taken together with McFadden's (1978) earlier suggestions that one need not consider all possible choices in a logit model – a randomly drawn sample would yield consistent parameter estimates – this framework offers an alternative approach for estimating the values for amenities.

A second version of the discrete choice model is the residential location model [McFadden (1978)]. In this model, we focus on estimating the probability that a particular housing unit yields the highest utility for a household, while, as mentioned above, the bid-rent model focuses on the probability that a given individual is the highest bidder. Estimation of the residential logit model also uses multinomial logit, but yields estimates of direct utility function parameters rather than bid-rent function parameters. An example of the use of residential location models for analyzing amenities is Friedman's (1981) model of factors influencing household choices of residential communities in the San Francisco Bay Area.

While these discrete choice models are interesting alternatives to the conventional hedonic model, they do not change the basic equilibrium process envisioned in a hedonic framework. Instead of focusing on a price function which assures a matching and can (in simplified cases) be shown to be a function of the parameters describing the distribution of demanders and of suppliers offered, the discrete choice approach specifies a distribution to distinguish demanders, assumes a fixed array of bundles are available for selection, and accepts a given functional form to describe household preferences.

Of course, the ability of a discrete choice model to recover household willingness to pay and benefits follows directly from the added information – the specific utility function and distribution of bidders that are assumed. If parameters of the utility function or bid function can be consistently estimated, then the marginal bid can be derived.

The most important contribution of this approach may not be as an alternative to the hedonic model's view of the process. Rather it may provide a basis for changing the equilibrium process or for dealing with site attributes that are not subject to continuous variation. Horowitz (1984a,b) has recently proposed modifications to the conventional bid-rent model that allow for the possibility that bidders are not necessarily matched to their highest valued housing units and some homes remain unsold. In his formulation sellers do not know the full set of bids for their units, but must decide sequentially on each bid, considering it in relationship to their asking price (which is the upper bound for bids). This type of model has many similarities to models in the larger literature on job search in the labor market.

Another possible modification to the basic hedonic model would involve using a mixed discrete/continuous framework in which some site characteristics were discrete, incapable of being altered continuously and outside the hedonic price function. Others would be a part of the hedonic equilibrium. Since both sets of characteristics could be assumed to contribute to household utility, a description of the household choice process would require both hedonic price functions *and* a discrete choice random utility framework.

At this point, very few papers (Horowitz, Friedman, Lerman, Williams) have implemented discrete choice models for valuing site amenities. Consequently, we do not see a basis for comparing the empirical valuations of amenities derived from these models with those derived from the conventional hedonic framework.

Another plausible method for valuing amenities would be to determine their effect on residential mobility relative to monetary factors. It would take us too far afield to review residential mobility models in any detail. But these models, despite their potential, have thus far shed little light on households' preferences regarding amenities. Despite the large literature discussing residential mobility models [see Porell (1982) or Quigley and Weinberg (1977) for reviews; Mills and Price (1984), Venti and Wise (1984) are recent examples of macro and micro models, respectively], few studies have found much of an effect of amenities on residential mobility.

In our view, the performance of residential mobility models may improve with better theoretical structure applied to micro-level data. A promising theoretical approach is to consider residential mobility to represent a type of discrete choice, in which the alternatives are different housing units and communities, including the household's current housing unit or community. Estimation of such a discrete choice model would be complicated by a type of selection bias. We know that the household preferred its current housing unit or community in the previous time period. Hence, the disturbance term for its current choice can not be considered to be independent of values of the observed variables affecting utility. The more strongly that observed variables indicate that the current choice is a poor one for the household, the more positive must be the effect of unobserved variables on household utility from its current choice.

2.5. Amenity supply in the hedonic housing model

Our description of models for valuing amenities thus far has implicitly treated amenities as either being exogenous or as being produced by individual housing suppliers. As we noted at the outset, a single specification of the process underlying the supply of amenities is unlikely to be very useful for most applications. The factors determining the supply of amenities vary rather substantially depending on the specific amenity under consideration. The examples we identified in the introduction were intended to illustrate the ways in which the public sector might influence this process, but also serve to reinforce this conclusion. It is somewhat surprising, given that concern over a public sector role in the supply process for amenities has motivated much of the research on valuation of amenities, to find that explicit analytical models of amenity supply are largely non-existent in the literature. Diamond and Tolley (1982), for example, define urban amenities as location-specific goods that are often non-excludable once access to their location is acquired (and therefore have some features of a public good), but suggest only that their supply can be influenced by private economic agents and the public sector in complex ways.

In most cases, it is probably reasonable to assume that the supply of urban amenities is fixed over the time horizon that is relevant to the market equilibrium described by the hedonic price function. Clearly, government expenditures on public services – education, law enforcement, fire protection, and the like – influence the supply of the amenities that are associated with these activities. However, the connection is neither direct nor sufficiently fast to warrant specifying a supply response mechanism. In other cases, where regulatory decisions or the joint decisions of groups of economic agents together influence the amenities available, this assumption is even more defensible. History will matter particularly for the latter of these influences. To assume otherwise would add significant complications to our model of the equilibrium process. That is, the decisions of demanders and suppliers of housing about their location, housing consumption, and supply levels are made subject to some maintained pattern of amenity supplies within the metropolitan area.[10] The households that select each neighborhood, and their behavior and characteristics, together with the housing

---

[10]This is the idea proposed by Tiebout (1956) as the basis for estimating the demand for local public goods.

production choices of neighborhood landlords, affect each neighborhood's amenity supply and a pattern of amenity supply for the metropolitan area (as the collection of these neighborhoods) is the result.

If we specify a framework in which amenity supply is endogenous then we must also describe the extent of information available to participants in the market. That is, if the available amenity supply results from the production decisions of firms, local governments, and landlords as well as from the location decisions of households we need to specify how much information each type of economic agent has about the others' activities. Asymmetries in the information available or differences in market power of each group would require changes in the equilibrium concepts. For example, if individual households or housing suppliers, or coalitions of such groups, perceived that their demand and supply choices or other actions could substantially affect the spatial pattern of amenities, a more complex hedonic model would be required. Some researchers may feel that such complexities are needed to model the market for some amenities. But for most amenities, the supply involves substantial time with long delays between the actions of economic agents and their realization in amenity supply changes. Furthermore, individual agents are unlikely to affect amenity supply, so the forming of coalitions would be needed for supply considerations to influence market behavior. For example, improvements in a local school system require years before they are realized and even longer before they are recognized by those outside the locality involved. Thus, most individual economic agents would not perceive a substantial effect of their individual actions on the schools, even in the long run.

2.6. Inter-city models of amenity sections

The preceding models have been intended to describe a subset of a household's possible decisions in that locational decisions were assumed to be made within a single metropolitan area. The most important aspect of this assumption is that the implications of a household's decisions concerning the site specific features of a housing choice would be confined to the housing market. Employment decisions were assumed to be unaffected by these selections. Of course, this was a simplification. In addition to choosing amenities by selecting a residential location within a city, individuals may also alter amenities by their choice of a city in which to live and work. The choice of a city is more complicated to analyze than the within-city locational choice for several reasons.

First, the choice of amenities across cities involves two hedonic markets, the labor and housing markets, not just the housing market. When we assume that locational decisions can involve movement among cities, the amenity choice problem facing individuals becomes more complex because the choice is now made subject to two hedonic price functions, one for the labor market and one for the housing market. These two functions arise as part of the requirements for an equilibrium matching involving both the housing and the labor markets simultaneously.

One of the most important issues that arises with this generalization is the extent to which inter-city amenity differences will be capitalized into wages versus rents. This depends largely on what is assumed about the response of labor demanders and housing suppliers. Each characterization of household adjustment in amenity selection has implications for both the capitalization issue and the proper interpretation of the partial derivatives of each hedonic price function in relationship to an individual's willingness to pay for changes in site specific amenities.

A second complication with an inter-city choice framework is how to incorporate the variation in amenities within cities into the model. As we implied, the model could consider the simultaneous choice by a household of a job and a residential site, given whatever pattern of amenity availability occurs within *and* across cities. However, characterizing the within-city variation is not an inconsequential task, especially because measures of amenity variables are often difficult to formulate. Consequently, the most common procedure in inter-city empirical studies has been to examine how wages and/or rents vary with the average amenity levels of each city, implicitly assuming either that the amenity levels are constant, or that they vary systematically within the city with another variable in the model, such as distance from the central business district [see Cropper (1981) as an example].

To date no model has fully addressed all these complexities. Roback (1982) and Rosen (1979) have proposed similar models of how amenities affect both sides of the labor and housing markets. However, both models ignore intra-city variations in amenities and assume a fixed city boundary.

Other researchers, such as Henderson (1982), and Clark, Kahn, and Ofek (1983), allow for intra-city variation in the amenity along with access to the central business district. In addition, these models allow for an endogenously determined city boundary. However, this second class of models does not develop how the firm's choice of a city will be affected by wage, rent, and amenity differentials.[11] The theoretical work of this second group of researchers implies that, controlling for commuting costs, inter-city amenity differentials will be reflected in wages.

A third type of model has recently been offered by Berger, Blomquist, and Hoehn (1985). This model is based on the Rosen–Roback model, but allows for a flexible city boundary. However, firms are assumed not to use land, unlike the Rosen–Roback approach.

---

[11]While the Clark, Kahn, and Ofek model analyzes the firm's problem, their actual empirical model is derived from the worker's maximization problem.

While all these models are incomplete, they do serve to illustrate the implications of joint consideration of the labor and housing markets as well as the assumed behavior of firms in describing these markets' equilibrium conditions. In order to understand their respective strengths and weaknesses, a brief outline of the essentials of each model will be discussed before turning to the empirical implementation.

Roback's model assumes that all workers have identical tastes, and a fixed labor supply, and all firms have identical cost functions associated with constant returns to scale (CRTS) production technologies. Workers' indirect utility functions can be specified in terms of the city's wage rate, land rental rate, and amenity levels, all assumed to be constant within the city. For equilibrium, worker's utility level realized must be constant (at k) across cities, as in (6).

$$V(W, r, A) = k \tag{6}$$

where w is the wage, r the land rental rate, and A the vector of amenities. Firms' costs are also assumed to depend on wage rates, land rents, and the amenity vector. For equilibrium, firms' units costs in each city must be equal to the product price, which is assumed to be a constant across cities. Normalizing this price to one yields (7).

$$C(w, r, A) = 1. \tag{7}$$

To describe the equilibrium wage and rent gradient, assume there is a single amenity and totally differentiate (6) and (7) with respect to A. Solving the resulting equations for $\partial w/\partial A$ and $\partial r/\partial A$ yields:

$$\frac{\partial w}{\partial A} = \frac{C_A V_r - V_A C_r}{V_w C_r - V_r C_w} = \frac{C_A V_r - V_A C_r}{L(A)V_w/X} \gtrless 0. \tag{8}$$

$$\frac{\partial r}{\partial A} = \frac{V_A C_w - V_w C_A}{V_w C_r - V_r C_w} = \frac{V_A C_w - V_w C_A}{L(A)V_w/X} \gtrless 0 \tag{9}$$

where all the subscripts indicate partial derivatives with respect to the subscript variable, $L(A)$ is total land in the city with an amenity level of A (assumed fixed), and x is total production in the city.

Several aspects of the Roback analysis are important to highlight. First, while the framework explicitly identifies a firms' production decisions with the specification of cost function given in (7), her framework is quite similar to that proposed by Rosen (1979).[12] His model postulated that households were self-

---

[12] Roback maintains that each firm's production function includes capital, labor, and land and that capital has been "optimized" out of the analysis. However, CRTS in capital, labor, and land, and this optimization process does *not* imply the CRTS in labor and land.

producers of a consumption good with a fixed capital stock and thereby attached the amenity and productivity effects directly to the household. In her framework the price of capital must be treated as fixed nationally, so that there are no locational advantages for capital. Thus, the effects of capital's price can be ignored and Roback's model specifies firms' production functions so that the burden of the proper assignment of resources is directed to the movement of households in response to the prices of location specific factors. While firms can, in principle, move, their decisions can be treated as complementary to the household selections.

We can also recast (8) and (9) to gauge the relative impact of a given percentage change in amenities for wages and property values (rents). Assume that amenities are neutral with respect to a firm's costs (i.e., $C_A = 0$). Using the duality properties of $C(\cdot)$ ($C_r = l/x$, $C_w = N/x$, with l the land used in production, and N the labor) we have:

$$\frac{\partial \ln w / \partial \ln A}{\partial \ln r / \partial \ln A} = \frac{\partial w / \partial A}{\partial r / \partial A} \cdot \frac{r}{w} = -\frac{rC_r}{wC_w} = -\frac{rl}{wN} \tag{10}$$

The absolute magnitude of the elasticity of the real wage response to amenities in comparison to the rent response is equal to the ratio of land's share of costs relative to that of labor. Thus, the responsiveness of wages to amenity changes relative to that of rents will depend on the assumed importance of land relative to labor (as a share of production costs net of capital). The most reasonable assumption is that labor will be much more important than land in production, and that rents are likely to be more responsive to amenity changes than wages.[13]

Finally, we can use the model to consider the implications of inter-city location decisions for the measurement of an individual's marginal willingness to pay for amenities. Recall in the intra-city model, the marginal bid was equal to the marginal price derived from the hedonic property value model. Now two markets must be considered and neither marginal price is equal to the marginal bid [as demonstrated in (8) and (9)]. Solving for the marginal willingness to pay (V_A/V_w) indicates that both functions' marginal price schedules must be considered to estimate the marginal bid.

$$\frac{V_A}{V_w} = y^* \frac{\partial r}{\partial A} - \frac{\partial w}{\partial A}, \tag{11}$$

with y^* the equilibrium residential land consumed by the household.[14] (11) indicates that the weighted sum (since $\partial w / \partial A < 0$) of the marginal price schedules

---

[13]This conclusion might change if city land area was endogenous. It would seem likely that land rents would go up less with an amenity increase if city land area expanded as amenities increased.

[14]The weight assigned to $\partial W / \partial A$ is unity because the model assumes that a fixed amount of labor time normalized to unity is supplied.

is equal to the marginal willingness to pay. However, this result should not be surprising. The model ties job and location decisions together. In effect, a job and a housing location are jointly supplied with each amenity level. Thus (11) parallels the familiar joint supply condition implying vertical addition of the marginal price schedules of the housing and labor markets. If this treatment of the decision process is plausible, then it implies that the issues associated with retrieving information on the marginal bid function can become more complex with inter-city models in that hedonic property value models will not provide point estimates of the marginal bids. Under ideal conditions, a hedonic real wage model, incorporating the effects of amenities on all prices that can vary with location and amenity levels will (for the ideal price index) yield a marginal price that equals the negative of the marginal willingness to pay for the amenity.[15]

By contrast to Rosen–Roback, the Henderson and Clark, Kahn, and Ofek models assume a flexible city boundary at which land rents must be equal to the agricultural land-rent. Controlling for commuting costs, at this boundary amenity differentials must be reflected in wage differentials. More formally, assume a monocentric urban model in which worker utility depends on wages, rents, amenities, and commuting costs. Commuting costs depend only on the distance of the worker's residence from the city center. At the city edge and a distance of $\bar{d}$, land rents equal the agricultural rent level r_a. In equilibrium, workers living at each city's edge must all have the same utility, or using a revised indirect utility function:

$$V(w, r_a, d, A) = k. \tag{12}$$

Differentiating (12) with respect to w, $\bar{d}$, and A, and re-arranging terms yield (13).

$$dw = -\frac{V_d}{V_w} d\bar{d} - \frac{V_A}{V_w} dA. \tag{13}$$

That is, holding the radius of the city constant, wages should vary with amenities. This framework stresses the importance of including some control variable for city size or area if one is estimating how amenities affect nominal wages. Most studies have implicitly done this by including a variable for population, which is strongly correlated with the city radius, or in some cases by including both population and population density as variables. However, these variables have usually not been interpreted as control variables for the commuting costs of the

---

[15]Izraeli (1977) used this interdependency to argue for a simultaneous equation model noting that: "Money wages and the goods' prices are not independent variables. Wages as the main component of firms' cost of production, help determine the price of goods, and the vector of prices of goods is a variable affecting labor supply, thus helping to determine wages" (p. 275).

We feel a connection is present but not a simultaneous determination. Labor is not the dominant component of cost for all industries. Indeed, for the manufacturing sector materials have the largest cost share. Of course, this relationship will vary with industry. Since adjustment is not instantaneous, the important implication is that the real wage is the relevant variable for a hedonic wage function.

resident at the city edge. Under this interpretation, any variable that is positively correlated with city radius would be expected to have a positive effect on wages simply because workers at the edge must be compensated for the higher commuting costs.

One problem with the Henderson and Clark et al. models is that the location decisions of firms are not examined. The derived conditions are clearly necessary for worker equilibrium. However, it is unclear why firms will be willing to pay a wage premium to compensate workers in large cities for higher commuting costs.

The Berger–Blomquist–Hoehn model relaxes the Rosen–Roback model by allowing for a flexible city boundary. Firm costs depend on wages, amenities and the population of the city (to allow for agglomeration economies or diseconomies). Firms are assumed to use no land, so the central business district is a point location, and land prices have no effect on profits. Workers' utilities depend on the price of land, the wage rate, amenities, and commuting costs to their city's central business district. Amenities are assumed to be uniform within a city. Land rents vary within and across cities, and wage rates vary across cities, so as to equalize utility for all workers and profits for all firms. The population and area of the city are determined endogenously. The city area includes all land in which the workers' bid for land exceeds the agricultural land-rent; the total population in the city depends on the endogenously determined density as workers at each location choose their land consumption in response to land prices at that location.

This model also tends to imply that inter-city variations in amenities are capitalized into land rents. In the absence of agglomeration effects or amenity effects on business, costs, wages must be the same across all cities to assure equal firm profits in all cities. Rents will then adjust within and across cities to equalize utility given differences in amenities. However, as in the Henderson–Clark et al. models, at each city's edge, where rents must equal the agricultural land-rent (assumed uniform nationwide), wages net of commuting costs compensate workers for amenity differentials. But the Berger–Blomquist–Hoehn model makes it clear this adjustment takes the form of higher commuting costs, not lower wages, in amenity-rich cities as population endogenously adjusts upwards in response to high amenity levels. If amenities or agglomeration affects business costs, then the relative effects of amenities on wages versus rents becomes much more uncertain.

All the models developed to date are partial descriptions of the inter-city amenity market. The Roback–Rosen model includes the demand side of the labor market, but ignores intra-city variations in amenities, commuting costs, and rents. The Henderson–Clark model allows for commuting costs and flexible city boundaries, but ignores firm behavior, incorrectly assumes city population is exogenous, and does not examine how average city rents vary with amenities. The Berger–Blomquist–Hoehn model allows for both flexible city boundaries and the demand side of the labor market, but ignores the effects of land rents on business costs and the implications of them for the behavior of average land/housing prices.

3. Empirical analyses of the role of amenities in household decisions

Implementing any theoretical model based on real world behavior and our available measures of the outcomes of that behavior is never easy. The informational requirements of models are rarely met, and thus the empirical work requires practical compromises. A standard of perfection is always a counsel of paralysis. To appraise the performance of hedonic models, we first consider some specific aspects of the estimation of hedonic price functions and marginal bid functions. Following this discussion, we review a selection of the hedonic housing price and wage models, discussing the types of data, models, and findings that have been obtained in practice. Finally, the section closes with a discussion of the qualifying assumptions and their likely impact on the usefulness of the models' results.

3.1. Estimating hedonic models

While there are many econometric issues that must be addressed in estimating hedonic models (and therefore might be considered here), we focus here on the specification of the hedonic price function. In Section 2, we already discussed the estimation of the marginal bid functions given a nonlinear price function.

Without theoretical guidance as to functional form, most empirical work has simply assumed some arbitrary functional form. In the hedonic housing literature, the most common functional form is the semilogarithmic, with the natural log of the housing price a linear function of the characteristics. This functional form assumes that a given change in characteristics has a constant percentage effect on housing prices.

Recently, a number of researchers have explored the use of the Box–Cox transformation procedure to develop the appropriate functional form for hedonic equations [Halvorsen and Pollakowski (1981); Sonstelie and Portney (1980); Bender, Gronberg, and Huang (1980); Linneman (1980a); Goodman (1978)]. The Box–Cox transformation of a variable y is:

$$y^{(\lambda)} = y^{(\lambda-1)/\lambda} \quad \text{if } \lambda \neq 0$$
$$= \ln y \quad \text{if } \lambda = 0. \tag{14}$$

This transformation can be applied to the dependent variable and/or to the independent variables in the hedonic equation. The transformation parameter, λ, is sometimes constrained to be the same across most of these variables, although this constraint is justified more by convenience than by theory.

The Box–Cox approach has the advantage of allowing for a more flexible functional form. This advantage is purchased at the cost of an additional set of parameters that must be estimated and difficulties in using the estimated price function in applications (see Cassel and Mendelsohn). Moreover, the Box–Cox maximum likelihood estimator has been recognized to be inappropriately defined. The transformation itself limits the range of dependent variable and therefore prevents the assumption of normality which is the basis of the "likelihood" function that has been proposed for estimating λ.[16] While the approach can be used despite this problem, one cannot appeal to ML theory for inference and interpretation of the properties of the estimates.

An alternative strategy for specifying a flexible functional form appeals to the notion of approximating any function with a Taylor-series expansion in all the characteristics. This approach can quickly become unmanageable if the number of characteristics is large, or if an expansion greater than second order is attempted.

Given the arbitrary nature of the specification for the hedonic price function, it is natural to consider the implications of mistakes. That is, how will misspecifications affect the performance of the hedonic framework? There are at least two ways to address this question. First we might consider the implications in a conventional statistical framework – such as that used to analyze specification errors generally. Alternatively, one might conduct controlled experiments – replicating the matching process envisioned in a hedonic equilibrium and evaluating the performance of alternative specifications for the price function in characterizing it as theory would imply it should. We will discuss both.

Any misspecification of variables in the hedonic function usually results in errors in measuring the marginal prices estimated from it, and hence the marginal bids. This measurement error is probably correlated with the right-hand side of the marginal bid function, resulting in a potential source of bias for ordinary least squares (OLS) estimates of the marginal bid function.

Consider the simple example of estimating the marginal bid function for z, which is assumed to depend on z, or

$$\frac{\partial W}{\partial z} = C_0 + C_1 z + \varepsilon \tag{15}$$

Since we do not observe the true marginal price, but some estimate of the marginal price, we cannot estimate (15), rather we can estimate only (16).

$$\frac{\partial \hat{p}}{\partial z} = \frac{\partial \hat{W}}{\partial z} = C_0 + C_1 z + \left(\frac{\partial \hat{W}}{\partial z} - \frac{\partial W}{\partial z} \right) + \varepsilon$$

---

[16]For a discussion of the implications of this problem for the properties of the Box–Cox transformation, see Amemiya and Powell (1980).

$$\frac{\partial \hat{p}}{\partial z} = \frac{\partial \hat{W}}{\partial z} = C_0 + C_1 z + M + \varepsilon. \tag{16}$$

where M is the measurement error. If M is correlated with z, OLS estimates of C_1 will be biased. This correlation should probably be treated as a likely outcome of most hedonic models. For example, suppose that the true marginal price function is

$$\frac{\partial p}{\partial z} = B_0 + B_1 z + B_2 S. \tag{17}$$

but the marginal price function we calculate is based on an estimated hedonic price function that omits an interaction term between S and z. The calculated marginal price function would then be given as (18).

$$\frac{\partial \hat{p}}{\partial z} = \hat{B}_0 + \hat{B}_1 z. \tag{18}$$

Under these assumptions, the measurement error term is given by (19).

$$M = (\hat{B}_0 - B_0) + (\hat{B}_1 - B_1)z - B_2 S. \tag{19}$$

This term will be correlated with the right-hand side term z in the marginal bid function, even though S is not an appropriate argument in the marginal bid function. Moreover, M can be correlated with z even if S is uncorrelated with z as a result of the term $(\hat{B}_1 - B_1)z$. B in this case is still biased because Sz, the omitted variable in the hedonic price function, is correlated with the z and z^2 term in the hedonic price function, even though S may be uncorrelated with z and z^2. Alternatively, if Sz is uncorrelated with z and z^2, S may be correlated with z, and the measurement error M term will be correlated with z even though B_0 and B_1 are estimated without bias. This last case may seem quite surprising: a hedonic that is estimated without bias may yield marginal price estimaters whose error is correlated with the level of housing characteristics. The key statistical problem is that a hedonic price function regression is designed to find the best prediction of prices, conditional on the right-hand side variables. Even if there is no omitted variable bias in the hedonic, this statistical approach is not focused on predicting the marginal price of a characteristic conditional on a set of variables.

Cropper, Deck, McConnell, and Phipps (1985) have recently reported the first attempt to simulate a hedonic equilibrium.[17] They use this approach to look at the accuracy of hedonic estimates of household marginal WTP. In theory, of

[17] Actually there have been two other studies reporting the simulation of a hedonic framework. The first by Ohsfeldt and Smith (1985) did not simulate a hedonic equilibrium. Rather it used a polynomial hedonic price equation and specified marginal rates of substitution equations to generate the data which were then used to re-estimate the model. Kneisner and Leeth (1985) used a multiple market simulation to investigate a hedonic wage framework as an approximation for the solution of the separate markets. Thus neither of these studies attempted an equilibrium matching as implied by the hedonic framework.

course, this should equal the hedonic marginal price, but they consider cases in which the assumptions of the hedonic models are not perfectly met or the hedonic is misspecified. Their analysis considers two basic structures. The first assumes households have linear utility functions with parameters for each site characteristic. Households are distinguished by the parameters for these attributes. A uniform distribution was assumed. The supply of these characteristics was also assumed to be uniform. These assumptions imply an exact solution for the hedonic price function – as a quadratic in the characteristics.

To simulate the market equilibrium the authors treat it as an assignment problem (paralleling the bid-rent models we discussed earlier). Their analysis with the linear model assumes three site attributes, and examines how the model's performance is affected by:

(a) the degree of variation in attributes;
(b) the degree of variation in tastes;
(c) the extent of collinearity in attributes;
(d) the introduction of a discrete attribute.

Each solution involved 200 households and 200 homes with a normal distribution of income.[18] Their second case modified both assumed utility functions and the characterization of the supply of sites.

Since the true marginal bids are known, the models are evaluated based on the difference between the partial derivative of the hedonic price function and each individual's marginal bid for each attribute with each computed at each individual's selected vector of attributes. Because the hedonic is correctly specified in this first case as quadratic, the discrepancies between marginal prices and marginal bids arise from the lack of perfect continuity in characteristics with only 200 homes in the model.

The results indicate good performance in the function summarizing marginal values. Variations in dispersion of attributes, collinearity or discreteness do not greatly affect the errors. Average absolute errors for narrow taste distributions were generally less than ten percent with the largest errors associated with the least important attributes. Increased dispersion in tastes had a marked impact on the average absolute errors. In most cases they were tripled (dispersion in tastes increased by a factor of two and one half) though there was not increased sensitivity to collinearity or discreteness.

The second set of experiments used constant elasticity of substitution utility functions and a multivariate normal distribution for the three attributes. Cases with both equal and normal income distributions were considered. In each case a variety of specifications for the hedonic price function were estimated including

---

[18]Two versions of the linear utility model were treated. The second utilized information from Baltimore to describe the distribution of attributes and income. These results were also consistent with our overall summary of the findings of the study.

the Box–Cox, semi-log, double-log, and various polynomials. In general, the Box–Cox provided the best estimates, with average absolute errors in estimating the marginal bids of less than five percent for both assumed income distributions.

While these findings are simply a beginning, they do indicate that if the equilibrium assumptions are satisfied the other assumptions of the hedonic framework may not be as limiting as previous theoretical discussions may have implied.

3.2. Hedonic housing price models

There have been an exceptionally large number of hedonic housing price models since the early contributions by Nourse (1967), Ridker and Henning (1967), Kain and Quigley (1975), and Anderson and Crocker (1971). It would be both impossible and not necessarily instructive to provide another summary of all of these studies in the space of a few paragraphs. Several detailed reviews have been prepared [see Ball (1973), Smith (1977), Freeman (1979a), Witte and Long (1980), and Ott (1982) as examples]. Based on these reviews, several general features of these studies should be discussed. They include: the unit of observation (and with it the implicit difficulty of observing actual market transactions), the problem of market segmentation, and the issues associated with measuring the amenity variables.

Early hedonic models were based on census information generally using the census tract as the observational unit, the median property value as the measure of price, and measures of the "average" characteristics of the owner-occupied units in each tract as if they adequately described each unit within the census tract. Examples of this type of study include Ridker and Henning (1967), Anderson and Crocker (1971), Polinsky and Rubinfield (1977), and Nelson (1978). Clearly, because of the data used, these studies pose significant problems for the interpretation of their estimated hedonic price functions. The measure of price is a summary statistic of what households report as their estimate of the value of their home not the market price. Such responses can be expected to be imperfect measures of the market prices. Moreover, the use of summary statistics for both the price and the characteristics implies the equilibrium condition must be assumed to apply to measures of the "representative" housing unit. Indeed, there may not exist a housing unit which corresponds to the characteristics used to represent structure in any tract.

The use of aggregate census tract data does not allow examination of the effects of some of the most interesting neighborhood amenities. For example, aggregate census tract data does not permit a distinction between the effects of a unit's own housing quality and neighborhood housing quality. This is potentially important because the effect of the physical condition of other housing in a neighborhood on an individual unit's value is quite relevant for federal and city community development policies.

A second class of studies has been based on the *Annual Housing Survey* with information on individual housing units, household reported property values (not market prices), characteristics of each unit, and household reported attitudes concerning the adequacy of neighborhood and town amenities (i.e. these are the micro counterparts to what was reported in Table 1). Linneman's (1980a) analysis of the prospects for a single national hedonic price function was, for example, based on these data. While an improvement on the census tract case, these studies rely on a price measure that the household perceives to be the current market price.

The final set of studies, and those with the best correspondence between the data and theory, is based on actual market transactions – such as rents paid by tenants, or the local multiple listing services' records for sales of homes in a community during a particular period. In these cases a market price is available along with the structural characteristics of the site. The samples generally contain recorded sales over some time span. In periods of inflation of the general price level, it is unreasonable to assume all transactions can be pooled to correspond to the same nominal price relationship. Since the sample size involved often has not permitted partitioning according to selling season in each town, a simple adjustment to the market price for movements in the overall price index is often performed and the data pooled to estimate a single function.

For any of these studies implementation of the model requires the determination of the extent of the housing market. It is customary to assume that the housing market coincides with the metropolitan area, but some observers have felt that the market might be segmented along racial lines or into smaller geographic units [Straszheim (1975), Sonstelie and Portney (1980), Goodman (1978), Schnare and Struyk (1976)]. On the other hand, as we noted above, Linneman (1980a) and Butler (1977) have investigated the possibility that the housing market and, hence the appropriate hedonic price function, might be national in scope.

Empirical problems can arise in detecting market segments. The usual procedure has been to divide the city into the proposed market segments, and then perform an F-test for whether the hedonic coefficients in the different segments are significantly different. But this procedure has difficulties. First, the hedonic coefficients could be the same or similar across different markets. Second, the nonlinearity of the hedonic budget constraint and our ignorance of its true form imply that specification errors, not the existence of separate markets, could explain any significant differences in hedonic coefficients across proposed segments. The omission of higher order, interaction terms, or any other omitted variable from the hedonic estimating equation would result in biased estimates of hedonic coefficients. These biased estimates are likely to differ across market segments that are chosen by the researcher, such as the ghetto sub-market versus the rest of the city.

These problems suggest that rather than relying exclusively on empirical methods for uncovering market segmentation, an examination of factors defining the conditions of access to the market may be more successful. Racial discrimination is the obvious example, but there can be others. Some sections of a city become "company towns". The enclave of housing surrounding a university often exhibits this characteristic. Neighborhoods within communities can become associated with the employees of particular firms and this association can reinforce perceived limitations of access.

Another major problem in empirical hedonic housing studies is the development of appropriate amenity measures. For most studies, site-specific amenity variables must be "attached" or matched with the records on housing units. As a rule, this attachment implies using city, neighborhood, or census tract averages as the measures of amenities. To the extent there is variation in the quality or character of the urban amenities at a lower geographic scale than can be identified in the matching, this procedure will lead to an errors-in-variables problem. Equally important, information on many of the amenity measures considered to be important determinants of housing prices may not be available. This can lead to an omitted variable bias. For example, the average income of neighborhood residents is often proposed as a proxy measure for the overall status of the neighborhood [Leven et al. (1977)]. However, average neighborhood income is likely to be positively correlated with many of the omitted neighborhood amenities. Hence, the estimated effect of this variable on housing prices is likely to be positively biased.

Finally, the analysis may have available multiple measures of what is believed to be the same amenity. For example, one might have available police measures of the neighborhood crime rate as well as residents' perceptions of the crime problem. Inclusion of both measures raises problems. The variables are likely to be highly correlated which reduces the prospect for deriving precise estimates of the individual effects of each variable. Equally important, the presence of a "technical" measure of the amenity along with an individual's perception of the amenity raises questions with respect to how they are to be interpreted. The hedonic price function will be influenced by what individuals perceive the amenities to be. Presumably, the technical measure is an indicator of the information available to individuals for forming these perceptions. A single summary index of the perceived level of amenities may be an inadequate measure of the effects of the distribution of perceptions on the price function. This is an important practical problem because the theoretical framework assumes all individuals have complete (and the same) knowledge of the attributes of a housing unit. In practice, this is not the case. Consequently, a reasonable procedure would seem to be to summarize the information contained in the various measures into one variable.[19]

Of course, the above discussion implicitly maintains that households recognize local amenities without difficulty (i.e. there is no error in their perceptions), but the analyst trying to understand their behavioral decisions has incomplete information. To the extent households also have difficulty, then other variables may serve as "predictors" of the amenities they desire. For example, individuals can easily observe the exterior physical condition of houses in a neighborhood in which they are considering purchasing a home. This exterior physical condition may be a good predictor of the average income level of the neighborhood, which may be valued in and of itself or as a possible cause of school quality or of the crime rate. As a result, any estimated positive effect of exterior physical condition of homes in the neighborhood on housing prices may reflect not only the aesthetic value individuals place on exterior appearance, but also the value of exterior condition as a predictor of other neighborhood amenities.

We now turn to an attempt to summarize the key points of consistency in the hedonic housing price literature. To keep this aspect of our review manageable, the studies have been limited to those with the most extensive amenity information. Specifically, only studies that use individual housing unit measures and that have at least some information on three crucial amenities: (1) neighborhood physical condition; (2) crime rate; and, (3) school quality are considered. Once these restrictions are imposed, surprisingly few studies remain out of the hundreds that have been done over the past two decades.[20]

A comparison of the effects of individual amenities is difficult because each amenity is measured in different units. Moreover, the selection of a basis for measurement even for a given amenity can vary across studies. To allow for some comparability, we have standardized our summary of the measured effects of each amenity by considering the impact of a one standard deviation change in each amenity variable (within each study's data set) on the natural logarithm of the housing price. That is, we are approximating their percentage effect on housing prices of a standardized change in the amenity variable. A further advantage of this approach is that it allows us to ignore differences in housing price levels between the studies, and the distinction between flow (rent) and stock (home value) measures of housing prices. However, this procedure does limit our review to studies on which we could obtain information on the mean and standard deviation of variables used in the hedonic analyses. For studies with multiple

---

[19]One possibility is to include in the hedonic only one of the available measures. A second possibility is to include the first principal component of the alternative measures. A more complex, but less ad hoc approach would be to use the multiple indicator-multiple cause (MIMIC) models that are extensively used in psychometrics [see Goldberger (1974) for more information on MIMIC models]. To our knowledge, MIMIC models have not been applied in the hedonic framework.

[20]For reviews of this literature, see Freeman (1979a), Smith (1977), Ott (1982), and Witte and Long (1980).

Table 2

A comparison across several studies of the percentage effects on housing prices of a one standard deviation improvement in each amenity variable

Study Author(s)	City	Tenure Type in Study	Physical Condition	School Quality	Crime	Racial Composition	Neighborhood Socioeconomic Status	Air Quality	Access to Work and Commerce	Noise	Overall Neighborhood Rating
Follain and Malpezzi	39 SMSAS	Owner	1.9%*	W	W	—	—	—	0.4%	W	3.5%*
Follain and Malpezzi	39 SMSAS	Renter	1.2%*	W	W	—	—	—	W	W	2.0%*
Kain and Quigley	St. Louis	Owner	4.3%*	3.0%*	0.8%	W	6.4%*	—	NR	—	—
Kain and Quigley	St. Louis	Renter	4.6%*	2.1%	W	W	2.0%	—	W	—	—
Barnett	Green Bay	Renter	2.6%*	NS	NS	NS	NS	—	3.0%*	—	—
Noland	South Bend	Renter	1.5%*	NS	NS	NS	NS	—	4.8%*	—	—
Merrill	Pittsburgh	Renter	2.8%*	NS	NS	NS	0	—	0.7%	—	—
Merrill	Phoenix	Renter	1.6%*	NS	NS	NS	0	—	1.7%*	—	—
Bartik	Pittsburgh	Renter	4.6%*	0.3%	1.6%*	W	—	—	W	0.5%	—
Bartik	Phoenix	Renter	1.2%	0.1%	0.6%	3.5%*	—	—	1.2%*	W	—
Li and Brown	Boston	Owner	9.4%*	1.7%	1.9%*	—	0.8%	0.5%	3.9%	—	—
Mark and Parks	St. Louis	Owner	1.4%*	W	0.1%	0.7%	15.3%*	—	NS	—	—

Key: * indicates variable is statistically significant at 10% level; W means variable has "wrong" sign; NS means variable is insignificant and coefficient is not reported; NR means variable's coefficient is not reported and significance is unclear – means variable in this category is not included in study.
Note: 1. For purposes of this Table, all the changes considered are improvements; that is, we consider changes that would be expected to positively affect housing prices, such as a one standard deviation decline in the crime rate.
2. All percentage effects are evaluated at the means of each study's data.

measures of the amenity variable, we only considered the measures with the largest percentage effects.

Table 2 reports the comparisons of the various studies.[21] This comparison is admittedly rough, but three general conclusions seem warranted. First, neighborhood physical condition usually has one of the largest percentage effects on housing prices of any neighborhood variable. This finding should be reassuring to the authors of current U.S. neighborhood policies, which primarily rely on physical improvement as the key to revitalizing neighborhoods. At the same time, we note that this larger effect of neighborhood physical condition than, for example, crime, does not necessarily mean that households place an enormous value on the appearance of the house next door. As we noted earlier, a neighborhood's physical condition may serve as a convenient visual signal to households of the overall quality of a set of neighborhood amenities.

Second, amenities seem to have smaller percentage effects on the price of rental housing than of owner-occupied housing.

Finally, the overall effects of amenities are within the range one might expect. Suppose that all neighborhood variables, both observed and unobserved, changed by one standard deviation. It seems unlikely, given the results in Table 2, for this to lead to less than a 10% change in housing prices, or more than a 50% change.

---

[21] The specific references to the studies, and the equations and variables on which Table 2 is based, are summarized below:

(1) Follain and Malpezzi (1980): Based on Mean Estimates, pp. 41 and 42; Physical Condition: V278; School Quality: School; Crime: Crime; Access: Shops; Noise: Traffic, Air; Overall Neighborhood Rating: V276.

(2) Kain and Quigley (1975): Based on Semilog Equation, pp. 100–201; Physical Condition: Adjacent units for owners; Block face for renters; School Quality: School Quality; Crime: Crime; Racial Composition: Proportion white; Neighborhood socioeconomic status: Median schooling; Access: Miles from CBD.

(3) Barnett (1979): Based on Table 4, p. 17; Physical Condition: Composite rating of neighborhood quality; Access: Generalized access to employment.

(4) Noland (1980): Based on Table 2, p. 11; Physical Condition: Composite rating of neighborhood quality; Access: Generalized access to employment.

(5) Merrill (1980): Based on Tables II–2 and II–4, pp. A–29, A–31; Physical Condition: Quality of blockface landscaping; Neighborhood Socioeconomic Status: Median income of census tract; Access: Distance from CBD.

(6) Li and Brown (1980): Based on Model 2, Table 2; Physical Condition: On-site visual quality; School Quality: Test scores for 4th graders; Crime: Percent 16–21 years old who are high school dropouts; Neighborhood Socioeconomic Status: Median income; Air Quality: Sulfur dioxides; Access: Distance to CBD.

(7) Bartik (1982): Based on Table 7–2, p. 184; Physical Condition: PHCON; School Quality: SCHOOL; Crime: CRIME; Racial Composition: PCTW; Access: ACCESS; Noise: CONG.

(8) Mark and Parks (1978): Based on eq. 4; Physical Condition: RENTPC; School Quality: EXPPUP; Crime: CRIMRATE; Racial Composition: ADJNONPC; Neighborhood Socioeconomic Status: MEDY; Standard deviations are calculated from Little (1976).

3.3. Hedonic wage models

The hedonic wage function has been a significant component of the empirical models of labor economics. In general these analyses have attempted to evaluate the effects of job characteristics on wage rates or earnings while taking account of the attributes of the employee.[22] More recently a parallel line of research has developed in which wage and earnings models were used to gauge the effects of site-specific amenities on compensation. As our analysis of the inter-city location model implied, we would expect both housing *and* labor markets to reflect the effects of amenities. Hoch (1972a,b, 1974, 1982) appears to have been the first to attempt to measure the association between wages and urban amenities such as crime. However, Fuchs (1967) and Tolley (1974) anticipated these arguments by noting that city size (including presumably the posivite and negative amenities that are associated with it) influenced money wages.

The type of data and measure of the dependent variables also serve to distinguish the wage models. For the most part these studies have used an average wage (or earnings) measure by occupation. These data were derived from BLS Area Wage Surveys or Census with the former reporting average hourly earnings and the later median annual earnings. Separate wage models were estimated by occupation with measures of urban amenities and labor market conditions. As a rule in these studies either a real wage measure was used as the dependent variable or an index of the cost of living was included as an independent variable in the wage functions. Most of these studies treat the estimated model as part of a simultaneous equation system. Hoch's work would be a notable exception in that his models are treated as reduced form equations.

Izraeli (1977) emphasizes the simultaneity in the determination of wages and the local price index; Getz and Huang (1978) argue that earnings, the cost of living, and the net migration are endogenous; and Cropper and Arriaga–Salinas (1980) interpret their estimated wage model as a labor supply function with real earnings, employment, and an index of air pollution as endogenous variables.

Overall the results of these studies are supportive but hardly overwhelming in the empirical evidence consistent with an inter-city model of household location and, with it, an association between real wages and urban amenities. The analyses can be criticized both on grounds that they are incomplete in their treatment of job and individual characteristics and too aggregative with their use of a summary measure of wages. Only the air pollution, crime, and climate variables (as measures of amenities) appear to have a detectable influence on wages. However, these effects are not upheld over all occupations. For example, Getz and Huang found the violent crime rate to be a statistically significant and

---

[22]For a review of the early literature on the use of hedonic wage models to estimate the effects of job characteristics, see Smith (1983). A more recent update to this can be found in Triplett (1983).

positive influence on earnings (after taking account of the cost of living) in four of the nine occupations considered. The measure used for air pollution (a principal component derived based on measures of particulates and sulfur dioxide) was a significant determinant in only one case and climate measures in three. The results for male laborers in Izraeli's (1977) analysis supported effects for air pollution and climate. Cropper and Arriaga–Salinas' study had similar findings with six of eight occupations exhibiting a significant effect for sulfur dioxide, five for a climate measure, and four for crime.

More recently four studies have considered the wage model with micro-level wage information – Rosen (1979), Roback (1982), and Smith (1983) and Berger, Blomquist and Hoehn (1985). The first three of these were based on the current population surveys – Rosen for 1970, Roback for 1973, and Smith for 1978. After controlling for individual characteristics, occupation, and industry characteristics, all three studies find clear support for effects due to crime, air pollution, and climate on wages. There are, however, some differences in the studies. Rosen's dependent variable was based on annual earnings deflated by a local cost of living index, while Smith's study used an hourly wage rate measure deflated by the cost of living index. Roback's model was based on nominal weekly wages.[23] Berger, Blomquist and Hoehn used the 1980 Decennial Census, estimating hedonic property value and wage models with a wide array of site characteristics. Site-specific amenities were more likely to be statistically significant and correctly signed in the property value than the wage model, for reasons that we discussed above.

Both types of hedonic wage studies support a role for amenities as influences to real wages. The findings based on the micro-level surveys with the possible exception of Berger et al. are more supportive than those with the aggregative measures. However, this is what we would expect both as a result of the superior information (and associated ability to control for related determinants of wages) and, equally important, the sheer impact of the larger sample sizes in assuring the isolation of even quantitatively small effects on wages.

3.4. Sizing up the assumptions and practice of hedonic models

Clearly, the general comments at the outset of this Section are relevant to the attempts to empirically implement the hedonic model. Freeman's (1979b) appraisal of the assumptions of the hedonic property value model provides a good starting point for describing some of these issues in generic terms. Based on his discussion as well as the subsequent literature, it is possible to highlight some of the most important of these concerns:

---

[23]Roback noted that a real wage would have been preferable, but indicated that the lack of availability of a local cost of living variable for all of the SMSAs in her sample prevented its use.

(1) Do households and firms have the information and a common basis of perception to permit the relevant markets to direct the locational assignment of activities and the implicit valuation of the site-specific amenities associated with those assignments?

(2) Is it reasonable to maintain the equilibrium assumptions required for the interpretation of the hedonic price function in housing markets where adjustment and transactions costs (which are ignored by the models) are substantial?

(3) The hedonic price function in either the housing or wage market is an equilibrium relationship. While analytical solutions for the equilibrium matching of economic agents have proved intractable for even moderately complex cases, there is now some encouraging work relying on simulations of the market that may hold the prospect for greater understanding of the limitations of the model. Nonetheless, the theoretical guidance available for the specification of hedonic price functions is quite limited. Therefore, it is reasonable to ask whether we can detect the structure of underlying behavioral functions with some assurance.

(4) All of the analytical descriptions of household and firm behavior used to develop hedonic functions have been static, ignoring a household's consideration of the future and the prospects for resale of the commodity. To what extent does the abstraction from these considerations affect the use of the model to isolate the effects of amenities and to estimate households' marginal valuations of them? And, finally,

(5) Uncertainty is likely to be an important part of the household's decision making. Yet the models of their behavior have largely ignored its effects. Uncertainty enters the analysis for at least two reasons. Households' information concerning housing or job characteristics may be quite imperfect. Equally important, the site-specific attributes may include risks – of health impairment due to exposure to air pollution or hazardous waste [see Harrison and Stock (1984)], of damage due to floods or other natural hazards [see Brookshire et al. (1985) and Nelson (1981)]. The ability to "insure" against these effects will affect the household's marginal bid. Is certainty a good enough approximation given our other empirical problems with implementation?

For the most part, the theoretical (or even the experimental) information does not exist to provide answers on the importance of any of these concerns. Thus, an evaluation of their importance for the usefulness of applied hedonic modeling in valuing amenities is at this stage a function of professional judgment. It can therefore be expected to vary with the analyst involved. Before offering our judgment, it is important to acknowledge that many, if not all, of the concerns we identified would also be raised with virtually all empirical models in economics.

Despite these limitations, empirical models based on the hedonic framework do seem to be providing, with increasing consistency, indications of what are the most important characteristics (and the site-specific amenities) to households. Where the amenity is difficult to perceive and/or measure these models' ability is correspondingly affected. Thus, at the level of detecting the clearly identifiable (to households) amenities, the models do seem to have had success. Where there is difficulty in perceiving the amenities, the results are nonetheless consistent with the framework. That is, when we consider air pollution, for example, the models perform quite well when the air pollution problem is a serious one [e.g. Los Angeles, see Brookshire et al. (1982)].

The issue of using hedonic models to estimate the marginal valuation of changes in amenities is a more difficult judgement call. To begin with, we will never know the true benefits of an amenity change. The available comparisons of property value models with direct questioning of individuals concerning environmental amenities has found agreement in that each set of estimates is within an order of magnitude of the other.[24] While this is not a high level of accuracy, it is as good or better than a large number of applied areas in economics. Ultimately, to evaluate the importance of inherent uncertainty in the estimates of the marginal values for amenities, we need to consider how they are to be used. It is probably fair to observe that for most policy-based uses, the level of uncertainty in other elements of the evaluation of a policy will be substantially greater than even fairly generous ranges accorded to these marginal willingness to pay estimates. For example, in evaluating an air quality standard for a criteria pollutant, analysis must "second-guess" what that standard implies for the set of state implementation plans intended to see that it is realized as well as estimate how these are likely to affect ambient air quality before the change in air quality attributed to the standard can be determined. Both are far more incongruous areas for analysis than the hedonic models.

A similar line of argument could be developed for evaluating policies designed to reduce crime, improve public education or enhance the physical character of neighborhoods. Thus, by this standard, our ability to value amenities has clearly outpaced our understanding of the process that delivers amenities to households, and particularly the role of the public sector in that delivery process.

4. Research issues

Amenities do play a central role in theoretical and empirical analyses of the spatial distribution of economic activities. Within the past two decades, there have been substantive advances in the modeling of individual and firm behavior,

---

[24]See Brookshire et al. (1982) and Smith and Desvousges (1986).

recognizing the role of amenities in their decisions and the prospects for estimating the implicit valuations of these amenities through hedonic models. In some respects theory has outpaced empirical practice. Nonetheless, the theoretical descriptions of the impacts of urban amenities on household and firm behavior have been supported in general terms with empirical models. One of the primary reasons for the lag between theory and practice seems to arise from the information that is available to implement empirical models. As a rule, the data used have been collected to serve other purposes and must be adapted to meet the needs of an empirical evaluation of the role of amenities. With such adaptation come compromises whose ultimate effects on the quality of the empirical findings are unknown.

Of course, in discussing the performance of empirical models designed to test theory or estimate key parameters for policy purposes it is too easy to call for more and better data as the "solution" for improving the empirical work. We think this is unlikely to be realized. Improved data will provide the basis for enhancing our understanding of the strengths and weaknesses of the hedonic framework. There are, however, some fundamental issues that require both theory and new data. In part, these were considered indirectly in the questions posed at the end of the last section. However, we believe four areas deserve repetition and emphasis. They involve: perception, equilibrium, empirical implementation, and policy uses of what we now have.

4.1. Perception

For the most part, the empirical analysis of amenities must rely on crude proxy variables, measured at an aggregate level, to estimate each amenity that is hypothesized to influence household or firm behavior. We have rarely asked how households learn of school quality, available recreation, crime, air quality, etc. Do they have key indicators that serve as proxies for these variables or do they rely on others' judgements (i.e. realtors, friends, business connections, etc.). Until we begin to realistically describe the process through which households (and firms) form these perceptions and acquire the information necessary to evaluate these descriptions, there will not be any resolution of the criticisms of the available proxy measures for amenities. Moreover, transferring estimates of the implicit valuation of these amenities to policy judgements will continue to be but a short step away from guesswork.

One would intuitively suspect that household misconception would tend to bias downwards hedonic estimates of household marginal bids and benefits of amenity improvements. But theoretical analysis of this problem has been lacking. This research gap is puzzling when compared to the vast research effort expended on how to identify marginal bid function and on the relationship of property value changes to benefits.

4.2. Equilibrium

The two markets used to estimate the effects of amenities are the housing and labor markets. For the most part past empirical studies have treated the former as local and the latter as national. Both types of studies have treated the markets as being in equilibrium where adjustment and transactions costs are negligible. We probably could not have picked cases where this is a less plausible assumption if some conscious effort had been devoted to the process. Nonetheless, the rather remarkably consistent track record of performance in both examples attests to the presence of the effects of amenities on market prices in these cases.

What remains is to judge how important departures from equilibrium will be to the theoretical interpretation and quality of empirical estimates of the implicit valuation of amenities. The hedonic model is a long-run model of household behavior. In some areas the average tenure in a home is three to five years, while in others it may be over a decade. It seems reasonable to expect that with existing empirical information and recent advances in modeling the role of adjustment costs for the dynamic behavior of the firm, our understanding of the equilibrium assumptions in this case can be enhanced.

4.3. Empirical implementation

To date there has not been an unambiguously correct implementation of the hedonic method for measuring the demand for characteristics. All past efforts can be criticized for their treatment of either the identification problem or the simultaneity posed by a nonlinear price function. Moreover, if the Rosen–Roback form of the inter-city model is accepted then the interpretation of the marginal prices are also incorrect. Clearly an attempt to build an application based upon the recent theoretical analysis and econometric methods discussed for these problems is warranted. Equally important, it also seems reasonable to call for experimental work where analytical solutions are intractable to gauge the impacts of the common mistakes of past empirical studies. Perhaps it would be possible not only to learn from our mistakes, but to interpret correctly the estimates that are available rather than to discard them.

One problem with learning from our past estimates of hedonic price functions is that there is no agreement on how to measure amenities. It would be helpful if journal editors would insist that standard deviations, means, and measurement methods be reported for all amenity variables in hedonic price models. Such practices are standard in disciplines (sociology, psychology) in which the units of measurement for most variables are arbitrary.

4.4. Prognosis for policy

Theoretical and empirical research on urban amenities is clearly at the stage where we can identify what are the important amenities to households. While there are a wide variety of studies reporting implicit marginal valuations of amenities, there remain substantive questions with all of these estimates. They have received the most direct use in the valuation of air quality changes as part of benefit-cost analyses of environmental regulations. It might be argued that this case poses (except for extremely polluted areas) one of the most difficult for households to perceive.

The available comparative evidence evaluating marginal valuations of air quality based on hedonic models with direct interviews suggests (as we noted earlier) that they fall within an order of magnitude of each other. While the hedonic results are often used as a benchmark for the survey, both are estimates conditioned on different sets of assumptions. In judging the value of estimates of the marginal valuations for amenities from hedonic models for policy purposes, one must consider the alternatives. Decisions that reallocate resources in an effort to change the amenities available will implicitly value these amenities even when these estimates are ignored. At this stage, there is no other "game in town" to replace them. Moreover, we feel their use is superior to nonuse. However, this does not imply that a strategy which treats these point estimates as reliable is warranted. Greater attention to incorporating the uncertainty due to the assumptions and statistical performance of the models is the only assurance that prudence will guide the interpretation of these valuation estimates, while research continues to improve their reliability.

References:

Abelson, P. (1979) 'Property prices and the value of amenities', *Journal of Environmental Economics and Management*, 11–28.
Amemiya, T. and J.L. Powell (1980) 'A comparison of the Box-Cox maximum likelihood estimator and the nonlinear two stage least squares estimator', Technical Report no. 132, Institute for Mathematical Studies in the Social Sciences, Stanford University.
Anderson, R.J. and T. Crocker (1971) 'Air pollution and residential property values', *Urban Studies*, 8:171–180.
Ball, M. (1973) 'Recent empirical work on the determinants of relative house prices', *Urban Studies*, 10:213–233.
Barnett, C.L. (1979) 'Using hedonic indexes to measure housing quality', R-2450-HUD Santa Monica, Calif.
Bartik, T.J. (1985) 'Measuring the benefits of amenity improvements in hedonic price models'. Unpublished paper, Vanderbilt University.
Bartik, T.J. (forthcoming). 'Estimating hedonic demand parameters with single market data: The problems caused by unobserved tastes', *Review of Economics and Statistics*.

Bartik, T.J. (1986) 'Neighborhood revitalization's effects on tenants and the benefit-cost analysis of government neighborhood programs', *Journal of Urban Economics*, 19:234–248.

Bartik, T.J. (1987) 'The estimation of demand parameters in hedonic price models', *Journal of Political Economy*, 95:81–88.

Bartik, T.J. (1982) 'Evaluating the benefits of neighborhood change'. Unpublished Ph.D. dissertation, Madison: University of Wisconsin.

Bender, B., T.J. Gronberg and H.-S. Huang (1980) 'Choice of functional form and the demand for air quality', *Review of economics and statistics*, 62:638–643.

Berger, M.C., G.C. Blomquist and J.P. Hoehn (1985) 'Valuing environmental amenities traded in implicit markets'. Unpublished paper, University of Kentucky.

Blomquist, G. and L. Worley (1979) 'Specifying the demand for housing characteristics: the exogeneity issue', in: D. Diamond and G. Tolley eds., *Economics of urban amenities*. New York: Academic Press.

Blomquist, G. and L. Worley (1981) 'Hedonic prices, demands for urban housing amenities, and benefit estimates', *Journal of Urban Economics*, 9:212–221.

Bresnock, A.E. (1980) 'Housing prices, income and environmental quality in Denver', University of Colorado.

Brookshire, D.S. M.A. Thayer, W.D. Schulze and R.C. d'Arge, (1982) 'Valuing public goods: a comparison of survey and hedonic approaches', *American Economic Review*, 72:165–178.

Brookshire, D.S., M.A. Thayer, J. Tschirhart and W.D. Schulze (1985) 'A test of the expected utility model: evidence from earthquake risk', *Journal of Political Economy*, 93:369–389.

Brown, G.M. Jr. and H.O. Pollakowski (1977) 'Economic value of shoreline', *Review of Economics and Statistics*, 54:272–278.

Brown, J.N. (1983) 'Structural estimation in implicit markets', in: J.E. Triplett, ed., *The measurement of labor cost*. NBER Studies in Income and Wealth, no. 48. Chicago: University of Chicago Press.

Brown, J. and H. Rosen (1982) 'On the estimation of structural hedonic price models', *Econometrica*, 50:765–768.

Butler, R.J. (1984) 'The effects of education on wages – hedonics makes selectivity bias (sort of) simpler', *Economic Inquiry*, 22:109–120.

Butler, R.J. (1981) 'Hedonic techniques in economics', unpublished manuscript, Cornell University.

Butler, R.V. (1977) 'Hedonic indexes of urban housing: theory and problems of cross-sectional estimation'. Unpublished Ph.D. Thesis, Massachusetts Institute of Technology.

Cassel, E. and R. Mendelsohn (1985) 'The choice of functional form for hedonic price equations: comment', *Journal of Urban Economics*, 18:135–142.

Clark, D., Kahn and H. Ofek (1983) 'Optimal city size in terms of compensating wage differentials', unpublished paper, Department of Economics, SUNY-Binghamton.

Cobb, S.A. (1977) 'Site rent, air quality, and the demand for amenities', *Journal of Environmental Economics and Management*, 4:214–218.

Court, L.M. (1941) 'Entrepreneurial and consumer demand theories for commodity spectra', *Econometrica*, 9:135–162, 241–297.

Cropper, M.L. (1981) 'The value of urban amenities', *Journal of Regional Science*, 21:359–374.

Cropper, M.L. and A.S. A.-Salinas, (1980) 'Inter-city wage differentials and the value of air quality', *Journal of Urban Economics*, 8:236–254.

Cropper, M.L., L.B. Deck, K.E. McConnell and T.T. Phipps (1985) 'Should the rosen model be used to value environmental amenities'? Paper presented at annual meetings of American Economic Association, New York City.

Daniels, L. (1979) 'The role of governments as suppliers of neighborhoods', in D. Segal, ed., *The economics of neighborhood*. New York: Academic Press.

Desvousges, W.H., V.K. Smith and M. McGivney (1983) 'A comparison of alternative approaches for estimating recreation and related benefits of water quality improvements', Environmental Benefits Analysis Series Washington, D.C.: U.S. Environmental Protection Agency.

Diamond, D. (1980) 'The relationship between amenities and urban land values', *Land Economics*, 51:1–32.

Diamond, D.B., Jr. (1980) 'Income and residential location: muth revisited', *Urban Studies*, 17:1–12.

Diamond, D.B., Jr. and G.S. Tolley, eds. (1982) *The economics of urban amenities*. New York: Academic Press.

Diamond, D.B., Jr. and B.A. Smith (1982) 'Simultaneity in the market for housing characteristics', unpublished paper.

Ellickson, B. (1979) 'Local public goods and the market for neighborhoods', in: D. Segal ed., *The economics of neighborhoods*. New York: Academic Press.

Ellickson, B. (1981) 'An alternative test of the hedonic theory of housing markets', *Journal of Urban Economics*, 9:56–79.

Epple, D. (1987) 'Hedonic prices and implicit markets: estimating demand and supply functions for differentiated products', *Journal of Political Economy*.

Fisher, A.C. and F.M. Peterson (1976) 'The environment in economics', *Journal of Economic Literature*, 14:1–33.

Fisher, A.C. and V.K. Smith (1982) 'Economic evaluation of energy's environmental costs with special reference to air pollution', *Annual Review of Energy*, 7:1–35.

Follain, J. and S. Malpezzi (1980) *Dissecting housing value and rent: estimates of hedonic indexes for 39 large SMSAs*. Washington, D.C.: Urban Institute.

Freeman, A.M. (1971) 'Air pollution and property values: a methodological comment', *Review of Economics and Statistics*, 53:415–416.

Freeman, A.M. (1974a) 'Air pollution and property values: a further comment', *Review of Economics and Statistics*, 56:554–556.

Freeman, A.M. (1974b) 'On estimating air pollution control benefits from land value studies', *Journal of Environmental Economics and Management*, 1:74–83.

Freeman, A.M. (1979a) *The benefits of environmental improvement: theory and practice*. Baltimore, MD: Johns Hopkins Press.

Freeman, A.M. (1979b) 'Hedonic prices, property values and measuring environmental benefits: a survey of the issues', *Scandinavian Journal of Economics*, 81:154–173.

Freeman, A.M. (1979c) 'The hedonic price approach to measuring demand for neighborhood characteristics', in: D. Segal, ed., *The economics of neighborhood*. New York: Academic Press.

Friedman, J. (1981) 'A conditional logit model of the role of local public services in residential choice', *Urban Studies*, 18:347–358.

Fuchs, V.R. (1967) 'Differentials in hourly earnings by region and city size, 1959', NBER Occasional Papers 101. New York.

Getz, M. and Y.C. Huang (1978) 'Consumer revealed preference of environmental goods', *Review of economics and statistics*, 60:449–458.

Goldberger, A.S. (1968) 'The interpretation and estimation of Cobb-Douglas functions', *Econometrica*, 36:464–472.

Goldberger, A.S. (1974) 'Unobservable variables in econometrics in frontiers', in: P. Zarembka, ed., *Econometrics*. New York: Academic Press.

Goodman, A.C. (1978) 'Hedonic prices, price indices and housing markets', *Journal of Urban Economics*, 5:471–484.

Greer, W. and M. White (1981) 'The effects of city size and moving costs on public project benefits', *Journal of Urban Economics*, 9:149–164.

Grether, D. and P. Mieszkowski (1974) 'Determinants of real estate values', *Journal of Urban Economics*, 1:127–146.

Griliches, Z. (1961) 'Hedonic price indexes for automobiles: an econometric analysis of quality change,' in: *The price statistics of the federal government*, General Series no. 73. New York: National Bureau of Economic Research 137–196.

Halvorsen, R. and H. Pollakowski (1981) 'Choice of functional forms for hedonic price equations', *Journal of Urban Economics*, 10:37–49.

Harrison, D. Jr. and D.L. Rubinfeld (1978) 'Hedonic housing prices and the demand for clean air', *Journal of Environmental Economics and Management*, 5:81–102.

Harrison, D. Jr. and J. Stock (1984) 'Hedonic housing values, local public goods and the benefits of hazardous waste cleanup', Unpublished paper, Harvard University.

Henderson, J. Vernon (1982) 'Evaluating consumer amenities and interregional welfare differences', *Journal of Urban Economics*, 11:32–59.

Hoch, I. (1972a) 'Income and city size', *Urban Studies*, 299–328.

Hoch, I. (1972b) 'Urban scale and environmental quality', in: R.G. Ridker, ed., *Population resources*, *and the environment*. U.S. Commission on Population Growth and the American Future, research Papers, III, Washington: U.S.G.P.O.

Hoch, I. (1974) 'Wages, climate and the quality of life', *Journal of Environmental Economics and Management*, 1:268–295.

Hoch, I. (1975) 'Variations in the quality of urban life among cities and regions', in: L. Wingo and R. Evans, eds., *Public economics and the quality of life*. Baltimore, MD: Lexington Books.

Hoch, I. (1982) 'Climate, energy use and wages', in: J.H. Cumberland, J.R. Hibbs and I. Hoch, eds., *The economics of managing chlorofluorocarbons, stratospheric ozone and climate issues*. Washington, D.C.: Resources for the Future.

Horowitz, Joel L. (1984a) 'Inferring willingness to pay for housing amenities from residential property values', Unpublished paper, University of Iowa.

Horowitz, J.L. (1984b) 'Bidding models of housing markets', unpublished paper. University of Iowa.

Houthakker, Hendrik S. (1952) 'Compensated changes in quantities and qualities consumed', *Reviewed of Economic Studies*, 19:155–164.

Izraeli, O. (1977) 'Differentials in nominal wages and prices between cities', *Urban Studies*, 14: 275–290.

Izraeli, O. (1979) 'Externalities and intercity wage and price differentials', in: G.S. Tolley, P.E. Graves and J.L. Gardner, eds., *Urban growth policy in a market economy*. New York: Academic Press.

Jud, G.D. (1980) 'The effects of zoning on single-residential property values', *Land Economics*, 56:142–154.

Jud, G.D. (1981) 'Schools and housing values', *Land Economics*, 57.

Kain, J. and J. Quigley (1975) *Housing markets and racial discrimination*. New York: Columbia University Press.

Kanemoto, Y. (1985) 'Hedonic prices and the benefits of public projects'. Discussion Paper no. 275, Institute of Socio-Economic Planning, University of Tsukuba, Sakura, Ibaraki 305, Japan.

Kneisner, T.J. and J.D. Leeth (1985) 'Simulating hedonic labor market models: computational methods and policy applications'. Working paper 85–2, University of North Carolina, Chapel Hill.

Krumm, R.J. (1980) 'Neighborhood amenities: an economic analysis', *Journal of Urban Economics*, 7:208–224.

Lerman, S.R. and C.R. Kern (1983) 'Hedonic theory, bid rents, and willingness to pay: some extensions of Ellickson's results', *Journal of Urban Economics*, 13:358–363.

Leven, C., J. Little, H. Nourse and R.B. Read (1977) *Neighborhood change*. New York: Praeger Publishers.

Leven, C. and J. Mark (1977) 'Revealed preferences for neighborhood characteristics', *Urban Studies*, 14:147–159.

Li, M.M. and H.J. Brown (1980) 'Micro-neighborhood externalities and hedonic housing prices', *Land Economics*, 56:125–141.

Lind, R.C. (1973) 'Spatial equilibrium, the theory of rents, and the measurement of benefits from public programs', *Quarterly Journal of Economics*, 87:188–207.

Linneman, P. (1977) 'An analysis of the demand for residence site characteristics', unpublished Ph.D. Thesis, University of Chicago.

Linneman, P. (1980a) 'Some empirical results on the nature of the hedonic price function for the urban housing market', *Journal of Urban Economics*, 8:47–68.

Linneman, P. (1980b) 'An empirical methodology for analyzing the properties of public goods', *Economic Inquiry*, 18:600–617.

Linneman, P. (1981) 'The demand for residence site characteristics', *Journal of Urban Economics*, 9:129–149.

Linneman, P. (1982) 'Hedonic prices and residential location', in C.D. Diamond and G. Tolley, eds., *The economics of urban amenities*. New York: Academic Press.

Little, J.T. (1976) 'Residential preferences, neighborhood filtering and neighborhood change', *Journal of Urban Economics*, 3:68–81.

Maler, K. (1977) 'A note on the use of property values in estimating marginal willingness to pay for environmental quality', *Journal of Environmental Economics and Management*, 4:355–369.

Manuel, E.H., Jr., et al. (1983) 'Benefit and net benefit analysis of alternative national ambient air quality standards for particulate matter', I–V, Final Report to the U.S. Environmental Protection Agency by Math Tech. Inc., Princeton, N.J. under Contract no. 68-02-03823.

Mark, J.H. (1980) 'A preference approach to measuring the impact of environmental externalities', *Land Economics*, 56:103–116.

Mark, J.H. and R.P. Parks (1978) 'Residential preferences, neighborhood filtering and neighborhood change: comment and corrections', *Journal of Urban Economics*, 5:535–537.

McConnell, K.E. and T.T. Phipps (1985) 'Identification of preference parameters in hedonic models: consumer demands with nonlinear budgets'. Unpublished paper, Department of Agricultural and Resource Economics, University of Maryland.

McCloskey, D.N. (1983) 'The rhetoric of economics', *Journal of Economic Literature*, 21:481–517.

McFadden, D. (1978) 'Modelling the choice of residential location', in: A. Karlqvist, ed., *Spatial interaction theory and residential location*. Amsterdam: North-Holland.

Mendelsohn, R. (1985) 'Identifying structural equations with single market data', *Review of Economics and Statistics*, 67:525–529.

Merrill, S.R. (1980) *Hedonic indices as a measure of housing quality*. Cambridge, Mass.: Abt Associates.

Mills, E. and R. Price (1984) 'Metropolitan suburbanization and central city problems', *Journal of Urban Economics*, 15:1–17.

Nelson, J.P. (1978) 'Residential choice, hedonic prices, and the demand for urban air quality', *Journal of Urban Economics*, 5:357–369.

Nelson, J.P. (1981) 'Three mile island and residential property values: empirical analysis and policy implications', *Land Economics*, 57:363–372.

Nelson, Jon P. (1982) 'Highway noise and property values – A survey of current evidence', *Journal of Transport Economics and Policy*, 16:117–138.

Noland, C.W. (1980) 'Assessing hedonic indexes for housing', N-1305-HUD. Santa Monica, Calif.

Nordhaus, W.D. and J. Tobin (1973) 'Is growth obsolete?' in: M. Moss, ed., *The measurement of economic and social performance*. Studies in Income and Wealth, 38, New York: National Bureau of Economic Research.

Nourse, H. (1967) 'The effect of air pollution on house values', *Land Economics*, 43:181–189.

Ohsfeldt, R.L. and B.A. Smith (1985) 'Estimating the demand for heterogeneous goods', *Review of Economics and Statistics*, 67:165–171.

Ott, D. (1982) 'Cross-section property values and the benefits of cleaner air'. American Petroleum Industry.

Palmquist, R.B. (1981) 'The demand for housing characteristics: reconciling theory and estimation', presented at the American Real Estate and Urban Economics Association Meeting, Washington, D.C.

Palmquist, R.B. (1982) 'Measuring environmental effects of property values without hedonic regressions', *Journal of Urban Economics*, 11:333–347.

Palmquist, R.B. (1985) 'Welfare measurement with nonlinear budget constraints'. Unpublished paper, North Carolina State University, revised.

Pines, D. and V. Weiss (1976) 'Land improvement projects and land values', *Journal of Urban Economics*, 3:1–13.

Polinsky, A.M. and D.L. Rubinfeld (1977) 'Property values and the benefits of environmental improvements: theory and measurement', in: L. Wingo and A. Evans eds., *Public economics and the quality of life*. Washington, D.C.: Resources for the Future.

Polinsky, A.M. and S. Shavell (1975) 'The air pollution and property value debate', *Review of Economics and Statistics*, 57:100–104.

Polinsky, A.M. and S. Shavell (1976) 'Amenities and property value in a model of an urban area', *Journal of Political Economy*, 5:199–229.

Porell, F. (1982) *Models of intraurban residential relocation*. Boston: Kluwer-Nijhoff Publishing.

Quigley, J.M. (1982) 'Nonlinear budget constraints and consumer demand: an application to public programs for residential housing', *Journal of Urban Economics*, 12:177–201.

Quigley, J.M. and D. Weinberg (1977) 'Intra-urban residential mobility: a review and synthesis', *International Regional Science Review*, 2:41–66.

Ridker, R.G. and J.A. Henning (1967) 'The determinants of residential property values with special reference to air pollution', *Review of Economics and Statistics*, 49:246–257.

Roback, J. (1982) 'Wages, rents, and the quality of life', *Journal of Political Economy*, 90:1257–1278.

Rosen, S. (1974) 'Hedonic prices and implicit markets: product differentiation in pure competition', *Journal of Political Economy*, 82:34–55.

Rosen, S. (1979) 'Wage-based indexes of urban quality of life', in: P. Mieszkowski and M. Straszheim, eds., *Current issues in urban economics*. Baltimore: Johns Hopkins Press.

Rothenberg, J. (1967) *Economic evaluation of urban renewal*. Washington, D.C.: Brookings Institution.

Roy, A.D. (1950) 'The distribution of earnings and of individual output', *Economic Journal*, 60: 489–505.

Sattinger, M. (1975) 'Comparative advantage and the distribution of earnings and abilities', *Econometrica*, 43: 455–468.

Schnare, A. and R. Struyk (1976) 'Segmentation in urban housing markets', *Journal of Urban Economics*, 146–166.

Scotchmer, S. (1985) 'The short run and long run benefits of environmental improvement'. Discussion Paper 1135, Harvard Institute of Economic Research.

Small, K.A. (1975) 'Air pollution and property values, further comment', *Review of Economics and Statistics*, 57: 105–107.

Smith, B.A. (1978) 'Measuring the value of urban amenities', *Journal of Urban Economics*, 5: 370–387.

Smith, R.S. (1979) 'Compensating wage differentials and public policy: a review', *Industrial and Labor Relations Review*, 32: 339–352.

Smith, V.K. (1977) 'Residential location and environmental amenities: a review of the evidence', *Regional Studies*, 11.

Smith, V.K. (1983) 'The role of site and job characteristics in hedonic wage models', *Journal of Urban Economics*, 11: 296–321.

Smith, V.K. and W.H. Desvousges (1986) *Measuring water quality benefits*. Boston: Kluwer-Nijhoff.

Smith, V.K. and T.A. Deyak (1975) 'Measuring the impact of air pollution on property values', *Journal of Regional Science*, 15: 277–288.

Sonstelie, J.C. and P.R. Portney (1980) 'Gross rents and market values: testing the implications of Tiebout's hypothesis', *Journal of Urban Economics*, 7: 102–118.

Starrett, D.A. (1981) 'Land value capitalization in local public finance', *Journal of Political Economy*, 89: 306–328.

Straszheim, M. (1973) 'Estimation of the demand for urban housing services from household interview data', *Review of Economics and Statistics*, 55: 1–8.

Straszheim, M. (1975) *An econometric analysis of the urban housing market*. New York: National Bureau of Economic Research.

Strotz, (1968) 'The use of land rent changes to measure the welfare benefits of land improvements', in: J.E. Haring, ed., *The new economics of regulated industries: rate making in a dynamic economy*. Los Angeles: Economics Research Center, Occidental College.

Thaler, R. and S. Rosen (1975) 'The value of life saving', in: N.E. Terleckyj, ed., *Household production and consumption*. New York: Columbia University Press.

Tiebout, C.A. (1956) 'A pure theory of local expenditures', *Journal of Political Economy*, 64: 416–424.

Tinbergen, J. (1956) 'On the theory of income distribution', Weltwirtschaftliches Archiv 77: 155–175.

Tolley, G.S. (1974) 'The welfare economics of city bigness', *Journal of Urban Economics*, 3: 324–45.

Triplett, J.E. (1983) 'Introduction: an essay on labor cost', in: J.E. Triplett, ed., *The measurement of labor cost*, NBER Studies in Income and Wealth, no. 48. Chicago: University of Chicago Press.

Violette, D.M. and L.G. Chestnut (1985) *Valuing reductions in risks: a review of the empirical estimates, environmental benefits series*. Washington, D.C.: U.S. Environmental Protection Agency.

Venti, S. and D. Wise (1984) 'Moving and housing expenditure: transactions costs and disequilibrium', *Journal of Public Economics*, 23: 207–243.

Witte, A.D., H.J. Sumka and H. Erekson (1979) 'An estimation of a structural hedonic prices model of the housing market: an application of rosen's theory of implicit markets', *Econometrica*, 47.

Witte, A.D. and S.K. Long (1980). 'Evaluating the effects of public policies on land prices in metropolitan areas: some suggested approaches', in: J.T. Black and J.E. Hoben, eds., *Urban land markets: price indices, supply measures, and public policy effects*. Washington, D.C.: Urban Land Institute.

Chapter 32

URBANIZATION IN THE DEVELOPING WORLD: PATTERNS, ISSUES, AND POLICIES

ANDREW M. HAMER and JOHANNES F. LINN*
The World Bank

1. The challenge of Third World urbanization

By the year 2000, over half of the population of the world will live in areas classified as urban by their respective national governments. The phenomenon of urbanization has a common cause across countries, regardless of the level of development; modern economic growth involves a shift in the composition of output away from primary activities and toward secondary and tertiary production, which tends to concentrate spatially. In turn, this concentration results from the benefits derived by industrial organization from physical proximity and from the technological opportunity to achieve high levels of output per unit of land.

Yet the present urbanization in developing countries does not merely recapitulate the past experience of today's developed nations. The shift from rural to urban is occuring in the context of far higher population growth rates, at much lower income levels, and with considerably fewer opportunities to colonize new frontiers, foreign or domestic. In the process, the absolute scale of urbanization is testing the ability of planners and decision-makers as never before. The developed countries expect their urban population to reach one billion by the year 2000, at which point four out of every five persons will live in cities. The population of the developing nations is only one-third urban, yet it has already reached the one billion mark. Furthermore, another billion will be added in the last two decades of the century. This increase will be fed by urban population growth rates, which, while declining, are three to four times higher than those experienced by the more advanced countries [United Nations (1985)].

Urbanization per se may seem a rather abstract concept. However, it finds vivid embodiment in the emergence of very large cities across all developing regions. Already, in 1980, there were 125 developing metropolises each with more than one million inhabitants, with a collective population in excess of 355 million.

* The views expressed in this paper are exclusively their own and do not necessarily reflect those of the World Bank or of any of its affiliates.

Handbook of Regional and Urban Economics, Volume II, Edited by E.S. Mills
© *1987, Elsevier Science Publishers B.V.*

According to U.N. estimates and projections, by the year 2000 the ranks of millionaire cities is likely to reach about 300, with a total population of close to one billion. The management challenge represented by this growth is best symbolized by the fact that 20 of the world's 25 largest urban agglomerations at the turn of the century will be found in 15 of the Third World nations. The Mexico City region alone is likely to contain up to 28 million residents, a level of concentration for which there is no precedent anywhere.

There are distinct regional differences in the degree of urbanization achieved to date. Two-thirds of the population of Latin America and more than half of the population of West Asia already live in cities. Elsewhere, in Africa, China, Southeast Asia, and South Asia, the proportions vary from just under one-quarter to just under one-third. In each of these broad regions, the population living in cities today will be matched or exceeded by the urban growth expected in the period 1980–2000. In Africa, where the problems of development appear the starkest, two persons will be added to the urban population for every one in place in 1980.

Urbanization patterns differ, as well, in other regards. In Latin America, for example, urban-to-urban migration is more important than rural-to-urban migration and natural population growth is more significant than either in shaping the city of the future. Elsewhere, especially where the degree of urbanization is relatively low, population growth *and* migration are likely mutually to reinforce one another in fueling urban expansion. There are also differences in urban settlement patterns. Very large urban areas, with populations in excess of 5 million, are characteristic of the largest countries of Latin America, Asia, and the Arab world. At the other extreme, most African countries do not contain an agglomeration of 500,000 or more residents. Regardless of how urban population is distributed across city size categories, however, the contribution of urban areas to national output exceeds their demographic share by a factor of two, three, or four. The efficient and equitable management of the urban sector is, therefore, vital to the achievement of macroeconomic objectives. Furthermore, whether because of intense pressure on agricultural land, recurring bouts of calamitous drought, or a legacy of political neglect and outright discrimination, it is clear across all regions that rural areas are worse off than urban areas, whatever the index of relative well-being utilized. Thus the pressure to deal with urban issues has developed against a backdrop of equally urgent demands for meeting rural basic needs.

Even in the best of circumstances, public decision-makers face difficult trade-offs in dealing with the cities of the Third World. Their problems are compounded, however, by the weaknesses of the analytical framework they typically bring to bear on the urban sector. In most countries the pattern of urban settlements is viewed with concern, often bordering on dismay. Large agglomerations are often seen as products of misguided entrepreneurs who concentrate the generation of output and wealth, and of "marginal" elements who migrate from rural areas, confusing the "bright lights" of the city for meaningful income opportunities. This apparently irrational behavior is seen not only to defeat common objectives of regional "balance", but also to generate a seemingly inexhaustible demand for infrastructure to achieve service levels which, it is asserted, could be provided in smaller quantities and at lower costs elsewhere. For these reasons, such cities are described as exceeding their optimal size and in need of direct measures to freeze or scale back their dimension. Symmetrically, "secondary" centers, varying in minimum threshold size from 10,000 to 100,000, are seen as vehicles for dispersing urban wealth generation, as less costly to equip, and as alternate magnets for rural migrants otherwise bound for large centers. Such cities appear ideal candidates for force-fed expansion, through a wide-ranging program to supply the "missing" prerequisites for growth.

The other set of urban problems facing policy-makers in developing countries involves the existing poverty and inefficiency found within cities. The problems created by the demands of large numbers of urban dwellers for housing, public services, and transportation are real enough. These issues are made more intractable by the tendency of planners to think of these problems in terms of "deficits" whose resolution require such an enormous infusion of public sector resources that despair and paralysis seem to be the only appropriate response. Confronted with the inability to provide each household with a high quality dwelling unit, to build extensive networks of sewers, or to lace an urban area with expressways and rapid rail transit systems, planners often are reduced to symbolic gestures or vain attempts to mandate that new employers and new workers go somewhere else. As in the case of urban settlement patterns, there are policies that can ensure a more equitable and efficient process of development within cities. Before such initiatives can be taken, however, the problems must be placed in perspective with the help of a more appropriate framework. The purpose of this paper is to summarize the findings of urban economists which can contribute to provide such a framework and some directions to policy makers in their efforts to deal with the challenges of urbanization in the developing world.

2. National urbanization: Determinants and policies

2.1. The determinants of urban settlement patterns: Conflicting orthodoxies

Behind much of the anxiety concerning urban settlement patterns in developing countries is the implicit notion of an optimal distribution of population. By that standard, the urban landscape would be covered with a dense network of small- and medium-sized centers, each growing at a similar, low rate. These centers, collectively, would generate at least as much output as the present configuration of cities. Great urban agglomerations would be largely absent, or at least irrelevant. The rural sector would evolve over time without the need to shift large groups of workers and their families to large or even intermediate size cities. Instead, the rural work environment would be enriched and diversified, as many modern activities located in villages. In the absence of startling shifts and discontinuities, all areas, urban and rural, could be upgraded in unison, receiving public services faster and at a lower cost than in the alternate, "real world" scenario.

Deviations from this "optimum" are thus understood as irrational, inefficient or inappropriate. All too often the policy response is to try to limit population and employment growth in large centers by means of regulations and licenses. The one fact that usually prevents this strategy from being applied fully and consistently is that national government authority is divided among competing groups. Ministries committed to giving spatial policy some priority are opposed by other ministries dedicated to fulfilling macroeconomic objectives. The latter tend to adhere to a different view of large cities. The concentration of economic activity in such agglomerations is accepted for an indefinite period because it appears to reflect the powerful impact of agglomeration economies associated with city size. In addition, forcible redirection of activity to other centers is seen to be disruptive and affect the achievement of such goals as rapid import substitution, increased industrial export activity, and the careful control and regulation of moderate and large size firms.

One can argue that both sets of policy-makers are operating within faulty frameworks. The optimum geography school misunderstands the determinants and consequences of migration. By extension, the key role played by the location of tradeable goods and services in shaping city size is also ignored. The concentrationists err in the opposite direction, confusing the type of urban settlement pattern that occurs under severe locational constraints with that operative under less constrained conditions [Renaud (1981), Richardson (1977), United Nations (1981)].

2.2. Migration and natural population growth: Some stylized facts

The role of migrants in city growth is more complicated than the optimalists believe. As a general rule, roughly 40–50 percent of urban growth is caused by immigration or the reclassification of previously rural population centers. The rest of the growth is due to natural increase, including the children born to migrant parents. Furthermore, there is regional variation; the percentage of the urban population born elsewhere is low in Latin America and South Asia, and high in Africa. Finally, the relative contribution of each component varies by place and, for any given location, over time.

There is also a consensus among students of migration concerning the de-terminants of relocation which differs from the views of the optimalists [Morrison (1983), Population Reports (1983)]. Migrants tend to move from places of lower economic opportunity to areas of higher economic opportunity. Migration levels originating from any area tend to reflect "push" factors related to the lack of local opportunities. Once set in motion, however, the characteristics of potential destinations, relative to those of the origin, are paramount. The possibility of choosing from among a variety of career paths is clearly very important in selecting a destination. So is the ease or difficulty of acquiring information about locational alternatives; distance acts as an impediment to relocation. Urban places may have an attraction over and above that reflected by narrow employ-ment considerations, but this is difficult to pinpoint with any confidence. Clearly, educational opportunities are important, especially for those migrants who have a relatively high level of education to begin with. Skilled and professional workers, especially those involved in urban-urban migration, also seem re-sponsive to the level of public services among competing alternative destinations. Unfortunately, the fiscal and planning mechanisms through which communities acquire, extend, and maintain infrastructure and education services may operate in such a way as to discourage moves to other than the larger centers of the country. In particular, secondary centers are rarely allowed to compete with one another for available central grants and urban development loans. Since local initiative is not usually rewarded, secondary centers have difficulty in getting access to the resources necessary to enhance their relative attractiveness through strategic infrastructure investments.

Other conclusions follow from the existing research literature. Contrary to melodramatic depictions of city-bound migrants, these individuals are among the most "upwardly mobile" in their area. They are primarily young (15–30), are better educated and better off financially than their non-migrant or rural-bound cohorts. They are likely to have nonagricultural skills and considerable linkages with destination-area households. Such linkages provide information on work and residence opportunities upon arrival. As a consequence, migrants tend to find jobs quickly after moving. Over time, there seem to be few employment-related differences between migrants and nonmigrants of the same age, sex, and educ-ational level. Similarly, migrants do not concentrate themselves dispropor-tionately among the ranks of the very poor or among the unemployed and underemployed. Most migrants believe they *and* their children are better off than if no move had taken place.

There are, of course, unsuccessful migrants, though studies suggest the pro-portion involved in rarely more than 10 percent. These move on to other cities or return to their place of origin. Even then, most origin areas appear to gain more than they lose. Population pressure is reduced, underutilized work time is cut, while remittances of migrants increase the living standards of relatives left behind.

None of this is meant to deny the optimalist contention that rapid city growth, whatever its source, is difficult to accommodate, especially in large centers. There, the higher costs for labor and land, the discontinuous nature of additions to infrastructure capacity, and the difficulty of performing public works in built-up areas, may offset potential economies of scale that come with higher densities and large city size; as a result the unit costs of infrastructure may be relatively high. Larger centers may require greater numbers of public services and more expensive types of services than smaller cities (e.g. sewer systems). Finally the income levels in such areas may encourage consumers to demand higher quality service than is the case elsewhere. Nevertheless, as detailed below, services can be provided, and at standards affordable to the beneficiaries, without necessarily drawing on subsidies paid by the nation as a whole. What is more, the available evidence indicates that public service provision, including education, health, clean water and sanitation, may on balance be as expensive, and possibly even more costly, to provide in rural areas and small towns, as in large cities [Linn (1982)].

There remains, then, the optimalist hypothesis that entrepreneurs who locate in larger centers are misguided because they could locate elsewhere, and receive similar or larger returns on their investment by operating in cities where public services, wages, and land are cheaper. There may be a small measure of truth to this assertion but, as demonstrated below, it in no way invalidates the initial or long-term net advantage of operating many businesses in large agglomerations.

2.3. The determinants of city size in the course of development

While the degree of urbanization appears closely associated with the levels of economic development, the link between urbanization and urban concentration is more complex. Empirical work, for example, suggests certain associations. One study of 44 countries [Rosen and Resnick (1980)] estimated Pareto distributions for the largest 50 cities or all cities over 100,000, whichever yielded the greater sample. The resulting Pareto exponents were found to vary as a function of at least two variables: per capita income and national population size. The wealthier and the more populous countries tend to have more evenly distributed populations, and are less likely to concentrate activity in a handful of very large centers. Henderson (1980) utilized an urban deconcentration index to explore city size distributions in 34 countries. He found that greater agricultural activity, more decentralized political system, increasing urban population, and larger proportions of resource-oriented to resource-independent activity, all are associated with decreased concentration. The ability of the labor force to manipulate modern technology, as measured by levels of education, also has an impact. At the initial stages of modern economic growth, concentration increases with improvements in education; thereafter, as educational opportunities continue to increase, more dispersed patterns of urban population are evident.

These associations can be blended together into a hypothesis about the determinants of urban settlement patterns within any country. For the sake of generality, it is useful to concentrate on countries or regions with the population and resource potential to support a diverse set of cities of different sizes at some point in their development.[1] Then the pattern of urban settlements appears to depend on two major factors: the impact of national or regional production patterns, and the public policies that affect the relative attractiveness of different cities as centers of production and consumption.

Urbanization under severe constraints.[2]   Cities and their size are molded by the tradeable goods and services they produce and "export" and, through such basic activities, by the demand they generate for locally consumed goods and services. The process of development that increases the level of urbanization also reshapes the composition of goods and services produced in the urban centers. This has implications for what types of urban areas are likely to grow relatively rapidly at each stage in a nation's development.

Early industrialization is built around resource-based tradeable activities. These include mining, agroprocessing, construction materials, beverages, textiles, repair activities, and the production of simple machinery and parts. Ports involved in interregional and international trade emerge, as do administrative and agrobusiness service centers. Activities which are dependent on physical proximity to natural resources tend to be scattered. Other production, facing no such impediments, tends to locate in large centers. The reasons are straight-forward. The supply of skilled labor is small and only large centers are likely to be assembly points for a diversified labor pool. Interregional and international transport is poor and only large centers are likely to have sizable, accessible markets or be well connected to the outside world. This is particularly important for any production using imported inputs which are available at port locations without the heavy costs of internal transportation. Urban public services are inadequate in quantity and quality, but large centers are better off than other locations. Industrial experience is limited, and large centers are usually the only places where knowledge of new markets and new technologies are readily available. Therefore, at early stages of national development, most plants that are not bound to a particular resource base will act as if urbanization economies, i.e. savings external to the firm that are associated with city size, are paramount in

---

[1]This is meant to exclude idiosyncratic cases like Chad, Lesotho, Bhutan, Yemen, Nepal, Mauritania, Burkina (formerly Upper Volta), Burundi, and Rwanda.

[2]Among contemporary examples of this phenomenon one can cite the Ivory Coast, Indonesia, the Philippines, Thailand, Pakistan, and Egypt. Empirical work on this issue is reviewed and extended in Parr (1985). Also useful is Wheaton and Shisido (1981).

location choices. City specialization in a related group of industrial activities is rare; thus, as argued below, the basis for extensive trade between cities suffers, as does the development of a vigorously expanding system of intermediate cities.

The cited constraints operate at another level as well. Those public policies that affect the relative attractiveness of different cities tend to favor large centers already playing a significant role in the economy. The public sector at early stages of development tends to be both relatively centralized and overwhelmed by the perceived public investment short-falls in interregional transport and communications facilities, and in urban services. National authorities are tempted to favor a few centers that are preeminent in some respect, including major ports, administrative capitals, and other large cities. This occurs because the central government, which controls the bulk of investable resources, is committed to taking as many shortcuts to achieve its modernization objectives as possible. By focusing on large cities, the public sector finds it possible to reduce the need for anticipatory physical and social infrastructure while achieving certain industrial targets. In effect, one or two cities become industrial and commercial city states, which can operate with only a fraction of the telephones, paved roads, power plants, and educational facilities needed to create the same environment at many points in space.

After this initial resource-oriented stage has passed, the most rapidly growing tradeable activities are associated with the emergence of engineering and metallurgy subsectors. Again, it is likely that the cited constraints will limit economic diversification to the largest centers, and that the agglomeration economies experienced by firms will continue to be linked to city size. Big cities act as economic supermarkets, providing a wide variety of inputs, services, skills, and clients for firms; and consumer goods, services and opportunities for workers of varying skill.

Urbanization in a less constrained setting.[3] The emergence of numerous intermediate centers, and of smaller centers that later grow into secondary cities, depends on a combination of factors. These factors tend to find full expression only in developed countries, but they can be detected in middle income developing countries as well. First is the growth of hinterland markets around urban centers that originally had a limited servicing role. This establishes an independent base for urban growth, in at least some activities. Second, as experience with consumer and producer goods' production processes becomes more extensive, much of this activity becomes routinized and is *potentially* available for profitable duplication in secondary centers. The reason, discussed below, is the shift in the nature of the relevant agglomeration economies, from those linked to

---

[3] This section reflects the conclusions of World Bank research work in Brazil, Mexico, Colombia, Taiwan, and Korea can also be cited as an example. Empirical evidence is available in Vining, 1985.

city size per se to those identified with local clusters of related activities, i.e. localization economies. Third, and critical to the full blossoming of the second factor, is the redirection of interregional and public service investments at the margin to modify the relative attractiveness of intermediate centers.

Hinterland markets can expand in one of two ways. First, improvements in agricultural practices, in infrastructure, and in public policies toward the rural sector can boost incomes and create new demands for local goods and services. Building upon this base, it becomes possible for area local entrepreneurs in the cities to initiate or expand production in a series of commodities to a scale at which longer distance exporting becomes possible. This expansion of the trade-ables base facilitates the growth of additional local-serving jobs, and permits the labor force to expand. Less often explored, but important, is the process of deconcentration across areas as distant as 100 kilometers from a large metropolis [Hamer (1985)]. For reasons that appear linked to decision-making under severe uncertainty, entrepreneurs in a developing metropolis generally will consider plant transfers or new branches only within the expanding region of influence of the home base. Within that region, some of the metropolitan dynamism gets transferred to free-standing communities which can offer proximity to the advan-tages of the original center at somewhat lower costs in wages, land, congestion, etc. Simultaneously, local entrepreneurs, who provide the basis for almost all expansion in secondary cities beyond the metropolitan region, also take advan-tage of the advancing edge of that larger market, finding new export possibilities. While this relatively easy form of decentralization is often viewed disdainfully, as a form of sprawl, it does contribute to enlarging the geographic area within which diversified industrial production takes place.

Clearly contributing to both deconcentration and decentralized development beyond the metropolitan region is a subtle shift in the nature of agglomeration economies operative for a widening number of industrial subsectors. Instead of merely reaping savings from the massing of large numbers of sectors in a metropolis, blocks of employment prosper in *specialized* secondary centers, where savings appear to depend on proximity to related industries. Among the benefits from these localization economies are: savings from information exchanged among related firms; cost reductions from the easy provision of intermediate inputs tailored to such firms; new opportunities for plant specialization within an area shared with establishments producing related commodities; and greater options for workers and businesses searching for specific job and skill combinations.

Empirical work suggests that the incremental savings that come from additions to industry output or employment in one city tend to become quite small once that local industry group reaches a total size which is moderate in absolute terms [Henderson (1986)]. Thus, where localization economies are operative, one expects that the affected firms maximize their advantage by growing in intermediate centers where one group of related activities is dominant and the rest of the workers are involved primarily in support or nontraded activities. Such specialization allows full exploitation of the dominant form of agglomeration effects for those firms while keeping the offsetting costs of doing business at more moderate levels than found in metropolitan centers. To expand those activities in the larger centers, once locational constraints are relaxed, yields few additional advantages while increasing the costs of many inputs.

Thus, in an environment where few locational constraints prevail, intermediate cities grow by specializing. Clearly, large metropolitan areas play a critical role and continue to expand, though less rapidly than secondary cities. But, at the margin, the key firms would now be in advanced technology items, in goods subject to volatile style changes, in national and international business services, in higher education, and in administration. The size of these metropolitan markets also ensures that a mix of market-seeking footloose industries attach themselves to the area.

In all this, there is a critical supposition that the policy environment is conducive. It is in this regard that the concentrationists operate from an incomplete perspective, by ignoring the impact of policies that inadvertently hold back decentralized development. These can be classified into two categories.

While the changing profile of national production provides a basis for the emergence of medium-sized centers, the speed at which this transformation takes place is dependent upon the improvement of local public services and of regional and interregional access. On one level this appears obvious. Until access is significantly improved across the system of cities, proximity to the main consumer markets, especially those in and around historically preeminent centers, dictates the location of producers who are neither resource-bound nor too small to cater to more than a very localized market area to begin with. Similarly, policies that ensure better city infrastructure in secondary centers reduce the costs of doing business there, even under price and tax policies that emphasize full cost recovery. Less apparent, however, is the important role these improvements play in attracting and retaining high-skilled workers, managers, and entrepreneurs. Work in both developed and developing countries suggests that high- and low-skilled labor are poor substitutes for one another. This means production of emerging tradeable commodities is associated with fairly rigid skill mix requirements. Decentralized development as described above thus depends on mechanisms which overcome the disamenities of secondary centers particularly from the vantage point of the skilled worker or entrepreneur. Many of these amenities are associated with the quantity and quality of public services, including education. Rising levels of amenities allow businesses at off-center locations to offer lower compensation packages to scarce types of workers and managers. These reductions may mean not only greater expansion possibilities for particular lines of production, but the difference between the existence or absence of certain kinds of activities.

Along with these initiatives, there are others whose importance is not as obvious and whose impact is harder to quantify; these are the so-called implicit spatial policies. Such policies are primarily macroeconomic or sectoral and they share in common a tendency implicitly to favor industrial development in some locations rather than others [Renaud (1981)]. They are also policies whose merit on strictly aspatial grounds is often dubious. One simple example can be found in the treatment of the rural sector in most developing countries during the last two decades. Very often governments taxed agricultural exports, controlled domestic food prices, placed heavy duties on imported inputs, ignored rural demands for credit, and in other ways restricted opportunity in rural areas. The result was that many secondary centers experienced long periods of stunted growth. Conversely, when the policy environment changed, the improved health of the hinterland was quickly reflected in the growth of secondary cities.[4]

Another common source of problems, was, and is, to be found in the nature and the administration of policies related to industrial promotion. Looking across industrial subsectors and across cities, it is clear that the input requirements of different production processes vary widely, as do the supplies of inputs at different locations. In the extreme, some inputs, such as easy access to government officials, to imported inputs, or to particular sophisticated services, may be available at only a few locations. Under these circumstances, promotion policies that affect subsectors which feel location-bound will result in long-term subsidies to particular urban areas.

Consider, for example, the impact of a heavily protectionist trade regime intended to impose a forced march to full-fledged industrialization. Research findings across developing countries suggest that many or most of the heavily favored sectors tend to locate in the largest urban areas, where they can satisfy their exceptional demand for imports, sophisticated factors of production, or access to discretionary favors [Renaud (1981)]. Under such a trade regime, the industrial value-added of major metropolitan areas is boosted by the artificial inducements. From this follow longer-term effects, which encourage additional growth over and above that recorded at one point in time.

As other locational constraints diminish, a neutralization of industrial promotion programs would allow production to restructure itself spatially over time. A less interventionist regime would tend to encourage sectors with fewer ties to the largest cities. With the passage of time, more cities would emerge that would be capable of accommodating the demands of sophisticated production. At that point, industrial modernization would no longer coincide with the growth of only one or two centers.

More generally, if any individual set of sectoral policies is ill-advised on

---

[4]Evidence exists that nonfarm rural employment is heavily linked to agricultural growth (e.g., Thailand and Colombia).

macroeconomic grounds, their differential spatial or urban impact is one more reason to consider reform. If the policies are justified but the economic environment is such that economic agents in urban centers, other than those initially benefited, are denied access to resources on reasonable terms with which to remedy locational deficiencies, then the public sector should act to remedy the matter. Among other measures, it is appropriate to modify the system of intergovernmental fiscal relations so that all urban centers can compete for matching grants and urban development loans on the basis of local performance in mobilizing resources through enhanced tax efforts and fuller cost recovery. Subsidizing services in selected, usually metropolitan, areas is counterproductive to any decentralization strategy. In the final analysis, however, central planners must take a hard look at sectoral policies before accepting the associated spatial consequences.

2.4. Public intervention in shaping city size: Limits and opportunities

Certain general principles apply when urban settlement policies are contemplated. Urban growth is the result of innumerable individual location decisions by households and businesses. These processes are complex; therefore, the probability is great that direct intervention through orders and prohibitions will prove counterproductive.[5] For this reason, policy-makers should avoid the temptation to assign optimal sizes to different cities and then set about forcing individuals to abide by them. Attempts to throttle the growth of particular cities above a certain size, by issuing edicts or by neglecting the infrastructure demand generated by new growth, are likely to harm national economic development and mire the bureaucracy and its subjects in red tape. Similarly, the central government must consider the large-scale replicability of any potential action to promote growth in secondary centers. For, at any point in time, only a few central initiatives are possible, and these must compete with all other demands for central financial and administrative resources. For example, it is not possible to declare that a large set of secondary centers are too small and then to attempt to flood those areas with costly, integrated packages of assistance meant to create the missing prerequisites of growth. Another, similarly unwieldy set of initiatives involves those meant to create regional balance by building new cities of particular sizes. Without exception this approach has meant a commitment of resources that cannot be sustained for very long.

In the end, the central decision-makers must realize that, to affect urban settlement patterns, they must concentrate on policies which have little of the

---

[5]There are several examples of this. Among others, one can cite Jakarta, Indonesia; the major metropolises in India; Seoul, Korea; Manila, the Philippines; and Buenos Aires, Argentina. A good review of the issues involved is found in United Nations (1981).

glamorous veneer of traditional spatial policies. Furthermore, they must apply their chosen measures consistently, and resist the temptation to modify policies repeatedly, thus muddling the signals sent to the individual economic agents who ultimately shape city size. This is no easy task, for little can be said about the precise way in which new outcomes will follow more appropriate policies. There is no available model of city size distribution which can be estimated with data and then used to predict changes in relative city sizes in the presence of policy changes. Nevertheless, even marginal changes in the growth rates of different city size groups will lead to the reallocation of millions of urban dwellers over time. The lack of precise estimates of policy change impacts is therefore no grounds for complacency in designing policies towards improved urbanization patterns.

Among the set of implicit spatial policies that require attention, to ensure consistency with spatial goals, one can list several as critical. The recommendations made share in common the fact that reforms are justified on nonspatial grounds alone. First, there is a need to ensure that the rural economy is not restrained by punitive price controls, heavy implicit or explicit export taxes, artificial constraints on the use of yield-boosting inputs, and poorly planned credit and technical assistance delivery systems. Market towns and regional centers can be stimulated simply by removing disincentives to rural production. In turn, this allows such centers to absorb a greater proportion of rural workers who seek better opportunities outside the countryside, as agricultural production restructures itself. Central decision-makers must also learn to accept the fact that, even in the best of circumstances, the modernization of the rural sector in the presence of population pressure requires urban policies that accommodate immigration at all city sizes. Thus, a reform of rural credit policies to remove a bias toward large-scale farmers will help to preserve opportunities in the countryside for paid labor and small producers. Yet, other policies meant to improve rural life, such as more and better schools and improved accessibility, stimulate outmigration. In fact, an effective family planning program in rural areas is probably one of the few mechanisms that can dampen migration flows without retarding other, worthwhile economic development objectives.

A second set of nonspatial initiatives is required, involving the environment in which industrial firms operate. Two major areas deserve attention. To begin with, measures should be taken to reduce unnecessary incentives to operate business near centers of government power. Too often, ongoing access to customs officials, tax administrators, regulators, government bankers, and sector policy-makers, especially those located in the capital, is made profitable. This type of implicit incentive to concentration rarely has any social benefits, and should be avoided by regulatory reform that stresses simplification, decreases uncertainty as to application, and encourages geographic decentralization of authority. Along with this change, another is necessary. This would involve modifying the implicit price signals that govern location behavior. A good example can be found in international trade regulation. A protectionist regime encourages the premature expansion of large cities by promoting the growth of inefficient, import-competing activities, many of which are dependent on inputs that are found in preeminent centers, and that are costly or impossible to acquire elsewhere. The adoption of lower, more uniform levels of protection is usually recommended on general, macroeconomic grounds. These same reforms will enhance decentralized growth, as well, by improving the *relative* level of promotion for many sectors that have excellent opportunities to grow in secondary centers. At the same time, reform would discourage the early emergence of domestic production in sectors which cannot avoid locating in big cities during earlier periods of national modernization.

Explicit spatial policies are also worth pursuing to improve opportunities for growth among secondary centers but they must be adopted with caution. As an example, location subsidies or tax breaks are often championed without sufficient regard for their limited effectiveness and serious fiscal costs. Firms searching for new plant sites tend to operate in an environment characterized by great uncertainty as to the pattern and future course of costs in different locations [Hamer (1985), Townroe (1979)]. They tend to avoid choices involving great distances from their home base, unless the firms are large enough to support major search costs and to sustain possible major cash flow problems for the first few years. Thus, the amount of interregionally mobile investment at any point in time is small and successful redirection of this will have limited implications for off-center communities. Add to this the lost revenue implications of such policies and it is doubtful whether they can be justified.

One can also argue that the location of public industrial investments should not be distorted to accommodate arbitrary regional objectives. Such enterprises may have a role in pioneering the development of non-traditional locations. However, this does not mean that public enterprises should accept sharp reductions in profits to promote regional goals. Since all too many public firms in developing countries are poorly managed, further departures from commercial objectives are probably unwise. Given the existing macroeconomic constraints in most developing countries, it is likely that such ventures will have to follow locational criteria not unlike those pursued by private enterprises.

What is needed, instead, is a set of policies which stress the importance of improved interregional access, on the one hand, and of improved infrastructure at the local level on the other. The steady improvement of transportation and telecommunications across the national territory is clearly justified by the large dividends which can be reaped by improving access to domestic and international markets. In fact, until access to secondary cities is significantly improved, *physical* proximity to the main consumer markets, especially in and around large cities, will dictate the location of most producers except those that are resource-bound or those too small to cater to more than a very localized market area.

Other central, infrastructure-enhancing, initiatives are probably sensible as well. The government should develop and expand the use of industrial zones and estates targeted selectively in areas of proven growth or well-documented potential. There is general agreement in the literature that the opportunity cost of underutilized public investment is so high that developing countries cannot afford to rely on "leading infrastructure" as an inducement for industrial dispersal. However, at most stages of development, there are areas outside the major urban centers where industrial growth and diversification can take place. It is in these areas where improved infrastructure is a critical condition for further growth. Elsewhere, the obstacles to industrial development are so many that even radical improvements in public services will not be cost effective and only gradual upgrading of infrastructure can be expected as economic development proceeds.

Finally, improved access to public services and education plays an important part in modifying the relative attractiveness of secondary centers over time. Such improvements reduce the operating costs of businesses and help attract skilled workers and professionals to off-center locations. Since the needs of rural areas and of large cities cannot be ignored, and since central resources are limited, intergovernmental fiscal relations must be modified. Local taxes and user charges must be exploited more fully and transfers of funds from the center to municipalities must be tied more explicitly to local resource mobilization efforts. In addition, local governments must take a larger role in planning, executing, and maintaining local investments, allowing an already overextended central bureaucracy to concentrate its resources in a more selective fashion.[6]

In the final analysis, urban settlement patterns are the indirect outcome of many policies interacting with the economic agents who must make locational decisions. These policies stress the development of a reformed macroeconomic environment backed by an orderly expansion of interregional investments. Cities must continue to extend and upgrade local public services, relying more heavily than before on local taxes and user charges. In turn, while some central government resources should be spent to provide services for the very poor, regardless of location, most national grants and loans to improve city infrastructure should be linked to local effort. Through the application of these policies, the constraints on the development of urban centers, regardless of size, can be systematically reduced.

---

[6]This emphasis on local resource mobilization in secondary centers is not meant to excuse subsidization of public services or heavy reliance on central funds in metropolitan areas. Besides straining central resources and limiting central support for rural areas and secondary cities, subsidized public service provision in metropolitan areas is one of the major policy distortions clearly fostering inappropriate location decisions, and thus excessive urban concentration.

3. Efficient and equitable development of cities: Issues and policies

3.1. The policy problem[7]

Improved policies towards urbanization will help to alleviate some of the pressures of growth on the cities of the Third World. Nevertheless, the problems now confronting policy makers in the management of those cities will remain for the foreseeable future as urbanization will continue apace in all developing countries. Urban policies at the city level are therefore of central importance in ensuring that the scarce economic, human and financial resources heavily concentrated in urban areas are utilized in as efficient and equitable manner as possible.

Analysis and experience show that, contrary to common perception, there is often no conflict between the twin objectives of efficiency and equity in the design of urban policies. Of course, this is not to imply that conflicts or tradeoffs never arise, in particular as many of the prevalent inefficiencies tend to result in benefits to the economic and political elite of a country. In fact, the biggest obstacle to urban policy reform may well be that a majority of the decision makers, who themselves are members of the urban elite, tend to have a particular view of the urban problem, which regards the growth of slums as an infringement on the beauty of their city; street vendors, pedestrians and overcrowded buses as a nuisance impeding the movement of automobiles; and education and health care needs as consisting of unmet requirements of higher education and modern hospitals. The policy prescriptions drawn from this diagnosis of the urban problem include the "beautification" of cities through slum removal and construction of high-cost public housing projects; the banning of street vendors from commercial districts; the construction of limited-access highways and high-cost rapid transit facilities without commensurate control over the use of private automobiles; and the expansion of subsidized universities and city hospitals.

An alternative view, which is advocated here, would take as basic objectives of urban policy an increase in the overall efficiency of urban growth and the alleviation of urban poverty placed in the context of the interaction between the forces of demand and supply of goods and services in cities (including transport, housing and public services) and labor, capital and land. The diagnosis of the urban problem would then, for example, include the observation that the demand for labor, and in particular for unskilled labor, is not expanding quickly enough to provide employment at rising wages to a rapidly increasing labor force, whereas the demand for land, capital transport, housing and public services are expanding more rapidly than their supplies, thus resulting in higher prices or

---

[7]Much of the subsequent analysis draws on Linn (1983) to which the reader is referred for details and documentation.

shortages for these important inputs or services. The policy analysis and pre-scription flowing from this diagnosis then would focus on efforts to match more effectively the demand and supply of labor, and to develop investment, pricing and regulatory approaches which lead to a more rapid expansion of supplies of urban land, capital and services while also rationing their demand in an efficient and equitable manner. The remainder of this paper develops this approach further by exploring the urban policy issues in the areas of employment, transport, housing, social services, and administration and finance.

3.2. Urban employment and labor market policies[8]

Cities in developing countries in effect represent the apex of employment growth and opportunities. As indicated above, urban employment growth is the primary factor inducing rural–urban migration, which in turn tends to equilibrate urban and rural wages for unskilled labor at a common low level, especially in informal sector activities. Urban unemployment, while not uncommon, tends to be re-stricted to the younger, more highly educated and relatively well-off groups among the urban labor force, who can afford to wait for desirable employment opportunities after leaving school, or who have been temporarily dislocated from their government or modern sector jobs during period of economic austerity. The truly poor are not able to afford periods of unemployment, but instead have to work long hours in low-productivity occupations.

The source of urban employment problems, as well as their solutions, may be found in three dimensions: labor supply, labor demand, and the interactions between supply and demand in the urban labor market. On the supply side, the rate of population growth is the most important underlying source of aggregate labor force growth. Countries which manage to contain and reduce population growth rates will, albeit with a lag of some 10–15 years, also see a significant slowdown in the rate of growth in the labor force which needs to find urban employment opportunities. Obviously, an effective national family planning and population policy is at the core of a longer-term effort to limit urban employment problems. There are no obvious appropriate policy interventions which might deal with two other factors contributing to the growth of urban labor supply: migration and increases in the labor force participation rate. Both reflect in-dividual households' reactions to employment opportunities, which are not easily controlled and where public intervention generally will contribute only to reduce efficiency in resource allocation and lower earnings, especially for poor house-holds. On the other hand, education and training policies have an important

---

[8]For a broader assessment of employment and labor market issues and policies in developing countries, see Squire (1981).

impact on the composition of labor supply, albeit also only in the longer term. In many developing countries, overextension of formal, liberal arts-oriented education, not geared sufficiently to the needs of agriculture, industry and service activities for applied technical and vocational training, and the use of formal education as a sorting device by public and private employers, have contributed to urban unemployment among the young, better-off, and relatively well-educated. More emphasis on basic education, complemented by on-the-job and other informal training in technical and vocational skills, can help upgrade the urban labor force and reduce the incidence of urban unemployment.

There is more scope on the demand side for effective urban employment policy than on the supply side, at least in the short and medium term. However, most labor demand policies need to be managed at the national, rather than at the city or project level, which limits the scope for intervention by city-level authorities. The single most important factor determing total (and thus also urban) labor demand growth is the overall growth rate of the economy. Successful macroeconomic and sectoral management which leads to sustained rapid economic growth, as has been the case for example in many of the East Asian economies, is central to maintain sustained growth in labor demand and earnings.[9] The growth of industrial, service and government activities, which as a general rule accompanies economic development, is obviously of greatest direct importance for urban labor demand growth, but indirectly the growth of rural labor demand, mainly in response to policies affecting agricultural growth and rural development, also plays a role in regulating the overall employment outlook for a country, and thus also for the urban areas.

In addition to affecting the pace of economic growth and thus labor demand, the macroeconomic, trade and sectoral policies also directly influence labor demand by affecting the labor intensity of economic growth. Such policies as overvalued exchange rates, trade regimes favoring import-substitution and inhibiting growth of export-oriented activities, interest rate and credit management, investment incentives, and tax and regulatory regimes in many developing countries have tended to provide powerful incentives to favor capital-intensive choices of technique, activities, and scale of operation and have militated against labor intensive activities which are generally carried out by export oriented and small to medium-scale enterprises. A reversal in these policies, besides fostering improved overall economic performance, can also support more labor intensive development, thus helping substantially to meet the urban employment challenge.

Imperfections in the labor markets have also contributed to some of the urban

---

[9]This is not the place for a more detailed assessment of the macro and sectoral policies which help explain the difference between more and less successful economic growth performance of developing countries. For a recent review of economic policy and management patterns and impacts, the reader may refer to World Bank (1983a).

employment problems. Most notable are institutional practices such as minimum wage legislation, public employment patterns, educational requirements unrelated to productivity evidence, ethnic and caste barriers to job access, and labor registration requirements. Lack of adequate information and access to jobs, or alternatively the often high cost of gaining information or of commuting have placed limits on the matching of labor demand and supply and have resulted in earnings differentials and in lower effective wage rates and earnings, especially for unskilled labor. Efforts designed to limit the distorting impacts of minimum wage legislation and of discriminating hiring practices and to reduce access and commuting costs can therefore also help in urban labor absorption and increasing labor earnings.

So far, macro and sectoral policies have been discussed which need to be pursued mainly at the level of the national authorities. Additionally, a number of policy instruments can usefully be employed at the city level, designed to improve labor supply and demand conditions and the working of the urban labor market. These include the elimination of frequent local administrative, tax and regulatory practices inhibiting small-scale and informal sector activities (such as bans on street vendors, neighborhood markets or traditional transport services, etc.), the consideration of labor-intensive techniques in urban public service provision, and the careful planning of the design and location of urban infrastructure investments with an eye to reduce commuting costs and facilitate access, especially by the poor, to educational, health and family planning facilities. These local- and project-level interventions cannot offset the impacts of national-level policies that discriminate against effective urban labor absorption, but they represent one of the elements of a broader strategy to support efficient and equitable urban growth.

3.3. Urban transport

Transport provides the essential link between urban activities, between residence, employment, and amenities, between and among urban producers and consumers. Intraurban transport demands, investment requirements and costs increase more than in proportion with city size, even as the agglomeration economies of cities reduce the interurban transport and communications requirements. The correct design, pricing, and regulation of intraurban transport therefore become more important with increasing city size as a factor determining the efficiency of urban resource allocation. In addition, the nature and design of urban transport systems in developing countries also has important impacts on such common important national policy objectives as energy conservation, foreign exchange and public resource saving and regional balance, since excessive growth of urban transport services tends to be highly intensive in energy, foreign exchange and public resource use, and tends to foster urban concentration through biases in national public investment and financing patterns in favor of the larger cities. Finally, urban transport policies have major implications for the distributional effects of urban growth. The urban poor are particularly affected by the inadequacy of the urban transport system in providing them with ready and affordable access to employment, educational and health care opportunities, as well as by virtue of the fact that the provision of other urban public service (such as fire and police protection, power and water supply, sewerage and garbage disposal) is frequently dependent on the road accessibility of a neighborhood.

Transport investment, pricing and regulatory practices in many cities of the developing world, however, besides often encouraging inefficient urban development patterns and resource use, have mainly benefited the wealthy and the middle-income groups by providing costly, but highly subsidized infrastructure primarily for use of private automobiles, very limited public transit facilities accompanied by restrictions in the development of low-cost private transit, and frequently inadequate road access in poor neighborhoods.

This brief overview of urban transport issues in developing countries can be complemented by a review of public policy options, contrasting commonly found policies which have tended to be both inefficient and inequitable with proposed alternative policies that avoid many of these shortcomings. Examples of successful application of the proposed policies may be found in the developing world, but much remains to be done in the majority of Third World cities if they are to come to grips with their growing transport problems. Since the urban transport system represents a highly interconnected system of competing and complementary activities, it is important to design a comprehensive strategy of policy action at the city level buttressed by supportive policies at the national or provincial level (including, for example, appropriate policies regarding domestic automobile production, taxation and registration, petroleum product pricing, etc.). In many developing countries this requires a significant change in policy perceptions at all levels of government, which obviously cannot be expected to happen overnight, especially as the beneficiaries of traditional urban transport policies, particularly higher- and middle-income car owners, bus users, and property owners are certain to be vigorously opposed to policies reducing their preferential and subsidized treatment. Much will therefore depend on a successful improvement in urban services for all major user groups in parallel with shifts in the distribution of the benefits of public intervention from the better-off to the poorer segments of the urban population.

In the area of transport investment, traditional investment policies have emphasized highway construction designed to meet the needs of private automobiles, matched by a neglect of access roads to poor neighborhoods and of facilities supporting buses, bicycling and walking, and, in an increasing number of cities, accompanied by very costly investments in high-technology rapid rail transit (especially subways). In contrast, more appropriate urban transport investment strategies have reduced the emphasis on general purpose arterial road construction mainly benefiting automobiles, stressing instead improved facilities for existing bus and minibus use (including reserved bus lanes, loading bays, terminals, etc.) and expanded neighborhood street-paving programs combining access routes for bus services and other public service vehicles with installation of bicycle paths and walkways. Only a few of the largest cities and along very limited routes are subways and other types of rapid rail transit systems likely to represent a cost-effective response to developing countries' urban transport problems. Their high capital and operating costs, substantial foreign exchange requirements and onerous needs for financial subsidies severely limit the scale at which they can be built in Third World cities, thus making only limited contributions to solving the urban transport problem. Moreover, because of overall economic and financial resource constraints, the huge capital outlays required reduce the scope for alternative solutions which would have broader benefits, particularly among the poor urban population groups.

Urban transport pricing, subsidies and taxes are another powerful policy tool often abused or underutilized. Subsidization of automobile use in highly congested and polluted cities is common, including in some cities even the provision of tax-exempt or subsidized central-city parking facilities [Linn (1981)]. Subsidized public urban bus and rail services are also common, generally provided by financially troubled state enterprises offering poor service of limited coverage. Privately owned transit operations (and even nonmotorized vehicles), in contrast, are often taxed and restricted by national or local authorities, if they are allowed to compete at all with their publicly owned counterparts [Walters (1979a,b)].

An alternative package of transport pricing policies could include congestion pricing for private automobiles using area and time specific license charges as applied successfully in Singapore, complemented by central city parking fees for on- and off-street parking [Watson and Holland (1978)]. General taxation of automobiles and gasoline, particularly when differentially higher in larger cities as compared with smaller towns and rural areas, is also an option for limiting private automobile ownership and use in urban areas, albeit second-best in terms of efficiency compared to the more specific congestion charges. Administrative ease, public revenue needs and a progressive incidence across income groups, however, make these taxes attractive fiscal instruments. Careful design of public bus fares to reduce widespread subsidization, to introduce distance-graduated tariffs, and to permit more frequent adjustments in line with cost increases, combined with a nondiscriminatory treatment for private transit operators, could go a long way in ensuring financially viable, reliable and broadly accessible urban bus service. Finally, the costs of urban road infrastructure investments could be more fully recovered from those reaping many of their benefits, i.e., from the landowners who find their property values enhanced by public investment.

Special assessments or betterment charges have been used successfully in Korea [Doebele (1979)] and Colombia [Doebele, Grimes and Linn (1979)] for this purpose; more effective urban property taxation is another possibility.

Finally, urban transport is frequently encumbered by misplaced regulatory restrictions, including those on privately operated transit modes including buses and minibuses, as well as traditional nonmotorized forms of public transport (e.g. rickshas and bekjas). Regulatory controls have limited private transit operations as well as the freedom to set fares, thus affecting the availability of privately supplied transport services directly as well as indirectly. In contrast, the use of private automobiles in congested areas is generally subjected only to insignificant and poorly enforced controls.

A preferable approach to urban transport regulation would rely more on control of the use of private automobiles in the congested areas, including daytime parking bans; would provide preferential treatment to transit vehicles (e.g. reserved bus lanes, which are now successfully used in a number of Third World cities); and would reduce the constraints on entry by private bus and minibus operators while easing limits on the fare structure, where these make private operations financially unviable [Walters (1979a)].

In implementing these and related urban transport policies a comprehensive approach to transport planning and administration and its integration into overall urban land use planning are important. The common fragmentation of responsibility for the urban transport sector among many public agencies often makes this difficult in developing countries. The successful design and implementation of a comprehensive transport policy in Singapore certainly owes much to the relatively clear assignment of public responsibility for the city's urban transport system.

3.4. Urban housing

An appropriate definition of housing is an important starting point for the correct diagnosis of the urban housing problem in developing countries. Housing should be defined to include not only the shelter structure as such, but also the residential plot of land with its on-site services (water, power, garbage collection, etc.) and the access it permits to off-site services (education, health, etc.), employment and other urban amenities. Thus broadly defined, housing is an important element of welfare and economic development in Third World countries, commonly accounting for a substantial share of household spending, fixed capital investment and even employment opportunities. In urban areas, housing problems are particularly important and visible, in view of the high population density, which requires higher service standards for public and environmental safety, and does not readily permit traditional building methods. Public intervention in the urban housing market is therefore very common, not only to regulate private activity in response to important externalities, but also through public investment in infrastructure and even housing structures. Despite these efforts, large slum areas in many cities of the Third World house more than half of the urban population, half of whom generally lack access to safe water supply and human waste disposal.

In beginning to address the urban housing problem, an understanding of the major determinants of housing demand and supply are crucial. Aggregate housing demand is the expression of many individual private preferences for suitable combinations of particular housing attributes (including access, space, tenure, services, and shelter structure), scaled according to the size of the urban population and its income level and distribution. Given the multidimensionality of housing and the heterogeneity in preferences and income levels, it is in practice very difficult to meet housing needs on a comprehensive basis through public intervention. Public housing programs generally have to rely on a small number of types or models of intervention, quite apart from administrative and financial constraints limiting their scope. Therefore, turning to the supply side, it is important to recognize the different roles which must appropriately be played by public and private agents in housing supply and the many constraints which public intervention often places on the private sector's ability to respond in meeting housing demand, especially those policies which restrict land conversion, provision of public services and construction of shelter.

The urban housing problem – whose symptoms include land invasion and illegal subdivision, overcrowding, lack of basic services, poor access to employment opportunities, and rapidly rising land and housing prices – can then be diagnosed as the result of a rapid increase in housing demand placing a heavy strain on an inelastic supply of housing, including the supply of accessible residential land, services, construction materials, contracting services and finance. As public intervention is often a major cause contributing to the low responsiveness of housing supply and since the poor, precisely because of their limited command over resources, are especially affected by the maladjustments in the urban housing market, correction of urban housing policies can make important contributions to greater urban efficiency and equity.

In the past, public housing policy generally consisted of attempts to build high-cost, subsidized housing projects, which usually ended up benefiting the higher income groups rather than the poor, and in any case could only meet a small fraction of total urban housing demand because of their high cost and the prevailing limits on public resources. In fact, these public housing programs have tended to limit the expansion of total housing supply since they tied up public and private resources which could more appropriately have been devoted to provide much-needed infrastructure and other services. Even more misguided, however, have been slum removal policies, involving, as they generally do, the destruction of valuable, if unsightly, housing stock providing shelter for the poor, and often representing the only assets owned by them.

Fortunately, these conventional approaches have slowly come to be superseded by more appropriate interventions, with public policies designed explicitly to assist in expanding those dimensions of the housing supply which the public sector is best equipped to provide. This means in practice some assistance in land assembly and subdivision, but mainly the provision of essential residential services which are best provided by the public sector to take advantage of economies of scale, to avoid private monopolies, and to allow effectively for health and environmental externalities. Even without subsidies, access to publicly provided services of water and electricity, for example, can provide substantial cost saving compared to the privately supplied substitute (water sold by water vendors, or kerosene and other fuels used for household purposes). Slum improvement – not removal – programs have been demonstrated to be an appropriate way in many cases to upgrade services without destroying housing stock [World Bank (1983b)].

Governments should generally not be directly involved in shelter construction, since experience has shown that the private sector tends to be more efficient in responding to the multiplicity of household preferences, particularly where it is the household's variable earnings profile. The success of large-scale public housing contracting and labor services, drawing on the financial resources of an extended family, and purchasing material inputs at intervals consistent with a poor household's variable earnings profile. The success of large-scale public housing projects in Hongkong and Singapore is explained by a number of exceptional factors, including relatively high average income levels, unusually capable institutions, acute land shortages, and cultural acceptability of high-rise, high-density living. Similar efforts elsewhere, for example, in Brazil, have not succeeded to replicate the success of these two cities [Linn (1983)].

Besides direct investment activities, the public sector influences urban housing demand and supply through pricing, taxation and regulation. Property taxation, although often hailed as an instrument with direct effects on urban land use, housing supply and demand, in practice probably has few such effects, at least at the relatively low effective rates generally found in developing countries [Bahl 1977)]. Its major use lies in its potential as a local fiscal mechanism to finance urban service provision in a reasonably efficient and equitable manner. In contrast, user charges and development fees can have a substantial effect in encouraging an efficient allocation of demand and investment patterns for urban public services. Estimates of marginal cost of service provision can serve as a guide to efficient pricing, although the cost of administration will limit the fine adjustments in the pricing structure. Subsidies, except those aimed selectively to small (and thus usually poor) consumers, should in general be avoided because of their detrimental efficiency, equity and financial implications.

Regulation and control of urban housing in developing countries have, on the whole, not been effective in achieving their stated goals, and often have in fact been counterproductive, partly because they are difficult to administer and partly because of their intrinsic design. Regulations regarding urban land use, subdivision and building standard are observed mainly in the breach, but nevertheless may result in clouded land titles, serve as an excuse for razing slums, or force the adoption of unnecessarily high building standards in public housing projects [Dunkerley et al., (1983)]. Rent control – although rarely very effective because commonly circumvented in practice – tends to limit housing supply growth, impedes mobility, and limits property tax revenues. In practice, therefore, less rather than more regulation and control of urban housing activity, and the careful evaluation, design and application of regulatory measures to ensure that they serve meaningful objectives effectively, should be aimed for.

3.5. Social services

It is commonly observed that the average urban dweller is better off than the average rural inhabitant as regards education, health, and nutrition, and that education and health care services are in much more ample supply in urban than in rural areas. However, research has shown that averages tend to hide the fact that in the cities of the Third World there are sizeable pockets of poor households which are much worse off than the urban average would suggest, and that the urban poor in many ways are comparable to their rural counterparts in regard to education, health and nutrition levels and access to social services [Basta (1977); Lee and Furst (1980); Linn (1983)]. The main problem for the urban as for the rural poor is, therefore, that they are caught in a vicious cycle of low incomes leading to poor education, health, nutrition and family planning, which in turn interact with and reinforce each other in producing continuing low productivity and incomes.

Public action can help to break this vicious cycle, but as often as not public interventions have been limited in effectiveness by poor design or implementation. As was mentioned above, the reliance on high-cost, advanced services in urban education and health care has limited access to the much needed basic education, technical training and preventive health services. This in turn has been compounded by the location of educational and health facilities primarily outside poor neighborhoods making physical access by the poor families difficult and costly. Efforts can be made successfully to focus educational and health services more explicitly on the priority needs of poor neighborhoods, to tailor them particularly towards high risk target groups (especially infants, young children and their mothers), and to ensure that physical and cultural obstacles to accessibility of social service facilities by the poor are minimized. Complementarities within and among social services should also be fully exploited. For example, school lunch programs can serve the goals of improved child nutrition and better school attendance among the urban poor, and a basic health care program can serve as a vehicle for disseminating information on nutrition and family planning. Improved integration of social service provision at the local level can go a long way in helping to attain this goal of exploiting complementarities, but, in the absence of significant efforts at improving local administration skills and capacities, local initiatives and involvement do not guarantee success.

Finally, consideration should be given to increase the extent of cost recovery for social services, particularly when they go beyond meeting the basic needs of poor population groups or where excessive use can be limited by even nominal fees. Given the limitations on financial resources of urban governments, any measure which helps to mobilize public resources in an efficient and equitable manner in support of worthwhile urban service provision should be exploited.

3.6. Urban public administration and finance

Public administration in urban areas faces difficult and important tasks. Some public sector involvement in the management of urban growth is unavoidable, and the role of the public sector probably grows as urban agglomerations increase in size, because of the increased need to manage the externalities of agglomeration and residential density which cannot be left entirely to the invisible hand of free market forces. The demand for public services and thus public expenditures certainly grows more than in proportion with city size and so does the size of the urban government [Linn (1981)]. With the pervasive role of urban government in managing urban growth, and the potential for positive as well as detrimental impacts of public policy amply demonstrated in the preceding sections, it is clear that the best urban strategy is substantially dependent on the quality of public institutions that are to implement it.

Considering the importance of urban government particularly in the largest cities of the Third World, and, in turn, the importance of efficient city growth to a country's overall economic performance, it is striking how, for all practical purposes, the local authorities administering urban areas are often treated with benign neglect, if not open hostility, by their national governments. Besides such neglect or even obstruction by higher-level governments, responsibility for urban public administration, which in principle involves a highly interrelated set of interventions in infrastructure and social service investment planning, implementation and financing, as well as in the control and regulation of urban land use and of many activities, is generally spread across a very fragmented set of public institutions. Responsibilities are usually divided along hierarchical lines among central, state and local government agencies, along geographic lines where urban areas are divided into a multiplicity of municipal jurisdiction, and along functional lines where autonomous state enterprises have responsibility for the investment, financing and regulating roles in particular urban service functions. Such an environment of fragmented responsibility virtually rules out a comprehensive and coordinated approach to urban development and planning, except under unusual circumstances, and then only for brief periods.

Another factor compounding the problems of urban government is that local public agencies often have insufficient authority to raise financial resources with which to meet their urban service responsibilities [Bahl and Linn (1983)]. In many cases the resulting "urban fiscal gap" is at least partly due to unrealistically high service standards previously alluded to; in many other cases, it has its origins in a mismatch between expenditure functions and revenue sources allocated to urban governments by higher-level authorities. While the demand for urban services tends to increase rapidly with city growth and generally has to be met by the local authorities, their revenue-raising authority is often restricted to relatively inelastic sources, such as property taxes, specific excises, fees and fines, and generally stagnant and erratic transfers from higher level governments. Even for those sources of revenue which are put at the disposal of local governments, high-level governments often restrict the local authority in the definition, scope and valuation of tax bases; dictate exemptions and the level and structure of tax rates and user charges; and limit local capacity for tax collection. These limitations on local revenue mobilization capacity, and the concomitant lack of administrative support and technical assistance in matters relating not only to tax administration, but also to management, budgetary and accounting practices, personnel training, and the intrinsic weaknesses of municipal governments resulting from low status and pay, all frequently add up to urban governments very poorly equipped to handle the large and rapidly expanding responsibility of urban administration and finance.

Under these circumstances, reform of urban administration is generally a difficult task, compounded also by the intricacies of local and national politics. The approach chosen in addressing the problems of urban administration and finance will depend to a large extent on whether one believes in the efficacy of a strong centralized (generally national level) authority, or whether one believes that local self-government is important in articulating and effectively meeting the demands for public action in a heterogeneous urban environment [Bird (1978)]. In the former case, preference will be given to strong central control and direction over urban policy, administration and finance. In the latter case, increased devolution of responsibility to local authorities will be aimed for, with fragmentation accepted as a necessary, but not always detrimental side effect.

Whichever of these two approaches is chosen, three general considerations apply equally across the board. First, whether entrusted with a large or small array of responsibility, urban governments should be given the leeway and encouragement to raise the financial resources commensurate with the responsibilities which they have been given. This is an important tool which helps ensure that urban areas are not subsidized by rural areas, thus also limiting incentives for excessive urban growth and concentration; but it also will tend to foster increased internal efficiency and equity of cities, and limits the drain on scarce national fiscal resources. The urban property tax, automotive taxation, user fees and development charges hold out the greatest prospect as efficient, equitable and administratively feasible financing instruments that can be used to finance urban public services.[10]

Second, technical assistance to the local authorities in the areas of financial management and administration of infrastructure planning investment, and operation and local regulatory and planning procedures can usefully be provided by higher-level government agencies or possibly through an autonomous municipal development authority, which could also act as a financial intermediary offering loan finance for major public investment projects of urban governments.

Finally, the adoption of the types of policy directions proposed in the preceding section in the areas of employment, transport, housing and social service provision can improve urban policy making and administration substantially, even in an environment of a relatively weak or fragmented urban government. Improvement is therefore possible even where the financial base of city agencies remains overextended, where administrative capabilities leave much to be desired, and where cohesive policy planning and implementation is out of the question. Even selective application of partial policies have been shown to succeed in facilitating the difficult job of managing rapid urban growth in developing countries. At a minimum, those policies and interventions which have commonly served to compound the urban policy problems can be eliminated. In fact, much progress has been made in recent years in many developing countries to replace counterproductive, conventional policy approaches with imaginative new departures even without substantially changing the entire existing structure of urban government. Nonetheless, the overall ability of urban government to constructively support urban growth ultimately is heavily influenced by a well-working administrative and financial structure and a set of mutually supportive relations between a city's local authorities and the national (and provincial) government agencies.

References

Bahl, R.W. (1977) 'Urban property taxation in developing countries', Occasional Paper no. 32. Maxwell School, Syracuse University, Syracuse, New York.

[10]See Bahl and Linn (1984) for a recent summary report on research findings in the area of urban finance and administration in developing countries.

1284

Bahl, R.W. and J.F. Linn (1983) 'The assignment of local governmen
countries', in: C.E. McLure, Jr., ed., *Tax assignment in federal countr*
National University Press.

Bahl, R.W. and J.F. Linn (1984) 'Urban finances in developing countries: res
World Bank Research News, 5:3–13.

Basta, S.S. (1977) 'Nutrition and health in low income urban areas of the
Food and Nutrition, 6:113–24.

Bird, R.M. (1978) 'Intergovernmental fiscal relations in developing count
Working Paper no. 304. Washington, D.C.

Doebele, W.A. (1979) 'Land readjustment as an alternative to taxation for the recovery of betterment:
the case of South Korea', in: R.W. Bahl, ed., *The taxation of urban property in less developed
countries*. Madison, Wisconsin: The University of Wisconsin Press.

Doebele, W.A., O.F. Grimes, Jr., and J.F. Linn (1979) 'Participation of beneficiaries in financing urban
services: valorization charges in Bogota, Colombia', *Land Economics*, 55:73–92.

Dunkerley, H.B. et al. (1983) *Urban land policy: issues and opportunities*. New York: Oxford University
Press.

Hamer, A. (1985) 'Decentralized urban development and industrial location behavior in Sao Paulo,
Brazil: a synthesis of research issues and conclusions', World Bank Staff Working Paper no. 732,
Washington, D.C.

Henderson, J.V. (1980) 'A framework for international comparisons of systems of cities', Urban and
Regional Report no. 80-3, World Bank, Washington, D.C.

Henderson, J.V. (1986) 'Methods of analyzing urban concentration and decentralization applied to
Brazil', in: G. Tolley and V. Thomas, eds., *Economics of urbanization and urban policies: the
developing countries*. Washington, D.C.: The World Bank.

Lee, C.-F. and B.G. Furst (1980) 'Differential indicators of living conditions in urban and rural places
of selected countries', Applied Systems Institute, Washington, D.C.

Linn, J.F. (1981) 'Urban finances in developing countries', in: R.W. Bahl ed., *Urban government
finance: emerging trends*. Beverly Hills: Sage Publications.

Linn, J.F. (1982) 'The costs of urbanization in developing countries', *Economic Development and
Cultural Change*, 30:625–48.

Linn, J.F. (1983) *Cities in the developing world policies for their equitable and efficient growth*. New
York: Oxford University Press.

Morrison, P. ed. (1983) *Population movements: their forms and functions in urbanization and development*. Liege, Belgium: Ordina Editions for International Union of the Scientific Study of
Population.

Parr, J. (1985) 'A note of the size distribution of cities over time'. *Journal of Urban Economics*, 18.

Population Reports (1983) *Migration, population growth, and development*, Population Information
Program, Johns Hopkins University Series M., no. 7, September–October.

Renaud, B. (1981) *National urbanization policy in developing countries*. New York: Oxford University
Press.

Richardson, H.W. (1977) 'City size and national spatial strategies in developing countries', World
Bank Staff Working Paper no. 252. Washington, D.C.

Rosen, K. and M. Resnick (1980) 'The size distribution of cities: an examination of the Pareto law and
primacy', *Journal of Urban Economics*, vol. 8, no. 2.

Squire, Lyn (1981) *Employment policy in developing countries: a survey of issues and evidence*. New
York: Oxford University Press.

Townroe, P. (1979) 'Employment decentralization: policy instruments for large cities in less developed
countries', *Progress in Planning*, vol. 10.

United Nations (1981) 'Population distribution policies in developing planning', Papers of the United
Nations/UNFPA Workshop on Population Distribution Policies in Development Planning,
Bangkok, 4–13 September 1979, New York, Department of International Economic and Social
Affairs, Population Studies no. 75.

United Nations (1985) 'Estimates and projections of urban, rural and city populations, 1950–2025: the
1982 assessment', New York: Department of International Economic and Social Affairs.

Vining Jr., D. (1985) 'Population redistribution towards LDC core areas, 1950–1980', *International
Regional Science Review*, vol. 10, no. 1.

Walters, Alan (1979a) 'The benefits of mini-buses', *Journal of Transport Economics and Policy*, 13: 320–34.

Walters, Alan (1979b) 'Costs and scale of bus services', World Bank Staff Working Paper no. 325. Washington, D.C.

Watson, P.L. and E.P. Holland (1978) 'Relieving traffic congestion: the Singapore area license scheme', World Bank Staff Working Paper no. 281. Washington, D.C.

Wheaton, W. and H. Shisido (1981) 'Urban concentration, agglomeration economics, and the level of economic development', *Economic Development and Cultural Change*, vol. 30.

World Bank (1983a) *World development report, 1983*. New York: Oxford University Press.

World Bank (1983b) *World bank lending for urban development, 1972–82*. Washington, D.C.

Chapter 33

CITY SIZE AND PLACE AS POLICY ISSUES

GEORGE TOLLEY
University of Chicago

JOHN CRIHFIELD*
Wake Forest University

1. Introduction

Questions have been raised perennially about the geographic distribution of economic activity, such as whether one part of some national economy is too small or too large, or whether particular regions or cities should develop more rapidly than others. Overurbanization, depressed regions, and balanced regional growth are a few of the expressions that have figured in policy discussion. Once mainly of concern only in high income countries, the issue of the best geographic distribution of population and economic activity has more recently become of pressing importance in low income and developing countries. Policy concerns have mounted as national populations all over the world have urbanized rapidly with emerging cities of unprecedented size and concentrations of urban poverty, along with attendant problems of urban management.

In most countries goals have been enunciated relative to the geographic distribution of population and economic activity. Planning and zoning, as well as direct and indirect taxes and subsides in a variety of forms, have been adopted as policies to influence location. In most cases these policies appear to have had rather limited effect.

Arguments about the desirability or lack of desirability of phenomena associated with urbanization, such as congestion and pollution, have been used in support of the policies. The arguments have been based on general impressions and beliefs. They have been stated almost entirely in qualitative terms, with few efforts to quantify the effects. This state of affairs has left room for debate involving more heat than light. In the absence of objective guidelines, more than usual scope has been left for the play of political considerations. For example, greater sensitivity in practice has been displayed toward effects of urban and

Handbook of Regional and Urban Economics, Volume II, Edited by E.S. Mills
© *1987, Elsevier Science Publishers B.V.*

regional development policies on wealth transfers in a political trading process, than toward broader goals affected by urbanization.

This chapter concerns the contribution of objective analysis to the problem of deciding what is a desirable distribution of population and economic activity. The aim is to analyze the problem in quantifiable terms. A central idea is that market outcomes respond to many, but not all, costs and gains of locating in one place as opposed to another. Starting with this idea, the quest becomes to find what effects are not adequately taken into account by market responses, and then to quantify their costs and gains as well as their implications for region and city size. From this endeavor come conclusions and insights useful to policy.

Labor markets are at the heart of decisions determining where people live and work, as well as how well off people are in different places. No attempt to understand optimum city sizes should proceed without building on this prerequisite behavior. A unifying hypothesis is that persons choose places to live and work such that the level of living across cities tends eventually to become equalized. In the long run the level of well-being taking into account local amenities and the local cost of living, becomes equal across cities for given types of workers. The approach is neutral as between developed and less developed economies. Local prices vary among cities in every country, developed or not. Few cities anywhere are spared the hassles of congestion, the struggles with pollution, or other desirable or undesirable effects associated with urbanization.

Following this introduction, the second section of this chapter considers the interaction between wages and local prices in a city. Labor costs affect prices of commodities produced in a city, and at the same time local living costs influence the wage required to attract labor to the city. City size itself often causes local costs to differ between cities. Thus, the tendency for real living costs to be higher in larger cities becomes magnified by a wage multiplier effect. The end result is that in a market economy either with or without distorting externalities, money wages will be different among cities even though real wages are the same.

The third section considers how to relate local productivity, local costs, and local externalities to city size, and defines in what sense a city may be too large or too small. A general formulation for the effect of externalities on city size is presented. Section 4 illustrates the spatial consequences of several externalities and presents ways to measure their effects. Suggestive measurements of effects on welfare and on city size are developed. the final section of the chapter considers policy implications.

2. The interaction between wages, local costs, and city size

In explaining spatial patterns in wages and prices, a distinction is needed between commodities which are produced and consumed locally and those which are traded between cities. The prices of a city's exports and imports are tied to prices of similar commodities in other cities. The price a local exporter charges or the price a local importer pays diverges from the destination or origin price at most by the amount of transportation costs. For many items, however, especially services which must be rendered on the spot, transportation costs are prohibitively high. Interregional commodity trade cannot be expected to govern local prices for these goods and services. Their prices are determined by demand and supply conditions within the city.

Let the price of a local good be $P_l = b_l w + R_l$, where P_l is the price of the local good, w is the local wage, b_L is the labor input per unit of local output, and R_L represents all nonlabor costs per unit of local output. Taking percentage differences between any two cities, a first relationship is obtained: $\hat{P}_l = s_l \hat{w} + r_l$, where the circumflex ( ) refers to percentage difference, $s_l = (b_l w)/P_l$ (labor's share in local revenue) and r_l equals $(R_l/P_l)\hat{R}_l$ or the difference in nonlabor costs as a percent of total costs. The term $s_l w$ on the right hand side of this equation suggests the cost-push effect that local labor costs have on local prices.

On the other hand, in the long run people choose among places to live according to how well off they will be. If the real level of living is higher in one city than another, all people may not move immediately, but some are likely to move. Younger persons just entering the labor force are generally the most mobile and are particularly alert to choosing places where their real earnings prospects are best. As they offer themselves for work in places where real earnings are higher than elsewhere, the resulting increased labor supply has a lowering effect on wages in those places. The process continues as long as there are real wage differences. Because of this process, real wages tend to be equalized among places over time, if not immediately. With real wage equalization, differences in money wages among cities in the long run must be proportional to differences in cost of living. Only then are real wages the same. The cost of living depends on the prices of local and traded goods. As before, let P_L be the price of local goods and w the nominal wage rate, i.e. payment for one unit such as an hour or year of labor input, and let P_T be the price of traded goods. Let L and T be the amounts of local and traded goods purchased with the worker's proceeds from one unit of labor input so that $w = P_L L + P_T T$. Then the condition for real wage equalization gives a second relationship: $\hat{w} = e_T \hat{P}_T + e_L \hat{P}_L$, where e_T and e_L are consumer expenditure weights. The analysis readily extends to cases where expenditure weights differ between cities.[1]

The two relationships that have been presented imply that the wage rate in a city influences local prices, while local prices in turn affect the city's wage rate. Substituting the expression for $\hat{P}_L$ from the first relationship into the second

---

[1] See Tolley et al. (1979, pp. 155–157).

relationship for $\hat{w}$ leads to the following result:

$$\hat{w} = \left[\frac{1}{1 - s_L e_L}\right][e_T \hat{P}_T + e_L r_L].$$

Since s_L and e_L are positive fractions less than one, the expression in the first set of brackets exceeds one. The first bracket is a multiplier on wages showing how nonlabor differences r_L and traded goods price differences $\hat{P}_T$ have a magnified effect on local wage differences. The more insular the local economy in the sense that local demand accounts for a large share of total expenditures (large e_L), or the more important are labor costs in producing local output (large s_L), then the larger is the multiplier. The feedback effects given by the first bracket multiplier under such conditions are relatively large. Expenditure shares also influence the second bracket. For example, holding nonlabor costs constant, the effect of an increase in traded goods prices $\hat{P}_t$ is greater, the smaller is e_L (since the coefficient of traded goods prices e_T equals $1 - e_L$). Therefore, even though a large e_L raises the multiplier given by the first bracket, at the same time it cushions local wages from effects of traded goods prices in the second bracket.[2]

The direction of money wage differences between any two cities depends on the sign of the second bracket, which in turn depends on whether the nonlabor cost difference r_L and traded goods price differences $\hat{P}_T$ are positive or negative. Some factors influencing $\hat{P}_T$ and r_L may have little to do with the city's size. However, several considerations suggest that nonlabor costs rise with city size, making r_L positive for larger cities. One consideration is that an individual's rent-plus-access expenditures rise as the city grows, since individuals at the city's edge must pay more in travel costs (value of time plus out of pocket expenses) to reach the city center than do residents closer in. This effect in turn increases the scarcity value of land between the edge and the center, so that the combined rent-plus-access cost, which must be the same for a person anywhere in the city if the land market is to be in equilibrium, rises throughout the city. There need not be any externality involved. Individuals on the edge pay higher real costs in travel because they travel farther than those closer in. The higher land rents paid by individuals living between the edge and the city center represent transfers to landowners.

In addition to this consideration, city size can be accompanied by negative technological externalities. These, too, will make r_L positive for larger cities. The actions of a first set of economic agents shift firm or household production functions of second parties. The extra commuter from the city's edge not only has father to go, but also adds himself to rush hour traffic, tending to slow everyone down, which is to say the time input required to go a mile is increased. Similarly,

---

[2]Evaluate $d(\hat{w})/d(e_L)$, setting $r_L = 0$.

the addition of each new immigrant to a city tends to result in increased concentrations of particulates in the air that affect everyone in the city. As a partially offsetting consideration, larger cities may enjoy scale economies. If these affect costs of local goods production, r_L is lowered.

In summary, as a city grows, local conditions affect the cost of living, P_L, in the city. Rent-plus-access costs and negative externalities raise r_L and thus raise P_L, thereby raising w through the multiplier process as shown in the centered equation above for $\hat{w}$. Scale economies tend to lower P_L and w.

If there were no externalities, there would be little or no reason for policy intervention on economic efficiency grounds. To the extent that externalities are large and pervasive, a question of intervention arises. The next section considers how externalities may lead to cities whose sizes could be improved.

3. Externalities and optimal city size

3.1. The basic framework

Effects associated with city size can be examined in Figure 1, which shows marginal products for different possible allocations of labor between two cities.

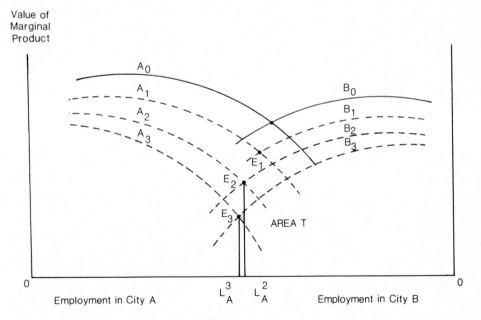

Figure 1. Private and social marginal product curves between a larger city and a smaller city.

Suppose we wish to compare the economy of a typical city of average size (city B) with the economy of a big city (city A), much larger than the typical city. Consider first the situation without externalities. A worker is assumed to receive his value of marginal product as his wage, moving to the city offering the highest real wage. Since he consumes both traded and nontraded goods, he does not compare gross wages between cities, represented by curves A_0 and B_0 in Figure 1. Local costs, such as from rent-plus-access, must be deducted from the gross wage. These deductions yield curves A_1 and B_1 in the diagram. With no externalities, their intersection at E_1 determines the levels of employment in each city, where real wages are equal. Production conditions prevent the large city from growing out of control. The diminishing marginal product of labor ultimately limits the wage a growing city can offer to the marginal worker. In addition, local costs increase as a city expands. Thus the vertical distances between curves A_0 and A_1, and between B_0 and B_1, increase with city size. Since A is larger than B, local costs are higher in A and are a consideration limiting its capacity to grow relative to B.

Now consider the situation with externalities. Distinctions between private and social marginal products become important. The curves defined above represent private marginal products. Externality creating activity can lead to a difference between private and social costs. For example, consider the extra congestion caused by each additional vehicle on a city's highways. The total or social cost of the congestion is borne by all travelers on the road. The new traveler is himself slowed down somewhat by his own added congestion, but so is everyone else. The part of the added congestion borne by the new traveler is a private cost. The remainder of the social cost is borne by others. If the traveler is one among 1,000 others on the road at the same time, then he bears $1/1,000$ of the extra travel costs, whereas $999/1,000$ of the imposition consists of costs borne by others.

For the big city, subtracting the private component from curve A_1 gives curve A_2, which becomes the marginal private product curve with externality. Further subtracting from A_2 the social cost component gives curve A_3, the marginal social product curve with externality. Curves B_2 and B_3 for the typical city are similarly defined. If agents do not fully bear the costs of their actions, real wages between cities become equal at point E_2. Unless the social costs per marginal worker at these levels of employment are identical between the two cities, the marginal social products per worker are unlikely to be equal between cities. In fact, the marginal costs of city externalities such as pollution and congestion tend to increase at increasing rates as cities grow. Low levels of pollution do minor damage, but increasingly higher amounts of pollution do major harm. In terms of the graphs, this means that curves A_3 and B_3 tend to fall at increasing rates. Since city A is larger, the vertical distance between A_2 and A_3 exceeds the vertical distance between B_2 and B_3. The intersection between A_3 and B_3 therefore occurs at E_3, to the left of E_2.

From the standpoint of maximizing the value of social product, optimal city sizes occur at E_3. At E_2 city **A** is too large because its marginal social product per worker falls below the like product attainable in city **B**. Reallocating $L_A^2-L_A^3$ workers from A to B would increase total social product by the value of area T in the diagram.

Figure 1 highlights essential features for metropolitan externalities. The following discussion extends the analysis of the simple case described above.

3.2. Generalization of the basic framework

Suppose we want to study how a city's private real wage changes if marginal taxes are imposed on the externality creating activities. Using the framework above, the private real wage in a city equals the money wage divided by the local cost of living. Define one unit of composite commodity for the city to consist of one unit of traded goods and k units of nontraded goods. The cost per unit of composite commodity then equals P_T+kP_L, where P_T and P_L are the unit prices of traded and nontraded goods. The private real wage in a city can then be represented as $w/(P_T+kP_L)$. Using the marginal product conditions that $P_TX_{TN}=w$ and $P_LX_{LN}=w$, where X_{TN} and X_{LN} are the marginal productivities of labor in the traded and nontraded sectors, allows one to rewrite the private real wages as

$$\frac{w}{\dfrac{w}{X_{TN}}+k\dfrac{w}{X_{LN}}}=\frac{1}{\dfrac{1}{X_{TN}}+\dfrac{k}{X_{LN}}}$$

To understand how taxing externalities might affect the private real wage, let the production functions for traded and nontraded goods be:

$$X_T=X_T(N_T,S_T,Q)$$
$$X_L=X_L(N_L,S_L,Q)$$

where N_T and N_L are resources including labor, capital and fuel employed in the city's traded and nontraded sectors. S_T and S_L represent activities which are productive to individual firms or persons, but which impose externalities upon others in the city. For example for an individual firm, S_T may be particulates emitted into the air from burning coal. Emissions S_T are subject to choice by the firm through varying the quality of coal burned and choice of pollution control devices. These choices affect outlays on N_T. There is a trade-off between S_T and N_T. In this sense emissions S_T are just like any other input. If the firm is not charged damages, fines or other payments for the act of emitting pollutants, the highest emission content coal will be used with no pollution control devices. Since the firm is not charged anything for emitting pollutants, the price of S_T is zero, so the firm makes no attempt to control emissions. Emissions are pushed to the point of zero marginal productivity. If there were a price or charge for emissions, the incentive would be to make expenditures on N_T reducing emissions until the marginal cost of emissions equalled the price.

A firm's productivity is also affected by Q, where Q itself is generated as follows:

$$Q = Q(S_T, S_L).$$

Q represents a production function shifter. For example, Q could be clean air which increases productivity by enhancing the health of workers. Q falls when S_T or S_L rises and is determined by physical considerations according to the equation just given for Q which is a representation, for example, of an air dispersion model showing how air pollutant emissions affect air quality. An increase in S_T, increases a firm's output, but the same increase in S_T lowers Q through the equation for Q, which in turn affects firm's (and everyone else's) productivity through the appearance of Q in the production functions for X_T and X_L. The total or social cost of an extra unit of emissions is determined by these indirect effects.

If a tax were imposed on emissions and were set equal to marginal social cost, the firm would have incentives to cut back on emissions just to the point where marginal productivity of emissions equalled marginal social cost. As an example the optimal tax on emissions S_T from traded goods production is the partial of Q with respect to S_T in the dispersion relation generating Q times the sum of the value of marginal products of Q in producing traded and nontraded goods as derived from their production functions, or $Q_T(P_T X_{TQ} + P_L X_{LQ})$.

A question becomes how relative wages between cities, and hence city sizes, are affected by an externality tax. To find the percentage effect on the private wage from the externality tax, differentiate the private real wage,

$$\frac{1}{\dfrac{1}{X_{TN}} + \dfrac{k}{X_{LN}}}$$

with respect to the emissions tax t, and then divide by the private real wage, to obtain the percentage change in the private real wage:

$$\frac{P_T}{(P_T + kP_L)X_{TN}}\left[\frac{dX_{TN}(N_T, S_T, Q)}{dt}\right] + \frac{P_L \cdot k}{(P_T + kP_L)X_{LN}}\left[\frac{dX_{LN}(N_L, S_L, Q)}{dt}\right]v$$

Expanding the expressions in brackets and writing the result in elasticity form gives the following expressions for the percentage change in the private real wage resulting from a one percent increase in t:

$$\frac{1}{t}\left\{e_T[N_{X_{TN}N_T}E_{N_{Tt}} + N_{X_{TN}S_T}E_{S_T} + N_{X_{TN}Q}E_{Qt}] + \right.$$

$$+ e_L [N_{X_{LN}N_L} E_{N_{lt}} + N_{X_{LN}S_L} E_{S_{lt}} + N_{X_{LN}Q} E_{Q_t}] \Big\} . \tag{1}$$

where as before, e_T and e_L are expenditure weights for traded and nontraded goods. The N's are elasticities of marginal products with respects to inputs, and the E's are elasticities of inputs with respect to the tax.

The upward shift in the city's private wage from the tax represents the private gain within the city from more efficiently allocating labor between the traded and nontraded sectors.[3] If the marginal private and social product curves shift proportionately upward more in city A than in city B, then there will be a tendency for city A to grow relative to B, as labor is drawn to the city of higher real wages.[4]

Consider the export sector. If there is complementarity in production, $N_{X_{TN}S_T}$ and $N_{X_{TN}Q}$ are positive (i.e., the marginal product of labor increases when another factor increases). With diminishing marginal productivity, $N_{X_{TN}N_T}$ is negative. The own price elasticity $E_{S_{Tt}}$ may be presumed to be negative with E_{Q_t} correspondingly positive in view of the effect of E in the air dispersion relation for Q. Only $E_{N_{Tt}}$ (the elasticity of labor demand with respect to the externality tax) is difficult to sign. Similar considerations apply to the local sector.

As an example, suppose city A were to impose a tax on auto emissions to counteract auto exhaust contributing to air pollution. If emissions S_L are highly sensitive to the tax t, so that $E_{S_{lt}}$ is large, then citywide Q may increase substantially, improving productivity in both sectors, and raising the private wage. An increase in the city's private real wage relative to that in other cities attracts workers to the city. How workers allocate themselves within city A depends on the elasticities in (1). Wages in city A's local and traded goods sectors must be equal. Employment rises in the traded goods sector because productivity of its labor increases from the increases in Q, thereby increasing this sector's demand for labor, when the local sector imposes its externality tax. However, employment in the local sector might rise or fall, depending on the net shift of labor demand in this sector.

---

[3]The city's wage earners become better off as t increases from 0 to t_L^* in the nontraded sector and from 0 to t_T^* in the traded sector, where t_L^* and t_T^* are the tax rates that maximize social product and need not be the same. Tax rates larger than these rates reduce social product. The analysis here assumes we begin near 0 where $t_L = t_T$, so that the gain from increasing t is, in fact, positive. The analysis holds the work force in the city constant, but permits workers to shift between the tradables and nontradables sectors in the city in response to the externalities taxes. The net effect is for the private and social marginal productivity curves A_2 and A_3 in Figure 1 to shift vertically upward.

[4]The geometrical analysis earlier implies that a tax on externalities caused by an additional worker would reduce the size of the larger city because these externalities are greater in a large city. The addition of workers is taxed, but the externalities themselves are not. They continue to be non-internalized. The tax considered in this section is a tax on externalities, not on the addition of workers to the city. The model is more complicated because now two sectors are included in each city. The tax on externalities causes a more efficient reallocation of resources between sectors within each city. As a result, the city's social and private marginal product shift curves upwards. The city which gains the most from the internal reallocation stands to grow relative to the other city.

Reducing local sector externalities increases productivity of local sector labor through the increase in Q. On the other hand, this enhanced productivity and increased demand for labor is offset partly or wholly by the complementarity-in-production elasticity $N_{X_{L}NS_{L}}$ since S_L falls. At the same time, if the cross-price elasticity E_{NU} is positive, then more labor is demanded at all wage levels when the externality tax is raised. In short, it is not clear what happens to employment in the local sector, because E_{Qt} and E_{NU} tend to increase it and E_{S_U} to decrease it. The smaller is this sector, the less likely are its externality reductions to cause productivity increases that create additional local sector employment.

If both cities A and B optimally reduce their externalities, then their marginal social product curves (such as A_3 and B_3 in Figure 1) shift upward. The new optimal allocation of labor between cities is determined by the intersection of the now higher curves, and favors the city whose curve shifts upward proportionately the most. Vernon Henderson and other authors have extended the type of framework presented in this section to further explore how taxing of externalities would affect city size, with the conclusion that city size might either increase or decrease.[6]

In the preceding section, the policy question was whether–taking externalities as given–welfare would be increased by policies such as zoning or entry taxes into a city which would operate directly on city size. On the presumption that negative externalities are greater in large than small cities, a corollary is that policies of this kind would likely result in restricting the size of larger cities. Using the more extended framework of the present section, a second quite different policy question has been asked: whether taxing externalities directly, rather than operating on city size, will increase or decrease the size of a city. The answer was found to be that traded and local goods production and city size might either increase or decrease.

It is to be emphasized that, as between the first policy of operating on city size without internalizing the underlying externalities and the second policy of directly internalizing the externalities, the second policy will make a greater contribution to total income. Under the first policy, some externality distortions are left while they are eliminated under the second policy.

4. Applications

The preceding sections lay out a conceptual framework for evaluating the relationships between city size, the local cost of living, and marginal private and social products of labor. These relationships can be given concrete meaning

---

[5] E_{Qt} represents the total effect on Q from changes in t, as t affects both S_L and S_T.

[6] See, Vernon Henderson, "Effects of Taxation of Externalities on City Size" in Tolley et al. (1979).

through some realistic examples. The discussion proceeds as follows. First, even without externalities, costs in a larger city tend to exceed those in a smaller city, and the annual wage differential between a worker in a typical larger city and a typical smaller city is calculated. Second, in addition to these costs, a new worker in the larger city imposes externality costs on everyone else in the city, and these costs are also calculated. Rough estimates are then made measuring, first, the extent to which the large city is too large or too small and, second, welfare costs from being too large. The analysis is applied to environmental externalities, various local and national fiscal and wage policies, and urban economies of scale.

4.1. Environmental externalities

Suppose that the large city has 6 million inhabitants, and that one in four works. Each of the 1.5 million workers earns $10,000 per year. Suppose also that it takes $\frac{1}{4}$ hour longer to get from the edge of this city to its center than it does in a city of average size. Based on 250 working days a year, two trips per working day, and travel time valued at $3 per hour, the worker in the larger city must pay $375 more in housing-plus-access than does the worker in the average size city.[7] The larger city will also typically have higher levels of environmental disamenities than the average city. For example, earlier work conservatively estimates the level of suspended particulates in a large city at 150 micrograms (μg) per cubic meter of air, and at 100 μg in a smaller city, and that $5 represents a rough estimate of the yearly cost per microgram per family reflecting damages to health, property and aesthetic quality of city life.[8] We are assuming here that the government has taken no action to control pollution in the large city or, if it has, that pollution still remains higher in the large city. The differential cost in environmental disamenity between the two cities therefore equals $5 \times 50 = \$250$, which is probably on the conservative side since other urban disamenities such as water and noise pollution and visual blight have been neglected.

The combined effect of the extra commuting and environmental costs comes to $625 per year. Since in equilibrium the marginal worker is indifferent between locating in the larger city compared to the average city, the real wage in the two tends to be the same. If the yearly money wage is $10,000 in the larger city, the lower commuting and pollution costs in the average size city will reduce the wage that must be paid there to $9,375.

The marginal social costs of commuting and pollution, however, are not fully characterized by the above discussion. In large and small cities alike each vehicle slows down all others through congestion, although the effects tend to worsen as

---

[7] $(\frac{1}{4}) \times 250 \times 2 \times \$3 = \$375$.
[8] See Tolley et al. (1979, p. 200).

city size increases. Similarly, as a city grows increments of pollution affect everyone, not just the new entrants to the city. The problem, then, is to estimate the marginal external costs of congestion and pollution from a new entrant to the city.

The following relationship is often used to estimate the impact on velocity of an additional vehicle: $v = \bar{v} - bq$, where $\bar{v}$ is congestion-free velocity, q is traffic volume, v is velocity, and b is a constant.[9] Suppose half the labor force in the large city commutes to work (750,000 workers) at an average speed of 20 miles per hour (mph), and that without congestion, velocity would be 35 mph. Under these circumstances b is found to equal 0.00002. If traffic volume increases by 1 to 750,001, and using the calculated value for b, traffic velocity falls to 19.99998 mph. The slowing seems inconsequential. But suppose the average trip is 5 miles. The marginal external cost on all other commuters then comes to about $280 per year.[10]

Others have estimated that the particulate level is likely to rise by $0.0004 \mu g$ per cubic meter when a single family enters a city.[11] The marginal external cost from this increased pollution then equals $300.[12] The total externality from a single family entering the city is therefore $580.

When there is equilibrium in the sense that a worker is indifferent between locating in the two cities, we have the following results. The nominal wage is $10,000 in the larger city and $9,375 in the smaller city. The marginal worker receives $625 more in the larger city because of its higher living costs. In addition the marginal worker imposes a $580 cost on everyone else in the larger city. Firms in the large city hire workers until their extra product is worth the $10,000 that must be paid to them, ignoring the $580 of costs that adding a worker imposes on everyone else in the city.

One can now roughly approximate the excess size of the large city. Paying workers according to their social marginal cost instead of private marginal cost would raise the cost from $10,000 to $10,590 or by 5.9 percent. Any estimate of elasticity of demand for labor is subject to a substantial error, but the elasticity is almost certainly above unity and may possibly be a quite high number in view of the many alternative places that industry may locate in an economy. If the elasticity of demand for labor equals -3, then the rise in cost will lead to a three-fold decline in employment or a 17.7 percent decline in employment in the city,

---

[9]This relationship is useful for studying the effect of an additional vehicle on the roads. However, since it is linear in traffic volume, it does not capture the increasing rate at which traffic slows as volume rises.

[10]The exact calculations is (mileage) × (difference in velocity) × (value of time per hour) × (number of trips per commuter per year) × (number of commuters) or $5 \times [(1/19.99998) - (1/20)] \times \$3 \times 500 \times 750,000 = \$281.25$.

[11]See Tolley et al. (1979, p. 201).

[12](Increase in micrograms) × (cost per microgram per person) × (number of people affected) or $0.0004 \times \$5 \times (1.5 \text{ million}) = \$300$ per year.

which is an indication of the excess employment due to pollution and congestion externalities.

A 17.7 percent decline in the number of people employed starting from the 1.5 million level of employment is a decline of 265 thousand workers. The social gain from eliminating the first worker is the $580 external cost of an additional worker calculated earlier. As workers are eliminated, the marginal social product of a worker rises to the point where for the last worker eliminated the gain is zero, providing the signal to stop reducing employment. The average gain on the workers eliminated is an average of the gradually falling gains between $580 or zero and may be approximated as half the maximum gain or $260. Multiplying the $260 average gain per worker times the 265 thousand decline in employment gives a total social gain from reducing the city from its actual size to optimum size of $69 million.

4.2. Local public finance

Local fiscal policies can also lead to disparities between private and social marginal products. If these disparities differ among cities, city size may again be affected, and there will again be welfare losses.[13]

Income redistribution occurs in a city when local services are provided on a per capita or per family basis without user charges to cover costs of providing the services. Police, fire fighting, streets, sanitation services, and in many places education, are provided freely or nearly freely on demand to any family in the city.

The costs are covered by local taxes. Some families will pay more in taxes than the cost of providing the services they use, and some will pay less. The net result of providing local services and paying for them through taxes rather than user charges is to redistribute income from those who pay more to those who pay less.

Those who pay more have an incentive to migrate out to other cities where they do not bear a redistribution burden, and those who pay less have an incentive to migrate into the city. If all cities follow the same system of taxation and provision of government services, the migration incentives will apply only to the differences in redistribution among cities. The present analysis is concerned with these differences.

The redistributions due to the method of paying for government services are influenced by the mix of skill levels and by nonhuman wealth subject to taxation, both of which may differ among cities. The outcome of the incentives resulting from the method of paying for local government services will be for the real

---

[13]Barton Smith contributed importantly to the analysis in this section and the next one. See "Fiscal Externalities, City Size and Suburbanization" in Tolley et al. (1979).

income of workers of a given skill level to be the same among cities, after adding to income from work the (positive or negative) difference between value of government services received and taxes paid.

Consider the cost of providing a given level of local government services costing s dollars provided at constant marginal cost to each of N residents. Total costs are sN which must be equal to total local government revenues. Dividing through by N, the cost s of the government services per person in the city must be equal to tax revenues as a fraction of wealth in the city times wealth per person. Let r_A and r_B be local tax revenues as a fraction of the wealth in City A and City B, respectively. If the sole form of taxation is property taxation, the property tax rates in the two cities are r_A and r_B. If there are other forms of taxes or local income taxes, revenues from them would be divided by wealth and added to property tax rates to arrive at r_A and r_B.

Let m_{jA} and m_{jB} be the proportions of workers in cities A and B with skill j, let V_j be the per capita taxable wealth for worker of skill j, and let Z_A and Z_B be the values per capita in cities A and B of commercial and industrial property. Then the average wealth per capita in city A equals $Z_A + \Sigma_j m_{jA} V_j$, and to cover costs of supplying government services the taxation rate r_A must equal

$$\frac{s}{Z_A + \sum_j m_{jA} V_j}.$$

A similar expression exist for city B. In equilibrium workers of a given skill are indifferent between locating in cities A and B. Thus, for workers of skill j equilibrium holds when $W_{jA} - r_A V_j = W_{jB} - r_B V_j$, that is, when the net of tax wage is equal across cities. By substituting in the values for r_A and r_B just obtained, the equilibrium percentage difference in wages between cities is found to be

$$\frac{W_{jA} - W_{jB}}{W_{jB}} = \frac{s}{W_{jB}} \left\{ \left[\frac{Z_A}{V_j} + \sum_i m_{iA} \left(\frac{V_i}{V_j} \right) \right]^{-1} - \left[\frac{Z_B}{V_j} + \sum_i m_{iB} \left(\frac{V_i}{V_j} \right) \right]^{-1} \right\}. \tag{2}$$

Building on the illustration presented earlier, let the work force of 1.5 million in the large city or City A be equally divided between high skilled and low skilled workers ($m_{HA} = m_{IA} = \frac{1}{2}$). High skilled workers earn \$13,000 per year, and low skilled workers earn \$7,000 per year, so that the average income is \$10,000, as before. In the average (smaller) city or City B, there are three times as many unskilled as skilled workers ($m_{HB} = \frac{3}{4}$, $m_{LB} = \frac{1}{4}$). The wealth ratios $V_H:V_L:Z$ are 3:1:3 in City A and 3:1:1 in City B. Let the wage of high skill labor be double that of low skill labor, and suppose that government expenditures per resident are one tenth of high-skilled earnings so $s/w_H = 0.1$ and $s/w_L = 0.2$. Substituting these values into (2) reveals that the high skilled wage is depressed 6% or \$780, and the low skilled wage is depressed 4% or \$280 in the large city, relative to what would occur in the absence of the local fiscal redistributions. Assuming labor demand elasticities of 3, there are 135,000 more high skilled and 90,000 more low skilled workers in a large city than would there be without the fiscal redistributions. Using triangular measures of welfare loss, these excesses translate into a $52.7 million loss for high skilled workers and $12.6 million for low skilled workers.[14]

It has been assumed that the level and cost of government services are identical among cities. In reality cities with larger proportions of high skilled workers and larger amounts of nonhuman wealth per capita may choose higher service levels, taxing themselves more to pay for extra services. Furthermore costs of providing a given level of government services could be higher in higher wage cities. These effects could be included in a more extended analysis.

4.3. Suburbanization in the United States

An addition to the foregoing local fiscal analysis concerns suburbanization. Given the fiscal redistributions occurring in cities, high income residents have incentives to form suburbs that exclude low income people through such devices as zoning to favor greater amounts of housing than low income people will demand.

As higher income people begin to suburbanize by moving outside the city limits, then as between the edge of the central city and adjacent land just over the line in a separate suburban taxing entity, land rents will be lower by the amount of the tax savings from living in the suburb. As a result of this attraction, the suburb will grow, resulting in commuting to farther distances. When the suburb is so large that the extra commuting cost to the far edge is equal the tax savings, incentives to suburbanize will have been exhausted. An explanation of the size of suburbs is provided by the balancing of tax savings against commuting costs.

The suburbanization lowers the tax rates for high skill people in the metropolitan area experiencing the suburbanization, while the tax rate for low-skilled workers, who remain within the city limits, is raised. As an order of magnitude, the wage depressing effect for high-skilled workers is lowered from 7 to 6 percent and for low skill workers is lowered from 4 to 3 percent. The national income loss is raised by an additional $35 million because of extra commuting costs caused by the flight to the suburbs.

With the exodus of some high income residents from the center city, land with access to jobs at low commuting costs becomes available in the center city. At prevailing wages, low-skill labor from other cities will find it attractive to move to the city which has experienced suburbanization. Assuming parameter values

---

[14]The excess of high skilled workers in $\Delta L = (\Delta W/W)(L)(3) = (0.06)(750,000)(3) = 135,000$. The welfare loss associated with this equals $(0.5)(135,000)(\$780) = \$52.7$ million. Similar calculations yield the indicated figures for low skilled workers.

along the lines of the preceding analysis, the population of the metropolitan area, including the city and surrounding suburbs, grows by an additional 4 percent.

Donald Haurin has extended the analysis of suburbanization taking account of property tax effects on the demand for housing, considering the combined spatial and housing distortions caused by local fiscal incentives.[15]

4.4. Developing country suburbanization

For many if not most developing countries, suburbanization differs from the example that pertained to rich escaping poor in the preceding section. The suburbanization example in the preceding section is applicable to large cities in the United States.

In contrast, in developing countries, especially in Latin America, the urban poor rather than higher income people are found living at the edges of the large cities. While land use supply and demand considerations over and above fiscal effects may play a role in explaining this phenomenon, there may also be fiscal effects, formally similar to those analyzed for suburbanization in the preceding section but acting on poor rather than rich people. The poor may find that within city boundaries, even with redistribution, they are still paying more through direct and indirect taxes for police, fire and street services than they choose to demand given their low incomes. They escape the burden by forming shanty towns where services and taxes are low. A full analysis remains to be developed.

4.5. Urban services in developing countries

The discussion of government-induced externalities so far has emphasized local fiscal policy effects in a nation of fragmented local jurisdictions responsible for financing a large portion of government services. In some national systems, especially in developing countries, the central government plays a larger role in determining service levels.

Policies may result in more pronounced differences in services as between large cities and other areas than occurs in high income countries. The provision of higher levels of health and education services in large cities in developing countries has effects expanding the size of cities by attracting migrants that are similar in nature to the local fiscal policy effects for high income countries examined above.

As an example, suppose policies in a developing country result in a higher than

[15]See Donald Haurin, "Property Taxes and Spatial Resource Misallocation", in Tolley et al. (1979).

average level of health, education and other personal services in a large city, with the excess over value of services available elsewhere being 5 percent of the income of a low skill worker, and with half the workers consuming the services (the other half preferring higher quality nongovernment services). Assume as before that the elasticity of demand for low-skill workers in the city is 3. Then the depressing effect of the services on money wages due to attraction of labor will result in a 5 percent times 3, or 15 percent, increase in unskilled workers. Under the assumption that they and their families account for half the population, the city will grow by 7.5 percent. While the assumptions could vary, the example is sufficient to show that provision of greater services in urban areas could have quite pronounced effects on city size.

Aside from human service levels emphasized so far, national government policies with regard to spending on other types of goods and service undoubtedly also have effects on the spatial distribution of population and economic activity. Whether these systematically favor or disfavor large cities is a subject for further investigation.

For developing countries, it is possible that infrastructure decisions, particularly those pertaining to intercity transportation, may reinforce existing patterns of urbanization, contributing to dramatic growth of one or a few primal cities relative to other parts of the economy.

Whether government policies alone are responsible for growth of primal cities is, however, moot. In many developing countries intercity transportation remains relatively expensive. Roads often do not have as high payoffs as other developmental activities. Neither the economies of transporting goods locally between businesses nor other economies of association realized in a big city are offset by decentralization economies. For example, the increasing costs including higher money wages due to higher cost of living encountered in the primal city would lead to decentralization of production of labor intensive transportable goods to smaller cities if less expensive intercity transportation were available.[16]

4.6. Minimum wages

To turn from government spending and taxing decisions to labor market policies, consider a minimum wage law setting a nominal minimum wage that is the same throughout the country. Given that money wages in the absence of the law would vary among cities due to cost-of-living differences brought on by differences in cost of producing local goods, then the law might be binding in only some cities or in all cities depending on the level of the minimum wages.

[16]For a more extended analysis of reasons for urbanization in developing countries, see Tolley (1986).

At a relatively low minimum wage, the law might be binding only in small cities. Unemployment would be caused in the small cities but not in larger cities where the market clearing money wage for the unskilled was above the minimum wage. As a result of unemployment caused in small cities, unskilled labor would be given incentives to migrate to larger cities, depressing wages there.

A formal condition is that the expected real wage, taking account of the probability of employment, should be the same in all cities. The real wage in the larger cities where the minimum wage was not binding would be equal to the real wage paid in the smaller cities, where unemployment was caused, times the probability of employment. The observed money wage differential for employed persons would narrow as between large and small cities.

A result of the adjustments is that the size of large cities increases relative to smaller cities as labor migrates to bring about equality of expected real wages. Suppose the prevailing wage in smaller cities is $2.75 an hour before imposition of a national minimum wage of $3.00. The nominal wage for unskilled labor in smaller cities would be raised by $0.25/$2.75 or 6 percent. With an elasticity of demand for unskilled labor of 3, the 6 percent rise in nominal wage of unskilled labor in the smaller cities would reduce unskilled employment by 18 percent.

Meanwhile the condition for equilibrium after imposition of the minimum wage is that the probability of employment times the nominal wages of $3.00 in smaller cities equals the money wage of $2.75 at which real wages in the smaller cities are equal to real wages in the larger cities. The implication is that the probability of employment or employment rate is $2.75 divided by $3.00, or 0.92. Since the unemployment rate is one minus the employment rate, the equilibrium unemployment rate of unskilled workers in the smaller cities would be 8 percent.

With employment of unskilled laborers declining by 18 percent and unemployment rising only 8 percent, equilibrium is achieved by 10 percent of the unskilled laborers in smaller cities migrating to larger cities. If one third of the unskilled workers of the nation originally resided in smaller cities, and if unskilled workers make up one fourth of the work force in larger cities, the number of unskilled workers in larger cities would rise about 3 percent.

The results would be further modified by taking account of the effect of the extra nonskilled labor in the larger cities reducing wages there, but this would likely be a second order effect. The results could be further refined by taking account of unemployment compensation differences between large and small cities. The refinements would not alter the basic conclusion that a universal nomimal minimum wage can have effects in increasing the size of larger cities through induced migration flows from areas where the minimum wage is binding.

National income costs of the minimum wage are incurred because of the lost product of workers who remain unemployed. In the example, if the wages of unskilled labor are one third that of skilled labor, the loss in national income from the 8 percent unemployment of unskilled workers in smaller cities is about

0.5 percent of national income and is sizable in comparison to national income costs in the other example in this chapter.

It should be emphasized that the national income costs are due to the minimum wage as such and not to the spatial reallocations resulting from it. Indeed the national income costs are reduced by spatial reallocations. Migration acts to reduce the unemployment that would take place if labor were forced to remain in the cities where unemployment was initially caused.

So far we have considered an example where the minimum wage is binding only in smaller cities. As the minimum wage is raised, a point is reached where it is binding in all cities. Unskilled workers in all cities are then receiving the same nominal wage, which will buy more in smaller cities. The probability of employment, or employment rate, will be inversely correlated with the cost of living in the cities and so will tend to be higher in smaller cities. However, proportionately more people become unemployed in smaller cities because the wage is raised relatively more above the market clearing level, increasing the likelihood that labor would be induced to migrate to larger cities as a result of the minimum wage.

Further investigation of spatial effects of minimum wages is clearly warranted. More sophisticated labor market models explaining where unemployed persons locate would be needed to refine the analysis above. A part of the investigation should have to do with the relation of unemployment in various places to government relief payments aimed at lower income persons. To the extent that minimum wages increase unemployment compensation and welfare payment, spatial effects of the minimum wages may be made more pronounced.

Furthermore, spatial differences in unemployment compensation and welfare payments may themselves become causes of migration. These effects are similar to local fiscal policy effects considered earlier, in that local variation in net benefits to different groups may give incentives to migrate. Concentrations of poor persons in large Northern cities in the United States may be increased by higher levels of unemployment compensation and welfare payments available there than elsewhere.

4.7. Protected employment

In some developing countries minimum wages apply selectively to employment that takes place in certain cities, or in cities as a whole with a large fraction of workers remaining in rural employment not covered by the minimum wage. Unemployment due to the minimum wage may then occur only in higher wage areas, opposite to the analysis of a more universal minimum wage in the preceding section which is applicable to a high income country.

The selective minimum wage arrangements just mentioned are an example of the broader phenomenon of protected employment, whereby wages of selected groups of workers are raised. Other examples are settling of wages through political or union agreements with government workers or selected private sector employees at above market clearing levels. Multinational corporations may hire labor at high wage rates for selectivity reasons.[17]

When there is protected employment, a queue may form among potential workers not in protected employment who are attracted by the hope of obtaining work at the high wage offered. Much attention has been given to protected employment as a phenomenon attracting workers from rural areas to cities in less developed countries. The mechanism envisioned is similar to that in the preceding section, whereby the expected wage as affected by the probability of being employed becomes equal to the wage available in alternative employment.

In the simplest formulation, the probability of obtaining employment is equal to the ratio of protected employment to total number seeking employment. The rationale is that each individual in the pool of people seeking work has an equal probability of becoming employed.

A first condition under this formulation is that labor mobility acting to equalize expected real wages will ensure that the probability of becoming employed, multiplied by the protected sector wage, equals the wage in unprotected unemployment. A rise in the protected sector wage must then be offset by a compensating decline in the ratio of protected sector employment to total number offering themselves for work in the protected sector. Taking differentials to express in terms of changes, a given percentage rise in the protected sector wage must equal the percentage increase in the total number offering themselves for work less the percentage increase in employment in the protected sector. Small order effects on wages in the unprotected parts of the economy are ignored here.

Meanwhile, a second condition under this formulation stems from the fact that the change in employment is governed by the elasticity of demand for labor in the protected sector. The second condition is that the percentage decline in employment will be equal to the absolute value of the elasticity of demand for labor times the percentage increase in the protected sector wage.

Combining the two conditions yields the result that the percentage change in the total number of people offering themselves for work in the protected sector is equal to the percentage increase in the protected wage times one minus the absolute value of the elasticity of demand for labor in the protected sector.

It might have been thought that protected employment occurring in cities unambiguously leads to increases in city size. However, as the result just stated brings out, raising the wage in protected employment will reduce employment

---

[17]This section builds on work reported in "Market Failure as the Economic Bases of Urbanization Problems," in Tolley and Thomas (1986).

because of the elasticity of demand for labor. If the elasticity of demand for labor in the protected sector is greater than unity, then raising the wage will reduce instead of increase the number of people employed and seeking employment, which is to say the total number of people in the city will be reduced.

Since the elasticity of demand for labor may well often be above unity for protected sector employment, we may conclude that it would not be unusual for an increase in wages in the protected sector to result in a decline rather than a rise in the total number of people in the city.

The discussion so far has referred to the simplest formulation where there is a pool of employed plus unemployed people each one of whom has an equal probability of being employed. However, in a more adequate formulation, it should be recognized that those in protected employment will be reluctant to leave their jobs in view of the prospects of unemployment or lower wage elsewhere. Turnover will tend to be low. Because of the low turnover, those without employment will have a lower probability of future employment than those already employed.

Furthermore, work experience, particularly if specific to particular jobs, will make those already working in protected employment jobs more valuable to employers than those without such work experience. Employers will be reluctant to consider unemployed persons on an equal basis with those who have the desired work experience. At an extreme, the pool of unemployed seeking protected sector work would consist of persons having no work experience and hence an extremely low probability of ever being hired in the protected sector. More realistically, the unemployed pool will contain people of various qualifications including different kinds of work experience affecting their probability of being hired. It is still reasonable to suppose that those who are unemployed are on average less well qualified than those already employed. The lower qualifications, like low turnover discussed in the preceding paragraph, act to make the probability of future employment in protected sector work less for the unemployed than for those already employed there.

People in the pool of unemployed seeking protected sector work without experience there will come to realize that their prospects are low. Starting from a situation where the protected sector wage for labor of a given skill is equal to the wage elsewhere, there will be an equilibrium amount of unemployment due to considerations such as turnover and search. As the protected sector wage is raised, people keeping themselves unemployed to search for protected sector jobs may increase or decrease.

The high protected wage attracts people, but the low probability of being hired acts to repel them. If the probability is low enough, it will more than offset the effect of the high wage, and people seeking work in the protected sector will actually decrease rather than increase. City size where the protected employment occurs could be reduced even if there were no labor demand elasticity effect acting to reduce employment.

A more general formulation consistent with these complications may be offered. As a first condition, let g be the elasticity with respect to the protected sector wage of the ratio of number of people offering themselves for work to the number employed. As a second condition, let b be the absolute value of the elasticity of demand for labor in the protected sector with respect to the protected sector wage. Taking percentage changes and substituting the second condition into the first condition gives

$$\dot{T} = (g-b)\dot{W}$$

where $\dot{T}$ is the percentage change in number of people offering themselves for work in the protected sector, and $\dot{W}$ is the percentage change in the protected sector wage.

The coefficient $g-b$ is the elasticity of number of people offering themselves for work with respect to the protected sector wage. The sign of this coefficient determines whether the number offering themselves, and hence city size where the protected employment occurs, will increase or decrease in response to an increase in the protected sector wage.

According to the simple formulation earlier, the number of people offering themselves for work is proportional to the protected sector wage, which implies a value of g of unity. The value of unity appears to be a maximum value that g might take on. The fact, that both turnover and the qualifications of those unemployed relative to those employed may decrease, suggests that the number of people offering themselves for work will rise less than in proportion to the protected sector wage. Thus g is likely to be less than unity. The discussion has implied that g could be negative if the probability of unemployed workers becoming employed declines by more than the increase in the protected sector wage.

A value of g less than unity reduces the absolute value of the elasticity of demand for labor needed for a rise in the protected sector wage to lead to a decrease in city size. A negative value of g would lead to a decrease in city size even if the elasticity of demand for labor were as low as zero.

People may be able to increase the likelihood that they or their family members will be employed in a protected sector without bearing the full cost of unemployment, by choosing to engage in unprotected economic activity within commuting distance of the protected employment. This consideration could act in the direction of increasing city size where protected employment occurs. However, it would be very difficult to establish that the location of unprotected economic activity is importantly influenced by the hope of obtaining protected employment. Unprotected activity sometimes takes the form of informal work by people who are difficult to distinguish from the unemployed. They may appear at first glance to be attracted to the area by the hope of protected sector employment, but they may only be producing local goods and services to meet the demands of protected sector and other workers, or they may be undertaking independent activity taking advantage of the same transport and other economies as attracted other activity to the area.

4.8. Economies of scale

To this point we have concentrated on reasons why large cities could be too large. There can, however, be advantages to large size. Indeed, if there were no advantage to size, it would be hard to discern an economic rationale for the existence of cities. Several considerations might lead to declining long run marginal cost curves in a city as it grows. As the city expands and the local market grows, producers of nontraded goods can lower unit costs through specialization of functions. In addition, as density of population and of economic activity increases, transactions costs between units fall, at least up to some point where congestion becomes a problem. For example, workers and employers can match skills and demands more precisely as the size and diversity of the labor market grows. Cost advantages specific to the firm as it increases output are ordinary economies of scale; cost advantages caused by positive technological externalities as a city grows are often called agglomeration economies. One hypothesis is that these economies are pronounced for towns and small cities, but gradually become exhausted at larger city sizes. A cost curve which describes this hypothesis could appear as a backward "Lazy J". Agglomeration and scale economies associated with city size are often referred to, but are difficult to specify and measure. Rough gauges of such economies are all we currently have. Izraeli found the elasticity of prices with respect to city population, holding other factors constant, to be about -0.03.[18] It is not clear whether such economies exist for very large cities. If they are small or nonexistent at the existing margin of city size, then they have little or no distorting effect on city size.

5. Conclusion

A framework has been provided for analyzing the effects of externalities on city size and for estimating the national income costs of the city size effects. Order of magnitude examples have been offered for several externalities. A recurrent finding is that effects on city size can be substantial, while the national income costs are quite small.

Pollution, congestion, local fiscal policies including suburbanization incentives,

---

[18]See Oded Izraeli, "Externalities and Inter-City Wage and Price Differentials", in Tolley et al. (1979).

and developing country policies that provide high service levels in cities all were found to make big cities too large. On the other hand, high wages in protected sectors in developing countries and economies of scale were found to have ambiguous or small effects on city size.

What are the policy implications of these findings? The question of whether policies toward city size and other overt policies to influence the location of economic activity are justified on the basis of externalities is in part a political question. A first best solution, to be strongly recommended, is to adopt policies that directly internalize the externalities. If externalities were internalized, there would be no departure of actual from optimum city sizes and hence no need for city size or other locational policies.

In a second best world, where externalities are not completely internalized, a case can be made in principle for indirectly attacking externalities through trying to influence the location of activity. If uninternalized externalities are greater in one place than another, there is a potential net gain from fostering a shift in location. However, the benefits from interventions aimed at capturing the national income gains have been found to be small, and they would require quite significant changes in city sizes. Ability to fine tune the policies in a practical policy setting is questionable. Political considerations come into play in devising spatial policies that could preclude actually making adjustments that would increase national income. Once the door was open to policies with teeth attempting to guide location, policies in a political process could go contrary to the adjustments aimed at capturing the national income gains and could instead have significant deleterious effects on national income.

In contrast to direct locational incentive policies, a more promising application of the analysis of this chapter could be to help improve government resource allocation decisions undertaken in fulfilling the normal public purposes of government. The analysis of this chapter is particularly applicable to government resource allocation decisions with pronounced locational effects, such as for roads, transit, water resources development, parastatal investments to promote national growth, other capital projects, national defense spending and location of government offices for supplying routine services that do not have to be produced in any one specified location. In deciding on where best to make these expenditures, consideration of benefits and costs of alternatives is needed, in order to arrive at the most desired alternative.

At present, evaluations of alternatives are carried out formally and informally, often subjectively, with great variation in the quality of evaluation from one type of expenditure to another as well as from one country to another. As part of needed improvement in evaluation, effects should be quantified objectively to the maximum extent possible. For the most part, the quantification will consist of estimating costs and benefits using market indicators as would a private firm. To this basic framework can be added allowance for the value of externalities, taking account of the difference between private and social benefits. In many cases, the difference will not be significant enough to merit quantification. For cases where a significant divergence is identified, the analysis of this chapter indicates methods for valuing the externalities.

In cases where the net benefits using market indicators are about the same if an expenditure is undertaken in one location as opposed to another, the value of the externalities could make the difference in indicating what the most efficient location is for the expenditure taking a social point of view.

Beyond externalities whose values are susceptible to valuation, that have been considered in this chapter, lie less quantifiable external values affected by locational decisions. These include the greater social than private value attached to integration of people of differing ethnicity and income, the value of the social and political consequences of lessening concentrations of low income people in large cities, the desirability of decentralization for strategic and defense reasons, and the desirability of preserving cultural identities of groups historically residing in regions that become depopulated as primal cities draw people from the rest of the country.

Conceivably, estimates could be made of values people attach to the foregoing externalities that are not susceptible to traditional means of quantification. Revealed behavior towards private goods that yield satisfactions similar to the externalities can provide evidence, as can contingent valuation interview techniques. But the time when serious estimates will be available does not seem close.

Important as the difficult-to-value externalities may be, optimism cannot be expressed about prospects for devising effective overall policies to deal with them. Bringing in these more ephemeral externalities often adds more confusion than light to policy discussion. They are too amenable to being overly emphasized in unbalanced ways, not so much because of laudable social goals but more because income will be redistributed to particular constituents.

In place of ill-conceived efforts to overtly guide location of activities, a more promising way for taking account of difficult-to-value externalities may again be in helping improve normal public purpose government resource allocation decisions. After having brought in externalities amenable to valuation as an adjunct to measures of benefits and costs based on market or private values, along the lines suggested above, systematic information for the difficult-to-value externalities could be developed in nonmonetary terms. For example, measures could be developed of effects on degree of integration, degree of decentralization, and the like, without attempting to assign monetary values to them. These measures in nonmonetary terms would be arrayed alongside the benefits and costs measured in monetary terms, with the intent of allowing them to be weighed subjectively.

A challenge would be to keep perspective on the effects expressed in non-monetary terms. A useful exercise is to ask what value is implicitly placed on the externalities which are measured only in non-monetary terms. A minimum estimate of the implicit value is the loss in measured net benefits when the externality is used as a reason to overturn a decision indicated by comparison of measured benefits and costs. Attempts could be made to seek reasonable consistency from one decision to the next in the value implicitly assigned to an externality.

References

Brueckner, J.K. (1981) 'Labor mobility and the incidence of the residential property tax', *Journal of Urban Economics*, 10:173–182.

Chappie, M. and L. Lave (1982) 'The health effects of air pollution: a re-analysis', *Journal of Urban Economics*, 12:346–376.

Cooley, T.F., and C.J. La Civita (1982) 'A theory of growth controls', *Journal of Urban Economics*, 12:129–145.

Cropper, M.L. (1981) 'The value of urban amenities', *Journal of Regional Science*, 21:359–374.

Cropper, M.L. and A.S. Arriage-Salinas (1980) 'Intercity wage differentials and the value of air quality', *Journal of Urban Economics*, 8:236–254.

Diamond, D.B., Jr., and G.S. Tolley, eds. (1982) *The economics of urban amenities*. New York: Academic Press.

Fare, Rolf, Groskopf, Shawna, and B.J. Yoon (1982) 'A theoretical and empirical analysis of the highway speed-volume relationship', *Journal of Urban Economics*, 12:115–121.

Fogarty, M.S. and G. Garofalo (1980) 'Urban size and the amenity structure of cities', *Journal of Urban Economics*, 8:350–361.

Graves, P.E. (1983) 'Migration with a composite amenity: the role of rents', *Journal of Regional Science*, 23:541–546.

Grieson, R.E. and R. Arnott (1981) 'Optimal fiscal policy for a state or local government', *Journal of Urban Economics*, 9:23–48.

Harris, J.R. and M.P. Todaro (1970) 'Migration, unemployment, and development: a two-sector analysis', *The American Economic Review*, 60:126–142.

Haurin, D.R. (1983) 'The effect of property taxes on urban areas', *Journal of Urban Economics*, 7:384–396.

Haurin, D.R. (1981) 'Local income taxation in an urban areas', *Journal of Urban Economics*, 10:323–337.

Haurin, D.R. (1984) 'The effects of output and factor subsidies or taxes on an urban areas', *Regional Science and Urban Economics*, 14:533–546.

Henderson, J.V. (1977) *Economic theory and the cities*. New York: Academic Press.

Henderson, J.V. (1982) 'Evaluating consumer amenities and interregional welfare difference', *Journal of Urban Economics*, 11:32–59.

Henderson, J.V. (1985) 'Property tax incidence with a public sector', *Journal of Political Economy*, 93:648–665.

Henderson, J.V. (1986) 'Efficiency of resource usage and city size', *Journal of Urban Economics*, 19:47–70.

Izraeli, O. (1977) 'Differentials in nominal wages and prices between cities', *Urban Studies*, 14:275–290.

McConnell, V.D. and M. Straszheim, (1982) 'Auto pollution and congestion in an urban model: an analysis of alternative strategies', *Journal of Urban Economics*, 11:11–31.

McDonald, J.F. (1983) 'An economic analysis of local inducements for business', *Journal of Urban Economics*, 13:322–336.

Porell, F.W. (1982) 'Intermetropolitan migration and quality of life', *Journal of Regional Science*, 22:137–158.

Power, T.M. (1981) 'Urban size (Dis) amenities revisted', *Journal of Urban Economics*, 9:85–89.

Rosen, S. (1979) 'Wage-based indexes of urban quality of life', in: P. Mieszkowski and M. Straszheim, eds., *Current issues in urban economics*. Baltimore: Johns Hopkins Press.

Tolley, G.S. (1974) 'The welfare economics of city bigness', *Journal of Urban Economics*, 3:324–345.

Tolley, G.S. and V. Thomas, eds. (1986) *The economics of urbanization process and policies in developing countries*. The World Bank.

Tolley, G.S., P.E. Graves, and J.L. Gardner, eds. (1979) *Urban growth policy in a market economy*. New York: Academic Press.

INDEX